Lennard Samson

The visitation of the county of Cornwall, in the year 1620

Lennard Samson

The visitation of the county of Cornwall, in the year 1620

ISBN/EAN: 9783337730437

Printed in Europe, USA, Canada, Australia, Japan

Cover: Foto ©ninafisch / pixelio.de

More available books at **www.hansebooks.com**

The
Visitation of the County
of Cornwall,

IN THE YEAR 1620.

EDITED BY

LIEUT.-COLONEL J. L. VIVIAN

AND

HENRY H. DRAKE, M.A., PH.D.,

MEMBER OF THE ROYAL ARCHÆOLOGICAL INSTITUTE OF GREAT BRITAIN AND IRELAND.

LONDON:

1874.

Preface.

The original drafts of the Heralds' Visitation of Cornwall in 1620 are preserved in the British Museum, and form part of the Harleian Collection, being MSS. 1162 and 1164. They are in the handwriting of Camden's deputies, Sir Henry St. George, when Richmond Herald, and Mr. Sampson Lennard, Blue Mantle; and the pedigrees are subscribed in most cases by the then representatives of the several families. The pedigrees in each of these MSS. have the word "Entered" written above them, in red chalk, shewing that they had been transcribed at the College of Arms; and those in MS. 1162 have an additional *mark* (thus #) in *black lead,* from which we presume that a second transcript was made, probably that in Harl. MS. 1079, by John Withie, Heraldic Artist of London,[1] in whose MS. the greater number of the pedigrees of MS. 1164 do not appear. The loose sheets on which the drafts were written were bound together by Mr. Sampson Lennard, whose arms were stamped on the cover. After his death they came into the possession of Mr. Parker, who added a few notes, and they then passed by purchase to Mr. Robert Fisher, and subsequently to the Earl of Oxford's library.

In editing this Visitation, we have endeavoured to reproduce these original drafts in printing type, scrupulously retaining all the inaccuracies, whether in orthography or in statement of fact, in order that the reader may be enabled to form a fair estimate of the nature and value of a Herald's Visitation. But the order of the pedigrees is not preserved. They are arranged alphabetically, according to the plan adopted for the 'Visitation of Devon,'

---

[1] Probably an accredited artist. Herald painters were (to ensure accuracy) obliged to obtain licence from the Heralds to pursue their occupation, and were punishable and punished for acting without such authority. Grim. Orig. Geneal., p. 83.

b

Harl. Soc. Pub., vol. vi. Where the Arms are given we have blazoned them in their places, and we have referred to the Harleian MSS.—chiefly MS. 1079—to supply the omissions in a separate list, at p. 301.

It is much to be regretted that Carew, the Historian, left his "painful collection of Cornish Arms" "unmentioned," from fear of doing his friends the Heralds wrong, "by thrusting his sickle into their harvest." He states that the Cornish appeared to change and diversify their Arms at pleasure, and further, that "The most Cornish gentlemen can better vaunt of their pedigree than of their livelihood, for that they derive from great antiquity, and I (R. C.) make question whether any shire in England, of but equal quantity, can muster a like number of fair coat armours, whereas this declineth to the mean." De Dunstanville edit., p. 179.

The County of Cornwall may be considered pre-eminent in the antiquity of its family Heraldry, since it was admitted in Court, during the memorable Scrope and Grosvenor controversy, that the same Arms, *azure a bend or*, had remained in the family of Carminow from the time of King Arthur! consequently it had been adjudged in a previous trial with Scrope, under the walls of Paris, that Carminow should continue to bear them entire, a fact at variance with the popular belief that a label was assigned to the Cornishman for difference.[1]

In point of family antiquity, Cleaveland, in his 'History of the House of

---

[1] Evidences of Arms of Carmynowe without the label. In addition to the seals quoted, p. 33. are the seal of Thomas Carmynow (Chapter Ho. Domestic Deeds. 7 R. II., No. 16), and the seal of Oliver Carmynow of Fentongollan, with the motto "Cala Raggi wethlowe" (Chapter Ho. Domestic Deeds, 35 Eliz., No. 25), both in good preservation. The seals of different deeds in the possession of John Jope Rogers, Esq., the present Lord of the Manor of Wyncanton, are without the label.

TESTIMONIES CONCERNING THE ARMS OF CARMINOW GIVEN IN THE SCROPE AND GROSVENOR CONTROVERSY.

(Misc. Rolls of Chanc., Nos. 311 and 312.)

John p' la gace de Dieu Roy DU CHASTELL & DE LYON DUC DE LANCASTRE, &c. Nous dions et tesmoignons q' a la derrain viage en France de notre tres redonte Sr & pier q' Dieu assoill' fuist moeve un debate des ditz armes p' entr' mons' Richard Lescrop susdit & un appelle Carmynau de Cornewale lequel Carmynau chalangea ses armes du dit mons' Richard le quele debate fuist toys en regard de sys chivalers and tielx sys chivalers jeo quide ne sont pas mayntenant en monde & la troverent p' lez tesmoignes verroies q' le dit Carmynau descendit delyne armez dazure ove un bende dor depuis le temps de roy Arthur encea. Et troverent q' le dit Mons. Richard descendut de droit lynee dauncestrie armez en memez lez armez dazur' ov un bende dor depuis le temps du Roy William Conquerour encea et issent fuist juggez q' *ambideux devont porter lez armez entiers!*

PREFACE.   vii

Courtenay,' mentions the still more astounding tradition that one of the Carminows led a body of troops to oppose the landing of Cæsar. Although the early history of this family is obscure, it was once classed amongst those related to the blood royal (Harl. 1074, fo. 320), and so many Cornishmen are proud to claim descent from it, that we select its example, at page 296, to shew the necessity of testing the truth of the Visitation Pedigrees by independent evidence.

Similar tests may be applied to the scarcely less distinguished Cornish family of Petit, and with similar results; and it must be understood from these examples, and our notes under Ley, Yorke, and others, that in reproducing the text of the Visitation we do not hold ourselves responsible for the errors it contains. The Records of the Heralds' Visitations are highly valuable in affording information which, but for them, would have been lost to the general public. These Visitations called moreover for the performance of two separate and distinct offices; the Heralds had to declare and record the Armorial cognizance of each particular family, to define the quarterings, differences, and due marks of cadency, while the *"Chief of the Coat Armour"* had to set forth his own pedigree, tracing from the last Visitation, and

Mons. Thomas Fychet, &c., dit coment il ad oy dir' dez ceux quex sont veillerds q' Thomas Carmynau de Cornwale qest mon p'ent estoit en debate ove le dit mons Richard et son lynage pr lez ditz armez en France dev^{a}nt le conte de Northampton luy quel Thomas Carmynau p'va cez armes du temps le Roy Arthur and le dit mons Richard du temps de Roy William le Conquerour p^r quell accorde le dit *Thomas Carmynau pur ce qil estoit dev^{a}nt le Q'quest il lez doit porter du droit.*

Nicholas Sabraham Esq. del age de lx ans. &c. Mes du chalange qi Carmynau fist a mons Richard Lescrop devant Parys lez queux estoient acordez p' le Roy and p' le duc de Lancast'r q' mort est q' *cheseun deux deyrent porter lez armez entiers.*

John Topclyffe Esquier del age de lx ans et plus. A la darrein voiage du Roy q' mort est un dez Carmynawe de Cornewale chalangeast le dit mons Richard et estoient acordez p' le count de Northampton adont conestable et p' le Count de Warwyk' adounc marshall et le duc de Lancastr' q' mort est q' p^r cause q' lun estoit de Cornewale et lautre estoit trovez adont del Conquest, &c. *Carmynawe lez doit porter pur ceo q' Cornwale estoit un grosse t're et jadys portant le noun dune roialme.*

John de Rither Esquier dage de lxvi ans, &c. Un Carmynawe de Cornwale q' chalangea le dit mons Richard a la voiage dev^{a}nt Parys & le Roy q' mort est & mons de Lancastr' q' mort est lez accorderent p' til man'e q' le dit mons Richard doit porter lez entiers armez & *le dit Cormynaue lez doit porter auxi.*

The evidence of Geoffery Chaucer was in favour of Scrope, and did not affect Carmynow.

(This memorable controversy lasted over four years. Among the witnesses appeared one Sovereign Prince, one Duke, three Earls, three Barons, three mitred Abbots, two Priors, eleven Bannerets, and more than one hundred and fifty Knights, Esquires, Gentlemen, and others, an array such as no other case has ever seen before or since. Chetham Soc.. The Amicia Tract.)

embracing such branches or members of his family as he thought fit to include for the Heralds' guidance and commemoration, and thus many genealogical errors occurred through indifference or lack of information on the part of the head of the house, and many omissions were due as much perhaps to a narrow or unamiable spirit as to forgetfulness.

It is only fair to exonerate the officials of the time, whom aggrieved persons are apt to blame for the trouble caused by an erroneous statement, for much had evidently to be taken upon trust, or upon evidence which would not now be accepted by their successors at the College of Arms; and modern Genealogists deem it necessary to prove every pedigree by wills, parish registers, and by searches at the Record Office, to which the public, through the liberality of the Master of the Rolls, has every facility of access.

The extracts from parish registers in the notes and appendix are intended not only to support the pedigrees, but to stimulate a taste for genealogical enquiries by assisting the cadets of a family to establish their connection with the main trunk, for, in the words of Richard Carew, " all Cornish gentlemen are cousins." They are extracted from large collections, commenced many years since, chiefly for private purposes, which will explain why they are not as uniformly given under each pedigree as we could have desired.

When availing ourselves of the opportunities, kindly afforded by the clergy, of searching their parish records, to curtail an intrusive visit, we have, like the Eastern pearl divers, hastily collected every thing within reach, without waiting to scrutinize; we cannot therefore guarantee the accuracy of every transcript made under these circumstances, and we recommend the reader who descries a pearl of value, to have it verified by the clergyman of the parish, by whose certificate alone it can be converted into legal evidence.

We have noted the varied spelling of the same name to encourage enquirers not to abandon their pursuit of a pedigree on account of the difficulty caused by such variations. About two hundred years since, the name Watts was spelt Oats, Woots, Wots in the Gwennap Registers.[1] A slight acquaintance with the Public Records will shew that family distinctions,

---

[1] Shortly after the earthquake of Lisbon, a considerable amount of personalty was lost to the family of Joll (one of whom had acquired wealth as a foreign merchant), presumably from the different spelling of the name in an advertisement. See variations under Jolliffe.

PREFACE. ix

based on the interchange of the letters i and y, such as in Vivian, Vyvyan, Williams, Wyllyams, are more imaginary than real.

The pedigrees of Arundel and Petit, given at pages 271 and 276, were evidently interpolations, and that of Vivyan is taken from Harl. MS. 1079, fo. 37. Several pedigrees, belonging more properly to Devonshire, were inserted by the Heralds among the Cornish. They are added in the Supplement, together with a list of the "disclaimed," taken from Harl. MS. 1079.

For the convenience of those among our Members who may desire to search further, we will repeat Sims' List of Heralds' Visitations for Cornwall (Manual, etc., p. 163).

S. D.				College of Arms.
1530.	Benolte			Brit. Mus. Add. MS. 14, 315.
„	„	(original)		Coll. of Arms MS. H 18.
„	„			„ „ MS. G 2 (1).
1573.	Cooke			Brit. Mus., Harl. MS. 1079.
„	„	(original)		Coll. of Arms MS. E 15.
„	„			„ „ MSS. G 6 (1); H 16.
„	„			Caius Coll., Camb., MS. 553.
1620.	Camden (By St. George and Lennard).			Brit. Mus., Harl. MS. 1079.
„	„	(part of original)		„ „ 1162.
„	„	(remaining part)		„ „ 1164.
„	„			„ „ 1142.
„	„			„ „ 1149.
„	„			Coll. of Arms, MS. C 1.
„	„	(with additions)		„ „ MS. E, D, N, No. 2.
„	„			Caius Coll., Camb., MS. 532.
„	„			Bodl. Lib. MS. 5054, f. 59.

To these we add the following from Sir N. Harris Nicolas' Catalogue, Harl. MSS. 891, 1956, 4632, 5827, 1482, 4031, 6252; and Cott. MS. Faust, E III.

We must here acknowledge our obligations to the indefatigable Historian of Trigg, Sir John Maclean, F.S.A., whose numerous contributions are distinguished by the initials J. M. affixed, and whose valuable co-operation throughout entitles him to be regarded as forming with ourselves an Editorial triumvirate.

HENRY H. DRAKE.
JOHN L. VIVIAN.

QUARTERINGS OF THE GRENVILLE SHIELD,
REFERRED TO ON THE FRONTISPIECE.

1. Grenville.
2. Wortham.
3. Whitleigh.
4. Esse ?
5. Winard.
6. Reprin, or Wroughton.
7. Bevil.
8. Waff ?
9. Tredignic.
10. Trefouis.
11. Mathedarva.
12. Tresithney.
13. Petit.
14. Fitz Yve.
15. Carminowe.
16. St. Leger.
17. Donet.
18. Butler, Earl of Ormond.
19. Rochford.
20. Hankford.
21. Stapeldon.
22. Bevil.
23. Trelowarren.
24. Tredignic.
25. Trefouis.
26. Mathedarva.
27. Bere.
28. Killegarth.
29. Udey.
30. Pengelley.
31. Becket.
32. Le Tailleur.
33. Nantion.
34. Delahay.
35. Lanhergy.
36. Fairford.
37.
38.
39.
40. Hungerford.
41. Berry.
42. Mallet.
43.
44.
45. Giffard.
46. Trecarrel al's Esse.
47. Ilcomb.
48. Kelloway.
49. Tregarthan.
50. Hender.
51. Cornwall.
52. Chamberlain.
53. Pever.

List of Visitation Pedigrees.

Name	Page	Name	Page	Name	Page
ALEIGH	1	COCK	43	GLYN	80
ARUNDELL of Lanherne	2	COKE	44	GODOLPHIN	80
ARUNDELL of Trerice	2	COLLING	44	GODOLPHIN	82
ARUNDELL of Camborne	3	COLQUIT	45	GODOLPHIN	83
ARUNDELL of Trerice (Add.)	271	CONNOCK	46	GOODE	83
AYRE	3	COODE of Morval	46	GRENVILE	84
BARRET	4	COODE of Menheniot	48	GREINEVELE	87
BARET	5	CORYTON	49	GRILLS	88
BASSETT	6	CORYTON	49	GRYLLS	88
BASTARD	7	COSWORTH	50	GROSSE	89
BATTERSBYE	7	COSSEN alias MADDERN	51	HALLAMORE	90
BEAUCHAMP	7	COURTENAY of Landrake	51	HARRIS	90
BEAUCHAMP	8	COURTENEY of Lanivet	52	HARVY	91
BEHE	9	COURTNEY of Penkivel	52	HATCH	91
BERE	9	COWLIN	54	HAWKE	92
BENNETT	10	CRAB	55	HELE	92
BILLINGE	10	CRESSEL	55	HENDER	93
BLAKE	11	CREWES	56	HERLE	94
BLIGHE	12	CROCKER	57	HEXT	96
BLIGHE	13	CROCKHAY	57	HICKES	96
BOGANS	14	CROSMAN	58	HILL of Hill Top	97
BOND	14	CULLOW	58	HILL	98
BOND	15	DAGGE	59	HILL of Truro	99
BONYTHON	16	DANDY	60	HILL of St. Keverne	99
BONYTHON	16	DARLEY	60	HYLL of Heligan	100
BOSAVARNE	17	DARRELL	61	HOARE	100
BOSCAWEN	17	DENYS	61	HOBLYN	101
BOSSAWSACKE	22	DEWEN	62	JENKYN	103
BOSUSTOWE	23	DODSON	63	JEYNENES	104
BRAY	23	EDGCOMBE	63	JOLLYFE	105
BULLER	24	EDGCOMBE	64	JOPE	108
BURELL	25	EDMONDES	65	KEKEWICH	108
BURGES	26	EDWARDES	65	KENDALL	109
BUSVARGUS	27	ELFORD	66	KENDALL	111
BYLL	27	ELLYOTT or ELIOT	66	KENDALL	112
BYRD	28	ENYS	67	KESTELL	112
CAREW	28	ERISEY	67	KESTELL	115
CAREW	33	ESTCOTT	69	KETE	116
CARMINOWE (Add. 296.)	33	FITZPEN alias PHIPPEN	71	KNYVETT	117
CARNSEWE	35	FLAMANKE	71	KYLLYOWE	117
CARTER	36	FLEMINGE	72	LAMPEN	119
CARY	37	FLETCHAR	73	LANGDON	119
CAVELL	37	FORTESCU	73	LANGDON	120
CEELYE	38	GAMON alias GAMBONE	74	LANGFORD	121
CHAMOND	40	GEORGE	75	LANGEFORD	122
CHEPMAN	40	GEIRVEIS	75	LANGHARNE	122
CHAPMAN	41	GEYRVEYS	77	LANYON	123
CHENOUTH	41	GLANVILLE	77	LAUNCE	124
CHIVERTON of Paul	42	GLANVILE	78	LEACHE	125
CHIVERTON of Trehunsey	43	GLYN	79	LEIGH	125

LIST OF VISITATION PEDIGREES.

Name	Page
LEVELIS	126
LEY	127
LEY alias KEMPTHORNE	129
LOVEYS	130
LOVEYS	131
LOWER	132
LOWER	133
LOWER	133
LYNAM	134
MANINGTON	134
MARKE	136
MARTYN	137
MATHEW	137
MATHEW	138
MAYNARD	139
MAYNARD	140
MAYOW	140
MENWYNICK	141
MICHELL	142
MICHELL	142
MOHUN	143
MOLESWORTH	147
MORTHE	147
MORTON	148
MOYELL	149
MOYLE	150
MUNDAY	151
NANKEVELL alias TIPPETT	153
NANSPIAN	154
NICOLL	156
NICHOLLS	157
NOYE	158
OPY	159
OUGHE	160
PARKER	161
PAYNTER	162
PENDARVES	163
PENDARVES	164
PENDARVIS	164
PENFOUN	164
PENHALLOW	166
PENHELLICK	167
PENROSE	169
PENROS	169
PENWARNE	170
PETIT (Add.)	276
PLUMLEIGHE	171
POLWHEILE	172
POLKINGHORNE	173
POLKINHORNE	175
POLLARD	176
POMEROY	176
POMEROY	177

Name	Page
PORTER	178
PORTER	179
POYLE	180
PYE	181
QUARME	182
RANDALL	182
RASHLEIGH	183
RESKIMER	185
ROBARTS	186
ROBERTS	186
ROBINSON	188
ROGERS	188
ROSCARROCK	189
ROSCARROCK	189
ROSCARROCK	190
ROSEWARAN	191
ROSKROWE	192
ROSKRUGE	192
ROSUGGAN	193
ROUS	193
SAMUELL	196
SAWLE	196
SAYER	197
SCAWEN	198
SCAWEN	199
SCAWNE	200
SCOBELL	200
SEARLE	202
SHORROCK	202
SKORY	203
SMYTH	204
SPARKE	205
SPARNON	205
SPOORE	206
SPREY	207
SPRY	208
SPRY	211
SEYNTAUBYN vel ST. AUBIN	212
STANBERYE vel STANBURYE	213
STEPHENS	214
STONE	215
TANNER (Add.)	278
THOMAS	215
THOMS	216
THOMS alias CARNSEW	217
TOINKEIN	217
TREBARFOOTE	218
TREFFRY	219
TREFRIE	221
TREFUSIS	222
TREFUSIS	222

Name	Page
TREOEARE	225
TREHANE	227
TRELAWNY	228
TRENANCE	231
TRENERTH	233
TRENGOVE alias NANSE	233
TRESAHER	234
TRETHEWY	237
TREUNWITH vel TRENWITH	238
TREVANION	239
TREVANION	240
TREVELYAN	242
TREVISA	244
TREWOLLA	244
TREWBODY	246
TREWREN	247
TUBB	247
TUCKER	248
VACYE	250
VERMAN	251
VIVIAN	252
VYVYAN	256
VIVYAN	257
WALLIS al's DARTE (Add.)	279
WEBBER	262
WHITE	262
WILLIAMS	263
WILLOUGHBY	265
WILLS	265
WODENOTE	266
WORTHEVALE	267
WREY	268
WYVELL	269
YORK	269

SUPPLEMENT.

Devonshire Pedigrees.

Name	Page
ARSCOTT	286
ARSCOTT	287
BARKLEY	287
BLACKALL	288
CALMADY	288
FOWNES	289
HUNKIN	290
ROLL	290
UPPETON	291
WYCHEHALSE	292
YEO	292

The Original Visitation of the County of Cornwall,

1620.

Aleigh.

ARMS.—*A Lion rampant is given in trick, without naming tincture or metal.*

Tho. Aleigh al's Leigh of Weke St Mary in Cornwall descended from Leigh of highleigh in Chesheire lived in time H. VI.
    |
Humphrie Aleigh al's Leigh =Da. of V .... & widow of ...
sonne and heire | Selman of ....
    |
Willm. Aleigh al's Leigh sonne & heire=Mary Da. of Andrew Pomeroy of Newton
of Leigh in Com. Cornw. | Ferreis in Com. Devon, Esq.
    |
Willm. Leigh of Leighe in Com. Corn=Elizab. Da. of Wymond Searle of
wall sonne & heire liveing 1620 | Anthonie in Cornwall
    |
John 2   Thomazin 1   Wymond Leigh sone &
—   —   heire æt. 18, 1620
Andrew 3   Agnes 2
—
Eliacan 4

WILLIAM ALEIGH.

Arundell of Lanherne.

Arondell of Lanherne in Cornwall Esq.[1]

Sr John Arondel of Lanherne 1 sonne Knight

Tho. Arondell of Lanherne 2 sonne = Elizab. da. & coheire of Tringove of Nance in Cornwall[2]

Tho. Arondell of Collomb Maior in Com. Cornw. liveinge 1620 = Rachell Da. of Monp'son & sist[r] to S[r] Giles Monp'son

Will[m] 2 sone   Cicilie 1 Da.   Tho. Arondell sonne & hey. liveing 1620   Jane 2 Da.

* THOMAS ARUNDELL, JUNIOR.

Arundell of Trerice.

Catherin da. & heire of Coswarth 1 wife[3] = John Arrundell of Trerise Esq. = Gertrude da. of S[r] Robt. Dennys of Holcombe Kt. 2 wife = Edw. Lord Morley 2 husband

1. Julian wife to Richard Carew of Anthony[4]
2. Alice wife to Henry Somester of Painsford
3. Dorothy wife to Edward Coswarth of Coswarth
4. Mary wife to Oliver Dynham

John Arrundell of Trerise Esq. living 1620. = Mary da. of George Cary of Clovelley Esq.

Thomas Arundell 2 sonn = Mary da. of Sr Gamaliell Capell

1. Ann wife to William Carnsew of Buckelley Esq.
2. Catherine wife to John St Albone of Clowans, Esq.[5]

John sonne & heir ætat. 7 annores 1620.

Richard 2   Agnes 1
William 3   Mary 2
Francis 4

Gertrude

JOHN ARUNDELL OF TRERISE.

---

[1] This was Sir John Arundell of Lanherne, who married Elizabeth, da. of Gerald Danet of Danet's Hall, Esq. *Vide* Pedigree of Arundell in Coll. of Arms.
[2] Nance in the parish of Illogan.
[3] Da. of John Cosworth, Esq. *Vide* Harl. MSS. 4031, fo. 77.
[4] Author of the Survey of Cornwall.
[5] John S[t] Aubyn of Clowance.

* These Pedigrees are considerably extended in Harl. MSS. 1079, fos. 78, 79 and 80.

Arundell of Camborne.

Robt. Arundell 2 son of Sr John = Elizab. Da. of Will'm Clapton Esq. of Stafford
Arundell of Camborne[1]

Christopher Arundell of Camborne = [3]Katherine Da. of Will'm Chiverton of Pawle in com. Cornub.[4]
in com. Cornwall[2]

[3]Thomas ob. s. p.

[3]Margery ux. John Bosavarne
—
[3]Elizab. ux. David Grosse

[3]John 2 son æt. 34 mar. Ann Da. of Alexander Pendarvis =

[3]Will'm Arundell of = Dorkis Da. of Zeakiell Grosse of Camborne in Com. Cornwall.
Camborne filius et heres æt. 36 living 1620.

Zeakiell Arundell filius et heres æt. 12 living 1620

2. Will'm æt. 11
—
3. John æt. 7

4. Robt. æt. 5
—
5. Francis æt. 6 mensis

Katherine a Da. æt. 13 living 1620

WILLIAM ARUNDELL.

Ayre.

Willim Ayre al's Eyre of St Cue in Cornwall. =

John Ayre al's Eyre of = Joane Da. of Jo. Jewell of Dewstowe in Cornwall.
St Cue in Cornw.

John Ayre Al's Eyre in com. Cornwall = Marg[t] Da. of Jo. Wotton of Ingleborne in com. Devon.
of Dewstowe liveing 1620.

Jane Da. & sole hey. ux[r] Phillip Crimes of Mevey in com. Devon leiveing 1620. =

John sone & heire æt. 9, 1620

Will'm 2

Phillip 3

Francis 4 sonne

Margaret a da. æt. 4, 1620

JOHN AYRE AL'S EYRE.

---

[1] This Robert was a bastard son of Sir John Arundell of Trerice, and is so described by him in two deeds dated 4 Jan., 1 Ed. VI., and 26 Jan., 2 Eliz. Vide Inq. P. M. Sir John Arundell of Trerice, 3 Eliz., No. 23 part 1.

[2] Mentioned in the will of John Arundell of Trerice, proved in London 26 Nov., 1580, of which his father Robert was one of the executors. There are several other children of Robert named in this will.

[3] Mentioned in the will of Thomas Chiverton of Paul, 26 August, 1604; proved in London 7 Feb. 1605.
Bur. at Camborne 1 March, 1617.

Barret.

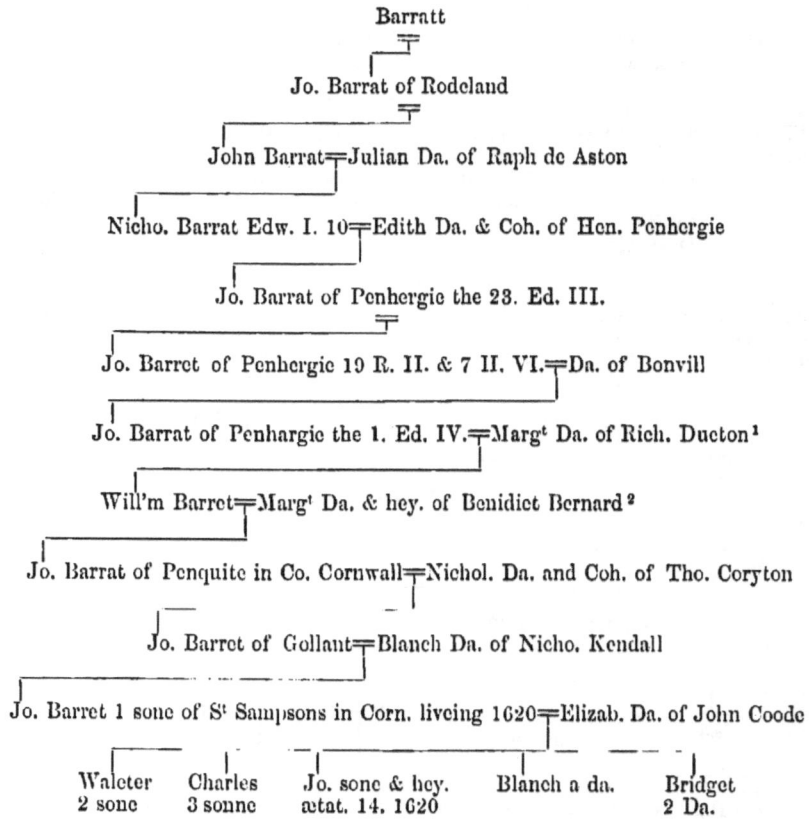

Not Signed.

---

[1] Rich. Becton in Harl. MSS. 4031, fo. 82.
[2] Of Penquite; she was heiress of Bernard Favell, Harl. MSS. 4031, fo. 82.

THE VISITATION OF THE COUNTY OF CORNWALL.   5

Baret.

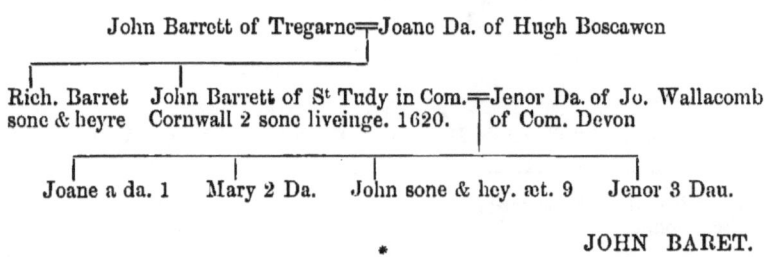

JOHN BARET.

Basset.

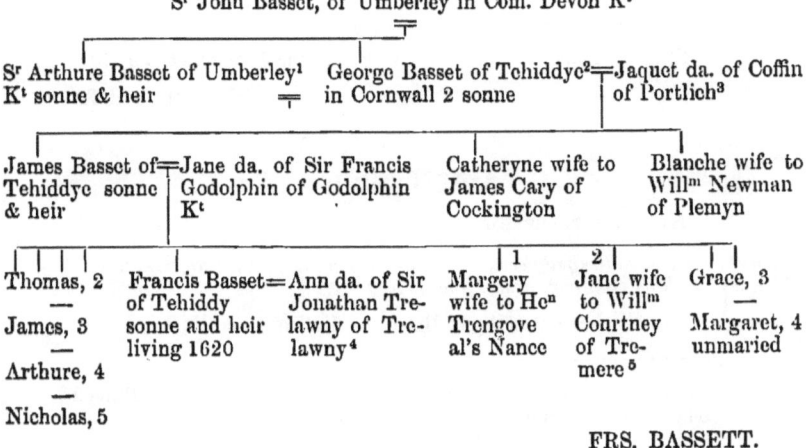

FRS. BASSETT.

---

[1] This Sr Arthur Basset was son of John Bassett, Esq., and grandson of Sir John; he was therefore *a nephew* of George Basset, *not a brother*, consequently his entry at this place was an error of the Herald. *Vide* Inq. P.M. 28 Eliz., No. 21, 1 part.
[2] M.P. for Launceston, 5 Eliz., and for Newport (Cornwall), 1 and 14 Elizab.
[3] John Coffin of Porthledge. *Vide* Visitation of Devon, 1620, p. 335.
[4] Mar. 31 Aug., 1620, at Pelint.
[5] Mar. at Illogan, 22 July, 1613.
* Pedigree extended in Harl. MSS. 1079, fo. 179.

Bastard.

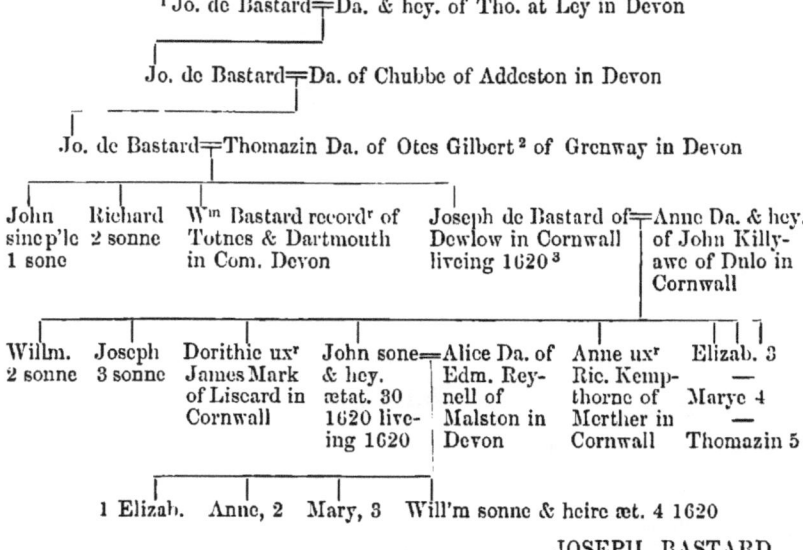

JOSEPH BASTARD.

Battersbye.

NICH. BATTERSBY OF HARRAVER P. R. S. NORREY, 1605

ARMS. Or : a saltire paly erm. and g. in chief a crescent for difference.
CREST. A Ram erm. trip. armed and ungued or.

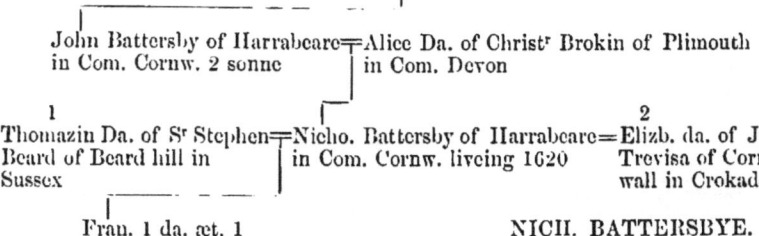

NICH. BATTERSBYE.

---

[1] Called Thomas in 'Visitation of Devon,' 1620, p. 19.
[2] Called Geffry Gilbert in 'Visitation of Devon,' 1620, p. 19.
[3] He acquired Westnorth in Duloe by this marriage.

* Joseph Bastard, gent, buried 1690 ⎫
Mrs. Elizb. Bastard   „   , ⎬ St. Veep. Par. Reg.
Mrs Dorothy Bastard   „   „ ⎭
Alice Bastard buried 1st Feb., 1635. ⎫ Lansalloes,
Thomas Helman married Mary Bastard 30th October, 1651 ⎬ Par. Reg.

Beauchamp.

ARMS. *Vairé Az. and Ar.*

Sciant p'sent' et futur' q^d ego Galfridus Beauchamp filius et heres Johis Beauchamp senioris Dom's de Binn'ton dedi concessi et p'senti carta mea indentata confirmavi Jacobo Beauchamp fri meo et Elizab. filie Nichi. Richowe et heredibus suis &c. totam placeam terre meam in Villa de Pensance &c. In cuius rei testimen. nos p'tes p'dictas. p'sentibz Indentur sigilla nra apposuimus hijs testibus Rico Browning cum alijs dat. apud Pensance quarto die Julij a° Reg. Regis Hen. VII. secundo.

Inquire for ye coate of Trefins.

```
Johes. Beauchamp senior de Binn'ton══Honor Da. et her. of Kenege de Keneg
         │                                    │
    ┌────┴─────┐                       ┌──────┴──────┐
Galfridus Beauchamp filius et heres══      Jacobus Beauchamp══Elizabetha fil.
mar Elizab. fil. Tregos de Tregos¹│        2 filius            Nich. Richowe
         │
    ┌────┼─────────┐                       ┌─────────────┐
    1    │         │                       │             │
John Beauchamp══Jana filia    Alice    Martin Beauchamp══Margered Da.
                W^m Carnsew    —       fil. et heres     & heir of Hen.
                            Margerie                     Trefyns²
    │                                       │
┌───┴──┐                              ┌─────┴────────┐
John Beaucha'══Maria 4 filia  Thomas  Willm. Beau-══Joane Da. of Willm.
              Rogeri Char-     —      champ fil et   Tubb of Gwenip 4
              fold Militis³ Margerie  heres          Son of Tubb of
    │                                                Trangoe in Com.
Margerie mariet to Rob$^t$ Yeo                       Cornwall

    │                         │                 │
John 3 fil.  Julian mar. to Peter Beauchamp  2 Margeret  Thomas 2 filius
ætat. 35     of Chiton in Cornwall            —          ætat. 37
                     ═                       3 Florence
             Walter Beawcham

Willm. Beauchamp filius══Katherin Da.  Richar. 4 son mar.    Sara youngest
et heres ætat. 38 de Tre-│ of John Tre- Florence Da. of Richard Da. mar. to
vince in P'ochia de      │ fuses of     Millionick of Glwvies   Hugh Trewike
Gwinop                   │ Trefuses     in Com. Cornwall            ═

John Beau-   2 Willm. æt. 7   1 Jane    Martin fil.     Katherin fil.   John fi'.
champ fil. et     —            —        primoge-        unica æt.       unicus ætat.
heres æt. 8  3 Francis 1      2 Maria   nitus ætat. 2   unius anni      2 annoru'.
annoru' 1620                            annoru'
                    *                                   W^M BEAUCHAMP.
```

---

¹ Da. of Rich. Tregose of Tregose. She afterwards married Wm. Carnsewe, who by his 1st wife Jane, daughter of Lawrence Sherston, had Jane married to John Beauchamp above, the son of his 2nd wife Elizabeth Tregose by her 1st husband, Galfridus Beauchamp. *Vide* Harl. MSS. 1079, fo. 201.
² Henry Trevince of Trevince in the Parish of St. Stythians.
³ Sir Roger Grenville of Stowe. *Vide* Pedigree of Grenville post.

* William Beauchamp, gent., married Mrs Elizab. Courteney of the Boro' of Truro, at St Kea, 9 April, 1695. *Vide* Gwennap Par. Register.

Beauchamp.

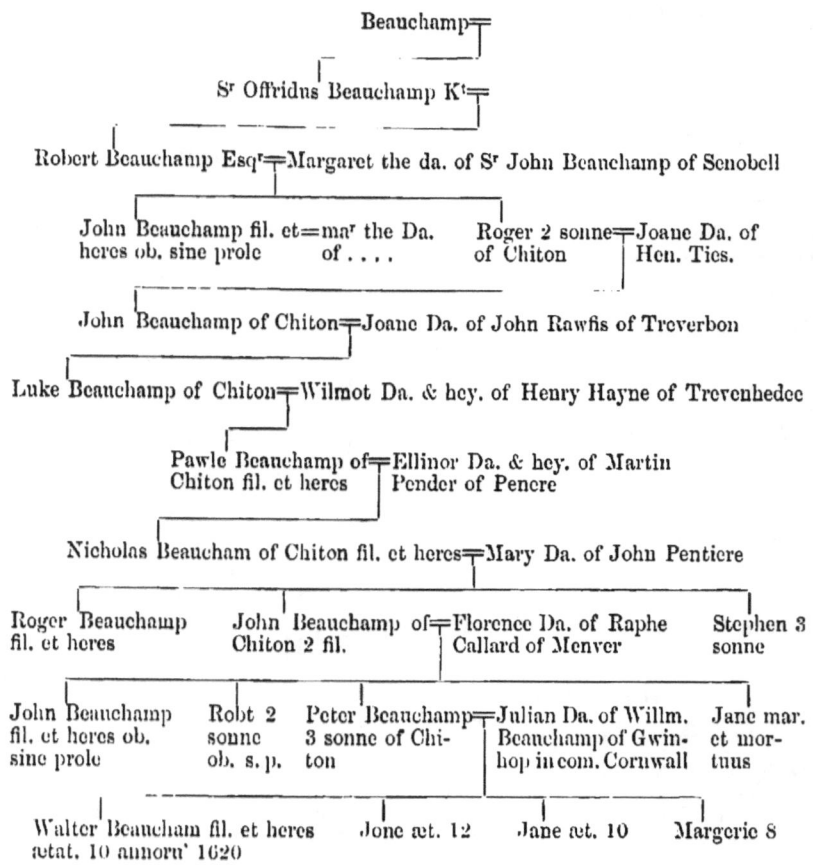

Beauchamp=

Sr Offridus Beauchamp K^t=

Robert Beauchamp Esqr=Margaret the da. of Sr John Beauchamp of Senobell

John Beauchamp fil. et=ma^r the Da. of . . . . | Roger 2 sonne of Chiton=Joane Da. of Hen. Ties.
heres ob. sine prole

John Beauchamp of Chiton=Joane Da. of John Rawfis of Treverbon

Luke Beauchamp of Chiton=Wilmot Da. & hey. of Henry Hayne of Trevenhedee

Pawle Beauchamp of Chiton fil. et heres=Ellinor Da. & hey. of Martin Pender of Pencre

Nicholas Beaucham of Chiton fil. et heres=Mary Da. of John Penticre

Roger Beauchamp fil. et heres | John Beauchamp of Chiton 2 fil.=Florence Da. of Raphe Callard of Menver | Stephen 3 sonne

John Beauchamp fil. et heres ob. sine prole | Robt 2 sonne ob. s. p. | Peter Beauchamp 3 sonne of Chiton=Julian Da. of Willm. Beauchamp of Gwinhop in com. Cornwall | Jane mar. et mortuus

Walter Beaucham fil. et heres ætat. 10 annorn' 1620 | Jone æt. 12 | Jane æt. 10 | Margerie 8

Not Signed.

Bere.

Tho. Bere of Trevedo.=Sibbell Da. & heire of Jo. Doyngle of Bencthewood

John sone & hey. mar. Jone Da. of Geo. Tubbe | Rich. 2 sone | Samsone Beare of Lante-glus in Cornwall = Phillip Da. of Ridgwaye of Devon

Jo. Beere of Trevedo in Com. Cornwall liveing 1620. = Margerie Da. of Tho. Hoblyn of St. Collom in Cornwall

Tho. sone & heire ætat. 5. 1620. | Elizab. æt. 3. 1620.* | Judithe ætat. half yeare
JOHN BERE.

Bere.

Sciant p'sentes & futuri q^d ego Anna Bere vidua nup. ux' Johis Bere de Pengelley dedi concessi et hac p'sent. carta mea confirmavi Johannæ Bere viduæ nup. ux'i Thomæ filio meo iam defunct' omnia messuag' terr' rev' reddit' et servicijs mea cum omibʒ p'tinentijs in Borlawren in p'ochia de Eglesheyle habend &c. Hijs Testibʒ Johis Flamank Armigero Willo Baret Nicho. Stephyn. et alijs. Dat' apud Borlawren 7 die Octobris A° 10 H. 8.

Omibʒ X'ri fidelibʒ &c. Johes Bevill de Killgath in Com' Cornub. armigero fil. & heres apparens Phelippi Arrundell vid. nup. relict' eiusdem Humf. Arrundell ar' defunct' salut' &c. Sciatis me presnto Johem Bevill dedisse &c. Tho. Bere de Egglosheile gen'ose ac consanguine meo totu' illud tent' meum cum omnibʒ suis p'tinentijs in Burlawren maior iacent et existent' infra p'ochia de Egloshele &c. Dat' apud Borlawren maior 16 die Augusti 1° Mariæ Reginæ.

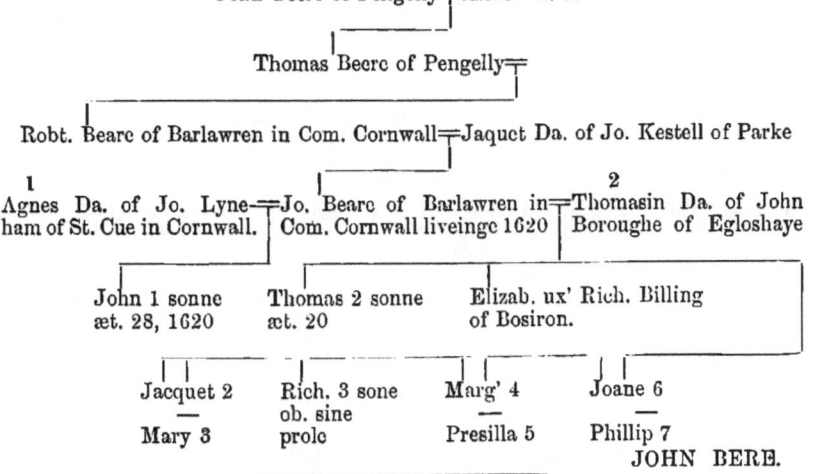

John Beere of Pengelly=Anne Da. of

Thomas Beere of Pengelly=

Robt. Beare of Barlawren in Com. Cornwall=Jaquet Da. of Jo. Kestell of Parke

1
Agnes Da. of Jo. Lyneham of St. Cue in Cornwall. = Jo. Beare of Barlawren in Com. Cornwall liveinge 1620 = 2 Thomasin Da. of John Boroughe of Egloshaye

John 1 sonne æt. 28, 1620 | Thomas 2 sonne æt. 20 | Elizab. ux' Rich. Billing of Bosiron.

Jacquet 2 — Mary 3 | Rich. 3 sone ob. sine prole | Marg' 4 — Presilla 5 | Joane 6 — Phillip 7
JOHN BERE.

* Extended Ped. in Harl. MSS. 1079, fo. 94.

Bennett.

Bennet of Sussex = Sist' of Broadbridge Bishop of Exiter

- Elles Bennet mar. & had issue
- Rob. Bennett of Lawhitton in Cornwall = Elizb. Da. of Rob. Couch of Lawhiton in Cornw.
- Rich. Bennet Drap. in Poules Church Yard =

Children of Rob. Bennett and Elizb:
- Elizb. ux' Thom. Nichol of Levante
- Willm. Bennet = Elizb. Da. of Huckmore of Devon
- Rich. Bennet of Lawhitton Esq. in Cornw. Councellor at Lawe = Mary Da. of Oliv' Cloberie of Bradstone
- Rich. Bennet mar. Lettice Da. of S' Jo. Haigham of Barowhall in Suff.

- Two Daught'.
- 2. Willm. æt. 8
- 3. Olver æt. 6
- Rob. sone & hey. æt. 15. 1620.
- Anne æt. 4
- Mary æt. 5

JOHN JOPE for ROB. BENNETT.

Billinge.

Richard Billing de Trevorder in Com. Cornw. =

- Rich. Billing de Trevarder fil. primogenitus = a Da. mar to Viall[1]
- a da. mar. to Kestell[2]
- Thomas Billing 2 fil. = John Billing fil. =

John Billing = Da. & Coh. of Blewet De com. Cornwall

Willm. Billing of Hanger in p'ochia de St. Tudy in Com. Cornw. = Elizab. fil. Bab. de Tindegrase in Com. Devon.

- Reginald Billinge 2 filius. = Eliz. Da. & hey. of .... Hockin of Brward.[3]
- Rich. Billing de Hanger in p'ochia de St. Tudy fil. primogenitus eschar & feodarie to Prince Charles temp. vite = Elizab. filia 2 Jo. Conock de St. Cleere in Com. Cornw.[4]

- 1. Willm.
- 2. John
- 3. Rich.
- Margaret
- 5. Lowday
- 6. Phillip
- Grace 4 fil.
- Margaret 3 filia
- Jane 1 Da. unmaried

A | B

[1] Elizabeth mar. Geo. Viell of Wood. *Vide* Ped. of Viell in Coll. of Arms.
[2] Margaret mar. John Kestell. *Vide* Kestell Ped. post.
[3] S' Broward.
[4] Called 3 daughter in Connock Ped. post.

THE VISITATION OF THE COUNTY OF CORNWALL. 11

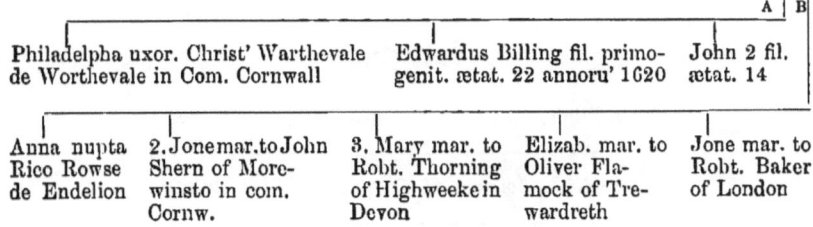

RICHARD BILLINGE.[1]

Blake.

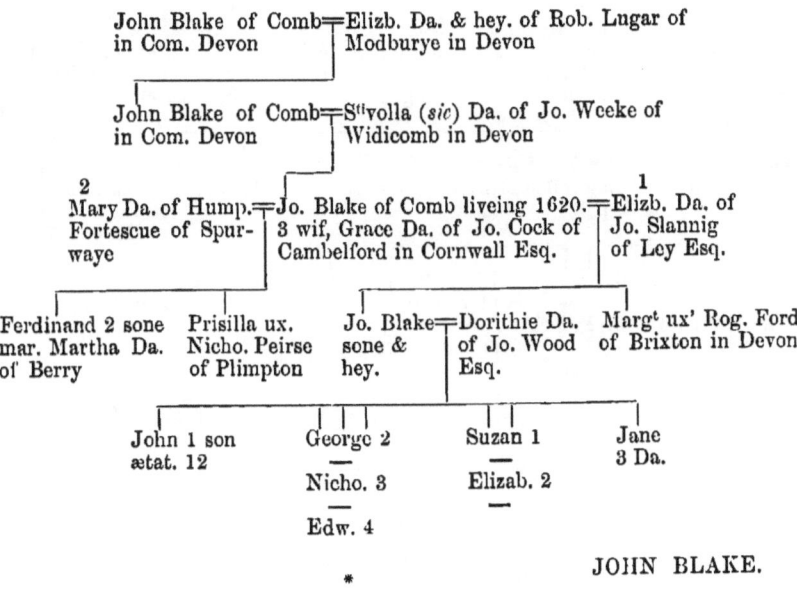

JOHN BLAKE.

---

[1] These Billings were commonly called Billing al's Trelawder, and are found thus described in numerous Inquisitions and Fines. A member of this family represented Cornwall in Parliament as early as Edw. II., and others of the name sat for Liskeard, Bodmin, and Helston.

* As an instance of peculiar spelling, as also of double entries in Parish Registers, tending to confuse, we give the marriage of the same persons in two parishes, as taken from the registers, viz. :—

Braddock (Broadoak) 15 June 1619 Henry Blake & Lowdye Helman.
Lanreth (Lanreath) 15 June 1619 Henry Blake & Louvdei Hollimau.

Blighe.

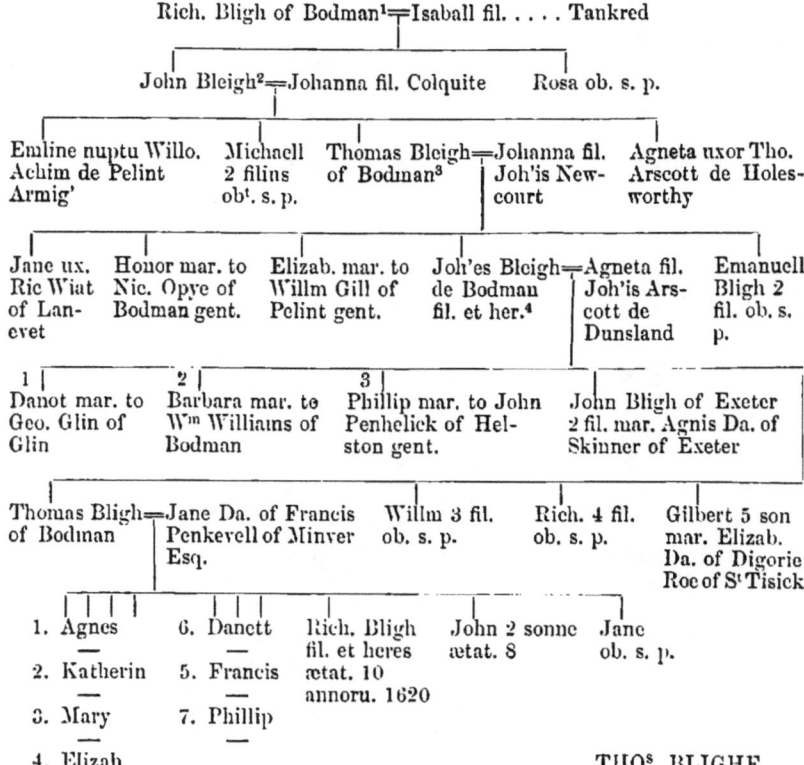

1. Agnes
2. Katherin
3. Mary
4. Elizab.

6. Danett
5. Francis
7. Phillip

Rich. Bligh fil. et heres ætat. 10 annoru. 1620

John 2 sonne ætat. 8

Jane ob. s. p.

THO^s BLIGHE.

---

[1] Mayor of Bodmin A.D. 1505 & 21.
[2] Mayor of Bodmin ,, 1531 & 39.
[3] Mayor of Bodmin ,, 1559 & 70.
[4] Mayor of Bodmin ,, 1582 & 88.

Blighe.

Sciant presentes & futuri q^d Joh'is Blygh & Johanna ux' mea dedimus concessimus & hac p^{r}senti carta n'ra indent' confirmavimus Waltero filio n'ro & Argentelle ux' eius medictatem unius orti cum p'tinentijs suis in Donheved, Burgh. &c. ex una p'te. et ortum Tho. Raynfrey ex altera p'te, &c. Hijs testibus Waltero Skinner et alijs Dat. A° 12. H. IV.

Sciant p^{r}sentes & futuri q^d ego Juliana Raynfry dedi concessi et hac p^{r}senta carta mea confirmavi Joh'æ filiæ mæ om'ia messuag' terr' et tenementa mea in Villa de Botathan cum om'b$_3$ suis p'tinentijs, &c. Dat. apud Launceston A° 7 R. II.

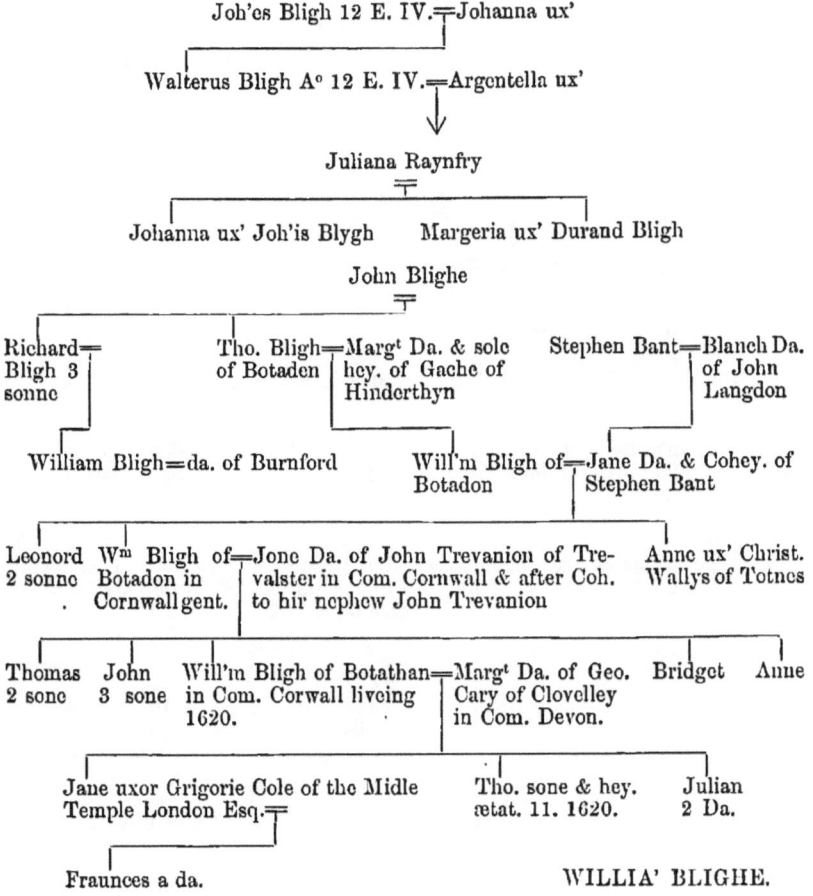

WILLIA' BLIGHE.

Bogans.

Jo. Bugan[1] of Helstone=Alice Da. of Allex. Penhellick of Helston in Com. Cornwall / in Com. Cornwall

Nicho. Buging[2] of S⁺ Keverne in=²Dorithy Da. of Haniball Vivion Com. Cornwall liveing 1620. / of Trelaworen in Cornwall

Fran. 2 — John 3

Katherin 1 — Jane 2

Haniball 1 sone ætat. 14, 1620

Phillip 3 Da.

Bridget 4 Da.

NICHOLAS BOGANS.

Bond.

ARMS. 1. *Arg., on a chevron sa.* 3 *bezants.* 2. *Arg., 3 stags' heads, 2, 1, couped sa, collar'd arg.* 3. *Maynard.* 4. *Coryton.*
CREST. *A demi Pegasus, Azure, winged and powdered with stars Or, with a crescent for difference.*

Rich. Bonde of Saltash in Com. Cornub.=Elizab. Da. & Coh. of Coriton.

John sans issue

Will'm Bond of Saltash mar. Katherin Da. of John Fitz of Devonsh.

Thomas Bond de Earth=Jone Da..... de Com. Cornwall 2 fil. / relicta T.... / Tome

Willmot filia Haughton de Haughton=Will'm Bonde of=Jane Da. of Tho. Sponre tower in Com. Lancash. relicta Phill. / Holewoode in / of Northill in com. Corn-
Stroud / com. Cornwall / wall ux. 1

Will'm æt. 12 — Peter æt. 10

Elianor uxor Hugonis Rositer de Ilmist' in Com. Som'set

Thomas Bond=Margaret Da. of Christo- of Holewoode / pher Savery de Shilston et fil. et heres / modo Viscomes Devoniæ

Margaret fil. unica æt. sex diern' 25 Septemb. 1620

Will'ms Bond fil. et hæres æt. 3 annoru'

Christopher 2 fil. æt. 2 annoru'

A

---

[1] This John Bogan came from Totnes. *Vide* Penhellick Ped. post.
[2] Named in Will of Haniball Vivian of Trelawarren, 30 Nov., 1608. Proved in London, 1609. Nicholas Bogan was one of the witnesses.

THE VISITATION OF THE COUNTY OF CORNWALL. 15

A |

John 2 fil. ætat. 34   Susanna ux. Petri   Anna ux. Ric. Roberts of
Hunt de Liskerd   Larack
Christopher 3 fil. æt 27

Richard 4 fil. æt. 24

*   THO. BOND.

Bond.

ARMS.   1. *Arg., on a chevron sa. 3 bezants.*   2. *Arg., 3 stags' heads, 2, 1, couped sa, collar'd arg.*   3. *Maynard.*   4. *Coryton.*
CREST.   A demi Pegasus, Azure, winged and powdered with stars Or.

Will'ms Bond ob. 20 H. VIII.

Ricus Bonde of Earth prope Salt Ash═Elizab. fil. et Coh. Coriton
ætat. 22 Annoru' 20 H. VIII.

Will'ms Bonde de Earth juxta═Katherina fil. Johis Fitz de Fitz Ford
Saltash in Com. Cornub.   in Com. Devon

Will'ms Bonde de Earth═Margareta fil. maxima et Coheres ... Fountaine
juxta Salt Ash   de Ugborough in Com. Devon

Margareta   Georg Bond═Argent Da. & Coh.   Joh'es Bond═Honora filia Johis
æt. 16   3 fil. de Salt-   of John Stronge of   fil. et heres   Carter de St Columbe
annor'   ash   Saltash Deceased   the higher in Cornw.

Margarete fil. unica   Will'ms Bond fil.   2. Johannes æt. 6   Dorothea 10
ætat. unius anni   primogenit æt. 11
annoru'   3. James æt. 2

Richard 4 fil.   Will'ms 2 fil. mar. Jone Sister to Sr Francis Crane═

Anthonie 5 fil.   Francisca fil. unica æt. 4

*   WILLIA' BOND.

---

* Extended in Harl. MSS. 1079, fo. 247 and 248.

Bonython.

Raphe Bonithan of Bonithan = Da. of Downe

- John Bonithan ob. s. p.
- Rich. Bonithan fil. et heres = Jane Da. & hey. of John Durant of Pensinans in Cornwall
- Edmond 2 son

Children of Rich. Bonithan and Jane:
- Jennet mar. to Tregolles
- Christian ux. Nich. Davy
- Bersaba ux. John Davy
- Elizab. 1 mar. to Condon after to Peter Cooke
- Isabell mar. to James Pawley
- Katherin — Margaret

- John Bonithan fil. et heres = Elianor Da. & Coh. of Willm Militon
- Jame Bonithon 2 filius = Margerie fil. Joh'is Melhuise of Truro merther

- Roskimer Bonithan sone & her.
- 2. Willm
- 3. John
- Elizab.
- John Bonithan de Cullum Minor fil. et heres = Margerie Da. of John Kerne al's Tresilian de Tresilian

- 1. Anne
- 2. Margerie
- 3. Mary
- 4. Prudence
- Willm Bonithon fil. primogenitus ætat. 6 annoru'
- John 2 fil. ætat. unius anni et dimidiu'

- Rob't 2 fil. mar.
- Nicholas 3 fil. mar. Anne Da. of Hugh Monday of Tregony
- Thomas 4 fil. now goldsmith in Chepeside mar. Alice Da. of Purforoy de Com. Leicter
- Anne unmaried

JO. BONYTHON.

Bonython.

Bonythan & Mileton to be quartered.

Raph Bonith'n. of Bonytham.

Rich. Bonyth'n. = Jane Da. & hey. of Jo. Durant of Pensinans in Cornwall.

John Bonytham sone and heire = Ellinor Da. & Coheyre of Wm Mylyton.
A

A

| Richard 2 — Edmond 3 | Anne ux' Walter Rosscarock | Elizb. ux' Hen. Pomeroy of Tregeny | Reskimer Bonytha' of Bony-tha'. high Shreife of the Countie of Cornwall liveing 1620. | =Lowday Da. of Wm Kendall of Lostwithan in Cornwall [1] |

Tho. Bonitha' sone & heyre=Fran. Da. of Erasmus Waller of London.

John sone & heire ætat. 2. 1620.

THO. BONYTHON.

Bosabarne.

Tho. Bossaverne of St. Just in Cornw.

Martin Bossavern of St. Just [2]=Jane Da. of Rich. Rob'ts. of Truro.

Tho. Bossaverne 2 filius mar.   John Bosseverne of St.=[3]Margerie Da. of Christop. Arundell Just first son   of Camborne

[3] Thomas fil. et heres ætat. 19 temp. visitacon's 1620   [3]John 2 fil. æt. 18   Mary æt. 15 — Anna æt. 14

JO. BOSAVARNE.

Boscawen.

Sciant present' et futuri q^d ego Alanus filius Henrici de Boskawen dedi et qui'te clamavi, &c. in Boscawen rose, &c. sans dat.

Sciant present' et futuri q^d ego Radulphus de Kerrise filius Mabile de Tresole dedi et concessi Henrico de Boscawen, &c. sans Dat.

Sciant p^rsent. et futur' q^d ego Martinus eger filius davidi de Helleston omnino remisi et quietu' clamavi p. me et heredes meis et p. meis assig' totu' Jus q^d habui et

---

[1] Lostwithiel.
[2] Martyn Thomas al's Bosaverne. *Vide* Roberts' Pedigree post.
[3] Named in Will of Thomas Chiverton of Paul, 26 August, 1604. Proved in London 7th Feb., 1605.

q^d habere potui aut debui in tota villa in Boscawen rose et in tota terra dicte ville c'm omn'bʒ pertin' suis in sicco et humido Henrico filio Rob'ti de eadem Boscawen rose, &c. sans Dat.

Sciant et p^{r}sent' q^d ego Will'ms. filius Nicholai Scutoris de Porthenes dedi quietu' clamavi et hac p^{r}senti carta confirmavi unam placeam qui habui in Brewory coram capite domus rectoris Sci Pawlia a parte superiori dictis (*sic*) domus' Henric' filio Henrici de Boscawen-rose, &c. sans dat.

Sciant p^{r}sent' et futur' q^d ego Tho. de Trewoof inspexi cartam quam Henricus filius Henrici de Boscawen rose habuit de Henrico de Boscawen rose et Havisia uxori eiusdem in hac verba, &c. sans Dat.

Reverend . . . . in Christo filio et hered. de Tresula ac suis . . . . Henrico de Boscawen rose salt. quia dedi Henrico filio et heredi meo totam terram meam in Landu de crouspoule cum pertin' &c. sans dat.

Pl'ita apud Westm' coram Robt. de Thorp et socijs suis Justic' d'no Regis de Banc' de termin Pasche Anno Regni Regis E. 3. 31.

Cornub. Johis de Boscawen Rose per Reginaldu' de 'Triwancamstell attornatu' suu' petit versus Thoma' Enedye duo messuagia et medietatem unius acre terre c'm p'ten. in Trevelli qui Henricus de Boscawen Rose p'oavus predict' Joh'is cuius heres ipse est dedit Rodulpho filio Phillippi de Trevilli Johanne filie Thome de Rosmodres et heredibus de corporibus ipsoru' Radulphi Johanne exeuntibus, et que post mortem predictorum Radulphe et Johanne ad p^{r}fatu' Johanne' reverti debent p' formam donationis predict' eo q^d predict' Radulphus et Johanna obierunt sine herede de corporibʒ suis exeuntibus, et unde dicit q^d predict'. Henricus de Boscawen proavus &c. fuit seizitus de tent' predict' cum pertin' in dominico suo de feodo et inde tempore pacis temp. dni Regis Edw. patris dni. regis nunc cepit ad val . . . . &c. et post modu' predict. Rodulphus et Johanna obierunt sine herede de corporibus eorunde' Radi' et Johanne exeuntibus. p' q^d terr. p^{r}dict. revertebantur p^{r}dicte Henric' ut Donatori et de ipse Henrico descendebat Jus cuidam Henrico ut filio et heridi &c. et de ipse Henric' descendebat ius cuidam Johanne ut filio et herid. et de ipse Johanni descendebat ius isti Johanni qui nunc petit ut filio et heredi A^o regni E. 3. 31.

Curia Henrici de Boscawen Rose fecit apud Boleth die sabbati prox post festu' beate Marie A^o Regni Regis E. 1. 30.

Sciant p^{r}sent. et futuri q^d ego Joh'es Boscawen Junior dedi concessi et hac p^{r}senti carta mea confirmavi Henrico Giffard Magro' D'nie [1] p'sone Ecc'lie de Lancfet Joh'i Tremain et Joh'i Boscawen patri meo o'nia maneria mea de Nansavallen, Trevaile, Trenancmoor ac o'nia messuag' terras et ten'te mea in Villa de Tregudon, Trenowre, Penwithes, Blaboll et Lamaelt, &c. a^o R. Rici 2 undecimo.

Sciant p^{r}sent. et futur' q^d ego Johes de Treguthnan dedi concessi et hac p^{r}senti carta mea confirmavi Johi de Boscawen rose et Johanne filie mei et heredibus de corporibus ipsoru' Johis et Johe exeuntibus o'nia messuagea mea et unam acram cornubicucijs terre in Treguthnan &c. una cum homgijs et Servicijs, &c. Johis Tully, Tho. de Prideis, &c. Dat. apud Tregothnan Octavo E. 3.

Hac Indentura facta inter Vivianu' Penrose Ch^r. et Margerie uxore' eius ex p'te una, et Joh'em Boscawen et Johanna' uxorem eius ex p'te altra testatu' q'd partes p^{r}dict. concordati sunt communibus amicis intervenientibus de om'ibus terris et ten'tes reditibus et servicijs que fuerunt Odonis de la Landa quondam viram predicte Margeria et patre predict' Joh'is, et que eidem Margere habet in dotem &c. a^o regni Regis H. 4. 5.

[1] ? Magister in Divinitate, a term used A.D. 1365. *Vide* Du Cange, Tom. 4, p. 481.

Osbertus de la Land cepit in uxorem Alicia' filiam Lawrencij Arundell, et habuerunt exitus Eurinu' de la Landa qui cepit in uxorem Aliciam filia' Odonis de Trevaile et Matilda' filie Johis de Reskimmer sorore Rogeri de reskimmer, qui Rogerus Reskimmer dedit duos partes omniu' terraru' suaru' in Tregiddin predictis Odonis de Trevaile et Matilde' sororis sue et heridibus de corporibus ipsoru' exeuntibus in perpetuu', et p^{r}dictus Eurinus habuit exitu' Odonem de la Land ex p^{r}dict. Alicia filie Odonis de Trevaile et Matilde sororis Rogeri de Reskimmer, et p^{r}dictus Odo de la Land cepit in uxorem Margeria' filia' Rad'i Raoll et habuerunt exitu' Johanna' que fuit maritata Johi Boscawen, et p^{r}dicti Johes et Johanna haberunt exitum Johannem, qui cepit in uxorem Roseam filiam Willmi Brett, et habuerunt exitu' Hugonam Boscawen qui cepit in uxorem Johannam filiam Rad'i de Trenouth et haberunt exitu' Richard'm Boscawenrose qui cepit in uxorem Matildam filiam et coheredem Lawrencij Trewonwall et Elionare Treville uxoris eius soror et hered. Willm's Treville A° E. IV. 19. et habuerunt exitum Joh'em Boscawen qui maritatus fuit Elizab. filie Nicholaij Lower de St. Wynow et habuerunt Hugonem Boscawen qui cepit in uxorem Philippam filie et heredem Nicholaij Carmino Armig' et Catherine filie et heredis Johis Wolvedon Armigeri et habuerunt exitu' Nicholau' Boscawen qui cepit in uxorem Aliciam filia' et heredem Johis Trevanion Armigeri et habuerunt exitu' Hugonem Boscawen, et Radagunda' nup. uxorem Will'mi Cooke de Hinam in Com. Glocestere Militis.

This bill indented made at Westm' the fourth daye of July the 20 yeare of o^r souvraing lo. King Henrie the VII. Witnesseth that Thomas Hobbes Clarke hath receyved in the name & for ye use and behouffe of o^r said souveraing lord of Rich. Boscawen in the Countie of Cornwall Esq. in redie monie V^{lb} of lawfull monie of England in full paiment of his fine made & given to ye Kings grace for his pardon to be released fro' the order of Knight of ye Bathe at ye creac'on of my Lo. Prince Henrie in wittnes whereof either partie interchangeablye have set their scales & subscribed theire names ye daye & yeare above rehersed.

p' me THOMA' HOBBES.

Decimo sext' feb. A° regni Regis E. VI. primo.

Cornub.
Recept de Hugonie Boscawen de Tregothnan Arg' p' fine suo milit' attachiat coram Rico' Rich. Ro' Southwell et Tho. Moyle Militibus Comissionarijs D'ni Regis in ea p'te assignatis Sum' 40^s.

p' WILL'M ALEXANDER.

Clericu'
WIMUNDI CAREW Armigero.

Be it known to all men by these presents y^t I John Arundell of Trerise K^t late sherief of the countie of Cornwall have receyved of Hugh Boscawen Esq. 4 Marks of Lawfull monie of England to the kinge & queenes maiesties uses for y^t he repaired not unto the Coronac'on of the queene, to receyve the order of Knighthood in Witnes whereof I the said John Arundell have subscribed my name, & set my seale the 18 of Januarie in the first & 2 yeare of King Phillip & Marie.

JOHN ARUNDELL of Trerise.

THE VISITATION OF THE COUNTY OF CORNWALL.

Boscawen.

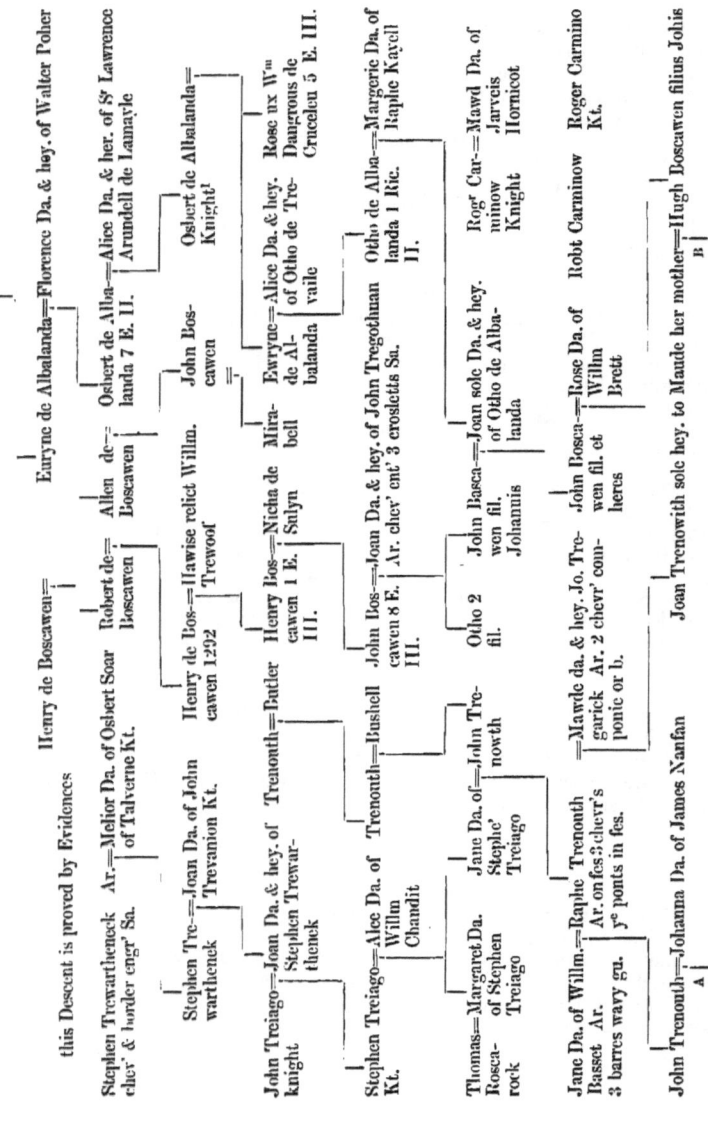

A | B

Trenouth = filia Penpons Ar. 3 Wolfes pas't B.

1 Elizab. Da. of Geofrey S[t] Aubin 38 H. VI. ux. 1 = Rich. Boscawen anno 6 E. IV. = 2 Mawde Da. & coh. of Lawrence Hallop of Trewonwall ux. 2 Or 3 bends Sa. & Elinor his wife Da. & hey. of Willm Treville

John Trenouth = Honor Da. of Willm Tregarthyn

Bennett ob. s. p.

John Boscawen fil. Rici = Elizab. Da. of Nicholas Lower 22 E IV.

All these descents were exactly proved by deedes

5 Grace ux Wm. Kempe de Blisland — 4 Elizab. ux Ric. Curteis sans issue

Lawrence ob. s. p.

John Boscawen son of John = Margaret Da. of Tho. Trethurf & Coh. of Edw. Courtney Erle of Devon

Hugh Boscawen 2 son heire to his Brother = Phillip Coh. of Nicholas Carminow

1 Jane ux Ric. Trevener[2]

2 Christian ux Tho[s] Ninnis of Ninnis[3] 2. Walter Burlace — 3 Isabell ux Samson Mannington

Thomas Bascowen ob. S. Prole

3 Petronell mar. to Peter Mayow

7 Katherin mar. Nanscaven 2. Ric. Gedy

5 Elizab. mar. to Richard Poyle 2. Ric. Trevilian

4 Mary mar. to Peter Coffin

7 Edward mar. Jane Da. of Will. White

1. John, 2. John } sine p'le

4. Willm sans issue

5 Hugh mar. Mary Da. of Tho. Tredinick

Mary mar. to Willm Bird de Foy

Hugh. fil. primogenit. æt. 24

6 Georg mar. Eliz. y[e] hey. of Tho. Carnarther

Nicholas 3 son of Hugh = Alice Da. & he. of John Trevanion of y[e] 2 house

1 Joan mar. to Walter Gav'gan 2. to John Barrett

2 Alice mar. to Richard Kendall

6 Marg[t] unmaried

Hugh fil. primogenit. æt. 23

2. Edward æt. 20

3. John

Grace ob.s.p.

Hugh Boscawen fil. et heres

Ric. Cole de Buckish in Com. Devo' vir primus = Radigan fil. 2 = Sr Willm Cooke of Highnam in Com't Gloucest[r] 2 Maritus

H. BOSCAWEN.

[1] This Osbert seems to have been entered in error as he does not appear in the narrative ped., pp. 18 and 19 ante., or De Banco Roll 50 Ed. III., Hill. Term, in which these descents are given.

[2] She afterwards mar. Lawrence Courtney, *vide* Harl. MSS. 4031, fo. 61 and 62.

[3] This is probably a mistake for Enis, as that name is inserted, and the first Ninnis altered to Innis, in the original Harl. MSS. 1164, apparently by another hand.

Bossawsacke.

Sciant presentes & futuri q^d ego Petrus Bosawsake dedi concessi & hac p'senti carta mea confirmavi Waltero Bosawsak heredibus & assignatis suis om'ia messuagio terr. in villa de Bosawsake &c. habend. et tenend. &c. Hijs testib₃ Johe Penans & alijs. Dat' apud Bosawsake A° 5 H. V.

Seal.

Pateat Univ'sis p' p'sentes me Petrum Bosawsake dedisse et concessi Joh'e Penpan & Joh'em Penwaren demisisse &c. Dat' apud Bosawsack A° 5 H. V.

Seal.

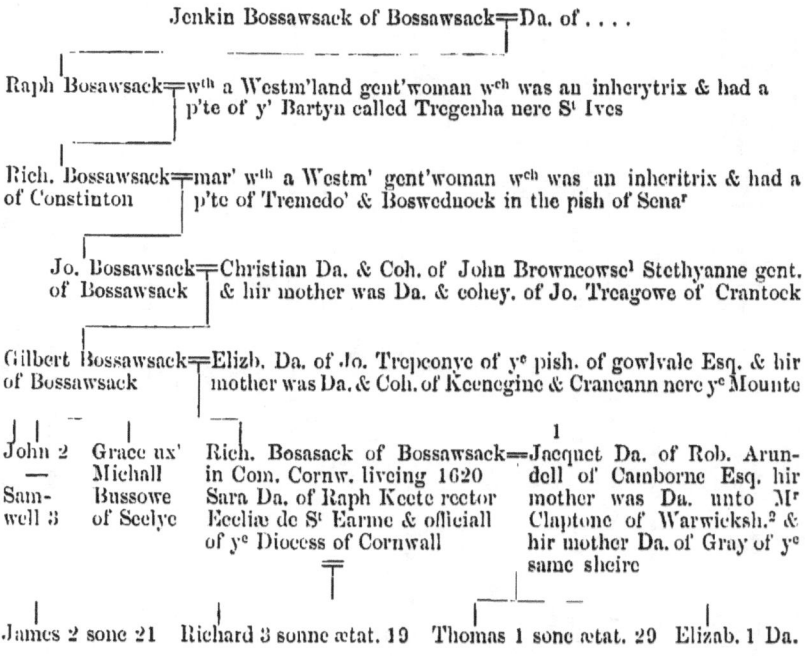

RICHARD BOSSAWSACKE.

---

[1] Burncoose in Parish of St Stithians.
[2] Willm Clapton of Stafford. *Vide* Arundell Pedigree ante.

Bosustowe.

Sciant presentes et futuri q^d ego Willms. de Dodustow dedi concessi & hac presenti carta mea confirmavi Rico. filio Radi. de Dodustow et heredibʒ. suis de corpore Johe. filie Johis. de Erisie exeuntibʒ omnia messuag. terr. et ten' mea in villis de Dodustow, Trevyan et Chinals, cum omnibʒ. p'tinentijs, &c.   Hijs testibʒ. Johe. de Trewethy Tho. Rosmorders, Rico. Pendre, Petro Erisi, Ric'o Vivian et alijs. Dat. apud Dodustow A° 50 Edward 3.

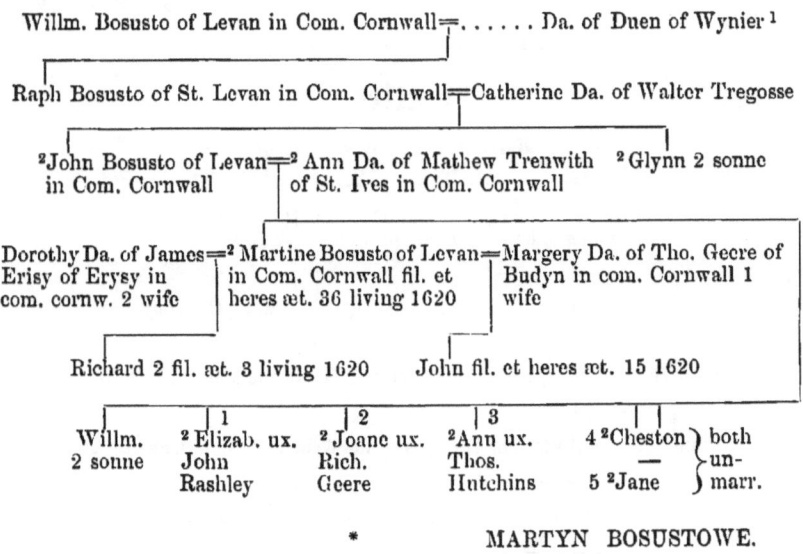

*   MARTYN BOSUSTOWE.

Bray.

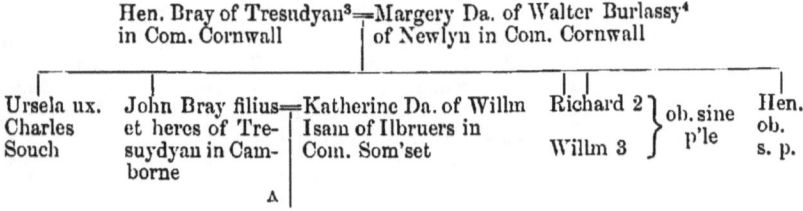

[1] Dewen of Gwinear.
[2] Will of John Bosustow 8 July, 1604. Proved in London 19 June, 1605. All so marked are named in the will ; also a brother William, of unsound mind, left in custody of his son Martin.
[3] Treswithen in Parish of Camborne.   [4] Burlace?
* Extended in Harl. MSS. 1079, fo. 115 and 116.

GEORGE BRAY.

```
                                          A
┌─────────────┬──────────────┬──────────────────────┬───────────────────┬─────────────┐
Mary ux.      Katherine      George Bray of Tre-=Elizab. Da. of Hen. Dan-   Willm 2
Peter         ux. John       suydyan fil. et heres  vers of Dancy in Com.   son mar.
Treunwith     James          æt. 54 living 1620     Wilts 2 Brother to Sr   ye Da. of
                                                    John Danvers           . . . .

┌──────────────────────────────────────┬────────────────────────┬───────────────────┐
Hen. Bray fil. et heres æt. 24 liveing 1620   Amies 2 son æt. 23    Willm 3 fil. æt. 22
```

Buller.

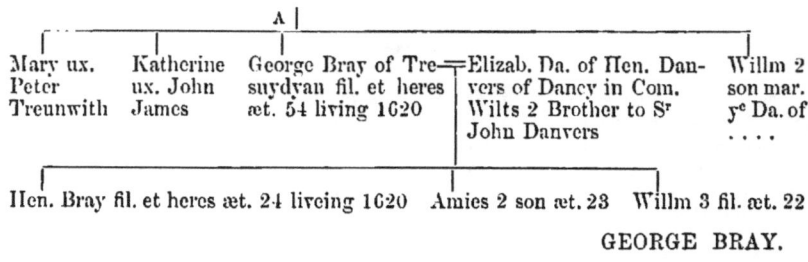

Ralfe Buller of Wood Esq.=

John Buller=Ann da. of Roger Staly. Argt
sonne & heir | a chev' betwene 3 ◊ B.

John Buller Esq. sonne & heir=. . . . da. of Gourney

John Buller Esq.[1]=. . . . da. & heire of Jo. Beauchamp of Lillesdon

John Buller of Lillesdon Esq.=Ann da. & heir of Nich. Chedington

John Buller of Lillesdon Esq.=Thamasine da. of Orchard

John Buller of Lillesdon=Alice da. of Sidnam of Brampton

Ann da. of Giles Lo.=Allexander Buller=Elizabeth da. of Sr John
Daubney 1 wife | 2 | Horsey Kt 2 wife

John Buller=Dorothy da. of Sr   Francis Buller of=Thomasine da.   Mary wife to
sonne & heir | Jo. Kellaway Kt   Shillingham 2   of Tho. Wil-   Thomas
A   sonne   liams Esq.   Wise of Sid-
                                                   B   enham Kt.

---

[1] He is called Nicholas Buller in the Pedigree in Coll. of Arms.

[2] A descent is left out here in the original MS., viz., Richard Buller, who married Margaret, daughter and coheiress of Thomas Tretherffe, and widow of Edward Courtney of Lanrake. It is entered in Heralds' College Pedigree, and Harl. MSS. 1079, and is proved by Inq. p. Mort. Alexander Buller, 18 Hen. VIII., No. 17. Richard Buller's will, dated in Nov., 1555, is recited in Inq. P. M. 2 and 3 Phil. and Mary, part 1, No. 5 ; his wife Margaret sole executrix ; he names his son Francis, daughter Mary, son-in-law Edward Courtney, son-in-law Peter Courtney, his cousin John Buller, 2d son of his nephew John Buller, his sister Abbyngton, and uncle Thos. Buller. Margaret, his widow, died 28 June, 1576 ; and Peter Courtney, Esq., her son and heir, was aged 40 years and more. Vide Inq. P. M. Margaret Buller, 18 Eliz., part 1, No. 22.

THE VISITATION OF THE COUNTY OF CORNWALL. 25

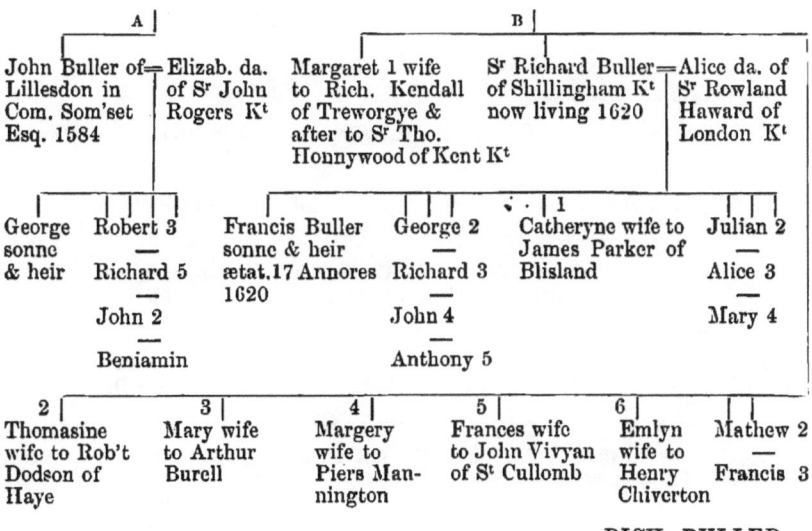

RICH. BULLER.

Burell.

ARMS.—*Ar. on bend Sa. 3 Stags' heds cabosed Or.*

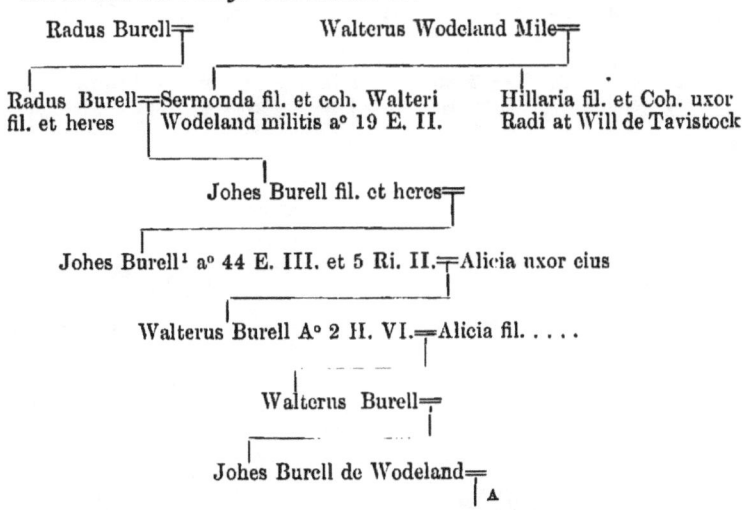

[1] Ped. Fin. 8 Hen. IV., No. 4. Lands in Trematon, Burrell, Saltash, &c.

THE VISITATION OF THE COUNTY OF CORNWALL.

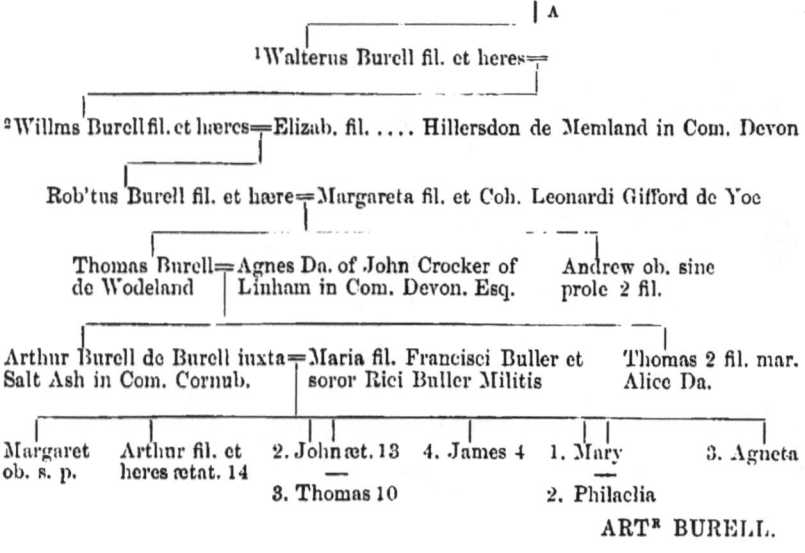

ART^R BURELL.

Burges.

Ellice Burgesse of Trwro in Com. Cornwall=
|
Tho. Burgesse of Trwro=Honor Da. of Hump. Sidnam of Tregonie

Humph. 2 — Rich. 3
Anne ux'. Rob. Trethewye
Hen. 2 sone=Jane Da. of Leiuftenant of Truro the foresaid Antho. Pye.
Tho. Bur=Elizb.⁴Da. gesse of Trwro living³ 1620 of Antho. Pye gent
Jane⁵ ux' Ephram Boniter

John⁶ 2 — Hen.¹⁰ 3
Calip — Josuah
Janes¹³ — Allicia
Rob.⁷ 1 sone æt. 18 1620
Honor 1 — Anne 2
Constance⁸ 3 — Elizb.⁹ 4

Humph.¹¹ 4 Twins¹²

THO. BURGES.

¹ Inq. P. M. 21 Edw. IV., No. 37. He died 13 Aug., 21 Edw. IV.
² Aged 8 years at time of Father's death.
³ M.P. for Truro 1 and 21 James I.
⁴ Mar. 27 Nov., 1598.
⁵ Bapt. 12 August, 1599.
⁶ ,, 3 Feb., 1604–5.
⁷ ,, 29 August, 1602.
⁸ Bapt. 13 Feb., 1613–4.
⁹ ,, 30 Dec., 1617.
¹⁰ ,, 12 March, 1606.
¹¹ ,, 17 Sept., 1612.
¹² ,, 8 Sept., 1611.
¹³ ,, 24 Nov., 1616.

Truro Parish Registers.

Busvargus.

John Busvargus of St Just in Com. Corw.=Jenefer Da. of Jno. Sparnon

    John Busvargus=Mary Da. of Tho. Randall of . . .

Alice mar. to Nich. Bolson of Paule | John Busvergus=Agnes Da. of John Hill of Gwendon in Cornw. | 2. Elizab. | 3. Tomazin

JOHN BUSVARGUS.

Byll.

ARMS.—*Azure three griffins' heads erased* 2, 1, *Arg. quartering Arg. a chevron Sa. betw. three estoiles gules.*

Edmond Byll[1] of Stoke in Com. Cornw.=Isaball Da. & hey. of John Skenoke

    Wm. Bile of St. Stephens in Com. Cornw. 2 sonne = Phillip Da. of Robt Hill of Helligam in Cornwall

Christopher Bill of Santon testified by Mr Estcott in the olde visitation (*an interpolation.*) | Christ' Bile of Santon in Cornwall liveing 1620 = Agath. da. of John Arondell of Bliston in Com. Cornwall

Gorge 2 — Barnard 3 | Grenvile sone & heire at. 9 1620 | Christopher 4 sonne | Marye 1 — Agathe 2

By mee
CHRYSTOP. BYLL.

---

[1] Sampson Byll, eldest son of Edmund, in a Chancery Suit, 12 June, 1578 (Elizb. B & A. S. s. 6. No. 36), names his brother John, whose wife was Mary, and da. Alice. Descents from Sampson Byll are also registered in the Coll. of Arms.

* There are numerous entries of the name of Becle in the Registers of the Par. of St. Ewe. This pedigree is much extended in Harl. MS. 1079, fo. 191-2.
        Roger Beyle, M.P. for Launceston, 6 Ed. III.
        Walter Byle of Lanccote, M.P. for Launceston 6 Ed. III.

Byrd.

Christ' Byrd of Stoke in Sussex but = Joane Da. of Holmes
came fro' Saffron Waldon in Esex | in Sussex

Tho. Byrd of = Joane Da. of Lick-   John Byrd of Aple- = Cicilye Da. of Adryan
Chichester | fald of Sussex   drum in Sussex | Mason of Southampton

Thomas = Ellinor Geo. Byrd of   Raph Byrd of   MaryDa. = Willm' = Grace da.
Byrd | Da. of Barne in Dor-   Tremeer in   of Hugh | Byrd | of Wm.
       | Beets   setsh. mar.   Cornw. maried   Bosca- | of | Frye of
       | of   Judith Da. of   Rebecka Da. of   wen of | Toye | Somer-
       | hert-   Seward of   Hen. Blaxton of   Tregow- | | setsheire
       | fordsh. Dowlans   Blaxton Halle in   non | |
                                   the Bish. of Dirw'
                                   Doctor of Divinitie

         Christop. Byrd   John Byrd

Not signed.

Carew.*

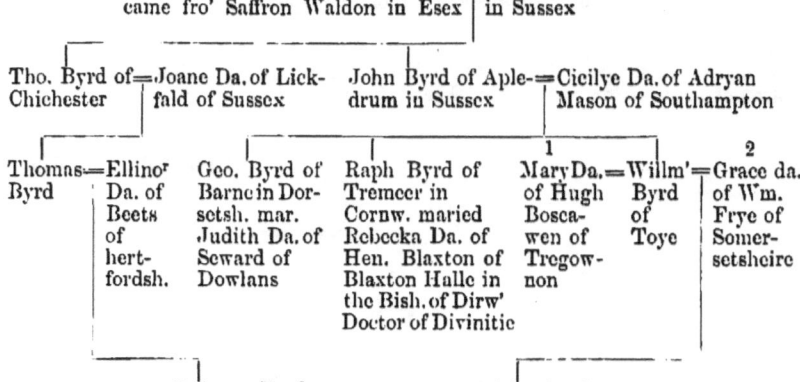

Tho. Carew of Anthony Esq. = Elizb. Da. of Sr Rich. Edgcomb
                           | of Edgcomb in Cornw.

Sr George Carew = Thomazin   Rich. Carew[1] = Julian Da. of John   Elizb. ux' Jam.
Kt. Mr of the | Da. of Sr   of Anthony | Arundell of Trerice   Erisy of Erisey
Court of Wardes| Fran.   Esq. liveing | & Cohey. to hir mo-   in Cornw.
               | Godolphin   1620 | ther Katherin Cos-
                                          | worth.
Fran. Carew sone & hey.
                                            A

---

[1] Author of the 'Survey of Cornwall.'

* Caerau pl. of Caer, a wall, mound, or fortress. Pugh. For Caerau, or the Camps, see Fenton's Pembrokeshire, p. 578. Kaeryw family, see Lewys Dwnn, by Sir Sam. Meyrick; and for Carrw, Karreu, Carru, Carrow, and other various spellings of the name on Deeds, see Harl. MS. 3288, fo. 131-2. See also Nicholas' Annals and Antiq. of Wales, vol. ii., p. 853. "*Caerau*, by helpless foreign tongues pronounced *Carew*."

THE VISITATION OF THE COUNTY OF CORNWALL. 29

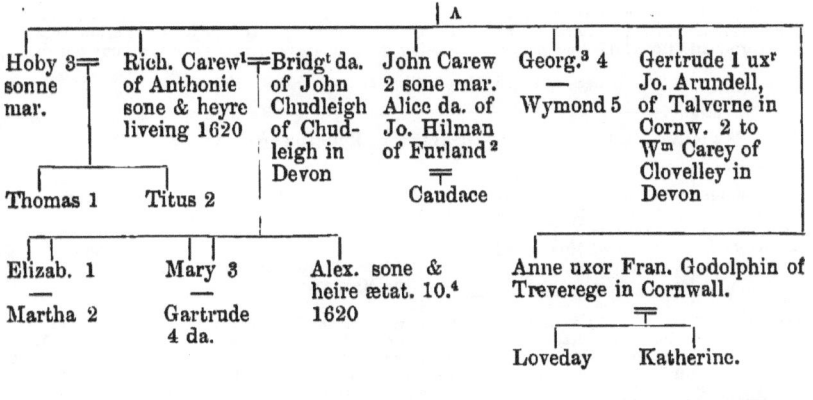

GEOR. CAREW.

---

[1] Rich. Carew mar. Miss Rolle of Heanton, as 2nd wife, and had by her two sons, John and Thomas of Barley near Exeter, from the latter the Sawles of Penrice descend, inheriting Barley.
[2] Al's Helman or Holman, mar. at St Thomas, Exeter, 9 Dec., 1615. This John Carew was styled the "One handed" from having lost his right hand at the siege of Ostend, A.D. 1601. He afterwards settled as a Merchant in Mevagissey. His son Richard died without issue, and his five daughters and coheiresses married into the Hoblyn, Tremayne, and Trevanion families.
[3] George Carew mar. Jane Hockin at Lanteglos by Camelford, 15 Feb., 1624-5, and his numerous descendants appear on the Parish Registers to this day. They contemplated laying claim to the Anthony estates about the commencement of the present century. Mr. William Carew, Mayor of Camelford, was buried 7 March, 1737.
[4] Born 30 August, 1609, and baptized at Anthony 4 Sept., 1609. Par. Reg.

* As the descendants of the distinguished family of Carew are still numerous in the Counties of Cornwall and Devon, a more extended notice than ordinary may not be out of place. The earlier generations have been somewhat confused, but the following extract from Sir Simon D'Ewes' Collection, vol. ii., fo. 87, Harl. MS. 380, may be relied on. It is entitled "The Copy of a Descent of Carew written on paper remaining in the Earl of Arundel's librarie being as followeth, which seemes to be the very truth faithfully transcribed out of and compared with the original A° D'n. 1646."
"Johannes Dei gratia rex Angliæ &c. sciatis quod reddimus et hac carta nostra confirmavimus Willo de Carrio Manerium de Mulesford, cum pertinenciis suis quod Henricus rex avus Regis Henrici patris n're dedit Geraldo filio Walteri, Avo Odonis patris predicti Williclmi de Carrio tenendum &c." (This confirmation is well known.)

> "Walter
> Gerald son of Walter
> William Fitz Gerold
> Odio de Carrio
> William de Carrio
> Nicholas de Carrio
> William de Carrio
> Nicholas de Carrio
> Nicholas de Carrio.'

THE VISITATION OF THE COUNTY OF CORNWALL.

The following Pedigree, compiled partly from Harl. MS. 1155, and partly from the Carew MSS., vol. 626, fo. 89, at Lambeth Palace (in the hand-writing of George Carew, Earl of Totnes), will throw additional light on the origin of other noble houses deriving from the same source.

Otheus, Constable of Windsor temp. Ed. Confess.
=
Walter Constable of Windsor=Gladys da. of Rywallon ap Conwyn Pr. of Wales.*

William, eldest son of whom the Lords Windsor descend.

Giraldus de Windsor 2nd son, was Constable of Pembroke, to whom K. Hen. I. gave the Manor of Moulesford in Berkshire.
=
Nesta dau. to Rees ap Theodor Maur Pr. of Wales, had children by Hen. I.
| Henry. sl'n in Anglesea of whom the Mylers descent.
=
Stephen Constable of Abertivi in Wales.

Dau. mar. Barry of whom the Lord Barry Viset. Butevant? descend

2 **David** Archdeacon of Cardigan and Bp. of St David's.

1 **William Fitzgerald** lived at Pembroke and there died 1173.

3 **Maurice Fitzgerald** went into Ireland with Earl Strongbow and died there, of whom the Geraldines are descended. Dermot Mac Morrough gave him Wexford Town.

Robert Fitz Stephen went into Ireland with his brother Maurice & had by the gift of King H. II. the one half of the kingdom of Cork at 30 knight's fees and died without issue, when his nephew Raymond possessed the same. Myles Cogan, another nephew of Robert, had the other half of Cork by gift of K. H. II.

Raymundus surn. le Gros bur. in the Abbey of Molana near unto Youghal, after whose death the Carews yt were issued fro' Odo Fitz Stephen. Of this Raymond's natural children the Lord Fitzmorice of Kerry, the Baron of Brentchurch, the families of Pendergast and Graces do descend.
=
Priscilla sister to Ric. Strongbow E. of Pembroke s.p.

Odo Carrio now called Carew in Pembrokeshire in Wales.

Willms Dn's de Carrio.(ª)=
to whom King John restored the Lo. of Moulesford in Berksh. wh. K. Hen. I. gave unto Walter the father of Gerald.

Marg' da. of Ric. son of Tancred.

Solomon. Walter.
Stephen. Tho.
Rob.
Tho.

Nicholas infra æt. 15. H. III.=**Kath'n** da. & coh. of Myles Lord Courcye.*

Morice.

William=

Maurice s. p.

Robert bur. at Kilkenny s. p.

Nicholas (ᵇ) Baron of Carew 5 E. II.
=
Avice da. & heir of Ric. Tuitt of Marston, renupta Willo Appledore. or Appeldryffeld. (Glover, Harl. MS. 245.)

Car. MSS., Vol. 635.

Sir **Nich.** Lord Carew=**Avice** da. & heyre of Digon Baron of Odrone in Ireland.

2 **Thos.** de C.

(1) **Elinor** da. & heir of Wm Mohun of Ottery.
=
John Carreu Lord of C. &c. ob. 17 E. 2.
=
(2) **Joan** da. of Sir Gilbert Talbot.

3 **Will** de Carrew Knt.

David de C.
|
David.
(Glover, Deeds Harl. MSS. 245.)

A   B

(ª) The MSS. differ here. The Harl. MS. 1155 states that this William de Carrio left a dau. & heyre, married to Adam de Montgomery, whose posterity assumed the name of Carew ; but the Earl of Totnes' MS. continues male line as given. The Inq. P. M. of Ada de Montgomerie, Aº 18 Ed. I., No. 5, gives Thomas, his son, æt. 30, and Robert, æt. 18, his son, by Isabel de Constantin, as his heirs.

(ᵇ) Vol. 626, Carew MSS., gives,—
Nich. de C. Lord of Mulesford, = Avice, sist. & heyr to John son to Carreu, and Idron.   Hugh Peverell.

Harl. 3288, cites the gift of the Manr Weston Peverell, jux. Plymº, by John Peverell, to his sister Amicia and her husb. Nich. C., followed by a note of "the Office of Wallingford, taken 2 E. III. 1328," wherein she was declared sister and heir of David Martyn, Bp. of St. David's.

THE VISITATION OF THE COUNTY OF CORNWALL. 31

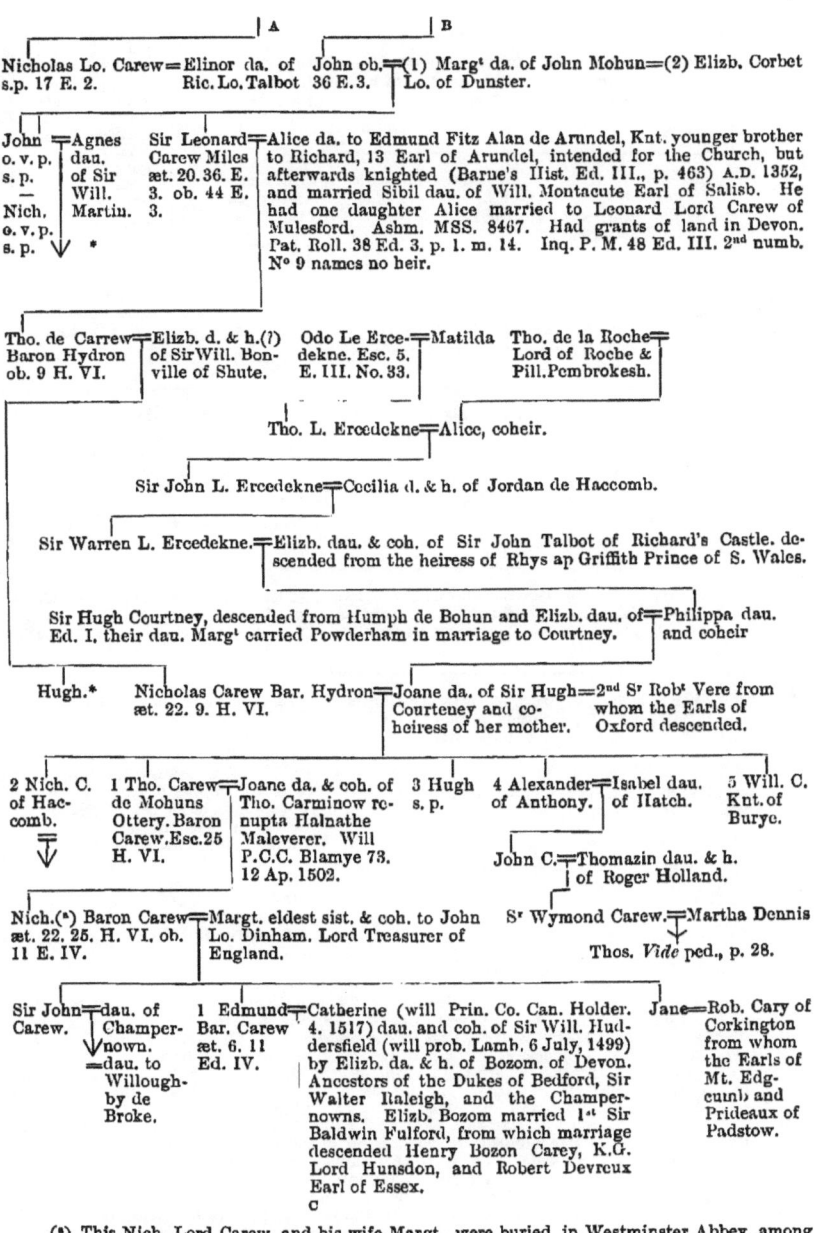

(*) This Nich. Lord Carew, and his wife Margt., were buried in Westminster Abbey, among the kings and queens of England. *Vide* Hals. Cornw.

* These are all from Sir John Maclean's 'Life of Sir Peter Carew.'

THE VISITATION OF THE COUNTY OF CORNWALL.

C

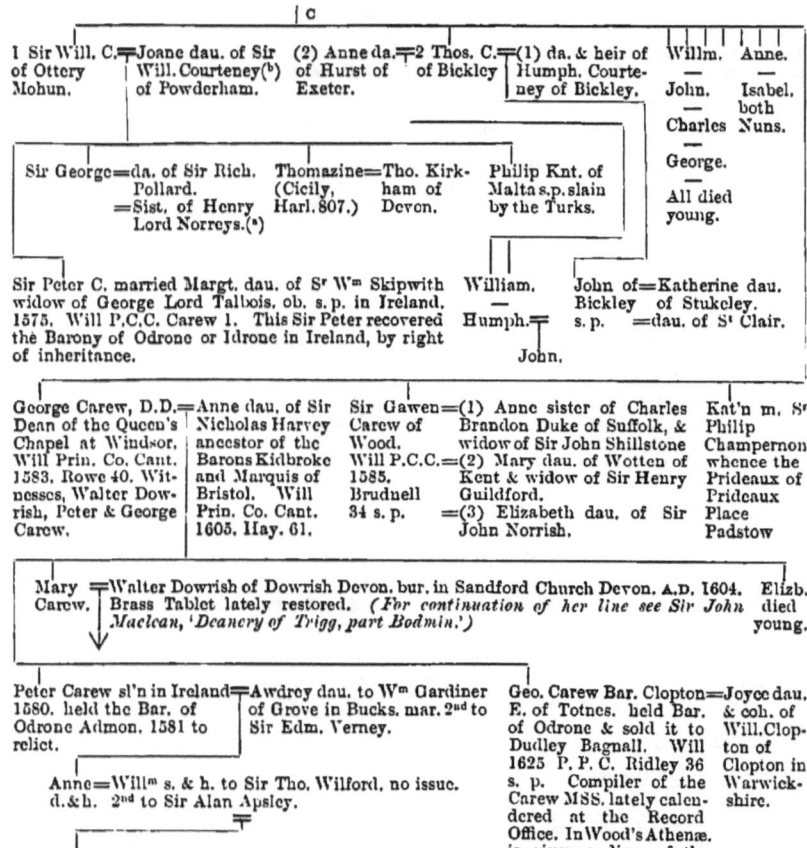

1 Sir Will. C.=Joane dau. of Sir Will. Courteney(ᵇ) of Powderham. | (2) Anne da.=2 Thos. C.=(1) da. & heir of Willm. Anne. of Ottery Mohun. | of Hurst of Exeter. | of Bickley | Humph. Courteney of Bickley. | John. Isabel, both Charles Nuns.

Sir George=da. of Sir Rich. Pollard. =Sist. of Henry Lord Norreys.(ᵃ) | Thomazine=Tho. Kirkham of Devon. (Cicily, Harl. 807.) | Philip Knt. of Malta s.p. slain by the Turks. | George. All died young.

Sir Peter C. married Margt. dau. of Sʳ Wᵐ Skipwith widow of George Lord Talbois, ob. s. p. in Ireland. 1575. Will P.C.C. Carew 1. This Sir Peter recovered the Barony of Odrone or Idrone in Ireland, by right of inheritance. | William. Humph.= John. | John of=Katherine dau. Bickley of Stukeley. s. p. =dau. of Sᵗ Clair.

George Carew, D.D.=Anne dau. of Sir Dean of the Queen's Chapel at Windsor. Will Prin. Co. Cant. 1583. Rowe 40. Witnesses, Walter Dowrish, Peter & George Carew. | Nicholas Harvey ancestor of the Barons Kidbroke and Marquis of Bristol. Will Prin. Co. Cant. 1605. Hay. 61. | Sir Gawen=(1) Anne sister of Charles Carew of Brandon Duke of Suffolk, & Wood. widow of Sir John Shillstone Will P.C.C.=(2) Mary dau. of Wotten of Brudnell Kent & widow of Sir Henry 34 s. p. Guildford. =(3) Elizabeth dau. of Sir John Norrish. | Kat'n m. Sʳ Philip Champernon whence the Prideaux of Prideaux Place Padstow

Mary Carew. =Walter Dowrish of Dowrish Devon. bur. in Sandford Church Devon. A.D. 1604. Brass Tablet lately restored. (For continuation of her line see Sir John Maclean, 'Deanery of Trigg, part Bodmin.') | Elizb. died young.

Peter Carew sl'n in Ireland=Awdrey dau. to Wᵐ Gardiner 1580. held the Bar. of Odrone Admon. 1581 to relict. | of Grove in Bucks. mar. 2ⁿᵈ to Sir Edm. Verney. | Geo. Carew Bar. Clopton=Joyce dau. E. of Totnes. held Bar. & coh. of of Odrone & sold it to Will. Clopton of Dudley Bagnall. Will 1625 P. P. C. Ridley 36 Clopton in s. p. Compiler of the Warwickshire. Carew MSS. lately calendered at the Record Office. In Wood's Athenæ. is given a diary of the principal events in the life of the Earl of Totnes, read before the Soc. of Antiquaries in 1794.

Anne=Willᵐ s. & h. to Sir Tho. Wilford. no issue. d. & h. 2ⁿᵈ to Sir Alan Apsley.

Peter Apsley, s. p. Adm. granted 1661 to Sir Alan Apsley, the half brother.

(ᵃ) Sir Simon D'Ewes, Harl. MS. 380.
The family possessions were very extensive in the Kingdom of Ireland. "In the book of the tenures called the White Book, remaynyng in the Exchequier at Dublin," it is thus recorded, that in Cork Robᵗ Carew held 30 Services." (Carew MSS., Vol. 635, fo. 41.) A list is given of "the landes wh. the Ancestors of Sʳ Peter Carewe did possess in the Countries of Cork, Desmond, and Kerry and by him claymed as his inheritance," representing 68 horse and 2600 foot. "Besides the lands here mentioned with the Countie of Cork the Carews at that tyme had landes in sundrye other Counties, viz. in Catherloghe, the Baronie of Odrone, and in Methe the Barony of Marston Tute, etc., Stellonorgan and other landes in Dublin, much lande in the Countie of Waterford and clls where." In A.D. 1568 (Rot. Pat. Banc. 14° Eliz., Dublin) it appears "that Sir Peter Carewe Knight was founde as trewe and lawful heyre to the Baronye of Odrone als Hydrone." (Carew MSS.) Sir Peter bequeathed this Barony by Will to his Cousin Sir Peter with remainder to George Carew, who successively entered into possession, and Geo. C., the last holder, sold it. The great extent of the Carew territories in Ireland was subject of disquietude to the State. King Edw. III. gave the Wardship of John Carew in respect to the Irish lands to his Queen Philippa. (Carew MSS.)

Carew.

Sr Mathew Carie [1] = Elizab. fil. et coh. Sr James Cromar of Tunsted in Kent — Willm 2 filius — first son

Eliza.[2] filia

Not signed.

Carminowe.

ARMS.—*Az. a bend Or, with a label of three Gules.*
CREST.—*A dolphin embowed Or.*

(The shield is drawn for twelve quarters, eleven left blank.)

Oliverus de Carmynowe Mile concessit om'ia Blada sua in terris crescentia ac etiam om'ia mobilia et immobilia Rogero de Carmynowe filio suo pro centu' Libris Stirlingeru.' Dat. apud Carmynowe A° regni Regis Edw. terrtij post conquest. Angliæ duodecimo A° Domini 1338.

SEAL.—*Circular, enclosing a shield charged with a bend only, inscribed* SIGILLVM. OLIVERI. DE. CARMYNOW.

Thomas de Carmynow præd le prendru Elizabeth filie Au Meunsier Raufe Beaupoll, Chivaler, a sa femme p' le Chart. fait au temps Edwardi tierce Le Ann. de son Reige 31 ann. 1357.

SEAL.—*Similar to the above, but inscribed* + SIGILLVM THOME CARMINOW.

Roger Carmynow [3] = Katherin Da. of Sherley
A

---

[1] Sir Matthew Carew, LL.D., father of this Sir Matthew, married Alice Ingpenny, widow of Sir John Rivers, Mayor of London; he was uncle of Richard Carew the historian, and was buried in London, at St. Dunstan's in the West, 2 August, 1618, where the inscription on his monument throws a different light on the story told by Richard Carew in his Survey respecting the quarrel between Joan Courtenay, heiress of Archedekne, and Thomas Carew, her eldest son. It states that the said Thomas Carew having been sufficiently well provided for by his patrimonial inheritance, out of maternal solicitude, and in no vindictive spirit, Joan distributed her own seventeen manors among her youngest sons. The inscription on Sir Matthew's tablet, names only three children,—Matthew, Thomas, and Martha; but in the Registers of St. Dunstan's we find the following entries of baptism, viz.—

Elizabeth, da. of Mr. Doctor Carye, — 13 Nov., 1580;
Wymond, sonne of Mathewe Carewe, Doctor, and one of ye Masters of the Chauncery — Dec. 11, 1586;
Walter, son of ditto — 8 July, 1588;

[2] Baptised at St Dunstan's in the West, London, 28 May, 1615.
[3] Oliver Carmino, father of this Roger, was son and heir of Roger Carmino, and æt. 30 et amplius 2 Ed. II. (Inq. p. mort. 2 Edw. II., No. 73), and it appears from an Inq. p. mort. 19 Rich. II., No. 15, that Johanna was daughter and heiress of Thomas Carminowe, and a Ward of the King, and that she died on the 21 Feb., 1396, when John Arundell, æt. 28, and John

F

34 THE VISITATION OF THE COUNTY OF CORNWALL.

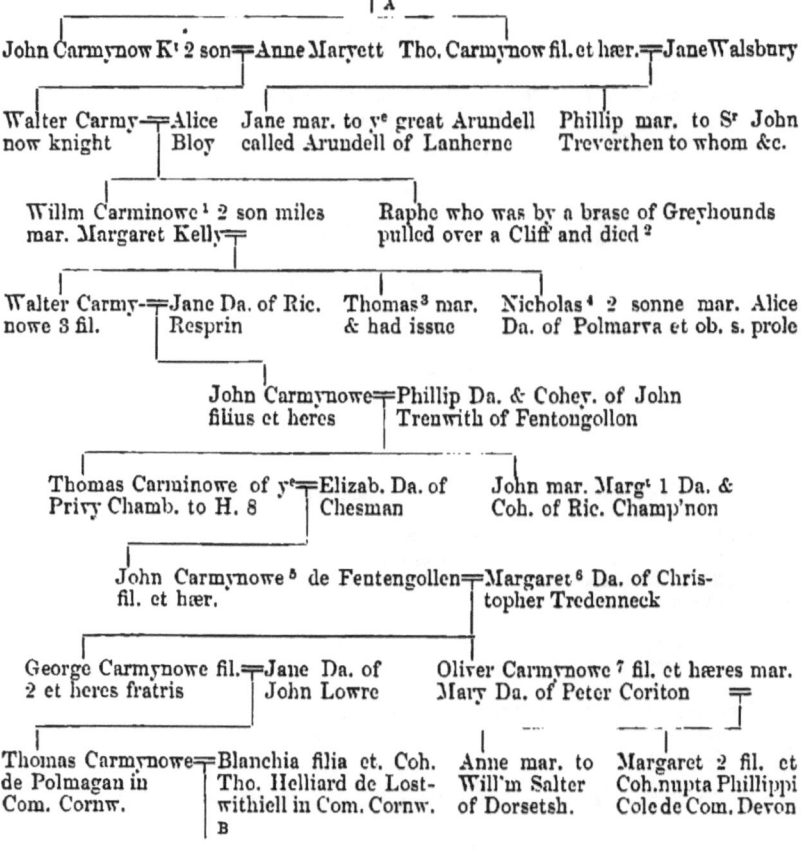

John Carmynow K[t] 2 son=Anne Maryett   Tho. Carmynow fil. et hær.=Jane Walsbury

Walter Carmy=Alice   Jane mar. to y[e] great Arundell   Phillip mar. to Sr John
now knight   Bloy   called Arundell of Lanherne   Treverthen to whom &c.

Willm Carminowe[1] 2 son miles   Raphe who was by a brase of Greyhounds
mar. Margaret Kelly=   pulled over a Cliff and died[2]

Walter Carmy-=Jane Da. of Ric.   Thomas[3] mar.   Nicholas[4] 2 sonne mar. Alice
nowe 3 fil.   Resprin   & had issue   Da. of Polmarva et ob. s. prole

John Carmynowe=Phillip Da. & Cohey. of John
filius et heres   Trenwith of Fentongollon

Thomas Carminowe of y[e]=Elizab. Da. of   John mar. Marg[t] 1 Da. &
Privy Chamb. to H. 8   Chesman   Coh. of Ric. Champ'non

John Carmynowe[5] de Fentengollen=Margaret[6] Da. of Chris-
fil. et hær.   topher Tredenneck

George Carmynowe fil.=Jane Da. of   Oliver Carmynowe[7] fil. et hæres mar.
2 et heres fratris   John Lowre   Mary Da. of Peter Coriton   =

Thomas Carmynowe=Blanchia filia et. Coh.   Anne mar. to   Margaret 2 fil. et
de Polmagan in   Tho. Helliard de Lost-   Will'm Salter   Coh. nupta Phillippi
Com. Cornw.   withiell in Com. Cornw.   of Dorsetsh.   Cole de Com. Devon
                  B

Trevarthian, æt. 36, were found to be her next heirs, viz. John Arundell, son of John Arundell, Kt., son of Elizabeth, da. of Oliver Carminowe. Kt., father of Roger Carminowe. Kt., father of Thomas Carminowe. Kt., father of Thomas Carminowe, Esq., father of the said Johanna Carminowe ; and John Trevarthian was son of Matilda, the other daughter of the aforesaid Oliver Carminowe, Kt. It would therefore appear by the reversions in this Inq. that John Carminow, Kt., given in the pedigree and leaving male issue, could not have been 2nd son of Roger Carminowe.

[1] Inq. p. m. William Carminow, 8 Hen. IV. No. 16, John son and heir, æt. 23.
[2] Inq. p. m. Ralph Carmynowe, 10 Rich. II. No. 11, William Carminowe brother and heir.
[3] Thomas was uncle and heir of John Carminowe, son of John Carminow in the writ named. Inq. p. m. John C., 8 Hen. V. No. 99.
[4] Inq. p. m. Nicholas Carminow, 11 Ed. IV. No. 44. A certain William Carminow, Ar., was father of said Nicholas, and Johanna, æt. about 40 [the widow of Sir Thomas Carew], now wife of Halnatha Maleverer, is next heir of said William, viz. da. & heir of Thomas, the uncle, and heir of John, son and heir of John, son and heir of said William Carminow.
[5] John Carminow bur. 1592.
[6] Margaret Carminow wid. bur. 1593.   } St. Michael
[7] Oliver Carmynowe, Esq., bur. 23 Dec., 1597.   } Penkivel
Juell Carmynowe. Gent., bur. 18 Dec., 1597.   } Par.
Mary widow of Oliver Carminowe, deceased, bur. 5 April, 1618. } Registers.
Margaret daughter of Oliver Carminowe bur.   }

THE VISITATION OF THE COUNTY OF CORNWALL. 35

| B

Thomas Carmynow fil. et   Will'ms Carminow 2   1. Jane   2. Blanch   3. Elizab.
hær. atat. 18 annoru' 1620 fil. æt. 11 annoru'   ætat.21   æt.   æt.

*   THO. CARMYNOWE.

Carnsewe.   1347126

Wᵐ Carnsewe of Sᵗ Kue in⹀Jane Da. of Edm. Stradlinge of
Com. Cornw.   Sᵗ Donnetts in Wales.

Will'm 1 sonne=Honoʳ Da. of Jo.   Geo. Carnsew 2 sonne⹀Thomazin Da. of John
of Sᵗ Kue   Fitz of Tavistock of Sᵗ Kue in Com.   Nicholl of Sᵗ Kue in
               in Devon   Cornwall   Com. Cornwall

                    1 | 2 | 3 |
Fran. Carnsew[1]=Mary Da. of   Honoʳ uxor   Anne uxor Hugh   Margᵗ uxor Jo. Lukie
of Philly in   John Webber   Jo. Joliffe   Prust of Hart-   of Helland in Corn-
Cornwall live- of Sᵗ Kue[2]   in Devon[3]   land in Devon   wall[4]
ing 1620.

                Geo. 1 sone ætat.   Mathew 2   Phillip   Mary
                16. 1620[5]   —   1 Da.[6]   2 Da.
                                     Francis 3
                                                              FRANCIS CARNSEWE.

[1] Bapt. 10 Nov., 1572.
[2] Mar. 26 Jan., 100¼. Bur. 29 Jan., 164⅜.
[3] Mar. 5 Nov., 1582.   } St. Kew Par. Reg.
[4] Mar. 4 June, 1599.
[5] Bapt. 2 March, 1602.
[6] Bapt. 9 June, 1606.

* Roger de Carminow, called to answer to the King for his Manor of Wynyanton, said that Richard, formerly Earl of Cornwall, gave to a certain Gervaise de Hornycote, his ancestor, the manors of Wynyanton, Merthyn, and Tamerton, to which the aforesaid belong, in exchange for the Manor of Bochym, etc., which exchange King Henry, father of this King (Ed. I.) ratified, and which same charter and deed Roger presents.—Assize Roll, M. }
                                                                           1 } 2 M. 32. 30 Ed. 1.
                                                                          20 }

Roger de Carmynow tenet man'ia Wynyenton & Mervyn in excamb. maner' de Bochym et Tyntagel que comes modo tenet.—Assize Roll, M. }
                                                 1 } 4 M. 14.
                                                20 }

Gervasius (Hornacote) Ped. fin. 40 Hen. III. Mich. 23. Gervas de Hornyngecote q. etc.

Sarra. dau. & heir to her niece Margery   Cenota dau. & h.
                 ⹀   ⹀   } Assize Roll, M. }   M. }
John s. & h.   Roger de Carminow bro.   Margery d. &   }   1 } 1 also 1 } 2 M. 21.
s.p.   and heir to John   h. s. p.   } Mich.30 Ed.1 21 }   21 }

Ibid. M. 14. Rog'us de Carmyno petit v'su' Pet'm de Lancuck decem acr. tre. etc. etc. in Est Dysart and West Dysart in quas id'm Petr'us no' h't. ingrm. nisi p. Will'm Lancuck q. inde injuste nec. diss Sarram de Hornyacote mr'm p'd'cti Rog. cui her. ipe est. Peter renounced claim and surrendered for himself and heirs to Roger C. and his heirs.

Walter Carminow afterwards held the Man. of Tamerton. The heirs of Sir John Arundel held Wynienton, and the heirs of Reskimer held Merthyn. Ralph, æt. 5, the son of Alan Bloyon, succeeded to the Manor of Polrode 34 Ed. I.

Carter.

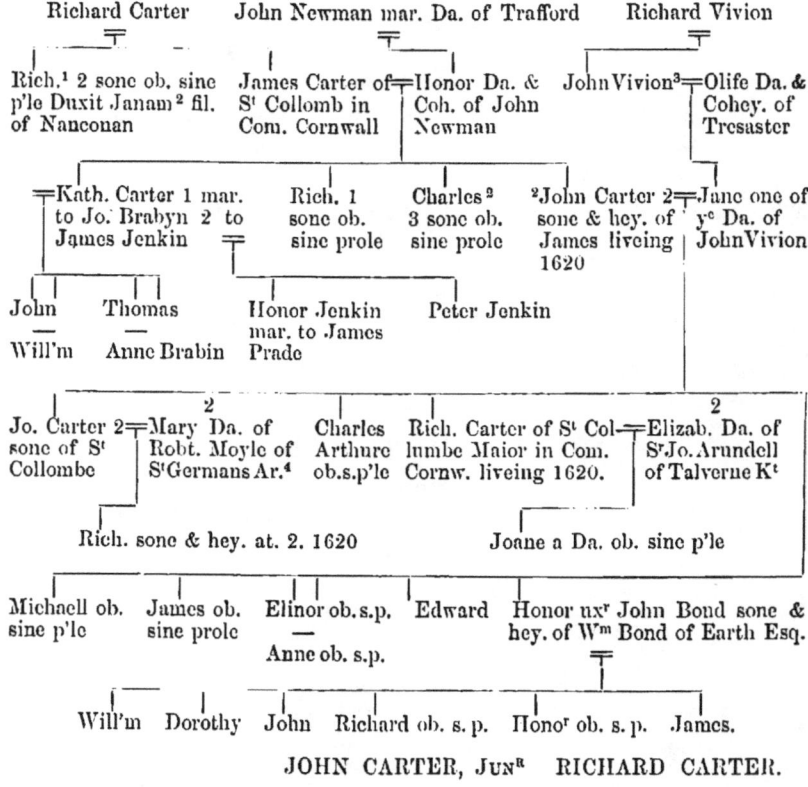

[1] Died at St. Columb Major, 4 August, 1581. Inq. p. m. 25 Eliz., No. 84. John, son and heir of James Carter, his nephew and heir, æt. 26. His will dated 27 Nov., 1578, prob. in Lond. 5 Feb. 1582.

[2] Named in the will of Ric. Carter, together with the following:—His sister Catherine Carter; his cousin Ric. Carter, the elder; Richard, John, and Elizb., children of the last named Richard; his Godson Richard, son of John Carter; Ric. Vyvyan of St. Meryn, and Jane Vyvyan, his wife, with John, Richard, and Olive, their children.

[3] Vivian of St. Columb.

[4] Married at St. Breock, 13 Sept., 1617. Bp. of Exeter's Transcripts.

Cary.

ARMS. *Argent, on a bend sable, 3 roses of the field.*
CREST. *A swan close Arg. beaked gu. legged sa.*

John Cary of Cary in Com. Devon. Esq.=Jane Da. & hey. of Edm. Devyok of
eldist sonne & heire of Robt. | Okehampton in Com. Devon [1]

Robt. 1 sone ob. sine pl'e | John 3 sonne ob. s.p. | Tho. Cary of Cary in Com. Devon 2 sone & hey. of John =Elizab. Da. of S^r Jo. Fulford of Fulford in Com. Devon K^t [2] | Mary ux^r Humphrie Stephens | Elizb. ux^r Thomas Walton in Com. Som'set | Alice unmar.

Grigorie 1 sone ob. sine p'le | Peter 2 sonne ob. sine p'le | Haniball 3 sonne ob. sin p'le | Andrew 4 sonne ob. s. ple

Hen. Cary of Launston in Com. Cornw. liveing 1620. 5 sone & hey. =Willmot Da. of Edm. Cann of Okehampton in Devon | Fulford 6 sonne ob. s.p. | Rich. 7 sone ob. s. p. | Mary ux^r Hen. Prost of Maryweeke in Corn.

Robt. 1 sone atat. 15. 1620 | George 2 sonne | Mary 1 Da. | Elizb. 2 Da. | Arminall 3 Da. | Alice 4 Da.

* HENRY CARY.

Cabell.

Roger Cavell=Anne Da. of John Bodulgatt Esq.

Stephen Cavell=Jone Da. & Coh. of Rob. Boniface Esq.

Rob. Cavell=Sibell Da. & Coh. of Jo. Trehaverock Esq.[3]

Nicho. Cavell=Alice Da. & hey. of Jo. Trecarren Esq.
& wdowe of Wm Carnsewe Esq.
A

---

[1] He is called Deviell 'Harl. Soc. Visit. Devon, 1620,' p. 49.
[2] She was widow of Humphry Arundell.
[3] By this marriage he acquired Trehaverock al's Treharrock, which came to Vivian of St. Columb, who married Mary, one of the coheiresses of Henry Cavell in 1615.
* Will'm Carye, gent., married Elizab. Gedye 4 Mar., 1621. Menheniot Par. Reg.
Nicholas, son of Will'm Carye, gent., bap. at Menheniot. Bp. of Exeter's Transcripts.

THE VISITATION OF THE COUNTY OF CORNWALL.

A |

Hen. Cavell=Da. of John Trevillian Esq.

Nicho. Cavell=Sole Da. & hey. of Wm Knight

Will'm Cavell=Thomazin[1] Da. of John Godolphin Esq.

John Cavell of Trehaverock=Phill. Da. of Lawrence Courtney Esq.

| Nicho. 1 sone ob. sine p'le | Mary | Will'm 2 sone & hey. of Treharerock liveing 1620[2] | Jane[3] Da. of Wm Pomeroy Esq.* | Elizab. 2 Fran. 3 Elizb. 4 | Dorithie 5 Thomazin 6 |

| Joane 2 Da. Jo. Hore of Trenouth[4] | | Mary 1 Da. & Cohey. nx^r Jo. Vivian of St Collomb[5] | | | |

Not signed.

Ceelye.

Thomas Ceely of Comesberic in Com. Som'set & 10 miles fro Bristow.[6]

Christopher Ceely of Plimoth=Avis Da. of ... Marchant & of his wife
in Com. Devon   da. & her. of Bullin of Dorsetshere

| Prisilla mar. to Rich. Joyce de Com. Wilts | Mary mar. to Will'm Eyres de | Thomas 2 son mar. Da. of Oliver Spry[7] of St Germans | Willm Ceely of St Ives in Com. Cornwall æt. 40 | Anne Da. of Tho. Penrose of Penrose in P'ochia de Scithney in Com. Cornwal | Christopher 3 fil. in partibus transmarinis |

| A | | | | B |

[1] She is called Elizabeth in Harl. MS. 4031, fo. 84, and Add. MS. 14135.
[2] Bur. at St. Kew 19 Dec., 1647.
[3] Bur. at St. Kew 26 June, 1652. } Bp. of Exeter's Transcripts.
[4] Mar. at St. Kew 10 August, 1618.
[5] Married at St. Kew 18 April, 1615.
[6] Bristol.   [7] Thomasin. *Vide* Spry Ped. post.

* Will. Cavell and Jane his wife, with their two daughters and coheiresses Joane and Mary, wife of John Vivian, are named in the will of John Pomeroy of St. Cleere, gent., prob. Lond. 12 March, 1619.
John Cavell married Jane Robins. 1623, at St. Mabyn. Bp. of Exeter's Transcripts.
Ped. fin. 5 Ric. II, No. 4. Int. Rad. Carmynewe Chivaler gu. Henry Cavel and Sibill his wife, and Wm Bray of Treworles and Elizabeth his wife, df.

THE VISITATION OF THE COUNTY OF CORNWALL.

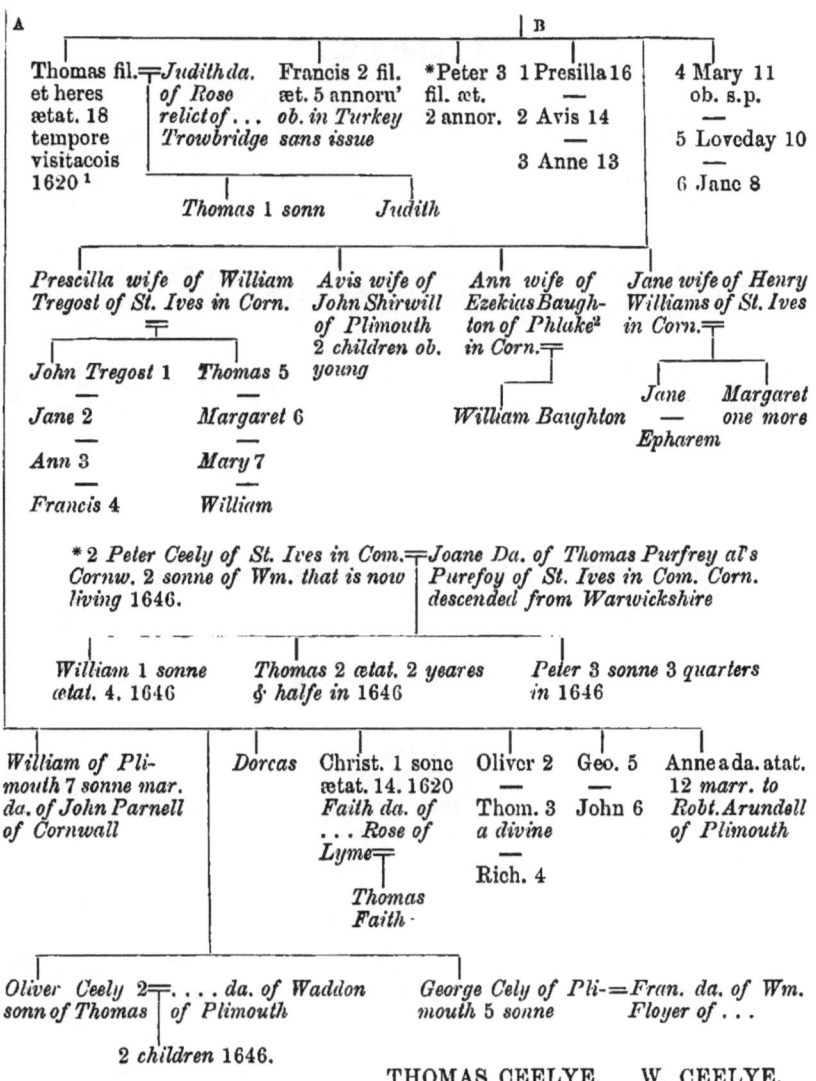

---

[1] A Thomas Ceeley commanded the Elizabeth Drake, 60 gun ship, against the Spanish Armada. Royal MSS. 14B, xiii.
[2] ? Phillack.

☞ The additions in Italics are in the hand of Parker.

Chamond.

ARMS. *Argent, a chevron betw. 3 fleurs de lis gu.*
CREST. *A Griffin sejeant Or.*

Alexr Chamond of Lancells in Com. Cornw. = Elizb. Da. & hey. of Tho. Treughans B. a chev'on ent. 3 Dalphins Ar.

Tho. Chamond of Lancells = Agnes Da. of Tho. Writhe.[1] Ar. an eagle displaied wth 2 heads armed & beaked Or.

Margt Da. and Coh. of Thom. Tregarthen. Ar. Chev'on ent. 3 Escallops Sa. 1 wife = S{r} John Chamond K{t} of Lancells in Cornwall = Jane late wife of Sir Jo. Arundell K{t2} Da. of Sr Tho. Grenvile K{t} Gu. 3 Sufflues or.

Rich. Chamond[3] of Lancells Esq. = Marg{t} Da. & Coheyre of Rich. Trevener. Ar. Chev'on Sa. ent. 3 Cornishe Dawes pp.

John Chamond of Lancells in Cornw. liveinge 1620. atat. 70. Esq.

*   *Not signed.*

Chepman.

John Chapman of Whetstone in Cornwall = Thomazin Da. of Ric. Gilbert Esq. of Northpetherwyn in Cornwall

Edw. Chapman of Liskard in Com. Cornw. liveinge 1620 & at this time Maior = Lore Da. of John Hantkin of Liskerd in Cornwall

| Beniamin 2 | Edward 4 | Jonathon 6 | Joseph 1 sone ætat. 16, 1620 | Rachell a da. |
| Jacobb 3 | John 5 | | | |

EDWARD CHEPMAN.

---

[1] Worthe of Washfield. See 'Harl. Soc.Visit. of Devon,' 1620, p. 316. [2] Of Trerice.
[3] High Sheriff of Cornwall A.D. 1544. 59, and 63.

* At fo. 84, in the Original MS., 1162, the Pedigree of Chamond, commencing four generations earlier, has been cancelled by the Heralds' pen.

Chapman.

Edw. Chapman of Hanckford in Com. === Jaquet Da. of Marwood of
Devo' descended out of the Northe | Westcott in Com. Devon

Seintleger Chapman 2 sonne ob. sine p'le

John Chapman of Hank- === Christian Dau. of Rob. Chichester
ford in Com. Devon | of Hall in Com. Devon

John 2 sone mar. Agnes Da. of Taylor of Westley in Com. Devon ==
A Dau.

Arthure 3 sone mar. Alice Da. of Jo. Salisburie of Buckland Bruer in Devon ==
A sonne

Edw. Chapman of === Elizb. Da. of
Resprin in Com. | Rich. Prediaux of Thewburie in Com. Devon
Cornwall liveinge 1620

Rich. sone & hey. atat. 21. 1620

Edw. 2 sone atat. 16

Nicholas 3 sonne at. 9

Sinobia 1 Da. at. 19. 1620

Grace 2 Da. atat. 14

Blanch 3 Da. atat. 9

Phillip 4 Da. at. 5 1620

| 1 | 2 | 3 | 4 |
| Jaquet uxor Stephen Hogge of Buckland Bruer in Com. Devon | Christian ux^r James Browneing of Kilkhampton in Cornwall | Anne uxor Shapley of Clovelley in Com. Devon | Julyan ux^r Daniell Colscot of West Putford in Com. Devon |

EDWARD CHAPMAN.

Chenouth.

The auntient name of this family of Chynoweth was called Trevelizek, & was changed upon this occation. one John Trevelizek had issue divers sonne unto one of the youngest named John he gave a certayne peice of Land whereon the said John built a new howse & alwais afterward was called Chinoweth which is in Cornish a new howse yet afterwards all the issue of th elder house failed, & the auntient land cam to this younger branch called Chinoweth whoe have the land & continew the same name to this day.

Trevelisick of St. Earth mar. Elizb. Da. of
John Tirrell of St. Earth & had issue John

Tho. Chenouth¹ of Mogion === Anne Da. of Tho. Tregose & one of his heires

Ellinor uxor Jo. Roskirke²

Antho. Chenouth === Grace Da. of Tho.
of Mogion | Spour of Trembath
A

¹ Mawgan in Menenge.   ² John Roskruge. See pedigree, post.

42 THE VISITATION OF THE COUNTY OF CORNWALL.

| A

Hen. Chenonth = Mary Da. of James Kestell of Monnaccon | John Chenouth of Mogion in Com. Cornw. liveing 1620 = Grace Da. of Henry Thoms als Carnsew of Budock | Temperence ux^r Walter Kestell
of Mogion 1 sone

Antho¹ sone & heyre atat. 4, 1620

Not signed.

Chiverton of Paul.

Tho. Chiverton of the parish of Paule = ... Da. of .... Whalisborough

James Chiverton of Pawle fil. et heres = Clarence Da. of John Cowling of Kirtheu

Willm. Chiverton de Com. Cornwall = Katherin Da. of Tho. Bevill²

Thomas Cheverton fil. et hæres = Johanna filia Robt. Butside

Willm. Cheverton de Pawle fil. et heres = Tomazin Da. of John Godolphin

1. Thomas³
2. Richard
ob. sine prole

Willm.⁴ Chiverton heire to his Brothers de Pawle in Com. Cornwall sup'stes 1620

= Mary Da. of Willm. Lanion Relicta Burlace

Jane ob. virgin

Elizab. mar. to John Trewren⁴

Katherin mar. to Christopher Arundell of Camborne in Cornwa.⁴

WILLYAM CHIVERTON.

---

¹ Baptized at St. Martin in Meneage 19 January, 1616. Bp. of Exeter's Transcripts.
² Beville of Gwarnake.
³ Will dated 26 Aug., 1604, proved in London 7 Feb., 1605.
⁴ Named in Will of Tho. Chiverton of Paule, 26 Aug., 1604.
   Richard Chiverton of Kerrys, in the Parish of Paul, High Sheriff of Cornwall, A.D. 1564. Henry Chiverton, Esq., M.P. for Cornwall 6 Edw. IV.; 1, 2, and 3 Philip and Mary; for Bodmin, 1 Mary.

THE VISITATION OF THE COUNTY OF CORNWALL.   43

Chiverton of Trehunsey.

ARMS.—*Arg. a castle tower triple-towered Sa. on a mound Vert.*

Hen. Chev'ton of Trehunsie=Alice Da. & hey. of Kindon[1]
in Com. Cornw.   of Trehunsie

[2] Hen. Chiverton sone & heyre mar. Mary   Rich. Chiv'ton of Tre-=Isaball Da. of
Da. of St G. aueu ob. sine prole   hunsie 2 sonne   Polewheele

Hen. Chiv'ton of Trehunsie in=Emlin Da. of Frau. Bullar
Com. Cornw. liveing 1620   Esq. of Shillingham

Francis 2 sone   Rich.[3] sone & heire atat. 4. 1620

HENRY CHIVERTON.

Cock.

Lewkis Cocke of Plimouth in Com. Devon=

Symon Cocke of Plimouth[4]=Grace da. of Sheere of Launston
in Com. Devon   in Com. Cornw.

John 2   Lewkis 1   Edward Cock of Plimouth in Com.=Amy da. of John Gubbes
sonne   son ob.   Devon mar. to his 2 wif Elizab. of Plimouth 1 wife
          s. p.   da. of Oswell Cooke of Launston

Lewkis Cock fil. et heres æt. 2. 1620   Grace 1   Christian 2   Joane 3
                       *   EDWARD COCK.

---

[1] Kingdon of Trehunsey in Quethiock.
[2] He mar. Mary, da. of John St. Aubyn of Clowance. *Vide* ped. of St. Aubyn, post. Zenobia, da. of Hen Chiverton, bur. 16 Oct., 1580. Gwinear Par. Reg.
[3] Lord Mayor of London in 1658, Knighted at Whitehall 12 Oct., 1663. *Vide* Le Neve's Pedigrees of Knights, Harl. Soc. pub., page 177. At page 256 of the same publication Le Neve has against Sir Richard's name " q^{re} of Sr John Coriton or write to my Lady."
[4] Symon had a son Francis, who also had a son Francis ½ year old 1620. Harl. MS. 1079, fo. 117.

* Capt. Cock of Plymouth, styled " A Cock of the Game," supposed to be of this family, was the only officer killed fighting against the Armada. Arms—Ar. a chev. engr. betw. 3 Cocks' heads Sa. a canton B. charged with an anchor Or.

Coke.

Christopher Cooke of Thorne == Margaret da. of Richard Garland
in Com. Devon | of Whitfeld

Christopher Coke of = Thorn sone & heir

John Coke of Trerice in Cornwall 2 sonne living 1620 == Prudence da. of William Godolphin of Trewarveneth

John Coke sonne & heir ætat. 14 Annores 1620

Edward 2

¹Jane 1

Margaret 3

Francis 3

Prudence 2

J. COKE.

Colling.

Geo. Collyng of Hampte in Cornwall

Jo. Collyng of Hampte of == Joane Da. of Rich. Burgoyne of

Geo. Collyng of Hampte == Kath' Da. & sole hey. of Hen. Mannington of Mannington in Cornwall

Geo. Collynge of Hampte in Com. Cornw. liveinge 1620 == Elizb. Da. of Pet' Mayowe of Torr in Cornwall

| Katherin 1 Da. atat. 11, 1620 | Radigund 2 Da. at. 9 | Judeth 3 Da. at. 7 | Margerie 4 Da. at. 4 | Anne 5 Da. at. 1 weeke 1620 |

GEORGE COLLING.

---

[1] Baptized at St. Allen 27 Sept., 1612. Bp. of Exeter's Transcripts.

* Exch. Inq. p. m. 14 Hen. VIII. No. 5. John Coke of Thorne, John Coke, son and heir, æt. 37 and more.

Colquit.

(*sic*) Quere:—ARMS. *Ar. fes b. frette or ent. 3 cinquefoils Gu.*

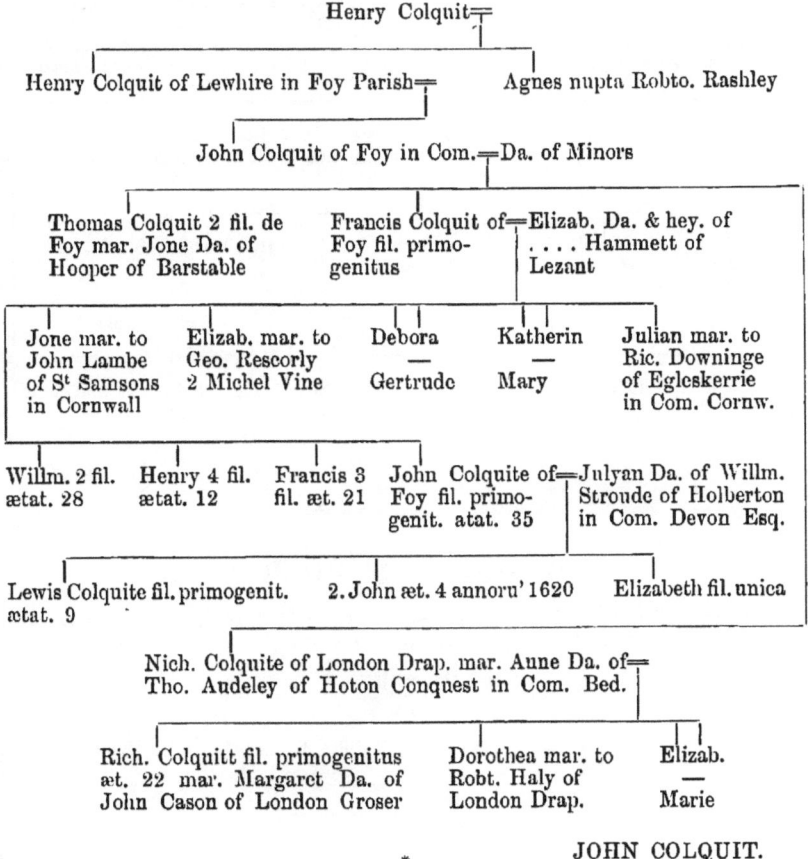

JOHN COLQUIT.

* *Fowey Par. Reg.*

26 Oct. 1543. John Colquite bapt.
14 Apl. 1558. Henry son of Thomas Colquite bapt.
1548. Henry Colquite bapt.
1559. Rich. Colquite. „
1564. Tho. Colquite.   „
1656. Wm. son of Mr. Lewis Colquite, bapt.

1660. Wm. son of Mr. Lewis Colquite. bapt.
16 May, 1568. Jno Colquite & Jone Rashleigh were mar.
1577. Jno Colquite & Alce Bewes   do.
1603. Henry Colquite buried.
3 May 1621. Elz[th] ux. Francis Colquite bur.
4 —— 1621. Francis Colquite her husband bur.

Connock.

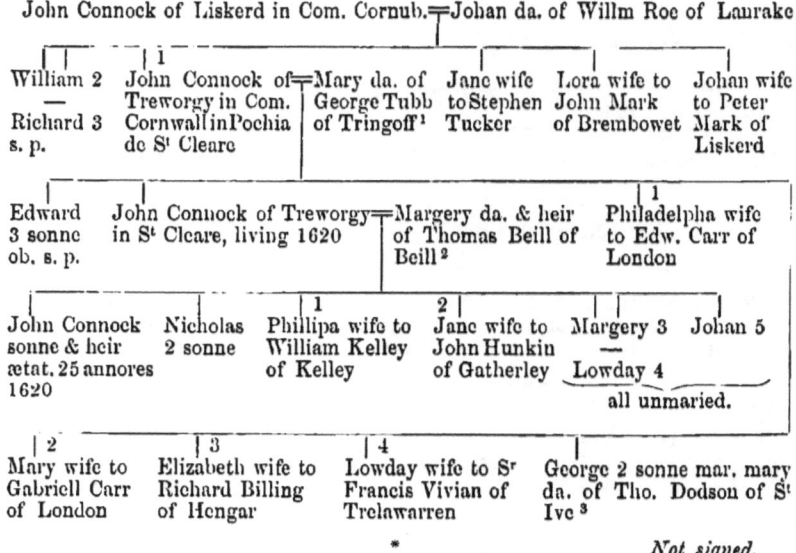

Coode of Morval.

ARMS.—1. [COODE.] *Argent a chevron Gules betw. 3 Cocks Sable, armed crested and jelloped of the second.* 2. *Gules 3 crescents Or.*

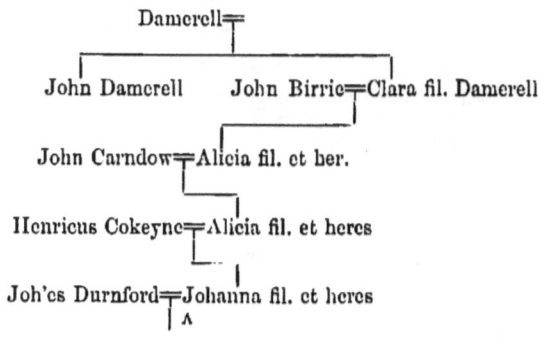

[1] In Gwennap Parish.   [2] Beele, Beyle, *vel* Byll.   [3] St. Ive, near Liskeard.
* John Connock, gent. M.P. for Liskeard 1 & 2 Phil. & Mary, & 13 Eliz.
  Nicholas Connock, M.P. for Bodmin 12 Jas. I.
  John Connock, gent. M.P. for Liskeard 31 Chas. II. & 1 Jas. II.
  John Connock of Liskeard, by deed dated 22 Jan., 1579, granted his Manor of Trewthand to John Nichols. *Sir J. Maclean.*

THE VISITATION OF THE COUNTY OF CORNWALL. 47

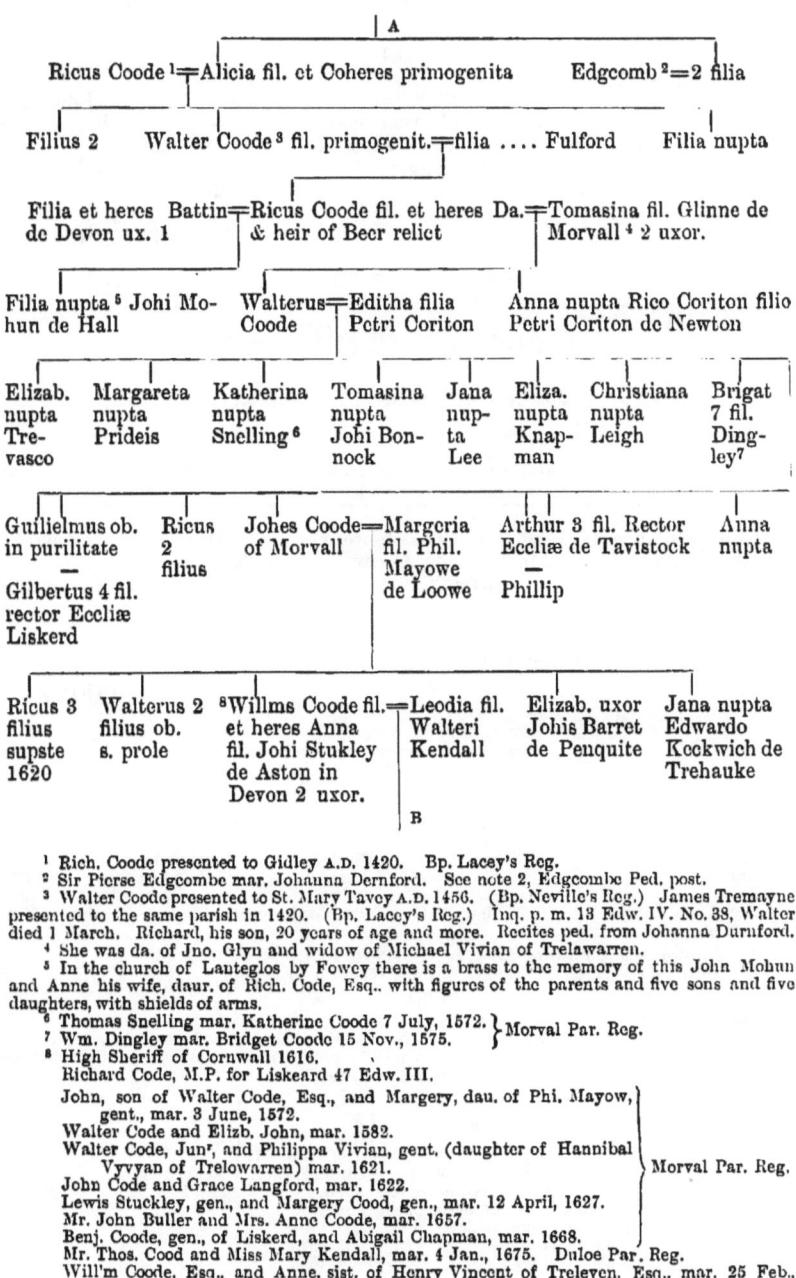

[1] Rich. Coode presented to Gidley A.D. 1420. Bp. Lacey's Reg.
[2] Sir Pierse Edgcombe mar. Johanna Dernford. See note 2, Edgcombe Ped. post.
[3] Walter Coode presented to St. Mary Tavey A.D. 1456. (Bp. Neville's Reg.) James Tremayne presented to the same parish in 1420. (Bp. Lacey's Reg.) Inq. p. m. 13 Edw. IV. No. 38, Walter died 1 March. Richard, his son, 20 years of age and more. Recites ped. from Johanna Durnford.
[4] She was da. of Jno. Glyn and widow of Michael Vivian of Trelawarren.
[5] In the church of Lanteglos by Fowey there is a brass to the memory of this John Mohun and Anne his wife, daur. of Rich. Code, Esq., with figures of the parents and five sons and five daughters, with shields of arms.
[6] Thomas Snelling mar. Katherine Coode 7 July, 1572. } Morval Par. Reg.
[7] Wm. Dingley mar. Bridget Coode 15 Nov., 1575.
[8] High Sheriff of Cornwall 1616.
Richard Code, M.P. for Liskeard 47 Edw. III.
John, son of Walter Code, Esq., and Margery, dau. of Phi. Mayow, gent., mar. 3 June, 1572.
Walter Code and Elizb. John, mar. 1582.
Walter Code, Jun[r], and Philippa Vivian, gent. (daughter of Hannibal Vyvyan of Trelowarren) mar. 1621.
John Code and Grace Langford, mar. 1622.
Lewis Stuckley, gen., and Margery Cood, gen., mar. 12 April, 1627.
Mr. John Buller and Mrs. Anne Coode, mar. 1657.
Benj. Coode, gen., of Liskerd, and Abigail Chapman, mar. 1668.
Mr. Thos. Cood and Miss Mary Kendall, mar. 4 Jan., 1675. Duloe Par. Reg.
Will'm Coode, Esq., and Anne, sist. of Henry Vincent of Treleven, Esq., mar. 25 Feb., 1685. Mevagissey Par. Reg.

} Morval Par. Reg.

[*Continued over.*

48   THE VISITATION OF THE COUNTY OF CORNWALL.

Elizab.	Maria[1]	Jana uxor.	Walterus Coode	2. John æt. 21	5. Edward
		Willmi	fil. primogenitus		ob. s. p.
Margerie	Anna	Ketchwich	ætatu 26 temp.	3. Willm 26	
		of Ketch-	visitacois 1620		6. Carolus
Leodia	Brigett	french		4. Phillip 18	ætat. 13

WILLIA. COODE.

Coode of Menheniot.

Jo. Code of Menhenet in Cornwall

Jo. Code[2] of Breage in Com. Cornw. 3 sone⹀Marg[t] Da. of Wm Lanion of Bereage

Elizb. ux.	Blanch ux. Edw.	Jo. Code of Breage⹀Jane Da. of W[m]	Lovedaye 3
Jo. Gere of	Noye of Paule in	in Com. Cornw. Prade of Uni Ie-	
S[t] Keverne	Cornw.	liveing 1620 lant in Cornwall	Thomazin 4

Willm. Code of . . . atat. 1, 1620.

*   JOHN COODE.

Morval Par. Reg.

Anne, da. of Walter Coode, Esq., bapt. 1544.   Richard, son of John Code, Esq., bapt. 1582.
John, son of   „   „   1546. Will'm,   „   Robert Code,   „   1589.
Arthur, son of   „   „   „   Philip,   „   Philip Code,   „   „
Philip   „   „   „   1550. John,   „   Will'm Code, Esq. „   1597.
Gilbert   „   „   „   1552. Philip,   „   „   „   1599.
Walter Code, Esq.,   bur. 1545. Phi. Coode, gent.,   bur. 1654.
John Code, an almes man,   „   1571.

Edward, son of Edward Coode, bapt. 29 Nov., 1601. St. Pinnock Par. Reg.
Gilbert Code, gent.,   bur. 18 Nov., 1676. } Illogan Par. Reg.
Joseph Coade,   „   1686.

[1] Bapt. 28 July, 1610. Morval Par. Reg.
[2] Inq. de Lunat. Inquir. 12 Jas. I., part 1, No. 35, Jurors find that John Code is of unsound mind, and that John Code, his son and heir, is aged 16 years and six months. Lands in Breage, Sithney, Constantine, St. Keverne, Cury, St. Anthony, and Truro.

* John son of John Coode, bap. 1578.
  Luke   „   „   „   1583.
  Peter   „   „   „   1585.
  John   „   „   „   3 Jan., 1610–11.   ⎫
  John Code, Jun., and Mary Ingram mar. 1602.   ⎬ Menheniot
  John Coode & Alse Eustys mar. 1580.   ⎥ Par. Reg.
  Elizabeth, wife of John Coode, bur. 1579.   ⎥
  Blanche Coode, widow   „   1594.   ⎥
  John Cood   „   1590.   ⎥
  John Cood the elder   „   1600.   ⎭

James Bath and Elizabeth, daughter of John Coode, were mar. 22 Feb., 1670. Stithians Par. Reg. The Baths are descended from Edmond Bathe, described in his will proved at Bodmin 20 Nov., 1633, as of Kenal, in the Parish of Stithians, Gent.

Coryton.

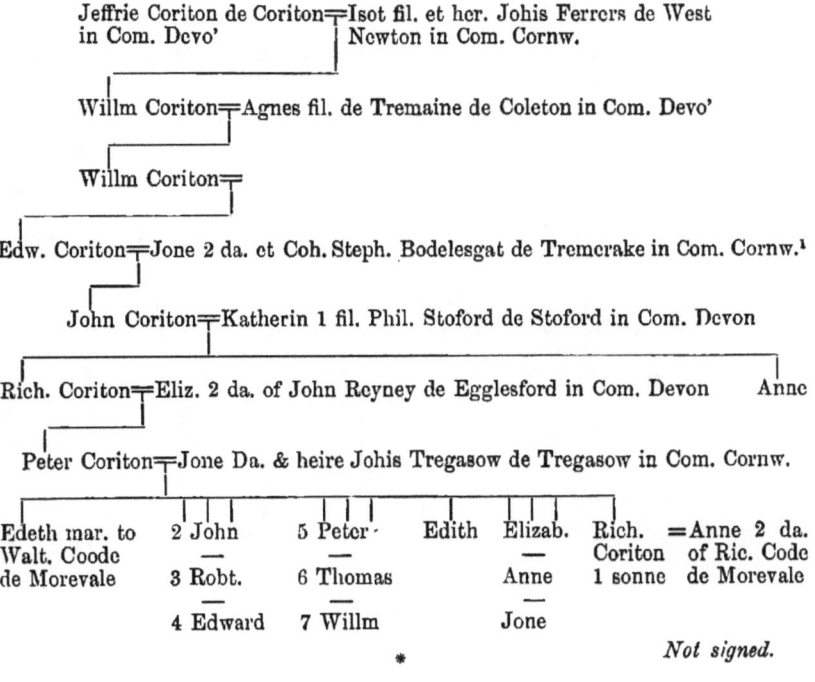

Jeffrie Coriton de Coriton in Com. Devo' = Isot fil. et her. Johis Ferrers de West Newton in Com. Cornw.

Willm Coriton = Agnes fil. de Tremaine de Coleton in Com. Devo'

Willm Coriton =

Edw. Coriton = Jone 2 da. et Coh. Steph. Bodelesgat de Tremcrake in Com. Cornw.[1]

John Coriton = Katherin 1 fil. Phil. Stoford de Stoford in Com. Devon

Rich. Coriton = Eliz. 2 da. of John Reyney de Egglesford in Com. Devon   Anne

Peter Coriton = Jone Da. & heire Johis Tregasow de Tregasow in Com. Cornw.

Edeth mar. to Walt. Coode de Morevale | 2 John — 3 Robt. — 4 Edward | 5 Peter — 6 Thomas — 7 Willm | Edith | Elizab. — Anne — Jone | Rich. Coriton 1 sonne | = Anne 2 da. of Ric. Code de Morevale

*

Not signed.

Coryton.

Willm Curington of Quethyock in Cornw. = Bridgett Da. of Burnell

Jo. Curington of St Ive in Cornwall = Prudence Da. of Prouse

John Curington sone & heire at. 23. 1620.

JOHN CORYTON.

---

[1] Inq. p. m. 2 Hen. VII., No. 51, John C., son and heir, æt. 40.

* This ped. is extended in Harl. MSS. 1079, fo. 22–23.

Mary, da. of Sir John Coryton, Bart., and Elizb., his Lady, bapt. at St. Mellion 11 Aug., 1664.
Katheryn, da. of the Worshipful Will. Coryton, Esq., and Elizab. his wife, bap. at St. Mellion 10 Nov., 1610.
Elizab., da. of John Coriton, gent., and Mary, his wife, bap. at St Ive 17 Nov., 1631.

Bp. of Exeter's Transcripts.

Cosworth.

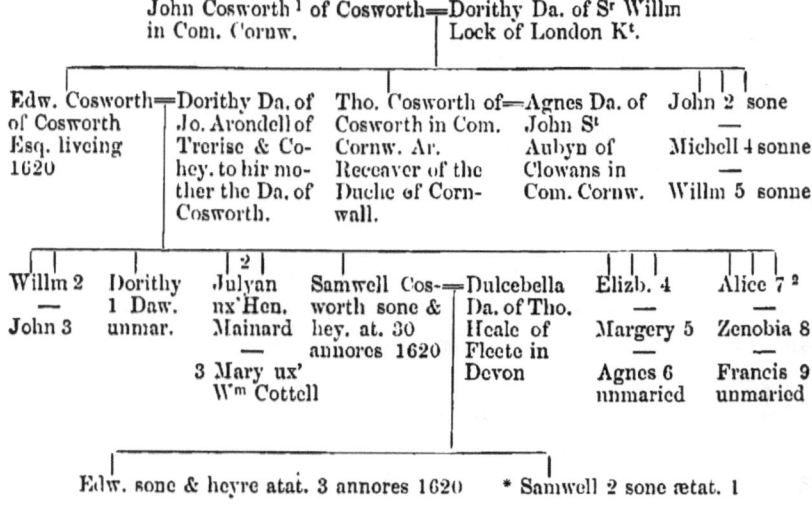

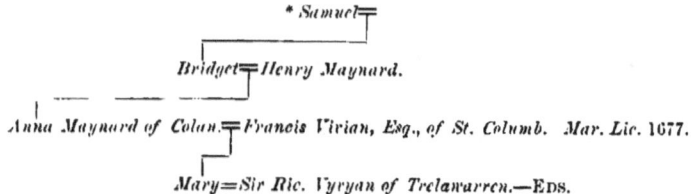

[1] Mercer of London, and Receiver General of the Duchy of Cornwall. Brass in Colan Ch. For more of Cosworth, see the 'Visitation of London. 1568,' Harl. MSS. 1096, fo. 56; and 1463, fo. 8, *b.* where the descent is continued from Nicholas (the elder brother of John C. of London) to the marriage of the heiress with Arundel. See Arundel Ped. *ante*.

[2] Thos. Hoblyn, Gt., and Alice Cosworth, mar. at Little Collan 7 Oct., 1634. Bp. of Exeter's Transcripts.

Francis Vivian's will, 1689, prob. St. Neott, dau. Mary executrix. He desired his father, his brother Vivian, brother John Vivian, and his cousins Richard and Francis Scobell of St. Austell, father and son, to manage his estate, and sell all, except the barton of Coswarth, to pay his debts.

Sir Richard Vyvyan and Mrs. Mary Vivian were married Nov. 9, 1697. St. Eval. Par. Reg. This marriage is said to have reunited the houses of Vyvyan or Vivian.

Ped. fin. 5 Ja. Mich. Ed. Coswarth, ar. qu. W. Vivian and o'rs def. ten't in Bossagran.
Jane, da. of Edw. Cosworth, Esq., bapt. at Little Collan 1 Aug., 6 King James, 1608. Bp. of Exeter's Transcripts.

Cossen alias Madern.

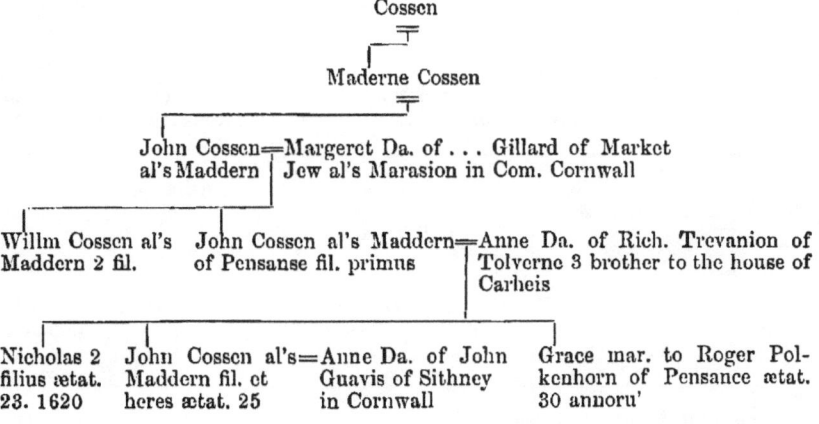

JOHN COSSEN ALIAS MADERN.

Courtenay of Landrake.

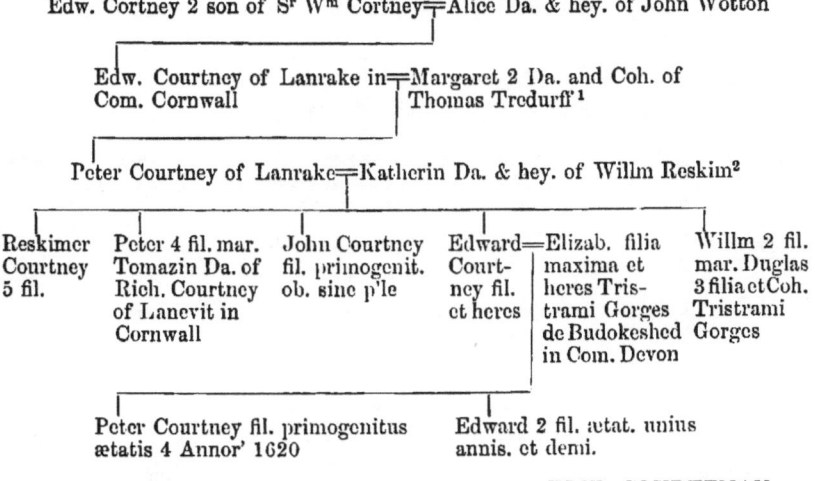

EDW. COURTENAY.

---

[1] Tretherffe; she afterwards mar. Rich. Buller. See Ped. post, and Inq. p. m.   [2] Reskimer.
* For fuller, though imperfect ped. of Courtenay, see 'Archæological Journal,' vol. x., p. 52.

Courteney of Lanivet.

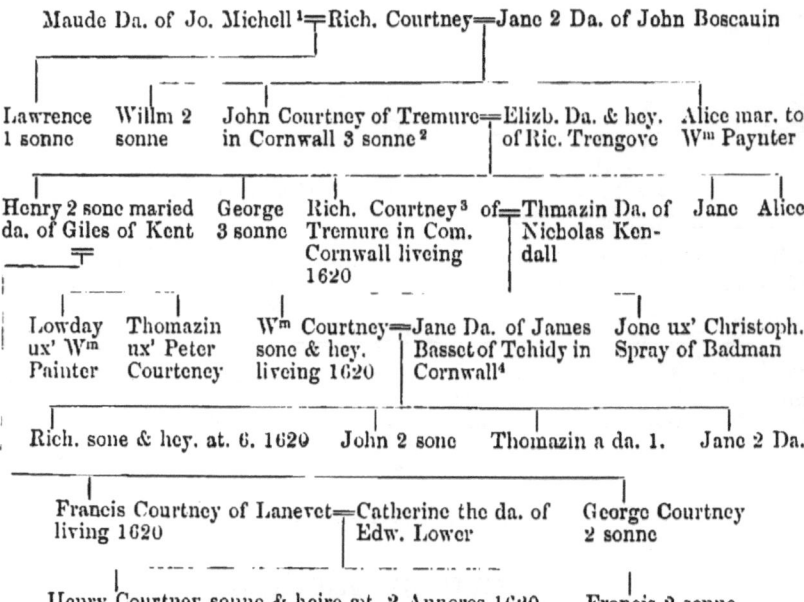

RICHARD COURTENEY.   WILLI. COURTENEY.

Courtney of Penkivel.

ARMS. 1. [COURTNEY] *Or 3 torteaux.* 2. [REDVERS] *Or a lion ramp. B.* 3 *Arg. a chevron engr. betw. 3 Does statant sa.* 4. *Quartered Crenellée Arg. and Sa.*
CREST. *A Panache Arg. rising from a Ducal Coronet Or.*

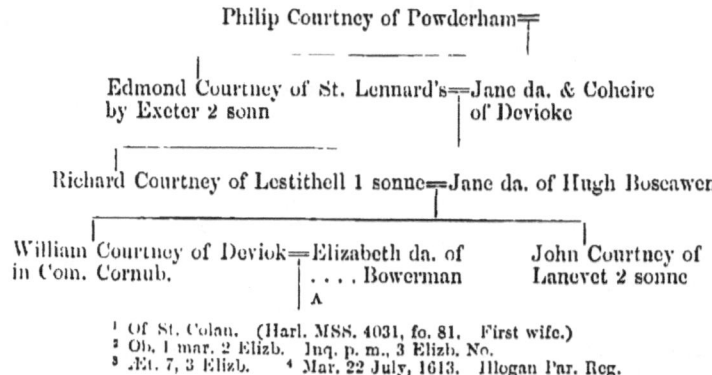

[1] Of St. Colan. (Harl. MSS. 4031, fo. 81. First wife.)
[2] Ob. 1 mar. 2 Elizb. Inq. p. m., 3 Elizb. No.
[3] Æt. 7, 3 Elizb.   [4] Mar. 22 July, 1613. Illogan Par. Reg.

THE VISITATION OF THE COUNTY OF CORNWALL. 53

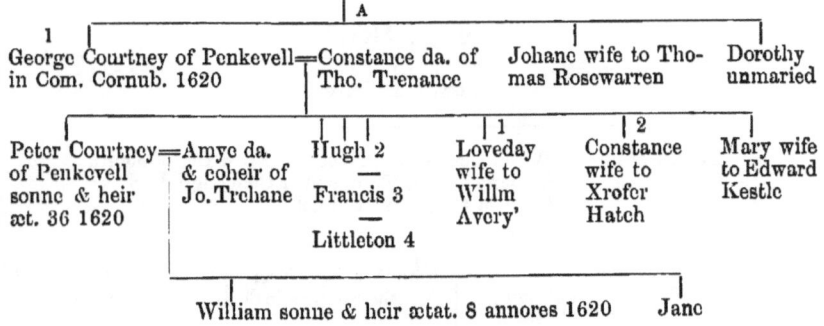

PETER COURTNEY.

	PARISHES.
Bishop of Exeter's Transcripts.	
Will. Courteney, Esq. did marry one of the daus. of Ja. Basset, Esq. (*sic*) 22 July,	1613. Illogan.
George Courteney, Esq. and Elizb. Mallet, mar. 5 Oct.	1609. Laddock.
Edw. son of Edw. Courteney, bap.	1619. ,,
Wm Bligh, Esq. and Elizb. Courteney, wid., mar.	1623. ,,
Lawrence, son of John Courteney, bp.	1622. Lanivet.
Humph. son of Ric. Courteney, gen. and Philippa, bap.	1641. ,,
Dorothy, dau. Edwd Courteney, gent. bap.	1610. Ruan Lanihorne.
George, son of Geor. Courteney, gent. bap. and bur.	1610. ,,
Honor dau. of John Courteney and Jane, bap.	1638. St. Austell.
Edw. Courteney, Esq. and Elizb. Gorges, gent., mar. 1 Aug.	1614. St. Budeaux, Dev.
Parish Registers.	
John Kempthorne, Gent., and Kath. Courteney, Gent. mar. 21 Jan.	1558. Chudleigh, Dev.
Mary, dau. of Peter Courteney, Esq., bapt. 6 Jan.	1639. Fowey.
Alice, ,, ,, ,, 29 Aug.	1641. ,,
Elizb., ,, Sir Peter Courteney, Knt., bap. 29 Dec.	1642. ,,
Anne, ,, ,, ,, 2 Feb.	1644. ,,
Mary, ,, ,, bur.	1655. ,,
Edw., son of Humphry Courteney, Esq., bap. 27 Dec.	1667. ,,
Wm Courteney, Esq., bur. 15 Jan.	1683. ,,
Will., son & heir of Rich. Courteney of London, Esq. and Jane, one of the daughters of Ja^s Bassett of Tehidic, Esq., mar. 22 July,	1613. Illogan.
John Courteney, bur.	1709. Laddock.
John Courteney of Tregellas in Probus, Gent., bur.	1718. ,,
Jno Courteney, bur.	1799. ,,
Peeter Courteney, of St. Erme, Gent., and Honnor, dau. of Ric. Courteney, Esq., dec., mar.	1673. Lanivet.
John, son of Will. Courteney and Patience, bap.	1695. Luxyllian.
Peter Courteney, bur. 21 Jan.	1699. ,,
Willm Courteney, bur.	1703. ,,
John Courteney and Jane Vyvyan, mar. 8 Oct., 1633; bur.	1633. St. Austell.
Will. Courteney and Grace Bice, mar.	1722. St. Enoder.
Reskimer, son of Peter Courteney, Esq., bur.	1673. St. Erme.
John Courteney and Dorothy Pendarves, mar. Jan.	1674. ,,
Anne, dau. of Peter Courteney and Honor, bap.	1674. ,,
Willm Courteney, of St. Erme, Gent., bur.	1725. ,,
Wm Averie, Gent., and Loveday Corteney, mar. 19 Feb.	1609. St. Mich. Penkivel.
Willm, son of Peter Courteney, bur. 31 Mar.	1665. ,,
Ric. Williams of Probus, Gent., was married to Mary, the dau. of Will. Courteney, Gent., dec^d, of this p'ish, 23 Dec.	1661. ,,
Peter Courteney, bur.	1698. ,,
Peter Courteney and Jane Olliver, mar. 28 Nov.	1671. St. Neott.
Joan, dau. of Peter and Jane Courteney, bap.	1673. ,,
Peter, son ,, ,, ,,	1679. ,,
Joseph, son ,, ,, ,,	1687. ,,
Willm ,, ,, ,, ,,	1683. ,,

[*Continued over.*

Cowlin.

Robt. Cowlin of Trevegles=

- Robt. Coulin fil. et heres ob. s. p.
- Willm Cowlin of Mathern in parochia de Trenguenthen[1] in Com. Cornw. fil. 2 = Ellen Da. of James Chanough de St Martin

Willm Cowlin 2 filius unmaried secns

Alice Da. of John Parmere of Sunner[2] in Com.Cornw.ux.2 = John Cowlin de Trenguenthen in pochia de Madern ætat. = Christian Da. of Robt Rosetor of Kestenton[3] ux. prima

- Anne — Alice
- John Colin fil. 2 ætat. 20 annoru. 1620
- Thomas Cowlin fil. et heres ret. 40 Annoru. = Katherin Da. of Willm. Levelis de Madern
- Gertrude mar. to Emanuell Blewet de Com. Devon

Robt. 3 fil. ætat. 2 annoru.

John Cowlin fil. et heres æt. 15

Willm Cowlin 2 fil. 10

1. Honor
2. Anne

3. Jone

       *   N

The M'ke of John Cowlin.

Parish Registers—continued.

		PARISHES.
Peter Courteney, bur.	1704.	St. Neott.
John Courteney and Mary Rawe, mar.	1709.	,,
John, son of John and Mary Courteney bap.	1716.	,,
Peter ,, ,, ,, ,,	1717.	,,
Will. ,, Will. and Jane Courteney, bap.	1742.	,,
John ,, ,, ,, ,,	1745.	,,
Willm, son of Peter C. Knt, by Alse his wife, bap.	1647.	St. Sampson's.
Ric. Courteney, gent., bur. 3 May,	1627.	St. Winnow.
Eleanor	1629.	,,
Allse, wife of Sir Peter Cortnye, bur. in the Church 25 Nov.	1659.	Tywardreath.
Mr Humphary Corteny and Mistres Allse Cortne, mar. 27 Dec.	1666.	,,
Edw., s. of Humphry Courteny, Esq., bapt. 22 Dec.	1667.	,,
Tho. Courteney and Jane Chely, mar. 26 May	1696.	,,

Marriage Licenses.

John Courteney, gen. de Lazack al's Ladock, and Anne St. Albin, dau. of St. Albyn of Crowan, ar.   10 Oct., 1595.

Edw. Courteney of Lazac, ar. and Elizb. Gorges of St. Budeaux   1614.

Will. Courtney of Butshed, in p'ish of St. Budoxe and Dorothy Gorg. of same gen.   1615.

Ric. Courteney of Lanivet, gen. and Philippa, dau. of Humphry Prouze of Chagford, mar.   17 May, 1637.

Peter Courteney of Lazack, ar. and Alice, dau. of Jonathan Rashleigh of Fowey, mar. 11 Dec., 1638.

Mr Wm Courteny of St. Mich. Penk. and Elizb. Crossman of Botesfleming, ,,   17 Dec., 1639.

---

[1] Treugwainton.   [2] Zennor ?   [3] Constantine ?

* Jeffery Cowlyn. gent., and Dorothy Courteney, mar. 17 Jan., 1561.—Chudleigh par. reg., Devon. John Cowling of Trewornon, and Joan ux. eius qu. Peter Burnand, def., names John, s. of Ju^n Cowling. Ped. fin. 32 Ed. III. No. 3.

Crab.

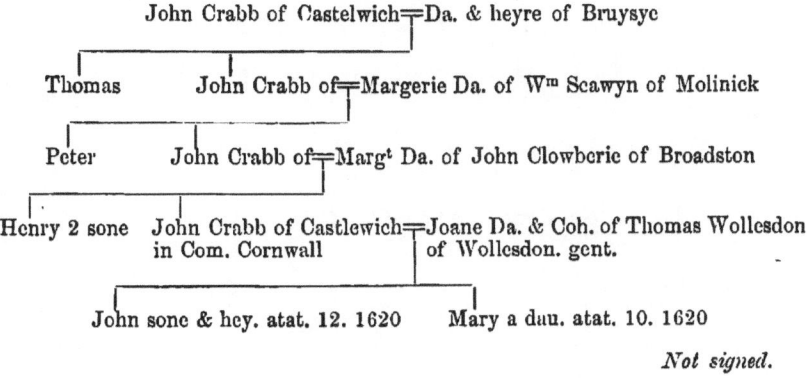

Not signed.

Cressel.*

Sciant presentes et futuri qd ego Nicholaus de Todiford dedi, concessi et hac p'senti carta mea confirmavi Robto fratri meo de Cressel unam acrum terræ Cornubiensis in Harelesdon &c. Hijs testibus Vinc de Poldresak Ermano de le Marquille Rico de Tregrilla, Waltero Doygnill et alijs sans dat

Sciant present. et futur' qd ego Ruwall de Cressol dedi concessi et hac present. carta mea confirmavi Robto de Treviwen p' homagio et servicio suo totam terram meam in Harelsdon &c. sans dat.

Sciant present. qd ego Rad'us de Cressel didi concessi et hac presenti Carta mea confirmavi Robto de Cressell totam terram meam in villa de Cressell &c. Hijs testibus Willo de Penquit Rico de la Brigge, Willo de Carballa et alijs. Dat. in festu Sti Lawrencij martiris anno regni Regis Edw. tercij a conquestu Angl. quinto

Sciant present' et futur' qd ego Walterus de Polhclon dedi concessi et hac presenti carta confirmavi Willo de Cressell Heredibus suis et assignatis &c. Dat. Die Sabbati prox post festu' Beati Joh'is ante porta' Latinam, A° regni regis Edw. III. a conq. Angli. nonodecimo

Hac Indentura facta inter Will'm Cressell et Isabell uxore' eius ex parte una et Joh'em Proseper et Margeria' uxore' eius et altra p'te testatur q^d predict. Will'mus et Isabella, Joh'is et Margcia &c. Hijs testibus Ric'o de Trochynock, Hen. Tresulgan, Johi Scawen et alijs. Dat. apud Sanctu' Gorna in die veneris prox post festum Sc'i Andrea Ap'li. A° regni regis Rici secundi tercio

Sciant presentes et futur' q^d ego Willms Cressoll et Isabella uxor mea dedimus concessimus et hac presenti Carta nostra confirmavimus Nicho. de Padarda et Thomo filio suo et heredibus de corporibus d'ci Thome excuntibus unam p'cellam terræ &c. Dat. apud Cressell die veneris prox post festu' S'ci Martini. Anno regni regis Rici secundi a conquestu Angli. decimo octavo

* Malger Cressel held Cressel, temp. K. John. Assize Roll, 8 John, Launceston.

THE VISITATION OF THE COUNTY OF CORNWALL.

Riwall de Cressoll sans dat.

Radus de Cressoll A° 5 E. III.

Willm's de Cressoll A° 19 E. III.

Willms de Cressell A° R. II. 3 et 18 = Isabella uxor eius

John Cressoll de Cressoll in Com. Cornb.

John Cressell de Cressell = Elizab. Da. of . . . Grills of
in Cornub.   Shevioke in Cornwall

John Cressell de Cressell = Agnes Da. of Edw. Scawen   James 2 fil. de
fil. primo.   of St Germins   St Germins

Jone æt. 30 Will'ms Cressell fil et heres = Amy Da. of Willm   John 2 fil.
—   æt. 40 Annoru' 1620   Andrew of St Germins   æt. 34
Parnell 19

Robt. Cressell fil. pri-   Thomas 2 fil.   John 3 fil. æt.
mogenitus ætat. 8   ætat. 5   3 mensis.

JOHN CRESSEL.

Crewes.

John Crwse[1] younger Brother of the house of = Jone[2] Da. of Baberie
Morchard lived at Liskerd in Com. Cornwall   in Com. Corny.

Rich. Crwse   Gilbert Crwse of = Jane Da. of James Humphrie   John Crwse 3 sone
fil. primoge.   St Garons in   of St Garrans in Com. Corn-   mar. Mary Da. of
ob. s. p.   Com. Cornwall   wall   . . . .
    A   B

---

[1] He was son of Anthony Crewes of Liskeard (who came from Cruse Morchard, Devon) by Johanna, wid. of Nicholas Glynn, and daughter of John Bealburye of Liskeard, Merchant, who died 28 July, 1581, and by Will (prob. at Exeter, 1583) gave unto John Crewes and the heirs of his body, lands in Burgh of Leskerd, Lyskeard Sanctuary, Trembrase, Trewidlonde, Trewen, Skynter, Trematon, Colewood in p'ish of St. Nightons, Bodmin, Easthendra in the p'ish of St. Kewe, and Bodinnick, co. Cornw.; rem. to Anthony Crewes, in default to rt. hrs. respectively of his three daurs., viz., Johan. ux. Anthony Crewes, and late wife of Nicholas Glynn, æt. 40; Alice, ux. Jn° Madocke, late ux. Jn° Petherbridge, æt. 37; and Thomazin, ux. Jn° Drake, and late ux. Tho. Ryder, æt. 30. Inq. p. m. 24 Elizh. John Bealbury purchased the advowson of Roche, Cornw. (Star Chamb. Ify. VIII.) Thomazin, dau. and cob., married John Drake; and the will of Will. Drake, Rector of Roche, was proved at Exeter 1597.

[2] Da. of Christf. Tredenick of St. Breock. Harl. MS. 1079, fos. 186 and 33.

THE VISITATION OF THE COUNTY OF CORNWALL. 57

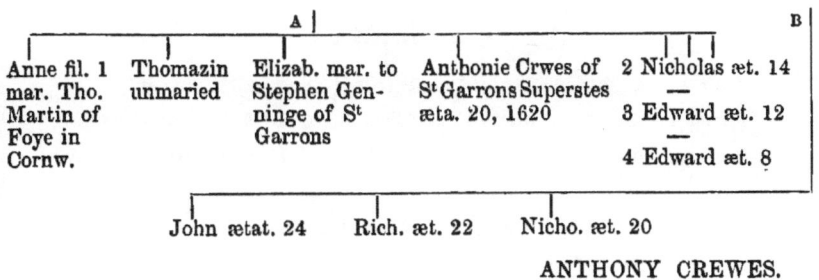

ANTHONY CREWES.

Crocker.

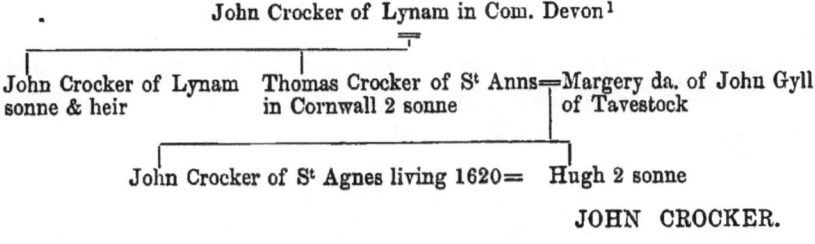

JOHN CROCKER.

Crockhay.

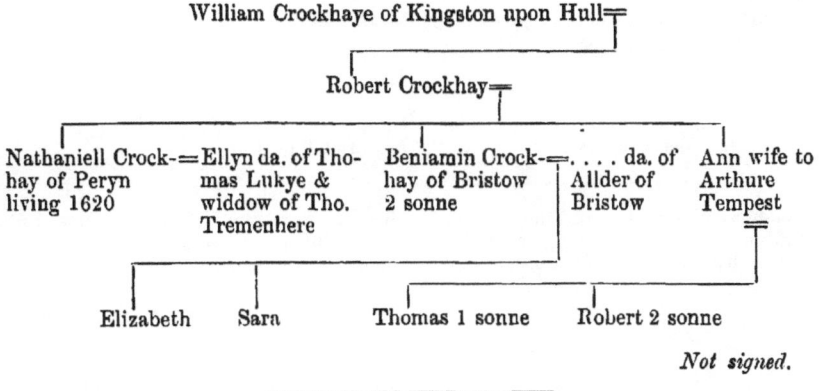

Not signed.

---

[1] Mary, dau. of John Croker of Lynham, married Hen. Knyvett of Cornwall, *vide* Ped. post, and Mary, 3rd dau. of John Croker of Lynham, mar. Tho. Southcott, *vide* Ped. 'Harl. Soc. Visit. Dev., 1620,' p. 269.

Crosman.

ARMS. *Sa. a chevr. Or. betw. 3 goats' heads erased Arg.*

James Crasman of Crose in Com. Corn. quere testified by Mr Estcote.

Jo. Croseman of Crosse in Cornwall gent. 24 H. VII.=Joane Da. of Louis

    Edw. Crosman of Crosse gent. 7 H. VIII.=Joane Da. of Brendon

        John Crosman [1] of Crosse=Phillip Da. of John Gifford of
        gent. 37 H. VIII.   Hallisburie in Com. Devon Esq.

[2] John Crosman of Crosse=Blanch Da. & Coh. of Edw. Couch of St. Stephens   Nicho. Crosman of St. Peniock in Cornwall=Marg^t Da. of Rich. Myners

[3] Rich. 2 sone of Crosse=Mary Da. of Rich. Trevanian   James Crosman of Crosse in Com. Cornwall liveing 1620=Elizb. Da. of Nicho. Skellton of Landilt   Phill. ux' Wm. Ede of St. Peniock   Elizb. uxor Jo. Eustace of St. Penioke

        Elizab. Da. & hey. at. half yeare

JAMES CROSMAN.   The marke of + NICHO. CROSMAN.

Cullow.

ARMS. *The Coate as they suppose is 3 garbes in pale.*

Henry Cullow of Tintagell=Walthen Da. John of Kelly

    John Cullow of Tintagell in Com. Cornwall=Jane [4] Da. & hey. of Rich. Facy of Winscott in the parish of Puerthy

[5] Honor 3 fil. mar. to [6] Edm. Painter of Lanreth in Cornwall   [7] Willm Cullow of Tintagell in Com. Cornwall ætat. 30 annoru' 1620   [8] Jane 4 Du. æt. 20 annor.   [9] Grace fil. primogenita ætat. 40 unmaried   Anna 2 fil. æt. 36 unmaried

            WILLIAM CULLOW.

---

[1] Ob. 4 Oct. 9 Eliz. Inq. p. m. 12 Elizb. No. 51, names his wife Phillipa, and John his son and h.
[2] Æt. 20 and 6 month, 12 Elizb.   [3] Married at Goran 28 Jan., 1617. Bp. of Exeter's Transcripts.
[4] Jane wife of Jno. Cullow bur. 10 Dec. 1621.   [5] Honor da. of Jno. Cullow bap. 28 Mar., 1595. ⎫ Tintagel
[6] (Edm) Painter and Honner Cullow mar. 20 Jan., 1618.   [7] Will. Cullow (ætatis 81) bur. 29 June, 1671. ⎬ Par.
[9] Grace da. of Jno. Cullow bur. 2 Aug., 1623. ⎭ Reg. (J. M.)
[8] Jane da. of Jno. Cullow bap. 29 Ap., 1597.

Dagge.

Sciant p'sentes et futuri q^d ego Willo Dagh de St Eth dedi concessi et hac p'sent carta mea confirmavi Warino Donand omnia messuagio &c. in Villa de St Eath &c. Dat' apud St Eath A° 45 Ed. III.

Sciant p'sentes & futuri q^d ego Lucea que fuit ux^r Joh'is Smith de Trewegett in pura viductate mea dedi concessi & hac presenti carta mea confirmavi &c. Rico Smith filio meo & Roesie filio Johis Cradock omnia messuagia terr. et tenement. &c. Dat' apud Trewegett A° Regni Regis Edw. post conquest. Angliæ Octavo.

Taken out of an old paper pedegre written in a very auntient hand, remaining in the custodie of John Dagg of Trewegett in Com. Cornub. the 2 of October a° D'ni 1620.

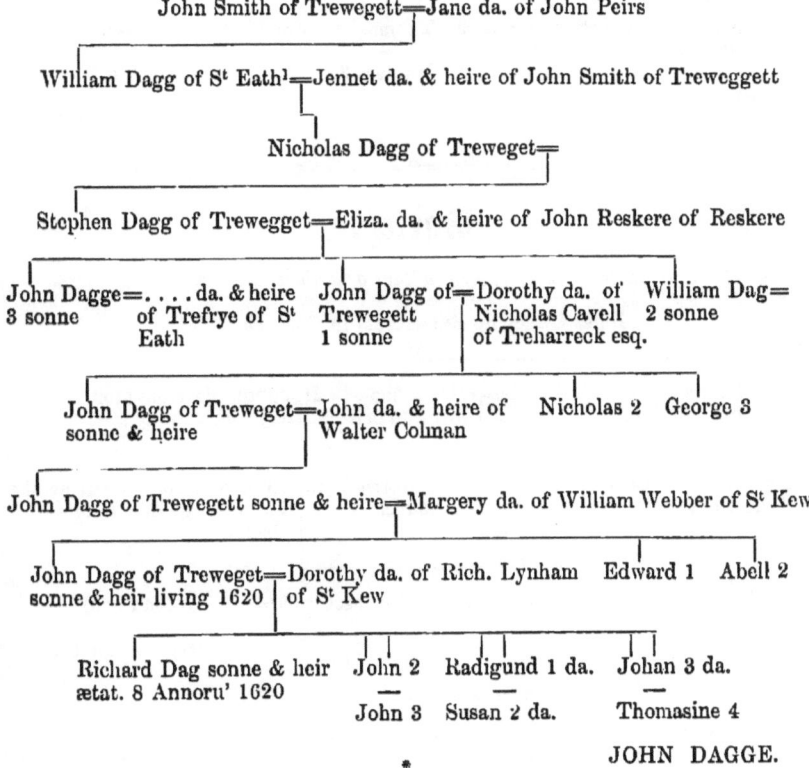

JOHN DAGGE.

---

[1] St. Teath.

* Several members of this family were Mayors of Bodmin. One, Digory Dag of St. Kew, son of Nicholas, before 1623 was a charitable benefactor, as appears on a Tablet in Bodmin Church. For a more comprehensive pedigree of Dagg, see Sir John Maclean's 'Hist. of Trigg,' vol. i., p. 296, and vol. ii., pp. 178, 179.

Dandy.

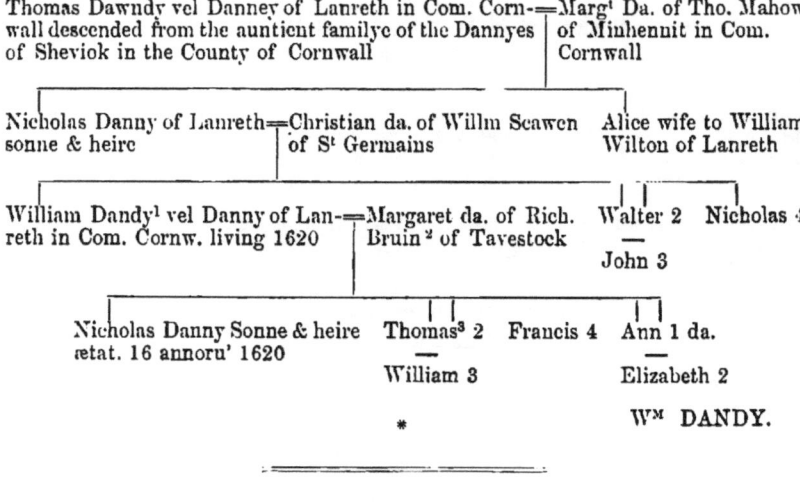

Darley.

ARMS. *Gu. 6 fleurs-de-lis 3, 2, 1, Arg. within a bordure Ermine.*

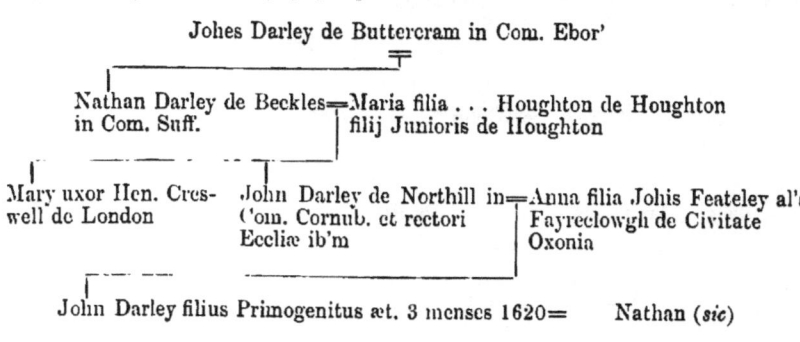

[1] Bur. 30 Mar., 1648; Margt., his wife. bur. 2 Aug., 1650. Mur. Tab. Lanreath Ch.
[2] Same as Browne of Brownlarsh. [3] Thos. Dandy, gent., bur. 1692. Lanreath Par. Reg.
* Inq. p. m. 6 Ed. III., 2nd Nos., No. 79, Nich. Dannay. John, his son and heir. æt. 30 and more. Inq. p. m. 20 Ed. III., 1st Nos., No. 33. John Daunee al's Dauney, Chivalier, ob. 4 Aug., 20 Ed. III. Emelyna, da. and heir, æt. 18 and more (she afterwards married Sir Edw. Courteney, and was mother of Edw. C., the blind Earl of Devon). Names Will. Daunee and John, brother of Nich. Daunee; lands in Sheviock, &c.
Ped. Fin. 36 Eliz. Hillary, Cornw. No. 16. Joseph Bastard, qu. Nicholas Dandy, gent., and others def. tent, in Rescradock.
Ped. Fin. 41 Eliz., Mich.. Cornw. No. 35. William Moulton, gen., and William Dandy, gen. qu. Edm. Dourich, gen., and Agnes, his wife, def. mess. aud tent. in Saltash.

THE VISITATION OF THE COUNTY OF CORNWALL. 61

Darrell.

To enquyre better for this descent of Brandon.

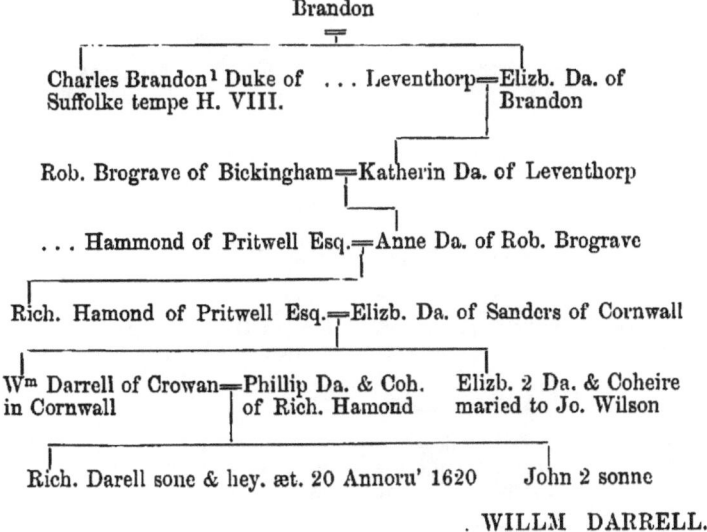

Brandon
|
┌──────────────┴──────────────┐
Charles Brandon[1] Duke of ... Leventhorp=Elizb. Da. of
Suffolke tempe H. VIII.   Brandon
                                   |
Rob. Brograve of Bickingham=Katherin Da. of Leventhorp
                                   |
... Hammond of Pritwell Esq.=Anne Da. of Rob. Brograve
                                   |
Rich. Hamond of Pritwell Esq.=Elizb. Da. of Sanders of Cornwall
     |
┌────┴─────────────────────┬───────────────────────┐
Wm Darrell of Crowan=Phillip Da. & Coh.   Elizb. 2 Da. & Coheire
in Cornwall   of Rich. Hamond   maried to Jo. Wilson
     |
┌────┴────────────────────────────┐
Rich. Darell sone & hey. æt. 20 Annoru' 1620   John 2 sonne
                                       . WILLM DARRELL.

Denys.

ARMS. 1. DENNYS. *Erm.* 3 *battle axes gu.* 2. DABERNON. 3. GIFFARD. 4. BREWER. 5. BOCKERELL. 6. *Ar., a chev. sa. charged with three acorns or, between 3 birds' h'ds erased of the second.* ? CHRISTENSTOW.
CREST. *A Griffin's head eras. erm.*
Ie le proveray vray.

Tho. Dennis of Holcomb=Jenn^or Da. of Phill. Lovday of Cheston in Suff.
     |
┌────┴──────────────┬──────────────────────────────┐
Sr Thomas Dennis 1 sonne   Hen. Dennis of Petroke Stowe=Alice Da. of Speeke
                             in Devon 4 sonne
                                   |
Tho. Dennis of Creede in Com. Cornwall=Marg^t Da. of Tho. Tremayne
                                      | A

---

[1] Anne, sister of Charles Brandon, D. of Suff., was widow of Sir John Shillston, and first wife of Sir Gawen Carew. Tomb in Exeter Cathedral. Named in will of Sir G. C. P. C. C. 34, Brudenell, 1585.

THE VISITATION OF THE COUNTY OF CORNWALL.

| A
| 1

Grace Da. of Wm Leigh = Tho. Dennis of Menheniot = Grace Da. of Jo. Polewheele
of St. Katherin's in   of Cornwall liveinge 1620   of Polewheele in Cornwall
Cornw.

Edmond   Mary   Tho. sone & hey.   Grace   Dorithie
2 Sone   3 Da.   atat. 16. 1620   1 Da.   2 Da.

*

THOMAS DENYS.

Dewen.

Raphe Dewin[1] of Gwinnier in Com. Cornwall = Da.[2] & Coh. of Tristram Culland

Katherin mar. to Willm Geare son of   Thomas Dewin[3] = Alice Da. of ... Geare
Geare Father of Alic wife to Tho.   of Gwinier   of Marrasow[4] in Com.
Dewin   Corn.

Thomas[5] 2 fil.   John Dewin[6] de = Marg^t Da. of John Thomas   Jane[7]   Blanch mar.
ætat. 30   Gwiner in Com.   of Crowan in Com. Corn-   virg   to Chapman
annor'   Cornwall   wall

4 Anna[8] ætt. 12   Thomas Dewin[11]   2 John[12]   1 Elianor æt. 20
                    sonne & heire   æt. 8
5 Elizab.[9] 7   atat. 17   2 Alice[13] æt. 18

6 Mary[10] 5   3 Charity 16

†   JOHN DEWEN.

* Edward Denys and Maria Thom's were mar. 25 Nov. 1581, St. Ewe Par. Reg. This Ped. is given at considerable length in Harl. MS. 1079, ffo. 177-8.

[1] Bur. 20 Aug. 1580.   [7] Bapt. 23 April, 1581.
[2] Ann, wife of Ralph. Dewin, bur. [8] „ 23 July, 1608.
    25 March, 1575.   [9] „ 31 Jan., 1610.
[3] Bur. 14 Feb. 1590.   [10] „ 20 Feb., 1613.
[4] Marazion.   [11] „ 7 Mar., 1608.
[5] Bapt. 13 April, 1589.   [12] „ 31 Jan., 1611.
[6] „ 1 April, 1571.   [13] „ 26 April, 1601.

† Grace, da. of Thomas Dewin, bapt. 17 Jan., 1573.
  Raffe, son of   „   „   19 Jan., 1574.
  Margery, da. of   „   „   1 April, 1582.
  Barbara, „   „   „   5 June, 1583.
  Jane,   „   „   „   10 May, 1607.
  Edward, son of   „   „   27 Aug., 1615.
  Peter,   „   „   bur. 24 Nov., 1577.
  Margery, da. of   „   „   20 June, 1582.
  Edward son of   „   „   10 Nov., 1615.
  Katherine daughter of Thomas Dewin
  and John Polkingborne, mar. 18 Feb., 1594.

Gwinear Par. Reg.

Dodson.

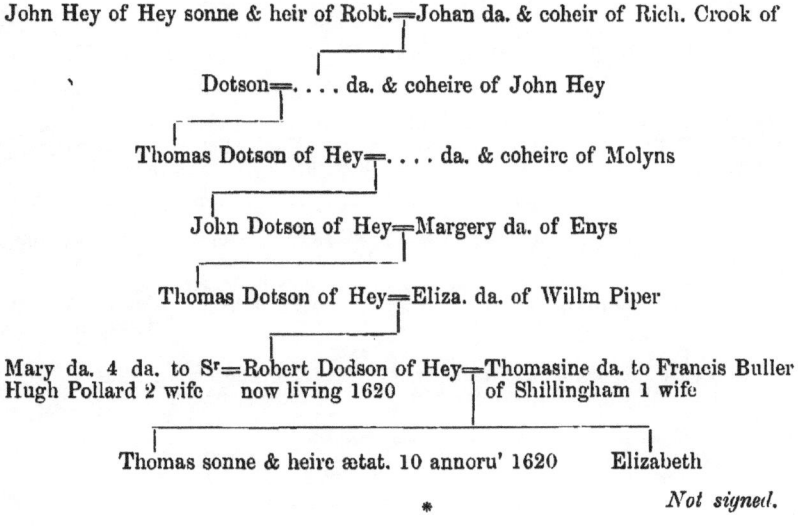

* Thomas Dotson, gener., buried 1610. Wendron Par. Reg.
John, son of Tho. Dodson, Esq., of Hay, in St. Ive, bur. 23 Sept., 1730, æt. 14, at Lansallos. Wm. Drake, cler., mar. Jane Dosten 3 Dec., 1598. Wm. Dosten mar. Honor Williams, 1604. Fra., s. of Wm. Dosen, bur. 1608. Truro Par. Reg.

Edgcombe.

ARMS. *Three shields are given :—*
   The first is impaled. BARON, *blank.* FEMME. *Or, a chev. betw. 3 escallops sa.*
   The second shield is of EDGCOMBE. *Gu. on a bend sa. cottised or, 3 boars' h'ds erased (? couped) arg.*
   Third shield, quarterly, 1 & 4, EDGCOMB. 2 & 3 (HOLLAND). *Sa. semée de fleurs-de-lis, a lion ramp. within a border engr. all arg.*
CREST. *A Boar's h'd couped prop.*

[1] Sr Richd Edgcomb. Kt. comptroler of the houshould to H. VII. ob. 1409. 8 Die Septemb.=

[2] Sr Pierse Edgcomb Kt. of Mont=Da. & hey. of Dernford
Edgcomb in Com. Devon
                                    A

[1] The date here given is incorrect. Hen. VII. began his reign 22 Aug., 1485. For more of Sir Rich. Edgcombe see 'Le Neve's Ped. of Knights,' Harl. Soc. Pub., p. 25.
   [2] Int. Wm. Courtency, and ors. qu. Peter Eggcombe, Kt., and Johanna his wife, def., East Stonehouse, Ashwater, Goodlegh, &c., Ped. fin., Cornwall, 7 Hen VIII., Mich. Term. No. 76.
   Inq. p. m. 19 Ed. IV. No. 35., James Dernford, son and h. of James, son and h. of Stephen Dernford. Johanna, da. and heir of said James, æt. 5 years and more.

THE VISITATION OF THE COUNTY OF CORNWALL.

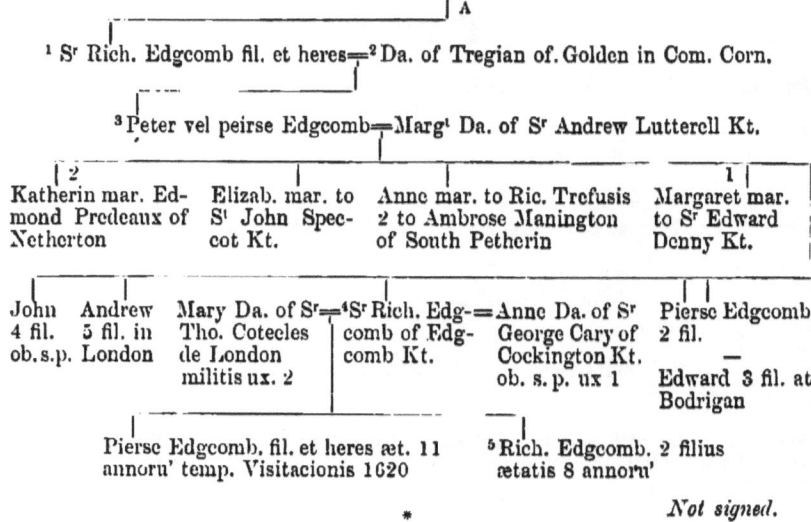

1 Sr Rich. Edgcomb fil. et heres=2 Da. of Tregian of. Golden in Com. Corn.

3 Peter vel peirse Edgcomb=Marg^t Da. of Sr Andrew Luttercll Kt.

| 2 Katherin mar. Edmond Predeaux of Netherton | Elizab. mar. to St John Speccot Kt. | Anne mar. to Ric. Trefusis 2 to Ambrose Manington of South Pethcrin | 1 Margaret mar. to Sr Edward Denny Kt. |

| John 4 fil. ob. s.p. | Andrew 5 fil. in London | Mary Da. of Sr Tho. Cotecles de London militis ux. 2 | =4 Sr Rich. Edgcomb of Edgcomb Kt. | =Anne Da. of Sr George Cary of Cockington Kt. ob. s. p. ux 1 | Pierse Edgcomb 2 fil. — Edward 3 fil. at Bodrigan |

Pierse Edgcomb, fil. et heres æt. 11 annoru' temp. Visitacionis 1620

5 Rich. Edgcomb. 2 filius ætatis 8 annoru'

Not signed.

Edgcombe.

Sr Rich. Edgcomb Kt. Mont Edgcomb=

Sr Peter Edgcomb=

Sr Rich Edgcomb. Kt.=
| A

1 Sir Richard died 1 Feb., 1562. Will dated 1 July, 1560, proved in London 24 April, 1562, names Richard, Henry, and Edward, his sons, a daughter mar. to Henry Champeruon, and his daughters Anne and Honor (Edward and the two last not of age). This da. Anne was wife of the Rev. Hugh Dowrish, Rector of Lapford; mar. lic. dated 29 Nov., 1580. She dedicated, in 1589, a book, now very scarce, to her loving brother Master Pearse Edgecombe of Mount Edgecombe, Devon, entitled 'A History of Bloody Broils,' &c. The dedication is a curious Acrostic on Pears Edgcomb's name. It is noticed in the Select Poetry of the Parker Society, 1845.
2 Inq. p. m., John Wyse, 34 Hen. VIII., No. 37, Sir Richard's wife is called Elizabeth [according to Edmondson Elizabeth was da. of Sir Jno. Arundell]; and in Inq. p. m., Sir Rich. Edgcombe, 4 Eliz. No. 29, the names of the children are given as in the will, but the Christian name of Champernon's wife is omitted.
3 Executor of his father's will, which he proved 24 April, 1562, as Peter Edgecombe. He was son and heir of Sir Richard, and aged 26 at his father's death. *Vide* Inq. p. m. 4 Eliz. No. 29.
4 Knighted at Whitehall 23 July, 1603.
5 Monument in St. Gorran Church. To Rich. Edgcumb of Bodrugan, Ar., a younger son of Sir Richard Edgcumb, erected by Piers Edgcumb, the eldest son, A.D. 1655.

* Sir Andrew Luttrell's wife was Marg^t, dau. of Sr Thomas Wyndham, the grandson of John Howard, 1st Duke of Norff. of that name. This match brought a Royal descent from Thos de Brotherton into the house of Edgcomb. Marg^t Luttroll's will P. C. C. 8 Butt. 1583. Peter Edgcumbe and his daughter Margaret his wife, Executors.

THE VISITATION OF THE COUNTY OF CORNWALL. 65

                        A

Peter Edgcomb.[1]=Marg^t Da. of Sr Andrew Luttrell Kt.

Sr Rich. Edgcomb. Kt.   Edw. Edgcomb. of Bodringham[2] in Cornw.
sone & hey.   3 sone of Peter liveing 1620

                                                EDWARD EDGCOMBE.

Edmondes.

Rich. Edmondes of Lidington in Com.=Margerie Da. of Rich.
Rutland who came out of the house of Knoles of Cold Ashby
Empingham in Lincolnsh.   in Com. Northampton

Roger 1 sone of Everard Edmondes=Jenephor Da. of Elizb. Margery
Lidington in   of Trwro in Com.   Michael Averie ux^r   ux^r Wil-
Com. Rutland   Cornwall liveinge of Trwro in   Haddon liames
liveinge 1620   1620 2 sonne   Cornwall

Edward Hugh Francis Hen. sone & hey. Margerie
2 sone   3 sone 1 Da.   atat. 7, 1620   2 Da.

                              EVERARD EMONDES. [*sic.*]

Edwardes.

Da. of Samford of   =Henry Edwardes of Lelant=Matilda Da. of
Coome florie de Com.   in Hund. Penwth Marg^t[3] da. John Launce of
Somerset relicta   of John Gavrigan of Gavri- St. Clemets iuxta
Stephens 2 uxor   gan in Com. Cornw. ux 3   Truro ux. 1

Willm William Tho. Edwards=Jane Da. of John Ros- Jenefer
—   de Lelant in   cruge de Roscrude in   —   }ob. infantes
Stephn.   Com. Cornwall Com. Cornwall   Elizab.

Jane   Margaret Henry Edwards Thomas Beniamin
—   —   fil. primogenitus 2 fil. 13 3 fil. æt. 7
Anne Prudence æt. 20, 1620
                           *
                                     THO. EDWARDES.

---

[1] Ob. 4 Jan. 4 Jas. 1606-7. Sr Rich. Edgcomb, son & h., æt. 30, et ampl. Misc. Inq. p. m. Eliz., Jas. & Chas., No. 109. Barton of Mount Edgcombe al's West Stonehouse, & other lands named.
[2] Bodrigan.   [3] She was widow of Wm. Bossavern. Harl. MS., 4031, fos. 61 & 62.
* Int. Ralph Edwards, gen. q. Michael Tresahar, gen., and Tho. Tresaher, gen., def. lands in Tregandallion al's Tregantallan and Mewan. Ped. fin. Cornw. 8 James I. Michm.

Elford.

John Elford of Shippester in Com. Devon=Margery da. of Roger Langefford

John Elford of Ship-=....da. of Gregory[1] | Thomas Elford of Mawnan in Com. Cornub. living 1620 =Alice da. of Benny & widdow of Edw. Spry
pesford sonne & heir

Walter Elford of Shippester living 1620=Barbara da. of John Crocker of Lynam

THOM'S ELFORD.

Ellyott or Eliot.

ARMS. 1. ELLIOT. *Argent, a Fess gu. betw. 4 cotises wavy, B.* 2. CUTLAND. 3. *Arg., a trefoil slipped vert.* 4. *B., a tilting spear palewise betw. 2 mullets or.* 5. PAWLHERMAN. 6. BREWIN. 7. KERSWELL. 8. DOWNE. 9. PRAWLE. 10. BRIXSTON. 11. *Arg. on a chief B., 3 mullets or.* 12. GILL.

CREST. *An Elephant's hd. coup. A., collared g.*

Edw. Ellyott of Cutland in Com. Devon.=Alice Da. of Rob. Gye of Kingsbridge

Marg.t Da. of Jo. Brjwyn of Plimouth =Jo. Elliot of St. Germayns in Com. Cornwall gent. =Grace Dau. of Jo. Fitze of Tavistock =Tho. Elyot of 2 sonne =Joane Da. of John Norbrooke of Exiter

Edward 4 sone | Hugh 2 sonne | Walter 3 sone | Richard 1 sone of Port Eliott[2] | =Bridget Da. & Cohey. of Carswell[3] of Hatch | Alice a dau.

A

---

[1] Elizabeth, daughter of Gregory of Plympton St. Mary. She afterwards married Thomas Drake (bro. and h. of the first Sir Francis D.) 'Visit. Devon, 1620,' Harl. Soc., pp. 105 and 96. And her will (as Elizb. Drake, wid.) proved P. C. C., 68 Audley, 23 June, 1632, mentions her son Sir Francis Drake, and other members of his family, her two sons, Will.m and Walter Elford, who are appointed overseers, and the following children of her son Walter: John (and Elizabeth his wife), Walter, Will.m, Frances, wife of Ric. Langworthy, gent. (and their dau., Elizab. I.), Anne, Joane, Elizb., Marie. Her da.-in-law, Barbara Elford. Her grandson, John, executor.

[2] Died 22 June, 1609. Inq. p. m., 7 James, part 2, No. 97. Names John, son and h., æt. 17, 11 April, 1609; and wife Radigund, da. of Rich. Gedye; also his own wife Bridget, and his uncle John E.

[3] A daughter of Nicholas Carswell, Ar. of Hatch Arundell, co. Devon. She ob. 5 March, 5 Jas. Jno. Elliott, son and h., aged 24 years and more. Inq. p. m. (16 Jas.) Eliz., Jas., and Chas., part 4, No. 124.

* For Extension of Elford, see 'Visit. Dev. 1620,' Har. Soc. Pub., p. 105.

THE VISITATION OF THE COUNTY OF CORNWALL. 67

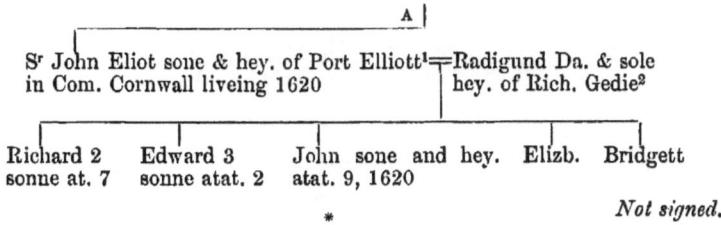

Sr John Eliot sone & hey. of Port Elliott[1]⹀Radigund Da. & sole
in Com. Cornwall liveing 1620 | hey. of Rich. Gedie[2]

Richard 2 sonne at. 7 | Edward 3 sonne atat. 2 | John sone and hey. atat. 9, 1620 | Elizb. | Bridgett

Not signed.

Enys.

The Coate of Enys is 3 Lizardes & must borne first [*sic*].

Tho. Enys of Eneys⹀Kath. Da. of John Reskimer
in Com. Cornwall | of Merthen in Cornwall

| Avis uxr Jo. Tre-thowen of Trethowen | Grace uxr Hen. Tyrack — Blanch 2 Da. | Jo. Enys of Eneys⹀Wynifrid Da. in Com. Cornw. | and Cohey. of liveing 1620 | Tho. Rise of Trewardrevah | Agnes uxr Mathew Woldridge | Sinobia uxr John Coffin |

[3]John 2
Samwell 3 | Thomas sone and heire atat. 15, 1620 | Richard 4 sonne | Katherina daughter

†

JOHN ENYS.

Crisey.

To remember to serch for the Coate that are to be quartered by Erysye, vidz.:—
1. ERYSIE.
2. EARE.
3. DURANT.
4. MILLETON.

Willm de Herisi sanz dat.⹀⎫
⎬ proved by a deed without date.
Ricardus de Herisi filius Willi Sanz date.⎭

---

[1] Aged 17 years, 11 April, 1609, Knighted at Whitehall, 10 May, 1618, died 27 Nov., 8 Chas. I. Inq. p. m., 8 Chas., part 3, No. 61. John, son & h., aged 20 years and 40 days at father's death.
[2] Inq. p. m., Rich. Gedy, 6 Chas., part 1, No. 90. Rich., son of Sir Jno. Elliot and Radigund his wife, &c., his heir.
[3] John, son of Mr. John Enys, was bapt. at Gluvias 4 April, 1610. Bp. of Exeter's Transcripts. (J. M.)

* William Ellyott, supposed to have been of this family, was the first Mayor of Falmouth when incorporated under the Charter of Chas. II. 1661.
† For earlier generations of this ped. see Harl. MS., 1079, fo. 201.

THE VISITATION OF THE COUNTY OF CORNWALL.

[1] John Erisy aº 19 E. III.=Johanna filia Allexanr D'ns de Godolghan.[2]

John Erysye aº 37 E. III.=

William Erisy aº 37 E. III.=

John Erisy aº 16 H. VI.=

Tho. Erisa of Erisa in Con. Cornwall Esq.=Alice Da. & hey.[3] of Ere of Grindreth.

James Erissa.=Margt Da. & one of heirs of Jo. Durant Pensinguns in Cornwall.[4]

Alice uxr Jo. Godolphin of Guinope.	Margerie uxr to Trenouth[6] of Trenouth.	[7] Katherin uxr Rich. Bonithon of Curklaw	James Erisa of Erisa.[5]	=Christian youngest Da. of Rog Grenvill of Stowe.	Julian uxr Jo. Arondel of Trerise.
Margt 1 da.	Philip wife to Cavell.	Honor uxr Wm Tucker of Exiter.	Rich.=Avce Da. & of Erisa. Coh. of Willm Milliton of Pengersey.	Dorothy wife to Pawle Hill.	Alice ux. 3 Da.	Julian wife to Specot of Hurledith.
Julian uxr Wm Wadda'8 of St Stevens.	Alice uxr Rog. Dolton of Ireland.	James Erisa of Errisa a sea Captayne.[9]	=Elizb. Da. of Tho. Carew of Anthonie.	Anne uxr Walt Tregost of Trewethock.

| Elizb. Da. of Petr Carew of Bickley in Devon. Esq.[10] | [1]=Rich. Erisa of Erisa in Com. Cornw. liveinge 1620 Esq. | [2]=Mary Da. of Sr James Ley of Westburie in Com. Wilts Kt & Baronet. | Dorithie uxor Martin Bosustow. |

James 1 sone æt. 4 1620.   Rich. 2 sonne atat. 5 weekes 1620.
A

[1] John Erisy, ob. 1328, married Joane dau. of Ric. Vivyan of Trevidren, ob. 1354. These were parents of John Erisy at the head of this ped. (*Vid.* Viviau ped., post.)   [2] Godolphin.
[3] In the Inq. p. m. 35 Hen. VIII., No. 8, of James Erisey, his grandmother's name is given as Elizabeth. His father James, grandfather Thomas E. and aunt Elizabeth Bonython also named.
[4] She died 1 January, 26 Hen. VIII., Jas. E., her son and h., æt. 34 years and more.' Esch. Inq. Cornw. 31 and 32 H. VIII., No. 3.   [5] Died 2 May, 33 H. VIII. Inq. p. m. 35 H.VIII. No. 8.
[6] Thos. Trenouth named in Inq. p. m. of Jas. Erisey, 35 H. VIII., together with Ralph Bonython and Elizab, ux., the da. of Tho. Erisey, and their sons John and Edmond B.
[7] She was wid. of Jno. Boys of Coswyn. See Inq. p. m. of her bro. James.   [8] Wadham.
[9] Commanded the White Lion under Sir Fra. Drake in 1585. and the galleon Dudley against the Armada, 1588. Ob. 3 Feb. 43 Eliz. Rich. son and h., æt. 10 years and no more 19 May. Misc. Inq. p. m., 43 Eliz. (temp. Eliz., Jas., and Chas.) part 7, No. 107.
[10] Rich. Erisey and Mrs. Elizb. Carew, mar. 9 April, 1615. Name of Parish obliterated. Bp. of Exeter's Transcripts. ? Bickley.
* Sir Nicholas Parker, Kt., mar. to Avis Erysye, widowe, 26 Jan., 1600, at Grade. Bp. of Exeter's Transcripts. (J. M.)
Elizb. da. of Ric. Erisey ar. bap. 3 Sept. 1623. Ruan Major Par. Reg.
Thomas, son of Ric. Erisey, Esq., bp. 1665.
Rich. Erisey, Gent., bur. 1700.
Charles Vivyan Ar. and Mary Erisey, da. of Rich. Erisey of St. Nyott Ar., mar. licence dated 11 March, 1674. } St. Neott Par. Reg.

| A |
| Kathr ux' Tho. Penwarne | Martha ux' Pet. | Geo. 2 | Gertrud uxr Harison |
| of Penorne 2 sonne. | Spry of [1] | sone. | 2d to Gravenor. |

RICHARD ERISEY.

Estcott.

Walter Estcott al's at Hole did graunt to Humphrie Beville Esq. & to John Pentier Esq. and to John Trevilian Esq. & to John Trenger Bastard, Tho. Viall, John Somaster, & Thos. Escott theire heires & assignes, all the lands lying in Davies w'thin the Mannor of Fenton & also all his lands in Tinnyo wch was lately the lands of Willm Blackdon, and also all his lands in Northdowne in the mannor of Westwillesworth. Dated at Fenton die lune prox ante festu Na'tis D'ni A° regni H. VI. 27.

SEAL.—*A shield charged with six escallops*, 3, 2, 1.

Willm. Totworthy the elder graunteth to Willm Davy & to Jone his wife & to Isabell their daughtr, one peece of land in Totworthy in the mannor of Northam, dated at Northam the monday next after the feast of the purificacion of the blessed Mary in the 10 yeare of H. IV.

SEAL.—*A shield charged with 3 plates on a fess betw. 3 griffins' heads erased.*

John Estcott the elder graunteth to Thos. Grenfeild Esq. & to John Estcott Junior all his lands in the p'ish of Holsworthy for ever according to the accustomed rent. Dated at Solden the 10 of Octob. in yᵉ 9 yeare of H. VII.

SEAL.—*Circular, having a gull, wings expanded.*

ARMS.—1. ESTCOTT. *Sa. six escallops Or*, 3, 2, 1.   2. *B. a fess Arg. charged with 3 roundlets B. betw. 3 griffins' h'ds eras. Arg.*   3. *Sa. a chev. betw. 3 trefoils slipped Arg.*   4. As 1. *An Escutcheon of Pretence, Gu. on a chief Arg. 2 Estoiles Sa.*

CREST.—*A gull erect, wings expanded Sa.*

This descent is proved downe by 25 auncient deeds whereof these are inserted yᵗ proveth the coate & creast.

| Ricus de Estcott | Willms Totworthy de | Walter at Comb. |
| sans date. | Totworthy Temp. R. I. | mar. Christian. |

Osbertus de Estcott duxit	Ricus Estcott	John Totworthy=Fil. et hæres
Basiliam fil. Willmi Laun-	Temp. R.	Temp. 5 R. II. Walteri at
celles.	Stepa.	Comb.

| Tho. Estcott duxit Asserian= | Thomas de Estcott de= | John Totworthy=fil. |
| fil. Adæ de Foye Militis. | Tamerton temp. E. III. | Temp. H. IV.   Noble. |

Richard Estcott mar.=	John Estcott at Hole in=	Willm Totworthy lived=
Jane da. of Gourdon.	Tamerton temp. H. V.	in the tyme of H. IV.
A	B	C

[1] Mar. at Ruan Major 10 Oct., 1614. (Par. Reg.) Henry Erisy, Esq., bur. 6 Ap. 1681. (Egloskerry Par. Reg.) Mrs. Frances Erissey, bur. 23 Ap. 1687. (Ruan Ma. Par. Reg.) Wm. Erissey, ob. 1688. Tomb. Egloskerry Churchyard.

* Ped. Fin. 4 King John, Corn. Pasch., No. 1. Inter Rich. de Trecarl q. Henry Heriz def. in Ebbeford, etc. Rob. de Heriz appears in the Assize Roll, Launceston, 8 K. John. Henry Erisey was seated at Tredidon, Egloskerry, A.D. 1676 (by deed in possess. of Ed.)

70 THE VISITATION OF THE COUNTY OF CORNWALL.

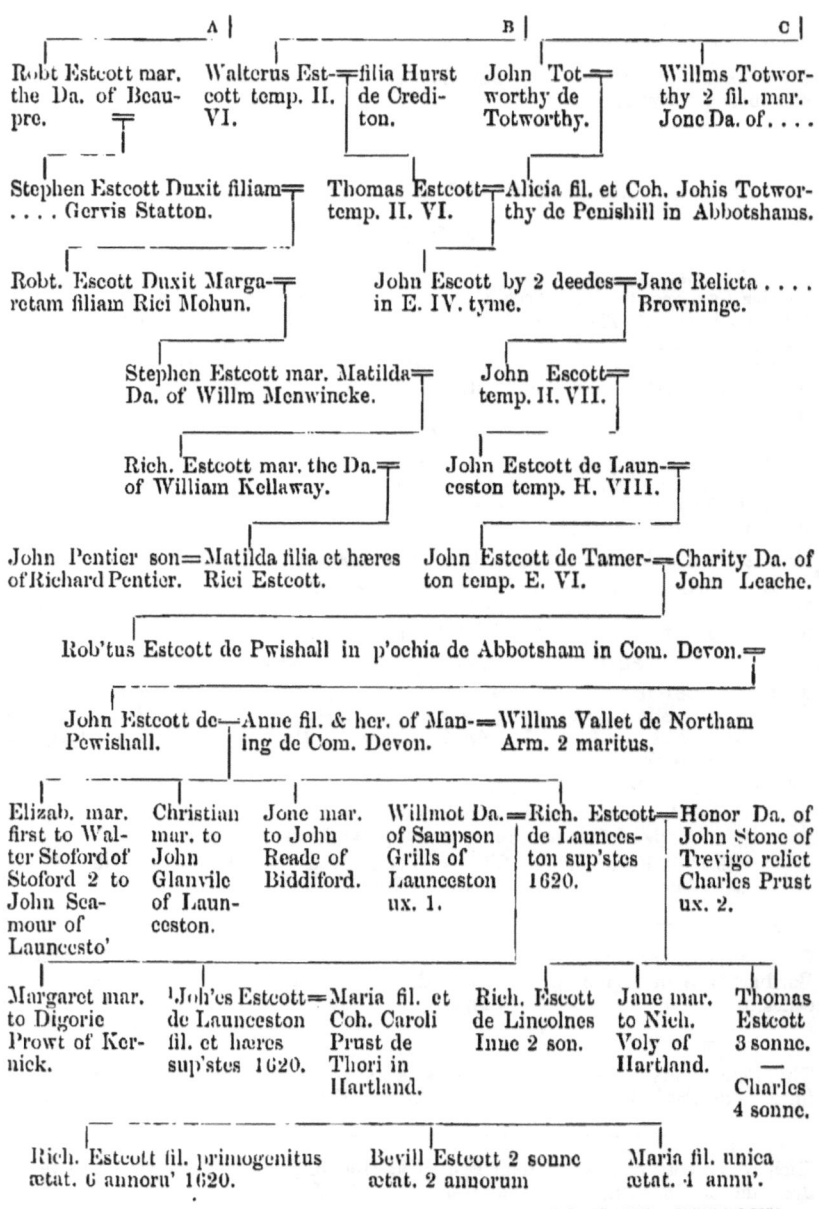

RICHARD ESTCOTT.

---

[1] In 1620, John Estcott of Launceston was Deputy to the Office of Arms for Devon and Cornwall (Bodl. Lib. Ashm. 836, fo. 513). (J. M.)

Fitzpen al's Phippen.

ARMS. *Arg. two bars, in chief 3 escallops, sable.*

Hen. Fitzpen of St. Mary Ov'y in Devon=Alice Da. of Peirse of Ireland
  |
  Jo. Fitzpen=. . . . Da. of . . . .
    |
    Robt. Fitzpen al's Fippen of=Cicilie Da. of Tho.
    Wamouth in Com. Dorset | Jordon of Dorsetsh.
    |
  ┌─────────────────┬──────────┬──────────────────────┬─────────┐
  Owen Fitzpen of   David   ²Geo. 3 sone of Trewro in Cicilie
  Ireland 1 sonne¹ 2 sone   Cornwall liveing 1620   a da.

GEO. FITZPEN AL'S PHIPPEN.

Flamanke.

ARMS. FLAMANKE. *Arg., a cross betw. 4 mullets, gu. pierced or, quartering* PEVERELL, *B. 3 garbs ar., a chief or.*

(The arms are trick'd in pencil, evidently by the Herald.)

Rich. Flamoke of Bukian in Cornw.=Margaret Da. of Peter Geirveis de Perin³

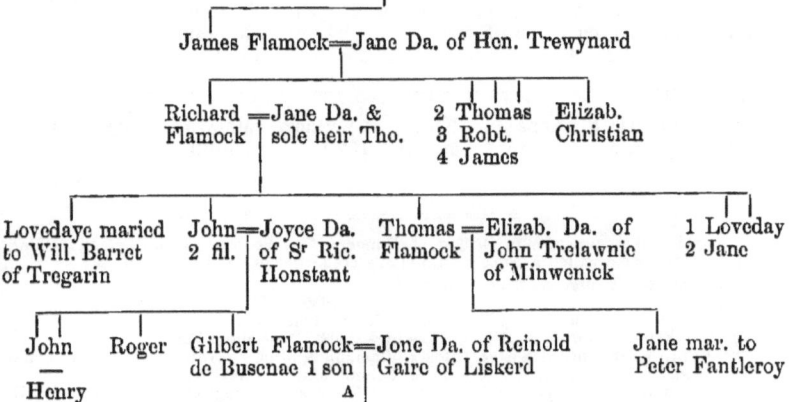

¹ There is a Monument to this Owen in Truro Church.
² Rector of Truro, 1636.   ³ Penryn.

THE VISITATION OF THE COUNTY OF CORNWALL.

A |

Willm Flamank = Mary Da. of John Carminow of
of Buscane | Fentengollen in Com Cornw.

- Hugo 6 fil. = Jane de Hellon fil. in Com. Corw.
- Charles ob. apud Yarmouth fuit Clericus
- Nicholas Flamank of Buscane in Com. Cornw. = Mary Da. of John Lipkencott of Wibberrie in Com. Devo'
- Oliver 2 fil.[1]
- John ob.

- Hugh Christop.
- Barnard Flamank of Buscane in Com. Cornw. ætat. 22
- Elizab. fil. unica

*

BER. FLAMANKE.

Fleminge.

John Fleminge of Monster in Ireland

John Fleminge who came into England & seated himselfe in Bristoll = Kath' Da. of Barry descended out of the house of the Lo. Barrye of Ireland

Nicho. Fleminge of Landith in Pochia de Maderne in Com. Cornwall = Elizb. Da. of Jenkin Keigwin of Paule in Cornwall

- John Fleminge Doct[r] of Divinitie & first Warden of Wadda' Colledge in Oxford ob. sine prole
- Tho. Fleminge of Landithe in Com. Cornw. liveing 1620 = Elizb. Da. & hey. of Tho. Cock of Bodmin in Com. Cornwall
- Elizb. ux[r] W[m] Treruf of Maderne in Cornwall
- Mary ux[r] 1 Tho. Crudge of Mderne 2 to Rob. Jago of St. Erme in Cornwall
- Clarence uxor Edw. Mundaye of Tregonic in Cornwall

- Thomas 2 sonne
- Francis 1 Grace 2
- Anne 3 Elizab. 4
- Nicho. sone & hey. atat. 18, 1620
- Mary 5 Phillip 6
- Jane 7 sone (sic.)

†

THOMAS FLEMINGE.

---

[1] He mar. Elizabeth, da. of W[m]. Billing, of Hanger. *Vide* Pedigree of Billing, ante. Mar. Lic. 22 Jan., 1596; she is called Elizabeth Billion al's Trelawder of St. Tudye. (J. M.)

* Will. s. of John Flamanck, gent., bap. 1631
John ,, ,, ,, and Anne, bap. 1639 } Padstow Par. Reg.
Rich. Vivian. gent., mar. Mary Flamock. 1601. St. Columb Major. Par. Reg.
Mr. Jno. Flamick mar. Mrs. Mileson Hockings, 1668. Lansalloes Par. Reg.
Ped. fin. 15 Elizb. Cornw. Easter. Roger Flamank & Jno. Vyvyan, gent., q. Otho and
John Merefield, gent., def. land in St. Columb Major. Luxyllion, &c.
For further and extensive ped. of Flamanke (which has been registered at Heralds' Coll. down to 1848), see Sir Jno. Maclean's 'Hist. of Trigg,' vol. i., pp. 283, 285.

† Thomas Fleming gent. and Mary Harris married, 1657. Gulval. Par. Reg.
Christabel da. of Will[m] Fleming, bapt. 1573. Fowey Par. Reg.
Nich. Flemyng, gent., and Anne, da. of Jno. Clese, gent., mar. 1629. } Madron Par. Reg.
Nich. Flemyng, gent., bur. 1668.

Fletchar.

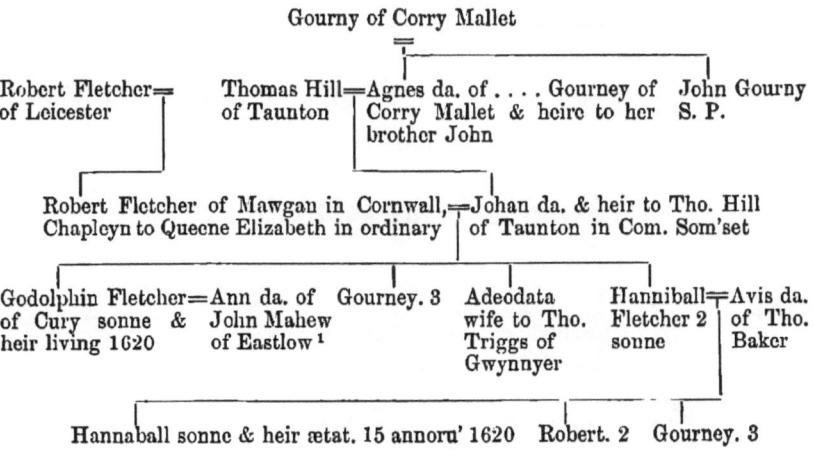

Gourny of Corry Mallet

Robert Fletcher of Leicester = Thomas Hill of Taunton = Agnes da. of .... Gourney of Corry Mallet & heire to her brother John — John Gourny S. P.

Robert Fletcher of Mawgan in Cornwall, Chapleyn to Queene Elizabeth in ordinary = Johan da. & heir to Tho. Hill of Taunton in Com. Som'set

Godolphin Fletcher of Cury sonne & heir living 1620 = Ann da. of John Mahew of Eastlow[1] — Gourney. 3 — Adeodata wife to Tho. Triggs of Gwynnyer — Hanniball Fletcher 2 sonne = Avis da. of Tho. Baker

Hannaball sonne & heir ætat. 15 annoru' 1620 — Robert. 2 — Gourney. 3

* GODOLPHIN FLETCHAR.

Fortescu.

Lewis Fortescue of Vallepit in Com. Devon

Nicholas Fortescue of Mawgan in Com. Cornub. 2 sonne = Jane da. of Robt. Hill of Hellegan and widdow Michaell Vivian

Eliza widow of Roger Sleman 2 wife =[2] William Fortescue of Mawgan now living 1620 = Christian da. of Jo. Vivian of Trelawarren 1 wife A — Lewis Fortescue 2 sonne = Lower da. of Jo. Samwell B — Agass wife to George Bowden — Margaret wife to William Prisk

---

[1] East Looe.
[2] Mr. William Fortescue of Skyberio was bur. at Mawgan in Meneage 1623. Bp. of Exeter's Transcripts.

* F. Fletcher was chaplain with Sir Francis Drake, and from his notes 'The World Encompassed' was compiled.

L

THE VISITATION OF THE COUNTY OF CORNWALL.

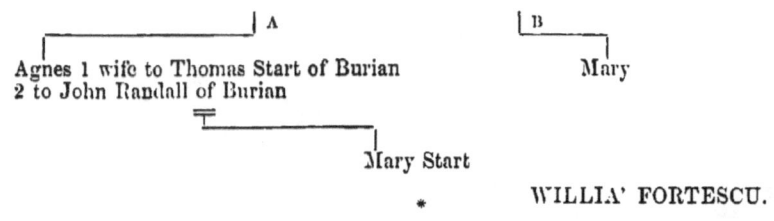

Agnes 1 wife to Thomas Start of Burian
2 to John Randall of Burian

Mary Start

Mary

WILLIA' FORTESCU.

Gamon alias Gambone.

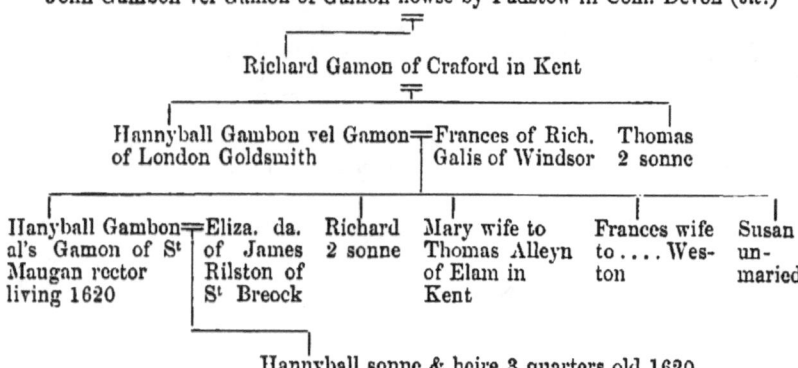

John Gambon vel Gamon of Gamon howse by Padstow in Com. Devon (*sic*.)

Richard Gamon of Craford in Kent

Hannyball Gambon vel Gamon = Frances of Rich.   Thomas
of London Goldsmith   Galis of Windsor   2 sonne

Hanyball Gambon = Eliza. da.   Richard   Mary wife to   Frances wife   Susan
al's Gamon of St   of James   2 sonne   Thomas Alleyn   to .... Wes-   un-
Maugan rector   Rilston of   of Elam in   ton   maried
living 1620   St Breock   Kent

Hannyball sonne & heire 3 quarters old 1620

HANNIBAL GAMON ALIAS GAMBONE.

---

* Mr. Fortescue, of Penwarne, Cornw., ar., and Anne Fortescue, of Wood Devon, spinster, mar. lic. 29 Oct. 1688.
    Peter Fortescue and —uye the Lady Courtney were mar. 21 Nov., 1669. Buryan par. reg.
    Robert Fortescue, Esq., and Grace Grenvile mar. 20 Feb., 1644. Kilkhampton par. reg.
    Xfer Fortescue of St. Wenne bur. 9 Oct., 1637. Menheniot par. reg.
    Ric. Fortescue and Jane Searle mar. 27 Oct., 1622.
    Hugh, s. of Arthur F. of Penwarne, Esq., & Barbara bap. 2d June, 1665. ⎫
    John, s. of Arthur F., of Penwarne, Esq., & Barbara, bap. 2 Sep., 1668. ⎪
    Arth., s. of Arth. Fortescue, bap. 1673. ⎪
    Joseph, s. of Arth. Fortescue, bap. 1675. ⎬ Mevagizzey par. reg.
    John Fortescue, gent., and Elizh. Keagle mar. 10 Jun., 1688. ⎪
    Arthur Fortescue. Esq., bur. 12 Ap., 1693. ⎪
    John, son of Arthur Fortescue, Esq., and Dinah, bap. 2 Sept., 1713. ⎪
    Arthur Fortescue, Esq., bur. 10 Oct., 1735. ⎭
    Mary, wife of Henry Foskew, bur. 1636. St. Issey par. reg.
    Margt., da. of Hen. Fortescue, of Filley, Esq., and Bridget, da. of the Rt. Hon. Hu. Boscawen, and the Lady Margt., born 1 Mar., 1693, bap. 3 Ap., 1694. St. Mich. Penk. par. reg.
    Onnor, wife of Mr. Fortescue, bur. 1641. St. Winnow par. reg.
    Ped. fin. Cornw, 50 Ed. III., No. 4, Willm Fortescue & Will Beere q. Ric. Prideux and Milicent ux. def. 10 Hen. IV., No. 5, Wm. Fortescue, Henry Fortescue, John Mareys and Tho. Stoke q. John Fortescue and Clarice ux. def. rem. to Hen. Fortescue.
    Ric. Fortescu held land in Lesnewth. 3 John. Coram Rege.

    For more see 'Visit. Devon. 1620,' Harl. Soc. Pub., p. 109, and '*Family of Fortescue in all its branches*,' by Thomas Fortescue Lord Clermont, Lond., 1869, 4to.

George.

.... George of Geo. Come in Com. Gloucester
 =
.... George of Gloucest' came to Osmondto' in Com. Dorset
 =
.... George of Osmondton in Con. Dorset = Da. of Hussie

Simon George came to Quo- = Thomazin Da. of Rich. Lanian
toule in Com. Cornwall   in Com. Cornw. Esq.

Simon 1 sone   Salathiell George of Trenouth = Agnes Da. of Jo. Trestrale
ob. sine ple   in Com. Cornw. liveinge 1620   of Verryan in Cornw. gent.

Anne 1   ¹Elizab. 2   Thomazin 3 Da.
Da. atat. 6   Da. atat. 4   atat. 2, 1620

SALATHIELL GEORGE.

Geirveis.

Peter Lo. of Antrewon Duxit fil. Hugonis Peverell
 =
Joseus de Antre- = Alicia fil. Rogeri le Archdecon
won sans Dat.   de Trewareton Hale Cornw.

Petrus fil. = filia   Gervasius de Antre- =
et heres   Basset   won in Cornub.

Michaell   John Gerveis ² de = Nicholea³ fil. et unica
fili. 2   Helston A° 17 E. II.   Heres Johis Benarklick

Michaell 2 fil.   Jacobus = Isabella³ filia et Coh. Rogeri   Thomas³
somtm' maior   Gerveis³   Treveglos died before hir   ob. s. p.
of Helston   A° 8 R.   husbond a° 7 H. IV.
                 II.   A

¹ Elizab., da. of Slenthiel George, gent., bapt. 3 March, 1616. ⎫
John, son of Roger George, bur. 22 Feb., 1563.   ⎬ Gwinear par. reg.
Thomazine George, bur. 19 Nov., 1587.   ⎫
Marie, wife of Thomas George, bur. 3 July, 1619. ⎬ St. Ewe par. reg.

² Ped. fin. Cornw. 6 Ed. III., No. 7, Jno. Bethever q. John Gerves of Helston Burgh & Nichola his wife def. ; names Alice wife of Jno. Banethlek ; remainder of Banethlek lands to Jno. Gerveis & Nichola ux.

³ Ped. fin. Cornw. 41 Ed. III., No. 3, Jacob Gerveys & Isabella his wife q. Thos. Gerveys def. Lands in Treveglas, etc.

76 THE VISITATION OF THE COUNTY OF CORNWALL.

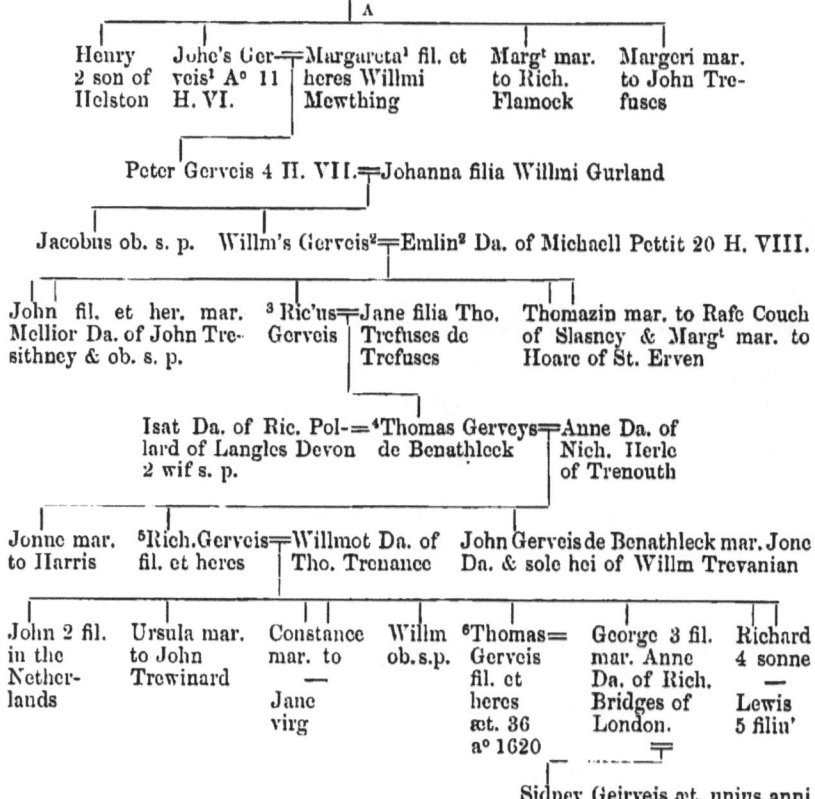

THO. GEIRVEIS.

Noverint universi p' p'sent me Johon Gerveys remisisse relaxasse & omnino imp'petue p' me et heredibus meis quietu' Clamasse &c. Hijs testibus Johe Skewys, Johe Keynwood tunc maiore ville de Helston Burgh, Rogero Jonwan, Johe Scler

[1] Ped. fin. Cornw. 2 H. IV., No. 2, John Gerveys & Margaret his wife q. Thos. Jon of Helston def.
[2] Peter Bevil married Thomazine. the widow of Michael Petit, and by his Will (prob. 1515 ; given more at length under Petit) he bequeaths to Willm Gervys his "best gowne lyned with Sasnet." Thomazine Bevil, the widow, by her Will, 1517, names her daughter Emlyn, and says, "I bequeath to Willm Gerves children begotten of Emlyn £6 : 13 : 4 between them."
[3] Brass in Constantine Ch. to mem. of Ric. Geyrveys, Esquier, and Jane his wyfe, Dowghter of Tho. Trefusys, Esq., bur. 2 Oct. 1574. Figures of Parents, with eight sons and eight daughters. Also Brass in same ch. to mem. of Melior, wife of Jn° Pendarvis and dau. of Ric. Gearveis, Esq. ob. 17 Mar. 1607.
[4] Bur. 26 Aug. 1616, at Constantine. Will prob. Arch. Cornw. 17 Mar. 1616–17. Names Wilmet, wife of his eldest son Ric., and Tho., Jno., Geo., Ric., Lewis, Ursula, Constance, and Jane, sons and daus. of sd. Ric. ; Jenophat. his dau., wife of Westcote of St. Issey, and several other daus. ; bro.-in-law Jno. Herle ; and Francis Gerveis, Executor ; Wm. Reskymer of Merthen, Esq., and Jno. Gerveis. his son, father of sd. Francis, overseers. (J. M.)
[5] Ric. G. 1608. Admon. granted 11 Jan. 1608, to relict Wilmet ; Jn° Gerveis of St. Gee's, one of the sureties. (J. M.)
[6] Tho. Gerveis by Deed dat. 25 Ap. 1612. 19 Jas., made over Benathlek, &c., to John G., his uncle, and Francis, son of John. (J. M.)

THE VISITATION OF THE COUNTY OF CORNWALL. 77

et alijs. Dat' apud Helston die sabbati prox post festu' S'ti Joh'is Ante portam Latinam. aº Regni Regis H. V. post conquest' Angl. secundo.

SEAL.—*A chev. betw. 3 garbs.*
Sig.—JACOBI GERVEIS.

*

Geyrveys.

Tho. Geirveis of Constenton=Anne Da of Nicho. Herle

John Geirveis of Constentin liveinge 1620=Joane Da. & sole hey. of Wᵐ Trevanion

Fran. 1 sone atat. 5   John 2 sonne   Richard 3 sone

JOHN GEYRVEYS.

Glanville.

ARMS. *Az. three saltires or.*
CREST. *A buck stat. ppr.*

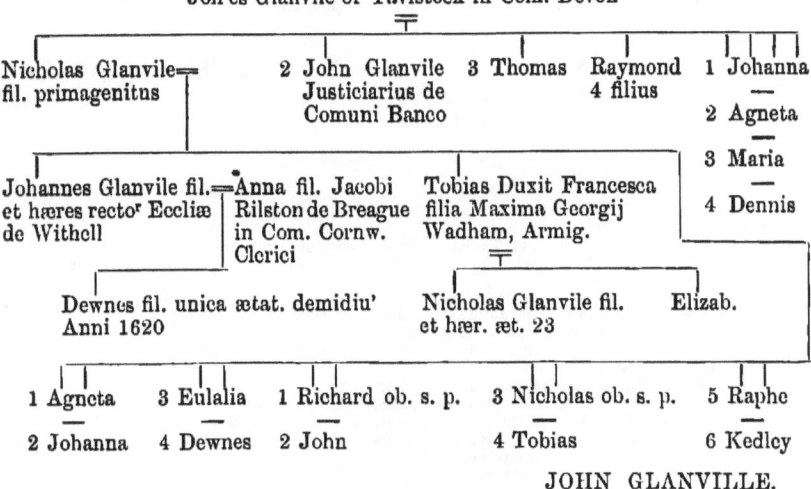

JOHN GLANVILLE.

---

* George, son of Richard Geirves, gent., and Wylemett, bapt. 22 May, 1592.
Johan da. of .... Gervys and Wilmett,   „   1593.
Elizab., da. of Richard Gerveis, gent., and Ann,   born 1654. } Constentin.
Richard Gerveis,   bur. 26 Nov. 1605. } (J.M.)
Thomas Gervies, Esq.   „ 26 Aug. 1616.

Glanvile.

ARMS. *Az. three saltires or.*
CREST. *A stag trippant ppr.* } (Tricked in pencil.)

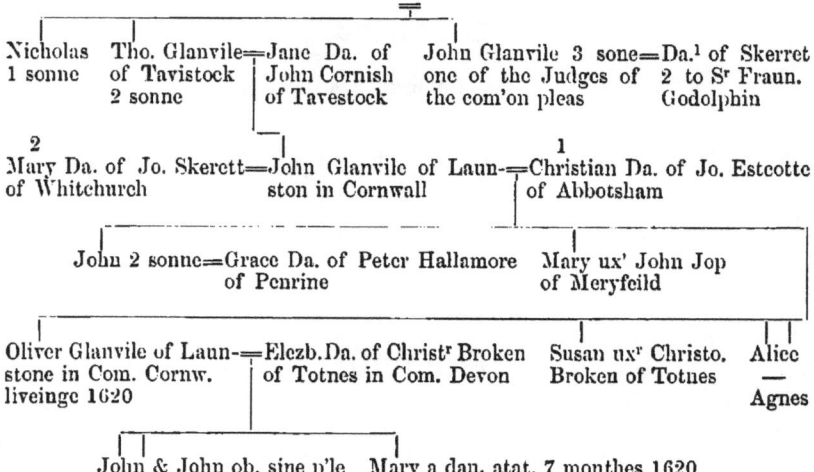

John Glanvile of Tavistock in Com. Devon

| Nicholas 1 sonne | Tho. Glanvile of Tavistock 2 sonne | =Jane Da. of John Cornish of Tavestock | John Glanvile 3 sone one of the Judges of the com'on pleas | =Da.[1] of Skerret 2 to S[r] Fraun. Godolphin |

2
Mary Da. of Jo. Skerett=John Glanvile of Laun-=Christian Da. of Jo. Estcotte
of Whitchurch   ston in Cornwall   of Abbotsham

John 2 sonne=Grace Da. of Peter Hallamore   Mary ux' John Jop
             of Penrine   of Meryfeild

Oliver Glanvile of Laun-=Elezb. Da. of Christ[r] Broken   Susan ux[r] Christo.   Alice
stone in Com. Cornw.   of Totnes in Com. Devon   Broken of Totnes   —
liveinge 1620   Agnes

John & John ob. sine p'le   Mary a dau. atat. 7 monthes 1620

* P. me OLIVER GLANVILE.

---

[1] Alicia, da. of John Skirritt of Tavistock, called wid. of Sir Francis Godolphin in Glanville Ped. 'Visit. Dev., 1620,' Harl. Soc. Pub., p. 130, where also the ped. is continued from this marriage.

* Oliver Sawel, Esq., and Mrs. Jane Glanville, da. of R[t] Worshipful Sir Francis Glanville, K[t], mar. 3 Feb., 1632, Sunday.
Jn[o] Dodge, Esq., and Dionyse, da. of the R[t] Worshipful Sir Fra. Glanvill, K[t], mar. 1635.
The R[t] Worshipful Sir Francis Glanville, bur. 1638.
Mr. Jn[o] Atwill, Minister, and Mrs. Grace Glanville, mar. 1675.
Francis Glandville Ar. & Elizab. Crymes, mar. 21 Sept. 1604. Buckl. Mon. Devon. Par. Reg.
Thomas Drake and Alice Glanville, mar. 23 Oct. 1634. Truro Par. Reg. In the Bp. of Exeter's Transcripts she is called Glanfield.
Johannes Glanville sac. Theol. bac., bur. 1615. Withiel.
Richard Glanville of Lelant was bur. 24 Apl. 1631. Probus.
Francis, son of Mr. Oliver Glanville, bap. 7 Dec., 1623. Launceston.
} (J. M.)
Miss Alice Glanvile, da. of the Lady Alice Godolphin, bur. at Tavistock, 14 Nov., 1608. Bp. of Exeter's Transcripts.

} Tavistock Par. Reg.

Glyn.

Tho. Glynn of Glynn═Alice Da. & hey. of Ric. Dennys

Nicho. 1 sone mar' to 1 Constance Da. & hey. of Joh. Brian ob. sine prole 2ᵈ to Elizb. Da. of John Talkerne of Golocotte and had issue

John Glynn of═Thomazin Da. of Nicho. Boyton 2 sonne Carlyon of Carlyon Key in Com. Corn- in Cornwall wall

John Glynn of Boyton 1 sonne═Mary Da. of Rob. Treweike of Stediens in Cornwall

¹Leonard Glyn 2 sone obijt sine p'le

²Willm. 3 sone

³John Glynn of═Anne Da. of Rob. Boyton in Com. Menwynnick of Cornwall live- Menwynnick in inge 1620 Cornwall

⁴Phillip ux. Tristram Peirse of Tamerton in Cornw.

⁵George 3 sonne

⁶Robert 2 sone now *heire* 1649

⁷John sonne & heyre═*Prudence da. of . . . . Risden of* atat' 11, 1620   *Aston in Com. Devon*

*

JOHN GLYN.

---

¹ Bapt. 11 Dec. 1578.   ² Bapt. 4 Aug. 1581.   ³ Bapt. 10 Feb. 1577.
⁴ „   10 Sept. 1582.   ⁵ „   23 Sept. 1612.   ⁶ „   30 June, 1610.
⁷ „   5 Aug. 1609. Boyton.

* Mar. Lic. Exeter, Leonard Glynn of Werrington vel Boyton, gent., and Johanna } (J. M.)
Noble of Boyton, 8 Jan. 1617.
Adm. of effects of Leonard Glynn, late of Boyton, co. Cornw., granted to Johanna, his relict, 11 Oct. 1639.

Nicholas, son of Walter Glyn, gt., and Agnes,		bapt. 1635.	
George,	„ „ „	„ 1637.	Lanreath Par. Reg.
Walter,	„ „ „	„ 1642.	
Mrs. Gartered Glynn,		bur. 1675.	
Denes Glyn, Esq.,		„ 14 April, 1705.	Cardinham Par. Reg.
Mr. Will. Glyn,		„ 1719.	
Will. Glyn, Esq., of Glyn,		„ 1727.	

Thos. Glynn of the Boro' of Helston, mar. Mary, the da. and heir of Otho Polkinhorne of Polkinhorne 22 April, 1662.
Otho Glynn, 3rd son of Thos. Glynn of Polkinhorne, gent., was mar. to Elizabeth, da. of Peter Pendarves of Bodriggey, gent., the 30 Dec., 1697.

Otho,	son of Thos. Glynn, gent.,	bapt. 26 Dec., 1667.	
Will.,	„ „	„ 11 Sept., 1669.	Gwinear Par. Reg.
Susanna, da. of	„	„ 7 Nov., 1671.	
Nicholas, son of	„	„ 4 Aug., 1673.	
Mary, da. of	„	„ 6 April, 1675.	
Phillip, son of	„	„ 3 April, 1677.	
Luce, da. of	„	„ 27 Dec., 1679.	
Margaret, „	„	„ 10 Aug., 1683.	
Mary, wife of	„	bur. 29 Nov., 1712.	

Edm. Herring of St. John's, gt., and Loveday, da. of Nich. Glynn of } St. John's Par. Reg.
St. Neot, gent., mar. 1712. He was bur. the same year, and she the year following.

Ped. fin. Cornw. 7 Edw. II. No. 5. Int. Peter, son of Ralph de Glen; qu. Ralph de Glen, def. In Boskennan and Treveniel.

☞ The additions in italic are in the hand of Parker.

Glyn.

Constance da. & heir of=Nicholas Glinn¹ of Glynn=Elizabeth da. of John Talkern
John Brian 1 wife s. p.   in Com. Cornub. Esq.   of Godacote 2 wife

²Willm. Glinn of Glinn sone & hey.=Anne Da. of Antho. Crewse

Nicho. Glinn of Glinn sone & hey.=Jane Da. of Walt' Kendall
in Com. Cornw. liveing 1620   of Pelyne

Walt' 2 sone   Willm.³ sone & hey.   Lovedaye ux' Tho. Hearle
at. 10   at. 21, 1620   of Trenonth Esq.
                *   NICH. GLYN.

Godolphin.

Edw. Godolphin=Matilda fil. Boteler de Camerton

Willm. Godolphin=Constance Da. of Willm. Wise of Grayston

Edwward Godolphin=Clare of Solgena

Alexander=Marrion Da. of John Tremrow

Willm.=Melior da. of John Cowlinge of Trewarnan

Elinor nupta Johi Rencie=
                        Thomas

[1] The ped. of Glyn is confused here. Compare Coles' Escheats, Note 1, under Crewes, p. 56, with the following extracts of wills :—Nicholas Glynne of Glynne, P'ish. of Cardinham, Cornw., 23 Nov., 1579, P. C. C. 21 Nov., 1580 ; names wife, Johane ; his son and heir, Will. ; his son Nicholas ; Rob., Sampson, Will., and John Trevethwane, his nephews ; Geo. and Leonard, sons of his bro. John Glynne ; his da. Mary, wife of John Harrye, and her 3 daus. ; and legacies to his Godchildren, not named. Prob. P. C. C., 1580. John Drake of Liskeard, mercht., dat. 30 June, 1582, prob. 1583 ; names wife Thomazine (Bealbery) to act as executrix, under advice of Nicholas Glin, Esq., and Rich. Myners, gent. Wm. Drake of Roche ; will 11 Feb., 1596 ; prob. 1597, Exeter ; makes his coseu Nich. Glinn. with o'rs, gardens (guardians) of his dau. till 18 years old ; Nich. Glinne, witness. Elizab. Drake of Lanlivey. spinster, died 17 Nov., 1621. Will prob. Bodmin, 1622. Names her " God Father and Gardeyn " Nich. Glyn, Esq., and Stephen Kendall.
Ped. fin. 32 II. VIII. Trin. Cornw. Jno. Bealbury, q. Jno. Glyn of Lanhydrok, def. ten. in Leskerde, &c., &c.
Inq. p. m. 23 Elizb. part 2, No. 14. Nich. Glyn, ob. 11 Oct., son and heir Will'm, æt. 46. Recites Deed dat. 18 Feb. 14 Elizb., enfeoffing Nich. Carminow, Rob. Treuereke, Wm. Courteney of Deviock, Jno. Crewes, Tho. Trevythvan, and Jno. Glyn of Boyton, gent., in behalf of his son Nich. Glyn.
[2] Phelip, da. of Will. Glinne of Glinne, mar. Jno. Incledon of Bratton. 'Visit. Devon, 1620,' Harl. Soc. Pub., p. 158.
[3] Will of William Glyn de Glyn in Cardinham, Ar. prob. Exeter, 1665. Nich. Glyn, son and exor.
* For extensive ped. of Glyn, see 'Hist. of Trigg,' vol. i., p. 68.

THE VISITATION OF THE COUNTY OF CORNWALL.

Sr William Godolphin Kt.=Margaret da. of John Glynn of Morvall

Elizabeth wife to Jo. Langdon	Honor wife to Willm. Meliton of Pengarsek	William Godolfin of Windsor 3 sonne to Sr Willm. of whome Guy Godolfin now living 1620 is descended	Sr William Godolfyn Kt sonne & heir =Blanch da. of John Langdon
			Margaret wife to Dennys — Grace wife to Sr John Sidenham Kt

da. of John Grenvile=Thomas Godolphyn 2 sonn=.... da. & heir of Edmond
& heire to his brother | Bonythan 1 wife

.... da. wife to Tho. Peters of Okhampton	.... da. wife to Fursman	Gentill Godolfyn¹ who lived in Devon' & had issue Will'm

Ann wife to Sr Jo. Arundell of Talvern Kt.	Sr Francis Godolphin Kt.	=Margaret da. of John Killigrew of Arwenneck	William Godolphyn of Treveneag 2 sonne	=Jane² da. & coheir of Walter Gaverigan Esq.

francis

Catheryn unmaried	Jane wife to James Basset	Thomasine wife to Sr Geo. Carew Kt.	Sr William Godolfyn of Godolphyn Kt. ob. 1613	=Thomasine³ da. and heire of Tho. Sidney of Wrighton in Com. Norff.

Francis Godolfyn⁴ sonne & heir ætat. 14, 1620. now in Warde | Sydney 2. | William 3. | Penelope 1.

John⁵ 2 sonne	=Judith da. of Edward Amerideth	Francis Godolphyn 3 sonne	Ursula wife to Jo. Crudge	Blanch wife to George Keckwich of Katchfrench

William sonne & heir ætat. 15, 1620 | Thomas 2. | John 3. | Elizabeth 1. | Margaret 2.

FRA. GODOLPHIN.

¹ Gentle, son of Gentle Godolphynne, bapt. 21 June, 1614, at Teingrace, Devon. Bp. of Exeter's Transcripts.
² William Godolphin and Mrs. Jane Gavrigan, mar. 11 Dec. 1587. St. Mabyn. (J. M.)
³ The Right Worshipful the Lady Godolphin was bur. 24 April, 1632. Tavistock Par. Reg.
⁴ Grandfather of Francis, Earl of Godolphin, who mar. Henrietta, da. and coh. of the great Duke of Marlborough. She was created Duchess of Marlborough by Act of Parliament.
⁵ Captain of Silley. 'Visit. of Devon, 1620,' Harl. Soc. Pub., p. 6.
* Francis Godolphin and Katherine Trevaniou mar. 8 May, 1622. Name of Parish wanting. Bp. of Exeter's Transcripts.
Sir William Godolphin and Mrs. Grace Barret, mar. 25 March, 1658. Sutcome, Devon. (J.M.)
Grace, the wife of Sir Will. Godolphin, Kt., died the 11 day of Oct., 1663, and was bur. the 13 day of the same month. } St. Mabyn Par. Reg.
Sir Will. Godolphin, Kt., died the 26, and was bur. the 27 Nov., 1663.
The will of Sir Will. Godolphin of St. Mabyn was proved at Bodmin 23 Dec., 1663. (Compare Edmondson, fo. 183.)
Francis Godolfyn and Frances Browne, mar. 20 March, 1684. St. Issey Par. Reg.

Godolphin.

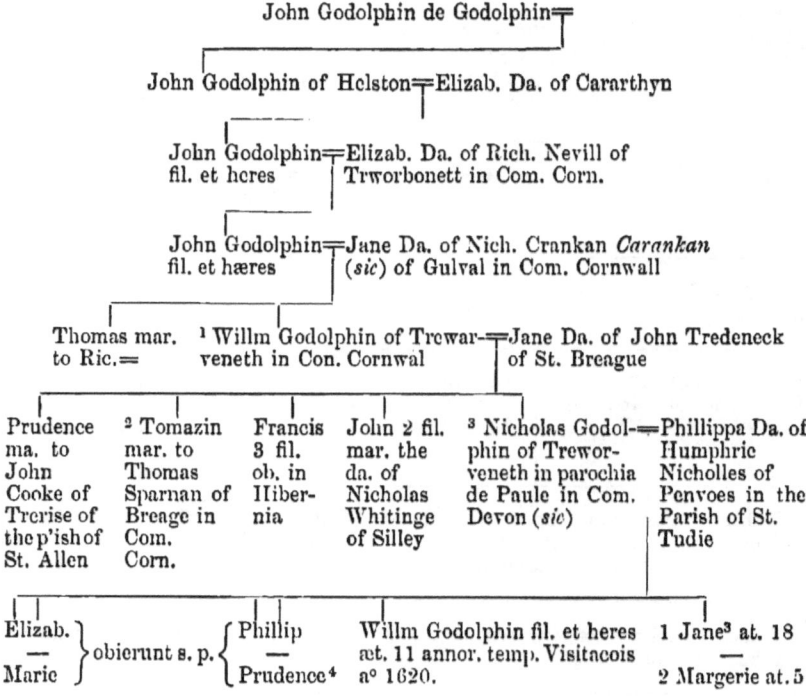

John Godolphin de Godolphin =

John Godolphin of Helston = Elizab. Da. of Cararthyn

John Godolphin = Elizab. Da. of Rich. Nevill of
fil. et heres   Trworbonett in Com. Corn.

John Godolphin = Jane Da. of Nich. Crankan *Carankan*
fil. et hæres   (*sic*) of Gulval in Com. Cornwall

Thomas mar. to Ric. = | ¹ Willm Godolphin of Trewar- = Jane Da. of John Tredeneck of St. Breague
                         veneth in Con. Cornwal

Prudence ma. to John Cooke of Trerise of the p'ish of St. Allen | ² Tomazin mar. to Thomas Sparnan of Breage in Com. Corn. | Francis 3 fil. ob. in Hibernia | John 2 fil. mar. the da. of Nicholas Whitinge of Silley | ³ Nicholas Godolphin of Trewor-veneth in parochia de Paule in Com. Devon (*sic*) | = Phillippa Da. of Humphrie Nicholles of Penvoes in the Parish of St. Tudie

Elizab. — Marie } obierunt s. p. { Phillip — Prudence⁴ | Willm Godolphin fil. et heres æt. 11 annor. temp. Visitacois a° 1620. | 1 Jane³ æt. 18 — 2 Margerie æt. 5

NICHOLAS GODOLPHIN.

---

¹ Mar. at St. Breock October, 1571. St. Breock Par. Reg.
² Mar. at Breage 10 July, 1598. Breage Par. Reg.
³ Named in the Will of Thomas Chiverton of Paul, 26 August, 1604. Proved in London, 7 Feb. 1605.
⁴ Bapt. at St. Paul, 1613. Bp. of Exeter's Transcripts.

Will., son of Will. Godolphin, Esq., by Ruth his wife, bapt. 1632.\
Ruth, da. of   „   „   born 7, „ 14 Oct., 1633.
Will., son of   „   „   „   2 Feb., 1634.
Ann, da. of   „   „   „ 12 Jan., 1641. } St. Mabyn.
Will., son of   „   „   bur. 29 Sept. 1631 (J. M.)
John Godolphin, gent., of St. Kew, and Honour Dennys, wid.,
     of same parish.   mar. 10 May, 1640.
John, son of Will. Godolphin, Esq.   bapt. 24 April, 1636.
Barnard, „   „   „   24 Feb., 1638. } St. Kew.
Margaret, da. of John   „   bur. 31 Oct., 1641. (J. M.)
Honour, wife of Mr. Godolphin,   „   15 May, 1642.
William Godolphin, Esq., and Elizab. Carrell, mar. April, 29, 1673. St. Winnow. (J. M.)

Godolphin.

S⁏ William Godolfyn of Godolfin Kᵗ = Margaret da. of John Glynn of Morvall

- S⁏ William Godolfyn Kt. = Blanch da. of Jo.[1] Langdon.
- .... da. of John Grenvile 2 wife = Thomas Godolfin 2 sonne & heire to his brother = ...[2] da. & heir of Edmond Bonythan of ....
  - Gentill Godolphyn[3] de Com. Devon
    - William Godolphin
  - S⁏ Francis Godolphin of Godolphin Kt. = Margaret da. of John Killigrew
    - [4] Francis Godolphin of Trevencag Esq. sonne & heir living 1620 = Ann da. of Rich. Carew of Anthony Esq.
      - Loveday 1 da. ætat. 2 annoru' 1620
      - Catheryne 2 da. ætat. 6 weekes the 9 of October 1620
  - William Godolphin of Trevencag 2 sonne = Jane da. & coheir of Walter Gaverigan of Gaverigan Esq.

* FRANCIS GODOLPHIN.

Goode.

ARMS. *A chevron* (unfinished).

Goode =

Rich. Goode of Whetston in Cornwall liveing 1620 = Da. of Penkevile

- Geo. 2 sone at. 50, 1620
- [5] Walter 3 sone at. 35 = Da. of ....
- Rich. Goode sone & hey. atat. 60, 1620
- Digorie 4 sonne at. 32
- Florence a dau. at. 45
- Margᵗ unmaried at. 40

Not signed.

---

[1] Robert in Langdon Ped., Harl. MS. 1079, fo. 63.
[2] Katherine Godolphin's name follows those of Tho. and James Bonythan in the Will of John Arundell of Trerice, Esq., proved in London 26 Nov., 1580.
[3] Mar. Cicily, da. of George Southcot of Calwoodley. 'Visit. Devon., 1620,' Harl. Soc. Pub., p. 269.
[4] Francis Godolphin of St. Hilary, near The Mount, gentleman, and Anne Carew, da. of Richard Carew the elder, Esq., of Anthony, married at Anthony 15 Nov., 1616. Bp. of Exeter's Transcripts.
[5] He mar. Alice, da. of Rich. de la More of Little Torington. 'Visit. Devon, 1620,' Harl. Soc. Pub., p. 194.
Rich Goode of Plymouth, mar. Joane, da. of John Downe of Pilton. 'Visit. Devon, 1620,' Harl. Soc. Pub., p. 90.
John Badcock, Parson of Whitston, and Dorothy Goode, mar. 4 Mar. 1656. Launcells. (J. M.)
John Goode of Whitston. and Dorothy Penkevil, mar. 20 June, 1648. } St. Kew.
Dorothy, da. of John Goode of Whitston & Dorothy his wife, bap. 15 Jan. 1648-9. } (J. M.)

* For pedigree of Godolphin more extended, see Harl. MS. 1079, ffo. 206 to 209.

Grenvile.

ARMS. (See Frontispiece.)

Ricus Grenvile filius Rici Grenvile sans Dat.=

Sr Thomas Grenvile fil. et heres=

Ricus Grenvile fil. Thomæ=

Sr Theobald Grenvile temp. Rici primi=Jana fil. Willm Trewent

Ricus Grenvile lived in=Isabell Da. of Josselin
the tyme of E. I. de Mont Tregomynion

Sr Willm Grenvile Kt. temp. E. II.=Johanna fil. et hæres Wortham

[1] Sr Barthomew Grenvile Kt. temp. E. II.=Joanna fil. Sr Viell Vivion militis

Sr Theobald Grenvile Kt. temp. E. III.=Jois Da. of Tho. Beaumont

Sr Theobald Grenvile Kt. temp. Ric. II.=Margaret Da. of Hugh Courtney

Sr John Grenvile   Willm Grenvile Brother and=Phillip sist' to the
ob. s. p.   hey. to Sr John temp. H. IV. Lo. Bondvile

Thos. Grenvile fil. et hæres=Elizab. Sist' to Sr Theobald de Gorges Kt.

Relicta Hill de=Sr Tho. Grenvile=Isabella fil. Otes   fil. nupta
Taunton ux. 2 Kt. temp. E. IV. Gilbert ux. 1 .... Yoe [2]

John Grenvile a priest	Jane mar. to Raleigh 2 to Batin	Phillip mar. to Francis Harris 2 to Stening	Da. mar. to Arundell of Lanherne	Honor mar. to Sr John Basset 2 to Arthur Plantaginet Lo. Lisly
Mary ux^r Ri. Blewet 2 to St. Aubin	Agnes ux. Johis Roscarick	Roger Grenvile fil. et hæres	Margaret fil. et Coh. Rich. Whitleygh A	Ricus ob. s. p.	[3] Jane ux. Jhon Arundell de Trerest

[1] Int. Bartholomew de Grenevill and Anna his wife, qu. Margery who was wife of Joceus de Dynham, def. Manor of Kilkhampton settled on Bartmw. and his wife for life. Rem. to Henry, son of Bartholomew, rem. to Johanna & Isabell, sisters of Henry. Ped. fin. Cornw. 10 Edw. II. No. 1.
[2] Ellin, mar. to Will. Yeo. 'Visit. Devon, 1620,' Harl. Soc. Pub., p. 322.
[3] She mar. Sir John Arundell of Trerice. Coll. of Arms.

THE VISITATION OF THE COUNTY OF CORNWALL. 85

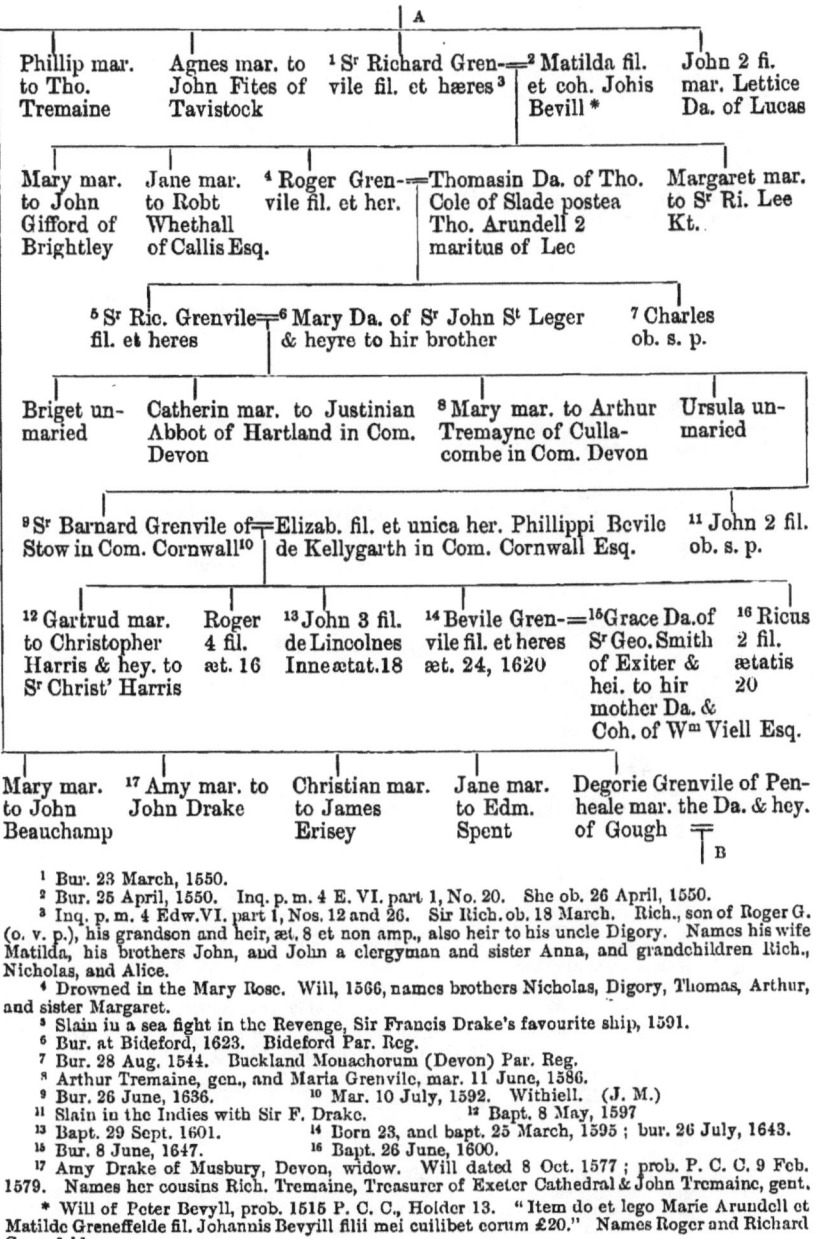

[1] Bur. 23 March, 1550.
[2] Bur. 25 April, 1550. Inq. p. m. 4 E. VI. part 1, No. 20. She ob. 26 April, 1550.
[3] Inq. p. m. 4 Edw.VI. part 1, Nos. 12 and 26. Sir Rich. ob. 18 March. Rich., son of Roger G. (o. v. p.), his grandson and heir, æt, 8 et non amp., also heir to his uncle Digory. Names his wife Matilda, his brothers John, and John a clergyman and sister Anna, and grandchildren Rich., Nicholas, and Alice.
[4] Drowned in the Mary Rose. Will, 1566, names brothers Nicholas, Digory, Thomas, Arthur, and sister Margaret.
[5] Slain in a sea fight in the Revenge, Sir Francis Drake's favourite ship, 1591.
[6] Bur. at Bideford, 1623. Bideford Par. Reg.
[7] Bur. 28 Aug. 1544. Buckland Monachorum (Devon) Par. Reg.
[8] Arthur Tremaine, gen., and Maria Grenvile, mar. 11 June, 1586.
[9] Bur. 26 June, 1636.   [10] Mar. 10 July, 1592. Withiell. (J. M.)
[11] Slain in the Indies with Sir F. Drake.   [12] Bapt. 8 May, 1597
[13] Bapt. 29 Sept. 1601.   [14] Born 23, and bapt. 25 March, 1595 ; bur. 26 July, 1643.
[15] Bur. 8 June, 1647.   [16] Bapt. 26 June, 1600.
[17] Amy Drake of Musbury, Devon, widow. Will dated 8 Oct. 1577 ; prob. P. C. C. 9 Feb. 1579. Names her cousins Rich. Tremaine, Treasurer of Exeter Cathedral & John Tremaine, gent.

* Will of Peter Bevyll, prob. 1515 P. C. C., Holder 13. "Item do et lego Marie Arundell et Matilde Greneffelde fil. Johannis Bevyill filii mei cuilibet eorum £20." Names Roger and Richard Greynfelde.

Digory, son of Rich. Grenville and Gertrude his wife, bapt. 1620. } St. Tudy. (J. M.)
Digory   „   „   „   bur. 1621. }

☞ When the name of the Parish is omitted here, the Registers are from Kilkhampton.

Rich. Grenvile mar. Florence Da. & coh. of Kelloway

George fil. et hæres mar. Julyan Da. & coh.   Willm. ob. s. p.   1 Mary   2 Jane
of Wm Viell
                                                                                3 ¹Martha
Sr Geo. Grenvile mar. Marie Da. of John Killegriewe of
Arwanick Esq.

Mary fil. unica ætat. 10

*   BAR. GRENVILE.

¹ Bapt. 8 Oct. 1555.
* *Kilkhampton Par. Reg.*
Rich., eldest son of the R. Wpfl. Bevill Grenvile, Esq., born at Tremeere in Lanteglos by Foye 19, and bapt. 25 Mar. 1621.

[The "Grenville Pew" in Lanteglos Church has on its panels a series of shields, containing in all nearly 150 quarterings properly blazoned. Among them appears the shield given in the frontispiece to this book. They were much injured by time, and were lately carefully restored in exact imitation of the originals under the supervision of the Editor, and at the expense of the Hon. Geo. M. Fortescue, the lay impropriator.]

Bevill, son of the R. Wpfl. Bevill Grenvile, Esq., born 23 June, bapt. 16 July, 1626.
John   „   „   „   „   29 Aug.   „   16 Sept. 1628.
Bernarde   „   „   „   „   4 and   „   20 Mar. 1630.
George   „   „   „   „   22 Aug.   „   2 Sept. 1632.
Roger   „   „   „   „   3 and   „   17 Nov. 1633.
Dennis   „   „   „   „   13 and   „   26 Feb. 1636.
Peter Prideaux, Esq., and Elizabeth Grenvile,   mar. 17 Nov. 1645.
Roger, son of Rich. Grenvile,   bur. 10 Dec. 1565.
John Greinvile, Rector of Kilkhampton,   „   5 May, 1580.
Roger Grenvile,   „   5 June, 1635.
Bevill Grenvile,   „   21 Feb. 1635.

Bishop Bronscombe's Registers at Exeter, 1257-1307, state that Gilbert de Clare, Earl of Gloucester, presented to Kilkhampton *ratione custodie Richardi de Greinvillâ*.

The Hon. Lady Mary Howard al's Grenfield, ob. 17 Oct., and bur. 10 Nov. 1671. Tavistock Par. Reg.

The match with St. Leger brought in the quarterings of St. Leger, Donnet, Butler, E. of Ormond, Rochford, Hankford, and Stapledon, given on the shield in the frontispiece; also numerous royal descents (both York and Lancaster), besides descents from the great Houses of Neville, Percy, Stafford, Beauchamp, Beaufort, Audley, De Burgh, Despencer, Clare, Fitz Alan, Knyvett, Montacute, Grandison, &c. (See Sir J. Maclean's 'Hist. of Trigg,' vol. i., p. 683.) The following Law Case from the Carew MSS. at Lambeth Palace, vol. 600, fo. 239, is curious as touching the relationship of Queen Elizb. :—

"*Mr. St. Leger's Case to his Title to the Earl of Ormond's lands.*"

"Thomas Butler, Earl of Ormond, took to wife Ann, daughter and heyre of Sir Richard Hankeforde, sonne and heire of Sir Will. Hankford, some tyme Cheefe Justice of the Court of the Common Pleas, and they had issue Anne and Margarett.

Thomas Earl of Ormond, had in his own right divers Mannors in fee and divers in tayle, he and his Lady in her right had sundry other Mannors in fee and in Tayle.

Anne the elder daughter was married to Sir James St. Leger, and they had issue Sir George St. Leger, and James died. Margaret was married to Sir Will. Bullen, and they had issue Thomas Bullen.

Thomas Butler Earle of Ormonde, and Anne his wife weare bothe dead, 7 H. VIII.

Anne the daughter and Sr George St. Leger her sonne. and Margarett, and Sr Tho. Bullen her sonne by indenture 10 H. VIII. did make partition. And p'te of the land of the Earl of Ormond was allotted to Margarett and to Thomas, her sonne. All the rest of the Father's and all the Mother's land was allotted to Anne and to Sir George St. Leger, her sonne.

[*Continued next page.*

Greinevele.

CREST. *A demi Griffin charged with a crescent for difference.*

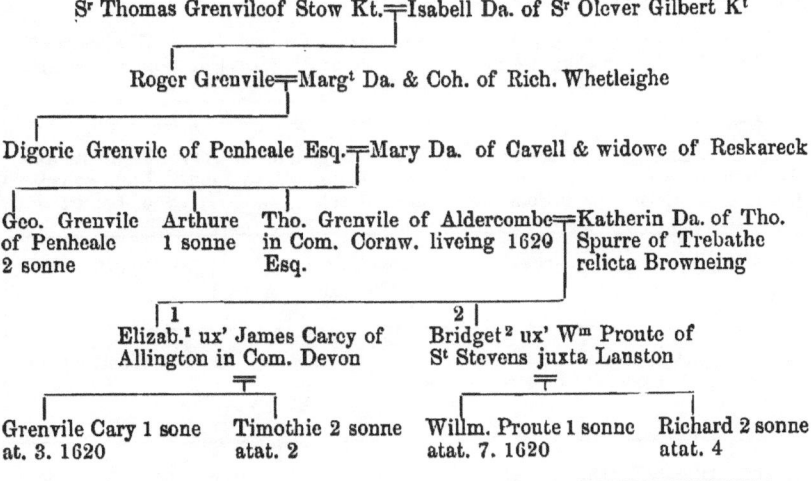

THOMAS GREINEVELE.

Anne St. Leger after died. Sir George St. Leger had issue Sʳ John St. Leger and died. Margaret became Lunatick the same yeare soone after this petition and died. Sʳ Thomas Bullen had issue Mary and Anne and died. Mary was married to Sir Wᵐ. Carey, and Anne to King H. VIII.

King H. VIII. had issue by Anne Queen Elizabeth of blessed memory, and Anne died. Mary had issue Henry Carey Lord Hunsdon, and she and her husband died. Henry Lord Hunsdon did alien that p'te wᶜʰ was allotted to his Auncestors and had issue Sir George Carey, and died. Sir George Carey had issue Elizabeth Lady Barkly, and died ; and Sir John St. Leger in the time of Queen Elizabeth alienated that which by the p'tition was allotted to his auncestors, and had issue John St. Leger that now is. Q. Elizabeth died without issue."

The case is summed up concisely, and opinion given in these words, followed by six separate reasons :—"I take it that John St. Leger hath good right to the moietie of the Mannors and hereditaments allotted unto Bullen."

St. Leger received with his wife, the Heiress of Ormond, 36 Manors in Engl'd, which estates were all wasted (see Ped. fin. repeatedly temp. Elizb.) and the descendant, Jno. St. Leger (the plaintiff above, and brother of Mary Grenvile), died in reduced circumstances s. p.

A very elaborate ped. of the St. Legers, with copious notes from authorities, has been compiled by Fras. Bayley, Esq., of Cambridge Terrace, Hyde Park, a portion of which was inserted by Charles Wykeham Martin, M.P., F.S.A., in his 'Hist. of Leeds Castle,' pub. 1869.

¹ Bapt. 5 Oct., 1589.
² „ 26 Jan., 1591 ; mar. 20 Aug., 1610.
* Bernard, son of Thos. Greinvile, gener., bapt. 5 July, and bur. 1 Sept., 1588. } Kilkhampton Par. Reg.
Thomas Grenvile, gent., bur. 10 July, 1625.
Rich., son of Rich. Grenville, gent., and Mary, bapt. 1689. } Poughill Par. Reg.
Chammond Grenville, gent., bur. 1689.
Rich Grenvil, Esq., and Mary Trewinnard, ye da. of Joseph Trewinnard, Rector of Mawnan, were mar. 1684. Mawnan Par. Reg.
Arthur Grenville, gent., bur. 1613. St. Tudy. (J. M.)

(For more of Grenvile, see 'Parochial Hist. of Cornwall,' vol. ii., p. 364.)

Grills.

ARMS. *Or, three bendlets enhanced gu.*
CREST. *A Porcupine pass. Ar.* } (Tricked in pencil.)

Da. of Leigh = Samson Grilles of Launceston = Dorothy Da. of Hunicome of
of Cawlstock | in Com. Corn. | Cawlstock in Com. Cornwall

| Joan uxor. Lawrene Trehayne of Southhill in Com. Corn. | Mary uxor Stephen Wardon of St Myett in Com. Cornwall | Marg^t u'or Gregory Hansam 2 to John Hocking | Willmott ux' Rich. Estcott of Launston |

Samson Grilles of Launceston = Katherine Da. of Will'm Smith
in Com. Corn. | of Stoke Clymsland

| Willm Grilles filius et hæres æt. 23. 1620 | Peteter 2 fil. ob. in the East Indies | 1 Christian æt. 22 — 2 Alice æt. 20 | 3 Wilmott æt. 17 |

| Marke Grilles = Martha Da. of of Calstock in | Tho. Bennet of Com. Cornub. | Launceston | John Grilles of Lincoln's Inne Esq. ob. sine p'le | Rich. Grilles mar. Anne Da. of Christ. Bligh of Treworgey in St Gennys in com. Cornwall |

| Samson fil. et hæres ob. sine Prole | 1 Mary æt. 22 — 2 Jane æt. 18 | 3 Tomizen æt. 16 | Wilmott ob. sine p'le. |

*

RICHARD GRILLS.

Grylls.

Willm. Grylles of Tavistock in Devon Esq.

Charles Gryles[1] of Lanrethoe in Cornwall Esq. = Agnes[2] Da. of Geo. Stubb Esq.

John Gryles of Lanrethoe in = Grace Da. & hey. of Wm Beare of
Cornw. liveing 1620 Esq. | St Nyott in Cornw. Esq. disceesd
A

---

[1] Bur. at Lanreath 2 March, 1611.
[2] ,, ,, 13 June, 1607. } Monument Lanreath Ch.

* Ped. fin. 40 Hen. III. No. 5. Int. Will. de Grelles and Millicent his wife, Pet., and Roger le Bere, def., a messuage in Bodmani. Thomas Griles bur. 23 Jan., 1587. Cuby Par. Reg.

THE VISITATION OF THE COUNTY OF CORNWALL. 89

| A

Charrles Griles   John ob. sin'   Jonathan   Grace 1   Elizab. 3   Joane 5
1 son atat. 8   p'le 2 sone   3 sonne
                                            Agnes 2   Mary 4
              *   JOHN GRYLLS.

Grosse.

Grosse who Came out of Norfolk and lived at Liskerd

Grosse of Liskerd

Ezechiell Grosse[1] of = Margaret Da. of Rich. Trelederis
Camborne 7 sonne   of Burian in Cornw.

Jone[2] mar.   Thomas 2   David[3] fil. pri-=Elizab. Da. of Christopher   Dorcas mar.
to Tho.   fil. æt. 30 mogenitus   Arundell of Menardarvy   to Willm.
Treunwith   ætat. 34   in Camborne   Arundell of
                                                                         Menadarvy

Ezechiell[4] fil. primogenitus æt. 10 annoru'

†   LAW. CALL
For MR. EZECHIELL GROSSE.

---

* Wm Can, gent., and Marie Grills were mar. at Lanreath, 1600. Bp. of Exeter's Transcripts.
Thos. Lower, gent., and Jane, da. of Charles Grills, gent., were mar.
14 June, 1652.
Elizb., da. of Methusela and Joan Grills,   bap. 1680.
Anthony, son of Mr. Nathaniel Grylles and Elizb.   „   „   } Lanreath Par. Reg.
Warwick   „   Charles Gryles, Esqr., and Elizb.   „   „
Methusela Grylls   bur.   „
Charles Grylls of Carwin, gent.,   „   1694.
For more of this pedigree, see 'Visit. Devon, 1620,' p. 134.

[1] Francis, da. of Ezechiel Grosse, Esq., and Margaret, bapt. 16 Aug., 1616,
at Probus.   } Bp. of Exeter's
[2] Tho. Trenwith of Trenwith, Esquire, and Joane, da. of Ezechiell Grosse, Transcripts.
Esquire, married at St. Ive's, 7 Mar., 1623.
[3] Elizabeth, da. of David Grose, bapt. 3 Nov., 1606. Camborne Par. Reg.
[4] Ezechiel Grose and Margaret Coryton were mar. at. St. Mellion 18 Sept., 1631. Bp. of
Exeter's Transcripts.

† Wm Grose, gent., and Alice, da. of Wm Nosworthy, mar. 1639. Madron Par. Reg.
Edward Grosse and Anna Huthnans mar. 7 April, 1611. Truro Par. Reg.
Jonathan Grosse, gent., & Kathn. Polsewe, widow, of Mevagizzy, mar. 1619. }
Joshua, son of Will. Grosse, gen^t, bap. 1581.   } St. Pinnock
Will.   „   „   „   1615.   } Par. Reg.
Ferdinando Grosse,   bur. 1643.

Hallamore.

John Halamore of=

Elynor da. of Bragdon=Walter Halamor of=Grace da. of Hen. Thomas
of Rye 1 wife | Penryn in Cornwall | al's Carnsew 2 wife

Peter Halamor of Penryn in=¹Ann da. of John   Rachell wife to   Petronell wife to
Com. Cornub. living 1620 | Trewolla   Thomas Trewolla   George Paynter

John Halamor sonne & heire æt. 19 Annoru' 1620   Grace 1   Alice 2

PETER HALLAMORE.

Harris.

Wᵐ Harris of Hayne in=Mary Da. of Sʳ Foulke Grevill of Beauchampe
Com. Devon. Esq. | Court in Com. Warrwick Kt.

Elizb. ux' Tho.   Brygdd sanz   Kath' uxor Tho.   Margᵗ ux' Wᵐ Grimes²
Stone of Minver   issue   Martin in Com.   of Buckland Monacorm
                          Som'set   in Devon

³Arthure Harris of Hayne=Margᵗ Da. & sole hey. of   Blanch uxor Tho. Kelley
in Com. Devon Esq. liveing | Jo. Davilles of Marland   of Kelley in Devon
1620   in Devon

John sone &   Will'm 2   Arthure 4   Mary ux' Tobias New-   Margart   Alice
hey. at. 34   —   —   court of Bickwel of
1620   Thomas 3   Henry 5   Devon Esq.   unmaried.
            Phillip 6

ARTHRE HARRIS.

---

¹ Agnes in Trewolla Ped. post.   ² Crymes.
³ Captain of St. Michael's Mount. Named in Will of Haniball Vivian of Trelowarren, 30 Nov. 1608.
* Mr. Arthur Harris and Mrs. Kath. Beard were mar. 1579. Ludgvan Par. Reg.
Wm. Harris, Esq., and Mrs. Jane St. Aubyn were mar. 4 Oct., 1685. Gulval Par. Reg.
Jno. Harris of Lanrest, gent., and Jane Harrys, gentlewoman, mar. 31 Jan. 1562. Menheniot Par. Reg. (She was sister of Sir Christopher Harris of Radford, co. Devon.)
Mr. John Harris and Mistress Mary Rashleigh, mar. 4 Feb., 1666. St. Breock Par. Reg.
John Harrys of Radford, Esq., and Amy Sawle were mar. 18 Aug., 1690. Tywardreath Par. Reg.
Mr. Ric. Harris and Mrs. Jane Webber were mar. 6 June, 1670. Padstow Par. Reg.
Jane, da. of Ric. Harrice, gent., and Jane ux., bap. 1672. Padstow Par. Reg.
John Harris (St. Breock.—Ed.) and Olivia Moyle were mar. 10 May, 1631. St. Austell Par. Reg.
Thos. Harris and Thomazin Viveau were mar. 27 April, 1681. St. Ewe Par. Reg.
Tho. Harryes of St. Issey and Jane Hart of Padstow, mar. lic. 1618.

THE VISITATION OF THE COUNTY OF CORNWALL. 91

Harvy.

ARMS. *Arg. a chev. betw. 3 harrows sa.*

John Harvy of Hale in pochiæ=Elizb. Da. of Baldwyne Grigorie of Trenyne in de Linkinghorne in Com. Cornw. | pochia de Mynver in Com. Cornw.

Baldwyne Harvy of Hale=Mary Da. of Jo. Somester of Peryn in Com. Cornw.

Marg^t mar. to Rich. Crabb   Jo. Harvy of Hale sone & hey. now liveinge 1620   Elizbeth unmaried   Mary unmar.

*   Not signed.*

Hatch.

Jeffery Hatch=

John Hatch=

Robt. 1 sone ob. sine p'le   Willm. Hatch=Jane. Da. of Willm. Worlington sone & hey. of Sr Mathew

Tho. Hatch=Mabell Da. of Tho. Leighe

Rob. Hatch=Guinthian Da. & hey. of S^r Jo. Murdoke of Northamptonsh.   Mabell   Beatrix   Jane

Rob. Hatch=Blanch Da. of Rowland Audley, sone of James Lo. Audley

John Hatch=Elizb. Da. & heire of Willm. Durwyn

John Hatch 2 sone mar. Alice Da. of Jo. Yeo of Branton=
      A   Willm' Hatch   John Hatch=   divers Daughters
                                                            B

* John Harvey, gent., bur. 16 Feb., 1617.   Lanteglos by Cam. Par. Reg.
   Francis Harvye mar. Xtian Bolytho   16 April, 1638. ⎫ Anthony in Mencage
   Francis Harvye   ,,   Alice Blanke, wid.,   1649. ⎭ Par. Reg.
   Richard Harvye   ,,   Anna Carthew   27 Nov., 1628. ⎫
   John Harvye   ,,   Jane Carthew   1605. ⎬ Breock Par. Reg.
   Tho. Harvey   ,,   Elizab. Trevail   1580. ⎪
   John Harvey   ,,   Jane Halke   1588. ⎭
   Walter Harvey and Anne Williams,   mar. 1599, at Feock. ⎫ Bp. of Exeter's
   Michael Harvey and Patience Williams,   ,,   ,,   ⎭ Transcripts.

THE VISITATION OF THE COUNTY OF CORNWALL.

```
        | A                                              | B
   John Hatch=Thomazin Da. of Wᵐ Selman    ¹ Tho. Hatch=
   _____|_____                         _____|_____
   Tho. Hatch=Mary Da. of Thomas Hellinge    Anne only Da. & hey. ux'
        |                                    Baldwyn Mallet
 _____|_____
Willm.  John  Rich.  Tho.  Willm Hatch=Mary Da. of Willm. Widdeslade of
                                      | Wideslade
                     _____|_____
                     Christ' Hatch of Busuistock=Constance Da. of Geo. Courtney
                     in Cornwall Esq.           of Penkevell Esq.
                          _____|_____
                          Prudence 1 Da.  Amye 2 Da.  Frances 3 Da.
                                                           Not signed.
```

Hawke.

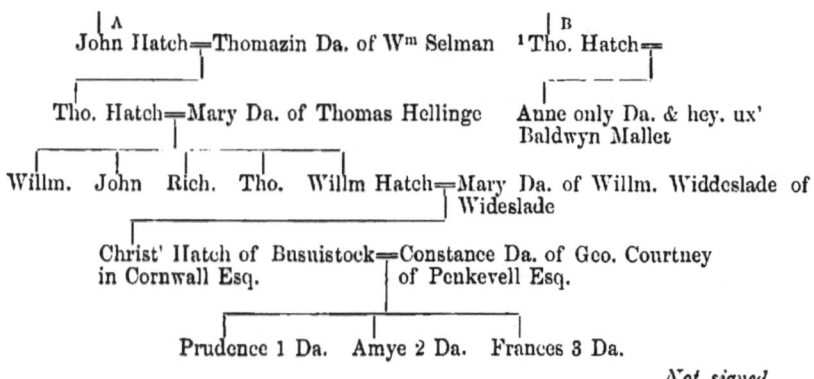

```
                         Hawke
                           =
   _____|_____
   John Hawke of Alternoon in Cornwall    Willm. Hawke of Alternon in Cornw. 2 sone
   _____|_____                      _____|_____
   .... Da. & heyre ux' Drew of   Tho. Hawke of Treriven=Cicily Da. & Coh. of Wᵐ
   Sᵗ Cleder in Cornw.            in Com. Cornw.         Heare of Treriven
                           _____|_____
                           Nicho. Hawke of Treriven in Com.=Temperance Da. & Coh. of Cha. Prust
                           Cornwall liveinge 1620          of Hartland in Com. Devon
   _____|_____
   Tho. 2    Mary a dat'    Rich. Hawke sone & hey.=Joane Da. & Coh. of Robt. Burden
   sonne     at. 1 yeare    atat. 20. 1620 liveing   of North Petherwyn in Devon
   at. 3     & half
                                            *         NICHOLAS HAWKE.
```

Hele.

```
         Nicho. Heale of Cornwood in Devon=Da.² of Done 2 wife
         _____|_____
         Tho. Heale³ of Fleete in Com. Devon=Julian Da. of Jo. Smith of Exiter.
                                            | A
```

¹ He mar. Agnes, da. of Sir John Bassett of Umberleigh.—Ed.
² Margeria, da. of Rich. Dune of Hollsworthy. See Hele ped. ' Visit. Devon, 1620,' p. 147.
³ Penelope, da. of Thos. Hele of Fleete, mar. Christopher Blackall (' Visit. Devon, 1620,' p. 31), and Joane, another da., mar. Robert Rolle of Heampton (' Visit. Devon, 1620,' p. 323).

* Mr. Peter Hawke and Mrs. Margaret Baker, mar. 1667. Tywardreath Par. Reg.

THE VISITATION OF THE COUNTY OF CORNWALL. 93

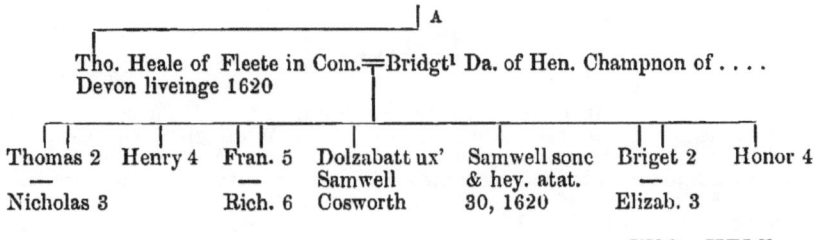

Tho. Heale of Fleete in Com. = Bridgt¹ Da. of Hen. Champnon of . . . .
Devon liveinge 1620

Thomas 2	Henry 4	Fran. 5	Dolzabatt ux' Samwell Cosworth	Samwell sone & hey. atat. 30, 1620	Briget 2	Honor 4
Nicholas 3		Rich. 6			Elizab. 3	

THO. HELE.

Hender.

Wᵐ Hender of Botriaux Castle = Agnes Da. of Jo. Newcourt
in Com. Cornwall   of Holisworthie

Jo. Hender² of = Da. of Thorne in Com.   Edw. Hender of Veriam = Elizb. Da. of Jo.
.... 1 sone &   Northampton   in Com. Corn. liveing Trefrie of Foye
heyre   1620, 2 sone   in Cornwall

Kath' ux' Jo. Molsworth   Mary³ ux' Ellys   Elizb. uxor   Fran. ux' Sʳ Rich.
of Breage   Heale of Devon   Cotton⁴   Rob.⁵ of Trwro

EDWARD HENDER.

---

¹ John Coswarth of Little Colan, gent., and Bridget Hele, widow, relict of Thos. Hele of Fleete. Mar. Lic. at Exeter, 1626.

* Samuel Hele and Elizabeth Stone,   mar. 28 Aug. 1631.
   Elizab., da. of Samuel Hele, gent., and Elizab., bap. 28 Oct. 1632.   St. Neot.
   Hannah,   „   „   „ 26 May, 1635.
   William, son of „   „   „ 23 Mar. 1636.
   William Hele, parsone,   bur. 25 June, 1624.   Landulph.   (J. M.)
   William, son of Samuel Hele, gent.,   „   6 Jan. 1636.
   Hannah, da. of   „   „ 21 June, 1637.   St. Neot.
   Samuel Hele, gent.,   „ 12 Mar. 1660.

For more extended pedigree of Hele, see 'Visit. Devon, 1620,' pp. 145–8, and 'Hist. of Trigg Minor,' vol. i., p. 42.

² John Hender, of Botreaux Castle, died 7 June, 1611 ; bur. at Minster, where is a monument to himself and wife, on which is a shield charged with the arms of Hender. Az. a lion ramp. within an orle of escallops or. Crest, a flaming sword erect, and impaling, Ar. a fess gu. betw. 3 lions ramp. difference, with a crescent for Thorne. There is also a monument in memory of Elizabeth, da. of the said John, and William Cotton her husband, Precentor and Canon of Exeter, eldest son of William Cotton, Bishop of that See. For more of this, and further memorials of Hender, see 'History of Trigg Minor,' vol. i.

³ Marriage settlement dated 16 Dec., 1 James. (J. M.)

⁴ William Cotton. See ped. 'Visit. Devon, 1620,' p. 341. [Marriage settlement dated 20 July, 5 James. (J. M.)]

⁵ Roberts.

Herle.

To all christen people these p^rsentez l'res to se & to heare. John, Prior of Durham, Willm, Abbot of Newminster, Thomas, Prior of Tinmouth, Robt. Whelpington, Mair of new castell on tyne, John Wodrington, knight, Rog. Wodrington, squire sherife of Northumb. gretinge in god. ffor that meritorie is to witnes truth to yor Universitie, we witnes & certifie of o^r verie knowing that one John Herle, Esq., y^t was Lo. of West Herle in Northumb. had issue in lawfull matrimonie one Tho. Herle his eldist son, & John Herle the elder knight his brother y^t dwelt in Cornwall & divers other children, & the said Thomas entered & peaceablie continewed his possession all his life, & had issue in lawfull matrimonie John Herle his sonne & heire, & died, & the said John his sonne entered & peaceablie possessed all his life, and had issue in lawfull matrimonie John Herle, his son eldest yet living, & Thomas his brother now dwelling in Cornwall of hale bloude, and then their said fader died, & the said John the brother of the last Thomas, entered as his sonne & heire, and continued his possession as right heire of the whole bloud to the date of the making of this, & where it is supposed that the said Thomas now dwelling in Cornwall should be bastard, we witnes and certifie y^t he is mulier and not bastar gotten & borne in forme & manner afforesaid, also we witnes & certifie that if the said John Herle knight & John Herle knight his sonne be dead w^thout issue of their bodies, that the same John Herle brother of the sayd Thomas dwelling in Cornwall is cosen & next heire to the sayde John Herle knight the sonne, that is to saye sonne & heire of the sayd John Herle his father, sonne & heire of ye said Tho. his father, sonne & hei. of the same John his father, whilke was father of the said John Herle knight the elder, father of ye said John Herle knight his sonne & heire by cause y^t ye same John died w^thout heire of him as before is specified. In witnes of whilke thinke we the said Priors, Abbot, Maior, the seales of o^r offices, & we the saide John Wodrington & Roger Wodrington o^r seales to these p^rsent l'res has .... set. At the Newcastell on Tine the first daye of Maye in the yeare of y^e raigne of King Henrie the 6 after y^e conquest of England the 14th.

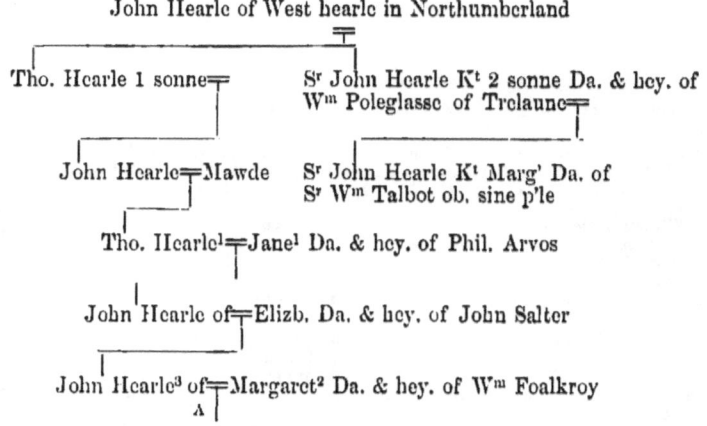

[1] Called 2 son of Jo. Herle, and mar. to Joane, da. of Rich. Arvos, Lo. of Pridieux. 'Visit. Devon. 1565 and 1620,' Harl. MS. 1080, fo. 104.
[2] She afterwards mar. Robert Cary. 'Visit. Dev., 1620,' p. 49. Mar. 1616. Luxyllian Par. Reg.
[3] His sister Margret Herle mar. Rich. Harrington, who was named with others on a commission directed to the Sheriff of Cornwall, to try Pirates (one of them named Glyn) at Fowey. Pat,

THE VISITATION OF THE COUNTY OF CORNWALL. 95

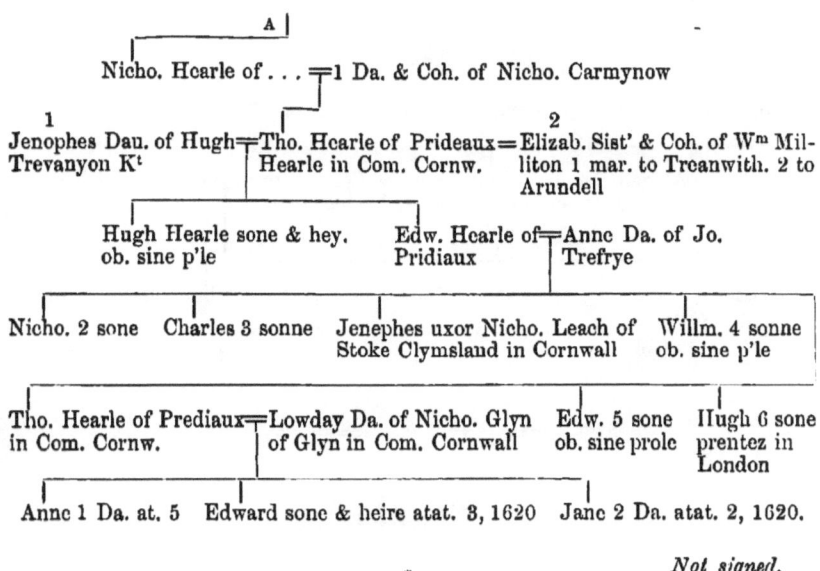

Roll 1 Edw. V. m. s. d. Carew, in his 'Survey,' relates that one Harrington of Fowey, was tried and hanged for Piracy about the end of Edw. IV. reign. While carefully searching the Record Office for confirmation of this, to no purpose, we lighted upon the Commission first named, and note the circumstance as one among many examples of distorted tradition. Anne, the daughter of Rich. Harrington, mar. Rob. Poyle (Harl. MS. 4031, fo. 78), and their only da. and heir mar. Thomas, the last male of the Petit family. Ped. fin. Cornwall 8 Hen. VIII. Trinity. Richard Harrington de Fowey, Mercat. qu. Tho. Glover and ux. def. lands in Fowey.

```
* Thos., son of Thos. Herle, Esq.,                    bap., 1622.⎫
  Bridget, da. of      „     and Loveday      „       1627. ⎪
  Charles, son of      „          „           „       1632. ⎪
  Thos.       „    Edward Herle, Esq., and Mary  „    1635. ⎪
  Edward     „         „          „           „       1643. ⎬ Luxyllian Par. Reg.
  Charles    „         „          „           „       1652. ⎪
  Edward Herle, Esq.                          bur.    1619. ⎪
  Will., son of Edw. Herle, Esq.               „      1653. ⎪
  Thos. Herle, gent.                           „      1666. ⎪
  Mrs. Mary Herle, wife of Edw. Herle, Esq.    „      1673. ⎪
  Edward Herle, Esq.                           „      1695. ⎪
  Charles Herle, gent.                         „      1697.⎭
  Nicholas Hearle and Richow Battin, mar. 21 Sept. 1617.    ⎫
  Stephen, son of Nicholas Hearle,    bap. 14 Mar. 1617–18. ⎬ St. Ewe Par. Reg.
  William        „             „       „   24 Oct. 1620.    ⎭
  Simon Clotworthy of Wembworthy, and Martha Herle of Tywardreth, Mar. Lic. at Exeter Nov. 1620.
```
Carlian, filius Carminois Herle, genosi, bap. 1584. Lanlivery Par. Reg.
Edw. Hearle, gen., and Maria Trefusis, mar. 1634. Buckland Mon. Par. Reg.

Duloe Par. Reg.

John Hearell & Marg. Sowden,	mar. 1668.	James, son of Tho & Dorothy. Hearle, bap. 1691.
Will. Hearl & Marg. Blake	„ 1686.	Ric., son of Ric. and Anstis Horrell, „ 1700.
Peter, son of Peter & Elizb. Hearle, bap. 1670.		Ric. Horrell, Sen., bur. 1695.
Peter Horrell,	bur. 1719.	Ric. Horwell, „ 1757.

[We insert the Duloe Regs. in further illustration of the note under Joliffe on change of name.]

Hext.

Jo. Hext of Stav'ton in Com. Devon=Phill. Da. of Wm Denham of Leviston

```
        2                                              1
John Hext   Abigall Da. of=Willm. Hext¹ of Constentin in=Jane¹ Da. of Wm Ri-
1 sone      Rob. Quarme    Com. Cornw. liveing 1620. 2 | chardes of Constantin
                        sonne
```

Thomas 3 sonne   Agnes a dau.   John 1 sone atat. 18   Willm. 2 sone at. 14
at. half yeare

*   WILLIAM HEXT.

Hickes.

Hen. Hickes of Luxillian of Cornwall

Rich. Hickes of Luxillian=Mary Da. of Wm. Grilles of Tavistock in Devon

² Walt' Hickes of Luxillian in=Elizb. Da. of Luke Bett of
Com. Cornwall liveinge 1620 | St. Tizey in Cornwall

Rich. son & hey.   Henry 2   Mary 1 Da.   Joane   Elizab.
at. 14. 1620   sone.   at. vi.   2 Da.   3 Da.

†   WA. HICKES.

---

¹ Will. Hext, gent., and Joan Richards, mar. at Constantine, 1601. Bp. of Exeter's Transcripts.

  * Emlin. da. of Geo. Hexte,   bapt. 1676. } Tywardreth Par. Reg.
    Thos. Hexed and Mary Chely, mar. 1671.
    Samuel Hext, gent., and Jane Moyle, mar. 19 Sept. 1668. St. Austell Par. Reg.

² Ob. 1636. Monument in Luxulyan Church.

† John, s. of Master Nicolas Hickes, by Jone, bap. 1688. } Tywardreath Par. Reg.
    Nicholas Hicks, gentleman, bur. 27 Sept. 1668.
    Robert Robins of the Parish of Blisland, gent., and Anne, da. of John } Zennor Par. Reg.
    Hicks of St. Ives, gent., mar. 28 Sept. 1693.
    David Hickst was one of the principal inhabitants of Lanlivery, and signed Register Book, 1654, electing Jno. Couch the elder as Registrar.
    Walter Hicks of Luxyllian and Frances Bersey, mar. 1747. St. Ervan Par. Reg.

THE VISITATION OF THE COUNTY OF CORNWALL. 97

Hill.

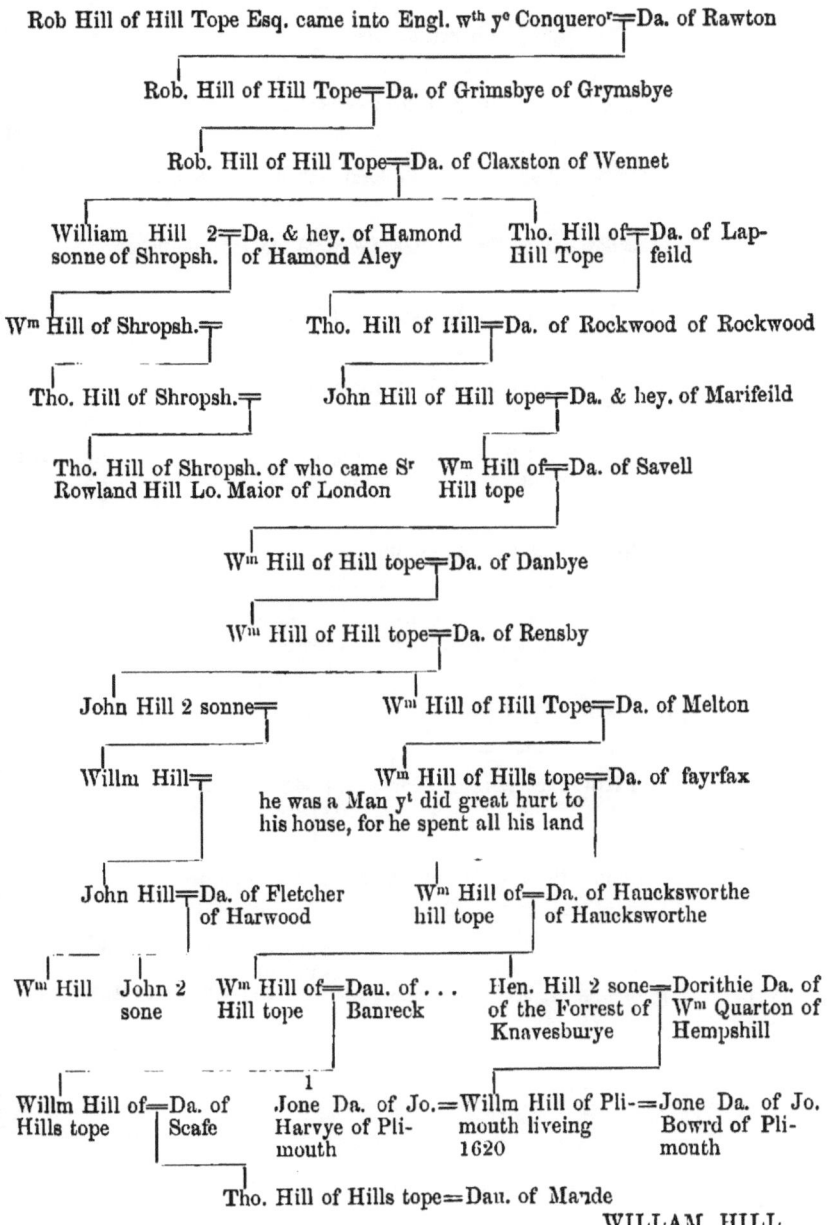

WILLAM HILL.

Hill.

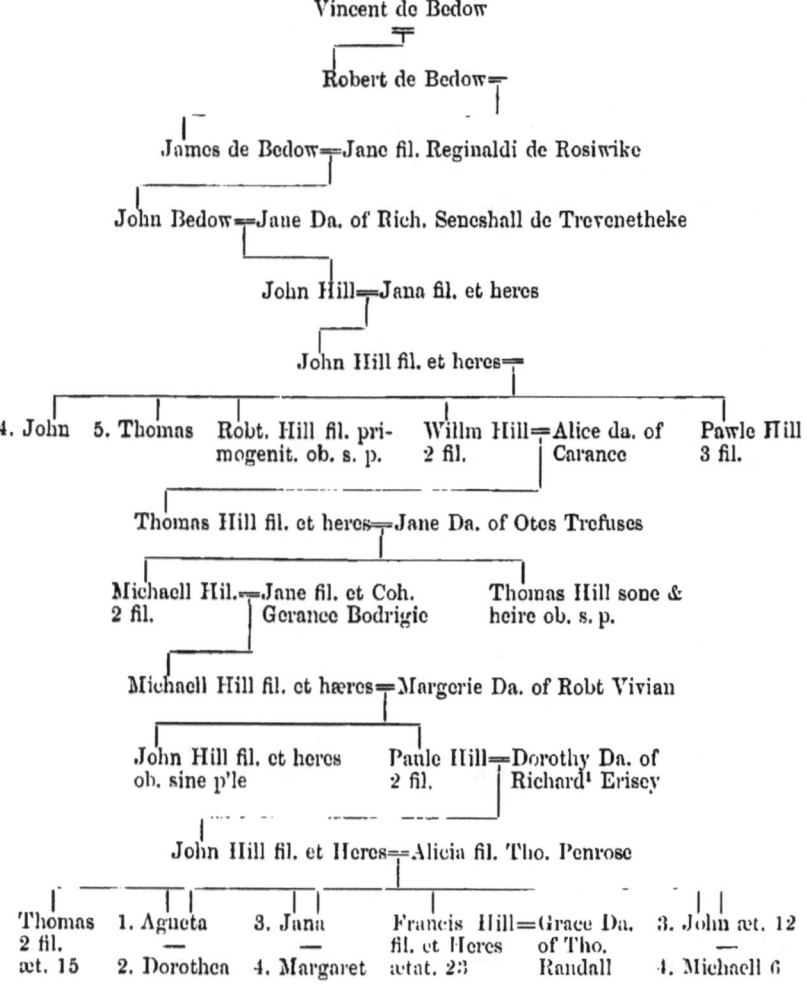

JOHN HILL.

---

[1] Called James Erisey in the Erisey Ped. *ante*.

Hill.

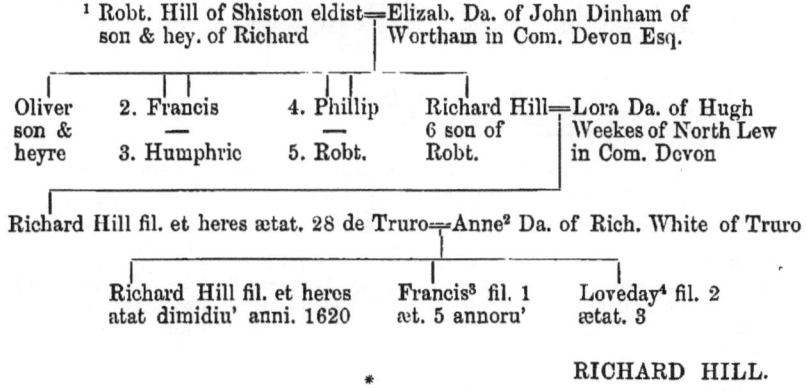

1 Robt. Hill of Shiston eldist = Elizab. Da. of John Dinham of
son & hey. of Richard | Wortham in Com. Devon Esq.

- Oliver son & heyre
- 2. Francis
- 3. Humphrie
- 4. Phillip
- 5. Robt.
- Richard Hill 6 son of Robt. = Lora Da. of Hugh Weekes of North Lew in Com. Devon

2 Richard Hill fil. et heres ætat. 28 de Truro = Anne² Da. of Rich. White of Truro

- Richard Hill fil. et heres atat dimidiu' anni. 1620
- Francis³ fil. 1 æt. 5 annoru'
- Loveday⁴ fil. 2 ætat. 3

RICHARD HILL.

Hill.

Oliv' Hill of Shilston in Com. = Agnes 2 Da. of Rog. Boduckshued
Devon Esq. sone & hey. of Robt. | of Budside in Com. Devon Esq.

- Rog. Hill 1 sonne
- Arthur Hill 2 sone of S⁺ Keverne in Com. Cornw. liveing 1620 = Marg⁺ Da. of Tho. Southcot of Bovye in Com. Devon

ARTHUR HILL.

---

¹ Son of Rich. Hill, by Joane, da. of Andrew Strechley of Hulberton, Devon. 'Visit. Devon, 1620,' p. 344.
² Mar. 16 Nov., 1613 ³ Bap. 13 July, 1615. ⁴ Bap. 31 Aug., 1617. } Truro Par. Reg.
Walter, son of John Hill of St. Clements, bap. 5 Jan, 1611–12.

* Jane, da. of Phillip Hill, bap. 10 Nov., 1610, at Helston.
William, son „ bur. 21 Nov., 1610,
Walter Hill and Elizb. Cowlin mar. 1632, at St. Stephen's, Saltash. } Bp. of Exeter's Transcripts.
For more, see Hill Ped., 'Visit. Devon, 1620,' p. 344.

Hyll.

Robt. Hill son &=Margaret Da. & hey. of Fantleroy & to hir
hey. of Giles Hill | mother who was Da. & heyre of Flamock

Giles Hill fil. et heres=Da. of Littlehor of Essex

Robt. Hill — Moris Hill of Helligan=¹Margaret Da. of John Carnsew
2 fil.   in Com. Cornwall   of Bokally of 2 House

| Katherin mar. to Peter Toker fratri Cristop. Toker | Honor mar. to Christoph. Toker of Hellond | Moris Hill 2 fil. ætat. 28. | ¹Humphrie Hill de Hellegan fil. primogenit. | Grace Da. of Peter Corriton of Newton in Com. Cornwall | ²Rich. Hill 3 fil. ætat. 25 |

Humphrie Hill fil. et Hæres ætat. 6 annoru' 1620

*   HUMPHRYE HYLL.

Hoare.

Eliza. da. to John=John Hore of=Catheryn da. to Phelip
Roskarock | Trenouth | Penkevell 1 wife

| ³Francis 4 | Dorithi 5 Da. | ³Richard Hore of Trenouth sonne & heir | Philip da. of Wynter A | Thomas 2 | Willm. 3 |

[1] In an Indenture dated 18 Oct., 1675, relating to lands in St. Mabyn, there is a citation of a lease which had been granted by Margaret Hill, widow, and Humphry Hill, son and heir apparent of the said Margaret. (Sir John Maclean's Collection.)
[2] Rich., son of Maurice Hill, Esq., bap. 2 Jan., 1595. Truro Par. Reg.

* Alexander Arundell & Catherine Hill mar.   21 July, 1568.
   John Loveales & Mary Hill were wedded   30 June, 1579.
   Antonie, son of Mr. Maurice Hill, was christened 27 Aug., 1583.
   John, son of Humphry Hill & Grace his wife bap. 12 July, 1621.   St. Mabyn Par. Reg.
   Humphry Hill, ye sonne of Mr. Robert Hill, bur. 1 Nov., 1576.   (J. M.)
   Mr. Robert Hill „ 4 Oct., 1578.
   Giles, ye sonne of Maurice Hill, Esq. „ 8 Feb., 1601.
   Robert Hill, gent. „ 22 Sept., 1611.

[3] Ped. fin. Cornw. Hill, 38 Eliz. Francis Hore qu. Rich. Hore def.
   Ped. fin. Cornw. 4 Hen. IV., No. 8. Int. Noel Paderda qu. Walter Hore and Alice his wife def. Lands in Pengelly, North Paderda, etc.
   Ped. fin. Cornw. 11 Hen. IV., No. 6. Int. John, son of Henry Hore, qu. and Warin Hore de Trewaythe and Nichola ux. eius def. Lands in Trewaythe, Trengale, and Fosnewyth settled on Warin H. and his wife by John.

THE VISITATION OF THE COUNTY OF CORNWALL. 101

| A

John Hore sone & hey.=Joane Da. & Coh. of Wm Cavill of
atat. 22 1620   St. Kue in Com. Cornwall

John sone & hey. atat. 1 1620   A da. at this p^rset unchristened

JOHN HOARE.

*

Hoblyn.

Richard Hoblyn=Margaret da. & coheire of John Daw of Lescarwell

John Hoblyn=Sibell da. & coheire of Edw. Ronnell of Boddrane

Anstace da. of Willm=Thomas Hoblyn=Agnes da. & heire of
Collard 1 wife   Willm. Kinge Treire

John Hoblyn=Eliza. da. of John   Reynald=Da. of   Peter Hoblyn mar. Tho-
2 sonne   Harrys of Lanrest   Hoblyn Hockin masin Da. of Hitchins

Richard=Phillip da. & co-   Katherin mar.   Anthonie 1. Kather. 3. Agnis
Hoblyn heire of John Pye   to John Pitt   ——   ——
                                            Robert   2. Elizab. 4. Jane

Dorothy da. of=Thomas Hoblyn of=Judith Da. of   Francis=Ephue Da. of
John Dynham   Nanswedon in   Edw. Trevals-   Hoblyn Tho. Hickes
2 wife   Cornwall living cois uxor   2 filius de Launceston
              1620   prima

Margeria uxor Edwardus Ho-=Mary Da. &   Thomas 2   2. Ricus   1. Dorothy
Johis Beare   blyn fil. primo- Coh. of   fil. de   2 fil.   æt. 18
de Trevedow   genitus ætatu. Robt. Apley medio   æt. 23   ——
inCom.Cornw.   33 a° 1620   of Barne- Templo   2. Susan
——   stable in Londo'   æt. 16
Agnes mar. to   Com. Devon ætat. 25
Charles Trwe-
body de Castell
A   B

* John Hocking and Johanna Hore mar. 10 May, 1569. St. Teath. ⎫
  Alexander Hore and Dorothy Cotton mar. 5 Nov., 1628. Poughill. ⎬ (J. M.)
  John Hore, Clerk, bur.   15 July, 1610. Blisland. ⎪
  Hugh, son of John Hore, gent., bap. 20 Jan., 1632. St. Kew. ⎭

102   THE VISITATION OF THE COUNTY OF CORNWALL.

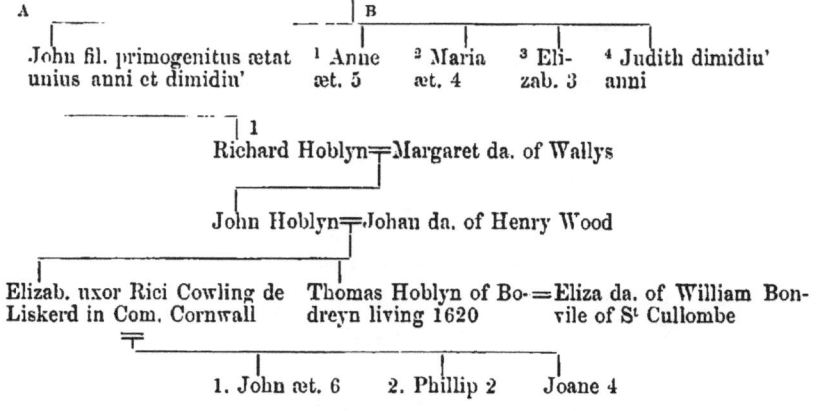

THOMAS HOBLYN OF BODRANE.
THO. HOBLYN OF NANSWHIDEN.

[1] Bapt. 19 Feb., 1614-15.
[2] Bapt. 22 Sept., 1616. } St. Columb Major Par. Reg.
[3] Bapt. 5 Jan., 1617-18.
[4] Bapt. 16 Oct., 1619.

* Reginald Hobling and Joan, da. of John Wenmouth of Quethiock, were mar. 1543. St. Pinnock Par. Reg.

Rachell, da. of Anthony Hoblyn and Joane his wife, bap. at Liskeard 12 March, 1624.
Robert, son of Edward Hoblyn, gent., and Marie his wife, bap. at Goran 6 June, 1624. } Bp. of Exeter's Transcripts.
Thos. Hoblyn, gent., and Alice Coswarth were mar. at Little Colon 7 Oct., 1634.

Thos. Hoblyne, gent., and Olyve Vivian, gen., were mar. 23 Nov., 1625. St. Winnow Par. Reg.
Anne. da. of Thos. Hoblyn, gent., and Grace, bap. 1665.
Will. Karkeek, gent., and Mrs. Grace Hoblyn mar. 13 March, 1687. } Goran Par. Reg.
Rich., son of Edw. Hoblyn, gent., bap. 31 May, 1696.   St. Stephen's in Brannel Par. Reg.
Edward Hoblyn, gent., son of Edward Hoblyn of Nanswhidden, Esq., dec. and Bridget, da. of John Carew of Penwarne, Esq., were mar. 8 August, 1659 (also entered in St. Col. Major Par. Reg.).   Mevagissey Par. Reg.
Francis Hoblyng and Elizab. Warne mar. 1685.   St. Issey Par. Reg.
Edw., son of Rob. Hoblyn, Clerk, bap. 1689. Colan Par. Reg.
Dorothea. da of Thos. Hoblyn, gent., and Alice his wife. bap. 16 Aug., 1637.
Judith, da.   ,,   ,,   ,,   8 Nov., 1638.
Alice. da.   ,,   ,,   ,,   6 Jan., 1640.
Judith, da. of Edw. Hoblyn. gent.   9 Oct., 1670.
Edward. son   ,,   ,,   ,,   21 Mar., 1674. St. Enoder
Alice. da.   ,,   ,,   ,,   1675.   Par. Reg.
John, son   ,,   and Joanna his wife,   ,,   30 Nov., 1683.
Mrs. Alice Hoblyn   bur. 1675.
Mr. Thos. Hoblyn   ,,   1699.
Francis Hoblyn   ,,   1710.
Peter Hoblyn and Elizab. Moyle   mar. 27 June, 1662.
Edw. Hoblyn, Esq., and Mrs. Barbara Hawkin mar. 27 Aug., 1726. } St. Austell Par. Reg
Mrs. Barbara Hoblyn bur. 1 Dec., 1739.

[*Note continued on next page.*

Jenkyn.

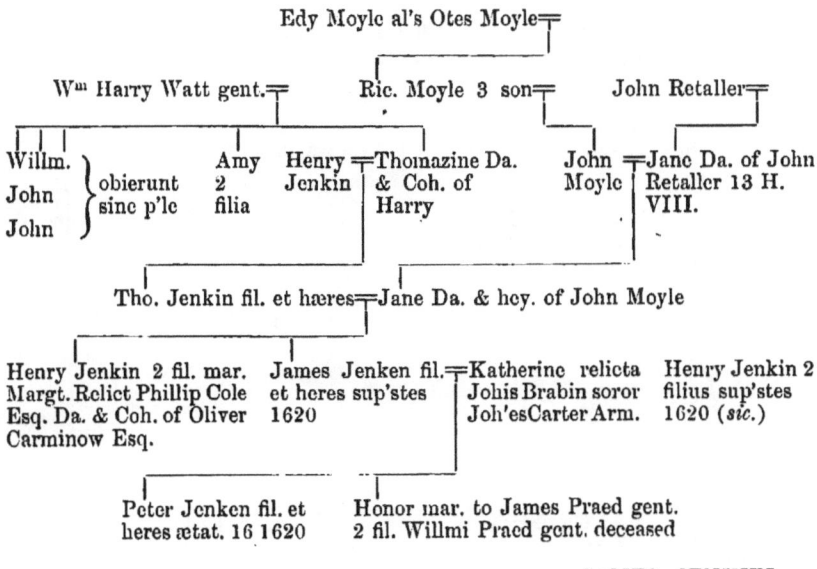

(Note continued.)
Rich. Hoblyn, Esq., and Anne da. of John Carew of Penwarne, Esq., were mar. 25 July, 1644.
Thos. Hoblyn, gent., and Mary, da. of Jno. Carter, Esq., were mar. 1 Sept., 1688.
Grace, da. of Thos. Hoblyn, bap. 23 Jan., 1697.
Judith, da. „ „ 1699.
Grace, da. of Mr. Thos. Hoblyn, „ 12 Nov. 1700.
Madam Grace Hoblyn, wid., bur. 1 June, 1693.
Edw. Hoblyn, Esq. „ 1684.

> St. Columb Major Par. Reg.

Mrs. Damaris Hoblyn. bur. 30 Dec., 1713.
Damaris, da. of Edw. Hoblyn and Damaris, bap. 18 Dec., 1683.

> Egloshayle Par. Reg.

John Hoblyn of St. Euoder, gent., and Anne Tub of St. Stephens, mar. 30 Jan., 1706. St. Mewan Par. Reg.
William Hobelyn held lands in Cornwall. De Banco Roll 50 Edw. III. Hillary. (Rob. Herres v. Will. Hobelyn.)
Ped. fin. Cornw. Mich. 28 Eliz. Int. Peter Marke qu. Richard Hoblynge, Thos. Hoblyng, and o'rs def.
The pedigree of Hoblyn has been registered in the College of Arms, and has been printed, with further extensions, in 'History of Trigg Minor,' vol. i. pp. 473–5.

* John Williams and Mary Jenking mar. 3 Aug., 1605.
Bartholomew Williams and Elizab. Jenkyn „ 8 Oct., 1610.
William Williams and Julian Jenkyn „ 23 Sept., „
William Williams and Agnes Jenken, both of Ladock, „ 8 Nov., 1642.

> St. Euoder Par. Reg.

Mar. Lic. between Peter Jenkyn of St. Columb Major, and Anne, da. of Andrew Pomeroy of the same, Esq., 20 Oct., 1628. (J. M.)

[*Note continued on next page.*

Jeynenes.

Rowland Jeynens of Bokonock in Cornwall⊤
descend of a familie of Shropsheire

Fran. Jeynens of Bosmawgan=Elizb. Da. of Hen. Spour of
in Cornwall | Trebarth in Cornwall

Hen. Jeynens of Bosmaw- Elizab. uxor   Mary 2   Lowdey 4   Anne 6
gan in Com. Cornwall   Nicho.   —
liveing 1620   Lavers of   Grace 3   Phillip 5

*   HENRYE JEYNENES.

(*Note continued.*)
John Jenken and Philip Vyvian	mar.	1 July. 1546.
John Jenken and Katherine Pube	„	7 Dec., 1549.
James Jenkin and Johan Francis	„	1573.
Thomas Jenken and Ursula Spraye	„	„
John Jenkyn and Elizabeth Nanconnan	„	20 April, 1602.
Anthony Jenkyn and Jane Bennett	.,	21 Aug., 1626.
Christopher Jenkins and Richo Dunn	„	1650.
John, son of Thomas Jenken,	bap.	16 March, 1553.
Thomas „ „	,,	1571.
John „ „	„	1574.
Richard „ . „	,,	1576.
Thomas „ „	„	1584.
Christopher „ Anthony and Jane Jenken	„	9 Jan., 1630.
Margery, wife of John Jenkin	bur.	4 May, 1542.
George, son of Thos. Jenkin	„	1 May, 1543.
Thomas Jenken	„	15 June, „
Peter Jenkyn, Esq.	„	19 Sept., 1663.
Mrs. Ann Jenkyn, widow	„	19 May, 1681.

{ St. Columb Major Par. Reg.(J.M.)

John Jenkyn and Margaret Basset mar. 15 Sept., 1611. Pyran in Powder. (J.M.)
Elizabeth, wife of Henry Jenkin, gent., bur. 5 Sept.. 1686. Lanivet. (J.M.)
John Seynt Auhyn, son of John Seynt Aubin, Esq., and Anne, da. of James Jenkyn, Esq.,
  deceased, were mar. 14 Nov., 1665, at St. Columb Major. (Bp. of Exeter's Transcripts.)
Sir Nicholas Slanninge, Kt. of the Bath and Bart., and Mary, da. of James Jenkyn, Esq.,
  did mar. 22 June, 1670. (St. Columb Major Par. Reg.)
Will of John Jenkyn of Penpons Alverton (Maddern), 14 Sept, 2 Jas. Names his wife
  Elizabeth, his son Edward, and Thomas, John. William. Mary, and Catherine, children
  of Edward ; also Richard, and Philip, son of William Noye, of Talcarn, his son-in-law.

  * Chancery Proceedings 27 June, 1579, Eliz. William Jennyngs of Padstow, thirty years
ago a soldier, he had two sons, William, o. s. p., and John Jennyngs of Tottin Mill, Co. Lanca-
shire. who had issue John, o. s. p., Elizabeth, mar. to Rich. Soughte, and Thomasine, mar. to
Robert Irishe.
  Rich. Symons and Lowdy Jennyngs. gent., mar. 9 May, 1629. St. Winnow.
  Thomas Jennynge and Elizabeth Horwell, mar. 10 Oct., 1624. St. Columb Major. } (J. M.)
  Ped. fin. 18 Jas., Easter, Cornw. Abraham Jennens qu. Edm. Dourishe, gent., and Agnes
ux. eius Elizeus Dourish and Johanna ux. eius def. Ten. in Saltashe.
  Ric. Williams and Jane Jennings were mar. 1600. St. Columb Major Par. Reg.
  For earlier and extensive ped. of Jeynenes, see Harl. MSS. 615, 1241, 1396, and 6172.

Jollyfe.*

Stephen Tredidon temp. Rici II.=Magdalena
|
John Tredidon temp. H. VI.=Joane fil. et hær. Rici Fowler de Twynyo
|
Tho. Tredidon temp. E. IV.=Elizab. fil. Willmi Penfound de Penfound
|
John Tredidon=
A

* The family of Erisey were seated at Tredidon in Egloskerry after the Visitation, and George Joll (i.e. Jolliffe) of Alternon and James Erisey married two sisters from Devonshire. John Erisey of Egloskerry, will prob. 1684 ; Ric. Erisey of St. Neot, will prob. 1707. (Bodmin.)
    Egloskerry. John Joll, clerk, and Ursula Prowse mar. Jan., 1610. In the mar. lic. he is called Jole.
    St. Enoder. Katherine, wife of Willm. Jollye, clerk, bur. 15 July, 1616. Will prob. 1628, Bodmin.
    Jno. Joll of Lewannick, miller, legacies to his bro. John J. of Egloskerry, clerk, and his bro. Thos. J. Will prob. 1624, Bodmin.
    George Jolliffe, clerk, Lewannick. Will prob. 1574, Bodmin, not found. Presented A.D. 1569, on death of Jno. Waye. Bp. Reg. Exon.
    George Jolliffe, Vicar of Lewannick. Will prob. 1593, Bodmin. Names children of his son Timothy.

    Timothy Jollif mar. Mary Martin,   1576. ⎫
    Tho. Joliffe mar. Eliz. Band,   1589. ⎪
    Tho. Jolly mar. Xtian Jane,   1602. ⎬ Fowey Par. Reg.
    Francis, son of Timothy Jolliffe, bap. 26 Dec., 1583. ⎪
    Will., son of Timothy Jolly,   ,,   1582. ⎭

    Hals mentions one Peter Jowll or Jouell, under clerk or deacon of Alternon, temp. Chas. II., who attained the age of 150 odd years. When 100 years old, new black hair sprung forth on his head, and new teeth grew in his jaws in place of those which had fallen out. The Rev. Peter William Jolliffe (B.A. 1789, M.A. 1792, St. John's Coll. Camb.), P. C. of St. James, Poole, died 22 Feb., 1861, in the seventy-first year of his incumbency, aged ninety-four ; the circumstance is alluded to in 'Notes and Queries,' vol. xi., second series. The families of Jolliffe, Jollowe, Jolle, Jollye, and Joll were evidently one and the same, and their tradition supports this view. They were seated in the same and neighbouring parishes, were landowners, yeomen, and clergymen there contemporaneously, using the same peculiar Christian names, Peter, Nicholas, and Digory, with the more ordinary ones, George, John, William ; and, according to Lysons, they were noted for their singular longevity. (The Lysons state they could not find any entry of the ancient Peter in the Parish Registers ; but Alternon registers have been much mutilated,—in fact all destroyed before the twenty-ninth page, beginning with 29 March, 1688—and the Editors have heard that they were cut up by their custodian, a tailor, to take measures. They here offer to the notice of the curious the following extract from the Parish of Broadock :—John Holman, 102 years old, was buryed the 8th of Dec., 1626.) In the folio pedigree of vol. i. 'Parochial Hist. of Cornwall' will be found the names of John Joll, from Alternon, who died aged 98, and of his three daughters, Honor, died aged 80, from the effects of a fall downstairs ; Catherine, died aged 86 ; and Mary, died aged 93, of injuries received in a field from the attack of a ram.
    It is of some import to the genealogist to note the corruptions and abbreviations of West Country names,—for instance, Joli, Jolla, Jowle, Joyl, Juyl, presumably the older forms, became Jolliffe, Jollow, Jollye, Joll (around Alternon and Egloskerry), Joll and Jolly, same persons (Landewednack), Gatliffe, Gatley (St. Clement's), Talbot, Talbutt, Talbord (Tavistock), Talver, Tabre, Tallbert (Lostwithiel), Mohun, Moon (St. Blazey), Bohun, Boon (Bp.'s Teignton), Carkeet, Terkick (St. John's and Sheviock), Hext, Hixt, Hix, Hicks (Lamorran) ; *cum multis aliis quæ nunc*, etc.
    Mr. Peter Jollife bur. 18 Mar., 1665. St. Thomas by Launceston Par. Reg.

Tho., son of John Joll, bap. 11 Sep., 1598. ⎫
Henry Rowe and Margt. Jolly mar. 1624. ⎬ Lewannick.
Nich. Jolle and Margt., da. of Arthur Dalley, were mar. at Michaelstow 1601. ⎫
John Jolliffe bur.   ,,   1616. ⎪
Jane, da. of Mr. Joseph Jolley, bap. at Kenwyn   1622. ⎬ Bp. of Exeter's Transcripts.
Francis Jolla bur. N. Petherwin.   1633. ⎪
Mary, da. of John Jollow, bap. at Jacobstow   1655. ⎭
Tho. Joll and Frances Pearne were mar. ,,
Ann, daughter of Peter Jolliffe, gent., baptized 26 Oct. 1623. Northill. (J. M.)

Tho. Windsor=Jone Da. and hei. of John Tredidon

John Joliffe de Pougwill=Maria fil. et hær. Tho. Windsor

John Joliffe temp. aº 28 H. VII.=

Willm Joliffe of Tredidon =Emma uxor eius

Nicholas Joliffe of Tre-=Elinor Da. Johis of (sic)
didon 24 H. VIII.   Trehanke de Trehauke
                    B

Henry Joll of Okehampton & Mary Howard of the same, spinst.,   25 July, 1695. } Mar. Lic.
Henry Jole of Okehampton, gentleman & Mary Collings of the same, spinst., 1737. }
John Jolliffe, gent., and Mrs. Agnes Cary were married 9 May, 1676.   West Pudford, Devon.
(J. M.)
Bridget, wife of Jno. Jolliffe, bur.   1609.
John Jolliffe bur.   1621.   Lanlivery
John, son of Gregory and Priscilla Jolly, bap.   1648.   Par. Reg.
Walter, son of Gregory and Priscilla Jolly, bap.   1650.
John Dowrish, son of George and Margaret Joll, bap.   6 Ap., 1677.
(„   „   bur. at Alternon 10 Aug., 1679. Archdcn. Transcripts.)
Anne, da. of George and Margaret Joll,   „   20 June, 1682.   South Petherwin
John, son   „   „   21 April, 1685.   Par. Reg.
(He was bur. at St. Budeaux, aged 98, 1 Jany., 1783.)
George Joll bur. 9 June, 1692.   } Alternon Par. Reg.
Dame Margaret Joll bur. 10 June, 1694.}
(She was the da. of Lewis Dowrish of Dowrish in Devon, et tandem hæres familiæ Dowrish.)
George Joll and Margaret Dowrish of Sandford.   Mar. lic. 2 Jany., 1674-5.
Nich., s. of Wm. Jolle, bap.   1602.
Nich. Jollie, Warden   1634.   Padstow Par. Reg.
Nicholas Jolly, gent., bur. 13 July,   1666.
Nich., s. of Nich. Jolly and Ann, bap. 1675.
Close Rolls.   30 Chas. II. pt. 3. Sir. Wm. Palmer and o'rs and Elizb. Clerk, wid. of Clerk, mercht. of Lond., one part, and John Jollife and Will. Jolly of London, merch'ts of London, of the other part.
  „   „   2 Geo. I. 12 pt. Sir William Jolliffe per Arabella Clark, wid.
  „   „   1657. Barney Morden 1st part. Tho. Jolley of Easton, Worcester, Esq., John Jolliffe, citizen mercht. of London, James Wainwright, cit. and haberdasher of Lond., and Will. Jolley of Ligorne in Italy beyond seas, mercht. Land in Great Woodstock St., p'ish of St. Michael's.
  „   „   2 Chas. I. pt. 10. John Jowle of Gray's Inu, co. Mid., gent., land in Kent.
  „   „   1658. Fra. Drake, of Walton on Thames, ar., before his Highness Rich. Lo. Protect. of the Commonw., acknowledgeth himself to owe unto George Joyliffe, of ye city of London, Doct. of Physic, £2800.
  „   „   7 Ed. VI. 2d pt. Int. Reve. Cotton and John Joll generosus, and Clemence ux. Ampthill in Bedfordsh., etc.
Ped. fin. 17 Elizb.   Easter, Cornw.   Will. Jollyffe al's Jollow q. Degory Beare gen. def. ten. in Penpole & Lesnewih.
  „   „   31 & 32 Elizb. Mich., Dev.   Jno. Jollowe & Wm. Trebarfoot q. Ric. Cleverton def. ten't in Cleverton Bradworthy.
  „   „   32 & 33 Elizb. Mich., Corn.   Degory Jollyffe gen. q. Jno. Harrys gen. def. ten. East Downend and Egloskerry.
  „   „   33 & 34 Elizb. Mich., Corn.   Degory Jollyffe gen. qu. Jno. Pearse def. tent. in N. Huish.
  „   „   36 Elizb.   East., Dev.   Jno. Jollowe gen. q. Tho. Vigurs gen. def. 400 acres in West Putford, Monk Okehampton, etc.
  „   „   37 Elizb.   East., Corn.   Nich. Jollowe q. Walter Cottell, Moorwynstow.
  „   „   38 Elizb.   Trin., Corn.   Nich. Jolyffe & al. q. Edw. Dassell gen. & Margt. Dassel wid. def. about 500 acres Egloskerry, etc., & St. Stephens.

THE VISITATION OF THE COUNTY OF CORNWALL. 107

| B

Degorie Joliff = Margaret Da. of Burden iuxta
of Tredidon | Biddiford relicta Nicolls

Nich. Joliffe de Tredidon in Com. Cornw. = Elizab. Da. of Tho. Risdon of Babligh

Peter Joliffe = Anna fil. Rici   Grace mar. to Nic.   [1] Mary wife of Nich.
de Tredidon | Spoure de   Mayow of Minhin-   Rutter of Costentin
               Northill   net   in cornwall

Elizab. fil. primogenita æt. 6 septimanes
PETER JOLLYFE.

[1] Nich., s. of Ric. Rutter, Vicar of Constantine, and Mary, da. of Nic. Joliffe of p'ish St. Thomas, Esquire, mar. 10 Feb., 1619. Constantine Par. Reg.

Ped. fin.	44 Elizb.	East., Dev.	Nic. Joliff gen. q. Hy. Spore & al. def. in Bridge & Knell.
"	" 2 James.	Mich.	Nich. Jolliffe q. Tremlet def. lands in Krabrill.
"	" 9 James.	Mich., Corn.	Wm. Jollye, clerk, q. Humph. Kemp ar. & al. def. Man. de Pencorse & lands in Bossiney, Cubert, Breock, Enoder, etc.
"	" 10 James.	Mich., Dev.	Nich. Jollyffe gen. q. Ric. Westlake & Xtn ux. def. land in Pyworthy.
"	" 13 James.	Dorset.	Humphry Jollif gen. & al. q. Wm. Holmes def. lands in Weymouth & Melcombe Regis.
"	" 16 James.	East., Corn.	Jno. Rawle gen. qu. & Wm. Jolle & Mary ux. def. lands in St. Juliott.
"	" 16 James.	East., Corn.	Wm. Jolle q. Emanuel Langford ar. def. lands in Alternon.
"	" 20 James.	East., Dev.	Nich. Prideaux mil. q. Peter Jolliffe gen. & Anna ux. def. 200 acr. land & 40/ rents in Bradworthic.
"	" 1 Cha.	East., Dev.	Geo. Small q. Peter Jolliffe gen. def. ten. in Blacktor-rington.
"	" 1 Cha.	Trin., Corn.	W. Rous ar. q. Wm. Jolly clerk & al. def. Manor of Pencorse, etc.
"	" 1 Cha.	Trin., Corn.	W. Jolley q. Ina Vivian wid. def. lands in Werrestone Aliscomb, etc.
			Jno. Seymour & al. q. Peter Jolliffe gen. def. lands in Downheved.
"	" 2 Cha.	Mich., Dev.	Tho. Burnevy gen. q. Peter Jolliffe gen. & al. def. lands in Devon.
"	" 2 Cha.	Mich., Dev.	Geo. Uglow q. Peter Jolliffe gen. def. Pyworthy, Bridgerule, etc.
"	" 2 Cha.	Mich., Dev.	Wm. Rous ar. W. Courteney gen. q. Wm. Jolley clerk Joseph Jolly gen. & Johan ux. & or. def. Pencorse, etc.
"	" 11 Chas.	Mich., Corn.	Nich. Jolly & al. q. Geo. Smyth ar. def. lands in Padstow, etc.
"	" 24 Chas. I.	East., Dev.	Henry Spoure ar. Peter Jolliffe ar. q. Wm. Mallett def. lands in Idderlegh, Monk Okehampton.
"	" 24 Chas. II.	Trin., Corn.	Benj. Jolly gen. q. Tho, Webb & al. def. land in Launcells
"	" 24 Chas. II.	Mich., Corn.	Spoore vid. q. Joseph Jollye & al. in Penryn Burrough.
"	" 28–29 Chas.II.	Hill., Cornw.	Sam. Kekewich ar. q. W. Jolley gen. def. lands in Kenwyn.
			(The name Joll is in Kenwyn Par. Reg.)
"	" 4 Jas. II.	Trin., Corn.	Arthur Fortescue ar. q. Wm. Jolley senr. gen. & Anne ux. Wm. Jolley jun. gen. def. St. Enoder, etc.
"	" 1653.	Hill., Corn.	Nich. Jeffery q. Peter Joll and Willm. Joll def. lands in Tredawle, Austell, Alternon, & Foy Moor.
"	" 1655.	Mich.	Rob. Couch q. Leonard Joll & Joan ux. def. land in Trewynt Alternon.

Cath. Joll al's Jolly bur. 7 Dec., 1731. Landewednack Par. Reg.
Inq. Nonar. 15 E. III. De nona garb vell. et agn. poch. Ecclie de Alternon etc. vend. Johi Yolla etc.

Jope.

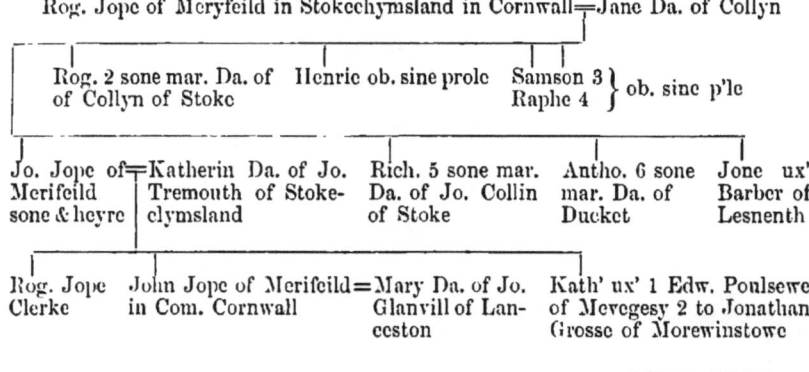

JOHN JOPE.

Kekewich.

ARMS.—*Shield of six quarterings:*—1 and 6. KEKEWICH. *Arg. 2 lions pass. in bend Sa. betw. 2 cotises Gu.* 2. *Arg. 3 bars gemels Gu.* 3. TOLKARNE. *Or on a fesse belw. 3 Cornish choughs prop. a garb belw. 2 cross-crosslets fitché of the first.* 4. BARDFIELD. *Arg. on a bend Az. 3 fleurs-de-lis Or.* 5. *Quarterly Or and Gu. on a bordure Sa. 8 escallops Arg.*
CREST.—*A leopard's head and neck affrontée Sa.*

p' ROB. COOKE.

Geo. Ketchwich[1] of Ketchfrench=Katherin Da. of Edw.
in Com. Cornwall Esq.   Courtney of Lanrack
                                                           A

[1] Ob. 26 June, 23 Eliz. Inq. p. m. 24 Eliz., 2 part, No. 13. George Keckwych, son & heir.

* Jno. Jope and Mrs. Ann Courteney were mar. 1772. Buckland Mon. Devon Par. Reg.
Margaret, dau. of John Jope, Glover, bap. 5 Aug., 1623.
Joane,   „   „   gent.   „   2 Nov., 1623.
Mary,   „   „   „   „   10 April, 1625. Stoke Climsland. (J. M.)
Thomazine, wife of George Jope, Sen. bur. 16 April, 1625.
Fortige ? son of John Jope,   ,.   6 Feb.,   „
Robert Jope of . . . . and Catherine Trigges (daughter of the Rector), mar. 3 May, 1706. Warleggan. (J. M.)
     Peter Lower of Treloske, co. Cornwall, and Thomas Lower, son and heir apparent of the said Peter, by deed dated 1 Jan., 1617, granted to Edward Reede of Wenbury, co. Devon, gent., and John Jope of Launceston, gent., a lease of certain lands in Alternon, etc., for the term of 99 years. Deed in the Collection of Sir John Maclean.
     Ped. fin. Cornwall 2 Hen. IV., No. 5. Int. John Jope, brother of Nicholas Bokelly. qu. Nicholas Bokelly and Alice his wife, def. in Tregorthian.

THE VISITATION OF THE COUNTY OF CORNWALL.

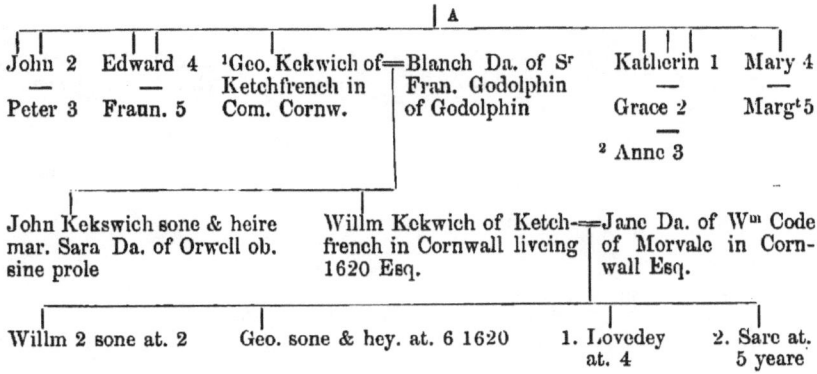

* WILLIAM KEKEWICH.

Kendall.

Nicholas Kendall[3] of Pelyn in Com. Cornwall = Loveday 1 Da. to John Kelow

Rich Kendall 3 sonne = Nicholas Kendall

Walter Kendall sonne & hey. of Pelyn mar. Agnes 2 Da. of John Bovele

Willm Kendall of Lostwithiell = Temperance Da. of Willm Waye of Lestidiall

Phillippa ob. s. p.

Walter 2 son ob. s. p.

Loveday mar. to Reskimer Bonithon of Bonithon in Cury in Com. Cornwall et nunc vicecom. Cornwall

Thomas Kendall of Pelenc in Tywardreth in Cornwall = Elizab. Da. of ArthurArscott of Titcott in Com. Devon

A

---

[1] Aged 24 years and more 26 June, 23 Eliz.
[2] She mar. Oliver Clobery. See 'Visit. Devon, 1620,' p. 60.

* Edward Ketchwich of Trethanke, mar. Jane, da. of John Coode of Morval. See Coode ped. *ante.*
   Peter Kekewich, gent., and Mrs. Ruth Williams, mar. 20 Ap. 1713.
   Peter, son of Peter Kekewich, gent., and Ruth, bap. 1714. Lanteglos by Fowey
   Mrs. Ruth Kekewich, bur. 1726. Par. Reg.
   Peter Kekewich of Hall, Esq., „ 16 Aug. 1728.
   Mr. Peter Kekewich of Lanteglos, and Mrs. Rebecca Williams, mar. 1741. Duloe Par. Reg.

[3] Inq. p. m. Walter Kendall of Pellyn 1 Ed. VI. No. 6. Nicholas, son and heir, æt. 36 et amp.; Lawrence Kendall, father of said Walter.

THE VISITATION OF THE COUNTY OF CORNWALL.

A

| Walter Kendall fil. et heres ætat. 12 annoru' 1620 | ¹ Thomas Kendall 2 fil. æt. 11 | Thomazin æt. 9 | Elizab. 2 fil. æt. 8 | Mary 3 fil. æt. 5 | Honor 4 fil. 1 ann. |

* WALTER ALLYN
For Mr. KENDALL.

¹ Bapt. 13 Aug. 1609, at Tywardreth. Bp. of Exeter's Transcripts.

* Avis, da. of Walter Kendall, gent.   bap.   1609.
 Lawrence, son of Lawrence Kendall, gent. „   9 Oct. 1609.
 James,   „   „   „   1612.   Anthony in Meneage
 Jane,   da. of „   „   „   1613.   Par. Reg.
 Agnes,   „   „   „   1614.
 William,   „   „   „   10 June, 1616.
 Lawrence Kendall and Furnifell Pollowyn, mar. 28 Dec. 1659. St. Colomb Major Par. Reg.
 Roger, son of Roger Kendall,   bap. 1650. St. Sampsons and Gollant Par. Reg.
 Sampson,   „   „   „   1652.   at Tywardreath.
 Mrs. Elizabeth Kendall,   bur. 1644. Tywardreth Par. Reg.
 Roger Kendall and Elizb. Vanson were mar. 1660.
 Anne, wife of Mr. Walter Kendall, bur. 1661. Truro Par. Reg.
 Jane, da. of Tho. Kendle,   bap. 21 Sept. 1628.
 Mary,   „ Tho. Kendall and Jone, „   1636.
 Geo., son of Thos. Kennall,   „   1638.   St. Pinnock Par. Reg.
 Anne, da. of Thos. Kendall,   „   1641.
 Francis, son of   „   bur. 4 Jan. 1640.
 Walter, son of John Kendall and Emeline, bap. 1626.
 Walter Kendall, Esq., and Jone Carew, his wife, were married to-
   gether the 17 July, 1650, in the Parish Church of St. Minver, by
   me William Collyer, Vicar of Lanlivery.
 Nich. Kendall, gen. et Emlina, uxor ejus, mar. 1623.
 Nich. Kendall, Vic. of Lanlivery, and Jane, da. of Tho. Carew, of
   Harroboro, Esq. decd. were mar. 14 Oct. by the Right Rev. Father Lanlivery Par. Reg.
   in God Jonathan (Trelawney), Lo. Bishop of Bristol, 1684.
 About this time (22 July, 1697), ye price of corn arose in ye marketts
   hereabouts: wheat to 35s. ye b's, barley to 24s., and oats
   to 12s. at 21 gallons to ye b's, which I sett down here as a thing
   never known before, and I hope never will be more. Nich.
   Kendall, Vic.
 Ric.,   son of Nich. Kendall, gent.   bap. 19 Mar. 1608.
 Walter, „   „   bapt.   1610.
 John,   „   „   „   1613.
 Nich.,   „   „   „   1617.
 Willm., „   „   „   1622.
 Loveday and Amye, daus. of Nich. Kendall, „   1626.
 Walter, son of Nich. Kendall, Esq., and Marie, „ 1630.
 Ric.,   „   Ric. Kendall, gent., and Anne,   „ 1655.
 Tho.,   „   „   „   „   1657.
 Nic. Kendall and Marie,   mar. 24 May, 1608.
 Allson Kendall, gent.,   bur.   1609.   Luxyllian Par. Reg.
 Ric. Kendall, gent.,   „   1620.
 Will. Kendall, gent.,   „   1640.
 Nich. Kendall, Esq.,   „ 21 Sept. 1649.
 Ric. Kendall, gent.,   „ 26 May, 1655.
 Mrs. Amy Kendall,   „   1656.
 Mrs. Marie Kendall, widow,   „   1666.
 Thos. son of Ric. Kendall, gent.,   „   1673.
 Ric.   „   John Kendall, gent.,   „   1679.
 Ric. Kendall, gent.,   „   1695.
 Ric.,   son of Tho. Kendall, gent.,   bap.   1603.
 Tho.,   „ John Kendall, gent.,   „   1628.
 Tho.,   „ Mr. Ric. K., gent.,   „   1637.   Morval Par. Reg.
 Walter, „ Walter K. and Agnes.   „   1662.
 Ric. Kendall and Philippa Treddenuick, mar.   1635.

THE VISITATION OF THE COUNTY OF CORNWALL. 111

𝕶𝖊𝖓𝖉𝖆𝖑𝖑.

[1] Nicho. Kendall of Pelyn in Com. Cornwall=Loveday Da. of Jo. Kellowe[2] of Lansells

[3] Walt' 1 sone of Pelyn mar. Agnes 2 da. of Jo. Bevill of Mellydar	W^m 2 sone mar. Tempance Da. of Wm Waye of Listidiall	Rich. Kendall of Medrose in Cornwall liveing 1620. Alie Da. of Hughe Bascoyne in Cornw. 2 wife	=Kath'[4] Da. & hey. of Tho. Trewolley of Trewolley

Nicho. Kendall sone & atat. 37 liveinge 1620 = Mary Da. & Coheyre of John Trehayne of Trehayne in Cornwall

Rich. sone & heyre at. 11. 1620	Walt' 2	John 3	Nicho. 4	Katherine a da. at. 6. 1620.

*   NICHOLAS KENDALL.

---

[1] Inq. p. m. 35 Eliz., 1 part, No. 52. Walter Kendall, son and heir.
[2] Killiowe of Lansalloes.
[3] Æt. 40, 35 Eliz. His da. Jane mar. Nich. Glinn of Glinn. See ped. *ante*. Phillipa mar. Rich. Michell of Bodmin. See ped. *post*. And Loveday (or Leodia) mar. Will. Coode of Morval. See ped. *ante*.
[4] In Chancery Proceedings, 9 April, 1583, Eliz. K. k. 2. No. 33. Rich. Kendall and Katherine his wife v. John Trewolla, she is called the dau. and hey. of Wm. Trewolla and great granddaughter of Rich. Trewbilla. See also Trewolla Ped. *post*.

* Tho. Kendall and Grace Robins,   mar.   1657.
Edw. Kendall and Philippa Crago,   „   1675.
Tho. Kendall, Esq.,   bur.   1600.
Mary, wife of Mr. John Kendall,   „   1637. } Morval Par. Reg.
Tho. K. of Cutparrot, Esq.,   „   27 Oct. 1638.
John Kendall of Treworgy, Esq.,   „   12 Jan. 1640.
Tho. Kendall, gent., Mearchant,   „   1676.
Mary, dau. of Thomas Kendall, Esq., bap. 11 Jan. 1614. Tywardreth.
Jane, dau. of Nicholas Kendall, gent., and Emeline, bap. 12 Oct. 1624. Lanlivery.
Jane, dau. of Walter Kendall, gent., bur. 23 Oct. 1683. } Lostwithiel.
Margaret Kendall,   „   15 July, 1696. }
William, son of Nicholas Kendall, bap. 1687. St. Cleer.
Jane, dau. of William Kendall,   bap.   1567.
Nicholas Kendall, son of Thomas Kendall and
   his wife Jone,   „   4 May, 1636. } St. Pinnock.
Mary, dau. of Thomas Kendall,   bur. 10 April, 1632.
Jone Kendall,   „   1643.   } (J. M.)
Alice, dau. of Thomas Kendall,   bap.   1600.
Elyal Kendall and Elizabeth Borlase,   mar. 22 Oct. 1699.
William, son of Nicholas Kendall, Esq., bur.   1604.   } Bodmin.
Capt. Kendall of Lostwithiel, (killed in a battle
   between the Royalists and Parliamentarians,
   fought in or near Bodmin, on or about 16 May,
   1643. See 'History of Trigg Minor,' vol. i.
   p. 222),   1643.   } St. Miniver.
Gualter Kendall, Esq., and Joane Carew were mar. 17 July, 1650.

John Kendall of Treworgey, Esq., was trustee named in settlement after marriage, dated 2 April, 1668, of John Anstis of Luna, and Mary, daughter and coheir of George Smith, which John Anstis and Mary were the parents of John Austis, Garter King of Arms, the first of that name. Deed in the Collection of Sir John Maclean.

Kendall.

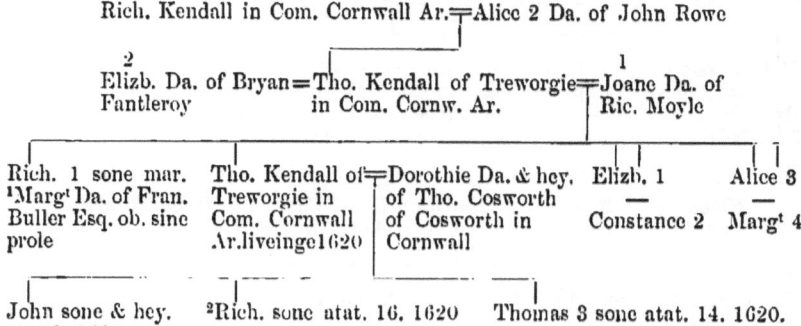

THOMAS KENDALL.

Kestell.

Sciant p'sentes et futuri q^d ego Willm's de Kestell fil. et heres Johis de Kestell, dedi concessi et hac p'senti carta mea confirmavi Joh'i filio meo primogenito et legittimo, &c. Dat' apud Kestell die Johis prox post festu' aploru' Petri et Pawli A^o Regni Regis Edwardi tertij post conquestu' Angliæ 25.

Sciant p'sentes et futuri q^d ego Joh'a Cammes filia Nici Russell et Heres Andrei f'ris mei dedi concessi et hac p'sent' carta mea confirmavi Petro de Kestell et Melior ux' sue una in Villa de Eggosheil. Hijs testibus Laurenc. de Arundell,

---

[1] She afterwards mar. Sir Thos. Honywood of Kent. See Buller Pedigree *ante*.
[2] Bapt. 1603. Morval Par. Reg.

* Ped. fin. Cornw. 40 Edw. III. No. 2. Int. Jno. de Kendale, qu. John Dubber of Bodmyn and Meranld his wife, def. Bridgend juxta Lostwithiell.
Ped. fin. Cornw. 40 Ed. III. No. 7. Int. Rich. de Kendale, qu. Walter Mayou, Junior, and Cecilia his wife, def. In Penquyt and Middelonde.
Ped. fin. Cornw. 18 Rich. II. No. 3. Int. Robert Kendall, qu. Michael Bettowe and Margery his wife, def. In Cayrowe and Porghol.
Ped. fin. Cornw. 6 Hen. VI. No. 1. Int. Stephen Kendall and Cristiana his wife, qu. Rich. Beate, def. In Lostwithiel, etc.
Ped. fin. Cornw. 6 Hen. VI. No. 3. Int. Thos. Kendale and Matilda his wife, qu. Will. Trewenhelek, def. Tregantallan, etc.
Ped. fin. Cornw. 16 Hen. VI. No. 2. Int. Stephen Kendall and Cristiana his wife, qu. John Malerbe and Cristiana his wife, def. Penquyt, Treworgey, etc.
Rich. Kendale, gen. of Treworgy v. Rich. Mareys and o'rs, in a plea of lands. De Banco Roll. 50 Edw. III., Hill., m. 139.
Ped. fin. Cornw. 28 Eliz. Int. Walter and William Kendall, qu. Francis Courtney and Philipa his wife, Nich., Rich., and Maria Courtney, and o'rs, def.

Rico de Crowan, Joh͡e de Kestell, Luck de Trenant, Nicho Trenchard et alijs. Dat' apud Eggloshcil die Lune prox' post festu' S'ci Vincencij Anno Regni regis Edwardi 34.

SEAL WITH ARMS.—*Two greyhounds ramp. combatant, on a chief three escallops.*

Sciant p̃rsentes et futuri q^d Ego Willmo de Kestell dedi concessi et hac p̃rsenti carta confirmavi Johi filio Galfridi de Eglesseil, &c.   hijs testibus Walt' Lap, Rico de Crowan, Johi Beorust et alijs.   Sans Dat.

SEAL WITH ARMS.—*A chevron betw. three birds.*

Sciant presentes et futuri q^d ego Joh'es Kestell filius et heres Willmi Kestell dedi concessi et hac p̃rsenti carta mea indentata confirmavi Joh'i filio meo unu' messuagiu' et totam terram meam cum omnibus suis pertin' in Villa de Trenart &c. hijs testibus Rob'to Post, Phillip Trevegan et alijs.   Dat' apud Kestell die Lune prox' ante festu' S'ci Mich'is Archangli anno regni regis Rici Secundi 15.

Sciant presentes et futuri q^d Ego Ric'us Crowan dedi concessi et hac presenti carta mea confirmavi Joh'i de Kestell in libero maritagio cu' Margeria filia mea totam terram meam in Pennaguinnell cum omnibus libertatibus d'ci terre spectantibus habend. predicti Johi et Margerie et heredibus de corporibus eorundem &c. Hijs testibus Rog' Treglethenek, Johi Billion de Egloshcil, Willo Francis et alijs. Dat' apud Eglosheile die lune prox' post festu' S'ti Lawrencij a° Regni Regis Ed'ri filij Regis Edwardi quint' et a° D'ni 1311.

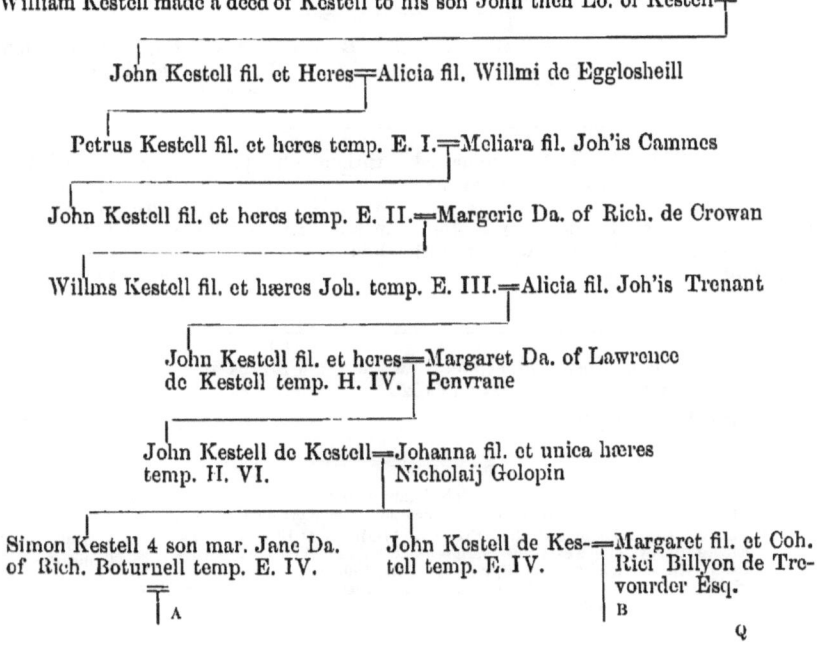

William Kestell made a deed of Kestell to his son John then Lo. of Kestell

John Kestell fil. et Heres=Alicia fil. Willmi de Egglosheill

Petrus Kestell fil. et heres temp. E. I.=Meliara fil. Joh'is Cammes

John Kestell fil. et heres temp. E. II.=Margerie Da. of Rich. de Crowan

Willms Kestell fil. et hæres Joh. temp. E. III.=Alicia fil. Joh'is Trenant

John Kestell fil. et heres=Margaret Da. of Lawrence
de Kestell temp. H. IV. | Penvrane

John Kestell de Kestell=Johanna fil. et unica hæres
temp. H. VI. | Nicholaij Golopin

Simon Kestell 4 son mar. Jane Da.   John Kestell de Kes-=Margaret fil. et Coh.
of Rich. Boturnell temp. E. IV.   tell temp. E. IV. | Rici Billyon de Trevounder Esq.

A   B

114   THE VISITATION OF THE COUNTY OF CORNWALL.

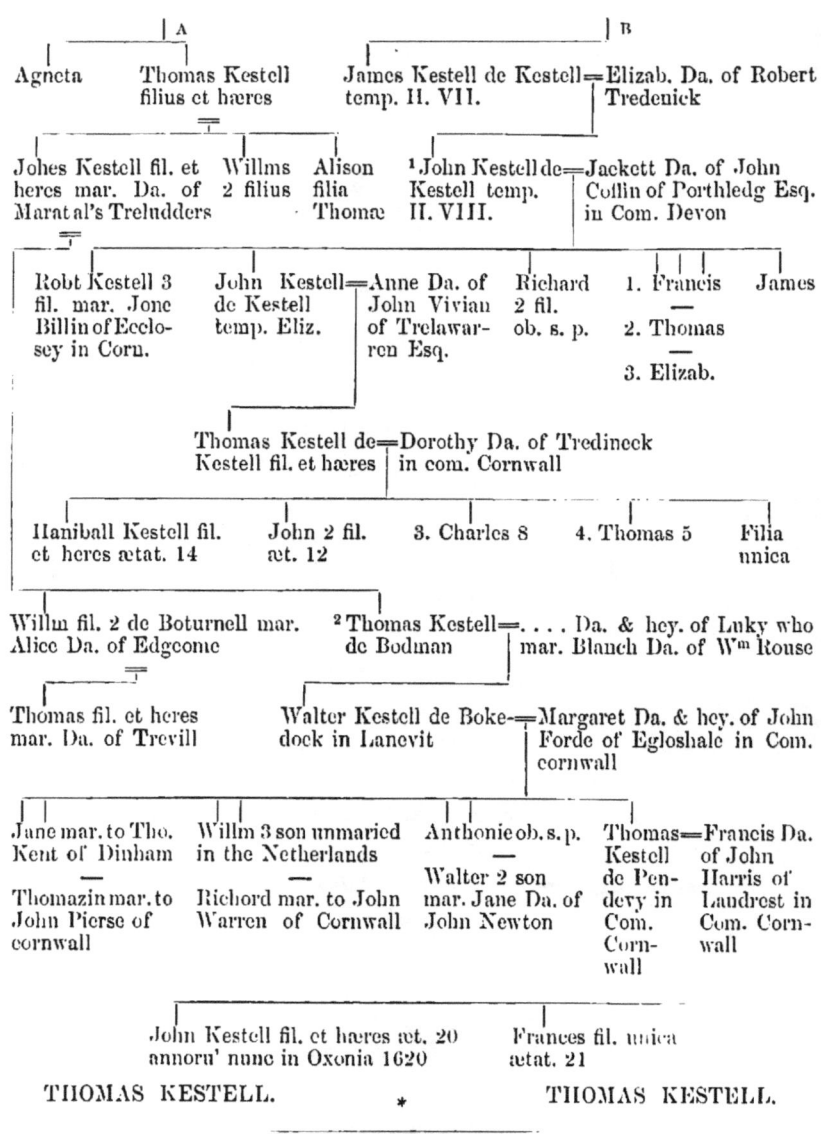

THOMAS KESTELL.   *   THOMAS KESTELL.

---

[1] He had also a da. Jaquet mar. to Rob. Beare of Borlawren. See Bere ped., *ante*.
[2] His da. Anstice mar. Christopher Worthevale. See Worthevale ped., *post*.
* Thomas, son of Thomas Kestell, Esq., bap. 14 March, 1612, at Egloshaile. } Bp. of Exeter's
  Elizab., da. of John Kestell of Trethannicke, bap. 27 Dec., 1612   „   } Transcripts.
  Hugh, son of Nicholas Kestell, bapt. 26 Feb., 1597, at St. Just
  Philippa, da. of Jno. Kestell, gentleman, bap. 1580. Mawgan in Men. Par. Reg.
  William Vyvian and Phillipa Kestell mar. 13 Jan., 1616. St. Austle Par. Reg.

𝕶𝖊𝖘𝖙𝖊𝖑𝖑.

Walter Kestle filius et hæres═Margᵗ da. of Robert Vivyon
│
Edward Kestle of Kestle═Jane Da. of John Tripconny
in Com. Cornwall   of Gulver

| Walter 2 son mar. Elizab. da. Ally in Devon | James Kestell of Kestle in Com. Cornwall liveing 120 [sic] ═ | Avis Da. of John Rashley of Foy in com. Cornw. | Sibbell ux. Tho. ¹Crnsew of Mabe in com. Cornwall |

1. Edward æt. 30
—
2. James æt. 20.
—
3. Willm æt. 18

Avis a da.

Walter filius═Temprance
et hæres æt. da. of An-
30 liveing   thony Che-
1620   nower²

1. Mary ux. Henry Chenoweth
—
2. Elizab. ux. Tho. Somer

3 Phillip ux. Tho. Edwards

4. Alice
—
5. Precilla

James filius et hæres æt. 4   1. Grace³   2. Avis⁴
            *   JAMES KESTELL.

---

¹ "Carnsewe" is written above this, but a pen has been drawn through it by the Herald.
² Chenoweth. See ped., *ante*.
³ Bapt. 29 Oct., 1612, at St. Martin in Meneage. } Bp. of Exeter's Transcripts.
⁴ Bapt. 6 Nov., 1615,   „   „   }

* Avis, da. of Walter Kestell, gent., bap. 1609. Anthony in Meneage Par. Reg.
Janet, wife of John Kestell, bur. at Constantine 14 Aug., 1597.
John Kestell al's Pengwin bur.   „   7 Nov., 1598. } Bp. of Exeter's Tran-
Edw. Coade of Breage and Jane, da. of Wm. Kestell, mar. 30 } scripts.
    Ap., 1599, at St. Pinnock.
Alice, da. of James Kestell, gent., bap. 1577. Fowey Par. Reg.
Will. Kestell & Johanna Roe   mar. 11 Aug., 1613.
Edward Kestell & Johanna Averie mar. 16 Sept., 1599.
Elizab., da. of Edward Kestell, bap. 10 July, 1604.
John, son   „   „   „   28 June, 1607.
Grace, da.   „   „   „   18 Dec., 1608.
Januaria, da.   „   „   „   17 Dec., 1609. } Truro Par. Reg.
Sara, da.   „   „   „   26 Feb., 1611.
Anna, da. Edward Castell   „   19 April, 1612.
Frances, da. Edward Kestell   „   25 Sept., 1614.
Henry, son Edward Castell   „   30 June, 1617.
Peter, son of Edward Kestle &
   Judith his wife   „   8 Feb., 1630.
John Kestell, Esq., bur. 1718. Manaccan Par. Reg.
Hugh Prust, gent., & Ann Kestill, wid., mar. 30 Sep. 1589. Poughill.
Walter Kestell, Esq., & Temperance his wife, mar. 14 Sept. 1610. } Manaccan.
Ann, dau. of Walter Kestell, gent.,   bap. 20 July, 1628.   }
Pentecost, dau. of Trevenard Kestell & Agnes his w., bap. 30 Jan. 1630. Lostwithiel. } (J. M.)
Mrs. Mary Kestell bur. 28 Dec. 1694. Fowey.
Leonard Yeo, gent., of North Petherwin & Margaret Kestell, mar. 18 Feby. 1670.
   Lanreath.

The pedigree of Kestell of Kestell in Egloshayle has recently been registered in the College of Arms down to the present time, and has been printed, with Extensions and Evidences, in Sir John Maclean's 'History of Trigg Minor.' Sir John has pointed out that two descents have been omitted in the old pedigree, between Rich. II. and Edw. IV. See 'Hist. of Trigg Minor,' vol. i. pp. 455-462. The Right Rev. Robert Kestell Kestell-Cornish, Missionary Bishop for Madagascar, is the present representative of this ancient family.

Kete.

Willm Kete of Hugborne in Com. Berkes = Da. of Angers

├─ Edward Kete of Lockage in Com. Berks 3 fil. = Jane Da. of Doc in Com. Berks
└─ John Kete of Chekington in Com. Berks first sonn = Da. of Oglethorp in Com. Berks

From Edward:
- 1. Edward first sonne
- 2. Willm

From John:
- Francis de Medio Templo London
- 2 filij

Raphe Kete of Whaddon prope Saru' in in Com. Wilts 2 fil. = Anne Da. of Clarke of Arrington in Com. Berks

Hugh Kete of Hugborne in Com. Berks
└─ Hugh fil. Hugonis

Raphe Kete of St. Colomb in Com. Cornwall Sephoronia Da. of Colman et relict Petri Beare ux. 2 = Anne Da. of Wm Arscott of Holsworthy in Com. Devon 1 wife who mar. Julyan Da. of Wm Hender of Botriux Castell

Willm 2 sonne de Heldrop in Com. Wilts = Da. of . . . .

- Gilbert p' 2 uxorem æt. 3 annorn'
- Rebecca mar. to Geo. Beare sonne of Peter Beare de Ervin in Com. Cornwall
- 2. Elizab. —
- 3. Anna
- Willm fil. et heres æt. 20
- John Kete 2 fil. ætat. 17 — Raphe 3 fil. ætat. 8
- 2 Children

John 3 son of Enodor in Com. Cornwall mar. the Da. of Coquit of Foy
- Willm 1 sone æt. 15

Gilbert 4 son mar. Jone Da. of Troblefeild of Kirton in Devon & hath issue
- George 2 sone æt. 13
- 3 Children

RALPHE KETE.

---

* Sara, da. of Ralph Kete, was second wife to Rich. Bossawsack. See ped. *ante*.
Edward Ashe, gent., and Anne Kete, mar. 8 June, 1631.
William, son of William Keet. gent., bap. 1625.
Ann, wife of Ralph Keat, gent, bur. 10 Nov. 1614.
John Keat,   „   1654.
John, son of John Keat,   „   6 April, 1658.
Owen Keat,   „   24 Nov. 1659. St. Columb Major. (J. M.)
William Keat, gent.   „   1 May, 1667.
Ralph Keate, gent.,   „   12 Mar. 1670.
Grace Keate, widow,   „   16 July, 1685.
Philip Keate,   „   26 June, 1688.
Jane Keate, widow,   „   28 April, 1699.
Anne, wife of Rob. Keate, gent. bur. 1 Feb. 1676. St. Columb Minor. (J. M.)
[*Note continued on next page.*

THE VISITATION OF THE COUNTY OF CORNWALL.

Knyvett.

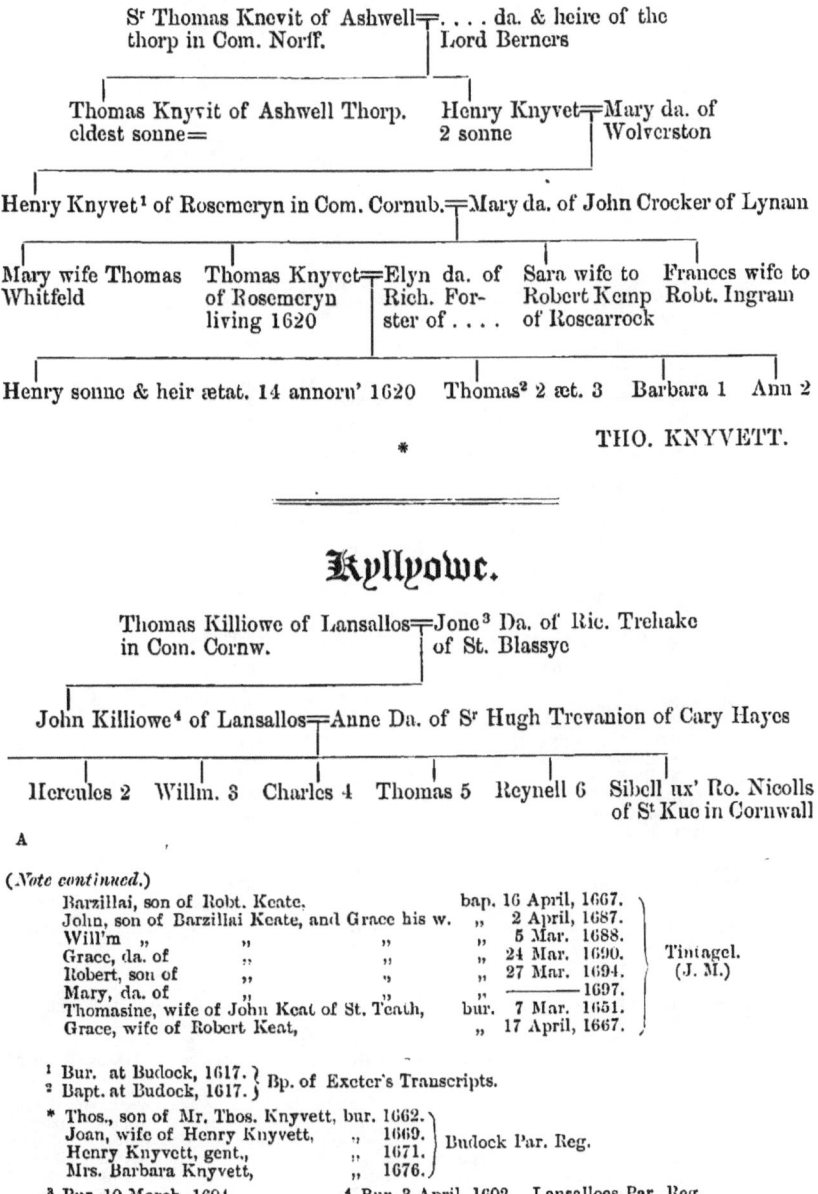

Sr Thomas Knevit of Ashwell=... da. & heire of the
thorp in Com. Norff. | Lord Berners

Thomas Knyvit of Ashwell Thorp. | Henry Knyvet=Mary da. of
eldest sonne= | 2 sonne | Wolverston

Henry Knyvet[1] of Rosemeryn in Com. Cornub.=Mary da. of John Crocker of Lynam

Mary wife Thomas | Thomas Knyvet=Elyn da. of | Sara wife to | Frances wife to
Whitfeld | of Rosemeryn | Rich. For- | Robert Kemp | Robt. Ingram
| living 1620 | ster of.... | of Rosearrock

Henry sonne & heir ætat. 14 annoru' 1620   Thomas[2] 2 æt. 3   Barbara 1   Ann 2

*

THO. KNYVETT.

Kyllyowe.

Thomas Killiowe of Lansallos=Jone[3] Da. of Ric. Trelake
in Com. Cornw. | of St. Blassye

John Killiowe[4] of Lansallos=Anne Da. of Sr Hugh Trevanion of Cary Hayes

Hercules 2   Will'm. 3   Charles 4   Thomas 5   Reynell 6   Sibell ux' Ro. Nicolls
of St Kue in Cornwall

A

(*Note continued.*)
Barzillai, son of Robt. Keate,   bap. 16 April, 1667. ⎫
John, son of Barzillai Keate, and Grace his w.   „   2 April, 1687. |
Will'm   „   „   „   „   5 Mar. 1688. |
Grace, da. of   „   „   „   „ 24 Mar. 1690.   ⎬ Tintagel.
Robert, son of   „   „   „   „ 27 Mar. 1694. | (J. M.)
Mary, da. of   „   „   „   „ ————1697. |
Thomasine, wife of John Keat of St. Teath,   bur. 7 Mar. 1651. |
Grace, wife of Robert Keat,   „ 17 April, 1667. ⎭

[1] Bur. at Budock, 1617. ⎫ Bp. of Exeter's Transcripts.
[2] Bapt. at Budock, 1617. ⎬

* Thos., son of Mr. Thos. Knyvett, bur. 1662. ⎫
   Joan, wife of Henry Knyvett,   „ 1669. |
   Henry Knyvett, gent.,   „ 1671. ⎬ Budock Par. Reg.
   Mrs. Barbara Knyvett,   „ 1676. ⎭

[3] Bur. 10 March, 1604.   [4] Bur. 3 April, 1602. Lansalloes Par. Reg.

118 THE VISITATION OF THE COUNTY OF CORNWALL.

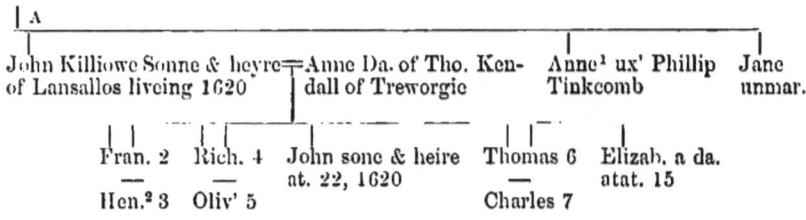

| A
John Killiowe Sonne & heyre ═ Anne Da. of Tho. Ken-   Anne[1] ux' Phillip   Jane
of Lansallos liveing 1620   dall of Treworgic   Tinkcomb   unmar.

Fran. 2   Rich. 4   John sone & heire   Thomas 6   Elizab. a da.
—   —   nat. 22, 1620   —   atat. 15
Hen.[2] 3 Oliv' 5   Charles 7

 * P' me JOHANNE KYLLYOWE.

[1] Mr. Philip Tingcombe and Mrs. Anne Killiow, mar. Nov. 1616. } Lansalloes Par. Reg.
[2] Bap. 13 June, 1602.   }

* Mr. Jno. Tippett and Florence Killowe mar. at St. Wenn 22 June, 1609. Bp. of Exeter's Transcripts.

Mr. Thos. Secom and Mistress Ann Kyllow. mar. 14 April, 1656.   Fowey Par. Reg.
Wm Killiow, gent., and Mrs. Joane Trejeagow, mar. 9 Feb. 1619. ╲
Mr. Oliver Killiow and Mrs. Sibilla Killiow,   „   Jan. 1655.
Richard Killiow and Mary Cock,   „   1685.
Will., son of John Killiow, jun., gent.,   bapt. 8 Jan. 1600.
John, son of Edward Killiow, gent.,   „   1610.
Will., son of Mr. Will. Killiow,   „   1622.
Sibilla. da. of   „   „   1632.
Ann, da. of Henry and Elizb. Killiow,   „ 22 Nov. 1650.
Solomon, son of Hen. and Elizb. Killiow,   „   1655.
Jonathan, „   „   „   1656.
Daniel,   „   Hen. Killiow, gent.,   „   1659.
Charles,   „   Oliver and Sybilla Killiow, „   1665.
Jonathan, „   Jonathan & Barbara Killiow, „   1698.
James,   „   „   „   „   1700.
Henry,   „   „   „   „   1702.   ⎫ Lansalloes Par. Reg.
Will.,   „   Jno. Killiow, gent.,   bur. 9 May, 1602.
John Killiow, senior, Esq.,   „   1632.
Mrs. Joane Killiow,   „   1634.
Frances, son of John Killow, Esq.,   „   1643.
John Killiow of Tresilian, Esq.,   „ 2 July, 1644.
Mrs. Ann Killiow,   „   1649.
Charles Killiow,   „   1651.
John Killiow, Esq.,   „   1660.
Mr. William Killiow,   „   1664.
Mr. Henry Killiowe,   „ 12 Mar. 1665.
Rich. Killiowe, gent.,   „ 28 Feb. 1671.
Edward Killiow, gent.,   „ 18 Sept. 1680.
Thos. Killiow, gent.,   „   1682.
Charles. son of Oliver Killiow, gent.,   „   1687.   ╱

Robt. Killiow of Anthony, and Jone Webb of this parish, mar. 15 Jan. 1673. Sheviock Par. Reg.

Ped. fin. Cornwall, 3 Hen. V. No. 4. William Killyowe de Trevordre, lands in Trevorder, Trevedowe, &c.

Ped. fin. Corn. 11 Elizb. Easter. Jno. Kyllyowe q. Jno. Karkycke (Carkeet), et al. def. Trethake, &c., in St. Cleer.

Ped. fin. Corn. 12 Elizb., Easter. Tho. Kyllyow ar. q. John Karkeke gen. et al. def.

John Killiowe, Cleric. A.B., presented to the Rectory of Lansalloes by Ric. Kilhowe of Roselion, Cornw. ar. 1681. Bp. Reg. Exeter.

Indenture dated 11 August, 44 Elizabeth, betw. Loveday Killiowe of Warleggan, spinster, of the one part, and Peter Sturbridge of Temple of the other part. Recites that Francis Courtency of Ethye, Esq., and Phillippa his wife. one of the daughters and coheirs of Phillip Dennis, by indenture dated 1 June 26 Elizb., had demised unto George Killiowe the younger, John Killiowe, and the said Loveday, certain lands in Temple, which by this indenture the said Loveday releases to the said Peter for the remainder of the said term. Deed in the Collection of Sir John Maclean.

Lampen.

John Lampene[1] of Lampene in Cornwall=Jane Da. of Nicho. Lowre

John Lampene of Padardaye in=Alice Da. & Coh. of Hen. Cloberie
Cornwall liveing 1620 │ of Salt Ashe in Cornw.

Katherin[2] a da. ux' Nicholas Trefuses │ John sone & heire=Wilmot da. of John Lan-
of Landew in Com. Cornwall │ atat. 15, 1620 │ drey of Wilcombe in Com.
│ │ Cornb.

John Lampen[3] of Padreda in=Jane da. of Anthony Rous Esq.
Com. Cornubia, Esq. │ of Wotton in Com. Cornub.

John sonn & h'r apparant
*
JOHN LAMPEN.

Langdon.

John Langdon[4] of Bicton in Com. Cornw.=Elizab. Da. of Sr Willm. Godolphin

Rich. Langdon[5] de Keverell Esq.=Agathe fil. Robti Hill de Helligan Esq.
△

[1] John Lampen, æt. 40, 23 Elizb., son and h. of John Lampen of Linkinghorne, who ob. 20 Feb., 23 Elizb. Inq. p. m. 24 Elizb. 2 part, No. 20.
[2] Mar. Lic. Nich. Trefusis of Lezant and Kath. Lampen of Linkinhorne, gent., 1615.
[3] Notes of Fines, 16 Chas. II., Trinity, Cornw. Anthony Rous and Ric. Killiowe, ar. q. John Lampen ar. and Jane, ux. def. Horwood, Northill and Linkinghorne, and Rectory of Linkinghorne.

* Edward Lampen and Redygan Renolds, mar. 7 Feb., 1614, at Kea. Bp. of Exeter's Transcripts.
John Husband and Hanna Lampen of Kea, mar. 10 June, 1655. Truro Par. Reg.
Richard Pomery and Jone Lampen, mar. 24 Sept. 1576. St. Neot Par. Reg. (J. M.)
Robert, son of Robert Lampen, bap. 15 Oct. 1618. ⎫
Anna, da. of Jno. Lampen, „ 5 April, 1619. ⎪ Truro Par.
Frances, da. of Rob. Lampen, and Thamasine his wife, „ 21 Dec. 1620. ⎬ Reg.
Anna, „ Jno. Lampen, „ 10 Jan. 1627. ⎪
Hannah, da. of Mr. Rob. Lampene and of his wife Thomasine, bap. ⎫
20 Dec. 1630, at Kea. Mr. Robt. Lampen, Churchwarden of Kea, ⎬ Bp. of Exeter's
1614. ⎭ Transcripts.
John, son of Edward Lampen, bap. 3 Dec. and bur. 4 Dec. 1617, at Kea.

Ped. fin. Corn. 14 Chas. Hill. Will. Lampen and John Knighton q. land in p'ish of Budeox.
„ 10 Chas. Mich. Geo. Pope q. Roger Lampen et al. def. lands in Milbrook, &c.
„ 16 Chas. II. Mich. Joseph Lampen, gent., and al. q. Jno. Trwbody et al. in Treworricke.
„ 31 & 32 Chas. II. Hill. Jno. Oliver and o'rs q. John Lampen, Sen., ar., and o'rs def. in Higher Millcombe, &c.

☞ The additions in italic are in the hand of Parker.

[4] John Langdon, æt. 40, son and h. of Rob. Langdon. See Inq. p. m. 4 Ed. VI., part 1, No. 10. Names his grandfather John Langdon of Keverell.
[5] Elizabeth, his sister, married Drake of Tavistock; Mary married Will. Whiddon of Chafford; and Margt. married John Cock. Harl. MS. 1079, fo. 63, where ped. of Langdon is enlarged.

THE VISITATION OF THE COUNTY OF CORNWALL.

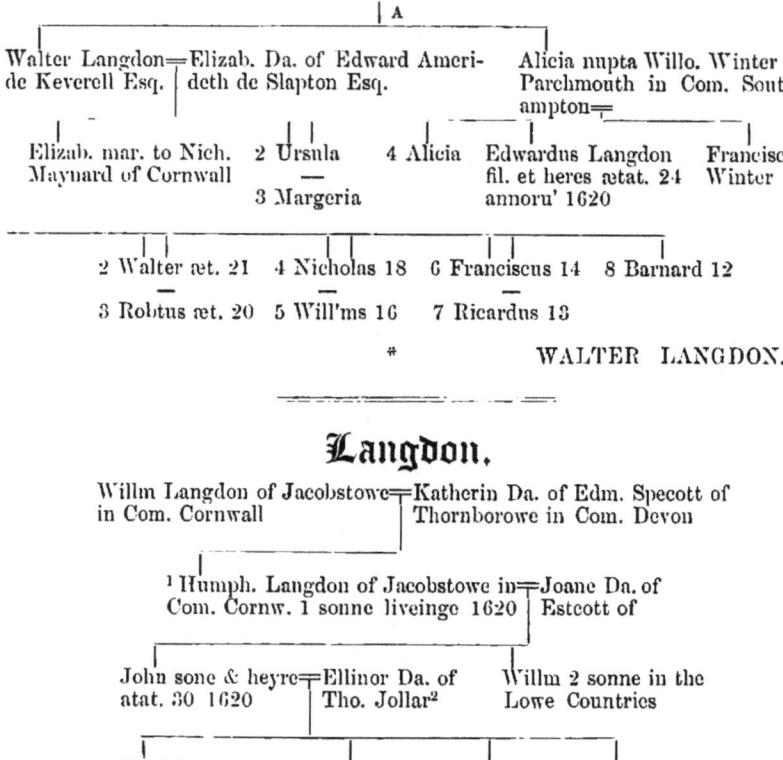

WALTER LANGDON.

Langdon.

Willm Langdon of Jacobstowe =T= Katherin Da. of Edm. Specott of
in Com. Cornwall | Thornborowe in Com. Devon

1 Humph. Langdon of Jacobstowe in =T= Joane Da. of
Com. Cornw. 1 sonne liveinge 1620 | Estcott of

John sone & heyre =T= Ellinor Da. of   Willm 2 sonne in the
atat. 30 1620 | Tho. Jollar[2]   Lowe Countries

Daniell 1 sonne   Digorie 2   Humph. 3   Jane a da.

II.

---

* Walter Langdon of Keverell and Wilmot Mathew of Endellion, wid., mar. Mar. Lic. 5 Nov. 1610.
John Langdon of St. Martin's, Cornw., and Hannah Hicks of St. Budeaux, by certificate of the banns being published in each of the said p'ish churches, mar. 29 Nov., 1715, at Egg Buckland. Bp. of Exeter's Transcripts.
Mary, da. of Will. and Margaret Langdon, bap. 1661. \
Walter Langdon, Jun., Esq.,   bur. 23 Feb. 1676. |
Walter Langdon, Esq.,   „   8 Sept. 1677. | St. Martin's by Looe Par. Reg.
Margaret Langdon,   „   1678. |
Wilmoth Langdon,   „   1688.   /
Tho. Langdon and Margery Lauyne mar. 1654. Truro Par. Reg.

Will. de Bortreus v. Thom. de Langdon, in a plea of Lands. Cor. Rege. Roll 3 John, No. 9.
Thomas and Roger de Langdon, held in Langdon. Assize Roll at Launceston, 8 John.

By Deed dated 1 June, 6 Elizabeth, John Langdon of Keverell demised to John Harrys of Carnworthy, in the parish of Warbstow, Honour, his wife, and William, their son, one tenement in Hendre to hold for their lives and the life of the survivor of them at the rent of 24s. 4d., and making suit at the Court of the Manor of Langdon, &c., "and ferder that the said John, Honour and William shall geve ther voyce at the eleccion of the knyghtes of the Shere for and with the said John Langdon and his heirs, or for and with any other person and persons at the appointment of the said John Langdon and his heirs." Deed in the Collection of Sir John Maclean.

[1] His sister Mary mar. Christopher Rogers of Lanke. See Rogers ped., post.
[2] ? Jollowe. (Kat., wife of Wm. Jollowe, bur. 1618. Jacobstow Par. Reg.)

Ped. fin. Corn. 42 Elizb. Hill. Will. Holman gen. & al. q. Will. Langdon def. ten't in Ventergon.

THE VISITATION OF THE COUNTY OF CORNWALL. 121

Langford.

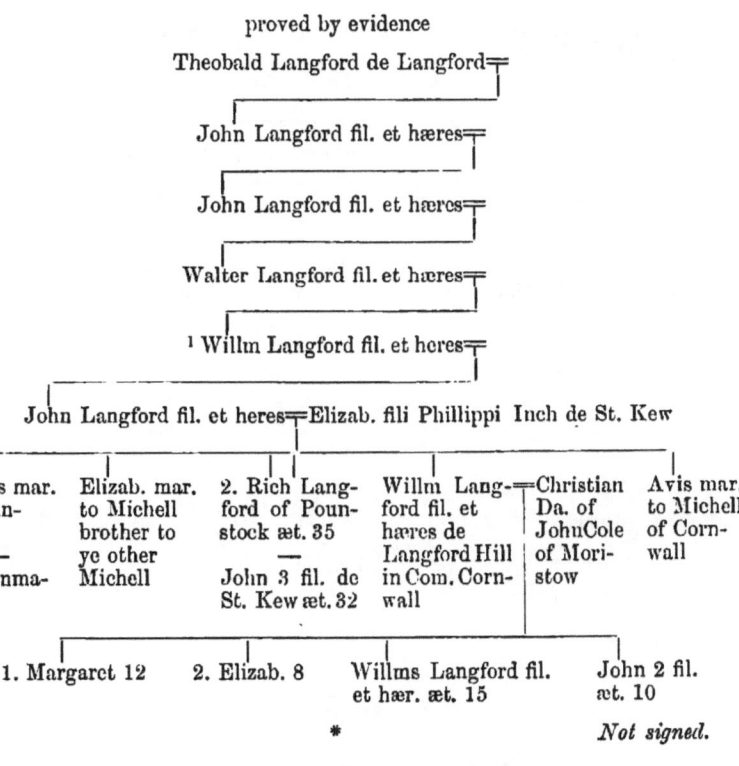

Not signed.

[1] Inq. p. mort. 6 Edw. VI. part i. No. 11. Will. Langford died 31 July, 1551. John Langford son & heir aged 10 years, and not more 1 May, 1551. (This Inq. is dated at Bodmin 12 Jan. 5 Ed. VI.)

* Lovegod, son of John Langford, gentleman, bap. 1580. Mawgan in Men. Par. Reg.
Walter Langford, gent., & Elizab. Langford, mar. 3 Aug., 1694. Marham Ch. Par. Reg.
William Langford and Christian Cooles   „   20 Dec., 1605.
Elizabeth, da. of John Langford, gent.,   bap. 20 March, 1586.
Elizabeth,   „   Mr. John Langford,   „   28 July, 1593.
Francis,   „   John Langford, gent.,   „   30 Mar., 1596.
Elizabeth,   „   William Langford,   „   17 Nov., 1606.
Elizabeth,   „   Mr. William Langford,   „   7 Aug., 1611.
John, son of   „   „   „   19 May, 1614.
Elizabeth, da. of John Langford, gent.   bur. 7 Jan., 1591.
William Langford, gent.,   „   7 March, 1633.
William Langford, Clerk,   bur. 1 May, 1642.
John Langford, gent.,   „   5 Mar., 1662. }-Week St. Mary Par. Register.
Elizabeth Langford, widow   „   12 Nov., 1665.
Roger Bloy, gent., and Dorothy Langford, mar. 1693. Constantine Par. Reg.
Henry Langford one of ye five clerks King's Bench, ob. 5 June, 1698, æt. 82, } M. I.
Loveday, wife of Hen. Langford and da. of Tho. Herle of Prideaux, Esq., } Morwinstow
ob. 14 Jan. 1691. } Church.

Gravestone in the Church of Marham Church:—Here lieth the Body of William Langford of Langford Hill, gent., who died the last male of his family, and was buried the 5 day of April, Anno Dom' 1686. (J. M.) Also of Elizabeth his wife, daughter of Hugh Prowse of Chagford, Esq., who was buried the 1st day of May, 1653. Arms, Langford impaling Prowse (EDS.)

Langeford.

ARMS.—*Paly of six Arg. and Gu., on a chief B. a lion passant guardant Or, a mullet for diff.*

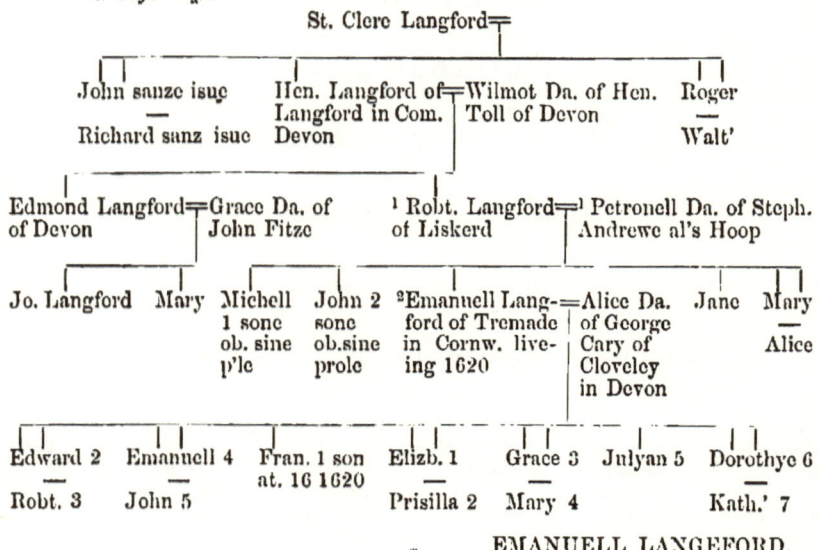

EMANUELL LANGEFORD.

Langharne.

Stephan Langhern of Tregovethan=┬

    ³ John Langhern=┬   Thomas Langhern=┬=Jane da. of Hum-
    1 sonne   2 sonne   phrey Danyell
    A   B

---

¹ At the East end of the South aisle of the Church of St. Cleer is a large tomb commemorating Robert Langeford, Esq., who died 23 Feby., 1614, aged 80 years, and also Petronilla his wife, Emanuel Langeford, his son, and Alice his wife, and four sons and five daughters of the latter, all of whose effigies appear on the tomb. The date of Robert Langford's death only is filled in, those of the others being left blank. Between the figures are the arms, Paly of six, on a chief a lion passant guardant. (J. M.) There is also a quaint inscription in St. Cleer Ch. relating to this Rob. Langford, given *in extenso* in the Parochial Hist. of Cornw. 1870, vol. i. p. 204. (EDS.)

"George Jagow, gent., and Grace, daughter of Robert Langford, were wedded at St. Cleare Jan. 8, 1599-1600. (Gerrans Parish Register.) (J. M.)

² Chan. Pro, Elizb. L. l. 6, No. 43 (A.D. 1595). Langford v. St. Aubyn and ors. Emanuel of Tremabe, and Robert his father are mentioned.

* Ped. fin. Cornw. 16 James, East. Will. Joll q. Emanl. Langford ar. def. 25 acres in Austle al's Hawsewell Park, Alternon, £41.

Ric. Langford, son-in-law of Francis Drake, bur. 2 June, 1608, at Tavistock. (Bp. of Exeter's Transcripts.)

³ Inq. p. m. 8 Eliz. No. 176. John Langhern ob, 17 March, 1566. John, son and heir, æt. 6 et amp.

THE VISITATION OF THE COUNTY OF CORNWALL.

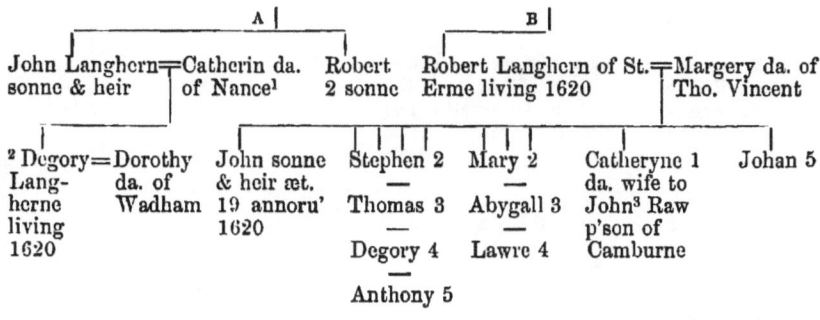

ROBART LANGHARNE.

Lanyon.

Rich. Lanian[4] of Lanyan Esq.=Marg[t 5] Da. & hey. of Tho. Treskillard

John Lanyon of Lanion in=Phill. Da. & Cohey.	[6] Edward Lann=Margery da. of
Com. Cornwall sone & heyre	of W[m] Myliton	yan 2 sonne	.... Chappell
Esq.			

Fran. Lanion of=Alice Da. of Jo.	[7] Willm	William Lanyan[8]=Eliza. da. of
Lanion sone &	Trewren of Sancret	2 sonne	of Wynyard	Rich. Lee al's
heire Esq.	in Cornwall		living 1620	Kimpthorne
A				B

[1] Da. of John Trengove, al. Nance, and her husband is called John Lawharne in Treugove ped., *post*.
[2] Rich., son of Digory Langherne, Esq., bap. 15 Oct., 1611, at St. Stephen's by Saltash. (Bp. of Exeter's Transcripts.) (J. M.)
[3] John Rowe, admitted Rector of Camborne 7 May, 1617, at the death of Doctor Flemmynge. Presented by Francis Bassett, Esq., true patron. Bp. Cotton's Reg., p. 108.

* Ind're made 20 Aug., 1630, between Katherine Langherne, of Roseverth, Co. Cornw., widow, and Katherine Langherne, her daughter, of the one part, and Edward Grosse, of Truro, gent., of the other part, witnesseth that in consideration that the said Edward Grosse shall surrender one lease dated 21 Dec. 30 Eliz., whereby John Langherne, Esq., dec'd, late husband of the said Katherine Laugherne, widow, demised to Gregory Foggins for a term of 99 years the premises hereafter mentioned, the same having been assigned to the said Edward Grosse for the remainder of the said term, etc. etc., hath granted to the said Edward Grosse all those three closes of land, etc., in the parish of Kenwyn, to hold to the said Edward Grosse for the full term of 99 years, if the said Edward Grosse, and Edward Grosse, and Susan Grosse, children of William Grosse, gent., brother of the said Edward Grosse, so long shall live. (Deed in the Collection of Sir John Maclean.) (J.M.)

[4] Mar. 11 June, 1581, bur. 18 Sept., 1592. } Gwinear Par. Reg.
[5] Bur. 28 Oct., 1579. }
[6] Edward, son of Mr. Edward Lanyon, bap. 5 Nov., 1592. (Gwinear Par. Reg.) Phillipa, da. of Edw. Lanyon, mar. Wm. Noye of Burian. (See Noye ped., *post*.)
[7] Will. Lanian of St. Breake mar. Susan, da. of Robert Burdon. 'Visit. Devon, 1620,' p. 39. Avis, da. of Mr. Will. Lanion, bur. at Morval 24 Sept., 1614. Bp. of Exeter's Transcripts. Margaret, da. of Will. Lanion of Breage, mar. John Code of Breage. See Coode ped., *ante*.
[8] Bap. 18 Nov., 1590. Gwinear Par. Reg.
Ezechiel Trenwith, gent., and Elizab. Lanyon, mar. 1614. St. Ive's Par. Reg.
John Williams, jun., and Katherine Lanion, mar. 16 May, 1668. Camborne Par. Reg.

124   THE VISITATION OF THE COUNTY OF CORNWALL.

A

- John 2 sonne
- Anne ux' Jo. Toinken of Penzance
- Rich. Lanion sonne & heyre of Lanion in Com. Cornwall Esq. liveinge 1620 = Jane Da. of Rich Mooringe al's De la More in Com. Devon
  - John sone & heire atat. 10
  - Francis 2 sone atat. 3

B

- [1] Tobyas sonne & heire ætat. 2 Annorn' 1620
- [2] Constance 1 — Margery 2 — [3] Johanna 3
  - Pasca 1 Da.
  - Phillip 2 Da.
  - Jane 3 Da.

*

RICHARD LANYON.

Launce.

the coate & Creast in the old visitacon.

John Launce of Penncare in Cornwall = Mary Da. of Polewheele of Polewheele

- [4] Tho. 1 sone ob. sine prole — John 2 sone ob. sine prole
- Rob. Launce of Penncare in Com. Cornwall liveing 1620 = Suzan Da. of Geo. Tubb of Tringoff in Cornwall
- Hen. sonne liveing in Lancashcire
- 4 = Ann da. & heire of .... Abraham of Abraham Hall in Com. Lanc.

- John sone & hey. atat 23 1620 = Isabell Da. of Sr Edw. Darsie of Dartford in Kent
- John 2
- Abraham 2

A   †

[1] Bap. 9 Mar., 1618-9.
[2] Bap. 3 Oct., 1613. } Gwinear Par. Reg.
[3] Bap. 27 July, 1617.

* Rich. Nance and Margaret Lanyne mar. 22 Oct., 1604. Truro Par. Reg.
Baldwin, son of Will. Lanyon,   bap. 1 Ap., 1561.
Blanche, da. of John Lanyon,   „   1582.
William, son of William Lanyon, gent.,   „ 18 Mar. 1620-21. } Gwinear Par. Reg.
Bawden,   „   „   bur. 24 Jun., 1563.
Tamson, wife of   „   „ 26 Jun.   „
John Lanyon   „ 22 July, „
Mr. Tobias Lanion and Jane Tresilian mar. 1670.
Mr. Will. Lanion of Sancret and Mrs. Keigwin of Mousehole mar. 6 } Buryan Par. Reg.
  March, 1672.
John Lanyon, gent., and Jane his wife mar. 13 June, 1625, at Madron. } Bp. of Exeter's
Susanna, da. of Francis Lanyon, gent., bap. 14 March, 1619,   „   } Transcripts(J.M.)
Francis Lanyne was mar. to Ales his wyffe 24 May, 1584. } Sancreed Par. Reg. (J. M.)
John, son of Francis Lanyne, bap. 10 Dec., 1587.
Ped. fin. Cornw. 28 Hen. III. Pasc. No. 2. Int. John de Linyine qu. Hugh de Bello Campo
def. Botnole Bichan and Over Bichan.

[4] Mar. Grace, daughter of Leonard Loveis. See ped. of Loveis, *post*.

† John Danyell and Phillippa Launce, mar. 11 May, 1609. Truro Par. Reg.

☞ The additions in italic are in the hand of Parker.

THE VISITATION OF THE COUNTY OF CORNWALL. 125

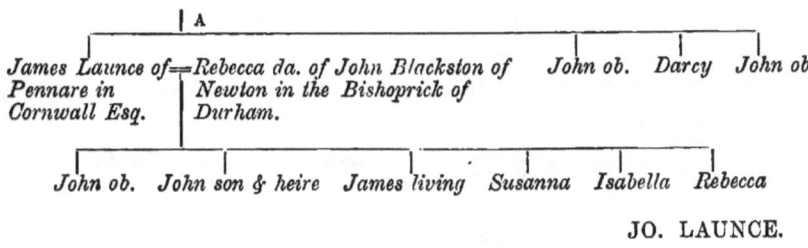

| A

James Launce of = Rebecca da. of John Blackston of   John ob.   Darcy   John ob.
Pennare in   Newton in the Bishoprick of
Cornwall Esq.   Durham.

John ob.   John son & heire   James living   Susanna   Isabella   Rebecca

JO. LAUNCE.

Leache.

ARMS.—*Ermine on a chief indented Gu. 3 ducal coronets Or.*
CREST.—*Issuing out of a ducal coronet Or a dexter fore-arm, grasping a serpent, all proper.*

John Leach of Exiter & = Elizb. Da. of Allex. Nappar &
Chauncell[1] of the Church   sist' to Baronet Napper

² Nicho. Leach of Stoke Clims- = Jenophah Da. of Edw.
land in Cornw. liveinge 1620   Hearle of Trenouthe

Martha a da. at. 2   ³ John sone & hey. at. 3 1620

*   NICHOLAS LEACHE.

Leigh.

This pedigree has the words "Not to be entered, but to be disclaimed" at the head of it. A pen has, however, been drawn through the sentence, and a note—"This must be entered"—added.

[1] Chancellor of St. Peter's, Exeter. Margaret, his da., mar. Robert Buryngton of Sandford. 'Visit. Devon, 1620,' p. 41.
[2] Nicholas Leach, gent., and Jenno (*sic*) were mar. 1616. } Luxyllian Par. Reg.
[3] John, son of Nicholas Leach, gent., bap. 1617.   }

* Sim. Leche of St. Columb, gent., and Dorothy Vivian, da. of Matthew Vivian of Advent, gent., deceased, mar. 23 Nov., 1700. St. Ervan Par. Reg.
Ped. fin. 9 Chas. Devon and Cornw. Simon Leach, mil. and o'rs qu. Emanuel Davy, ar. def. Crediton, Dev., and tent. in Advent Cornw.

John Leach of Crediton =

Simon Leach of Crediton, s. and h., Blacksmith. = Elizab. da. of John Roe of Crediton.

Elizab. Borowe. = Symon de Cadley, knighted at Forde 26 Sept. 1625. = Katherine Tuberville.
                  Harl. MS. 6062, fo. 34 b.   Coll. of Arms.

THE VISITATION OF THE COUNTY OF CORNWALL.

John Leighe of Leigh in Cornw.=Da. & hey. of Isseck of Cornwall

Willm Leigh of Leigh=Jane Da. of Code[1] of Morle in Cornw.

Hen. Leigh of Leigh=Sibell Da. of Hearle of Trenouth in Cornw.

Nicho. Leigh of Leigh in Cornw. liveing 1620 =Barbara Da. & Coh. of Fardinando Lower of

Barbara 1 Da. at. 4 *

Anne 2 Da. at. 3

NICHOLAS LEIGH.

Levelis.

Tho. Levelis of Castle Horneck in Com. Cornw.=Elizab. Da. & hey. of Edw. Bosvennon

Willm Levelis=Joan Da. & hey. of Renold Trerise of Sancred

James Levelis=Joan fil. et Coh. Johis Archar of Lizard   Jane

Jane Da. of Tho. Bond 2 wife=Tho. Levelis=Joan Da. of Trewooffe first wife

Elizab. — Jane | Robt. 2 sonne | John Levelis sonne & heire=Katherin Da. et coh. Nancoras | Jane | Jacobus 2 fil. | Amy — Marg't

Hugh 2 fil. ob. s. p.   John Levelis fil. et heres=Jane Da. of Robt. Poile

Willm — Hugh | John | [2] Arthur Levelis fil. et heres =Anne Da. of Tho. Herle Esq. | Jane mar. to Roger Hall | Elizab. to Tho. Glason | Alice

---

[1] Walter Coode of Morval. See ped. *ante*.
* Ped. fin. Cornw. 23 Edw. I. No. 1. Int. Rich. de Leghe qu. Jno. de Thurlbere def. lands in Yalwelegh.
Ped. fin. Cornw. 49 Edw. III. No. 2. Int. Will. son of Robert Leygh qu. John Harry and Joan his wife def. Dunheved Burgh.
Ped. fin. Cornw. 50 Edw. III. No. 1. Int. Robert de Tresilian qu. John Leygh def. Landreyth, &c.

[2] Arthur Lavelys of Trewoof and Hugh his son sold Hewgose Wood in Kea to Wm. Beauchamp, junior, of Gwennap. Indenture dated 1 Nov., 1616. (B.M. Add. Chart. 15379.)
Chan. Pro. Elizb. L. 1. 7, No. 44 (A.D. 1602). Arthur Lavelis, Esq., v. Hen. Thoms al's Carnsew and o'rs, names John L. the father, & John L. the grandfather of said Arthur Lavelis of Buryan.

THE VISITATION OF THE COUNTY OF CORNWALL. 127

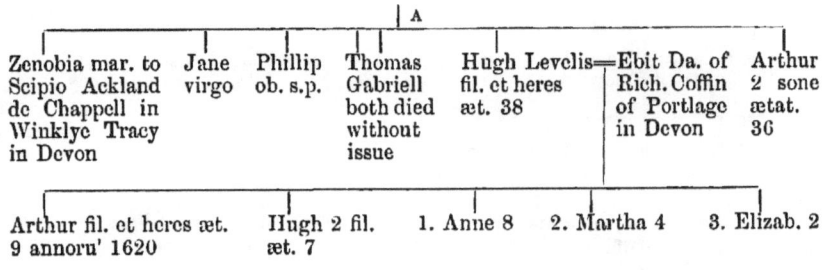

| A

| Zenobia mar. to Scipio Ackland de Chappell in Winklye Tracy in Devon | Jane virgo | Phillip ob. s.p. | Thomas Gabriell both died without issue | Hugh Levelis fil. et heres æt. 38 | =Ebit Da. of Rich. Coffin of Portlage in Devon | Arthur 2 sone ætat. 36 |

Arthur fil. et heres æt. 9 annoru' 1620

Hugh 2 fil. æt. 7

1. Anne 8   2. Martha 4   3. Elizab. 2

*

ARTHUR LEVELIS,
for Mr. ARTHUR the elder his father.

Ley.

Crest given in Trick, *a Lion Sejant*.

Robert Ley of Kempthorn in Com. Devon⚌

John Ley of Kempthorn⚌

John Ley al'as Kempthorne=Thamazin[1] Da. & hey. of
of Tonacombe   Jordon of Tohacambe

John[2] Ley=Kath' Da. of Sr Peirse   Three   Rich. Ley al's Kempthorne
1 sonne   Courtney ob. sine p'le   Daughters   of Merther⚌

                                                  Two Sonnes Two Daughters
                                                                           A

* Robert Lavelis, gentleman, bur. 1583. }
Margaret, wife of Tho. Levelis, gent., bur. 1638. } Madron Par. Reg.
Hanibal Levelis and Mary Chenalls mar. 28 April, 1634, at Zennor. }
Honour, dau. of Hanibal Levelis and Mary his wife, bap. 23 Jan. } Bp. of Exeter's
1634, at Zennor.   Transcripts.
Ind're dated 19 Sep., 1653, betw. Thomas Levelis, of Penzance, gent., of the one part, William Godolphin, of Trewarveneth, Co. Cornw., Esq., and Arthur Levelis, of Trewoofe in the said Co., Esq., of the other part. Settlement by said Thomas Levelis upon Honour Levelis, spinster, daughter of Hanibal Levelis, gent., dec'd, brother of the said Thomas, upon the marriage of the said Honour and David Grosse, son of Thomas Grosse of Penzance, gent., of certain messuages in Penzance, to hold to the said Honour and the heirs of her body, in default remainder to Thomas Cowling, son of John Cowling of Trengwenton, gent., and Ralph Lanyon, son of Thomas Lanyon, gent., sisters' sons of the said Thomas Levelis, etc. etc. Sealed with the arms of Levelis—*Ar.* 3 *calves' heads couped Gu.*
Prudence, sole heir of Arthur Levelis of Trewoof, married Richard Vosper of Liskeard. Their son, Arthur Vosper, left two daughters and coheirs,—Elizabeth, married Joseph Marke of Woodhill, and Prudence, married George Dennis of Liskeard, gent. (J. M.)
[1] Bur. 7 Jan. 1585.
[2] Ob. 1 Mar. 1592. Mr. John Kempthorne, Justice and the only stay of Morwinstow, bur. 2 Mar. 1592. Inq. p. m. 36 Elizab. part ii. No. 79. John, of Lyffney al's Luncy, nephew and heir, æt. 22.

THE VISITATION OF THE COUNTY OF CORNWALL.

A |

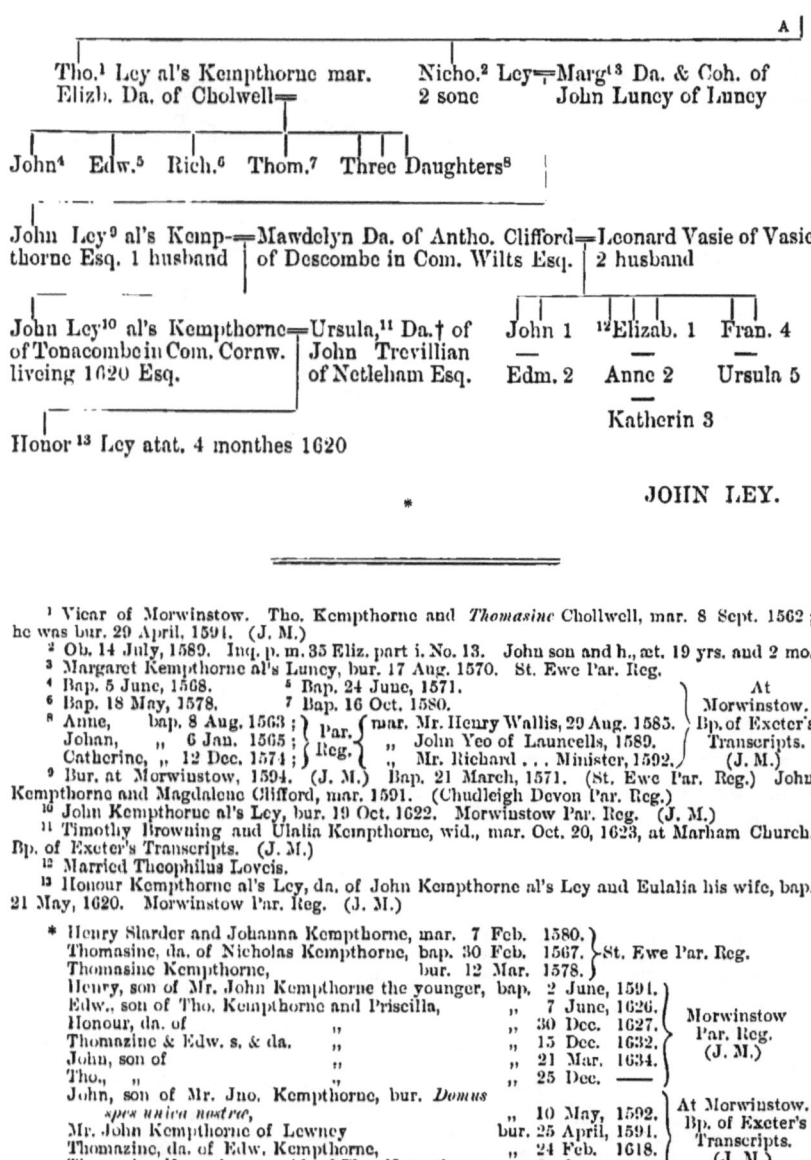

Tho.[1] Ley al's Kempthorne mar. Elizb. Da. of Cholwell==

Nicho.[2] Ley=Marg[t 3] Da. & Coh. of 2 sone   John Luncy of Luncy

John[4]   Edw.[5]   Rich.[6]   Thom.[7]   Three Daughters[8]

John Ley[9] al's Kemp-==Mawdelyn Da. of Antho. Clifford==Leonard Vasie of Vasie
thorne Esq. 1 husband | of Descombe in Com. Wilts Esq. | 2 husband

John Ley[10] al's Kempthorne==Ursula,[11] Da.† of   John 1   [12]Elizab. 1   Fran. 4
of Tonacombe in Com. Cornw.   John Trevillian   —   —   —
liveing 1620 Esq.   of Netleham Esq. Edm. 2   Anne 2   Ursula 5
                                                          Katherin 3

Honor[13] Ley atat. 4 monthes 1620

*   JOHN LEY.

---

[1] Vicar of Morwinstow. Tho. Kempthorne and *Thomasine* Chollwell, mar. 8 Sept. 1562;
he was bur. 29 April, 1594. (J. M.)
[2] Ob. 14 July, 1589. Inq. p. m. 35 Eliz. part i. No. 13. John son and h., æt. 19 yrs. and 2 mo.
[3] Margaret Kempthorne al's Luncy, bur. 17 Aug. 1570. St. Ewe Par. Reg.
[4] Bap. 5 June, 1568.   [5] Bap. 24 June, 1571.   } At
[6] Bap. 18 May, 1578.   [7] Bap. 16 Oct. 1580.   } Morwinstow.
[8] Anne,   bap. 8 Aug. 1563;) Par. (mar. Mr. Henry Wallis, 29 Aug. 1585.   } Bp. of Exeter's
   Johan,   „   6 Jan. 1565; }   „ John Yeo of Launcells, 1589.   } Transcripts.
   Catherine, „ 12 Dec. 1574;) Reg. („ Mr. Richard ... Minister, 1592.   } (J. M.)
[9] Bur. at Morwinstow, 1594. (J. M.) Bap. 21 March, 1571. (St. Ewe Par. Reg.) John
Kempthorne and Magdalene Clifford, mar. 1591. (Chudleigh Devon Par. Reg.)
[10] John Kempthorne al's Ley, bur. 19 Oct. 1622. Morwinstow Par. Reg. (J. M.)
[11] Timothy Browning and Ulalia Kempthorne, wid., mar. Oct. 20, 1623, at Marham Church.
Bp. of Exeter's Transcripts. (J. M.)
[12] Married Theophilus Loveis.
[13] Honour Kempthorne al's Ley, da. of John Kempthorne al's Ley and Eulalia his wife, bap.
21 May, 1620. Morwinstow Par. Reg. (J. M.)

* Henry Starder and Johanna Kempthorne, mar. 7 Feb. 1580. }
  Thomasine, da. of Nicholas Kempthorne, bap. 30 Feb. 1567. } St. Ewe Par. Reg.
  Thomasine Kempthorne,   bur. 12 Mar. 1578. }
  Henry, son of Mr. John Kempthorne the younger, bap. 2 June, 1591. }
  Edw., son of Tho. Kempthorne and Priscilla,   „   7 June, 1626. } Morwinstow
  Honour, da. of   „   „ 30 Dec. 1627. } Par. Reg.
  Thomazine & Edw. s. & da.   „   „ 15 Dec. 1632. } (J. M.)
  John, son of   „   „ 21 Mar. 1634. }
  Tho., „   „   „ 25 Dec. — }
  John, son of Mr. Jno. Kempthorne, bur. *Domus*
  apos unica nostræ,   „ 10 May, 1592. } At Morwinstow.
  Mr. John Kempthorne of Lewney,   bur. 25 April, 1594. } Bp. of Exeter's
  Thomazine, da. of Edw. Kempthorne,   „ 24 Feb. 1618. } Transcripts.
  Thomazine Kempthorne, wid. of Tho. Kempthorne „ 21 June, 1619. } (J. M.)
      For more of Kempthorne, see 'Hist. of Trigg,' vol. i., p. 314.

† She is called Eulalia in the Pedigree at the end of Part III. of the Trevelyan Papers
(printed by the Camden Soc. 1872), also at the baptism of her dau. Honour, in the Morwinstow
Par. Reg. 1620, and Ulalia Kempthorne, widow, on her second marriage at Marham Church; yet
it would appear that her husband testified that her name was Ursula!

Ley al's Kempthorne.

John Ley al's Kempthorne of ═ Thomazin Da. of Rob. Jordon of
Kempthorne in Com. Devon │ Tonycomb in Com. Cornw.

- John 1 sone
- Nicho 2 sone
- Thomas 3 sonne
- Rich Ley al's Kempthorne of Merther in Cornwall ═ Constance Da. of Tho. Kendall of Treworga in Cornwall

Rich. Ley al's Kempthorne of Merther living 1620 ═ Anne 2 Da. of Joseph Bastard of Westmarker in Dwlo in Cornwall

- Tho. 1 sonne atat. 9 1620
- John 2 sone
- Willm 3 sone

RICHARD LEY AL'S KEMPTHORNE.

*

* John, son of Ric. Kemptborne by Sarah, ux., bap. 4 Sep. 1694. ⎫
John, ,, ,, ,, ,, 1696. ⎪
Tho., ,, ,, ,, ,, 1698. ⎬ Cury Par. Reg.
Richard, ,, ,, ,, ,, 1700. ⎪
Samuel, ,, ,, ,, ,, 1701. ⎪
Thomas, ,, ,, ,, ,, 1702. ⎭
John, son of Edw. Kempthorne, bap. 28 Nov. 1622. ⎫
Sarah, da. of ,, ,, 28 Jan. 1626. ⎪
Elizb., ,, ,, ,, 1629. ⎪
Grace, ,, ,, ,, 1631. ⎪
Elizb., ,, ,, ,, 1633. ⎪
Samuel, son of Samuel Kempthorne and Jane, ,, 1630. ⎪
James, ,, ,, ,, 5 Nov. 1633. ⎪
Ursula, da. of ,, and Florence, ux. ,, 1636. ⎪
Thos., son of ,, ,, ,, 3 Feb. 1638. ⎪
John, ,, Will. Kempthorne and Constance, ux. ,, 16 Aug. 1640. ⎪
John, ,, Samuel Kempthorne and Florence, ,, 1642. ⎪
Renatus, ,, Renatus Kempthorne and Elizb. ,, 23 May, 1643. ⎪
Elizb., da. of Edw. Kempthorne and Mary, ux. ,, 1640. ⎪
Rob., son of Edw. Kempthorne and Jane, ,, 1652. ⎬
Rich., ,, ,, ,, ,, 1657. ⎪ Mullion
Edw., ,, James Kempthorne and Elizb. ,, 1670. ⎪ Par. Regs.
Grace, da. of Renatus Kempthorne and Loveday, ux. ,, 24 Sep. 1672. ⎪
Renatus, son of ,, ,, ,, 7 June, 1674. ⎪
Chas., ,, Will. and Jane Kempthorne, ,, 1673. ⎪
Edw., ,, Renatus Kempthorne and Loveday, ,, 19 Mar. 1675. ⎪
Ambrose, ,, William Kempthorne, ,, 1677. ⎪
Edw., ,, Ric. and Sarah Kempthorne, ,, 1692. ⎪
Will. Kempthorne and Constance Parnell, mar. 1639. ⎪
Renatus Kempthorne and Elizb. Hickinge, ,, 7 June, 1641. ⎪
Edw. Kempthorne and Jane Stewert (?) ,, 1649. ⎪
James Kempthorne and Blanch, ,, 1650. ⎪
John Kempthorne and Anne Robinson, ,, 1666. ⎪
John Kempthorne and Anne Tonken, ,, 1670. ⎪
Ric. Kempthorne and Sarah Kempthorne, ,, 1691. ⎪
Renatus Kempthorne and Jane Tonken, ,, 1699. ⎪
Edw., son of Edw. Kempthorne, bur. 1631. ⎭

[*Note continued on next page.*

Loveys.

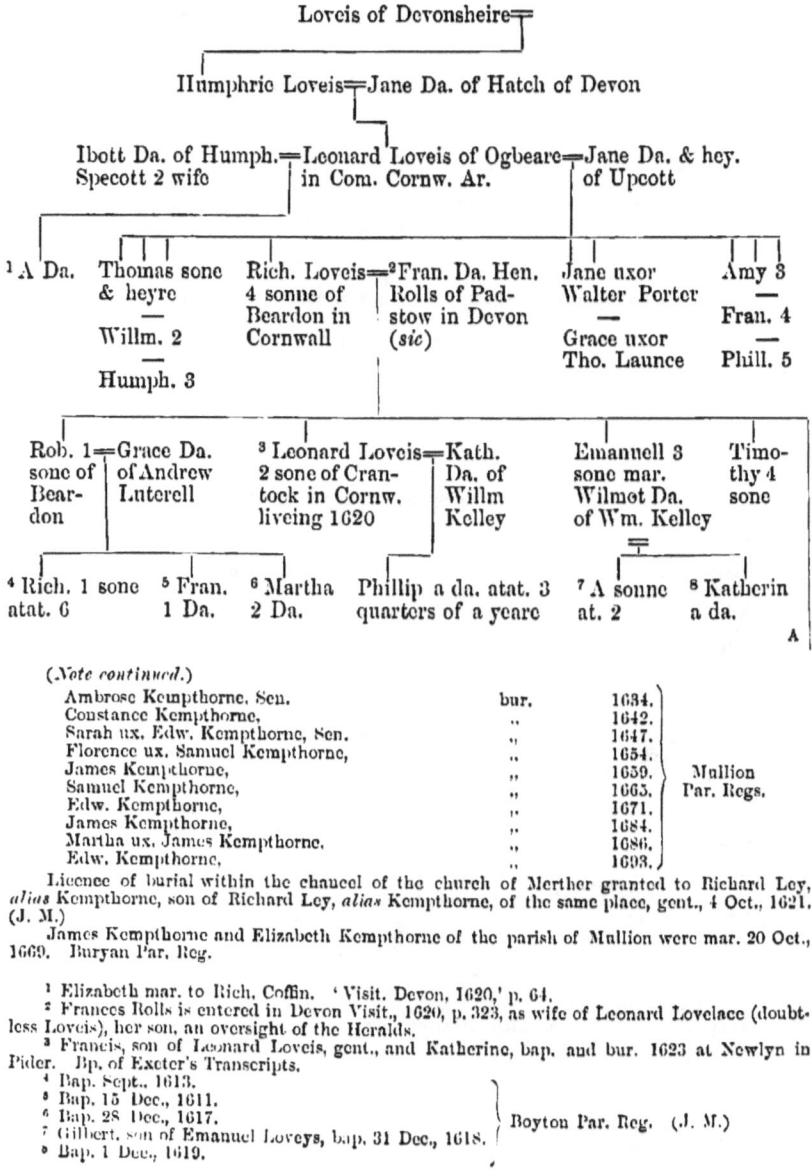

(*Note continued.*)

Ambrose Kempthorne, Sen.	bur.	1634.
Constance Kempthorne,	,,	1642.
Sarah ux. Edw. Kempthorne, Sen.	,,	1647.
Florence ux. Samuel Kempthorne,	,,	1654.
James Kempthorne,	,,	1659.
Samuel Kempthorne,	,,	1665.
Edw. Kempthorne,	,,	1671.
James Kempthorne,	,,	1684.
Martha ux. James Kempthorne,	,,	1686.
Edw. Kempthorne,	,,	1693.

Mullion Par. Regs.

Licence of burial within the chancel of the church of Merther granted to Richard Ley, *alias* Kempthorne, son of Richard Ley, *alias* Kempthorne, of the same place, gent., 4 Oct., 1621. (J. M.)

James Kempthorne and Elizabeth Kempthorne of the parish of Mullion were mar. 20 Oct., 1669. Buryan Par. Reg.

[1] Elizabeth mar. to Rich. Coffin. 'Visit. Devon, 1620,' p. 64.
[2] Frances Rolls is entered in Devon Visit., 1620, p. 323, as wife of Leonard Lovelace (doubtless Loveis), her son, an oversight of the Heralds.
[3] Francis, son of Leonard Loveis, gent., and Katherine, bap. and bur. 1623 at Newlyn in Pider. Bp. of Exeter's Transcripts.
[4] Bap. Sept., 1613.
[5] Bap. 15 Dec., 1611.
[6] Bap. 28 Dec., 1617.
[7] Gilbert, son of Emanuel Loveys, bap. 31 Dec., 1618.
[8] Bap. 1 Dec., 1619.

Boyton Par. Reg. (J. M.)

THE VISITATION OF THE COUNTY OF CORNWALL.   131

A |

Theophilus=Elizb. Da.		1 Elizb. uxor	2 Amy ux' Wm.	3 ¹Martha uxor	³Mary
5 sone of	of Leonard	Ric. Carwy-	Upcton of	Coland Blewet	uxor Rich.
Beardon	Vesie of	tham of	Newton	of Litlecollom	Goddard of
	Tamarton	Panston in	Ferris in	in Cornwall	.... in
		Devon	Devon		Com. Wilts

³Mary 1 da. atat. 3   Martha a dau.

*   p' me LEONARD LOVEYS.

Loveys.

Humph. Loves=Jane Da. of Hatch of Devon

Leonard Loves of Ogbeare in Com. Cornw. Esq.=Jane Da. & hey. of Upcote

Tho. 1   Willm 2   Humph. 3   Rich. Loves of Bere-=Fran. Da. of Hen. Rolles
                                  don 4 sonne   of Heamton

Rob. Loves of Berdon in Com.=Grace Da. Andrew Luttrell
Cornw. liveing 1620   of Hartland

Fran. a dau.   Rich. sone & hey. at. 9   Martha a dau.
      †   ROBERT LOVEYS.

---

¹ Bapt. 27 Nov., 1589. Boyton Par. Reg. (J. M.)
² Rich. Goddare and Mrs. Mary Loveis mar. 25 March, 1613. North Tamerton. Bp. Trans.
³ Bap. 18 Oct., 1618.
* Theophilus, s. of Theophilus Loveys and Elizab. his wife, bap. ⎫
    9 Nov., 1623.   ⎪
  Elizab., da.   „   „   „ bap. 1 Dec., 1626. ⎬ Boyton Par. Reg.
  Francis, s.   „   „   „ „ 15 Mar., 1628. ⎪
  Rich., s.   „   „   „ „ 17 May, 1636.   ⎭
  Ric., s. of Ric. Loveys, bap. 4 Feb., 1646.
  Leonard Loveys of Lifton and Zenobia Thorne of Sheepwash, mar. lic. 1 Oct., 1615. ⎫ (J. M.)
  Humph. Loveis of Black Torrington and Philippa Morecombe of Sheepwash, mar.   ⎪
     lic. 29 Sept., 1629.   ⎬
  Samuel Loveis, gent., and Elizb. Matthew, dau. of Wm. Matthew, gent., mar. 2   ⎪
     Aug., 1649. St. Kew Par. Reg.   ⎪
  Joseph Hankyn, gent., and Frances Loves, mar. 30 Mar., 1630, at Boyton. Bp.   ⎭
     of Exeter's Trans.

† Ped. fin. Cornw. 15 Rich. II. No. 2. Int. William Lowys and Simon Lowys qu. Simon
Gunmaylek and wife def.
  Ped. fin. Cornw. 9 Hen. IV. No. 7. Int. Simon Lowys and Nicholas Gerlyn qu. Robt. Bray
and Alice his wife and Thos. Porter and Christian his wife def.
  Andrew Loveys mar. Avis da. of John Gaverigan and wid. of Robert Kestle. Kestle Ped., *ante*.
  Theophilus Loves mar. Elizabeth da. of Leonard Vacey. See Vacey ped., *post*.
  For further ped. of Loveys *vel* Lowis, see ' Visit. Devon, 1620,' pp. 171-2.

Lower.

CREST.—*A unicorn's head erased*, tricked in ink over a quartered shield tricked roughly in pencil, but evidently the same as is given detailed under Lower in Harl. MS. 1079, fo. 54.

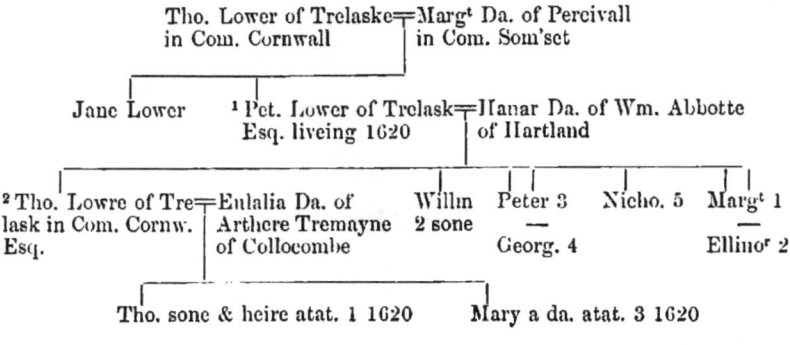

*

Not signed.

---

[1] James I., Ind're betw. Peter Lower of Trelaske, Esq., and Honor his wife. Tho. Lower, Esq., s. and h. appar., and Eulalia his wife, Sir Will. Wrey, Arthur Tremayne of Collocombe, Esq., Edmund Tremayne, s. and h. appar. of said Arthur, etc. (J. M.)

[2] Thos. Lower of Lewannack, gent., and Ulalia Tremayne of Lamerton, mar. lic. 13 Oct., 1613. Ezechiel, son of Thos. and Eulalia Lower, bap. at Lewannack 1614. (Bp. of Exeter's Transcripts.)

* Hercules Lower and Lore Alee (Alcigh Bp. Trans.) mar. 1 Jan., 1597.
Lore, da. of Hercules Lower, bap. 1604.
Thos., son „   „   „ 1607.
Thos., son of Rich. Lower, gent. „ 1630. } Lanreath Par.
William, „   „   „ 1631. } Reg.
Lore, da. of Hercules Lower bur. 1626.
Hercules Lower, gent., „ 4 Mar., 1639.
Thos. Lower, gent., and Jane, da. of Chas. Grills, gent., mar. 14 June, 1652.
Tho. Lower of Trelaske bur. 1687. Lewannick Par. Reg.
John, son of John Lower, gent., and Elizb., bap. 1677. Michaelstow Par. Reg.
John Eustic and Elizb., da. Tho. Lower, gent., mar. 24 Ap., 1688.
Ric., s. of Hercules Lower, bap. 24 June. 1601.
Nycholas, s. of Ric. Lower, gent., and Philadelphia „ 24 Nov., 1633.
Elizb., da. „ „ „ 29 June, 1636.
Frances, da. „ „ „ 4 Nov., 1638.
Thos., s. of Thos. Lower, gent., and Jane „ 6 Dec., 1653. } Lanreath
Elizb., da. „ „ „ 19 May, 1655. } Par. Reg.
Elizb., da. „ „ „ 8 Oct., 1657.
George, s. of Wm. Lower, bur. 15 Jan., 1572.
Lore Lower .. 1 Ap., 1617.
Elizb., da. Ric. Lower, gent., ,. 10 Feb., 1641.
Elizb., da. Tho. Lower, gent.. „ 28 Mar., 1656.
Justinian Cocke *alias* Lower bur. 16 Apr., 1662. St. Breward Par. Reg.
Loare, wife of Justinian Lowre, bur. at St. Just, Roseland, 28 Feb., 1611.
Rich. Haydon and Agnes Lower mar. at Alternon 3 Sept., 1611. } Bishop of Exeter's
James, son of Ric. and Elizb. Lower, bap. at St. Germans 17 } Transcripts.
Feb., 1632.

(J. M.)

Ped. fin. Cornw. 9 Edw. IV. No. 1. Int. Nicholas Loure qu. Margaret, Lady Hungerford and Botreaux, wid., da. and h. of William, late Lo. Botreaux, def. Manor of St. Wynowe.
The ped. of Lower is given more extensively in Harl. MS. 1079, ffo. 53, 54.

THE VISITATION OF THE COUNTY OF CORNWALL. 133

Lower.

To enquire whether Lower did not mary with Elynor, da. & heir of Pentire, which if he did then may he quarter the Coate.

Wm. Lower of St. Wynnow = Agnes Da. of Tho. Trefry of Foye
in Cornwall

- Tho. Lower 1 sonne
- Hen. 2 sone mar. Elizab. widow of Antho. Fox. of highhampton in Devo'
- Edw. Lower[1] of St. Tudy in Com. Corn. liveinge 1620 = Mary[2] Da. of Humph. Nicholls of St. Tudy
- Ferdinando 4 — Walter 5

- [3] Willm 2 — [4] Edward 3
- [5] Nicholas 4 — Phillip 5
- [6] Hump. sone & hey. atat. 21 1620
- [7] Katherin ux' Fran. Courtney of Lanivet
- Agnes 2 — [8] Elizab. 3
- [9] Grace 4 — Janor 5

HENRYE LOWER.   *   EDWARD LOWER.

Lower.

Willm Lower of Winnow = Agnes Da. of Tho.
in Com. Cornw.   Trefrye of Foye

Ferdinando Lower of Lesaunt in Com. = Lore Da. of Wm. Kelley of
Cornwall liveing 1620 5 sonne   Northlew in Com. Devon

- 1. Jane ux' Tho. Grose of Liscard in Cornw.
- 2. Barbara ux' Nicho. Leighe of Quethiock in Cornw.
- Elizab. ux' Nicho. Cock of South Pederwyn Esq.

†   FERDINANDO LOWER.

---

[1] Mar. 22 April, 1594, bur. Aug. 1627. [2] Bur. April, 1626. [3] Bap. 1598.
[4] Bap. 1600. [5] Bap. 1604. [6] Bap. 1597.
[7] Bap. 1595. [8] Bap. 1602. [9] Bap. 1609.

* Francis Courteney and Kat. Lower, gent.,   mar.   1617.
Will. Hocken of St. Advent and Jane Lower of St. Tudy   „   1634.
Rich. Lower and Elizb. Trelawney   „   17 Sep., 1656.   St. Tudy
  (She was da. & h. of John Billing of Hengar, and relict of Sam.   Par. Reg.
  Trelawney. See Biding ped., 'Hist. of Trigg.' vol. i. p. 389.)   (J. M.)
Mr. Edw. Lower and Elizb. Prideaux   „   Apr., 1678.
Anne. da. of Edw. Lower, gent.,   bap.   1601.
Jane, da.   „   „   „   1610.
Rich.. son of Mr. Humphrey Lower,   „   29 Jan., 1631.
Tho.. son of Humphrey Lower of Tremeer, gent.,   „   11 Aug., 1633.
John Lower, Esq.. son of Dr. Ric. Lower.   „   19 Nov., 1679.
Elizb.. widow of Rich. Lower. Dr. of Physic,   „   22 Feb., 1703.
Thos. Lower bap. 27 Jan., 1543. Fowey Par. Reg.
Will., son of Mr. John Lower and Mary, bap. 1608 at Constantine.   } Bp. of Exeter's
Rich. Lower, gent.. and Philadelphia Searell. wid., mar. 1630 at Lanreath. } Transcripts.
Tho. Lower and Mary Packer mar. 1670. St. Winnow Par. Reg.

† Walter, son of Will. Lower, gent.,   bapt. 1611, at Madron.   } Bp. of Exeter's
Will., „   Mr. John Lower and Mary „   1608, at Constantine. } Transcripts.
Mr. Will. Lower, bur. 20 Aug. 1615, at Madron. Bp. Transcripts. (J. M.)

Lynam.

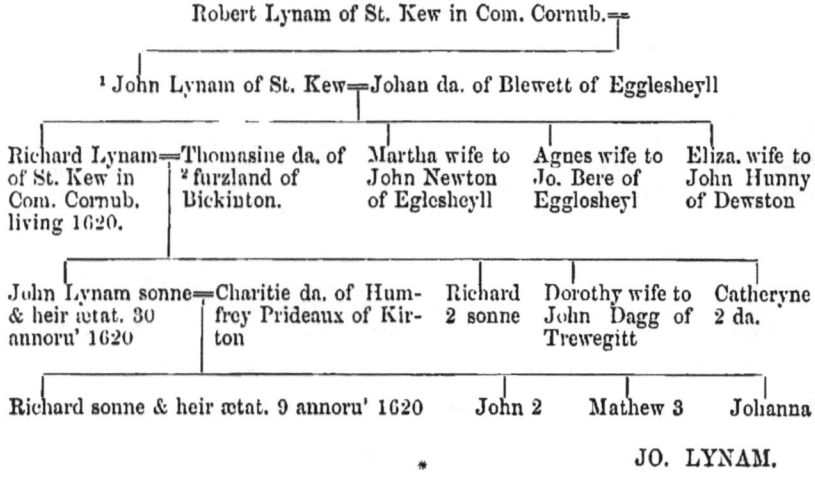

JO. LYNAM.

Manington.

ARMS.—*Arg. on a bend Sa. 3 mullets Arg. pierced of the first.*
CREST.—*A demi-unicorn Sa., crined and ungued Arg., with a crescent Or, on shoulder, for diff.*

Sampson Manington, of Manington in Com. Corn., p. R. C. Clarent., but the creast testified by Mr. Philpott.

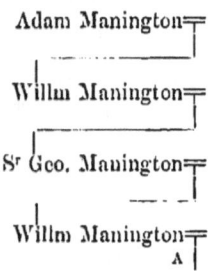

---

[1] He married secondly a da. of Tresungar, and by her had issue; she afterwards married Will. Matthew. Rich. Mathew, gent., of Tresungar, in his will dated 2 June, 8 Jas., P. P. C., names Sara and Ursula Lynam, and his cousin George Lynam.
[2] John Fursland. 'Visit. Devon, 1620,' p. 122.
* This pedigree will be found fully extended in the 'History of Trigg Minor,' vol. ii., pp. 258, 263.

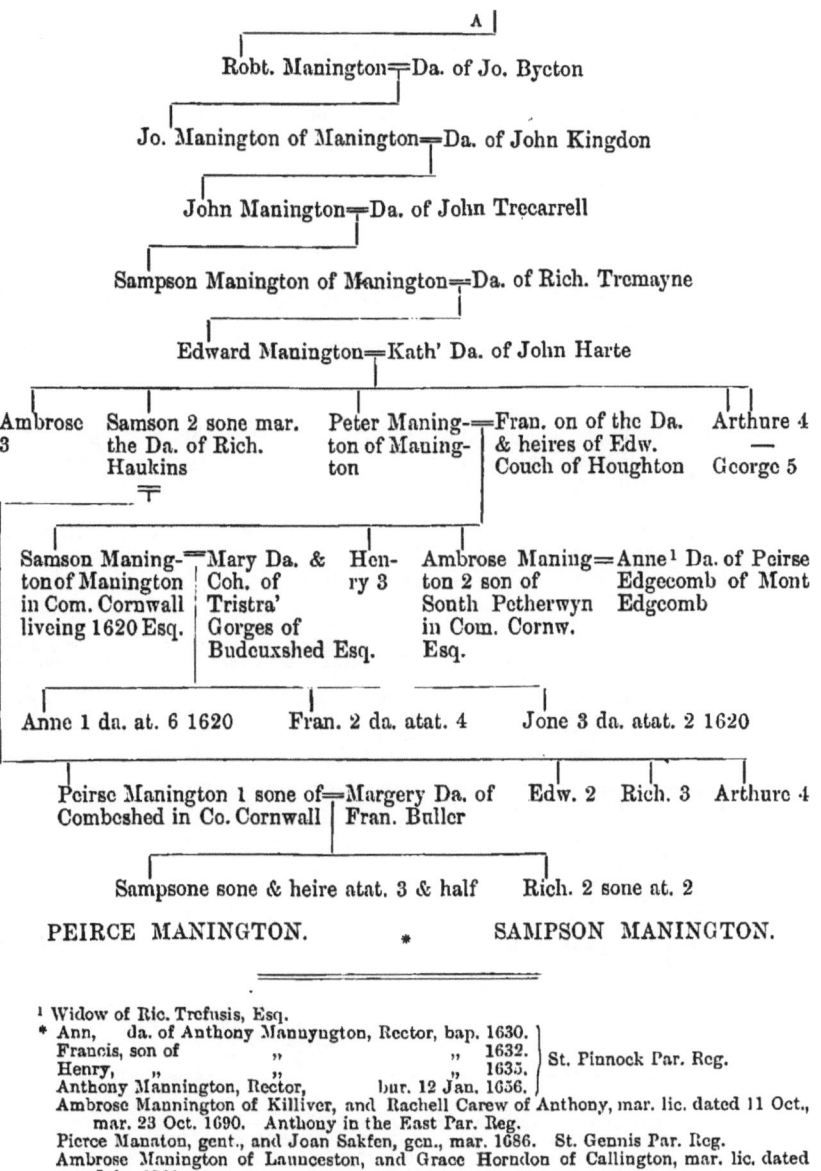

PEIRCE MANINGTON.   *   SAMPSON MANINGTON.

[1] Widow of Ric. Trefusis, Esq.
* Ann,   da. of Anthony Manuyngton, Rector, bap. 1630. ⎫
  Francis, son of   „   „   1632. ⎬ St. Pinnock Par. Reg.
  Henry,   „   „   „   1635. ⎪
  Anthony Mannington, Rector,   bur. 12 Jan. 1656. ⎭
  Ambrose Mannington of Killiver, and Rachell Carew of Anthony, mar. lic. dated 11 Oct.,
     mar. 23 Oct. 1690.   Anthony in the East Par. Reg.
  Pierce Manaton, gent., and Joan Sakfen, gen., mar. 1686. St. Gennis Par. Reg.
  Ambrose Maningon of Launceston, and Grace Horndon of Callington, mar. lic. dated
     July, 1721.   *
  Philippa, da. of Mr. Peter and Mrs. Philippa Manaton, bap. 1665, at Stoke Climsland.
     Bp. of Exeter's Transcripts.
  Martha Manaton (Mannington) of Calstock, widow. (Will, Bodmin, 1707.) To Mr. Jno.
Fursman (after Chancellor of Exeter Cathedral), silver watch and all the books of her late husband, and a gold ring. All the rest of her property to her niece Martha Radcliffe, sole executrix
[*Note continued on next page.*

Marke.

Willm Marke of Liscard in Com. Cornwall=Joane Da. of Andrew of Liscard

John Marke of Liscard=Emlene Da. of Tho. Vivian of
in Cornwall — St. Culme in Cornwall

Willm 3	Margerie 1 — Marye 2 — Olve 3	James Marke of Liscard in Com. Cornwall liveinge 1620	=Dorithie Da. of Joseph Bastard of of (sic) Dulo in Cornwall	Rich. Marke of Michelstow 2 filius	=Francis Da. of Francis North of Michelstow
		Josephe 2 sonne at. 3	Willm 3 sonne half yeare old 1620	John sone & heire at. 6 1620	Humphrie Marke fil. primogenitus atat. 2 Septimanes 1 Octob. 1620

JA. MARKE. * RICHARD MARKE.

(*Note continued.*)

—said Martha "not to sell my chariot nor coach horses, but to keep them for her own use." Funeral not to exceed £30. A leaden coffin to be carried to the p'ish of Tintenhall in Somerset, and there buried at twelve at night. (John Fursman, Curate of Calstock, Rector of Trevalga, Vicar of Lamerton, and Chancellor of Exeter, married the above Martha Radcliffe, St. Thomas, Exeter, May 18, 1721, Par. Reg.) And among other heirlooms was a portrait of Sir Fra. Drake, which remains with the representatives of Fursman. Ambrose Mannington commanded the bark Mannington, 160 tons, in the squadron serving under Sir F. Drake against the Armada. Roy. MSS. 14 B. xiii.

License of marriage between Anthony Mannington, Clerk, Rector of St. Pinnock, and Joanna Wills of Saltash, 15 May, 1623.
Penelope, wife to Mr. Richard Manaton, bur. 1670. Bodmin Par. Reg.
Edward Manaton, gent., and Abigail Ally,   mar. 25 April, 1670.
Christopher, s. of Edward Manaton, gent., & Abigail, bap.   April, 1673.
Mary, dau. of   ,,   ,,   23 Sep. 1674.   St. Breward
Christopher, s. of   ,,   ,,   bur. 30 April, 1673.   Par. Reg.
Abigail, wife of   ,,   ,,   22 April, 1691.
Elzabith Maniton,   ,,   8 Nov. 1699.
Degory Pearce, gent., and Jane Mannington.   mar. 1657.
Christ. Elford, of Modbury, gent., & Elyzabeth Mannington, da.
   of Anthony Mannington, late Rector of this p'ish,   ,, *1657.   St. Pinnock
Elzabeth, da. of Anthony Mannington, Rector. bap. 20 Jan., 1627.   Par. Reg.
Jane,   ,,   ,,   ,,   14 Jan. 1637.
Henry, son of   ,,   ,,   bur. 16 April, 1636.
Jane Mannington,   ,,   10 Jan. 1639.
Thomasine, dau. of Pierce Manyngton, gent., bap. 10 April, 1625, at Stoke Climsland. Bp. Exeter's Transcripts.

(J. M.)

* Thomas, son of Marten Marrake, bap. 10 April, 1607, at Paul.
Jane, da. of Thos. Marrake,   ,,   25 Sept. 1625, at Newlin in Pider.
Prudence, ,, Rich. Marck,   ,,   5 April, 1613, at Paul.
William, son of Rich. Marke,   ,,   8 July, 1617.   ,,
Rich., ,, John Marrak,   ,,   8 June, 1619.   ,,   Bp. of Exeter's Transcripts.
Henry, ,, John Marrke,   ,,   20 April, 1621.   ,,
William, ,, George Mark,   ,,   28 June, 1737.   ,,
William Mark,   bur. 20 June, 1737.

[*Note continued on following page.*

Martyn.

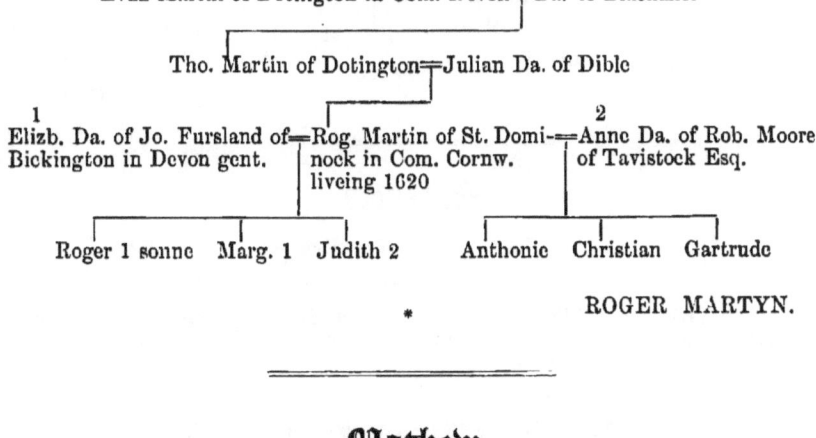

Evan Martin of Dotington in Com. Devon=Da. of Blackaller

Tho. Martin of Dotington=Julian Da. of Dible

1
Elizb. Da. of Jo. Fursland of=Rog. Martin of St. Domi-=Anne Da. of Rob. Moore
Bickington in Devon gent. | nock in Com. Cornw. | of Tavistock Esq.
liveing 1620

Roger 1 sonne Marg. 1 Judith 2   Anthonie Christian Gartrude

*   ROGER MARTYN.

Mathew.

Edm. Matthew of Dodbroke in Com.=Anne Da. of Tho. Parker of North-
Devon sone & hey of Edm. | molton in Com. Devon

James Matthew of Dodbroke=Da.¹ of Courtney of Molland in Devon

Edmond Matthew of Dodbrooke=Justian Da. of Weekes
in Com. Devon 1 sonne | in Com. Somerset
A

(*Note continued.*)
Paule Marke and Maria Husband, mar. 23 Oct. 1608. Truro Par. Reg.
Licence of marriage between John Markes of Liskeard, and Joanna Brendon of St. Dominick, 7 Oct. 1620.
Philip Marke of Liskeard and Joanna Howsaye,   mar. 1606.
John Marke of Liskeard, and Gartred, da. of Christopher
   Polland, gent., of St. Mabon   „ 1635. St. Pinnock
Anthony Markes of Liskeard, and Jane,   „ 1664. Par. Reg. (J. M.)
Henry Markes of Liskeard, gent., and Elizabeth,   „ 1666.
William Gabriel to Dorcas, da. of Philip Marke of Liskeard, „ 1682.
Stephen Pomery and Pasca Marke, mar. 22 July, 1593. St. Neot Par. Reg.
Dorothy, wife of Rich. Roberts, Mayor of Liskeard, and da. of Joseph
   Marke of Woodhill, Esq., died 13 Aug., and bur. 16 Aug. 1697.
John Marke, son of Will. Marke of Woodhill, bur. 28 Feb. 1614.   Mon. in Liskeard
Margery, wife of Walter Tregasse, da. of John Marke, of Woodhill, died   Church.
   1 Dec. 1629.
Emblyn Mark, gent., bur. 13 June, 1629.
The Paul and Newlin Registers are inserted to shew the difference in the spelling of proper names.

  * Nich. Martin and Joan Cole were mar. 1628. Tavistock Par. Reg.
  ¹ Ursula, da. of Phillip Courtney.

138   THE VISITATION OF THE COUNTY OF CORNWALL.

A |

John Matthew of Milton in Com. Corn-=Mary Da. of Tho. Plumley
wall liveing 1620 of Lalivery P'ish | of Dartmouth

| John 2 | Thom. 3 | Anne 1 Da. | Rebecka 2 | Bridget 3 | Edm. sone & hey. at. 14 1620 | Mary 4 Dau. |

*

JOHN MATHEW.

Mathew.

John Mathew of St. Kew=

| [1] Da. of Vivian of=Willm Mathew of Penetenny Da. & hey. of=Emlin Da. of
Trenouth ux. 2 | Tresungar relicta Johis Linan ux. 3 Willm | Rouse 1 wife
Mathew=

| Dorothy mar. to Rich. Foote | [2] Rich. ob. s. p. | [3]Elizab. mar. to Jo. Sharock of Creed | [3]Willm 3 fil. mar. the Da. of Wellington= |

[4] John Mathew of Penytenny=Winifred[5] Da. of John Stone of Trevigo

| Andrew 5 fil. unmaried | Degorie 4 fil. unmaried | Edward 3 fil. mar. Rebecca fil..... Jones de Com. Devon | John Mathew 2 fil. ob. s. p. | Willm Mathew=Sibilla filia of Peniteny now Johis Rosof Treshungar carrock de in Com. Cornwall Roscarock in Com. Cornw. |

| 1. Sibella æt. 6 | 2. Katherin 5 | 3. Lady Mathew 2 | [6] John Mathew fil. primogenitus ætat. 4 annoru' 1620 |

| | 2 Jone mar. to _ Raphe Lawse of Dewstock | | 3 Phillip mar. to Nicholas Canno of St. Kew | | 4 Tamazin mar. to Robt. Lampen | Mary unmaried | 1 | Dorothy mar. to Grigorie Tom de Little Petherick |

A

* This pedigree is much extended in Harl. MS. 1079, fo. 70.
[1] Emlyn, da. of Rich. Vivian of Trenouth.—Eds.
[2] He mar. Wilmot. da. of James Nanspyan of Gurlyn (see Nanspyan ped., *post*). His will, dated at Tresonger 2 June 8 James, proved in London 30 July, 1610, names Wilmot his wife, his bro. John Sharrock and wife, his cousins John, Anne, and Phillip Sharrock, Sara and Ursula Lynam and his cousin George Lynam, Richard, son of his brother Nicholas Mathew of Tregildren, bro. William Mathew, cousin John Foote, and his brother Foote's children.
[3] Named in Rich. Mathew's will, preceding note.
[4] Mar. 3 Nov., 1573 (St. Minver), bur. 29 Oct., 1606. } St. Kew. } (J. M.)
[5] Bur. 11 June, 1634.
[6] Bur. 31 Oct., 1688. Endellion.

THE VISITATION OF THE COUNTY OF CORNWALL.   139

| A

¹Nicholas² mar. Jone³ Da. of John Randal

⁴Richard 3 son ata. 28 in Oxonia¹ | ⁵Dorothy ætat. 24 | ⁶Mary mar. to Walter Webb of Tintodgwell in Com. Cornw. | ⁷Willms Mathew fil. primogenitus mar. Susan⁸ Da. of John Parsons of Black Torrington | ⁹Sidrack 2 fil. mar. Jane Da. of Savory of . . . . & widow of John Rashley

¹⁰John Mathew fil. et hæres 5 annoru'   ¹¹Dorothy æt. unius anni   ¹²Willm 2 fil. æt. 3
DEGORY MATHEW.   *   WILLIAM MATHEW.

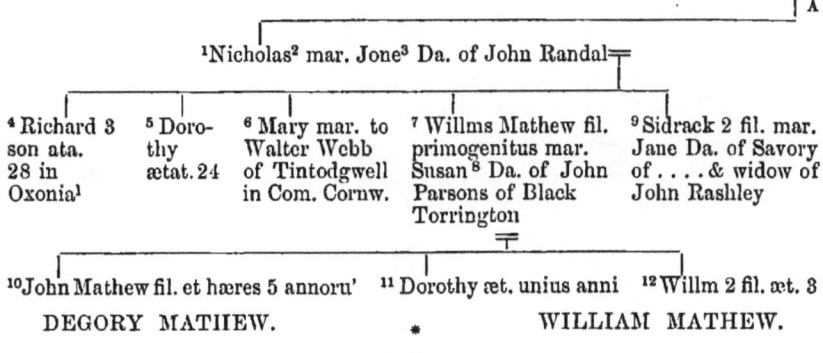

Maynard.

Henry Maynard of Milton in Com. Devon=Johan da. of Jackman

Constatyne=Agnes da. of Maynard of | John Hawkyns of Milton | Tavestock | Oliver 2 — William 3 | Johan wife to Chapman | Mary wife to Wodman | Alice wife to Robyns | Philip wife to Edgcomb

Nicholas Maynard of Milton=Eliza. da. of Walter Langdon of Keverell 2 wife | Henry=Julyan 2 da. of living ¹⁴Coswarth 1620 | John 3 — Bartholomew 4
sonne & heir Living 1620 mar. Jane da. of ¹³Michell 1 wife

Philippa | Charles sonne & heir ætat. 3 annoru' 1620 | Rebecka — Elizabeth | Henry sonne & heir æt. 6 annoru' | Samuell 2 sonne | Barbara 1 — frances 2
                                                  †   NICHOLAS MAYNARD.
                                                                       HENRY MAYNARD.

¹ Named in Rich. Mathew's will.
² Bur. 21 Feb., 1608.   ³ Bur. 4 June, 1641.   St. Kew.
⁴ Bap. 28 May, 1592.   ⁵ Bap. 8 Aug., 1596.   „
⁶ Mar. 28 April, 1609.   St. Kew.   ⁷ Bur. 4 Aug., 1661.   „   (J. M.)
⁸ Bur. 9 Aug., 1655.   ⁹ Bur. at Tintagel 4 Oct., 1625.
¹⁰ Bur. 1701.   ¹¹ Bap. 3 Jan., 1619.   ¹² Bap. 12 Dec., 1617.   St. Kew.
Henry, son of Will. Mathewe of St. Clements, bap. 6 June, 1610.   Truro Par. Reg.
    * For continuation of the ped. of Mathew, registered at Heralds' College, see certified copy in 'Hist. of Trigg,' vol. i. pp. 564, 573.
¹³ Gilbert Michell.   See ped., post.   ¹⁴ Henry Cosworth.   See ped., ante.
    † Ped. fin. Cornwall 34 Edw. I. No. 4. Rich., son of John le Tailleur of Bodmin, qu. Bernard Maynard and Matilda his wife def. Messuage, etc., in Bodmin.
         Francis Vivian of St. Columb and Anna Maynard of Colon, mar. lic. dated 1677.
         Ric. Vyvian and Maria Mynars mar. 2 Nov., 1614.   St. Austell Par. Reg.
         John Vivian and Margaret Minerd mar. at St. Mewan 1666. Bp. of Exeter's Transcripts.

Maynard.

Alexander Maynard de Tavistock et de = Honora filia Arthuri
Medio Temple 4 filius Johis Mainard | Arscott de Tetcott

| 1 Arthur | 4 Allan ob. s. p. | John filius et heres ætat. 16 annoru' 1620 de medio Temple | Joseph 2 fil. æt. 13 |

*

Not signed.

Mayow.

Phillip Mayow of Lowe in Com. Cornwall = Marg[t] Da. of Snith of S....

Phillip Mayow[1] of Lowe = Da. of Webb of Tavistock in Devon

John Mayow[2] of Lowe = Joane Da. of John Rashley of Foye

Phillip Mayow[3] of Brey of Morvell = Edeth da. of Haniball Vivion
in Com. Cornwall liveing 1620 of Trelawarren in Cornwall

† PHILLIPPE MAYOW.

---

* Arthur Maynard and Johan Hitchings mar. 1618. ⎫
Oliver Maynard and Elinor Troute   ,, 1622.
Jonathan Maynard and Thomazin Bickford ,, 1644.
Joseph, son of John Maynard, Esq.,   bap. 1639.
Alexander, ,,   ,,   ,,   ,, 1642. ⎬ Tavistock Par. Reg.
Arthur Maynard   bur. 1628.
Andrew, son of John Maynard, Esq.   ,, 1635.
Andrew, ,,   "   "   ,, 1641.
Elias,   ,,   Elias Maynard   ,, 1672. ⎭
Philip Maynard and Joanne Crypse mar.   1571. ⎫
John, s. of John Mainerd,   bap. May, 1538.
Agnes, wife of John Mainerd, bur.   1543. ⎬ Buckland Mon. Par. Reg.
Will. Mainerd, son of John,   bap.   1546.
Agnes Mainerd, wife of John M., bur.   1551. ⎭

[1] Margerie, da. of Phillip Mayow, mar. Jno. Coode, son of Walter Coode, 3 June, 1572. (Morval Par. Reg.) See also ped. of Coode, *ante*.
[2] Anne, da. of Jno. Mayow, mar. Godolphin Fletcher. See ped. of Fletcher, *ante*.
[3] Named in will of Haniball Vivian, dated 30 Nov., 1608, but his wife is called Judith, not Edith.

† Philip, son of Philip Mayow, gent., bap. 1639. ⎱ Morval Par. Reg.
Stephen Mayow bur. 1668.   ⎰
Philip Mayow of Morval and Martin Burthogg of Totnes, spinster, mar. lic. dated 1700.
Wm. Jolley and Phillip Maybow mar. at St. Columb Major 8 July, 1617. Bp. of Exeter's Transcripts.
Phil. Mayow, gent., and Dorothy, da. of Mr. Will. Mohun, mar. 1710. St. Ewe Par. Reg.
[*Note continued on next page.*

THE VISITATION OF THE COUNTY OF CORNWALL. 141

Menwynick.

Roger Menwynnick of Menwynnick =

Willm Menwynick of Menwynick in Com. Cornwall =

John Menwynick of Menwynick = Da. of Thorne of Thorne in Com. Devon

Rob. Menwynick of Menwynick in Cornwall = Barbara Da. of Wolcott of Cornwall

1		
Elizb. Da. of Giles Pawlet = Wm Menwynnick of Menwynnick = Agnes Da. of Tho. of Swandrop in hampsh.	in Com. Cornw. liveinge 1620	Roscorrock of Roscorock in Cornwall

Lewis sone & heyre atat. 15, 1620

				|1	
Nicho. 2 sone mar. Nathaniah Da. of Leonard Jolle	John 3 sone mar. Anne Dau. of Bartholo. Hatherley	Robt. 4 sone	Radigund ux' Alex' Tripcunny of St Tue in Cornwall	Anne ux' John Glyn of Boyton in Cornwa.

* WILLIAM MENWYNICK.

(*Note continued.*)
    Joseph Mayow and Elizb. Greby mar. 1677. Tywardreath Par. Reg.
    John Mayow, gent., and Phillip Roberts mar. at Lezant 31 March, 1614. Bp. of Exeter's Transcripts.
    Grace, da. of Jno. Mayo, gent., bap. 1605.
    Philip, son of Philip Mayow, gent., „ 1639.
    John Mayow, gent., bur. 1615. } Menheniot Par. Reg.
    Peter Mayow, gent., „ 1645.
    Stephen Mayow bur. 1668.
    Philip Mayow and Frances Stuckley, da. of Jno. Stuckley of Afton, } Morval Par. Reg.
Esq., mar. 22 Nov., 1635.
    Davis, son of John Mayowe, bap. 30 Ap., 1570.
    George, son of „ „ 3 Feb., „
    Johanna, widow of John Mayowe, bur. 5 May, 1559.
    Matilda Mayowe, widow, „ 18 Oct., „ } St. Pinnock.
    Milsom, dau. of William Mayowe, „ 18 Jan., 1569.
    John Mayowe „ 15 June, 1579.
    William Mayowe „ 14 Mar., 1588.
    Penta (Pentecost?) dau. of John Mayow, „ 1589.
    Richard Bligh, gent., and Ann Mayowe mar. 29 Feb., 1619. (J. M.)
    John, son of Thomas Mayowe, bur. 3 July, 1562.
    Wm., „ „ „ „ 6 Ap., 1564. } Lanreath.
    John, „ „ „ 10 Jan., 1565.
    Katherine, wife of Nicholas Mayowe, „ 18 Aug., 1596.
    Nicholas Mayowe „ 11 May, 1616.
    Charles Harry and Margery Mayowe mar. 10 Nov., 1612. St. Kew.
    John Mayow, gent., and Philip Roberts mar. at Lezant 31 March, 1614. Bp. of Exeter's Transcripts.
    There is another pedigree of Mayow or Mayhowe in Harl. MS. 1079, fo. 4, 5.

    * Johannis Moone filius Willmi Monne p'ochie Lyskeard et Joanna Menwynecke conj. fu. 1540. St. Pinnock Par. Reg.
    Ped. fin. Cornw. 29 Hen. VI., No. 3. Stephen Kendall and Wm. Menwynyk qu. and Wm. Horde and Johanna ux. lands in Polkinghorne, etc.
    Ped. fin. Cornw. Mich., 1655. Rob. Couch qu. Leonard Jolle and Joan ux. def. lands in etc. Alternon.
    Leonard Jolle bur. 1689. Alternon Par. Reg. Will. Bodmin.

Michell.

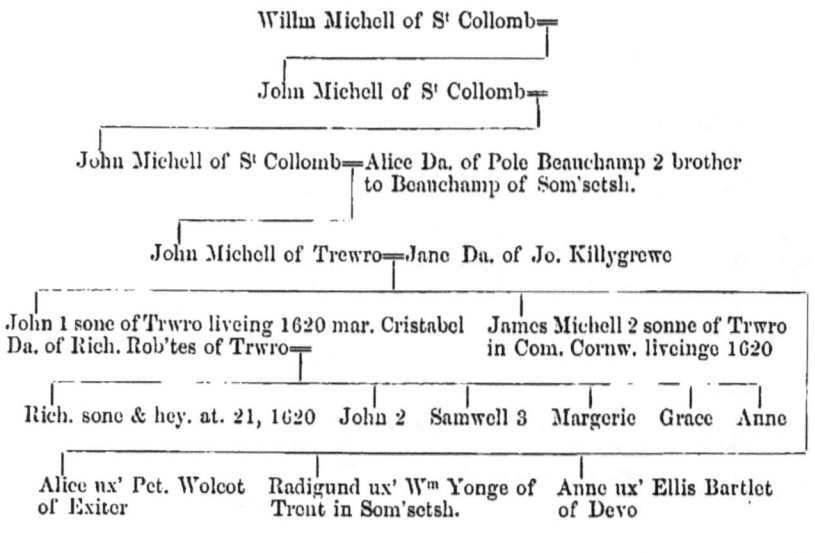

JAMES MICHELL.

Michell.

ARMS. *Sa., a falcon close in fesse Or. betw. 2 cotises Ar.; in chief, 2 falcons close of the second.*

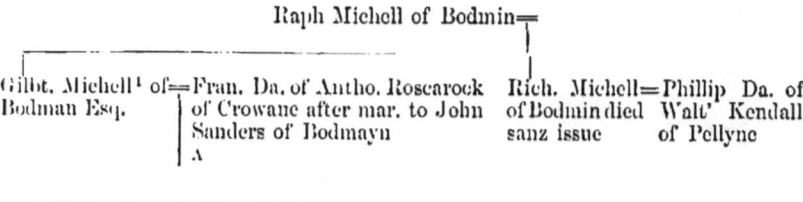

   * Hercules Michell and Bethseba Sampson mar. 1621.
   Rich., son of Hercules Michell,   bap. 1635.
   George, ,,   ,,   ,,   ,, } Truro Par. Reg.
   David, ,,   ,,   ,,   1645.
   William Carter and Margery Michell mar. 12 Nov., 1553. St. Col. Maj. Par. Reg. (J. M.)
  [1] Inq. p. m. 11 Jas., part 3, No. 198. Gilbert died 28 March, 1615; Phillip son and heir.

THE VISITATION OF THE COUNTY OF CORNWALL. 143

A |

Jane ux' Nicho. Maynard of Mylton Abbott in Com. Devon = Phill.[1] Michell Bodman now liveinge soe & heire Raph 2 — Gilbert 3 Richard 4 sonne Joane died

Phillip Maynard

*   PHILLIP MICHELL.

Mohun.

Willms de Mohun cam into England wt w. Conqueror =

Willms de Mohun =

Willms de Mohun vocatus Comes Som's. =

Willms de Mohun vocatus Meschines =

Reginaldus de Mohun D'ns de Dunster = Alicia fil. de Brewer   Willmi = Willms Paynell D'ns de Bampton Primus Vir. ob. s. p.

Willms Mohun habuit ex dono matris manoru' de Torry ob. sine herede 1265   Anelina uxor Patricij Frisell Comitis de Anegos   Alicia ob. sine hered.   Gilbertus = Isabella = Reginaldus de = Hawisia
Basset 1 maritus ob. s. p.   filia Willi[2] Comitis Darbiæ   Mohun fundator Abbatiæ de Newham in Maneria de Axmist' 1246 ob. 1257   soror Johis filij Galfridi Prima uxor. ob. 1260

Willms Mohun fil. 2 dictus = Beatrix filia Reginaldi fil. Petri   Sibilla   Isabella
de Mohun Otery ob. 1280

Reginaldus de Mohun ob. s. p.   Maria ux. Johis Meriett ob. s. p.   Alinora fil. et heres nupta Joh'i filio Nich'i Carew

A

---

[1] Æt. 19 et amp. 11 Jas.

* John Drake and Johan Michell mar. 28 June, 1601, at Lanreath. Phillip Michell, gent., and Blanche Carmenowe mar. at St. Winnow 16 June, 1625. } Bp. of Exeter's Transcripts.

    Walter Kendall of Lostwithiel inscribed a stone in Bodmin Ch. to the memory of the above Blanch, who died 13 Sep., 1673, having survived her husband 15 years.

[2] William Ferrers.

```
Reginaldus      Lucia uxor      Joh'es de Mohun══Johanna fil.¹    Alicia nupta    Juliana
de Mohun        Johis Grey      de Dunstar fil. 1 │ Comitis de    Beauchamp       de
ob. s. p.       de Codner       ob. 7 E. I.      │ Ferrarijs     de Hatch        Ilstor
                                                 │ Soror Isabellæ miles et Baro
                                                 │ Basset        Angliæ
```

```
    Reginaldus          Joh'es de Mohun ob. in Gas-══Alinora filia      2. Rob'tus
    de Mohun            conia evocatus ad parliament │ Reginaldi          —
    ob. s. p.           A° 28 E. I.                  │ filij Petri²     3. Jacobus
```

³ Joh'es de Mohun ob. A° 4 E. III.══Ada filia D'ni Pagani Tiptoft

```
Joh'es de Mohun ob.══Christiana fil.   Rob'tus 2 fil. Duxit Elizab.   Alinora uxor
in vita patris sepelitur │ D'ni Johis  fil. Rogeri occisus p' mali-   D'ni Rad'i de
apud Eborn'             │ Segrave ob.  ciam uxoris suæ 1332           Willington
                        │ 1341                                        ob. s. p.
```

```
Joh'es de Mohun fuit in minori══Johanna ⁴ filia   Margareta       Elizabetha
etate et custodia avi eius et p' │ Bartholomei    uxor D'ni       ob. s. p.
cum venditur p' sex centis mercis│ Burwash 1343   Johis Carew
Dno. Bartholomeo de Burwash
```

```
Elizab. uxor Willi Montague      Matild. fil. et     Phillippa uxor Edwardi Ducis
had issue Willm slaine in his    her. ux. Johis      Eboru' et postea uxor Walteri
father's life                    D'ni Strange       fitz Walter
```

```
6. Paganus        8. Patricius     Reginaldus 4 filius Duxit    Baldwin        Thomas 3
   —                 —              Elizab. filiam Johis Fitz    5 filius       filius ob.
7. Lawrentig⁵     9. Henricus       Williams militis                             s. p.
                                    ══
```

Johannes de Mohun══Johanna fil. St. Aubin

Thomas de Mohun fil. et heres══Elizab. fil. et hær. Rici Hayre

Willms Mohun fil. et hæres══Johanna fil. Cavell
                                │ A

---

¹ William, Earl Ferrers.
² Afterwards mar. to Sir William Martin, and called da. of William Fitz-Pierse in Mohun ped., 'Visit. Devon, 1620,' p. 185, which see for further information.
³ Inq. p. m. 4 Edw. III. No. 35. Johes de Mohun ob. 4 Edw. III. John de Mohun, his grandson, and heir.
⁴ Inq. p. m. 6 Hen. IV. No. 33. Elizabeth, Matilda, and Phillipa, her dau'rs and coheirs.
⁵ From him descended Mohun of Tavistock. See 'Devon, 1620,' p. 185.

THE VISITATION OF THE COUNTY OF CORNWALL. 145

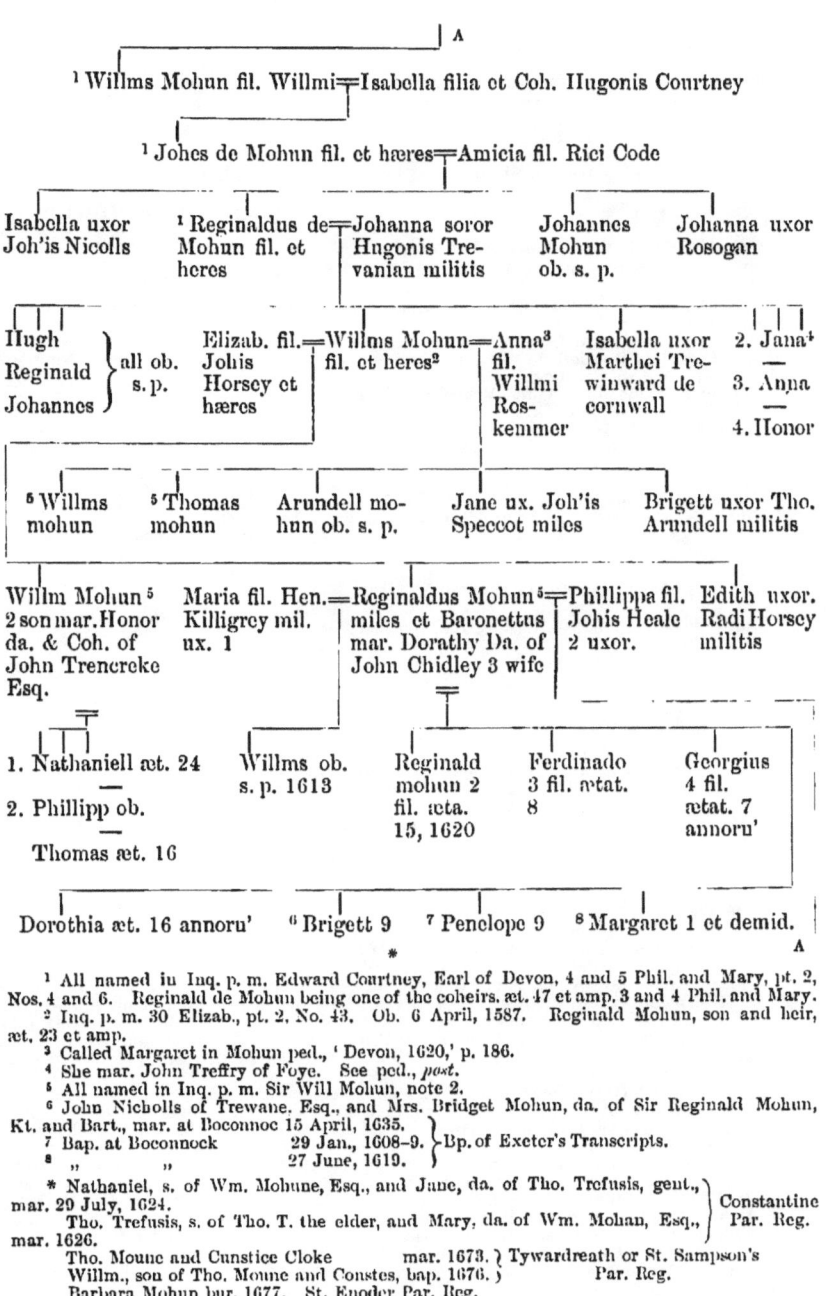

[1] All named in Inq. p. m. Edward Courtney, Earl of Devon, 4 and 5 Phil. and Mary, pt. 2, Nos. 4 and 6. Reginald de Mohun being one of the coheirs. æt. 47 et amp. 3 and 4 Phil. and Mary.
[2] Inq. p. m. 30 Elizab., pt. 2, No. 43. Ob. 6 April, 1587. Reginald Mohun, son and heir, æt. 23 et amp.
[3] Called Margaret in Mohun ped., 'Devon, 1620,' p. 186.
[4] She mar. John Treffry of Foye. See ped., *post*.
[5] All named in Inq. p. m. Sir Will Mohun, note 2.
[6] John Nicholls of Trewane. Esq., and Mrs. Bridget Mohun, da. of Sir Reginald Mohun, Kt. and Bart., mar. at Boconnoc 15 April, 1635.
[7] Bap. at Boconnock 29 Jan., 1608-9. } Bp. of Exeter's Transcripts.
[8] „   „   27 June, 1619. }

* Nathaniel, s. of Wm. Mohune, Esq., and Jane, da. of Tho. Trefusis, gent., } Constantine
mar. 29 July, 1624.
Tho. Trefusis, s. of Tho. T. the elder, and Mary, da. of Wm. Mohan, Esq., } Par. Reg.
mar. 1626.
Tho. Moune and Cunstice Cloke   mar. 1673. } Tywardreath or St. Sampson's
Willm., son of Tho. Moune and Constes, bap. 1676. }   Par. Reg.
Barbara Mohun bur. 1677. St. Enoder Par. Reg.

U

THE VISITATION OF THE COUNTY OF CORNWALL.

A |

Johannes Mohun fil.=relicta Rogeri et hæres æt. 25 | Aston militis

¹ Elizab. nupta Johi Trelani of Trelani in com. Cornwall

Joh'es Mohun fil. et hæres æt. 5

2 filiæ

* RAYNOLD MOHUN.

¹ Bap. 10 Feb., 1593. St. Pinnock Par. Reg.
* Charles, son of John Mohun, Esq., bap. 25 Aug., 1622. } Mevagissey Par. Reg.
Philippa, da. " " 1623. }
Warwick Mohun of Boconnock and Anna Addis of Plymouth, spinster, mar. lic. dated 23 Nov., 1704.
Guarvicus Mohun de Luny Armiger et Anna Addis hoc anno etiam nempe Decembris Octavo in Ecclesia Parochiali de Stoke Damerel juxta Plimothia in agro Devoniensi Nuptias inierunt 1704. St. Ewe Par. Reg.
Johannis Moone, filius Willmi Moune, Pochiæ Lyskeard, et Joanna
   Menwynecke were   mar. 1540.
Thos. Moune of Liskeard and Alicia Wood   ,,   1562. | St. Pinnock
Ann,   da. of Cornelius Moone, gent., and Jane,   bap. 1666. | Par. Reg.
Mary,   ,,   ,,   ,,   ,,   1667.
Beatrice, ,,   ,,   ,,   ,,   1673.
Edw., son of Thos. Mohun,   bap.   1617.
Thos. Moohun, gent., and Johan Harris mar. at Peter Tavy 1614.
Wm. Moore and Frances Mohune   ,,   1617. } Tavistock Par. Reg.
Josias Mohune   bur.   1626.
Mr. Thos. Mohun   ,,   12 Dec., 1644.
Willm. s. of John and Emma Moone,   bap. 1653.
John,   ,,   "   "   ,,   1657.
Ambrose Moon and Jane Harding of Fowey mar. 1685. St. Veep Par. Reg.
Will. Moone   bur. 1655.
Delia,   da. of Will. Mohun,   bap.   1667.
Warwick, son of ,,   Esq. ,,   8 Dec., 1668.
Warwick Mohun   bur. 12 March, 1714. } St. Ewe Par. Reg.
Ann Mohun   ,,   6 Jan., 1714.
John Mohun, Esq.   ,,   1719.
Warwick Mohun, Esq.   ,,   27 Oct., 1733.
Rob. Morshead and Mary Moone mar. 1639. Menheniot Par. Reg.
Edith,   da. of Will. Mohun, gent., bap. 15 Aug., 1566.
Will.,   son of ,,   Esq. ,,   1 Sep., 1571.
Arundell, ,,   ,,   ,,   ,,   16 Sep., 1575.
Bridget, da. of Mr. Will. Mohun   ,,   1579. } Fowey Par. Reg.
Margt., ,,   ,,   ,,   ,,   1608.
Will., son of Will. Moon,   ,,   1611.
Tho., ,,   ,,   Mohun,   ,,   1613.
Tho. Clark and Pascoe Moone mar. 13 Nov., 1687. } Lanteglos by Fowey
John, son of Philip Moone, bap.   1687. } Par. Reg.
Nicholas, son of Simon Mohoon, bap. 1709. Wendron Par. Reg.
Charity, da. of Matthew Moon and Jane his wife, bap. Oct., 1719. { St. Blazey
Philip, son of Matthew Mohun and Jane his wife, bur. 6 Ap., 1721. (Par. Reg.
(In Bishop's Teignton Par. Reg., Devon, appears a parallel change from Bohun to Boon.)
In St. Ewe's Church is a monument with a bust to the memory of William Mohun, Esq., "The last of that Ancient Name and Noble Family," who died 2 Dec., 1737, æt. 32.
Margaret, sister and coh. of Reginald Mohun, married Charles Roscarrock of Roscarrock. Vide ped. of Roscarrock, 'Hist. of Trigg, vol. i., p. 562.
To all, etc., Sir John Grenville of Stowe, Knt., sends greeting, etc. Know, etc., I, John Grenville, have remised, etc., to the Rt. Hon'ble Warwick, Lord Mohun, Baron of Okehampton, son and heir of John Mohun, dec'd, being in full possession, all my estate, etc., in the Manors of Bodmin and Bocarren, etc., sometime the lands of inheritance of Sir William Bevill, Knt., Philip Bevill, Esq., John Bevill, Esq., Sir Bernard Grenvile, Knt., and Sir Bevill Grenvile, Knt., some or one of them, which said premises the said Sir Beville Grenvile, father of me, the said Sir John Grenvile, did sell to John, Lord Mohun, father of the said Warwick, Lord Mohun, etc., etc. Dated 18 Oct., 1657.—Deed among the muniments at Boconnoc. (J. M.)
William Mohun & Thomasine Langson mar. 26 Oct., 1607. St. Breward Par. Reg. } (J. M.)
Johan, the wife of Robert Mohan, was buried 2 Dec., 1582. St. Mabyn ,,
Wm. Mohun, Esq., bur. 24 Dec. 1707, at Creed. Archd. Trans.
For extensive ped. of Mohun, see Harl. MS. 3288.
The Moon family is dispersed about the county, some following the occupation of basket makers.

Molesworth.

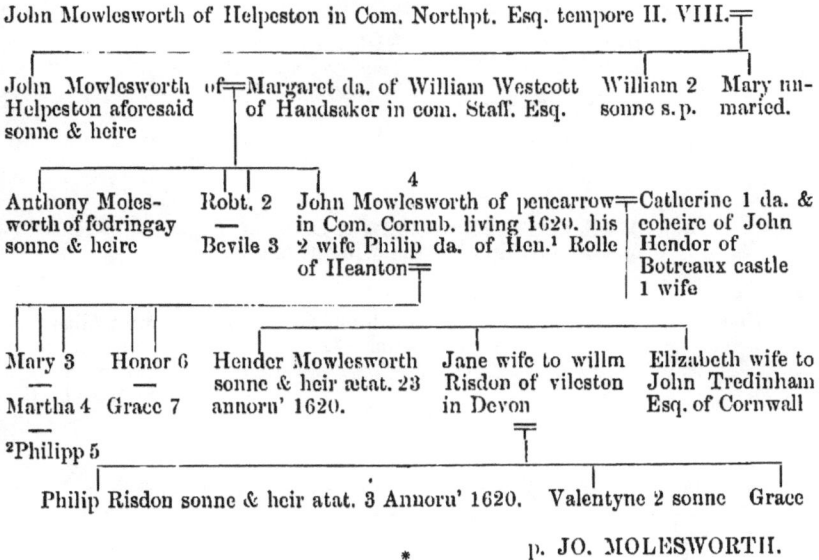

John Mowlesworth of Helpeston in Com. Northpt. Esq. tempore H. VIII.=

- John Mowlesworth of Helpeston aforesaid sonne & heire
- =Margaret da. of William Westcott of Handsaker in com. Staff. Esq.
- William 2 sonne s. p.
- Mary nu- maried.

- Anthony Molesworth of fodringay sonne & heire
- Robt. 2 — Bevile 3
- 4 John Mowlesworth of pencarrow in Com. Cornub. living 1620. his 2 wife Philip da. of Hen.[1] Rolle of Heanton=
- =Catherine 1 da. & coheire of John Hendor of Botreaux castle 1 wife

- Mary 3
- Martha 4
- Honor 6
- Grace 7
- Hender Mowlesworth sonne & heir aetat. 23 annoru' 1620.
- Jane wife to willm Risdon of vileston in Devon
- Elizabeth wife to John Tredinham Esq. of Cornwall

²Philipp 5

Philip Risdon sonne & heir atat. 3 Annoru' 1620.   Valentyne 2 sonne   Grace

*   p. JO. MOLESWORTH.

Morthe.

Rich. Murthe of Murthe=Isabell Da. of John Andrew
in Cornwall   of Michellstowe in Cornw.

John Murth=Isabell Da. of Jo. Carver of Carver in Cornw.
of Murth   Sistr & Coh. of Rich. hir brother

John Murth of Murth=

John Murth of Murth=

Hugh Murth of Murthe=Constance Da. of Jo. Kt. of Treganaw
A

---

[1] Called Moris Rolle, 'Visit. Devon, 1620,' p. 244.
² Bap. at Egloshaile 22 Nov. 1612. Bp. of Exeter's Transcripts.
* For memoir and extended pedigree, see 'History of Trigg Minor,' vol. ii., pp. 463, 472.

A

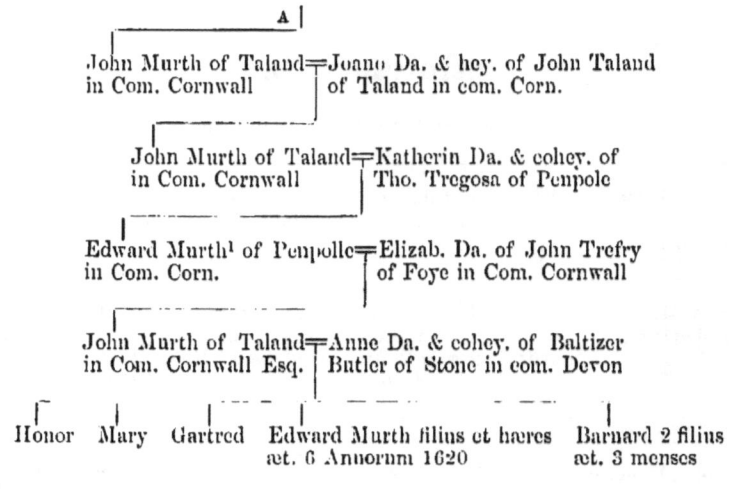

John Murth of Taland ⊤ Joano Da. & hey. of John Taland
in Com. Cornwall   of Taland in com. Corn.

John Murth of Taland ⊤ Katherin Da. & cohey. of
in Com. Cornwall   Tho. Tregosa of Penpole

Edward Murth[1] of Penpolle ⊤ Elizab. Da. of John Trefry
in Com. Corn.   of Foye in Com. Cornwall

John Murth of Taland ⊤ Anne Da. & cohey. of Baltizer
in Com. Cornwall Esq.   Butler of Stone in com. Devon

Honor   Mary   Gartred   Edward Murth filius et hæres   Barnard 2 filius
                         æt. 6 Annorum 1620   æt. 3 menses

*   JO. MORTHE.

Morton.

William Morton of Launceston ⊤ Mawd da. of John Squire

Thomas Morton now Maior =   Oliver Morton of ⊤ Margery da. of William
of Launceston living 1620   Stitheans living Kendall
                                 1620

John Morton sonne & heir ætat. 3 annoru' 1620   Temporance 1 da.   Martha 2

                                        OLYVER MORTON.

---

[1] Mr. Edward Murth was buried 27 Jan. 1602, at Anthony in Meneage. Bp. of Exeter's Transcripts. (J. M.)

* Thomas Morthe, gent., bur. 1606. Anthony in Meneage Par. Reg.
 Ped. fin. Cornwall, Eliz. Edward Morthe, gent., qu. Thomas Vyvyan, gent., def. quarter part of lands in Penpolle-Melyn, Manoid al's Manor Mylls, Carne Greowe. Toba al's Gyllyn Wollas, Trelege Vean, St. Anthony, St. Keverne, and Mannaccan. Edward paid Thomas £40.
 Pet. to Parl. 12 and 13 Ed. IV. John Vivian of Trelowarren, gent., and Anor his wife, set forth that on the 2nd Aug., 12 Ed. IV., Jas. Gerves, Jno. Mayowe, jun., late of Fowey, Rob. Toker, and o'rs, servants unto Tho. Trethewe, Esq., Coroner of Cornw., "arraied in maner of werre." with bows and arrows, swords, bucklers, etc., did lay awaite to murder him and his on their way to the Chapel of St. James, Tregours (Tregoney?), on pilgrimage, and maimed Vivian, his wife and son Richard, and murdered "oon John Morthure, gent., nevewe and servaunte" to the said John Vivian. Rot. Parl. vol. vi., p. 54.
 For continuation of this ped., see Couche's 'Hist. of Polperro,' Lond., 1871.

Moyell.

¹Rich. Moyle of St. Austle in Cornw.=Mary² Da. of Lawrence Kendall³

- Lowdy uxor Hen. Ashe of Sowton in Devon
- ⁴Rich. Moyle of Austle=Emlin⁵ Da. of Tho. Vivion of St. liveing 1620 | Collomb in Com. Cornwall

- Davy 2 sonne
- John sone & hey. ætat. 11, 1620
- ⁶Olive 1 Da.
- ⁶Barbara 2
- Mary 3

RCH. MOYELL.

---

¹ Rich. Moyle, gent., bur. 17 Aug., 1589. } St. Austell Par. Reg.
² Maria, wife of Rich. Moule, bur. 5 Dec. 1573. }
³ By his wife Katherine, niece of Tho. Munday al's Wandsworth, last Prior of Bodmin (see note under Munday).
⁴ Rich. Moyle, gent., bur. 14 June, 1654. (St. Austle Par. Reg.) Will 1 Nov., 1653, prob. P. C. C. 1 July, 1654. Alchin. 144. Of the p'ish of St. Austell, gentleman, to be bur. near my auncestors in the South Chauncell of the p'ish Ch. of St. Austell. Bequests to poor of said p'ish £100 ; to poor of St. Mewan, £3 ; to poor of Meragizy. £12.

    To my daughter Olave Trebarfett, £5. (She was relict of Harris of St. Issey, see note p. 90.)
    „ „ Barbara Carlyon, £5. (For her descendants, see 'Hist. of Trigg,' vol. i., page 319.)
    „ my grandchild Richard Harris, £30.
    „ „ Barbara Carlyon, £10. (She married Rich. Scobell of Menaguins. See 'Hist. of Trigg.')
    „ „ Richard Moyle, £5.
    „ „ Samuel Moyle, the Manor of St. Austell prior within the p'ish of St. Austell.
    „ Jane Moyle, £10 ; to Ann, Philip, Mary, and Emblen Moyle, each £100.
    „ my sister Loveday Ash's two grandsons, £10 each, and her five granddau'rs, legacies.
    „ Ric. Moyle of St. Columb Major, £5.
    „ John Moyle „ „ £10. (A weaver.)
Son David Moyle, Executor.
John Vivian of St. Columb Major, Esq., and Walter Moyle of St. Germans, gentleman, to be overseers of the will.
⁵ Rich. Moyell, gent., and Emblin Vivian, mar. 30 Jan. 1606. St. Columb Major Par. Reg.
Emblyn, wife of Rich. Moyle. gent., bur. 21 July, 1648. St. Austell Par. Reg.
⁶ Both named in the will of Rich. Moyle, note 4.

* This ped. is carried four generations earlier in Harl. MS. 1079, commencing with Odo Moyle of Rosegrence, whose grandson John Moyle mar. Agnes, da. of Jno. Vivyan of Chipons. Probably Moyle obtained Rosegrence through an early marriage with Vivyan, for by Ped. fin. 21 Hen. VI. No. 1, Odo Vyvyan and Matilda his wife held Rosegrense among other lands. For another short descent of Moyle, see ped. of Jenkyn, *ante*.

Thomas Moyle and Honor Landare, mar. Feb. 1672. } St. Winnow Par. Reg.
Mary, da. of Posen (? Parson) Moyle and Tamsin, bap. 1638. }
John, son of Samuel Moyle, gent., and Minister, bap. at Liskeard, 1630. } Bp. of Exeter's
James Moyle and Elizab. Vivian, mar. at St. Columb Major, 1615. } Transcripts.
Jane Moyle, widow, bur. „ „ 9 Feb., 1634. }
Jno. Moylle and Johan his wife, mar. 5 May, 1555. }
Rich. Moylle and Johan Barne, „ 1576. } St. Columb Major Par. Reg.
Rich. Moyle and Maria Bray, „ 1582. }
David, son of Rich. Moile, gent., bap. 23 April, 1620. }
John Moyle, bur. 1 Feb., 1566.
Elizab., da. of Rich. Mule, „ 9 Aug., 1572.
John, son of David Moyle, „ 1654.
Charles, „ „ „ 1662. } St. Austell Par. Reg.
Nich., „ „ „ 10 June, 1664.
Jno. Moyle, gent., „ 16 Dec., 1670.
Joseph, son of David Moyle, gent., „ 24 Aug., 1672.
David Moyle, gent., „ 5 May, 1672.

[*Note continued on following page.*

Moyle.

Edw. Tredinick Lo. of Tredinick in Com. Cornwall

- Rob'tus Moyle Sanz date
- Christian uxor Adam de Bath (Bark?) 10 Ed. III.
- Rog. Tredinick
- Alice ux^r Rich. Hallacombe

Children:
- Reginald Moyle
- Thomas
- Thomas
- Richard
- Alice ux. Tho. Windsor

- Roger Moyle 29 Ed. I.
- John
- John

- William Moyle 1 Ed. III.
- Willm Bake
- Richard
- Agnes uxor Rich. Fortescue
- Isabell ux^r John Ritt

- [1] John Moyle = da. & heir of Palford — 1 sonne
- Roger Moyle 2 sonn to Willm Moyle = Johanna filia et heres ux^r
- Nicholas — John sanz issue
- Richard

- John Moyle = Elinor da. & coheir of Willm Tirrell
- John Moyle of Bake = Agnes Da. & hey. of Rich. Fortescue of Hollocombe

- Johana ux. Edw. Burnbury
- .... wife to Keate
- .... wife to Tregasaw
- Margaret wife to Kelley of Southweek
- Rich. Moyle of Bake in Cornwall = Eliza. da. of willm fortescue of preston in com. Devon

(Note continued.)

St. Austell Par. Reg.:
- Ann, da. of Rich. Moyle, gent., bur. 1683.
- Mary Moyle, widow, „ 1685.
- Rich., son of Rich. Moile, gent., „ 23 May, 1686.
- Emlin, da. of „ „ 1687.
- Mrs. Alice Moyle, „ 1714.

St. Merryn Par. Reg.:
- Frances, da. of Samuel Moyle, Vicar, and Hester, ux., bap. 1689.
- Walter, son of Mr. Samuel Moyle, clerk, deceased, „ 1690.

Gulval Par. Reg.:
- Elizb., da. of David Moil, bap. 1695.

Lansalloes Par. Reg.:
- Rich. Moyle and Martha John, mar. Feb. 1609.
- Daniel Moyle and Anne Pike, „ Oct. 1674.

Truro Par. Reg.:
- Ann, da. of Mr. Samuel Moyle and Dorothy, bap. 1673.
- David, son of „ „ 1675.
- Ann, da. of „ bur. 1676.
- David, son of „ „ 1679.
- Samuel, „ „ „ 1681.
- Dorothy, wife of „ „ 1687.
- Mr. Samuel Moyle, bur. 25 Jan. 1717.

Gwennap Par. Reg.:
- Martayn Moile and Ellenor John, mar. 1681.
- Richard Moile and Willm. Perrow, „ 1687.
- George Moile and Susan Perrow, „ 1689.

[1] Ped. fin. Cornwall 41 Edward III. No. 4. Int. John Moil and Matilda his wife qu. Ralph Padreda of Lostwithiel and Matilda his wife def. Lands in Polscoth, &c. Moil paid 100 silver mares.

Ped. fin. Cornwall 5 Rich. II. No. 11. Int. Stephen Bony qu. John Moyle de Bodmalgan, Junior, and Johanna his wife, def. Bodmyn, Lostwythiel, Bonathalek, etc.

THE VISITATION OF THE COUNTY OF CORNWALL.   151

```
                                                           A
Willm. 3 sonne    Robt. 1 sone    ¹John Moyle=Anne Da. of   Jone ux. Tho. Kendall
ob. sine p'le     ob. sine p'le   2 sone & heire | Tho. St.  of Treworgey
                                                  Tavy¹

              ²Robt. Moyle sone & heire=Anne Da. of Hen. Lock
                 of Bake in Cornwall     of Acton in Midd.

              ³John Moyle of Bake in=Admonition da. of Edm. Predieux
                 Cornw. liveing 1620    of Netherton in Devon Esq.

   John sonne & heire atat. 6, 1620    Anthonie 2 sonne    Anne 1    Bridgett 2

                                  *                       JOHN MOYLE.
```

Munday.

Munday=

```
⁴Thomas Munday    John Munday who being a younger brother of=Joan Da. of J...
Prior of Bodmin   the family of Munday in the County of Derby | Man of ....
temp. Hen. VIII.  cam into Cornwall about 80 yeares since &
                  lived at Rialton, who cam through the meanes
                  of his Brother Tho. Prior of Bodmin
                                                                A
```

¹ Ob. 28 Sept. 28 Elizb. Inq. p. m. 30 Elizb., pt. 2. No. 70. Rob. Moyle, son and heir. (His wife was a da. of St. Aubyn.)

² Æt. 30, 30 Elizb. The ped., Harl. MS. 1079, fo. 196, gives him two bros., Geo. and Will., and three sisters, Joane, Elizabeth, and Ann, wife of John Prideaux.

³ John Moyle of St. Germans, ar., and Admonition Prideaux, da. of Edmond Prideaux of Farway. Mar. lic. I Sept. 1612.

* Admonition, da. of Nathaniel Moyle, Esq., bap. 29 July, 1670; bur. 1672. ⎫
  John,   son of   „   27 Aug. 1672. ⎪ Egloshay'e
  Nathaniel,   „   „   1673.   ⎬ Par. Reg.
  Mrs. Sarah, wife of Nathaniel Moyle, gent. bur.   1702.   ⎭
  Tho., son of Tho. and Dorothy Moyle, bap. 1672. ⎫ Ruan Minor Par. Reg.
  Tho.,   „   „   and Priscilla Moyle, „   1693. ⎭
  Francis, son of Charles Tredeneeke, Esq.,   bap. 20 Nov. 1565. ⎫
  Wm. Godolphin and Jane Tredeneek,   mar. Oct. 1571.   ⎪
  Warren Williams and Constantia Tredinnick,   „ 1606.   ⎬ St. Breock.
  Nicholas Tredinick, gent., and Francisca Brabin,   „ 1616.   ⎪ Par. Reg.
  John Carter, gent., and Maria Moyle,   „ 1616–17.   ⎪
  John Tredennick, gen., and Alicia Randall,   „ 1626.   ⎭

Ped. fin. Cornw. 33 Edw. III, No. 3. Int. Radulphus de Tredynek and Amiciam, ux. eius qu. Ric'um Baldewyne Capellanus, def. Lands in Carnewynck Wartha and Trepack settled on Ralph and Amicia, and their heirs.

⁴ Tho. Mundye al's Wansworth, will dat. 17 Feb. 1548; P. P. C. 16 Feb. 1554. More 19, mentions intended marriage between his nephew Will. Mundy and Elizb. da. of Humphry Prideaux, "when and as soon as she came to lawfull age according as I certified the King's Councill by my writing what time I was judged to dye." Also mentions his nephew Lawrence Kendall, and Katherin Kendall his wife.

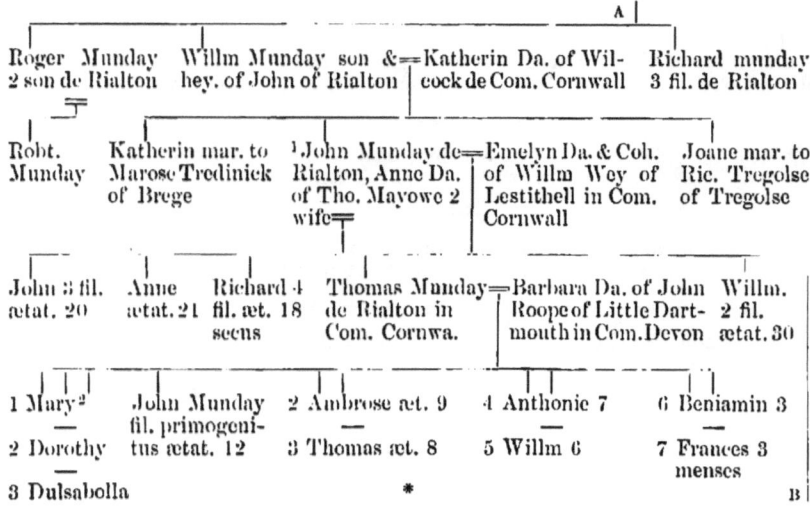

[1] John Munday of Rialton, Cornw., gent. (collated wills Exeter). to be bur. in Ch. of St. Columb the Lower. To eldest son Tho. M. Ryalton and Peterwthk in Bailiwick of Hund. of Pider, lands in Porthveau and Perin; to son Will. M.. £100. and tent. of Penrose and part of Manor of Ryalton; to dau's. Dorothy, Carthart. Loveday, Philippa, Margery. and Emilin the youngest, each £100; to Anne my now wife, 200 marks. Tho. M., the son, ex'or. Overseers, Walter Kendall, Esq., Hen. Courteney. Esq.. Jno. Courtis. and Ric. Crossman.

[2] Bap. at St. Columb Minor, 5 Jan., 1609-10. Bp. of Exeter's Transcripts.

* John Munday, gent., and Anne Mayow. da. of Mr. Thos. Mayow of Trey, mar. 2 Jan., 1596. Menheniot Par. Reg.
Anthony Munday of Penryn, gent., and Anna Boyle of St. Wenn. Mar. lic. dated 15 Nov., 1614.
Anthony Munday bur. 1677. St. John's Par. Reg.
Nan, wife of John Munday, gent., bur. 9 Jan., 1614. } Tywardreath Par. Reg.
John Munday. gent., " " }
Jane, da. of Mr. Edw. Munday, gent., bap. 1620. Madron Par. Reg.
Will., son of Hugh Munday, bur, 11 Dec., 1598, at St. Ewe. Bp. of Exeter's Transcripts.
Mary, da. of Nich. Munday, gent., and Mary. bap. 1658.
Nich. Munday of Mawnan, gent.. son of Thos. Munday, dec'd, and Mary, da. ⎫
of Sam. Trefusis of Constantine. gent., were mar. 9 Nov., 1657. (Also ⎬ Mawnan
in Constantine Par. Reg.) ⎭ Par. Reg.
Sam. Pentire, son of Rich. Pentire of the Boro' of Tregoney, gent.. and
Julian Munday, da. of Thos. Munday, gent., were mar. 13 April, 1670.
Will., son of Will. Munday and Temperance his wife, bap. 2 Mar. 1645. Mullion Par. Reg.
Thos. Munday and Florence John of Mullion, mar. 1719. Ruan Major Par. Reg.
Elizb., da. of Will. Mundaye,   bap. 1575.
Malachi, son of   „   „   „   1590.
Henry,   „   „   „   „   1592.   Fowey Par. Reg.
Will.,   „   „   „   „   1596.
Thos.,   „   Will. Munday, Mariner, .. 1703.
Will., son of Hugh Munday, bur. Dec. 11, 1589. Cuby Par. Reg.
Jane, da. of   „   „   bap. 1608, at Cuby.   Bp. of Exeter's Transcripts.

Deed, date omitted, settlement by Robt. Keste of St. Neott. yeoman. on his son and heir. George Keste, who married Joan. da. of Robt. Munday of Penryn, merchant. Harl. MS. 6243, fo. 37.

Lawrence Kendall married Katherine, dau. of John Munday, and niece of the Prior, who settled on them certain Priory lands. Observe the recurrence of the names Lawrence Kendall with that of Munday in Menenage; see notes under Kendall.

William, son of Humphrey Prideaux, married Johanna, another da. of John Mundy. Augmentation, Hill. 34 Hen. VIII.

¹ Dorothy mar. to Francis Rawle of St. Gilt Cornw.
Gartrud. mar. to John Ede of Bodmin
Lowday mar. to Rich. Kensham of St. Keverne
² Phillip mar. to John Martin of St. Erven Cornw.
Margerie 5
Emlin 6

THO. MUNDAY.

Nankebell alias Tippett.

Nankevill of Collomb Maior or St. Wenn.

Tipett Nankevill of Collomb Maior in Cornwall

John Nankevill of Collomb Maior

Jenkin Nankevill of Collomb Maior

Marke Nankevill of Collomb Maior

Rich. Nankevill of St. Wenn in Com. Cornwall = Mary Da. of John Gaveregan

¹ Francis Rawle and Dorothy Munday,	mar. 29 Oct. 1605.	
² John Martyn, gent., and Phillip Munday,	„ 20 Nov. 1607.	
* John Turnavyne and Honour Mundaye,	„ 22 Oct. 1622.	
Thomas Munday of Ryalton, gent., and Gillian Carnsewe, gent.,	„ 4 Feb. 1625.	
John Ugler and Rebecca Munday,	„ 4 Feb. 1627.	
Nicholas Langmaid of East Allington, Devon, gent., and Mary Mundaye of Ryalton, dau. of Thomas Munday, gent.,	„ 29 April, 1633.	St. Columb Minor (J. M.) Par. Regs.
Robert Munday and Jane Roberts,	„ 7 Nov. 1637.	
Thomas Munday, gent., and Margaret Cooke,	„ 1 Feb. 1639–40.	
Ambrose Munday, gent., and Elizabeth Carne,	„ 1 June, 1640.	
John Andrew, gent., and Mrs. Julian Munday,	„ 6 Feb. 1642.	
William Pitts and Dunsabella Munday,	„ 11 Ap. 1687.	
Lawrence Michell and Elizabeth Munday,	„ 19 Aug. 1690.	
Nicholas, son of Thomas Munday, gent.,	bap. 1 May, 1622.	
Emlyn, dau. of „	„ 2 Oct. 1633.	
Roger Carne and Dorothy Munday,	mar. 22 Sept. 1634.	
Thomas Crossman and Emlin Munday,(*)	„ 20 Nov. 1621.	Bodmin.

An, dau. of John Munday, gent., bap. 3 Oct. 1636. Fowey Par. Reg.

William Munday of St. Columb the lower. Will dated 29 Nov., 1650, names Brother Carnes, eldest daughter, and his younger children ; brother Ambrose Munday's daughters ; brother Longman's children ; John Munday and Thomas Munday, sons of his brother Thomas ; Ann, dau. to John Munday, his ex^or ; his father Thomas Munday (dec'd) ; Magdalen, daughter of John Munday ; brother John Munday, Exr. Appoints his uncle John Munday of Tretharas, brother Ambrose Munday, and Roger Carne, Overseers. Probate 29 Nov. 1650. (Pembroke 181.) (J. M.)

(*) See Ped. of Crossman, 'Hist. of Trigg Minor,' vol. i., p. 298 ; see also notice of Munday family in the same work, p. 309.

154   THE VISITATION OF THE COUNTY OF CORNWALL.

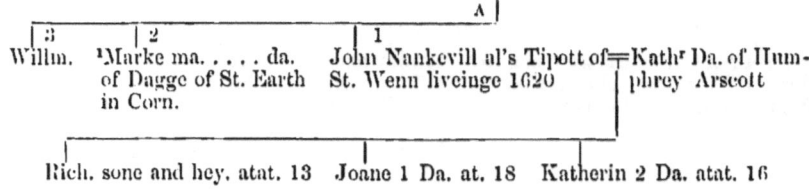

|3 |2 |1
Willm.   ¹Marke ma. .... da.   John Nankevill al's Tippett of=Kath^r Da. of Hum-
          of Dagge of St. Earth St. Wenn liveinge 1620   phrey Arscott
          in Corn.

Rich. sone and hey. atat. 13   Joane 1 Da. at. 18   Katherin 2 Da. atat. 16

JOHN NANKEVELL
Al's TIPPETT.

Nanspian.

John Nanspyan=Joane Da. & hey. of Tho. Tregose

|3 | |1 |2
Edward   Elizab. ux. James Nanspyan=Grace Da.   Hen. Nanspyan=Marg^t Da. of
ob. s. p. Walter   of Garlyn in com. | of John of Crowen in Rich.
          Anyon   Cornwall   Penrose Com. Cornwall Roberts of
                                                                  Truro

²Catherine ux. Michell   Zenobia ux. Rich.   Cheston ob.   Wilmot mar. to Rich.
Vivion of Phillick in   Predinx of Gur-   sine p'le   Mathew 2 to Walter
com. corn.   land in Cornwall   Langdon of Keverl in
                                                           St. Martines in com.
                                                           cornwall
                                                                            A

¹ Mar. Phillip, da. of Dagg. The names of their children are given in Harl. MS. 1079, fo. 156.
* Mr. John Tippett and Florence Killowe were mar. at St. Wen 22 June, 1609, Bp. of Exeter's Transcripts.

    Ursula, da. of James Nankevell,   bap. March 23, 1540. ⎫
    Thomas, son of John Nanskevell,   „   1548. ⎪
    John Vyncent and Johan Nanskevell,   mar. Nov. 29, 1551. ⎪
    Richard Nanskevell and Agnes Hamblie,   „   Oct. 4. 1555. ⎪
    John Nanskevell and Elizabeth Howse,   „   1577. ⎪
    Thomas Nankevell and Wilmot his wife,   „   1582. ⎬
    Ursula, dau. of James Nanskavell,   bur. April 15, 1540. ⎪ St. Columb Major
    Harry, son of James Nanscavell,   „   July 24, 1543. ⎪ Par. Reg.
    Johan Nankevell,   „   April 10, 1578. ⎪ (J. M.)
    Catherine, dau. of Umfry Nankevell,   „   Aug. 24, 1582. ⎪
    Umfry Nankevell,   „   May   9, 1586. ⎪
    Elizabeth Nankevell, widow,   „   June 1.   „   ⎪
    John, son of John Nankevell,   „   April 8. 1587. ⎪
    Thomas Nankevell.   „   Aug. 13,   „   ⎪
    John Nankevell,   „   June 17, 1590. ⎭
    George Tooker (of Minster) and Dorothy Nankivell, mar. 26 Sept., 1677. Michaelstow
Par. Reg. (J. M.)

² Mr. Michael Vivian and Kath. Nanspian, one of the dau.'s of James Nanspian, Esq., mar.
14 Oct., 1603. St. Erth Par. Reg.

THE VISITATION OF THE COUNTY OF CORNWALL. 155

A |

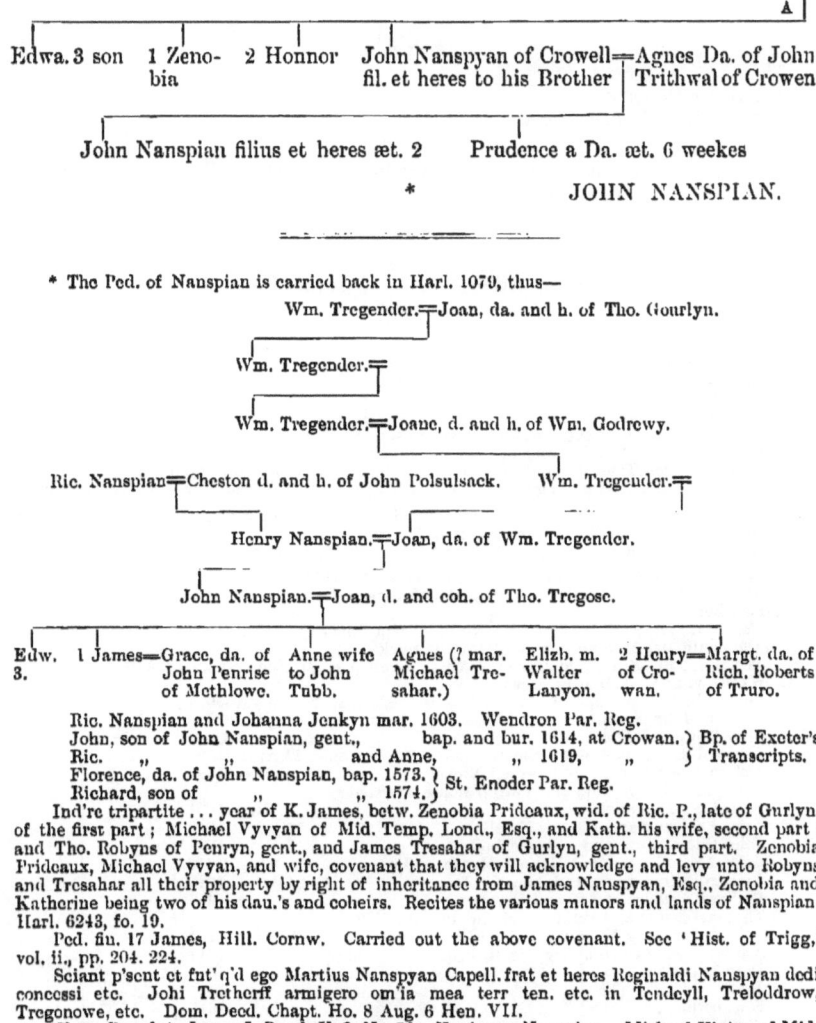

Edwa. 3 son 1 Zeno- 2 Honnor John Nanspyan of Crowell==Agnes Da. of John
              bia   fil. et heres to his Brother │ Trithwal of Crowen

John Nanspian filius et heres æt. 2   Prudence a Da. æt. 6 weekes
                           *   JOHN NANSPIAN.

---

* The Ped. of Nanspian is carried back in Harl. 1079, thus—

   Wm. Tregender.==Joan, da. and h. of Tho. Gourlyn.

    Wm. Tregender.==

    Wm. Tregender.==Joane, d. and h. of Wm. Godrewy.

Ric. Nanspian==Cheston d. and h. of John Polsulsack.   Wm. Tregender.==

    Henry Nanspian.==Joan, da. of Wm. Tregender.

   John Nanspian.==Joan, d. and coh. of Tho. Tregose.

Edw. 1 James=Grace, da. of   Anne wife   Agnes (? mar.   Elizb. m.   2 Henry=Margt. da. of
3.   John Penrise   to John   Michael Tre-   Walter   of Cro-   Rich. Roberts
                of Methlowe.   Tubb.   sahar.)   Lanyon.   wan.   of Truro.

Ric. Nanspian and Johanna Jenkyn mar. 1603. Wendron Par. Reg.
John, son of John Nanspian, gent.,   bap. and bur. 1614, at Crowan. ⎫ Bp. of Exeter's
Ric.   „   „   „   and Anne,   „   1619,   „   ⎬ Transcripts.
Florence, da. of John Nanspian, bap. 1573. ⎫ St. Enoder Par. Reg.
Richard, son of   „   „   „   1574. ⎭
Ind're tripartite ... year of K. James, betw. Zenobia Prideaux, wid. of Ric. P., late of Gurlyn, of the first part ; Michael Vyvyan of Mid. Temp. Lond., Esq., and Kath. his wife, second part ; and Tho. Robyns of Penryn, gent., and James Tresahar of Gurlyn, gent., third part. Zenobia Prideaux, Michael Vyvyan, and wife, covenant that they will acknowledge and levy unto Robyns and Tresahar all their property by right of inheritance from James Nanspyan, Esq., Zenobia and Katherine being two of his dau.'s and coheirs. Recites the various manors and lands of Nanspian. Harl. 6243, fo. 19.
Ped. fin. 17 James, Hill. Cornw. Carried out the above covenant. See 'Hist. of Trigg,' vol. ii., pp. 204. 224.
  Sciant p'sent et fut' q'd ego Martius Nanspyan Capell. frat et heres Reginaldi Nanspyan dedi concessi etc. Johi Tretherff armigero om'ia mea terr ten. etc. in Tendeyll, Treloddrow, Tregonowe, etc. Dom. Deed. Chapt. Ho. 8 Aug. 6 Hen. VII.
  Chan. B and A, James I. Bund. U. 3, No. 70. Vyvian v. Nanspian. Michael Vivian of Mid. Temp., gent.. orator. Whereas James Nanspean of Gurlyn, co. Cornw., Esq., was seised in his demesne as of fee of the Manors and Bartons of Gurlyn, Tregender, Penpons, Gurlyn Rebah, Mellyn, Gurlyn Lountha al's St. Earthe Ch. Town, etc., etc. (a long list), in co. Cornw., "worth to be bought and sold at least £6000," and having issue four daughters, viz., Willmot, Cheston, Katherin (wife of Orator), and Zenobia. With forethought said James N. settled his lands on self and his wife Grace for life, rem. to his four daughters, of whom Chester is dead s. p. Wm. Mathew of St. Kew, Cornw., gent., about nine years last past, took to wife said Willmott the eldest da., and shortly after Ric. Prideaux, Esq., took to wife Zenobia the youngest da., and yo. Orator Michael Vivian did, with consent and liking of said James N. and Grace his wife, take to wife the said Katherine. The said Ric. Prideaux was indebted to Humfry Yorke, gentleman, and John Carvaddres in the sum of £400, and his goods were taken in execution, and your Orator at earnest request of said Ric. P., did sell to Humph. Yorke one third part of an estate called Pulsack
                  [*Note continued on next page.*

Nicoll.

ARMS. *Sa. a Pheon Arg.*
CREST. *A Cornish chough proper.*

[1] Humph. Nicholl of Penvos in Com. Cornwall gent. = Jane [2] Da. of Rich. Roscarock
|
Humph. Nicholl of Penvos in Com. Cornw. liveing 1620 = Phillip Da. of Sr Antho. Rowse K^t.
A

(*Note continued.*)
on three lives, and did procure Mathew and Willmott and James Nanspian and Grace to likewise sell their interest, etc.
From the answers, we learn that Cheston died s. p.; that James Nanspian was indebted some moneys, partly on his own account, and partly as surety; was arrested by the Sheriff of Cornw. and imprisoned in her late Majesty's prison in Bodmin; that James Nanspian leased Gurlyn to William, son of Rich. Prideaux and Zenobia; and the said daughter Katherine Nanspian married Michael V. out of affection, and against the will of her parents. Taken at Mawnan 2 June, 4 James.

[1] He had two daughters,—Isabell, mar. to Robert Seawen (see ped., *post*), and Phillipa, mar. to Nicholas Godolphin of Trewarveneth (see ped., *ante*).
[2] Widow of William Tremayne of Upcott. See ped. of Roscarrock.
* Margt., da. of Herculaus Nicoll, bap. at Gwennap, 1614. Bp. of Exeter's Transcripts.
John Nicholas of Sendy and Jane, da. of Steven Rosewarne, mar. 27 May, 1547. Camborne Par. Reg.
Ped. fin. Cornwall 19 Rich. II. No. 4. John Nicol qu. John Hogge of Bodrennck and Mabilla his wife, da. of John Nichol. def. Bodrennck.
Ped. fin. 29 Cha. II. Mic. Cornw. Anty. Nicoll gen. qu. Jno. Vivian ar. and o'rs in Gorwena in Cornw. in Scobell et al. Devon.

John Nicoll. gent., and Mrs. Anne Russell, widow, mar. 1 July, 1656.		St. Maben Par. Reg.
Captain John Nicoll	bur. 2 Sept., 1685.	
Mrs. Bridgett Nicoll	„ 20 Nov., 1696.	
Edward Lower and Mary Nicoll	mar. 22 April, 1594.	
Robert Seawen, gen., and Isabell Nichol	„ 3 Feb., 1599.	
Humphry Nicoll, Esq., and Phillip Rouse married at St. Dominick	„ May, 1604.	
John Prideaux and Abigail Nicolls	„ 20 Sept., 1610.	
John Sillye, Esq., and Philip Nicoll	„ 4 Jany., 1639.	
John Nicholl, gen., and Honour Moyse. widow	„ 1640.	
Richard Sillye. gent., and Ann Nicoll, gent.	„ 25 Jany., 1649.	
Richard Archard. gent., and Dorothy Nicolls. gent., „	24 May. 1656.	
Thomas Turner of Exeter, merchant, and Ann dau. of Humphry Nicholl, Esq., dec'd	18 May, 1704.	
Anthony, son of Humphry Nicoll, Esq.,	natus 14 Nov., 1611.	
Dorothy, dau. ,,	bap. 1613.	St. Tudy Par. Reg. (J. M.)
Jane, „ „	1614.	
Elizabeth. „ „	1615.	
Richard. son of „	(nat. 26 Feb.) March, 1619.	
Augustine, „ „ and Phillippa his wife nat. 20 June, 1622.		
Bridget, dau. of Hump. Nicoll, Esq., and Phillippa	1624.	
Degorie ? son of „ „	22 March, 1627–8.	
Anthony, son of Anthony Nicoll, Esq.,	1649.	
John, „ Anthony Nicoll, gen.,	1651.	
Peter. „ Anthony Nicoll. Esq., and Amy, born 3 Sep., 1654.		
Anthony, „ Anthony Nicoll, Esq., and Amy, born 7 Jany., 1656.		
Anthony, „ Hump. Nicoll, Esq., and Rebecca. baptized in London 10 Dec. and born the same day he was baptized.	1678.	
Humphry. son of Humphry Nicoll of Tremeere. Esq., born 18 March, 1680.		

This pedigree is carried back five generations, to John Nicholls of the Isle of Guernsey. Harl. MS. 1079, fo. 91.

THE VISITATION OF THE COUNTY OF CORNWALL.

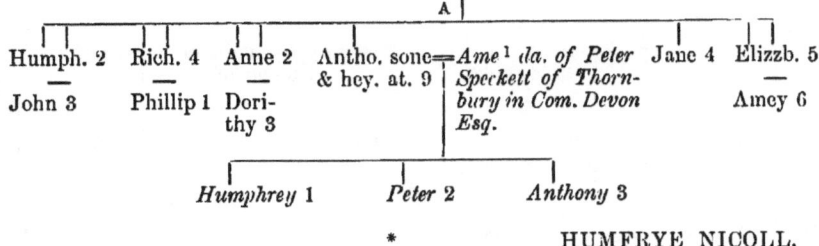

Humph. 2	Rich. 4	Anne 2	Antho. sone = Ame¹ da. of Peter	Jane 4	Elizzb. 5
John 3	Phillip 1	Dorithy 3	& hey. at. 9 / Speckett of Thornbury in Com. Devon Esq.		Amcy 6

| Humphrey 1 | Peter 2 | Anthony 3 |

*   HUMFRYE NICOLL.

Nicholls.

² John Nicholls of Trewane in the p'ish of St Kew in Cornwall

John Nicholls = Catheryn da. of John Trobridge
of Trewane   of Trobridg in Com. Devon
                A

¹ Amy, afterwards mar. to John Vivian of Trewan at St. Tudy, 4 May, 1671, as Amy Nichols (Bp. of Exeter's Transcripts), and registered at Heralds' Coll. as dau. of Peter Spccot.

* John Nicoll, son of Humphrey Nicoll, born and bap. 1 March, 1681.
Rebeccah, da. of Humphry Nicoll and Itcbeckah, born 19 Sep., 1685.
Mary,   „   „   „   „   2 Aug., 1687.
Philippa,   „   „   „   „   28 Jan., 1688.
Joseph, son of   „   „   „   1694.
Mary,   da. of Humphry Nicolls   28 July, 1615.
Amath,   „   „   Nov., 1618.
Benjamin, son of Humph. Nicoll, Esq., by Rebecca, 15 Sept., 1696.
Bridget, da.   „   „   1 July, 1698.
Isabell, da.   „   „   bur. 1570.
Jane,   da.   „   „   „   1607.
Mrs. Jone Nicolls   died 7 May, bur. 27th, 1615.   St. Tudy
Mathew Nicoll, clerk,   „   1625.   Par. Reg.
Humphry Nicoll of Penvose, Esq.   „   1642.
Richard, son of Humphry Nicoll, Esq., of Penvose „ 1646.   (J. M.)
Anthony, son of Anthony Nicoll, Esq.   „   1649.
John,   „   „   „   1652.
The Worshipful Anthony Nicoll of Penvose, Esq.,
    dyed Feby. 20 in the Savoye parish in London
    and was bur. 22 in the Savoye   1658.
Phillippa Nicholl, widow, who died at Helligan in St. Mabyn
    and buried at St. Tudy   1668.
. . . . son of Humphry Nicoll, Esq.   bur.   1679.
Dorothy, da. of Humphry Nicolls, Esq.,   „   25 Jany., 1609.
Bridget, da.   „   „   14 Aug., 1698.
Will of Anthony Nicoll of Penvose, dated 13 Feby., 1658. names his mother Phillip. wife Anne. sons Peter, Anthony, eldest son Humphry, brother John Nicoll, cousin John Barrett. Probate to John Nicoll, uncle and guardian of Humphry Nicoll during minority, 7 October, 1662.
Inq. p. m. 43 Elizab., pt. 1, Nos. 148 and 155. Humphry Nicoll, late of Penvos, died 27 Dec., 40 Elizab. Humphry Nicoll, son and heir, aged 20 years, 21 weeks, and 5 days, and no more, at his father's death.

☛ The additions in italic are in the hand of Parker.

² His da. Thomasin mar. Geo. Carnsewe of St. Kew. See ped., *ante*.

158   THE VISITATION OF THE COUNTY OF CORNWALL.

| A

Thomas 4 | Nicho. 5 | John Nicholls of Trewane=Eliza. da. of Edmond fortescue of Vallepit
living 1620

John sonne & heire | francis | Sibill 1 | Grace 2 | Mary 3
æt. 7 annoru' 1620 | 2 sonne

Roger Nicholls=Sibell da. of John | Robert Nicholls=Constance da. of Hugh
2 sonne. | Killiow of Lausallers | 3 sonne | Pomeroy of Trigney

*

JOHN NICHOLLS.

Noye.

Willm Noy of Burryan=Phillip Da. of Lenyne of
in com. Cornwall | Gwynier in Com. Corn.

[1] Edward filius | [2] Willm Noy of Buryan 3 filius=Sara [2] Da. of Humpfry | John 2
et heres | æt. 56 living 1620 | York of Fellick | filius

Anne 2 Da. | Humphry Noy filius | [3] Phillip 2 sonne | Joseph 3 | [4] Barbara 1
æt. 2 | et heres æt. 11 | æt. 8 | son æt. 4 | Da. æt. 6

†

WILLIA. NOYE.

---

* For memoir of the family of Nicholls of Trewane and exhaustive pedigree, see 'History of Trigg,' vol. ii., pp. 164, 166.
 Ped. fin. Cornwall 18 Rich. II, No. 1. John, son of Rich. Nicholl of Lostwithiel qu. John Hora and Johana his wife def. Lostwithiel, Bryggond, and Nether Polscoth.
 Ped. fin. Cornwall 8 Hen. VI, No. 2. John Nicoll of Bodmin qu. Thos. Lycheborowe and Johanna his wife def. Trenale. Tregearchapell, Drannck.
 Ped. fin. Cornwall 17 Hen. VI, No. 10. Oto Nicoll and Jno. Colyn of Hellond qu. Jno. Lukey of Wadefast and Johane his wife def. Tregagelwales and Tregagelwortha.
 James Nicolls, gent., and Dionis Erisey mar. 27 Nov., 1683. St. Neott's Par. Reg.
 John Nicolls of Trewane, Esq., and Mrs. Bridget Mohun, da. of Sir Reginald Mohun, Kt. and Bart., were mar. 15 April, 1635, at Boconnoc. Bp. of Exeter's Transcripts.
 Thos. Nicolls and Annys   were mar. 1 July, 1565, ⎫
 Robert Tubb and Jane Nicholls   „   20 Sept., 1565, ⎬ St. Ewe Par. Reg.
 Charles Williams, Esq., of St. Twin (Wenn) and Jane Nicholls of Gulval, mar, 27 Feb., 1676-7, Gulval Par. Reg.

[1] Father of Wm. Noye, the Attorney-General under Chas. I. See Harl. MS. 1079, fo. 113 b.
[2] Wm. Noy, gent., and Sarah, da, of Humphry York, gent., mar. 26 Nov., 1606. ⎫ Phillack and
[3] Philip, son of Will. Noy, gent.,   bap.   1612. ⎬ Gwithian
[4] Barbara, da. of Will. Noy, generosus,   „   21 Aug., 1608. ⎭ Par. Reg.

† Edward, son of Edward Noie,   bap. at Paul 9 May, 1619. ⎫
  Henry,   „   Martin   „   „   „   16 Jan., 1619-20. ⎪
  Robert, „   Werter   „   „   „   17 Jan., 1619-20. ⎬ Bp. of Exeter
  Jone, wife of John   „   bur.   „   9 June, 1619.   ⎪ Transcripts.
  Ann, da. of Werter   „   „   „   10 Nov., 1619.   ⎪
  Mary, da. of Edward Noy, gent., bur. at Mawgan in Pider   1612. ⎭

[Note continued on next page.

Opy.

¹Nicholas Opy de Badman = ²Ebit Da. and hey. of Willm. Heydon

³Thomas Opy de Bodman = ⁴Alicia 2 fil. et Coh. Willm. Way de
in Com. Cornwall   Lestwithiell in Cornwall
A

(*Note continued.*)

Will. Harris, gen., and Philippa Noy mar. 4 June, 1625. } Gulval Par. Reg.
John Noy, generosus,   bur.   1634. }

Esct. Eliz. Ja. and Chas. pt. 21, No. 41. Inq. p. m. taken 27 May, 11 Cha., at Truro, John Noy, Esq., ob. 29 Ap. 10 Chas., lands in Sancreed, Zenuor, Paul, St. Ives, Ludgvan, and in Buryau Ch. Town, which latter he held of Edw. Noy, Esq., as of his Manor of Buryan. Philippa, wife of William Harris, sole da. & heir, aged 21 years and 10 months at father's death.

Ric., son of Daniel Noie,   bap. at St. Paul   1635. } Bp. of Exeter's
Mary, da. of Edw. Noy, gentleman, bur. at Maugan in Pider 1612. } Transcripts.
Adrodata, da. of John Noye, Esq., bap.   1629. }
Edw. Noye, Esq. and Ane Bluett mar. 28 June, 1617. } St. Columb Minor Par. Reg.
Philip, wife of Edw. Noye   bur.   • 1697. }
Will., s. of Sampson Noy,   bap. 13 Oct., 1611.
Tho., s. of Will. Noy,   „   1646.
William Noy and Margaret   mar.   1596.
Sampson Noy and Anne   „   1601.
Ralph Noy and Margaret   „   1604.   } Madron Par. Reg.
Walter Noy and Margaret   „   1645.
James Noy and Jane   „   1649.
Arthur Noy and Alice   „   1647.
Will. Noy and Margaret   „   1652.

Edward and Blanche Noy bur. at Paul in Penwith 1668. Bp. of Exeter's Transcripts.
Mar. lic. dated 1682 between Henry Drake of Barnstaple and Anna Noye, of the City of Exeter, widow.

John Jenkyn of Penpons Alverton (Maddern), in his will, 14 Sept. 2 Jas. I., P. P. C., names Richard and Philip, sons of William Noye of Talcarn, his son-in-law.

Philip Noie and Honor Crudge   mar.   28 May, 1613. }
Edm'd Noye and Blanche Code   „   29 April, 1616. } Breage Par. Reg.
Michael Noy and Parker Harry   „   2 April, 1627. }
Thos. Noy and Rachel Peard   „   6 June, 1631. } Constantine Par. Reg,
Will., son of Thos. Noy by Rachel, bap. 14 July, 1631.
Edward, son of Edward Noy by Elizab., bap. 18 June, 1649.
Martha, dau. of   „   „   „   19 Mar., 1654. } Padstow Par. Reg. (J. M.)
Elizabeth, dau. of „   „   „   bur. 16 Apl., 1656.

Will of Edward Noye of Maugan in Pyder. gent, dated 25 Oct., 1621, names wife Jane, sons Thomas, Edward, John, Philip, William (eldest). daughter Jane Penkevell. Wife Jane and son Edward ex'rs. Prob. 27 July, 1622. Saville 65.

Humphry Noy was included in the Commission of Array for the King, and his estates were sequestrated by the Parliament. In his petition, dated in 1646, he prayed to be admitted to compound, and sets out the particulars of his estate, claiming an allowance of £1500 due on mortgage of the Manor of Lanowemore, etc., and annuities of £60 given by the will of his brother Edward Noy, dated 16 March, 1635, proved 7 April, 1636, which is fully set out. He was fined at a tenth under the Articles of Truro, 6 Feby., 1646.—Royalist Comp. Papers, 2nd Series, vol. xxxvi. ff. 253-280. (J. M.)

¹ Inq. p. m. 8 Elizab. No. 177. Thomas Opye died at Bodmin 19 Jan. 1565. Nicholas, son and heir, aged 46 and more.
² Bur. 1576. Bodmin Par. Reg.
³ Chan. Pro. Eliz. O. o. 2, No. 36, 1579. Opye v. Kestell. Names Thomas Opye of Bodmin, with Radigan and Patience, daughters of his late brother Nicholas, whose wife Honor (daughter of Thos. Bligh of Bodmin) was married to William Kestell.
⁴ Mar. to Thos. Opie 9 Sept. 1566. Bodmin Par. Reg.

A

¹Nicholas 2 fil. de Plimouth in Com. Devon Duxit Jana fil. Johis Waade² of Herston in Devon═ | Thomas fil. primogenit. ob. s. p. | Edward 4 fil. | Eliza. mar. to Patrick Jenkin of Lanivet in com. cornwall | Mary mar. Ric. Pierse 3 son of Wm Pierse

Thomas sonne and heir ætat. 14 annoru' 1620.　　Nicholas 2　　Edward 3

Emelin 2 filia unmaried | Will'ms Opy ═Maria filia Johis de Penborgard in Courtier de Devon Com. Cornw. | Tho. 3 fil. de London in Bread Street, Linendrap' mar. . . . . . Da. of Palm^r London

1 Maria 14　　4 Felip 6　　Thomas Opy fil. primogenit. ætat. 22, 1620　　Will'ms 2 fil. æt. 21　　3 John æt. 20　　5 Edward 10
2 Elizab. 13　　5 Grace 2　　　　　　　　　　　　　　　　　　　　　　　　　　4 Nicholas 18　6 Richard 4
3 Jana 12　　6 Emmalin 1

*

WILLM OPY.

Oughe.

Willm Oughe of St. Cleare in Cornwall═Marg^t Da. of Wm Samwell of Restormell in Cornwall

Christ' Oughe of St. Cleare in Cornwall liveing 1620═Prisilla Da. of Tho. Woodnott of Linkinghorne in Com. Cornwall

Theophilus sone and heyre æt. 10, 1620　　Bridget æt. 8, 1620

CHRISTOP. OUGHE.

---

¹ Sarah, da. of Nicholas Opie of Plymouth, mar. Christopher Warren of London. 'Visit. Devon, 1620,' pp. 300 and 354.
² Woode. 'Visit. Devon, 1620,' p. 314.
* Chan. Pro. Eliz. O. o. 3, No. 15. Thomas Opye v. Otes Trelother. To recover deed and possession of Manor called Parke in Bodmin and Egloshaile.
John Opie, gent., and Margaret Hole, mar. 1660. Egloshayle Par. Reg.
William Opie of Boconnoc, gent., and Anne Stuart. Mar. lic. dated 1670.
Phillip, da. of Robert Opey of Cornwall, mar. Hugh Luttrell of Marshwood, co. Somerset. 'Visit. Devon, 1620,' p. 175.
Thos.,　 son of Thos. Opie, gent., bap. 1568. ⎫
Emline, da. of　　 "　　　　 "　　 1570. ⎪
William, son of　 "　　　　 "　　 1572. ⎬ Bodmin Par. Reg.
Nicholas,　"　　　 "　　　　 "　　 1574. ⎪
Thos.,　　　"　　　 "　　　　 "　　 1575. ⎪
Edward,　　"　　　 "　　　　 "　　 1577. ⎭

For a particular account of the family of Opie, with extended pedigree of Opie of Bodmin and Penhargard, and Pedigree of Opie of Parke, see ' Hist. Trigg,' vol. ii., pp. 47–55.

𝔓𝔞𝔯𝔨𝔢𝔯.

Rob'tus Parker de Brousholm in=Elizab. filia Georgij Chaterton de
Bolland in Com. Eboru' | Nuthurst in Com. Lancast.

Thomas Parker fil. primogenitus de Brusholm in Com. Eboru'

Willms Parker de Blis-=Johanna filia
land in Com. Cornwall | .... Pan-
et Archidiaconus de | chard de Com.
Cornwall 3 fil. | Wiltes

Rogerus Parker 2 fil. Decanus de Lincolne

Jacobus Parker filius=Katherin filia Rici
et hæres ætatis 30 | Buller de Com.
annoru' | Cornub. Militis

Willms Parker 2 filius ætat. 28 de Academia Cantab.

Katherina filia maxima etat. 2 annoru' temporere visitacois 1620

Alicia filia 2 ætatis dimidiu' anni 1620

* WILLIAM PARKER.

---

* Wilmot, da. of Jno. and Mary Anstis   bap.   1671.
  Mary,   „   Jno. and Eliz. Anstis   „   1698.
  Rachel,   „   Jno. Anstis, Esq., by Elizab., was born 6 June, 1700, Xtened at St. Clement's Danes in London, dyed Feb. 3, 1701, and bur. at St. Marie's Bermondsey in Southwark, as appears by the Registers of these Parishes, and removed hither yᵉ 14 Aug., 1706.
  Jno., son of Jno. Anstis, Esq., born 1703-4, Xtened at St. Martins in the Fields, dyed at Fulham and there bur.
  John, s. of John Anstis, bap. St. Clements, dyed in Essex Street, Lond., 2 May, and bur. at Duloe.
  Will., son of Jno. Anstis by Eliz., born in Arundell Street 1713, bur. in Dulo 1714.
  Rich.,   „   Jno. Anstis, jun., Esq.   Duloe
  Edward Anstis   bur.   1671.   Par. Reg.
  Mary Anstis   „   1671.
  Jno. Anstis, senior   „   9 June, 1692.
  Mr. Jno. Anstis of St. Nyot bur. in Dulo Church   26 Jan., 1713.
      (Styled Jno. Anstis Seig'r, gent., in the Archd. Transcripts.)
  Philip, son of Jno. Anstis, Esq., Garter Principal King at Arms, bur. here 1 Oct., 1719.
  Jno. Anstis, Esq., Garter Principal King at Arms, died at Mortlake in Surrey and was bur. here 23 March, 1743.
  Mrs. Anna Anstis of Mortlake, Surrey,   bur. 14 Oct., 1749.
  John Anstis, Esq., Principal Garter King of Arms, died at Mortlake in Surrey and was bur. here 30 Dec., 1753.
  Roger, son of John Anstis, gent., bap. 1675. } St. Neott Par. Reg.
  Mary, wife of John Anstis, gent., bur. 1669.
  John Anstis, gent., of Cornw. and Elizab. Cudlip mar. (by licence) 23 June, 1695. } Tavistock
  Hugh, s. of Hugh Anstis. bur.   } Par. Reg.

For memoir of the family of Parker, and continuation of pedigree to John Anstis, Garter King of Arms, see 'History of Trigg,' vol. i., pp. 67, 69.

Paynter.

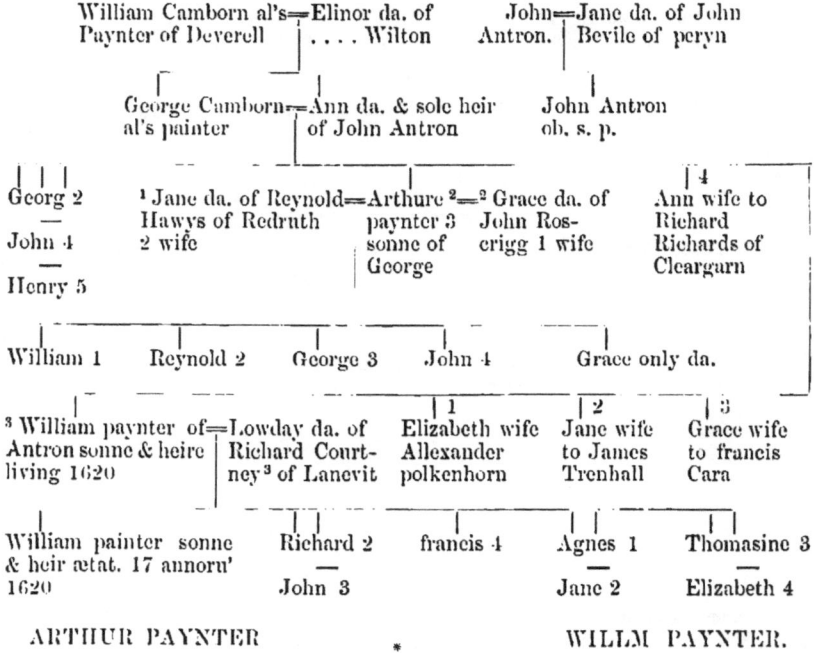

ARTHUR PAYNTER.   WILLM PAYNTER.

---

[1] Bur. at St. Erth 24 Jan., 1619-20. Bp. of Exeter's Transcripts.
[2] Grace da. Mr. J. Reskreek and Mr. Arthur Penter of St. Earth mar. at Anthony 2 Feb., 1597. Bp. of Exeter's Transcripts. (J. M.)
[3] By Indre. 22 May, 1555. Rich. Courtney of Tremere and William Paynter of Antorne in the Co. of Cornwall Esquires bound unto Hugh Bawden of the parish of Ken gent. in the sum of £120 to fulfil Indentures bearing same date made between the same parties (signed by Rich. Courtney only, seals gone). B. M. Add. Chart, No. 15,386.
* Balthazer Williams and Anna Paynter mar. at Stithians 24 Nov., 1630. Bp. of Exeter's Transcripts.

Francis Paynter of St. Earth, gent., and Margaret, da. of Francis Paynter of Boskenna St. Buryan, gent., mar. 8 July, 1706. Buryan Par. Reg.

George Painter and Petronell, da. of Walter Halamore,	mar.	30 Sept., 1602.	
Rachell, da. of George Painter, gent.,	bap.	9 April, 1604.	
Thomas, son	,,	7 July, 1610.	Gwinear
Alice, da.	,,	10 March, 1615-16.	Par. Reg.
George, son	,,	21 Feb., 1617-18.	
Rich., ,,	,,	29 Oct., 1619.	

Tristram Bath and Petronell Painter mar. 1696. Stithians Par. Reg.
Matthew Rutter and Loveday Painter mar. 11 May, 1669. Constantine Par. Reg.
William Paynter of Antron, Esq., named as a trustee in the settlement upon the marriage of Richard Gerveys of Benallack, gent., and Sara, daughter of George Yeo of Huish, Esq. Dated 14 April, 1653. Deed in possession of S. M. Grylls, of Lewarne, Esq. } (J. M.)
For. ped. of Antron, and more of Paynter, see Harl. MS. 1079. f. 236.

Pendarves.

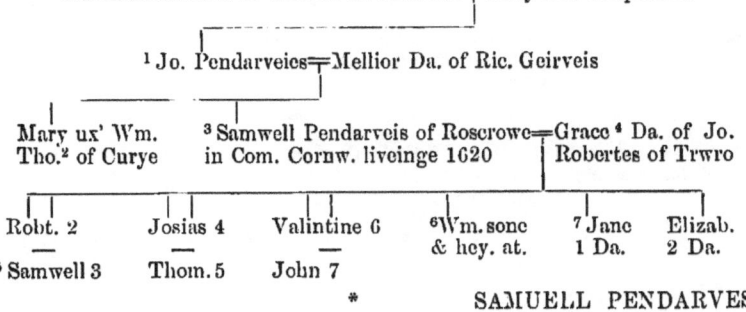

SAMUELL PENDARVES.

[1] Bur. 18 July, 1616. Constantine Par. Reg. (J. M.) Inq. p. m. 14 Jas., part 2, No. 85, Samuel Pendarves son and heir.
[2] William Thoms or Thomas.
[3] Æt. 43 and more 14 Jas. Mar. at Constantine to Mrs. Grace Roberts 24 June, 1598 (Bp. of Exeter's Transcripts); died 5 Sept., 1643; M. I. St. Gluvias Ch., and named with his wife and their son William in the will of William Roberts of St. Allen, merchant, 30 Jan., 1604, proved in London 1605.
[4] Bur. 23 July, 1662. M. I. Gluvias Ch.
[5] Bap. 13 July, 1603. } Truro Par. Reg.
[6] Bap. 20 July, 1600. }
[7] Jane, da. of Samuel Pendarves, gent., & Grace, bap. 11 June, 1611. Constantine Par. Reg.
* John, son of Samuel Pendarves, gent., bap. at Constantine 1599.

Thomas, son of Samuel Pendarves, bap. 18 Aug. and bur. 16 Sept., 1612, at Constantine.
Samuel Enys, gent., and Mrs. Elizab. Pendarves mar. 1647.
John Pendarves of Roscrowe, Esq., and Mrs. Bridget Carew ,, 6 May, 1658.
John, son of Samuel Pendarves, bap. 1619.
Mrs. Bridget Pendarves bur. 15 June, 1625.
Walter, son of John Pendarves of Roscrowe ,, 1663.
Madam Bridget Pendarves ,, 29 Mar,. 1701.
Mrs. Melior Pendarves .. 1715.
Walter, son of John and Bridget Pendarves, ob. 20 June, 1663.
William, ,, ,, ,, ,, ,, 14 Oct., 1693.
William Pendarves of Roscrow, Esq. ,, 4 June, 1673.
Anne, wife of do. ,, 3 Oct.. 1643.
Steven Pendarves, gent., bur. 12 Dec., 1676. Padstow Par. Reg.
Thos. Pendarvis bur. 1638. } Wendron Par. Reg.
William Pendarves ,, 1696. }
To Bridget Pendarves, da. of William Pendarves of Roskrow, Esq., a legacy under the will of John Tresahar of Constantine, prob. 1661. Bodmin.
Jane, da. of John Pendarves, gent., and Mellyor his wife, bap. 3 Sept., 1581. Constantine Par. Reg.
William Thomas, gent., and Mary Pendarves mar. 19 Nov., 1598, at Wendron. Bishop of Exeter's Transcripts.
Henry Pendarves, clerk, and Mrs. Mary Pearse, widow, mar. 8 Aug., 1701. Sancreed Par. Reg.
Thomas Pendarves, Rector, bur. 18 Mar.. 1703. St. Columb Major Par. Reg.
Rich. Pendarves, Esq., bur. 7 July. 1706, at St. Columb Major. Bp. of Exeter's Transcripts.
Mar. lic. between Randolph Pendarves of .... gent. and Elizabeth Boone of the same, 13 July, 1639. Exeter Act Books.

(Bp. of Exeter's Transcripts.) Gluvias Par. Reg. M. I. Gluvias Ch.

(J. M.)

Pendarves.

Tho. Pendarvis of Pendarvis in Camborne in Com. Cornub.=

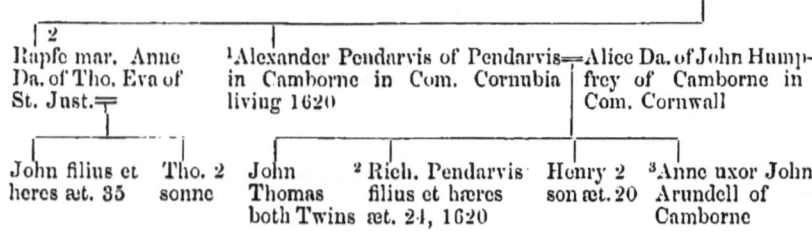

| 2 Rapfe mar. Anne Da. of Tho. Eva of St. Just.= | ¹Alexander Pendarvis of Pendarvis=Alice Da. of John Humphrey of Camborne in Com. Cornubia | Com. Cornwall |

| John filius et heres æt. 35 | Tho. 2 sonne | John Thomas both Twins | ² Rich. Pendarvis filius et hæres æt. 24, 1620 | Henry 2 son æt. 20 | ³Anne uxor John Arundell of Camborne |

* RICHARD PENDARVES.

Pendarvis.

David Pendarvis of Camborn in Com. Cornwall=

| Willm Pendarvis 2 son of david of Crowen in Com. Cornwall æt. 67 liveing 1620 | John Pendarvis of Constantine in Com. Cornwall son & hey. mar. Mellior da. of Rich. Jarvis of Constantine |

† RICHARD POLKENHORNE.

Penfoun.

Penfoun of Penfoun in the Parish of=Da. of Trevillian Pounstock in the hund. of Lesnuth

A

¹ Bur. 29 July, 1624. (Camborne Par. Reg.) Inq. p. m. 2 Chas. 1., Esch. Eliz., Jas., and Charles. part 20. No. 84. Alexander Pendarves, gent., died 28 July, 1624. Richard, his son and heir, aged 26 and more.
² Rich. Pendarves, gent., and Katherine Arundell, mar. 13 April, 1629.
³ John Arundell and Ann Pendarves, „ 29 Oct., 1617.
* John Williamsof Probus and Florence.da.of....Pendarves. „ 28 Sept., 1549. ⎫ Camborne
John Vavian and Ellyzabeth Pendarves wedded ye 26 Mar., 1570. ⎬ Par. Reg.
Will., son of Rich. Pendarves, gent., and Admonition, da. of Edw. Prideaux, ⎭
Esq., mar. 23 May. att Padstow, as per Register doth there appear, 1667.
Blanch, da. of Stephen Pendarves of London, merchant, bap. 1666. Phillack Par. Reg.
Sir William Pendarves, Knight, and Madame Powley Hoblyn were mar. 1714. St. Enoder Par. Reg.
Mar. lic. between John Courteney de Tregellas, ar., and Dorcas Pendarves, dated 1674.
Master Richard Pendarves, bur. 30 Dec. 1667. Truro Par. Reg.
Inq. p. m. 22 Jas, Esch. Eliz., Jas., and Chas., part 4, No. 24. Ralph Pendarves, gent., died 10 April, 22 Jas. John Pendarves, son and heir, aged 21 and more at the time of his father's death.
For more of Pendarves, see Harl. MS. 1079, f. 115.
† Raphe. son of John Pendarves, bapt. at Crowan 18 May. 1617. ⎫ Bp. of Exeter's
Rich., son of John Pendarvis and Blanche, bap. at Crowan 1619. ⎬ Transcripts.

THE VISITATION OF THE COUNTY OF CORNWALL.

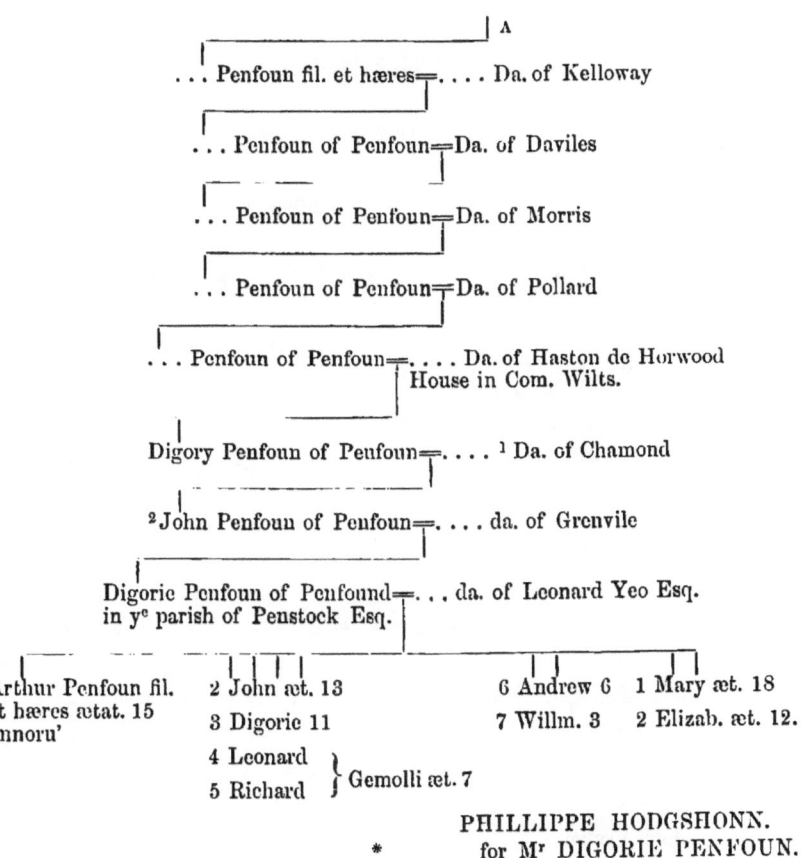

PHILLIPPE HODGSHONN.
for Mʳ DIGORIE PENFOUN.

---

[1] Jane, da. of Sir John Chamond. Harl. MS. 1079, fo.
[2] Had two daughters; Maria mar. to Hugh Corry, and Jane mar. to Andrew Corry. 'Visit. Devon, 1620,' p. 73.
* Chancery Proceedings, Eliz., P. p. 16, No. 4. John Penfownd v. Edward and Richard Penfownd (his brothers). Names Willyam Penfownd, Esquire, their father, to whose will defendants were executors. John Penfownd, complainant, son and heir, lands in Whitston.
Chancery Proceedings, Eliz. M. m. 14, No. 2. Benett Myll v. Richard Penfowne and Elizabeth his wife, widow of Nicholas Wykkett. Land in St. Gennys.

License of marriage between Arthur Penfound of Poundstock, gent., and Sibella Nicholls of St. Kew, 24 October, 1634. ⎫
License of marriage between John Penfound and Ann Pollexfen of Sherford, 25 August, 1673. ⎬ Exeter Act Books.
Anne, da. of Alexander Penfounde, bap. 23 Oct. 1621. ⎫
Jane,   ,,   ,,   ,,   26 Feb. 1622. ⎬ St. Columb (J. M.)
Humphry, son of Alex. and Margaret Penfound, ,, 3 Mar. 1624. ⎪ Par. Regs.
Grace, da. of   ,,   ,,   ,,   13 Jan. 1632. ⎭
Mr. George Wills and Mrs. Ebbott Penfound, mar. 3 Oct. 1682. Minster Par. Reg.
Degory Penfound, gent., bur. 22 Jan., 1671-2. Poundstock. Bp. of Exeter's Transcripts.

Penhallow.

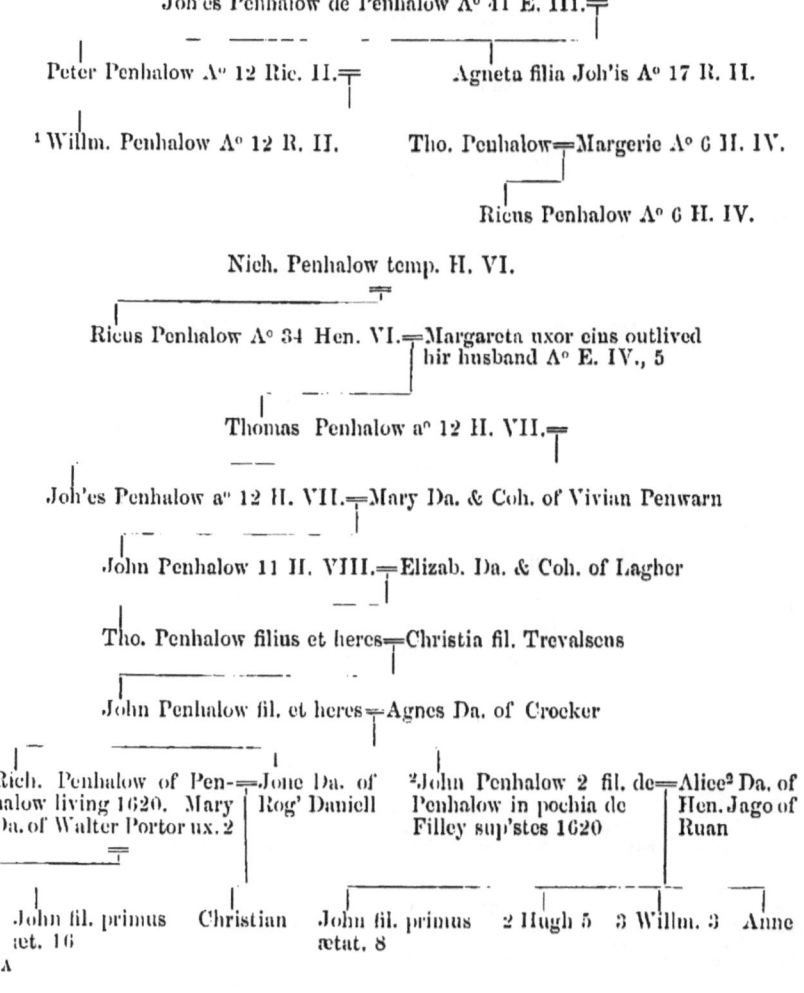

[1] Margareta Penhalow, A° 2 H. V.=Ricus Penhaloo. } (This is a marginal note in the original.)

[2] John Penhallow, gent., and Alyce Jagoe, mar. at Ruan Lanihorne, 1608. ⎫ Bp. of Exeter's
Hugh Penhallow, gent., and Elizab. Free, „ St. Clements, 18 Nov. 1641. ⎭ Transcripts.

THE VISITATION OF THE COUNTY OF CORNWALL. 167

| A

Chamon Pen-   3 Richard   4 Hugh   5 Emanuell   1 Elizab.   2 Mary   3 Susan
halow 2 son
                                    *   p' me JOHANE PENHALLOW.

Penhellick.

Walter Penhelleck of Penhellick=Margaret Da. of John Bosuysa

Walter Penhelleck fil. et heres=Alice Da. of John Trehey

John Penhellick of Illogan=Thomazin Da. of Jenken
in Com. Cornw.   Killivorne

John Penhelick of Penhelick fil. primogenitus=Mary Da. of Edm. Bee

Katherin mar. to Henry Nangothan=

Penhelek Nangothan

John Penhellick=Elizab. Da. of John Nancothan
2 sonne

John 1 son mar. Alice   Tho. Penhellick 2 sonne Ellinor Da. of
Da. of Boweyr=   Rich. Dowse of Totnes Devon=

Elizab. Da. & hey.   Christo-   John 2 son   Florence   Mary   Thomas 3 fil.
mar. to John   pher fil.   mar. Phillip   mar. to   ob.   ætat. 25 1620
Herbert of Helston   primog.   Da. of Tho.   John   virgo   —
                     ob. s. p.   Bligh of   Cock of   Humphrie 4
                                   Bodmin   Helston   fil. ætat. 22

Alexander Penhellick 3 son of John=¹ Florence Da. of Willm Tone
                                    | A

---

* Sara, da. of Jacob Penhallow, gent., bur. 1667. Madron Par. Reg.
  Will. Penhallow. gent., Filley,   Prob. 8 Mar. 1679. ⎫ Archd. of Cornw. ⎫
  Chamond Penhallow, gent., Filley, Adm. 30 Ap. 1690. ⎬   Bodmin.   ⎬(J. M.)
  Chamond Penhallow, gent., bur. at Fowey 19 Feb. 1689. Archdeacon's Trans. ⎭
  Ped. fin. 11 Will. East. Cornw. Hugh Boscawen qu. Baker, Penhallow, and o'rs, def. in
Tregoney Burg.

¹ Chancery Proceedings A.D. 1582, Eliz., P. p. 4, No. 36. Florence Penhellicke of Helston,
widow, v. Tho. Lukey, John Penhellick the younger, and o'rs. One-third part of Gweek wood.

THE VISITATION OF THE COUNTY OF CORNWALL.

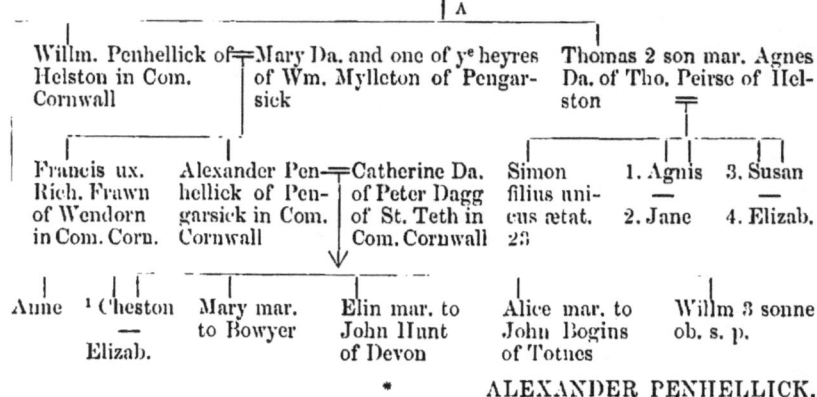

Willm. Penhellick of=Mary Da. and one of yͤ heyres | Thomas 2 son mar. Agnes
Helston in Com. | of Wm. Mylleton of Pengar- | Da. of Tho. Peirse of Hel-
Cornwall | sick | ston

Francis ux. | Alexander Pen-=Catherine Da. | Simon | 1. Agnis | 3. Susan
Rich. Frawn | hellick of Pen- | of Peter Dagg | filius uni- | — | —
of Wendorn | garsick in Com. | of St. Teth in | cus ætat. | 2. Jane | 4. Elizab.
in Com. Corn. | Cornwall | Com. Cornwall | 23

Anne | ¹ Cheston | Mary mar. | Elin mar. to | Alice mar. to | Willm 3 sonne
— | — | to Bowyer | John Hunt | John Bogins | ob. s. p.
 | Elizab. | | of Devon | of Totnes

ALEXANDER PENHELLICK.

Penrose.

Jo. Penrose of Secny in Com. Cornwall=

Barnard | ² John Penrose of Manacon=Nora Da. and sole hey. of John
1 sone | in Cornwall 2 sonne | Tregetho of Monacon

Edw. | Elinor uxor | Jo. Penrose of=Blandane Da. | Alice ux' | Grace ux'
2 | James Chris- | Monacon in | Abraha. Baker | Michaell | John
sone | topher of St. | Com. Cornw. | of Kilkhampton | Tanner of | Nicholl of
 | Erth inCornw. | liveing 1620 | in Cornw. | Monacco | St. Keverne

¹ Cheston mar. Gilbert Staplehill of Dartmouth. 'Visit. Devon, 1620,' p. 275.

* John Williams and Ann Penhillick mar. 31 Jany., 1665, at Helstone. Bp. of Exeter's Transcripts.
  John Penhellick and Phillip Bligh mar. 15 June, 1620 (see *ante*, page 12). Bodmin Par. Reg.

Alexander, son of Mr. John Penhellick	bap.	20 Oct., 1622.
Ann, dau. of Mr. Simon Penhallick,	„	27 May, 1632.
Humphry, son of Humphrey Penhallick,	„	2 Oct., 1634.
Elizabeth, da. of Mr. Humphry Penhallick	„	1 Nov., 1635.
Martha, dau. of Mr. Humphrey Penhellick, Mayor of Helston	„	28 July, 1638.
Thomas, son of Mr. Humphrey Penhellick	„	6 Jan., 1640.
Humphrey Penhellick and Grace Bolithoe	mar.	27 Nov., 1623.
John Penhellick, gent., bur.	bur.	Aug., 1603.
John, son of Mr. John Penhellick,	„	12 April, 1621.
Mr. Thomas Penhellick, jun.,	„	23 Jan., 1624.
Anna, wife of Thomas Penhellick, gent.,	„	18 Feb., 1627.
Mr. Symon Penhellick	„	20 Dec., 1635.
Mr. Thomas Penhellick	„	7 Feb., 1635.

Helston Par. Reg. (J. M.)

  John Penhellick of Helston, merchant, named in the marriage settlement of
Thomas Glynn the younger, of Helston, and Mary, dau. of Otho Polkinhorne, of the
parish of Gwynier. Dated 14 April, 1662. Deed in possession of S. M. Grylls, Esq.

² Chancery Proceedings A.D. 1592, Eliz. R.r. 2, No. 39. Roscrowgye v. Roscrowgye. Names
John Penrose of Tregethowe, gent., and Nora his wife.

THE VISITATION OF THE COUNTY OF CORNWALL. 169

Willm 2   James 3   Walter 4   John sone & hey   Avis ux^r Tho. Treourne
                                at. 18 1620   of Monacco
                                    *   JOHN PENROSE.

Penros.

Johes Tretherf Armig^r 2 vir.=Filia Trenowith Armige'

Reginaldus Trethref   Johes Treveno'=Filia Johis Tretherf

Willm. Trevenour=   Ricus Metheros

Johannes Penros=Phillippa fil.   Thomazin fil. et heres nupta Nicho. Enis

[1] Rich. Penros fil. et heres=Florence Da. of Tho. Erisey   John Enis sone & hey.

John Penros=Agneta fil. Johis   Thomas Enis=Christian Da. of
            Killegrew   John Boscawen

Bernard Penros=Elizab. Da. & hey. of Tho. Enis de Com. Cornw.

[2] Agneta fil. Emanuell=Tho. Penros of Penros Metheley=Agneta fil. Joh'is
Drwe de Com. Devon   in Com. Cornwall sup'stes 1620   Rashley de Foy
ux. 2   ux 1
                              A

* William Carlyan and Ann Penrose mar. 1619.   Ladock Par. Reg.
  James Williams and Jane Penrose mar. 1670.   Newlin in Pider Par. Reg.
  Edward, son of Jno. Penrose, gent., and Elizab. ux. bur. 1689.   Manaccan Par. Reg.
  John,   „   Thos. Penrose, gent.,   bap. 15 Sep., 1620.   Mullion Par. Reg.
  Edw.,   „   Jno. Penrose, Esq.,   bap. 1670. ⎫
  Barnard,   „   „   and Mary his wife „ 1672.   ⎬ Sithney Par. Reg.
  John,   „   „   „   „   „ 1674.   ⎪
  John Penrose, Esq.,   bur. 1680.⎭

Chancery Proceedings, Eliz., P. p. 9, No. 56.   Henry Penrose al's Nicholas and Margaret his wife v. Jno. Vyvyan al's Cooke.   Messuage called Trethias in St. Merryn and Porthvyan in Lower St. Columb claimed by Henry in right of his wife Margaret, da. of Mellyar, da. of Jno. Trethias.

Chancery Proceedings A.D. 1586, Eliz., M. m. 2, No. 52.   Peter Mark of Liskeard v. Martin Diggow and or's.   Claims Manor of Tredinnyal by purchase from Raphe Penrose of St. Syney (son of Bennett P., son of Joce Penrose), who granted a lease to defendants in Botallack in St. Just, part of said manor.

Chancery Proceedings, Elizab., R. r. 7, No. 19.   Resuygan and o'rs v. Trerraffe al's Treruthe. Romfray Penrose and Milyscnt his wife, da. of Thomas Cocke, are named as plaintiffs.

[1] Inq. p. m. V. O. 33 Hen VIII., No. 197.   Rich. Penrose ob. 19 Jan., 31 Hen. VIII.   John Penrose, his son and heir, æt. 21 and more, mar. to Agnes, da. of John Kyllygrew.

[2] Agnes, da. of Mr. Emanuel Drew, bap. 1552.   Kenne Par. Reg., Devon.

z

170 THE VISITATION OF THE COUNTY OF CORNWALL.

A |

3	4	5	6	7
Anne mar. to Wm Coley	Katherin mar. to Wm Robinson	Edy mar to Phil. Champ'non of Berie in Devon	Marg^t mar. to John Davy of Crediton in Com. Devon	Francisca unmaried

			1	2
Thomas æt. 40 — Edward æt. 38	John Penros fil. et heres ob. 1617	=Jane fil. Johis Trefuses of Miler	Alice mar. to John Hill of Gwendron	Marie mar. to Tho. Lukie of Perin

| John Penros fil. et heres ætat. 9 annoru' 1620 | Franciscus fil. 2 ætat. 4 annoru' | 1 Jane | 2 Mary | 3 Agnes[1] |

*

THOMAS PENROS.

Penwarne.

Thomas Penwarren of Penwaren=

John Penwarren of Penwarren=Margery da. to Vivian Penwaren of Mevagesye

Richard Penwaren of Pen-=Margaret da. of Rich.
warren in Mawnan   Bonythan of Kerclew

A

[1] Agnes, da. of John Penrose. Esquyre, bap. 24 Nov., 1616. Helston Par. Reg.
* Henry Penrose al's Trevenre & Christian Peryam, wid., mar. 20 Nov., 1605. Truro Par. Reg.
Richard Penrose and Cheston his wife were mar. 28 Sept. 1618. Gwinear Par. Reg.
Alex. Penrose and Judith Coterell mar. at Ruan Lanihorne 22 July, 1610. Bp. of Exeter's Transcripts.
Philip, son of Henry Penrose, gent., and Elizb. his wife, bap. 1688.⎫
Henry, „ „ „ Margery „ „ 1707. ⎬ Anthony in Menenge
Tho. Penrose, gent., and Mary Kestell, gent., mar. 1706. ⎪ Par. Reg.
Henry Penrose, gent., bur. 1703.⎭
Inq. p. m. 33 Edw. I., No. 120 b. Reginald. son of Richard de Penrees.
Inq. ad quod damp, 20 Edw. III., 2 Nos., No. 32. Roger de Penros. Lands, etc., in St. Berian. Joceus de Penros one of the Jury.
Inq. de ext. terr. 5 Hen. V., No. 68. John Penrose. a Prisoner. Manor of Penrose Methle.
By Indenture dated at Trewond 6 Sept., 8 Hen. IV.. John Penrose Methele gave to Jno. Boswathek and Katherine his wife, and their heirs, all his lands and tenements in Villa de Trewand and Tr . . . . , remainder to the heirs of said John Penrose Methele for ever. No seal. B. M. Add. Chart. No. 15,352.
⎡Penelope, da. of John Williams al's Boswathick, bap. 1695. Falmouth Par. Reg.⎤
⎣Frances Williams and Marg. Boswarthick   mar. 1697. Wendron Par. Reg.⎦
6° Elizab. Fine. Barnard Penrose Armiger qu. Henry Earl of Huntingdon, &c., and Katherine his wife, def. de medictat. manor of Harvena al's Harmena, &c., in Parish of St. Enoder. Barnard paid the Earl and his wife £40 sterling. B. M. Add. Chart. No. 15,370.
Richard Penrose was buried 25 Mar., 1608, at Fcock.
John Penrose & Prisella his wife, mar. 29 Oct., 1627, at Manaccan. ⎫
Mary, dau. of John Penrose, gent., bur. 28 Dec., 1628, ⎬ Bishop's Trans.
John Merrifield and Agnes Penrosse, mar. 14 Feb., 1550. St. Columb Major Par. Reg. ⎭
William Penrose and Dorothy Catcher, both of St. Clements, mar. 8 July, 1708. (J. M.)
Fcock Par. Reg.
Joane, dau. of John Penrose of Sythney, Esq., mar. 1 Mar., 1634. ⎫ Helston
Mr. George Phippen, Pastor of Lamoran, and Mrs. Mary Penrose. ⎬ Par. Reg.
mar. 20 June, 1648. ⎭

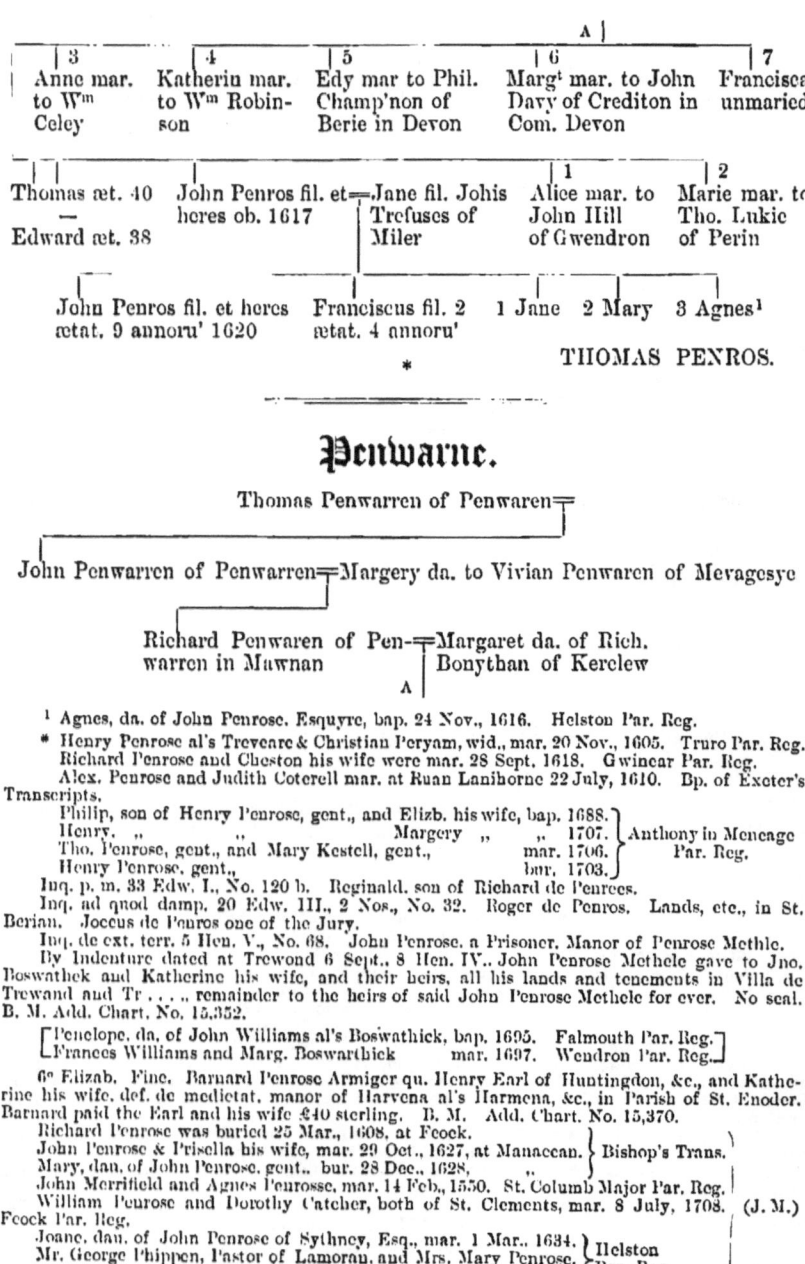

THE VISITATION OF THE COUNTY OF CORNWALL. 171

A

Richard Penwarren[1] of Penwarren in Mawnan = Jane[1] da. & coheir of Robt. Trencrecke of Treworgan | John 2 sonne | Robert 3 sonne

[2] Robt. Penwaren of Penwaren in St. Mawnan living 1620 = | Thomas Penwaren 2 sonne living 1620 of Mullion = Catherine da. of James Erysie | Grace 1 Ann 2 | Mary 3

Richard sonne & heir ætat. 1 yeare 1620 — ROBT. PENWARNE. * Mary 1 Eliza. 2 [3] frances 3 — THO. PENWARNE.

Plumleighe.

[4] John Plumleigh of Dartmouth in Com. Devon = ... Da. of Fortescue of Falopit in Com. Devon

Tho. Plumleigh of Townstall iuxta Dartmouth = Elizab. Da. of Robt. Shapleigh of Dartmouth

John Plumleigh of St. Mabin in Com. Cornwall gent liveinge 1620 = Jone Da. of John Sture of Huish in Com. Devon

Gilbert sone & hey. atat. 16 1620 | [5] Raphe 2 sonne atat. 10 . | Elizab. 1 Dau. at. 13 | [6] Grace 2 Da. at. 8 | [7] Joane 3 Da. at. 5 1620

† JO. PLUMLEIGHE.

---

[1] Rich. Penwarne, gent., and Jane. — mar. 1 Sept., 1572.
[2] Rob. Penwarne, Esq., — bur. 1658.
[3] Frances, da. of Tho. Penwarne, gent., — bap. 1618.
} Mawnan Par. Reg.

* Will. Arundell of Milcr, & Elizabeth, da. of Thos. Penwarne, mar. 1651.
Rich. Penwarne and Johana Deuse, mar. 7 Feb., 1606.
Penticoste, da. of Rich. Penwarne, bap. 27 May, 1607.
Margareta,   „   „   „   30 May, 1610.
} Truro Par. Reg.
John, son of Thos. Penwarne, gent., bap. 15 Sep., 1620. Mullion Par. Reg.
Richard Penwaren, witness to will of Tho. Poyle. P. P. C. A.D. 1502.
Nicholas Penwaryu, Lo. Willoby de Broke, Peter Bevyl, etc., Exors. to the will of Sir John Treffey. P. P. C. A.D. 1500.
Ped. fin. Cornw. 34 Edw. I, No. 7. Auger de Firsdon and Margery his wife qu. John de Penwarren and Isold his wife, def. Wadeford, etc.

[4] His 1st wife was a da. of Eastchurch, the 2nd was Ann, da. of John Foscue of Vallopit. ' Visit. Devon, 1620,' p. 211, which see for an extended pedigree.
[5] Bap. 13 May, 1611.   [6] Bap. 20 Sept., 1612.   [7] Bap. 9 July, 1615. } St. Mabyn Par. Reg. (J. M.)
† John, son of John Plumleigh, gent., and Jane his wife, bap, 15 March, 1620.
Joane, dau. of Ralph Plumleigh, gent., and Grace „   4 July, 1639.
Grace, dau. of   „   „   6 Mar., 1651.

[*Note continued on next page.*

Polwheile.

John Polewheele of Polewheele in the time H. VI.=Eizb. Da. of

Otes Polewheele of Polewheele=Alice Da. & sole hey. of Otes Lukye

Otes Polewheele of Polewheele=Margerie, Da. & sole hey of Walt' Killigrewe

Stephen Polewheele of Polewheele=Mary Da. of Erisse

John Polewheele of Polewheele=Da. & hey. of Tresoye of Tresoye

John Polewheele of Polewheele=Grace Da. of Lowre of Trelaske

Digorie Polewheele of Polewheele=Kathe' Da. & Cohey. of Rob. Trencreke
A

(*Note continued.*)

Mary, dau. of John Plumleigh by Anna,		bap.	April, 1652.	
John, son of John Plumleigh		,,	1652.	
John, ,, ,, gent., by Ann		,,	1 April, 1658.	
John, ,, ,, ,,		,,	18 Nov., 1659.	
Willm. ,, ,, ,,		,,	19 Nov., ——	
Charles, ,, ,, ,,		,,	5 June, 1662.	
William, ,, ,,		,,	14 July, 1611.	
Grace, dau. of ,,		,,	20 Sept., 1612.	
Mary, ,, John Plumleigh, gent., and Jane		,,	12 July, 1627.	
John, son of Ralph Plumleigh, gent., and Grace		,,	20 April, 1638.	
Thomas, ,, John Plumleigh, gent., by Ann		,,	10 Oct., 1634.	
Joseph, son of John Plumbleigh, gent., by Ann		,,	6 June, 1656.	
Wm. Hendar of Tintagell and Joane Plumbleigh		mar.	20 Jan., 1633.	
Giles Petty and Grace Plumbleigh		,,	1641.	
William Parnell and Jane Plumbleigh		,,	20 Jan., 1664.	
John Oliver, gent., and Mary Plumbleigh		,,	11 May, 1665.	St. Mabyn Par. Reg. (J. M.)
John Helman of Lanlivery and Honour, dau. of Ralph Plumleigh, gent.,		,,	18 Nov., 1675.	
Henry Stevens and Joan, dau. of John Plumleigh, gent.,		,,	12 Oct., 1682.	
Margaret, dau. of John Plumleigh, gent.,		bur.	20 Mar., 1610.	
Wm., son of ,,		,,	25 Sept., 1611.	
John, ,, ,,		,,	31 Aug., 1620.	
Thomas Plumleigh, gent.,		,,	24 July, 1615.	
John, son of Ralph Plumleigh,		,,	20 April, 1638.	
Ralph Plumbleigh, gent.,		,,	16 Aug., 1658.	
John Plumbleigh, gent.,		,,	7 Feb., ——	
Wm., son of John Plumbleigh, gent.,		,,	19 Jan., 1659.	
Thomas, ,, ,,		,,	12 Mar., ——	
Elizabeth, dau. of Ralph Plumleigh, gent.,		,,	5 April, 1660.	
Joan Plumbleigh, widow,		,,	7 Nov., 1667.	
Charles, son of John Plumbleigh, gent., by Ann,		,,	16 April, 1685.	
John Plumbleigh, gent.,		,,	4 Sep., 1689.	
Mrs. Anne Plumbleigh, relict of John P., gent.,		,,	20 Jan., 1694.	
Grace Plumbleigh		,,	24 Jan., 1697-8.	

Adm'n of the goods, etc., of Ralph Plumleigh, late of St. Mabyn, dec'd, granted 27 Oct., 1658, to Grace Plumleigh, relict of dec'd.—P. C. C. (J. M.)

		A				
Susan ux' Jo. Webber of St Kue	Mary ux' Jo. Chatley of Truro	¹Tho. Polewheele of Pole-wheele in Com. Cornw. liveing 1620		¹Dionesst Da. of Judge Glanvile of Tavistock		

John sone & hey. at. 14 1620	Fran. 2 sone at. 12	Tho. 3 sonne at. 10	Alice at. 9	Digorie at. 4	Rob. 2	Anne half yeare

John 2 — Phillip 3	William 4 sonne of London	Otes 5 sone	Digorie 6 sone liveing in London	Jonathan 7 sonne	Anne ux' Wm Hearl of Bericon erber in Devon

* THOMAS POLWHEILE.

Polkinghorne.

Sciant p^{r}sent. et futur. q^d ego Rogerus de Polkenhorne dedi concessi et hac presenti carta mea confirmavi Johi filio meo un'm messuag. in Truru etc. Dat' apud Polkenhorne die sab' prox. ante festu' circumcisionis D'ni anno Regni regis E. III. a conquestu primo.

Sciant present. et futur. q^d ego Willmus fil. Joh'is de Polkenhorne dedi concessi et hac p^{r}senti carta mea confirmavi etc. hijs testibus D'no Michael Vicarie Ecclie de Wyniore, Joh'ne Bois et alijs. dat' apud Polkenhorne die Dominico prox. post festu' sc'i etc. A° regni regis Rici. II. 8.

Sciant p^{r}sent et futur. q^d ego Willm's de Polkenhorne dedi concessi etc. Dat' apud Polkenhorne a° Regni regis R. II. 15.

---

¹ Thos. Polwheele, filius Digorii Polwheele de Parochia Scti Earme Armigeri et Duena Glanvill (filia Johis Glanvill defuncti olim unus ex Justiciarys Domini Regis de curia Common Plees), nupti fuere Tercio die Marcii 1606. Breage Par. Reg.
"*Dionisia nupta Thomæ Polwheile, Ar.*" Inscription on Judge Glanville's Tomb, Tavistock Church.

* Katherine, da. of Thomas Polwheele, bap. 1608. Breage Par. Reg.
    Ped. fin. 4 James, Mic., Cornw. Edw. Skirrett, gen., Edw. Vivian, gen., Edm. Dowriche, gen., qu. Digory Polwhele ar. et Katherine ux. ejus. Tho. Polwhele, gen., def. 30 mess., etc. ; 40 gard. and orch., 1000 acr. ter., 300 mead., 100 past., 40 wood, 2000 Down, 100 more, 40 sh. reddit. in St. Herme, Clements, Truro Burg., Kenwyn, Key, Gwendron, Gwynyer, Helston Boro', Cuthbert, Newlyn, Probus, and Tregoneyboro. £400 paid.
    Ped. fin. 21 James, East, Cornw. John Drake, jun., and Will. Polwheile, qu. ; Jo. Gerry, def. Land in Tavistock.
    Stephen Trewbody and Anne Polwhile, wief of Stephen P., dec., mar. 4 July, 1597. St. Clement's Par. Reg.
    License of marriage betw. Stephen Polwheele, gent., and Susan Lauder of Kenwyn, 14 May, 1662.
    Francis, son of John Polwhele, Esq., bur. 1678. Tavistock Par. Reg.
    License of marriage between John Polwheele, Clerk, Vicar of Whitechurch, and Elizabeth Browne of Tavistock, 9 June 1623.
    License of marriage between Gregory Stubley and Anne Polwheele of Treworgan, 21 June, 1673.   Exeter Act Books.
    Margaret Polwhele, widow, buried 25 Mar., 1612, at St. Allen. Bishop's Trans.   (J. M.)
    Mr. Francis Polyheil (Polwhele ?) bur. 8 June, 1678. Lanhydrock Par. Reg.
    Mr. Philip Polwheele, Clerk, buried 9 Mar. 1663. St. Kew Par. Reg.
    Margaret Polwheele, Probus 27 Sept., 1683, Adm. Archdeaconry of Cornwall, Bodmin.

174 THE VISITATION OF THE COUNTY OF CORNWALL.

Sciant p'sentes et futur. q^d nos Rob'tus Tubba et Ricus Roscreek dedimus et concessimus Nicho. Polkenhorne et Elizab. uxori eius filio Johis Renolds etc. Dat' decimo die mensis Julij Anno Regni regis Ed. IV. post conq. Angl. 19.

Roger Polkinhorne a° 1 E. III.⊤

Johannes Polkinhorne⊤

Will'ms Polkinghorne A° 8 R. II. et 15=

Nicholas Polkinhorne A° 19 E. IV.=Elizab. filia Johis Renolds

Bowdon Gascoyne of St. Ives in Com. Cornwall⊤

John Gascoyne=Da. & heyre of John Hell

John Hell=Joane fil. et her. Johis Gascoyne

Nicho. Hell⊤

Willm Hell⊤

Rich. Nancothon=Jewunnt Da. & hey. of Wm. Hell

Robt. Nancothon⊤

Jo. Nancothon=

Thomas Polkinghorne of Polkinghorne mar. the Da. of Opy of Bodmin⊤

3 |
Raph. Polkinghorne of Guiniard in Cornw. bought the Mann' of Dynasia & porthin of Jo. Nacothon being his Kinseman
=Katherin Da. of Tho. Coswyne of Guinerby whome he had landes

1 |
John Polkinghorn of Polkinghorne mar. the Da. & hey. of Olver of Bodmin

2 |
Willm. Polkinghorne of Breague mar. the Da. of Cowling

1
Kath' Da. of Tho. Dewen
=John Polkinghorne of Gwiner in Com. Cornw. liveing 1620
=Kath' Da. of Tho. Wolcott

Thomas Polkinghorne sone & heyre mar.⊤

Henry Polkinghorne fil. primogenitus.

John sonne & heire

Roger Polkinghorne fil. et haeres

p' me JOHN POLKINGHORNE.

THE VISITATION OF THE COUNTY OF CORNWALL.   175

Polkinhorne.

Tho. Polkinhorne

John Polkinhorne[1] of Polkinhorne = Elizab. Da. & hey. of Tho. Oliver of
in Com. Cornwall   Bodmin in Com. Cornwall

Tho. Polkinhorne[2] of Polkinhorne* = Catherine Da. of Rich. Pella-
in Com. Cornwall   mounter in Com. Corn.

Thomas 2 sonne æt. 40	2 Grace unma^r æt. 34	1 [3] Mary ux^r Warne Pryor of Gwendier	John Polkinhorne of Polkinhorne in Com. Cornwall filius et hæres æt. 44	Alice Da. of Otes Edy of Bodmin in Com. Cornwall	3. Richard æt. 38 — 4. James æt. 33

Otes Polkinhorne filius et heres æt. 20	Catherine 1 Da. æt. 13 — [4] Margery 2 Da. æt. 4	[5] Tho. 2 son æt. 18 — John 3 son æt. 16 †	4. Willm æt. 15 —. 5. Roger æt. 14	6. Raphe [6] æt. 12 — 7. Stephen [7] æt. 6

JOHN POLKINHORNE.

[1] Bur. 19 March, 1565-6.
[2] Mar. 11 Jan., 1564-5 ; died 4 Dec. and bur. 6 Dec., 1610.
[3] Bap. 15 Aug., 1582.
[4] Bap. 7 Feb., 1616-17.   } Gwinear
[5] Bap. 10 Feb., 1601-2.   Par. Reg.
[6] Bap. 15 May, 1609.
[7] Bap. 20 May, 1613.

* Chancery Proceedings A.D. 1581, Eliz., P. p. 4. No. 93. Thomas P. claimed a tenement and four acres of land called Traytor in parish of Padstowe as his by right of descent from Thomas Olyver, father of Elizabeth, his mother.

† Esch. Eliz. Jas. and Chas., part 25, No. 77. John Polkinhorne, gent., died 20 Oct., 1638. Otho P., son and heir, aged 30 and more.

John Polkinhorne and Catherine his wife   mar.   14 Jan., 1584-5.
Mr. John Polkinhorne and Catherine   „   18 Feb., 1594-5.
Thos. Glynn of the Boro' of Helston mar. Mary the da.
 and heir of Otho Polkinhorne of Polkinhorne   22 April, 1662.
Margaret, da. of Mr. Thos. Polkinhorne, bap.   June and bur.   6 Aug., 1571.
Elizabeth, „   „   „   „   20 Aug., 1572, bur. 17 Sept., 1572.
John, son of Thos. Polkinhorne,   „   11 Nov., 1573.
Blanch, da. of Mr. Thos. Polkinhorne,   „   15 Mar., 1574-5. bur. 30 Sept., 1580.
Grace,   „   „   „   „   25 Sept., 1583.   Gwinear
William, son of Thomas   „   „   8 Oct. and   bur. 12 Oct., 1583.   Par. Reg.
Avis,   da. of   „   „   „   1587,   „   7 Dec., 1610.
Katherine, „   „   „   „   7 Jan., 1586-7.
Jane,   „   Mr. John Polkinhorne,   „   1 Feb., 1600.
Katherine,   „   John Polkinhorne, gent., bap.   1610.
Elizabeth,   „   John Polkinhorne of Polkinhorne,
                                        bap. 25 June. 1615, bur. 3 Oct., 1616.
James, son of Mr. John Polkinhorne, „   6 Aug., 1619, bur. 26 Nov., 1619.
Nicholas, „   John Polkinhorne, gent., „ 18 Aug., 1608, bur. 6 Oct., 1608.

[*Note continued on following page.*]

Pollard.

Christopher Pollard filius=Jana fil. Rici Erlesman in Insula Victis in Com. South.

¹ Christop. ob. s. p. | ² Benjamin Pollard fil. ætatit unius anni | 1. Anna³ 6 | 2. Gertrud 4 | 3. Jane⁴ 2

* CHRISTOPHER POLLARD.

Pomeroy.

John Pomeroy of Colliton in pochiæ=Da. of Strowd de Newton Ferrers in Co. Devon | of Pardnon

Andrew Pomeroye of Colliton=Anne Da. of Sr Geo. Mathewe in Com. Devon | of Wales

A

(*Note continued.*)

Zenobia, da. of Thos. Polkinhorne,	bur.	16 Sept., 1575.
Jane, ,, ,,	,,	20 March, 1578-9.
Thomas, son of Mr. Thomas Polkinhorne,	,,	17 May, 1586.
Catherine, wife of John Polkinhorne,	,,	28 Feb., 1588-9.
James, son of John Polkinhorne, gent.,	,,	8 Feb., 1600-1.
Katherine, wife of John Polkinhorne, gent.,	,,	16 March, 1610-11.
Otho Polkinhorne, gent.,	..	1665.

Gwinear Par. Reg.

Nicholas Polkinghorne and Jane Stephen mar. at Breage 28 Nov., 1601.   Bp. of Exeter's Transcripts.

Jas. Williams and Margaret Polkinghorn, mar. 15 April, 1644.   Breage Par. Reg.

Otho, son of John Polkinhorne, gent., baptized 1599.   Bodmin Par. Reg.
Mary, dau. of Pascho Polkinhorn   bap. 1582. } St. Columb Major
Richard Tregennowe and Jane Polkinhorn mar. 1632. }   Par. Reg.   (J. M.)
License of marriage between Roger Polkinhorne of Maddern, gent., and Blanche Elise of the same, 25 January, 1626.

¹ Christopher, son of Christopher Pollard, gent., bap. 28 Nov., 1616, bur. 20 Aug., 1620,					
² Bengymyn,	,,	,,		..	19 April, 1633.
³ Amy,	dau. of	,,		bap.	4 Sept., 1613.
⁴ Jane,	,,	,,		,,	15 Oct., 1617.
Christopher, son of	,,	and Jane,		,,	24 May, 1624.
Gilbert,	,,	,,		..	May, 1627.
Margaret,	dau. of	,,	,,	..	16 Oct., 1628.
Mary,	,,	,,		..	30 Dec., 1626.
Edward,	son of	,,	and Jane,	..	12 Dec., 1628.
Jane,	dau. of	,,		..	1 Nov., 1628.
John Toker, jun., gent., and Protesia Pollard				mar. 17 Dec., 1683.

St. Mabyn Par. Reg. (J. M.)

* Chancery Proceedings A.D. 1593, Elizab., P. p. 7 No. 55.   Pollard v. Chiverton and o'rs. Names Alexander Pollard of St. Hillary and Thomas Pollard, his son.

Charles Pollard and Frances Godolphin mar. 19 Nov., 1698.   Tywardreath Par. Reg.

Lewis Pollard, Esq., and Mistris Mary Fortescue mar. 9 May, 1611, at Filleigh.   Bp. of Exeter's Transcripts.

THE VISITATION OF THE COUNTY OF CORNWALL. 177

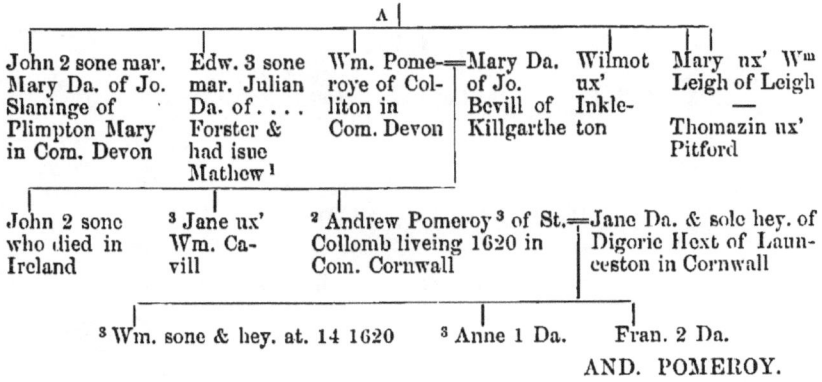

AND. POMEROY.

Pomeroy.

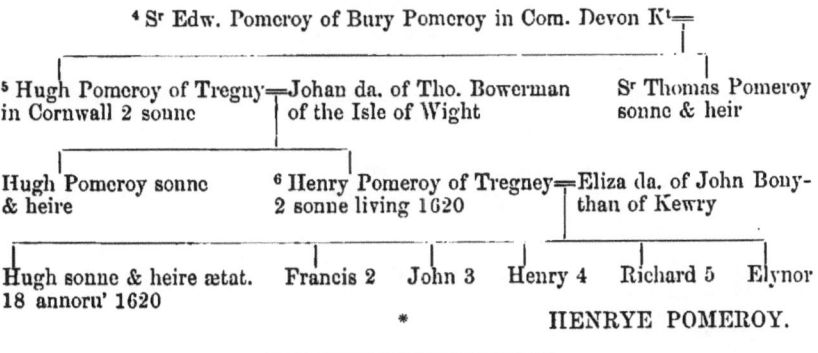

HENRYE POMEROY.

---

[1] Bur. 31 May, 1634.
[2] „ 22 Nov., 1639. } St. Columb Par. Reg. (J. M.)
[3] Named in the will of John Pomeroy of St. Cleere, gent., 16 June, 1618, in which is also named Matthew, son of *Ellis* Pomeroy, deceased (qy. Edward). Proved in London 12 March, 1619. Witnesses Pascowe Vivian, Pascowe Vivian, jun., and Rich. Vivian.
[4] Son of Sir Rich. Pomeroy, Sir Edw. died 21 Oct., 30 Hen. VIII. Thomas Pomeroy, his son and heir, aged 35 and more. Esch. Inq. p. m. 30 and 31 Hen. VIII., Cornw., No. 7. Names his wife Johanna, da. of Sir John Sapcot, and the Manor of Tregoney.
[5] Ob. 23 Sept., 7 Eliz. Inq. p. m., 8 Eliz., No. 50. Hugh Pomeroy, son and heir, æt. 11. Names Sir Thomas Pomeroy, his brother.
[6] Mar. 15 Apr., 1600. St. Columb Par. Reg. (J. M.) Mayor of Tregoney, 1620.
* Walter Jenkyn and Ann Pomeroy, mar. 27 Oct., 1628. St. Columb Par. Reg. (J. M.)
Gregory Pomeroy and Joane Broade, mar. 17 Nov., 1617.
Rich., son of Gregory Pomerie, bap. 14 Jan., 1617–18. } St. Ewe Par. Reg.
Grace, da. of „ „ 22 Oct., 1620.
Cor. Reg. King John, No. 6. Hen. de la Pomeroy v. John Russell and Rohaysia de la Pomeroy, his wife, plea of dower. Rohays de la Pomeroy for her husband John Russell v. Henry de la Pomeroy, her son, in a plea of dower.
Inq. prob. æt. 15 Edw. I., No. 72. Henry, son of Henry de la Pomeroy, born at Tregoney, and baptized in the church of the said town, 22 years of age on the Friday after Feast of Pentecost, 15 Edw. I.
Inq. p. m. 27 Ed. I., No. 32. Henry de la Pomeroye and Peter Corbet consang. et hæred. of Roger de Valle Torte.
Ped. fin. 29 Eliz., Ea. Rich. Carveth qu. Hen. Pomeroy gen. def. Ten't in Penwarne Chidown, etc.

2 A

Porter.

[1] Walt' Porter of the Counties of Cornwall = Gartrude Da. of Rich. Chamond

- Peter Porter 2 sonne of Launcells = Suzun Da. of [2] Digory Grenvile
  - John 1 sone atat. 16 1620
- Rich. Porter of Lancelles in Com. Cornw. liveing 1620 atat. 44
  - Rich. 2 sone at. 14

* *Not signed.*

---

[1] Inq. p. m. 24 Eliz., No. 7. Walter Porter died 17 Jan., 24 Eliz. Rich. Porter, son and heir, æt. 5 years 7 July last. Recites will of Walter, dated 14 Jan., 1581, in which are named his wife Gertrude, sons Peter and John, da. Mary, and his bro. Emanuel Chamond. Richard Porter, his son, sole Ex'r.

[2] Will of Barnaby Leigh of St. Catherine's, Devon, dated 20 Aug., 1616, proved London, 15 May, 1618. Names his sister Porter (probably this Susan) and his mother, Mrs. Phillip Grenville ; and we find, 'Visit. Devon, 1620,' p. 226, that Phillip, da. of Hugh Prust, mar. 1, Wm. Leigh, and 2, Digory Grenvile.

* Inq. p. m. 8 Eliz., No. 175. John Porter died 24 August, and Walter, son of Walter Porter, bro. and heir of said John, and aged 10 years and more.

Mr. Richard Porter, Esq., and Mrs. Mary Mollesworth.	mar. 21 Aug., 1628.	Egloshayle Par. Reg.
Mary, dau. of Richard Porter, Esq., of the parish of Launcells,	bap. 14 May, 1637.	St. Kew Par. Reg.
Mr. Thomas Porter was presented to the Rectory of this parish	15 June, 1629.	
Thomas, son of Thomas Porter, Rector of St. Malyn, by Sarah his wife,	bap. 15 Mar., 1639.	
Mary, da. of Christ. Porter, gent., by Elizab.,	,, 1 Jan., 1670.	
Thomas, son of ,, ,,	,, 28 Dec., 1671.	
Lucy, da. of ,, by Eliz.,	,, 13 Oct., 1673.	
Thomas, son of ,, ,,	,, 20 Aug., 1683.	
Christopher, ,, ,, ,,	,, 20 Jan., 1686.	
John, ,, ,,	,, 19 June, 1688.	
Charles, ,, ,,	,, 17 June, 1690.	
Endymion, ,, ,,	,, 1 Oct., 1692.	St. Malyn Par. Reg.
Walter Langollen, gent., & Mrs. Ann Porter,	mar. 15 June, 1658.	
Thomas Fornell, gent., & Mrs. Mary Porter,	,, 30 Dec., 1658.	
Mr. Charles Porter & Mrs. Mary Caffin, of Launceston,	,, 24 June, 1711.	(J. M.)
John, son of Thomas Porter, Rector, by Sarah,	bur. 5 July, 1639.	
Thomas Porter, gent., son of Mr. Thomas Porter, Rector,	,, 23 Jan., 1666.	
Sarah Porter, wife of Thomas Porter, Rector,	,, 12 May, 1668.	
Thomas Porter, Rector,	,, 30 Sep., 1668.	
Christ., son of Christ. Porter, gent., by Elizab.,	,, 15 Oct., 1681.	
Elizab., wife of Mr. Christ. Porter,	,, 17 May, 1701.	
William, son of ,, ,,	,, 14 May, 1706.	
Wm., son of Robert Porter, gent.,	bap. 1665.	
George, ,, Wm. and Grace Porter,	,, 1688.	
Mr. Robert Porter and Alice Taverner,	mar. 21 Feb., 1663.	
Wm. Porter and Grace, dau. of George Bastard, of Lanteglos,	,, 1688.	St. Teath Par. Reg.
Robert Porter, gent.,	bur. 1676.	
Alice Porter, widow,	,, 1682.	
George, son of Wm. Porter,	,, 1691.	
Grace, wife of William Porter, gent.,	,, 1699.	

Porter.

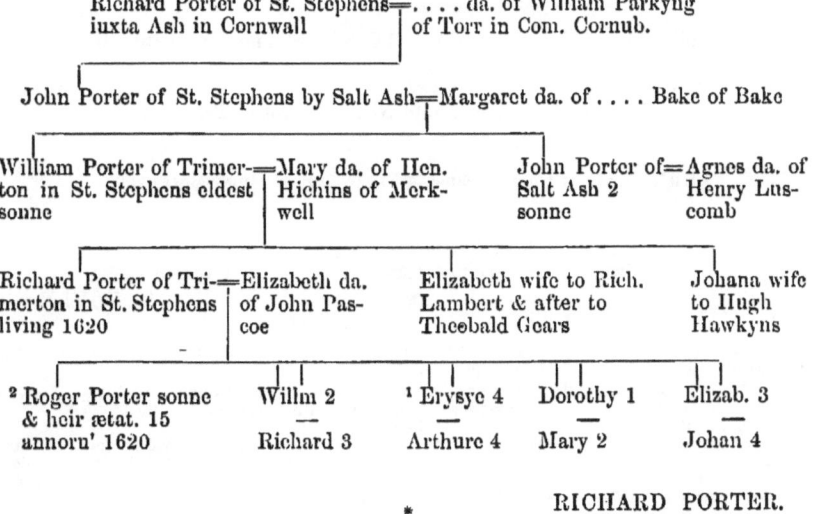

RICHARD PORTER.

[1] Erisye, son of Richard Porter, gent., bap. 5 Jan., 1615, at St. Stephen's by Saltash.
[2] William, son of Roger Porter, gent., „ 9 Oct., 1633, „

} Bishop's Trans.

* Christopher Osmond, gent., and Marye Porter, mar. 26 Mar., 1627. Kilkhampton Par. Reg.

St. Stephens by Saltash. William Porter, gent., prob. 23 Sept., 1675.
                                   Roger Porter, gent., „ 31 Oct., 1677.
                                   Elizabeth Porter, „ 2 May, 1679.
St. Mabyn.   Thomas Porter, „ 19 Sept., 1666.
St. Teath. 1677. Robert Porter. W.
Plymouth. 1672. Francis Porter, clerk. W.

} Wills: Archdeaconry of Cornwall.
} Wills: Principal Register, Exeter.

(J. M.)

Will of Thomas Porter, Rector of St. Mabyn, dated June, 1668. To be buried in chancel of St. Mabyn Church. Names daughters Alice Porter, Sarah Elford, Mary Howell, Ann Langollan, and son Christopher Porter, who he makes sole executor. Probate 20 Jan., 1668-9. Coke, 9 P. C. C.
Inventory of the goods of Richard Porter of Launcells, 2/6, 24 June, 1631.
License of marriage between Michael Porter of Launceston, clerk, and Alice Jennings, widow, of Plymouth, 22 July, 1642. Exeter Act Book.
Ped. fin. Cornw. 38 Hen. III., No. 1. Henry le Porter, qu. Reginald le Porter, def. A knight's fee in Treseles on the death of Reginald to remain entirely to Henry and his heirs, as held of Reginald and his heirs for ever by payment of 2s. annually at Michaelmas.
Chancery Proceedings, A.D. 1579, Elizab. P. p. 3, No. 11. Porter v. Battin. Names William, Richard, Bartholomew, and Jane, children of Thomas Porter and Agnys his wife, who afterwards mar. defendant, John Battin. Will of Thos. Porter dated 29 Aug., 1558; proved before Thos. Fuyge, Official of the Archdeaconry of Cornwall, 10 Oct., 1558.

Poyle.

ARMS.—*Argent a Brake Sa.*

Rob. Poyle of Tregney=

John Poyle of Tregney=Da. and Coh. of Sr Tho. Tregarthan K{t}

Jo. Poyle of Tregney=Da. of Nicho. Barrat of Tregardon

¹ Rich. Poyle of Castlecesanse=Elizb. Da. of Hugh Boscawen

Nicho. Poyle of Castlezance in=Elizb. Da. of Hugh
Com. Cornw. liveinge 1620 Monday of Tregney
*   NICH. POYLE.

---

¹ Rich. Poyle, ob. 9 July, 35 Eliz. Nicholas, son and heir, æt. 14 at time of father's death. Castlesans, etc. Inq. p. m. 36 Eliz., 2 pt., No. 43.

* Nicholas, the son of Mr. Poyle, was buried 9 Nov., 1563. St. Mabyn Par. Reg. ⎱ (J. M.)
John Hender and Willmet Poyle mar. 1657. St. Teath Par. Reg. ⎰
Ralph Poyle bur. 1626. Padstow Par. Reg.
Tho. Poyle of Tregoney. Will, many bequests to Churches, Tregony, Bodmin, etc. Residue to wife Joan. Names sons Robert, Richard, and Martin, who were appointed exors. in succession after Joan. Henry Pester,(*) Ric. Penwerin.(*) and o'rs. witnesses. P. P. C. A.D. 1502. Blamye, 163.
Robert Poyle.(*) Will, 10 Sept., 1502 ; to be buried in the Church of St. Frembaron of Fowcy.. to the building of the said Church, " all my part of a ship called the De le An of Fowey ;" legacies to Tho. Trevroi (Treffry) and the Vic. of Fowey. Residue to Ric. Haryngton,(*) his father-in-law, and Tho. Poyle, his brother, whom he appointed executors for the protection of his daughter Joane. He bequeathed to each son of his brother a silver cup. Hen. Pester,(*) Supervisor. P. P. C. at Lambeth, Dec.. 1502. (Blamye, 163.)
Ped. fin. 1 and 2 Ph. and Mary. East. Cornw. John Tremayne and o'rs. qu. ; J. Poyle, def. ten. in Tregoney and Cornelly.
Ped. fin. 22 Elizb. Hil. Cornw. Jno. Dallamayne, qu. John Poyle and o'rs, def. Ten't in Tregarrock, etc.
Ped. fin. 43–4 Eliz. Mich. Cornw. Ric. Coga, qu. ; Nich. Poile, def. tent. in Trevalla Vean.
.. 16 James. East. Cornw. Andrew Avent and Hugo Munday, qu. ; Nicholas Poyle, gen., def. Lands in Castlesins al's Castellzens, Elerkie al's Verian, Trewolla-Vean. Goran, Helligan al's Heligan, Kestell, St. Ewa, Benga-Cubie, Penboghe. Saynt Stephen's in Brannell, Oxford Park, and Clements, etc. £120 paid.
Richard Harrington of Fowey. Ped. fin. 8 Hen. VII.=Margaret, da. of Jno. Herle of Prideaux Trin., Cornw. Commissioned to try Pirates at Fowey. | Herle and Anne his wife, da. and h. of Pat. Roll. 1st Edw. V. | Jno. Salter of Foye.(*)

Anne=Robert Poile.

Jane Poile, so. da. and h.=Thomas Petit, 2nd husb. (in whom the male line of Petit ended.)

Alice, so. da. and h.=James Tresahar of Trevethan.

(Harl. 4031. fo. 78 and 72. Add. MSS. 14315. Benolt's Visit. of A.D. 1531. Treffry MS. at Place Fowey, and Sir John Maclean's ' Hist. of Trigg.' vol. i. p. 683.)
In the list of knights summoned from Cornwall, A.D. 1277, to attend King Edw. I. at Worcester, on service against Llewellyn ap Griffith, we find the names of Walter de la Poylle, Ralph Bassett, Tho. le Ercedekne, Rob. D'Aumarle, Henry de Ralegh, Robt. de Dyneham, Robert Malet, etc., knights. For Sir Walter de la Poyle, John de la Poyle, his son, offered to perform the service of half a fee in Hampton (Hampton, Poyle, Oxfordsh.) "qui idem Walterus est de familia Com. Cornub." Cott. Claud. C. II., fos. 52, 55.
Inq. p. m. 27 Ed. I. No. 41. Walter de la Poyle. John, s. and h., æt. 25.
In a window of the Manor Ho. of Sutton Valence were the arms of De la Poyle.—*A. a saltire Gu. with a bord. Sa. bezantée.* Hasted's ' Kent.' vol. ii.. p. 412 n. Presumably of Cornish origin, from the border Sa. bezantée.
Coram Reg. Ro. 30 Ed. I. Cornw. Roger de la Poylle named.
(*) Named in the will of Sir John Treffry P. P. C. 19 Feb.. 1500. (Moone. 20.) See Treffey. *post*.

Pye.

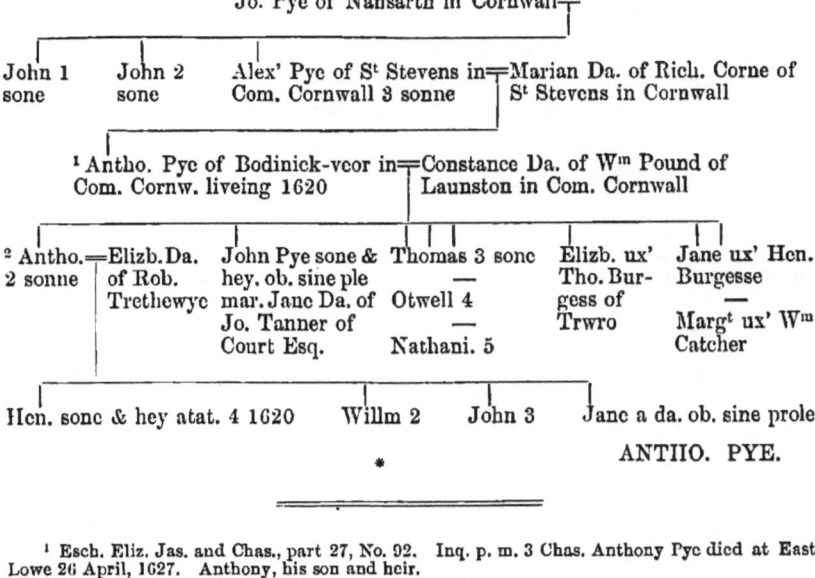

ANTHO. PYE.

---

[1] Esch. Eliz. Jas. and Chas., part 27, No. 92. Inq. p. m. 3 Chas. Anthony Pye died at East Lowe 26 April, 1627. Anthony, his son and heir.
[2] Aged 30 and more at the time of his father's death.
* Chancery Proceedings, Eliz., P. p. 14, No. 13. Anthony Pye v. Rich, Pengelley. Lands, etc., in Grampound.

William Tremayne and Anna Pye mar. 13 Aug., 1579. Entered also in St. Ewe Par. Reg. }
Robert Benett and Betonia Pye „ 26 Oct., 1600. } Truro Par. Reg.

Ped. fin. 10 James, Hill., Cornw. Anthony Pye gen. and Hugh Trevanion gen. qu. Tho. Tresahar gen. and Anna Tresahar vid. def. Lands in Govyly Vean, Fentongocock al's Fentongocth, Tresoren al's Soren, and Kebye (Cuby); one-third part of the Manor of Trelowyth with its appurt's, a part of Trelowith the lower, Naphissick, Tregantallan al's Tregandallen, Bossinver, Mewan, Saynt Tewe alias Eva, etc.

Ped. fin. 12 James, East. Cornw. Ant. Pye gen. qu. John Carveighe gen. and Barbara ux. and Ric. Carveigh def. Lands in Tregerthick, Trenynnock, Rayles, Streete, l'ortheast, &c., in Saynt Goran.

Ped. fin. 3 Chas. Mic. Cornw. Hen. Boscawen, qu. Jno. Hoare and Joane ux. Anthony Pye, jun. gen. def. Manor of West Langdon, etc. St. Stephen's in Brannell and Feock.

John, son of Anthony Pye, bur. 29 May, 1617, at St. Stephen's in Branel. } Bp. of Exeter's
Robert, son of Anthony Pye, bap. 21 March, 1623, at do. } Transcripts.
Mr. Anthony Pye and Phillippa Andrew mar. 8 Sept., 1684. Archdeacon's Transcripts at Probus.

Will of Susannah Pye of St. Stephen's in Brannel, co. Cornw., dated 16 Nov., 1712, prob. 1719. Names Philippa and two grandsons, Henry and Pye Harris.

The following wills of this family are lost :—
St. Stephen's in Branwell. Alexander Pye, 14 Feb., 1569.
Do.   John Pye,   30 Mar., 1582.
Do.   John Pye,   12 Decr., 1607.

Nathaniel Pye of St. Stephen's in Branwell, gent., and Jenofesse his wife held lease of lands at Terris in that parish. Deed dated 6 January, 1654.

By deed dated 1 Aug., 12 Charles I., Anthony Pye of St. Stephen's in Branwell, gent., conveyed lands at Hallivick in that parish to Thomas Hoblyn and his heirs.

By deed dated 25 June, 7 Chas. I., Anthony Pye of St. Stephen's in Branwell conveyed lands called Terrys to John Vivian. } Deeds in Collection of Sir John Maclean.

} (J. M.)

[*Note continued on next page.*]

Quarme.

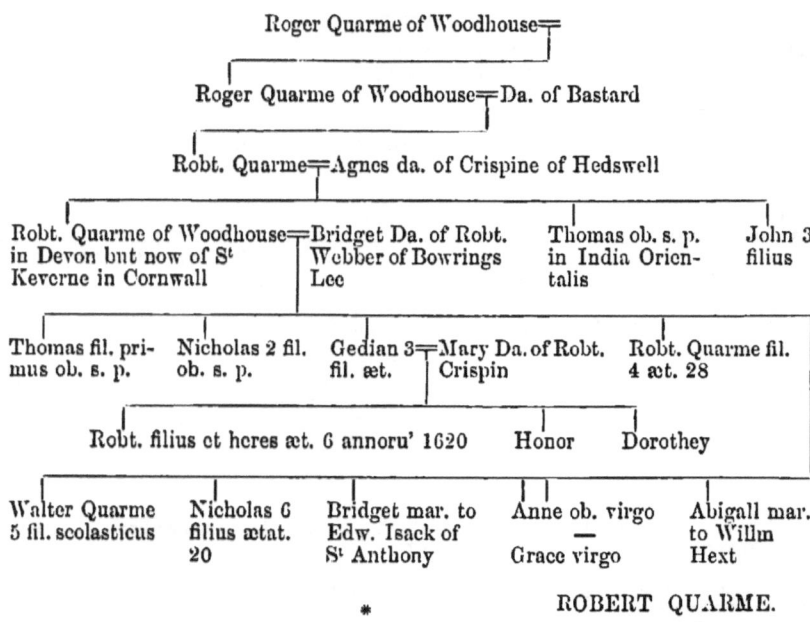

Captaine Quarme = Da. of Crispin Lo. of Woodhouse

Roger Quarme of Woodhouse

Roger Quarme of Woodhouse = Da. of Bastard

Robt. Quarme = Agnes da. of Crispine of Hedswell

- Robt. Quarme of Woodhouse in Devon but now of St Keverne in Cornwall = Bridget Da. of Robt. Webber of Bowrings Lee
- Thomas ob. s. p. in India Orientalis
- John 3 filius

- Thomas fil. primus ob. s. p.
- Nicholas 2 fil. ob. s. p.
- Gedian 3 fil. æt. = Mary Da. of Robt. Crispin
- Robt. Quarme fil. 4 æt. 28

Robt. filius et heres æt. 6 annoru' 1620 | Honor | Dorothey

- Walter Quarme 5 fil. scolasticus
- Nicholas 6 filius ætat. 20
- Bridget mar. to Edw. Isack of St Anthony
- Anne ob. virgo — Grace virgo
- Abigall mar. to Willm Hext

*   ROBERT QUARME.

Randall.

To Inquire for ye Coate of Randall.

Da. of Eyre = Tho. Randall of Peryn in Com. Cornw. liveing 1620 Gertrude da. of Nic. Penticost 3 wife = [2] Grace Da. of Rich. Geirveis of Constenton in Com. Cornwall

A   B   C

(*Note continued.*)

    Adm'n, etc., of Otwell, alias Atwell P'ye. Probus, granted to Jane P'ye, his relict, 19 Sept., 1683.
    Adm'n, etc., Nathaniel P'ye of St. Stephen's in Branwell granted to Jenefer P'ye, his relict, 10 Sept., 1669. } Bodmin. } (J. M.)
    Humphry P'ye and William P'ye witnesses to the will of Constantine Moyle of St. Minver, dated 16 Decr., 1618.

   * Robert Quarme, gent., and Katherine Trefusis, da. of Thomas Trefusis, mar. 1633. Constantine Par. Reg.
    Mrs. Dorothy Quarme bur. at Creed   1668. } Bp. of Exeter's Transcripts.
    Grace, da. of Rob. Quarme, gent., bur. at do. 1668.
    Joseph May (Clerk) and Judith Quarme mar. 1688. St. Ewe Par. Reg.
    The register books of Mawnan contain several entries of the family of Quarme about the date of this Visitation.

THE VISITATION OF THE COUNTY OF CORNWALL. 183

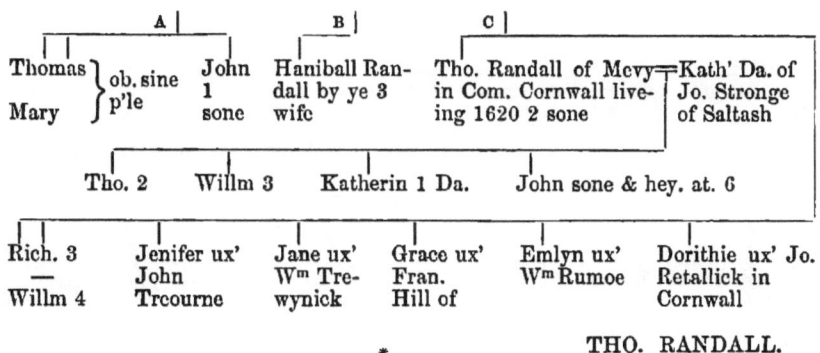

```
    A |                    B |            C |
  | |              |              |              |                    |
Thomas ⎱ ob. sine  John     Haniball Ran-  Tho. Randall of Mevy=Kath' Da. of
Mary   ⎰ p'le      1        dall by ye 3   in Com. Cornwall live-  Jo. Stronge
                   sone     wife           ing 1620 2 sone          of Saltash

     |            |              |                 |
   Tho. 2      Willm 3      Katherin 1 Da.    John sone & hey. at. 6

  | |            |              |              |              |              |
Rich. 3     Jenifer ux'   Jane ux'      Grace ux'     Emlyn ux'     Dorithie ux' Jo.
—           John          Wm Tre-       Fran.         Wm Rumoe      Retallick in
Willm 4     Trcourne      wynick        Hill of                     Cornwall

                                            *               THO. RANDALL.
```

Rashleigh.

¹ Phillip Rashleigh of Fowye═Genet Da. of Tho. Leighe

```
        |                          |
² Robt. Rashley         ³ John Rashleyghe═Alice Da. of Wm
sone & heyre              2 sonne           Hanyon
```

```
  | |              |                  |              |              |
⁴ Agnes ux' Mar-  ⁵ John Rash-═Alice⁶ Da. of  Avis ux' Kes-   Emlyn ux. J. Ape-
tin of Devon      ley sone &  Bonithan of   tell of Cornw.    ley of Devon
—                 heire of    Kertleowe     —                 —
Jone uxor Jo.     Fowye in    in Cornwall   ⁷ Joanne un-      ⁸ Mary uxor Sim.
Mayo of Lowe      Com. Corn-                  maried           Clotworthie of
                  wall liveing                                  Rashleigh
                  1620
                              A       †
```

* Ped. fin. Cornw. 4, Edw. IV., No. 1. Henry Courteney, son of Thos. Courteney, late Earl of Devon, qu. Thos. Sele and Margaret his wife def. Names John Randell of Merther.

¹ Inq. p. m. 4 Edw. VI., part I., No. 23. Philip Rayssheligh died 14 June, 4 Edw. VI. Robert R., son and heir, aged 30 and more.

² Inq. p. m. 30 Elizb., pt. I., No. 12. Robt. Rayshlegh ob. 27 March. John Rashlegh, son and heir, aged 20 years, 7 mo., 24 d. at father's death, and had married Elizabeth, the da. of Rich. Trevanion, ar.

³ Inq. p. m. 25 Eliz., No. 163. John Rashleigh died 10 Aug., 20 Eliz. John, son and heir, aged 27 and more.

⁴ She is called Joane, wife of Will Martin of Totnes, in Martin ped.,'Visit. Devon, 1620,' p. 182.

⁵ Jno. Rashleigh and Alice Bonython mar. 10 Feb., 1575. ⎫
⁶ Alice, wife of John Rashley, son of Robert R., his next heir, æt. 10 Ap., 1607. ⎬ Fowey Par. Reg.

⁷ Named in Inq. p. m. John Rashleigh, note 3.

⁸ Simon Clotworthy and Mary Rashleigh mar. 2 Mar., 1583. Fowey Par. Reg.

† Inq. p. m. 21 Eliz., part I., No. 15. Thomas Rashleigh of Foye died 20 May, 18 Eliz. John Rashleigh, his nephew, son of Robert R., his next heir, æt. 18 y'rs 2 months.
Inq. p. m. 20 Jas., part I., No. 92, John Rashleigh. Robt., s. and h., aged 24 at father's death.
Jonathan Rashleigh of Menabille, Esq., and Madam Jane Carew, da. of Sir ⎫ Anthony in
John Carew, Bart., were mar. 12 Dec., 1681. (Entered also at Lan- ⎬ the East
livery.) ⎭ Par. Reg.

184 THE VISITATION OF THE COUNTY OF CORNWALL.

	A		
Jonithan 2 sonc mar. Anne Da.of Sr Robert Bassct K^t	John Rashley sonc & hey. at. 34 liveinge	Alice ux' Nicho. Sawle of Cornw.	Debora ux' John Spark of Devon

* JONATHAN RASHLEIGHE.

* Johan Rashleigh	bap.	3 Aug. 1544.
Joan Rashleigh	,,	26 Jan., 1546.
Letty Rashleigh	,,	8 July, 1548.
John, son of Jo. Rashleigh,	,,	11 May, 1550.
John, ,,	,,	27 Nov., 1554.
Joan Rashleigh	,,	5 May, 1558.
John, son of Rob. Rayshley,	,,	14 Jan., 1563.
Margaret Rashleigh	,,	1564.
Robert, son of Mr. Jno. Rashlegh of Coombe,	,,	29 June, 1585.
Jno., ,, ,, ,, gent.,	,,	22 Dec., 1588.
Jonathan. ,, ,, ,,	,,	4 July, 1591.
Philip, ,, ,, ,,	,,	11 Nov., 1593.
Thomas, ,, ,, ,,	,,	7 Sept., 1595.
John, son of Robert Rashley,	,,	21 Jan., 1619.
Jno., ,, Jonathan Rashlegh,	,,	22 Apl., 1621.
Jonathan, ,, ,,	,,	15 Jan., 1631.
Jonathan, ,, John Rashley of Menibilie, Esq.	,,	23 July, 1642.
Philip, ,, John Rashley of Coombe	,,	19 Nov., 1643.
Jno., ,, John Rashley, gent., of Menabilly,	,,	20 Nov., 1644.
Rob., ,, John Rashley of Coombe, gent.,	,,	1645.
Absalom, ,, Robert Rashleigh,	,,	21 Jan., 1655.
Thos., ,, ,, gent.,	,,	1660.
Thos. Rashleigh and Elizab. Trevanion	mar.	30 June, 1573.
Francis Vivyan and Elizab. Rashleigh	,,	13 Jan., 1605.
Mr. Robert Rashlegh and Jane Maior (qy. Maioe)	,,	16 Dec., 1619.
John Rashleigh. gent., and Elizab. Rashleigh	,,	5 Dec., 1642.
Rob. Rashlegh and Grace Biggs	,,	Jan., 1652.
Kath., ux. Mr. John Rashleigh of Coombe,	bur.	1614.
John Rashlegh	,,	20 Aug., 1619.
John Rashlegh, gent., of Coombe	,,	21 Nov., 1621.
Mr. Jno. Rashleye, Esq.	,,	16 May, 1624.
John, his son,	,,	22 May, 1624.
Jonne, ux. Rob. Rashlegh of Coombe	,,	Jan., 1643.
Thos., son of Jno. Rashley of Coombe, gent.,	,,	1648.
John Rashley of Coombe, the elder	,,	1654.
Thos., son of Jno. Rashley,	,,	1660.
Rob. Rashley, Esq.,	,,	1666.
Thos. Rashley of Coombe	,,	1661.
Mrs. Joane Rashley, wid.,	,,	1668.
Mrs. Mary Rashley	,,	1674.
Phil. Rashley, gent.,	,, in the Church	1681.
Mrs. Jane Rashley	,,	1681.
Mrs. Joan Rashey	,, 2 March,	1682.
Mrs. Mary Rashey	,,	1683.
Mr. Jno. Rashey	,, in the Church	1691.
Jno. Rashley of St. Katherine's, Esq.,	,,	1693.
Jane, ux. Jonathan Rashley, Esq.,	,,	31 Aug., 1700.

Fowey Par. Reg.

Stephen, son of John Rashleigh, bap. 26 Feb., 1630. Mawgan in Men. Par. Reg.
Mr. Jonathan Rashey, Esq., and Nan Courtney were mar. 11 March, 1672. Tywardreth Par. Reg.
Phil., son of Jno. Rashley, Esq., by Joan, bap. 1647. St. Sampson's and Golant Par. Reg.
Francis, s. of W^m. Rashleigh (of Gunwalloe) & Jane his wife. bap. 1690. } Cury, Par.
Joane, da. of Peter Rashleigh and Mary. bap. 14 Oct., 1690. } Reg.
Several entries of Rashleigh appear in the Par. Reg.'s of Gunwalloe and Cury.
Chan. Pro., Eliz., R. r. 4, No. 52. John Rashleigh of Menabilly v. W^m. Achym and or's. Right of water at Penhellick in parish of Pelynt. John Rashleigh, father of Orator, named.
Ped. fin. Cornw., 6 Edw. VI., pack. 9. John Rashley gent. qu. Stephen Vyvyan gent. and Maria his wife def. Pennyllyke, Foxchall, and Holewood, in the parishes of Pelynt and Quethyock. John paid Stephen £80 sterling.
For more extended ped. of Rashleighe, see Harl. M.S. 1079, fo. 200.

Reskimer.

John Reskimer of Marthen in Com. Cornub. Esq.

- John Reskimer sonne & heir ob. s. p. = Grace da. to John St. Aubyn of Clowans Esq.
- William Reskimer 3sonne & heire to his brother of Merthen = Elynor da. of Henry Spurr of Northill in Com. Cornub.
- Richard Reskimer 2 sonne = ...
- Catherine wife to Thomas Enys of Enys
- Jane wife to John Conch of Penryn

Children of William:
- Henry 2
- William 3
- James 4
- Nicholas 5

- John Reskimer of Marthen Esq. living 1620 = [1] Margaret da. of George Gifford of Tiverton

- Grace 1 d.
- Mary 3
- Johan 4
- Catherin 5
  all unmaried

- Philippa [2] wife to Jo. Trithwall of Trink

- John Reskimer sonne & heir ob. s. p.

HENRY RESKIMER.

---

[1] Mary in the Gyfford Ped. See 'Visit. Devon,' p. 135.
[2] Compare ped. of Thomas of Crowan, *post*.

* John, son of John Trelawney, Esq., and Anne Reskymer, gent., da. of Alse Reskymer, mar. 11 Dec., 1562. Menhenniot Par. Reg.
  This marriage carried the quarterings of Reskymer, Trevarthian, and Carminow, to Trelawney; John Trevarthian having been proved one of the heirs of Joanna Carminow, Inq. p. m. 19 Ric. II., No. 15, as son of Matilda, the daughter of Sir Oliver Carminow. The subsequent descent through the main line of Reskymer is given in the 'History of Trigg,' vol. i., p. 555.
  Rich. Reskymer, bur. 1597.
  John Reskymer, Esq., „ 1601. } Constantine Par. Reg.
  Will. Reskymer, Esq., „ 1616.
  Arthur, son of Mr. Will. Reskymer, bur. 27 Dec., 1601. Gluvias Par. Reg.
  Alice Reskymer, gent., bur. 1563. St. Tudy Par. Reg.
  John Treuthall, gent., and Phillis, da. of Wm. Reskymer, Esq., mar. 10 Feb., 1615. } (J.M.)
    Constantine Par. Reg.
  Inq. p. m. 5 Ed. IV., No. 19. Ralph Reskymmer, ob. 14 April last. Will. Reskymmer, son and heir, æt. 28.
  Inq. p. m. 11 Ed. IV., No. 45. William Reskymmer, ob. 11 Feb. last. Names Elizabeth, his wife, da. of Thos. Arundell, militis; John Reskymmer, son and heir, æt. 14, et amp.
  Inq. p. m. 6 Elizb., No. 15. Alice Reskymer, wid., ob. 14 Jan. Anne, ux. John Trelawney, aged 21, 26 July last; Katherine, aged 16; Francisca, aged 13; and Johanna, aged 12, her daughters and heirs.
  Inq. p. m. 15 Jas., part 1, No. 96. John Reskymer al's Creber of Merthen, ob. 2 Feb. last past. An Ind're, 3 Ap., 44 Elizb., between John Reskymer al's Creber of Merthen, first part, and Tho. St. Awbyn of Clowance, Esq., and Tho. Enys of Gluvias, gent., second part, recites a demise by John Reskymer, Esq., of Merthen, dec. dat. 1 Mar., 4 Elizb., of certain lands to John Reskymer al's Creber, rem. to Will. Reskymer al's Creber, rem. to John Reskymer al's Creber, son of Richard Reskymer al's Creber, rem. to right heirs of John Reskymer al's Creber first named, rem. to right heirs of John Reskymer of Merthen, Esq., dec. William Reskymer, bro. and heir, aged 50 years and more.
  Ped. fin. Cornwall, 20 Hen. III., No. 2. Abbas de Bello Loco, qu. Ric. de Riskemere, def. In St. Kavaron.
  Ped. fin. 32 Ed. I., No. 2, Cornwall. John de Reskemmer qu. Roger de Carmynou, def Lands in Lannergh, Trevagethyghan, Trevagetnur, etc. £10 sterling paid.

Robarts.

ARMS (tricked in pencil).—*B. on a chev. Arg. three mullets pierced Sab.*
ARMS.—HENDER *in trick. A lion ramp. within an orle of escalops.*

Rich. Robts of Trwro in Com. Cornw. esq. =
|
├─ John Robertes 1 sonne ma. Phillip 2 da. of John Gaveregan, Esqr
└─ Rich. Robertes of = Margerie Da. of Willes Trwro 2 sone │ of Saltashe esq.

Rich. Lo. Roberts Baron of Truro = Frances da. & heyre of Ed. Hinder of Botreaux Castle Corn. Esq.

¹Josias Roberts of = Barbara Da. of Edw. Noye esq. of Carnington in Cornwall Tregaso in Com. Cornw. esq. liveinge 1620 │ by Jane da. of Crabbe father & mother of Wm. Noye of Lincolnes In. esq.

John Lo. Roberts Baron of Truro mar. Lucy da. of ye Lord Rich Earle of Warwick

Hugh 2 —
Phillip 3 —
Rich. 5

Willm 4 mar. Elinor da. of Richard Hekinson of Islington in Midd. gent. by Jane daughter and coheyre to John Wilson of Bednall Greene gent. by his wife Katherine daughter of .... Muschamp of Peccam in Surry esq.

²Edw. 1 sone at. 22

Frauncis, a dau.

JOSIAS ROBARTS.

Roberts.

Richard Roberts of Truro in Com. Cornub. = ¹Johan da. of Geffrey of St. Breage

1	2	3		
Jane wife to Martyn Thomas al's Bosaveron	Ann wife to Roger Tucker of Illmester in Com. Som'set	Elizabeth wife to Balthazar Williams of Trevorvoe in Pochia de Probes	Christabel wife to John Michell of Truro	Margaret wife to Henry Nanspian of Crowan

These 2 last daughters weare Twinns

Richard = Margery da. Roberts of Wills of 2 sonne Blowfleming

John Roberts of = ²Philip 2 da. of John Gaverigan Truro Esq. sonne │ of Gaveregan in Com. Corn. & heire │ Esq.
A

---

¹ See Truro Par. Reg. *opp.*   ² Bap. 29 Nov., 1598. Truro Par. Reg.
* Ped. fin. 17 Edw. IV., No. 1. Peter William and John Roberds qu. Johana Coty of Tresula, widow, def.
¹ Johan Robartes, wife of Mr. Rich. Robarts, Senior, bar. Xmas. day. 1608. } Truro Par. Reg.
² Philip, wife of John Robartes,   ,,   1603.
☞ The additions in italic are in another handwriting.

THE VISITATION OF THE COUNTY OF CORNWALL.

A

Sr Richard Roberts of Truro Kt *and Baronett* = Frances da. & coheire of living 1620 & *created Baron of Truro by K.* John Hender of Botriaux *James 26 of January 26 Ja. R. A° 1624* Castle Esq.

| John Roberts sonne & heir ætat. 14 annoru' 1620 | [1] Mary wife to [2] William Rowse of Halton sonne of Ambrose Rowse desceased whoe was sonne & heire Sr Anthony Rouse of Halton Kt | Jane 2 daughter *ma. to Charles Lo. Lambert of Cavan in Irelande* |

Francis a da.   *Tho.* 3 sone   *Anthonie* 1 son   *Richard* 2 son   *Richard* 1 son

Not signed.

*

---

[1] Maria, da. of Richard Roberts,   bap. 28 Jan., 1599–60. ⎫ Truro Par. Reg.
[2] William Rowse and Maria Robarts,   mar. 24 Apr., 1617.   ⎭

* Samuel Pendarves, gent., of Constantine, and Mrs. Grace Roberts of Truro, mar. at Constantine 24 June, 1598. Bp. of Exeter's Transcripts.
Will of William Roberts of St. Allen, Merchant, 30 Jan., 1604, proved in London 1605. Names his sister Grace Burgess, and her son William when 21; Samuel Pendarves and Grace his wife, with their son William; John, son of Symon Roberts, when 21; Maria Lanyon. His bro. John Roberts and wife Jane, Exors.

John Robarts and Johana Brende,   mar. 11 July, 1612.⎫
Edward, son of Josia Roberts (*see opp. page*)   bap. 29 Nov., 1598. ⎮
Jane, da. of Richard Roberts,   „   21 Dec., „
Josias, son of Josias Roberts (*see opp. page*)   „   22 Sept., 1600.
Frances, da. of Mr. Richard Robartes, jun.,   „   1611.   Truro Par. Reg.
Reginald Robartes, senex,   bur.   1605, ⎮
Maria, wife of Simon Robartes,   „   1605.
Frances, da. of Rich. Robarts, militis,   „   1618.
William Roberts and Mary Calmadow   mar.   1663.⎭
Richard, son of The Hon. John Robartes, bap. 29 Dec., 1630.
John,   „   „   „   „ 29 Jan., 1631–32.
Hender,   „   Lord Robartes,   „ 28 Nov., 1635.
Richard,   „   „   „   „ 24 Feb., 1648–9.
Francis,   „   „   „   „ 6 Jan., 1649–50.
Letitia, da. of John Lord Robartes, bap. at . . . . in Essex, 1651.
Charles,   son of   „   bap. 20 Sept., 1653.
Diana,   da. of   „   „ 19 Oct., 1654.
Aramintha, „   „   „ 18 Oct., 1655.
John,   son of   „   „ 2 Dec.,   1656.
Olympia,   da. of   „   „ 10 Dec., 1657.
Henry,   son of   „   „ 22 Feb., 1658.
John, son of the Hon. Robert Robartes, Esq.,   ⎫
   born Feb. 10, 1658, bap. in London.   ⎮ Lanhydrock
Mary, da. of Lord Robartes, born 31 May, 1661,   ⎬ Par. Reg.
   bap. at Chelsea.   ⎮
John,   son of Lord Robartes,   bap. 14 Oct., 1662.
Warwick, „   „   „   born at Chelsea, April 21, 1667.
Enese, da. of   „   „   April,   1669.
The Right Hon. Lord Francis Robartes was bur. 28 Oct., 1626.
Richard, son of Lord Robartes, bur. the last day of Dec., 1630.
Richard, Lord Robartes,   bur. 4 July, 1634.
   (Richard, Lord Robartes, dyed the 19th day of Aprill,
   Anno D'ni 1634, and was buryed the 4 July the
   next following. Bp. of Exeter's Transcripts.)
John, son of John, Lord Robartes,   bur. 23 Feb., 1657.
Diana, da. of   „   „ 26 Jan., 1672.
John, Lord Robartes, died at Chelsea,   July 17, 1685.   ⎭

Robinson.

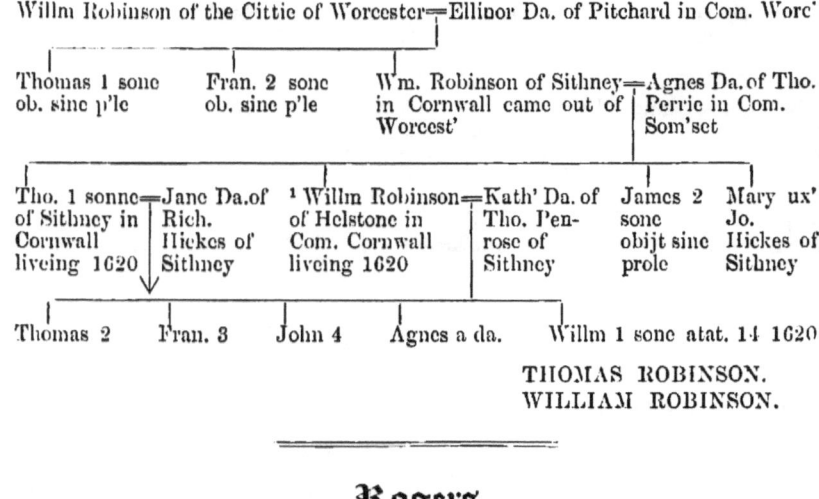

THOMAS ROBINSON.
WILLIAM ROBINSON.

Rogers.

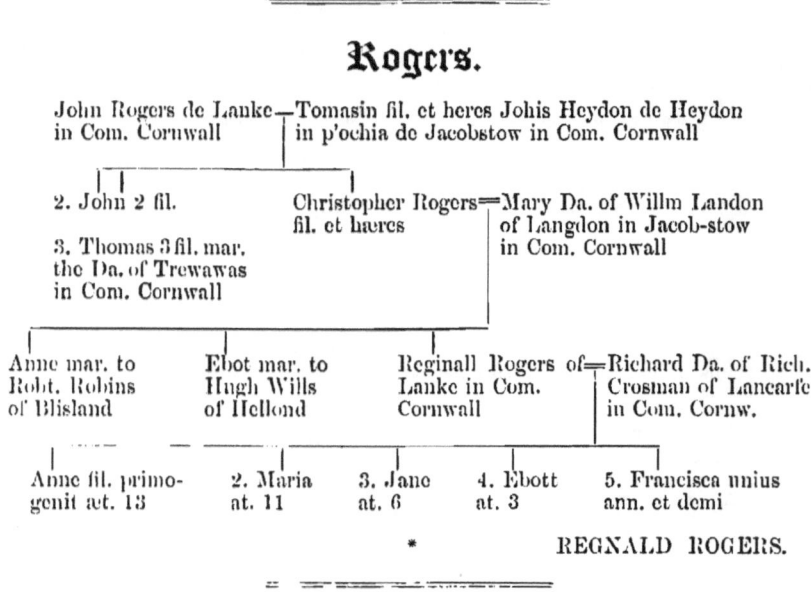

REGNALD ROGERS.

---

[1] William Robinson signed the return of Arms of the Borough of Helston at the 'Visitation of Cornwall, 1620.'

* For account and ped. of Rogers, see 'Hist. of Trigg,' vol. i., p. 392.
Chanc. Proc. Elizab. R. r. 11, No. 37. Christopher Rogers v. Hu., Riche, Wm. Bathe, and o'rs re Penrose, St. Breward.
Inq. p. m. 25 Eliz., part 1, No. 109. Wm. Rogers ob. at Trebigh in Eggloskerry 26 Nov., 1582. Edward Rogers, son and heir, aged 21 on 20 June, 1583.
John, son of John Rogers, gent., bap. at Crowan, 1690. Archd. Transcripts.

Roscarrock.

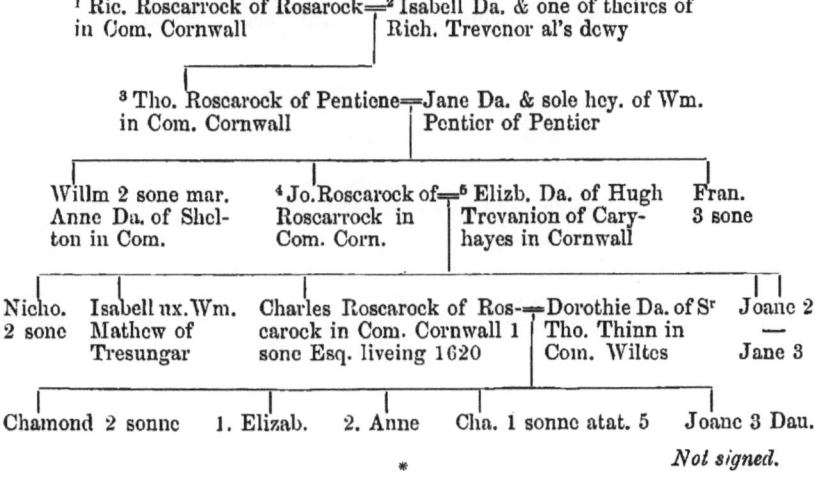

* Charles, son of Charles Roscarrock, Esq., bur. 1647. St. Neott Par. Reg.
Dorithye Roscarrocke, gentlewoman, bur. at Trevalga 20 Dec., 1613. Bp. of Exeter's Transcripts.

Roscarrock.

Thomas Roscarrock=Jane da. & sole heir of William
of Roscarrock Pentier of Pentune
A

[1] Son and heir of John Roscarrock, Esq., and aged 30 and more at his father's death, 26 Oct., 29 Hen. VIII. (Esch. Inq. p. m. 28 and 29 Hen. VIII., Cornwall, No. 4.) Ob. 26 Oct. 17 Elizab. Thomas, son and heir, aged 44 and more. (Inq. p. m. 18 Elizab., part 1, No. 9.)
[2] One of the sisters and heirs of Will. Trevener, defunct. Inq. p. m. 29 H. VIII., No. 30. See also note 3, p. 190.
[3] Ob. 13 Feb. 29 Eliz. John, s. and h., aged 30 and more. Inq. p. m. 30 Eliz. pt. 1, No. 82.
[4] Ob. 24 Nov., 6 Jas. Charles, son and heir, aged 18 and more. Inq. p. m. 6 Jas., 2 part, No. 66.
[5] In a pedigree given at fo. 62, Harl. MS. 4031, she is called Katherine, da. of Hugh Trevanion, which agrees with the entry on the next page.

Ped fin. Cornw. 12 Hen. VI., No. 1. Benedict Hamle qu. Thos. Roscreck and Annora his wife, def. Lands in Karlunyck, Helston Burgh, Truro Burgh, etc. Names also John and William Pennance, sons of Annora.
Ped. fin. Cornw. 15 Eliz. Jas. Humfry qu. Robert Roscowrak al's Roscoryck, gener., and Ann his wife, and John Arundell of Treberthes (? Treverthes), gener., and Margaret his wife, def. Lands in Nauspellye in St. Gerans.
Ped. fin. Pasch. 1 and 2 Phil. and Mary. No. 6. Rich. Roscarrock, Esq., and Rich. Chamond, qu. Stephen Vyvyan, gent., and Maria his wife, def. Lands, etc., in Trenans Austell, St. Austell, Castell Gotham, Tregorrck, Trethyrgy, and Roscovey, called also Roscavevyon in St. Austell and St. Blazey. Item. to John Vyvyan, bro. of Stephen, rem. to Francis Bluett, Henry Chiverton, and John Courteney, and in default rem. to right heirs of said Stephen Vyvyan for ever.
Inq. p. m. 3 Hen. VII., No. 117. Isabella Rescarrek. John R., son and heir, aged 40 and more.
Chanc. Proc. Elizab. R. r. 3, No. 27. Humphry Rescarrock v. Richard Mathewe. Lands in Endellion.

THE VISITATION OF THE COUNTY OF CORNWALL.

A

William Roscarrock of Padstow 2 sonne living 1620 = Ann da. of .... Shelton of London | Francis 3 sonne living | Eliza wife to Lewis Dart | Agnes wife to William Menwinnck | Catherine wife to Jo. Tanner | Margaret wife to Littleton Trenance

Jane unmaried

John Roscarrock of Roscarrock sonne and heir =[1] Catheryne da. of Hugh Trevanyan of Carryheys

Charles Roscarrock of Roscarrock living 1620 = Dorothy da. of Sr John Thynn of Wilt' Kt. | Nicholas 2 sonne | Sibell wife to William Mathew of Tresunger | Johan unmaried

Charles Roscarrock sonne and heir ætat. 4 ann.

*   *Not signed.*

Roscarrock.

[2] Richard Roskarrock of Roscarrock in Com. Cornwall =[3] Isabell da. and coheir of Rich. Trevennor al's Dewy

[3] Thomas Roscarock of Roscarrock sonne and heir = Jane da. and sole heir of Willm Pentier of Pentune | Hugh Roscarrock 2 sonne mar. the da. and heire of Boswaro | Anthony Roscarrock of Crowne 3 sonne = Isabell da. of John Stone

John Roscarrock of Crawne in Com. Cornub. Esq. living 1620. = Eliza. da. of Thomas Hinckston of Parkgate & of Durworthy | Frances 1 first maried to Gilbert Michell & after to John Sanders of Bodman

William sonne and heir ætat. 8 Annoru' 1620 | Humfrey 2 | John 4 | Frances 1 da. | Philipp 2

Thomas 3

JOHES SAUNDERS.

[1] See note 5, p. 189.
* Roger Roscowreake, bur. 24 Feb., 1561. St. Ewe Par. Reg.
[2] Chan. Pro. Eliz. R. r. 11, No. 61. Roscarrocke v. Trevanyon and o'rs. Names Richard Roscarrocke & his sons Humphry & Nicholas R. John R. is named as a def. re Deliobell, St. Tethe.
[3] Inq. p. m. 34 Elizb., part 1, No. 32. Isabella Roscarrock, widow, died 17 Aug. last past. John Roscarrock, aged 30 years and more, was next heir, viz., son of Thomas, son of said Isabella. See n. 2, 3, and 4, p. 189.
Ped. fin. 3 John, No. 8, Cornw. Matthew de Egloshei, qu. Walter de Roskarco, def. Havenant, etc. Pipe Roll, 1 Ric. I. Walter de Roscharet. Lands in Cornwall.
For fuller and continued ped. of Roscarrock, see 'Hist. of Trigg,' vol. i., p. 563.

Rosewaran.

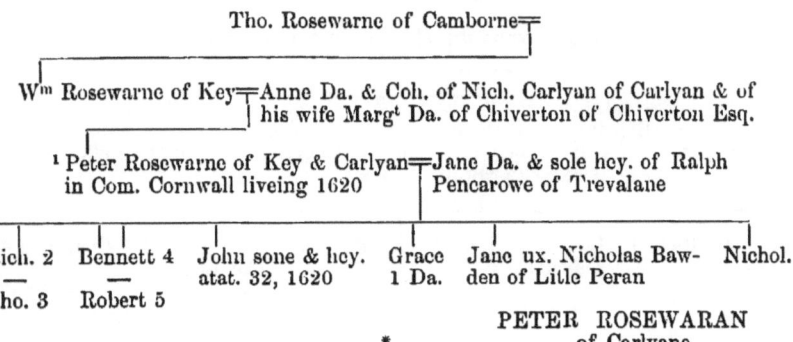

Tho. Rosewarne of Camborne═┬═

Wᵐ Rosewarne of Key═┬═Anne Da. & Coh. of Nich. Carlyan of Carlyan & of his wife Margᵗ Da. of Chiverton of Chiverton Esq.

1 Peter Rosewarne of Key & Carlyan═┬═Jane Da. & sole hey. of Ralph Pencarowe of Trevalane in Com. Cornwall liveing 1620

Rich. 2 — Tho. 3 | Bennett 4 — Robert 5 | John sone & hey. atat. 32, 1620 | Grace 1 Da. | Jane ux. Nicholas Bawden of Litle Peran | Nichol.

PETER ROSEWARAN of Carlyane.

1 Ind're 8 July, 4 Chas., betw. Peter Rosewarne of Carlighan, gent., and John R., son and h. appar't of s'd Peter, of the first part, and Rich. Hendra, p'ish of Feock, yeom., other part. Conveyance of certain lands in Feock, sometime the heredit. of Thomazin Glyn, dec'd, and of Anne Rosewarne, wid., mother of s'd Peter—two of the dau'rs and coh's of Nich. Carlighan, gent., decd.,—now in occup. of Rich. R., son of s'd Peter R., and o'rs. Names Will. Rosewarne. gent., sometime husb. of s'd Anne, and Judith, wife of John Rosewarne, son of Peter R. Signed by John and Peter Rosewarne. *Dors.*—Sealed by the within-named John Carlyan (? John Rosewarne) in presence of Jno. Haweis, Sam. Davyes, Rob. Rosewarne, and Tristram Moore.

* John Killigollan and Jane, da. of Thos. Roswarne, mar. 21 June, 1550.⎫
Jno. Evah and Ann Rosewarne, „ 26 Jan., 1617. |
George Rosewarne and Ann Mason, „ 20 June, 1619. |
John Nicholas of Sendy, and Jane, da. of Steven Rosewarne, „ 27 May, 1547. ⎬ Camborne Par. Reg.
Katherine, da. of Rich. Rosewarne, bap. 1 Sept., 1605. |
Jane, „ George Rosewarne, „ April, 1622. |
Rich., son of „ „ 19 Aug., 1627. |
Bennett Rosewarne and Jane his wife, mar. 2 Nov., 1603.⎫
Grace, da. of Bennett Rosewarne, bap. 9 Mar., 1561. |
Mary, „ „ „ 1565. |
Rich., son of „ „ 20 Aug., 1567. |
John, „ „ „ 16 Aug., 1572. |
Jane, da. „ „ 26 July, 1573. |
Bennett, son „ „ 17 July, 1582. |
Thomas, „ Thomas Rosewarne, „ 27 Oct., 1594. |
Rich., „ „ „ 24 Jan., 1595. |
Marke, „ „ „ 7 April, 1598. |
John, „ „ „ 28 Sept., 1600. |
Bennett, „ Thomas Rosewarne, „ 1603. |
Richard, „ „ gent., „ 14 Dec., 1606. |
Will., „ „ „ „ 28 May, 1609. |
Edward, „ Bennett Rosewarne, „ „ 30 Jan., 1604. ⎬ Gwinear Par. Reg.
John, „ „ „ „ 29 May, 1607. |
Phillip, „ „ „ „ 2 Mar., 1613. |
Gyllian, da. „ „ „ 29 Oct., 1615. |
Arthur, son „ „ „ 10 June, 1610. |
Thomas, „ Thomas Rosewarne, gent., ,, 27 Aug., 1620. |
Mary, da. William Rosewarne, bur. 28 Mar., 1566. |
John, son Bennett Rosewarne, „ 26 Oct., 1571. |
Jane, da. „ „ 29 Aug., 1574. |
William, son of Mr. Rosewarne, „ 6 Jan., 1578. |
Richard Rosewarne, „ 20 July, 1591. |
Katherine, wife of Bennett Rosewarne, „ 14 Feb., 1598. |
Richard, son of Thomas Rosewarne, „ 14 Feb., 1603. |
Bennett Rosewarne, gent., „ 26 April, 1604. |
Thomas, son of Bennet Rosewarne, „ 8 Feb., 1618. |
Jane, wife of „ ,. 5 June, 1619.⎭

Roskrowe.

```
1                                                              2
Da. & heire of Trewynnard = Tho. of Roscrowe in = Jane Da. of Tho.
                            Com. Cornw.          Gerratt
```

| Tho. 1 sone ob. sine p'le | Richard 2 sonne ob. sine p'le | Rich. 3 sone = Da. of Dedicott of Gluvias in of Worcest' Cornwall | John 2 sone ob. sine p'le | John 3 sone |

| Peter 1 — Tho. 3 | Rich. 4 | Elizb. ux' Hen. Kelverth | Jane ux' Josias Perne | Sibell ux' Tho. Lugie | W^m 2 sone mar. = a da. |

*   PETER ROSKROWE.

Roskruge.

Tho. Roskruge of St. Anthony in Com. Cornw. =

¹ John Roskruge of St. Anthony = Ellinor Da. of Tho. Chinoweth
in Com. Cornwall   of St. Martin

| Jane ux Tho. Edwards of Uny Lelant | Anthony Roskrug of St. Anthony fil. et heres æt. 47 liveing 1620 | Dorothy Da. of John Davy of Samford in Com. Devon | Christian ux Peter Spry of Mawnon in Com. Cornwall |

| John Roskrug fil. et heres æt. 14, 1620 | 1 Ann æt. 16 — 2 Elinor æt. 15 | 3 Susan — 4 Elizab.² | 5 Lowday — 6 Alice | Grace — Sinobia |

†   ANTHONY ROSKRUGE.

---

* Chanc. Proceed. Elizab. R. r. 1, No. 9. John Roskrowe v. Peter Hallamore and Phi. Tonckin, respecting tenement, etc., at Peryn al's Penryn.

¹ John Roskruge, gent.,   bur. 1605.
² Elizab., da. of Anthony Roskruge, gent.,   bap. 1608.
† Rich. Roskruge, gent.. and Rebecca Phillips were mar. 1666.
   James, son of Jno. Roskruge, gent., and Grace, bap. 1634.
   John,   ,,   ,,   ,,   ,, 1636.
   Francis, ,,   ,,   ,,   ,, 1636.
   Benjamin, ,,   ,,   ,,   ,, 1646.
   Anthony, ,,   Anthony Roskruge,   ,, 1620.
   Henry, ,,   ,,   ,, 1627.
   John Roskruge, gent.,   bur. 1665.
   Anthony Roskruge, gent.,   ,, 1707.

} Anthony in Meneage Par. Reg.

Chanc. Proc. Elizab., R. r. 2, No. 39. James Roscrowgye of St. Kevern v. Gilbert Roscrowgye, his bro. Names Nowell R.. son of James. and Rich. R., son of Gilbert. Gilbert states that long since he took to wife Margaret, and complainant James took to wife Nicholla. dau'rs and coheirs of Rich. Rysgrowgie, deceased, etc.

THE VISITATION OF THE COUNTY OF CORNWALL. 193

Rosuggan.

ARMS.—*Ar. chev. ent. 3 roses, gu. seeds and leaves pp.*

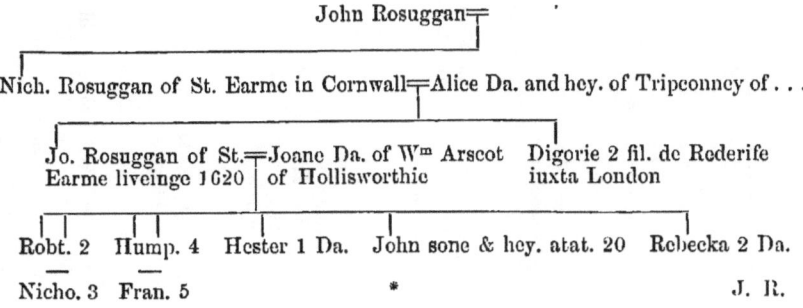

Rous.

ARMS.—1. ROUS, *Or an eagle displayed B. armed Gu.* 2. EDMERSTON. 3. RAMES-LAND. 4. HILL. 5. REVELL. 6. LEIGH. 7. BARNHOUSE. 8. BRIGHTRIXTON. 9. KERKHAM. 10. WRAY.

CREST.—*An eagle displayed.*

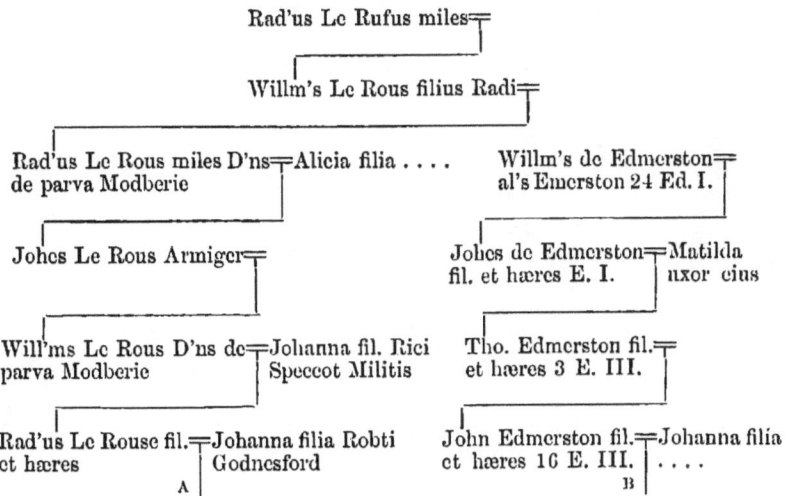

* Chanc. Proc. Elizab. R. r. 7, No. 19. Resuggan and o'rs v. Trerruffe al's Treruthe. Names Robert Resuggan and Katherine his wife, one of the dau'rs and coh. of Thomas Cocke.

2 C

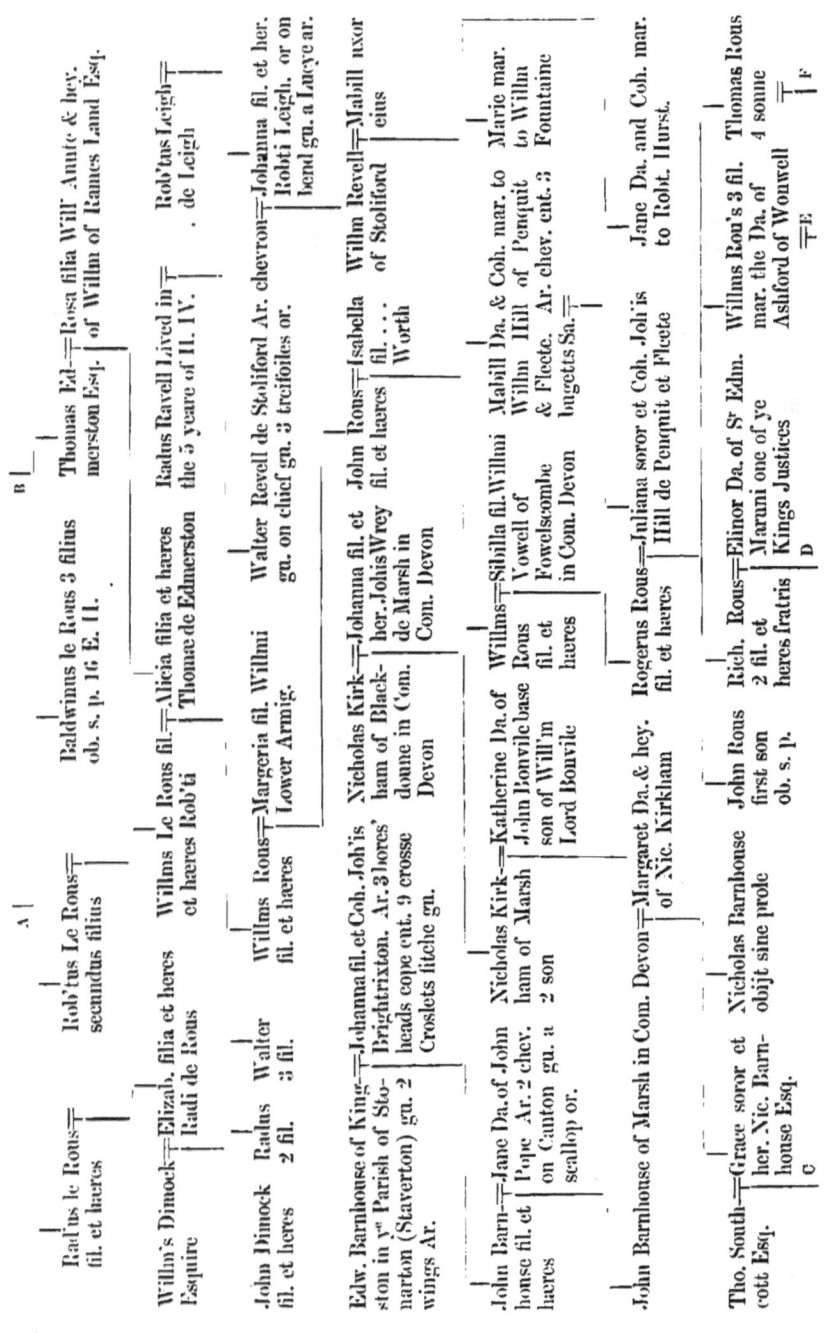

THE VISITATION OF THE COUNTY OF CORNWALL. 195

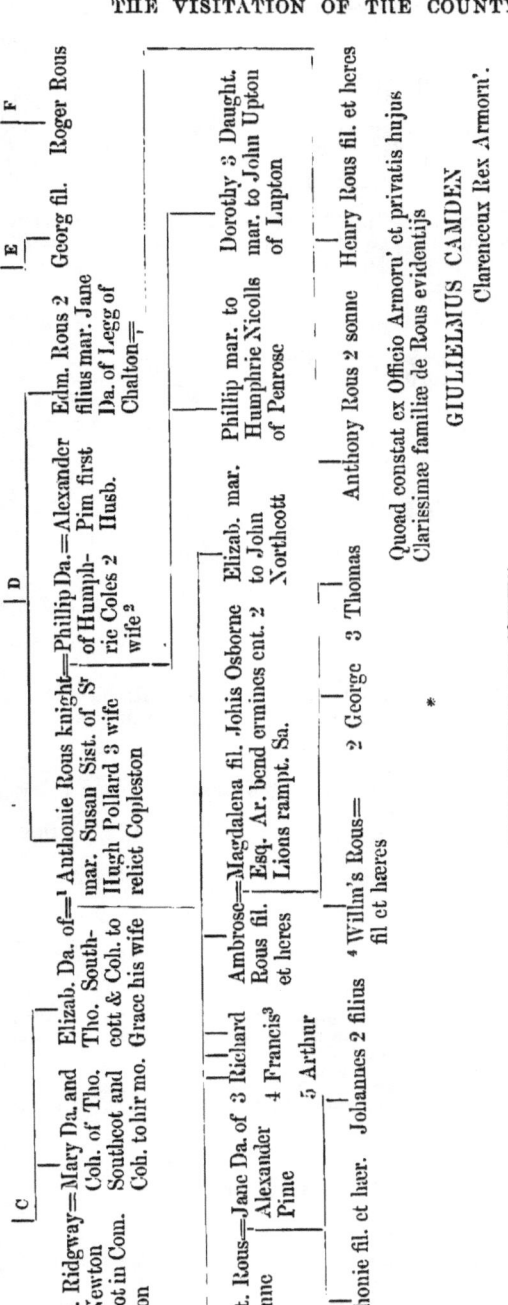

GUILIELMUS CAMDEN

Clarenceux Rex Armorn'.

[1] Executor to the will of Sir Francis Drake, the Circumnavigator.
[2] She was the relict of Alexander Pym. See 'Visit. Devon,' Harl. 1080, fo. 360.
[3] Francis Rous, gent., son of Sir Ant. Rous, Knt., and Ebbot Greynvile, the da. of Geo. Greynvile, Esquier. of Penheale, mar. 2 Ap., 1612. (Menhenniot Par. Reg.) He was M.P. for Truro 1643, Speaker of Barebones Parliament, and afterwards Provost of Eton, where he died 7 Jan., 1658, and was interred in the College Chapel. He and his brother Richard wrote commendatory verses prefixed to the Rev. Charles Fitzgeffery's 'Life of Drake.'
[4] William Rowse and Maria Robarts, mar. 24 Ap., 1617. Truro Par. Reg.

* Marten Rous of Holbeton in Devon, bur. 1623. Menhenniot Par. Reg.
Francis Rows and Martha Carew, mar. at Antony, 26 Dec., 1639. Bp. of Exeter's Transcripts.
Francis Rous of St. Dominic, Cornw., gent., and Honor Coppleston of Boskerin, in Bodmin, wid., mar. lic. 29 Aug., 1610.
Ped. fin. 7 Ric. I. No. 2, Cornw. Rich. Ruffus and Marina ux. qu. Ric. fil. Wybd. def. Lands in Tredewi.
„ 30 Ed. I. No. 10, Cornw. Rich. le Rous de Tregaminion and Belisentam ux. qu. Rad. de Boskenman, def. Treguminion juxta Lesard.
„ Cornw. 33 Hen. VIII. No. 7. Odonem Rous and William Rous his son, and Johana his wife, qu. Michael Rous, bro. of William. def.
Pipe Roll 31 Hen. I. Osbt. Ruffs. held in Cornwall.
Chan. Proc. Eliz. R. r. 9, No. 11. John Rowse v. Will. Kendall, claim by descent.

196   THE VISITATION OF THE COUNTY OF CORNWALL.

Samuell.

Wm Samuell of Shevyock=Mary Da. of Tho. Tremayn
in Com. Cornwall   of Collocombe

Marg^t 1	1		2	Lorew 3	Honor 5
Elizab. 2	Honor Da. of=Jo. Samuell of=Mary Da. of Jo.			Margery 4	Grace 6
	Ric. Halse of Rostormell in Chichester of				
	Keneton in Com. Cornwall Hall in Devon				
	Devon liveing 1620				

John 2 sone   Willm sone & hey.   Elizab. 1   Anne
at. 7   atat. 17, 1620   a da.   2 Da.

                            *

                                        JO. SAMUELL,

Sawle.

Richard Sawle of Lavaren=Rose, da. of .... Sallamon

¹ Oliver Sawle of Lavaren=¹ Jane da. of Nich. Kendall

¹ Richard sonne and   ¹ Nicholas Sawle of=Alice da. of John Rashley
heire ob. s. p.   Penrise Living 1620 | of Foy in Com. Cornub.

² John sonne   ³ Oliver 2   ⁶ Jonathan 5   ⁸ Willm 7   ⁴ Jane 1
& heir ætat.
21 annoru'   Nicholas 3   ⁷ Richard 6   ⁹ Joseph 9   ⁵ Elizabeth 2
1620
               Francis 4   Robert 8   Alice 3

                            †   NICHOLAS SAWLE.

---

* For additions to ped. of Samuell, see Harl. MS. 1079, fo. 195.

¹ Oliver Sawle. Will. Harrington, 79. To Parish Stocke of Sanestell (St. Austell). 20s.; names his brother Marmaduke, wife Jane; to son Rich. his best brass Crock. Second son Nicholas, Brother Kendall, and Cousin Rich. Tremayne to be overseers.

² John, son of Nicholas Sawl. bap. 13 May, 1599. Fowey Par. Reg.
   Mr. John Sawell and Mrs. Mary Putt. mar. 13 Mar., 1627.   St. Austell Par. Reg.
³ Oliver Sawel, Esq., and Mrs. Jane Glanville, da. of the Rt. Worshipful Sir Fras. Glanville, Knt., mar. Sunday. 3 Feb., 1632. Tavistock Par. Reg.
⁴ Jane.   da. of Nich. Sawl, bap.   Mar.. 1598.
⁵ Elizb.,   „   „   „ 11 Oct., 1603.
⁶ Jonathan, son of „   „   „ 17 Sept., 1609. } Fowey Par. Reg.
⁷ Richard,   „   „   „ 17 Feb., 1611.
⁸ Will.,   „   „   „ 7 Mar., 1613.
⁹ Joseph,   „   „   „ 3 Jan., 1619.

† Rychard Sawell witnessed the will of the Rev. Edmund Drake, Vic. of Upchurch, Kent, father of the Admiral Sir Francis Drake. Testator requested " Rycharde Sawell to stande my good frynde." Prob. at Canterbury 16 Jan., 1566.

[*Note continued on next page.*

Sayer.

Sayer & Bond

Sayer & Vivcon

Sayer & Kendall.

Hugh Sayer of Michaell Penkevell=[1] Margaret da. of .... Digby of Colshull

[2] Richard Sayer of Michaell Penkevell=Ursula da. of Hugh Trevillian of Yarnescomb

Edward Sayer of Michaell Penkevell living 1620 ætat. 20   Richard 2 sonne

*   EDWARD SAYER.

(*Note continued.*)
Elizab., da. of Oliver Sawle, Esq., bap. 1638, at Tavistock.   Bp. of Excter's Transcripts.
Henry Sawle and Elizb. Peck,   mar. 1678.   Lansalloes Par. Reg.
John Sawlle and Jonne,   mar. 1615.   Luxyllian Par. Reg.
Ric. Sawell of the parish of Gerrenst and Sibill Michell, mar. 1615. } Mawnan Par. Reg.
Rich., son of Rich. Sawell and Sibilla, ux.,   bap. 1628. }
Alice, da. of Mr. Oliver Sawel,   bap. 1633, ⎫
John Sawle and Mary Hooper,   mar. 1637, ⎪
John Sawle and Thomazin Trevillian,   „   1670. ⎬ Tavistock Par. Reg.
Rich. Saule,   bur. 1667. ⎪
Mary Saule, wid.,   „   1677. ⎭
Will. Saule of St. Austell,   bur. 14 May, 1659.   Truro Par. Reg.
John Harrys of Radford, Esq., and Amy Sawle, mar. 31 May, 1661. ⎫ Tywardreath
Temperance, wife of Mr. Nich. Saull,   bur. 2 April, 1658. ⎬ Par. Reg.
Mr. Nich. Saule,   „ 30 Nov., 1667. ⎭

Ped. fin. 6 Ed. VI. East. Rich. Sawle, gen., qu. Tho. Drake and Margaret, ux., John Ernectle and Joan, ux., def. Lands in Hawcombe, p'ish of Beer Ferris. Ernsettle Estate is on the left bank of the Tamar, above and near Saltash Bridge.

Ped. fin. 16 Elizb. Mich. Cornw.   William Kendall, qu. Oliver Sawle, def. Lostwithiel.
„   34   „   „   ,,   Nicho. Sawle, gen. qu. Jno. Loure, sen. gen. and o'rs, def. Ten't in Penryse, etc.
„   40   „   „   Dev.   Jno. Glanville, qu. Tho. Sawle, def. Tavistock.
„   2 Jas. II. Trin. Cornw.   Jos. Sawle ar. and o'rs, qu. Bridget Maynard vid Vivian and o'rs in Cosewarth, etc.

The following notes relate to the issue of Joseph, son of Oliver and Joan Sawle :—
Joseph Sawle of St. Austell and Amy Trevanion of Pendennis or St. Allen. Mar. lic. 21 Mar., 1660.
Timothy Shoote, Rect. of Lawhidon, and Garthryd, da. of Joseph Sawle of St. Austell, Esq., mar. 29 Jan., 1700.   St. Mewan Par. Reg.
John, son of Jno. Vivian, Esq., of St. Columb Ma., and Mary, da. of Joseph Sawle of St. Austell, mar. at St. Mewan, 1684.   Archd. Transcripts.
Will of Mrs. Jane Williams (da. of Joseph Sawle) of St. Austell, wid., 3 Feb., 1732. Names sisters Ann and Mary Beauford; brother Francis Sawle, and his son Rich. and da. Mary; brother Joseph Sawle and his son John; nieces Polly and Agnes Sawle; sisters-in-law Mary Sawle and Jane Carthew and her husband John Carthew; nephews John Harris and Tho. Shute; cousin Tho. Vivian; brother-in-law Hugh Williams; sister Mary Vivian. To Ch. of St. Austell her best and largest silver salver. Bodmiu Prob. Co.

For more of Sawle, see ped. 'Parochial Hist. Cornwall.' Lond., 1667. Vol. i., p. 44; and Harl. MS. 1079, fo. 204.

[1] Margaret, wife of Hugh Saier, Esq., bur.   1608. ⎫
[2] Rich. Saier, Esq.,   „ 11 Sept., 1603. ⎬ St. Michael Penkivel Par. Reg.
* Anthony, son of Rich. Saier, Esq.,   ,, 29 Oct., 1599. ⎭
Tho. Sayer and Elizb. Weeks, mar. 1665.   Probus Par. Reg.

Scawen.

Sciant present et futur q^d Ego Joh'es de Kilquite dedi concessi et hac p^{r}sent Carta mea confirmavi Sibille que fuit uxor Will'mi Scawen de Meleneck, matris Joh'is Scawen filij et heredis d'ci Will'mi Scawen, etc., A° 8 Rici II.

Sciant p^{r}sent' et futuri q^d ego Joh'es Scawen de Meneleck dedi concessi et hac presenti carta mea confirmavi Nico Strike omnia mesuag. et totam terra' meam de Kilquite cum suis p'tn' etc. hijs testibus Thoma Paderda Joh'e Tolcarn, Willo Cressell, Johe Harlisdon, Waltero Smith et alijs. Dat. apud Melenck die Jovis prima post festu' Aploru' Johi et Jacobi A° regni Regis Henrici quarti post conq. nono.

(Seal of John Scawen—*A chev. betw. 3 Griffins' heads erased.*)

Sciant p^{r}sent' et futuri q^d ego Thomas Scawen dedi concessi et hac presenti Carta mea indentata confirmavi Rogero filio meo omnia, etc., A° 10 H. VI.

Omnibus Christi fidelibus ad quos present scriptu' indentatu' p'ven'it Rogerus Scawen de Meleneck salt'. Dat. apud Stoketon quartodecimo die Junij A° regni regis Edw. quarti vicessimo.

Sciant present et futur q^d ego Tho. Scawen dedi concessi et hac p^{r}senti carta mea confirmavi Waltero Scawen filio meo et heredi et Anastacie filie Robti de Wenemonth quem idem Walterus ducit in uxorem etc. Anno regni regis Hen. VII. vicesimo primo.

Sciant p^{r}sent et futur q^d ego Willms Scawen filius et heres Walteri Scawen defuncti etc. Dat. apud Belenick vicesimo die octob. A° regi Regis Hen. VIII., 32.

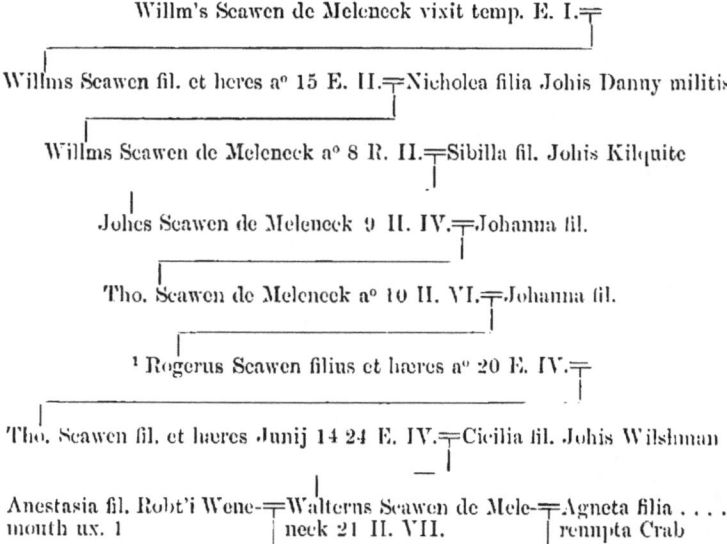

Willm's Scawen de Meleneck vixit temp. E. I.=

Willms Scawen fil. et heres a° 15 E. II.=Nicholea filia Johis Danny militis

Willms Scawen de Meleneck a° 8 R. II.=Sibilla fil. Johis Kilquite

Johes Scawen de Meleneck 9 H. IV.=Johanna fil.

Tho. Scawen de Meleneck a° 10 H. VI.=Johanna fil.

[1] Rogerus Scawen filius et haeres a° 20 E. IV.=

Tho. Scawen fil. et haeres Junij 14 24 E. IV.=Cicilia fil. Johis Wilshman

Anestasia fil. Robt'i Wene-=Walterns Scawen de Mele-=Agneta filia . . . .
mouth ux. 1 | neck 21 H. VII. | renupta Crab
A | | B

[1] Ped. fin. Cornw. 36 Hen. VI. No. 1. Roger Skawen and John Talkarn. bastard, qu. John Talkarn and Johanna his wife, def.

THE VISITATION OF THE COUNTY OF CORNWALL.

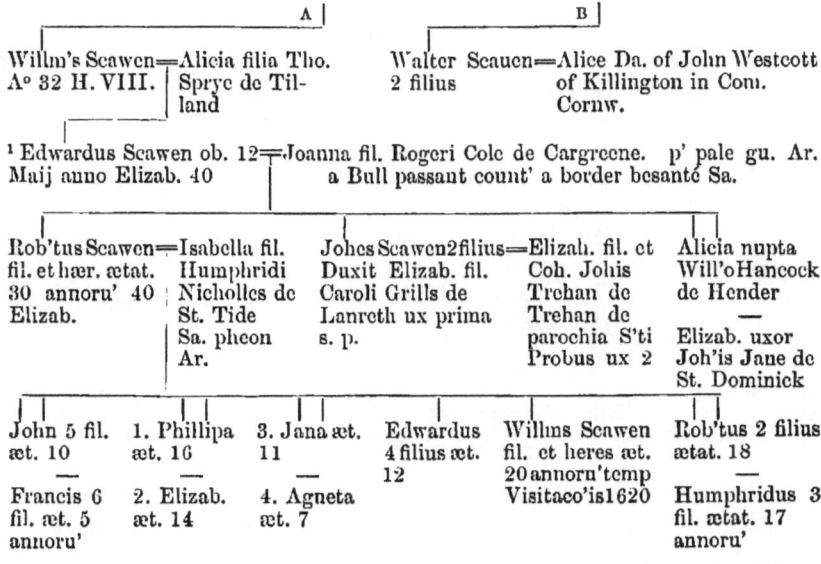

ROBERT SCAWEN.

Extract ex diversis evidentijs et record. in officio Armoru'
Rob'tus Treswell, Somerset.
mense Junij A° D'ni 1601.

Scawen.

Edwardus Scawen Inq.=Johanna filia Rogeri Cole de Cargreene per pale
capta 4 Sept. 40 Elizab. gu. Ar. a Bull pass^t counter border Sa. besanté

Robtus Scawen fil. | Joh'es Scawen 2 fil.=Elizab. fil. | Elizab. nupta Johi Jane
et heres ætat. 30 | de Trehane Elizab. Caroli | de S'to Dominick
annoru' Ar. mar. | fil. et Coh. Johis Grilles de | —
Isabella fil. Hum- | Trehane de Trehane Lanrath | Alicia nupta Willo Han-
phridi Nicholles de | de p'ochie de ob. s. p. | cock de Hender
St. Tyde | Probus uxor 2 |

1. Elizab. | 3. Anna | Trehane Scawen fil. primo- | John 2 fil. | 3. Peter æt.
— | | genitus ætat. 8 annoru' | ætat. 5 | unius anni
2. Katherin | | temp. visitac'ois 1620 | |
 | | † | JOHN SCAWEN.

[1] Inq. p. m. 40 Elizab. No. 26. Edward Scawen died 12 May, 40 Eliz. Robert Scawen, son and heir, aged 30 and more.
* Thomas Scawen Generoso and Anna Urban were mar. at Werrington 4 March, 1608. Bp. of Exeter's Transcripts.
† Ped. fin. 36 Elizb. East. Dev. Wm. Holman, gen. and Rob. Scawen, gen. qu. Tho. Drake, gen. Rich Wylles, gen. Wm. Predyaux, gen. def. Manor of Strete al's Trevervyn, Blackawton, Stoke flemynge.
Ped. fin. 42 Elizb. Mic. Cornw. Wm. Holman, gen. and Rob. Scawen, gen. qu. Geo. Harvey, gen. def. Lands in Kilkhampton.

𝔖𝔠𝔞𝔴𝔫𝔢.

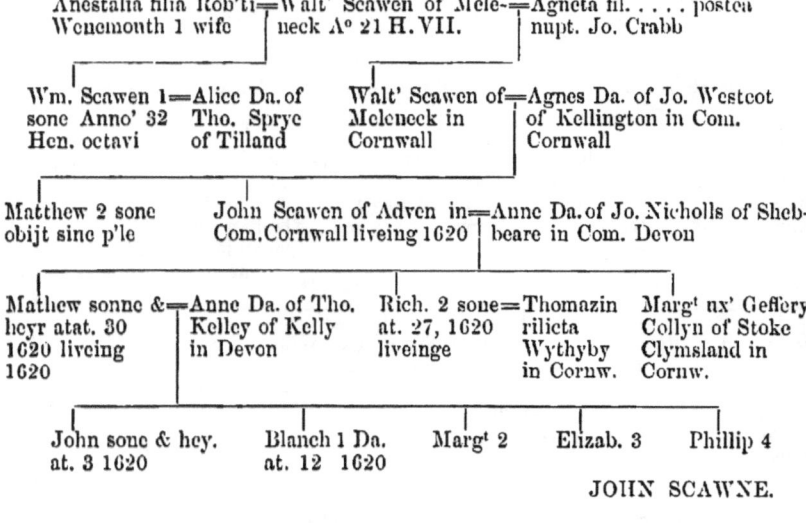

JOHN SCAWNE.

𝔖𝔠𝔬𝔟𝔢𝔩𝔩.*

Sʳ Robt. Scobbell who heyres generall were maried to severall families

Margerie Da. of Willm Webber al's Gilbert⹋Vincent Scobbell⹋Jone Da. of
de Chestow in Com. Devon ux. 2 ┃ of Plymouth ┃ ux. 1
            A ┃ B ┃

---

* The above pedigree properly belongs to Devon, and was intended for insertion under that county, as the word "Devon" was written in pencil at the top of the original. For more of the Cornish Scobels see 'Parochial Hist. of Cornwall,' under the articles St. Ewe, St. Austell, and St. Blazey, and 'Hist. of Trigg,' vol. I. Several families derive from the Cornish branch. Francis Vivian of Coswarth (will prob. 1689, Archd. Co. Cornw.) names his cousins Rich. and Francis Scoble of St. Austell, father and son. John Cosgarne of St. Austell, will 1698, names his uncle Rich. Scobell. Rich. Scoble of St. Austell, gent., will 1716 (Bodmin), names his daughters Mary Hawkins and Barbara Hawkins, sons Francis, Henry, and Rich. Scoble, and his kinsman John Anstis (Garter?). The son Francis was M.P. for St. Mawes, and married Mary, the da. and heiress of Sir Joseph Tredenham, by Mary, dau. of Sir Edw. Seymour. The male line becoming extinct, Mary and Barbara Hawkins inherited the estates, which still remain with their descendants.

Franciscus Scoble duxit uxorem Johan Bennet vidua, prima die Feb., ⎫
 1601. Name of parish torn off.   ⎪
Rich. Scoble, bur. at Milton Abbot, Dev., 1614.   ⎪
Wm., son of Rich. Scobbell and Grace, bapt. at St. Cleer, 1599.   ⎬ Bp. of Exeter's
Francis, son of Tho. Scobble, bapt. 30 Oct., 1631, at Buckl. Mon. Dev. ⎪ Transcripts.
Francis, „ John „ „ 29 Apr., 1628, at Tavistock.   ⎪
Loveday, da. of Rich. Scobble, „ 28 July, 1626, at St. Blazey.   ⎪
John Scoble & Argent Bruyne, mar.   1626, at Lamerton.   ⎪
Rich. Scoble,   bur. 16 Mar., 1622, at St. Blazey.   ⎭

[*Note continued on following page.*

THE VISITATION OF THE COUNTY OF CORNWALL. 201

A | B

Ellin	Athanasius Scobbell	John Scobbell de=Elizab. Da. of	Jone mar.
—	fil. 2 æt. 20 annoru'	Plimouth fil. pri-	Willm Perrye	to John
Diana	aº 1620	mogenit.		Lewis

John Cole Witchampton in=Jone fil. unica mar. to John Trlawny
Com. Dorset 2 maritus   ob. ille s. p. first husb.

John Cole fil. primogenitus   2. Lawrence 5   3. Thomas 2   Elizab.
ætat. 7 annor' 1620
                              *
                                            JOHN SCOBELL.

* Mr. Jno. Prideaux and Dorothy Scoble, mar. at St. Ive, 17 Aug., 1691. ⎫ Archdeacon's
  Mrs. Dorothy Scoble bur. at Quethiock,   1682. ⎭ Transcripts.
  John Scoble and Alice Facie,   mar. 22 Aug., 1543.⎫
  Rich. „   and Richarda,   „   1563. |
  John   „   and Agnes,   „   1567. |
  John   „   and Jone Hamlyn,   „   1572. |
  Rich. „   and Richarda Warren,   „   „ |
  Robt. „   and Xtn. Harwoode,   „   1586. |
  Robt. „   and Joan Tapson,   „   „   ⎬ Buckland Mon. Par. Reg.
  Tho.   „   bur. · 1546. |
  John   „   „   1548. |
  John   „   „   1551. |
  John, son of Richard S.,   „   1552. |
  Nich. Scoble,   „   1553. |
  Gabriel „   „   1556. ⎭
  Rich., son of Fras. Scoble, by Priscilla, bap. 22 Feb., 1633.⎫
  Francis,   „   Rich Scoble, by Barbara,   „   24 Aug., 1664. |
  Barbara, da. of   „   gent.,   „   „   21 May, 1669. |
  Elizb.,   „   „   „   „   „   31 Oct., 1671. ⎬ St. Austell Par. Reg.
  John Cosgarne and Elizb. Scobell,   mar. 28 Jan., 1672. |
  Francis Scobell, gent.,   bur. 31 Mar., 1664. |
  Priscilla   „   wid.,   „   3 Aug., 1670. ⎭
  Mrs. Barbara Scobell,   „   16 Mar., 1712.⎫
  Francis Scobell, Esq.,   „   3 Dec., 1740. ⎬ St. Ewe Par. Reg.
  Mary   „   wid.,   „   26 Aug., 1742. ⎭
  Francis, son of John Scoble, bap. at Tavistock,   1638. ⎫
  Loveday, da. of Rich. Scoble,   „   St. Blazey,   1622. ⎬ Bp. of Exeter's Trans.
  Rich. Scoble,   bur. at   „   16 Mar.,   „   ⎭
  Rich., son of John Scoble,   bap.   1661. ⎫
  Philip Scoble and Emma Bodman,   mar.   1614. |
  Oliver   „   Elizb. Rowe,   „   1617. |
  Philip   „   Wilmot Soper,   „   „ |
  John   „   and Mary Palke,   „   1618. |
  Walter S'obbell and Johan Hooper,   „   1620. ⎬ Tavistock Par. Reg.
  Roger Scoble and Joan Peeke,   „   1647. |
  John   „   Mary Martin,   „   „ |
  Tristram „   „   Hilman,   „   1700. |
  Oliver   „   bur.   1619. |
  Walter   „   „   1626. ⎭
  Mr. Richard Skobell and Barber Carllyone, mar. 24 April, 1660. Tywardreath Par. Reg.
  Mr. Henry Scoble, bur. 23 Aug., 1655. Kenwyn Par. Reg.
  Rich. Scobell and Joane, mar. 9 July, 1611. Luxyllian Par. Reg.
  John Scoble and Joan Carveth, mar. 1574. St. Columb Ma. Par. Reg.
  Chas. Fortescue and Dorothy Scoble of Plympton St. Mary, 1685. Mar. lic.
  Lic. to erect monument in Church of St. Blazey granted to Fra. Scoble ar. 16 Mar., 1730.
    Exeter Act Book.
    Ped. fin. 20 Jas. East. Cornw. Rich. Scobell qu. Edw. Retallack and Elnr. ux. def. Heybullien,
Heywartha, Polmeder, St. Austell.
    Ped. fin. 1651, Hill. Cornw.   Francis Scoble qu. Chas., Philip, and Lewis Dart and Lewis
Tremaine def. Polruddan Port, Pentewan, St. Austell.
    Ped. fin. 26 Chas. II. Trin. Cornw. Ric. Scoble and o'rs qu. Chas. Trevanion ar. def. Man.
of Tregarthen and ten'ts.   2 D

Searle.

ARMS.—*Arg. a chev. Sa. betw. 3 wood doves proper.*
CREST.—*A Greyhound Arg. collared Gu. sejant on a bank Vert.*

Anthonie Searle of Thanks, p. w. C. C. the 44 of 2 Eliz. a° D'm. 1602

Rich. Searle of Thaukes in Cornwall lived in the time R. III.

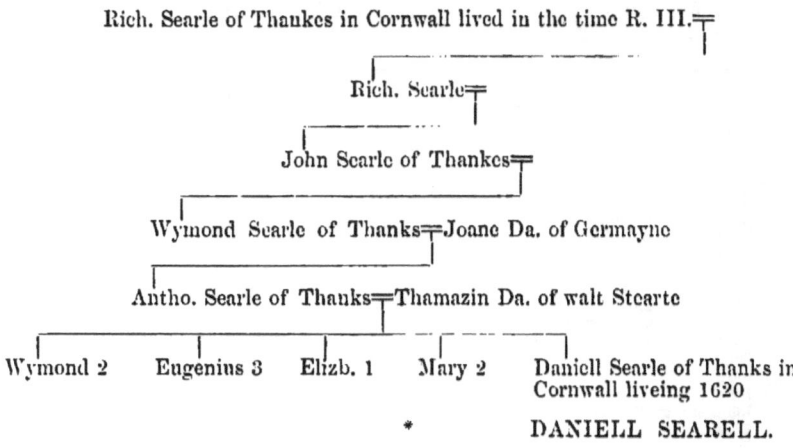

Wymond 2	Eugenius 3	Elizb. 1	Mary 2	Daniell Searle of Thanks in Cornwall liveing 1620

DANIELL SEARELL.

Shorrock.

Shorrockes of Ribbelsdale in Com. Lanc^r, first of wch name was Raphe Shorrock of Shorockhayes, wch in the Barons' Wars was advanced to be a Captaine and therein lost his life. his descent grewe poore, and when the Scotts overan the Northrne borders & parte of Lancasheire and Chesheire, the most parte of this familie fled unto Dublyn in Ireland, where by Corruption of the Irish Ideoam the were termed Sharlock, wch name of necessitie they were constreyned to hold in the time of King Henrie the Seventh.

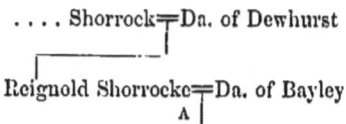

* Ped. fin. Cornw. 27 Hen. VI. No. 1. John Serle of Leskyrd and Isabella his wife def.
Henry, son of John Sorrell, gent., bap. at Lanston 18 Oct., 1608.
Richard Lower, gent., and Philadelphia Searell, wid., mar. at Lanreath 1630. } Bp. of Exeter's Transcripts.
John Dyer and Claris Searle   mar. 19 Feb., 1581-2.
Martin Searle   bur. 7 March, 1581.   } St. Ewe Par. Reg.
Edward Searle   „   19 March, 1607.
Mr. Walter Searle, Minister.   „   28 Nov., 1677.   } Lanhydrock Par. Reg.
Letitia Isabella, da. of Mr. Edw. and   (J. M.)
    Elizabeth Searle,   bap. 27 Jan., 1671.

THE VISITATION OF THE COUNTY OF CORNWALL. 203

A |

Robert Shorrock=Da. of Adams in Com. Midd.

¹ John Sharrock of Tregon-John in=¹ Elizb. Da. of Wm. Matthew of
Com. Cornwall liveing 1620   St. Kue in Com. Cornwall

¹ John sone   Rob. 2 sonne at. 23   Matthew 3   ¹ Anne mar. to   ¹ Phillip   Elizb.
& hey. at.   Mastʳ of Arte in   sonne atat.   John Tucker of   unma-   unma-
32, 1620   Exiter Coledge in   15, 1620   Kingsale in Ire-   ried   ried
   Oxford   *   land

Not signed.

Skory.

Sʳ Rich. De la laune=Da. of ....

Edm. De la laune=Maud da. of Sʳ Rich. Bluett Kᵗ

Robt. De la laune=Alice Da. of Sʳ Tho. Boscawen Kᵗ

² John Skorie of whals-=³ Mawde Da. and one of the hires
borowe Esq.   of Rob. De la laune

John Skory of Whalsburye=Margᵗ Da. and one of the heires of Rob. Lanion

Rob. Skorie of Whalsburye=Grace Da. of Hugh Trevenor Esquire

⁴ John Skorie=Grace Da. and one of the heires of Robt. Redris

John Skorie=Kathʳ Da. of Hen. Trevisa Gent.

Rich. 1 sone   ⁵ John Skorie 2 sonne   Rob. Skorie   Henric 4   Tho. 5   Michaell
had 2 Da.   Da. of Trewynt   3 sonne   sonne   sone   6 sonne
   A=

¹ Named in will of Rich. Mathew of Tresunger 2 June 8 James, proved in London 1610.
* William Sharrock, Vicar of Gluvias, bur. 22 Nov., 1612. Gluvias Par. Reg.
² Son of John Skory of Whallesburgh, Ar.
³ Alice was the other daughter and coh.   } Harl. MS.
⁴ His wife is called Jane, dau. of Rich. Kendall, and the arms of Kendall { 1140, ffo. 23, 24.
of Pelynt are annexed.
⁵ Married Maria, da. of Tho. Shelton of Norff. *B. a cross Or.* Harl. MS, 1545, fo. 34.

¹ Tho. Skorie sone of John=Jane Da. of Callard

Tho. Skorie=Alice Da. of John Tregonell

Stephen Skorie of Treworgie Skorie in Cornw.=Elizb. Da. of Jo. Trubodie

John Skorie of Lanliverie in=Elizb. Da. of Wm.
Com. Cornw. liveinge 1620 | Samuell

Bridgett a da. atat. 24, 1620 — Walt^r 2 sone atat. 18 — John sone & heire atat. 22, 1620

*

JOHN SKORY.

Smyth.

Rob. Smithe of Tregonake in the=Joane Da. & hey. of Rob.
p'ish of St. Germayns | Killegrew 1 wife

Wilmot Da. & hey.=Thomas Smith of Tregonake=Mary Da. of S^r ... Lentall of
of Roger Tremayne | sone & hey. | Latchford in Com. Oxford

John Smith sone & hey. of Tregonok

Robt. Smith of Trewynt in Blysland P'ish in Com. Cornw. atat. 35, 1620

† **ROBT. SMYTH.**

---

¹ His brother John Skory Bp. of Hereford, ob. 1585, whose wife Elizb., da. of Robt. Clement of Surrey, ob. 1592. The descent is continued, in the MSS. quoted, 3 generations below the bishop.
  "John Scory, Byshop of Hereford, ignorant of his descent, procured this coat above tricked to be granted to him" (*Party per chevron embattled Or and Sa., 3 pelicans' heads erased counterch., vulned (iu.. on a chief B. a fleur-de-lis betw. two estoiles of the first*) "as appeareth by the pattent, 6 March A° Reginæ Elizabethæ. But his posteritie, findeing as it seemeth better proofe, left this and doe nowe bear as in the pedigree before set downe,—Or, on a saltire Sa. 5 cinqfoils Or" (quartering DE LA LANDE, *Arg. a chevron betw. three billets (iu., and* LANYON). Harl. 1140, fo. 25. Crest, *Medusa's head*, Harl. 1545, in which MS. is a note that the Bishop's ped. was subscribed by Clarenceux Camden.

* John Beale and Jane, filia Thos. Score, mar. 28 Jan., 1606-7. St. Ewe Par. Reg.
John Skore and Elizabeth Grilles mar. at Laureath 12 Jan., 1600. Bp. of Exeter's Trans.
† Ped. fin. Cornw. 5 Rich. II. No. 9. Walter Smyth and or's qu. John Cok and wife def. Trelay, etc.
Ped. fin. Cornw. 20 Rich. II. No. 2. Lawrence Smyth of Fowey, gent. qu. Wm. Carpenter def.
  „   19 Hen. VI. No. 7. Thomas Smyth of Crofthole qu. John Estcote of Atte hole def. Trithell juxta Crofthole.
Honor da. of John Smith gent. bap. at St. Columb Major 19 Feb., 1614. Bp. of Exeter's Trans.
Jno. Smith, gent., bur. 5 Aug., 1656. Blisland Par. Reg.
Christopher Pomeroy of Plymo., and Anne Smith of Blisland, mar. lic. 7 Nov. 1617. ⎫
Jno. Smith of St. Germans, and Elizb. Carter of St. Columb Maj., wid., mar. lic.   ⎬ (J. M.)
  28 Nov.. 1631.   ⎭
For Smith of Blisland, see 'Hist. of Trigg,' vol. i., pp. 47, 48, etc.

Sparke.

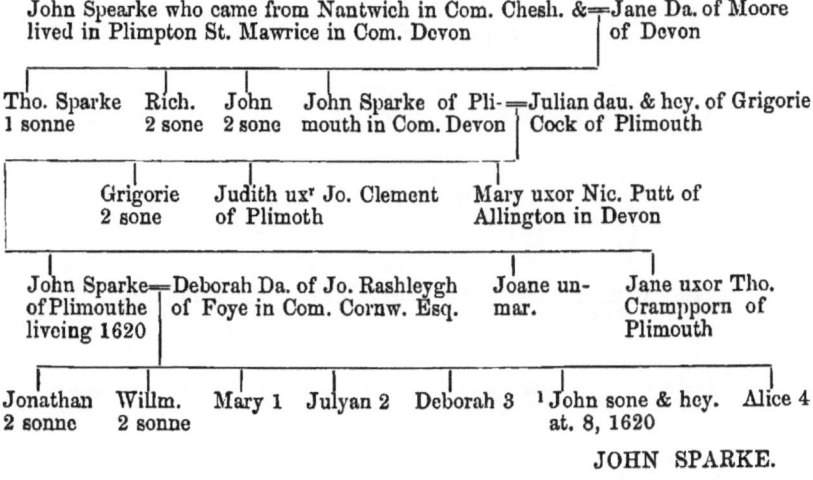

JOHN SPARKE.

Sparnon.

Sim. Sparnon of Sparnon in Cornwall=

John Sparnon of Sparnon=Margt Da. of John Martin of Breage

Edw. Sparnon of Sparnon=Elizb. Da. of John Toule of Dalverton in Somrsetsh.

1
Jane Dau. of Pasco Kerne of=Tho. Sparnon=² Thomazin Da. of Godolphin of
Tresilian in Cornwall | of Sparnon | Trewarvenner in Cornwall

John | Edw. Sparnon of=Anne Da. of edw. Bugges | Thomas 3 | Fran. 4 | Anne
2 sone | Spernon in Com. | of Harlow in Essex | — | | a da.
 | Cornwall liveing | | Beniamin 5
 | 1620

Thomas 2 sone | Fran. sone & hey. | John 3 sone | Mary 1 Da. | Anne 2 Da.
 | atat. 5, 1620

EDW. SPARNON.

---

¹ John Sparke was born in Nov., 1602, died in Fowey, and there buried March, 1633.
M. I. Fowey Church.
² Thomas Spernon gent. and Thomasin Godolphin mar. 10 July, 1598. Breage Par. Reg.

Spoore.

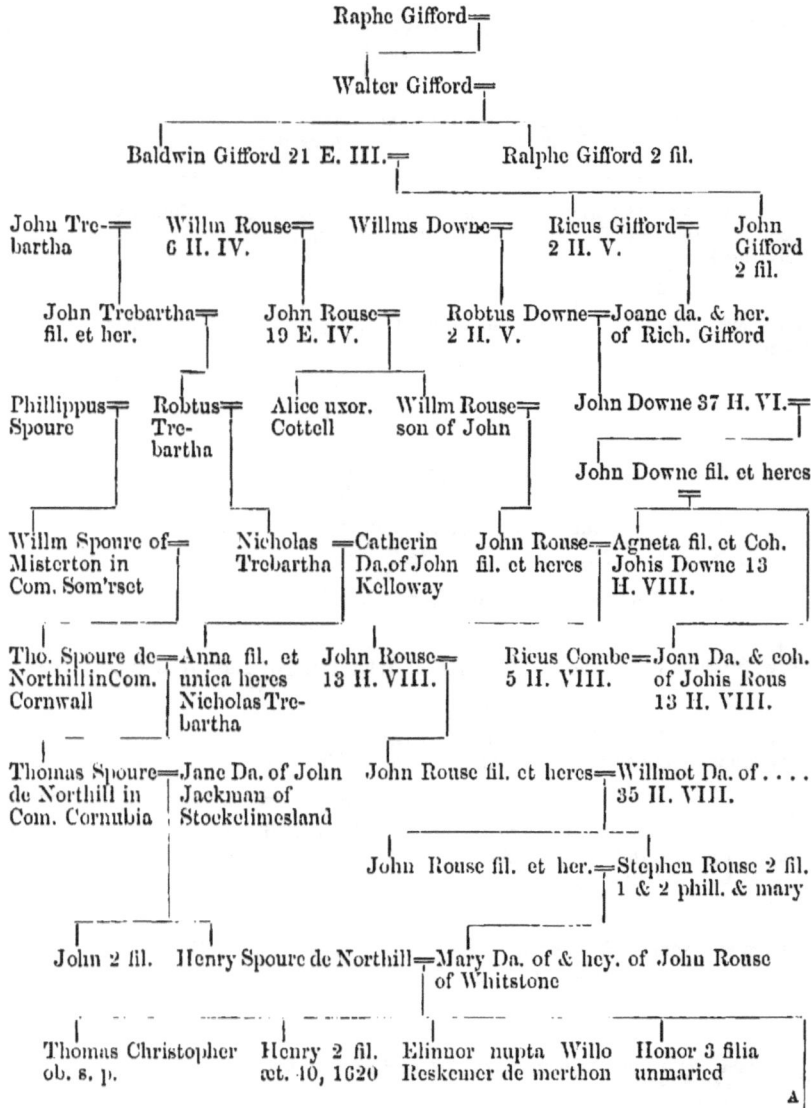

THE VISITATION OF THE COUNTY OF CORNWALL. 207

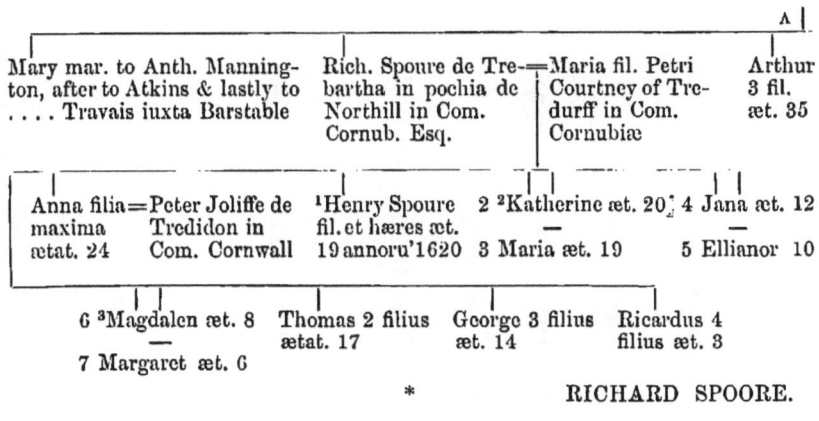

RICHARD SPOORE.

Sprey.

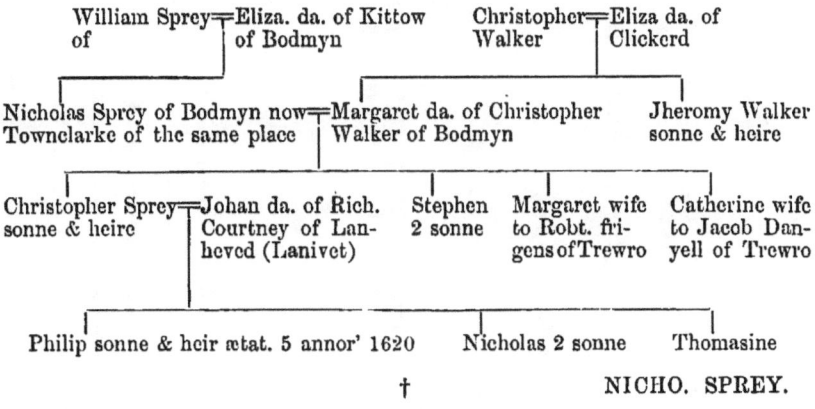

† NICHO. SPREY.

---

[1] Lic. to marry Gertrude, da. of Humph. Bury of Culleton, p'ish of Chumleigh, Esq., 14 Sept., 1622.
[2] Lic. to marry Tho. Cooke of Forde, p'ish of Hartland, 16 July, 1630.
[3] Bur. 15 April, 1687. Whitstone Par. Reg.
* Mar. lic. to Pet. Spoure, gent., and Joanna Short of Ashwater, 19 Oct., 1674 ; Edm. Speur and Mary, da. of Jas. Rodd of Exon, 6 Oct., 1675 ; Wm. Hooper of Linkinghorne, and Fras. Spoure of Northill, sp., 14 Sept. 1667.   (J. M.)

Ped. fin. 44 Elizb. East. Cornw.   Nich. Joliff, gen. qu. Hen. Spore and o'rs def.   Bridge, Knell, etc.
„   1 Chas. Mich. Cornw. Rich. Spoure ar. qu. Peter Jollyffe, def. Manor of Dodacomb, etc.
„   24 Chas. East. Devon.   Henry Spoure ar. and Peter Jolliffe ar. qu. Wm. Mallett, def. Iddeslegh, Monkhampton.
„   1657, Hill. Cornw.   Henry Spoure, Esq., qu. Jno. Carkeete, def.   Brown Park, etc.

† For account of this family and contin. of ped., see ' Hist. of Trigg,' vol. i., pp. 293–4.

THE VISITATION OF THE COUNTY OF CORNWALL.

Spry.

ARMS.—SPRY. B. 2 bars and a chev. in chief Or. TRENOWITH. Arg. on a fess Sa. 3 chevronels palewise, points to dexter of the first. TREWARTHENIK. Arg. a chev. within a bord. engr. Sa.

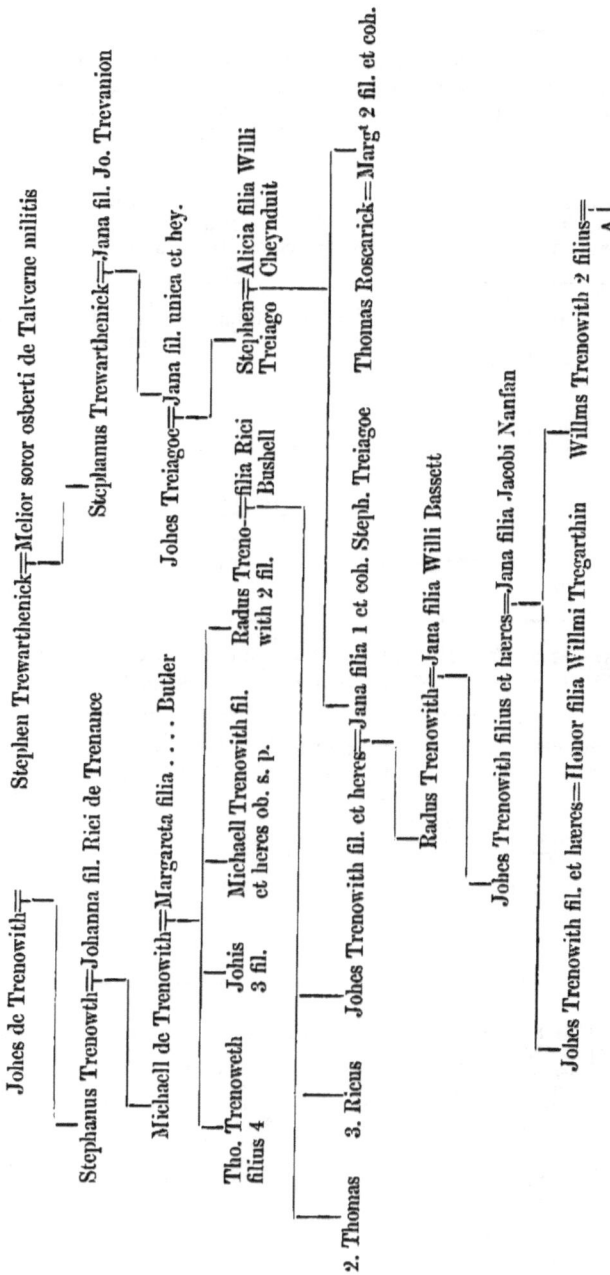

THE VISITATION OF THE COUNTY OF CORNWALL.

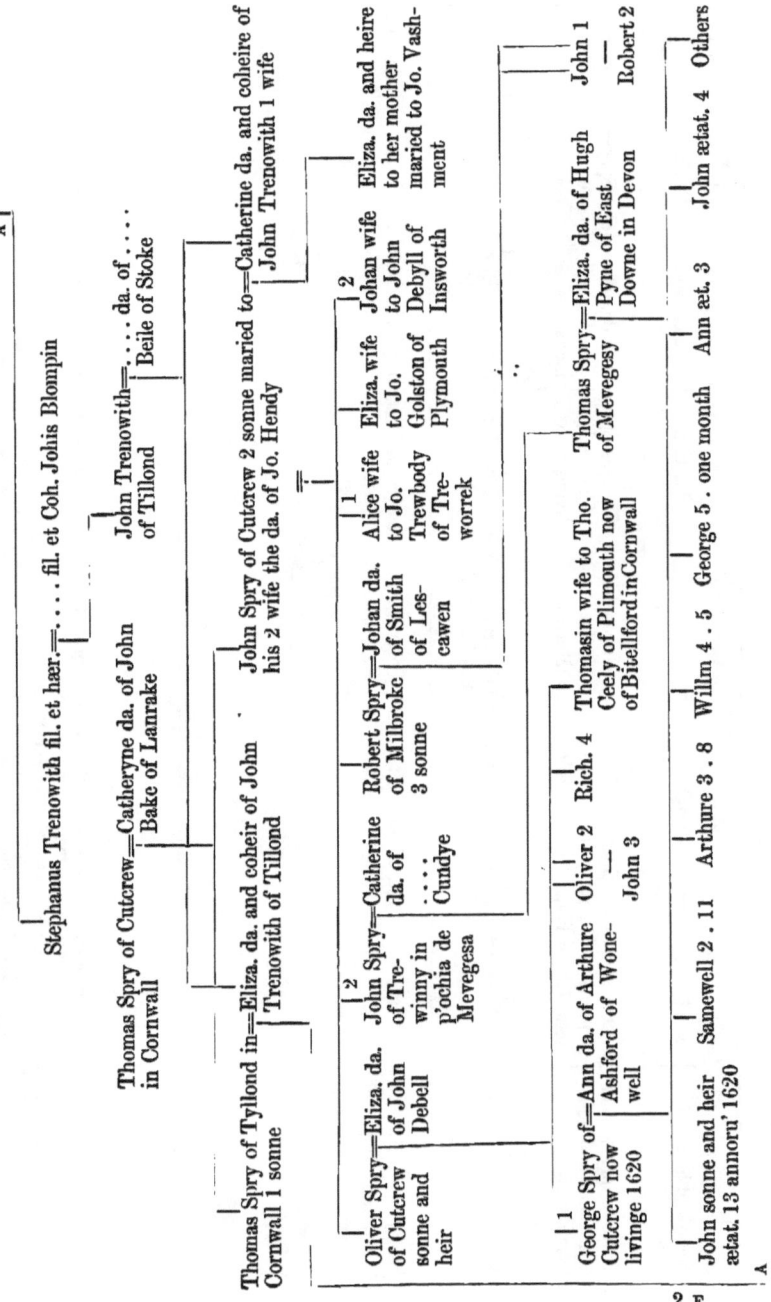

210   THE VISITATION OF THE COUNTY OF CORNWALL.

Hugh Spry of Tillond=Margaret da. of John | Edward Spry of Ten- =.... | Catherine wife | Agnes wife to Robert
sonne and heir | Debyll of Inswerth | creke 2 sonne | to Jo. Kemp | Trelawny
                                                                  | Johan wife to | John Spry=Ann da. of
                                                                  | Peter Burden | 2 sonne | .... Ten-
                                                                                              | creke
                                                                                  | 2 sonnes

Thomas Spry of Bod-=Catherine da. of Arthure | Hugh 2 | Johan wife | Thomas Spry=Ann da. of | George ∴ | Elizabeth wife | ... a da. mar.
myn sonne and heir | Ashford of Wonwell in | —— | to Jo. | of Tenereke | John Vash- | | to .... | to Stiler
living 1620 | Com. Devon Esq. | Edw. 3 | Meriet | living 1620 | ment | | |
                                                                                                                            | ¹.... da. of ...
                                                                                                                            | Erisye 2 wife

Arthure Spry sonne and | Thomas 2 | Henry 3 | Robt 4 | John sonne and heir | Edward 2
heir æt. 18 annorū 1620 | | | | ætat. 18 annorū 1620 |
                                                                                                                            | Issue
² | ³
Henry Spry a Captaine of Foote | .... da. of Rich. Prediaux=Peter Spry of Mewden in Mawnan=¹.... da. of ...
in the Low Countryes | of Thewborow 1 wife | his 3 wife da. of Castle

                                 | Issue
                                   *
                                                                                                                            Not signed.

¹ Peter Spry and Martha Erysey mar. at Ruan Major 10 Oct., 1614. (Bp. of Exeter's Transcripts.) A Peter Spry of Mawnan also mar. Christian, da. of John Roskruge of Anthony. Compare ped. of Roskruge, *ante*.
* Richard Heunah and Elizab. Spry, mar. 1700. St. Ewe Par. Reg.
Ped. fin. 30 Eliz⁵. Cornw. Nich. Skelton and Glinn Spry, gen., qu. Wm. Fortescue, ar. def. Lands in Millbrook, Insworke, and Maker.
„ 21 Chas. I.¹ Trin. Cornw. Arthur Spry qu. Stephen Robins def. Trebisker, etc. St. Eval, St. Ervan.

Spry.

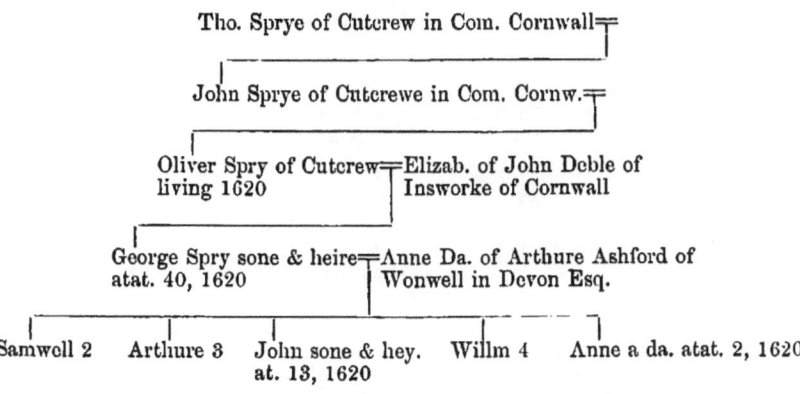

Samwell 2	Arthure 3	John sone & hey. at. 13, 1620	Willm 4	Anne a da. atat. 2, 1620	

*

GEORGE SPRY.

---

* There are two lines in form of a **X** drawn though this pedigree.

Peter Spry, gent., and Anne da. of Rich Penwarne Esq. mar. at Mawnan 1681.
Tho. Holman and Susannah Spry, both of Maker, by lic. from Plymo. dat. 1 7ber, 1721, mar. at Maker. } Archd. Transcripts.

Agnes, da. of Wm. Sprie of Ramsham, bap. 1614 at Tavistock. } Bp. of Exeter's Transcripts.

Will Spry and Alice Elford	mar.	1611. } Buckland Mon. Par. Reg.
Rich. Knighton and Maria Spry	,,	1611.
Elizb. da. of Lewis Spry	bap. 12 Feb., 1624. } Fowey Par. Reg.
Ric. son of Ric. Spry	,, 26 Ap., 1625.
Tho. Elford and Alis Spry	mar.	1585. Menheniot Par. Reg.
Elizb., da. of Rich. Spry,	bap.	1646.
Honor, da. of Will. ,,	,,	1667.
Mary, da. of Anthony ,,	,,	1671.
James, son of Mr. Will. Spry,	,,	1682.
Mary, da. of ,,	,,	1695.
Anthony Spry and Joan Edgcombe	mar.	1631. Tavistock Par. Reg.
Richard Spry and Honor Hillman	,,	1632.
Rich. Spry of Tavistock and Honor Hilman of Anthony, mar. lic.	7 Dec., 1632.
Francis Edgcumbe, gent., and Honor Spry	mar.	1658.
Anthony Spry and Abigail Abbott	,,	1671.
Will. Spry and Mary Vivian	,,	1680.

Holman, Helman (Helman Tor, Lanlivery), Hillman, indifferently. See ped., 'Visit. Devon, 1620,' p. 150.

Grant by Ralph de Valletorta to Roger Derwyn, clerk, Sibil his wife, and Joan, the da. of Roger, of lands that Fulke Holman held in p'ish of Maker. Deed dat. 19 Ed. III., 1345. } Communicated by Deeble Boger, Esq.

See corrected ped. of Spry, 'Hist. of Trigg,' vol. i., pp. 72, 73.

Seyntaubyn vel St. Aubin.

John St. Albone of St. Clowins =[1] Blanch Da. & Coh. of Tho. Whittington
in Com. Cornw. | of Pawntley in Com. Glouc.

Tho. St. =Zenobia Da.	Mari mar.	Grace mar.	Agnes to	Avis mar.
Albin	of John	to Hen.	to John	Tho.	to Corri-
de St.	Mallet of	Chiverton	Reskemer	Coso-	ton
Clowins	Wolley			worth	

John St. Albin=Katherin Da. of | Thomas 2 fil. de Helston | Anne mar. to John
fil. et heres | John Arundell | mar. Katherin[2] Da. of | Courtney of La-
| of Trerise | John Bonithon of Cal- | sack in Com. Corn-
| | clew | wall

1. Gartrude 15	4. Blanch 6	John fil.	2. Thomas æt. 9	Henricus	Thomas
—	—	et her.	—	fil. et	2 fil. æt. 3
2. Anne 14	5. Catherin[3] 4	æt. 10	3. Willms 7	heres	annoru'
—	—	annoru'	—	ætat. 3	et 3 men-
3. Zenobia 12	6. Margaret 3	1620	4. Henry 6	annoru'	sis
			—	et demi	
			5. Nicholas 4		

THOMAS SEYNTAUBYN.   ANTHONIE STEPHENS X mark
for his Mr THO. ST. AUBIN.

*

---

[1] Inq. p. m. Thos. Whittington, 38 Hen. VIII. Blanche, da. and coh., æt. 22.
[2] Mar. 13 April, 1615. Milor Par. Reg.
[3] Bap. at Crowan 18 Sep., 1614. Bp. of Exeter's Transcripts.
* John Seyntaubyn, Esq., bur. 20 Aug., 1684, at Crowan. ⎫
Sir John Seynt Aubyn, Bart., „ 24 June, 1679, „ ⎪
Mrs. Blanch St. Aubyn „ 2 Jan., 1680, „ ⎬ Archd. Transcripts.
Sir John St. Aybyn, Bart., and Catherine, da. of Sir Nicholas Morice, ⎪
Bart., mar. by lic. 3 Oct., 1725. ⎭
(Sir Nich. Morice bur. 7 feb., 1725.)
John Seynt Aubyn, son of John Seynt Aubyn, Esq., and Anne, da. ⎫ Bp. of Exeter's
of James Jenkyn, Esq., dec., were mar. at St. Columb Major 14 ⎬ Transcripts.
Nov., 1665. ⎭
Henry, son of Sir John St. Aubyn, Bart., born 4 June, bap. 12 June, ⎱ Crowan Par. Reg.
1703. ⎰
Francis St. Aubyn, Esq., of Crowan and Maddren, and Mrs. Anc ⎱ Gulval Par. Reg.
Arundell mar. 29 Sept., 1690. ⎰
John Courtenay, of Lazack or Laddock, and Annie St. Abin, da. of ⎫
St. Ablyn of Crowan, ar., 10 Oct., 1595. ⎪
John St. Aubyn of Crowan and Catherine Godolphin, da. of Fras. ⎬ Mar. Lic.
G. of St. Illary, 29 Mar., 1637. ⎪
James St. Aubyn, of St. Agnes, gent., and Mary Sleeman of Lower ⎪
St. Columb 1728. ⎭
Mr. Harrie Sintabin's mother, of Carminowe, bur. 21 Jan., 1595. ⎱ Mawgan in Men.
Hen. Saintawbin of Carminowe. Esq., „ 17 Aug., 1617. ⎰ Par. Reg.
Ped. fin. Cornw. 6 Edw. III., No. 6. Guy de Sancto Albino and Margareta his wife qu.
Walter de Sutton def. Argalles, Medeshole, Wyk St. Mary, and Whitstone, to Walter for life,
rem. to Guy and his heirs.

[*Note continued on following page.*]

Stanberye vel Stanburye.

ARMS. *Quarterly* STANBERYE. *Party per pale B. and O. a lion ramp. Sab.* and ESTCOTTE. *Sa. six escallops Or*, 3, 2, 1.

John Stanbery of Stanbery in Morewinstow in Com. Cornwall=⊤

⎯ Walter Stanbery son & heyre of John=Cicily fil. . . . .

Rich. Stanbery 2 son was Bishop of Hereford

Robt. Stanbery 3 son who dwelt at weststanbery =⊤

Willm Stanbery 4 son who dwelt at Cliff =⊤

John Stanbery sone & heyre=⊤

John Stanbery son & hey.=⊤

John Stanbery sone & heyre=⊤

Willm Stanbery sone & heyre=⊤

Willm Stanbery of Morwinstowe

Nich. Stanberie=Margaret Sister & of Cliffe | Coh. of . . . . E

Willms Stanbery of Tamerton =Jone 1 Da. & hey. of Robt. Dawe of Broadwood

Tho. Stanberie of=Phillip Da. of Hugh Manning Morewinstow or | of Dassell in Morewinstow in Cliffe | Cornwall

Nich. 2 fil. mar. Anne da. of Robt. Cutting of Tam'ton =⊤

Willms=Jane Da. & Coh. of Stan- | Willm Salisberie bery of | of Buckland Tamer- | Brewer ton

Tho. Stan-=Willmot Da. of John bery fil. | Clowter of South primogenit | Petherwin Com. | Cornub.

1. Margerie
2. Maria
3. Magdalen

Willms Stanbery fil. et hæres æt. 10 annoru' 1620

Roger 2 fil. ætat. 6

Abigall — Maria Elizab.

Thomas fil. et hæres æt. 2 annoru'

John Stanbery fil. primogenitus=Rosa fil. . . . .
A

(*Note continued.*)
    Inq. p. m. 8 Ric. II., No. 32. John de St. Aubyn chev. Guido filius æt. 7. (Somerset and Cornwall.)
    Inq. p. m. 14 Rich. II., No. 46. John St. Aubyn, Kt., ob. 7 Rich. II. Guido St. Aubyn, son and heir, æt. 13 et amp. Names Johanna, wife of Sir John, and Elizabeth, wife of his son Guido.
    Inq. p. m. 7 Hen. V., No. 39. John St. Aubyn and Katherine ux., heir of Sir Robt. Challons. Joan, æt. 8, da. and coh., after married Otho de Bodrugan. Margaretta, æt. 4, da. and coh., after mar. Reginald Trethurff.
    (For this line of St. Aubyn, consult Sir Wm. Pole's Devon.)
    Inq. p. m. 1 Hen. IV., 1 part, No. 77. Philipa, wife of Rich. Sergeaux. Alice, born at Kilquite in Mabin and bapt. in the church of St. Mabin, one of the das. and heirs of Philipa, mar. to Guido de St. Aubyn. Prob. æt. Sep. 1 Hen. IV.
    Mrs. Isabella Saintaubyn is named in will of Dame Elizabeth, wid. of Sir Jno. Arundell of Lanherne, 12 June, 1564. P. P. C. 9 Nov., 1564.
    Jane Arundell of Lanherne, will 2 Sept., 1575. P. P. C. 31 Oct., 1577. Names her goddaughter Elizabeth St. Aubyn.

214   THE VISITATION OF THE COUNTY OF CORNWALL.

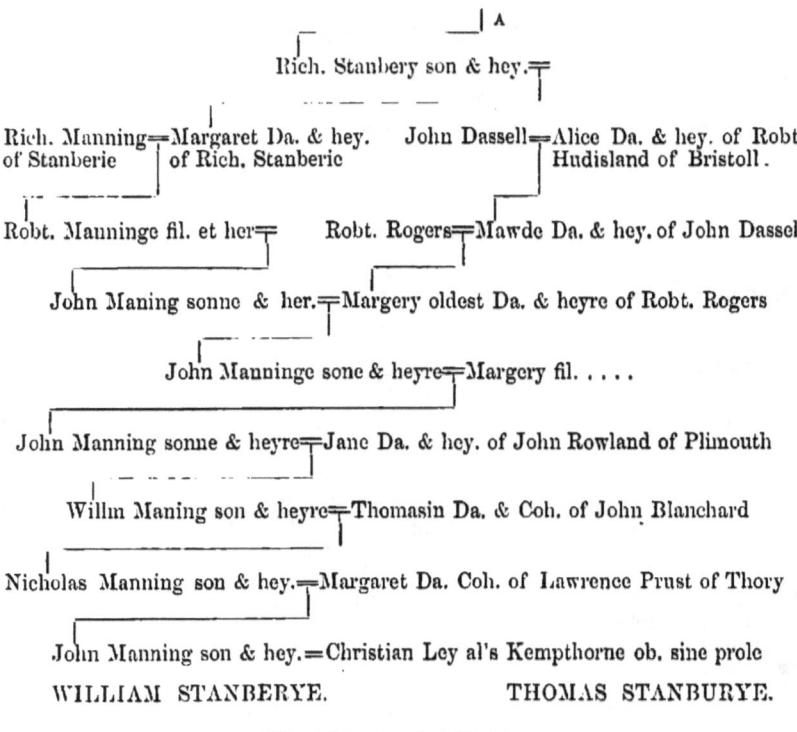

```
                              | A
                    Rich. Stanbery son & hey.=

Rich. Manning=Margaret Da. & hey.    John Dassell=Alice Da. & hey. of Robt.
of Stanberie  of Rich. Stanberie                  Hudisland of Bristoll.

Robt. Manninge fil. et her=         Robt. Rogers=Mawde Da. & hey. of John Dassell

        John Maning sonne & her.=Margery oldest Da. & heyre of Robt. Rogers

                John Manninge sone & heyre=Margery fil. . . . .

        John Manning sonne & heyre=Jane Da. & hey. of John Rowland of Plimouth

                Willm Maning son & heyre=Thomasin Da. & Coh. of John Blanchard

        Nicholas Manning son & hey.=Margaret Da. Coh. of Lawrence Prust of Thory

                John Manning son & hey.=Christian Ley al's Kempthorne ob. sine prole
        WILLIAM STANBERYE.                    THOMAS STANBURYE.
```

Stephens.

```
                        Jo. Stevens of . . . .=

                Tho. Stevens of Dulo in Cornwall=Joane Da. of Collicotte

                Tho. Stevens of Tregony=Jane Da. of Tho. Cock of Bodmin
                liveing 1620            in Com. Cornwall

Hen. sone &     John 2    Arther 3    Elizb. 1    Agnes 2    Rafe 3    Richard 4
hey. at. 18                              *
                                                         THO. STEPHENS.
```

* John Stephen of Godolphin   bur.   1584. ⎱ Breage Par. Reg.
  Will. Williams   and Xtian Steven mar. 12 Nov., 1642. ⎰
  Thomas Stephens and Miss Vivian   mar. 27 June, 1674.   St. Ervau Par. Reg.
  John Treffry, Esq., and Katherine Stephens mar. 22 Dec., 1675.   Fowey Par. Reg.
  Henry Vyvyan and Jane Stephens mar. 1682.   St. Austell Par. Reg.

[*Note continued on following page.*

Stone.

ARMS. P'tie p' pale Or and V't chev'on engraled ent. 3 birdes countercharged, quart'r with Sa. & fesse ent. 3 Beares Or, as in the old Visitacon of Cornwall.

Stephen at Stone in the old Visitacon.

[1]Jo. Stone of Trevigo in Cornw.═Jane Da. of Callard of Callard in Devon

Elizb. ux' Antho. Roscarrock	Jone ux' Oliver Collyns of Launston	Tho. Stone═Elizb. Da. of Wm. of Strevigo │ Harris of Hayne

John 2 sonne mar. Suzan Da. of Tho. Moor Doct. of Divinitie	Dorithie ux' Wm. Lennard of Favant in Com. Wilts Docter of Divinitie	Wm. Stone of Stre-═Mary Da. of Jo. vigo in Com. Cornwall liveing 1620	Newcort of Pickwell in Devon Esq.

Wynifrid ux' John Mathew of St. Cue	Honor ux' 1 Cha. Prust 2 to Rich. Estcot of Lanston	Anne ux' Digorie Hixt of Lanceston	Marg't ux' James Bagg of Plimouth

*

WILLIA STONE.

Thomas.

John Thomas of Crowan in Cornwall═Margerie Da. & hey.

Jo. Thomas of Crowan═.... Da. of....

John Thomas of Crowan═Ellino'r Da. of Wm. Paynter of St. Earth
| A

(*Note continued.*)

    Rich. Carter, St. Columb the Lower, will 27 Nov., 1578, P. P. C. 5 Feb., 1582. Names Tho. Stephens, the elder, of Trenythen, and Tho. Stephens of Trenythen in Probus, an overseer.
    Ped. fin. Cornw. 13 Hen. IV., No. 3. John Stephen, Vicar of St. Peter's, Bodmin, qu. Rich. Wyket and Johanna his wife def. In Grampound, etc.
    Ped. fin. Cornw. 18 Hen. VI., No. 12. Nicholas Stephen and John Kympe qu. Rob. Brewys and wife def. In Leskyret.
    Ped. fin. Cornw. 19 Hen. VI., No. 1. Thos. Dawe, cl'icus, and Henry Stevens, cl'icus, qu. John Thomas and Alianor Lovell def. Names Johanna, wid. of Will. Thomas, Padestowe. etc.
    Ped. fin. Cornw. 28 Hen. VI., No. 2. Thom. Bertelot qu. Robert Stephen and Alice his wife def. In Truruburg, etc.
    Ped. fin. Cornw. 16 Edw. IV., No. 1. Jno. Carowe, cl'icus, and William Stephyn, capellanus, qu. Thos. Tregose and wife def. Kenegy, etc.
    [1] Called John in Bagg pedigree 'Visit. Devon, 1620,' p. 16.
    * Michael Williams and Joan Stone mar. 29 Sept., 1676. Kenwyn Par. Reg.
    Ped. fin. Cornw. 2 Hen. VI., No. 1. Rich. Fortescue and Agnes his wife qu. Margaret, who was wife of John Stone, def. Littlecote, etc. Rem. to Margaret and her heirs if Rich. and Agnes died without issue.

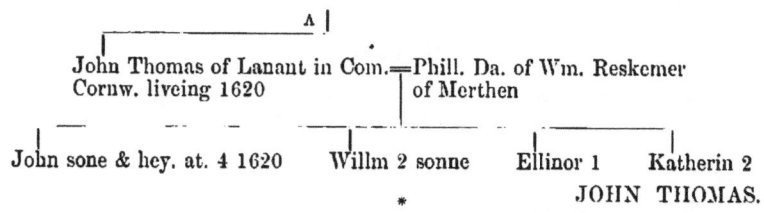

Thoms.

This coate of P' pale nebule Ar. B. was ye coate armor of Sr Willm ap Thomas, from whome this familye chalengeth to be descended.

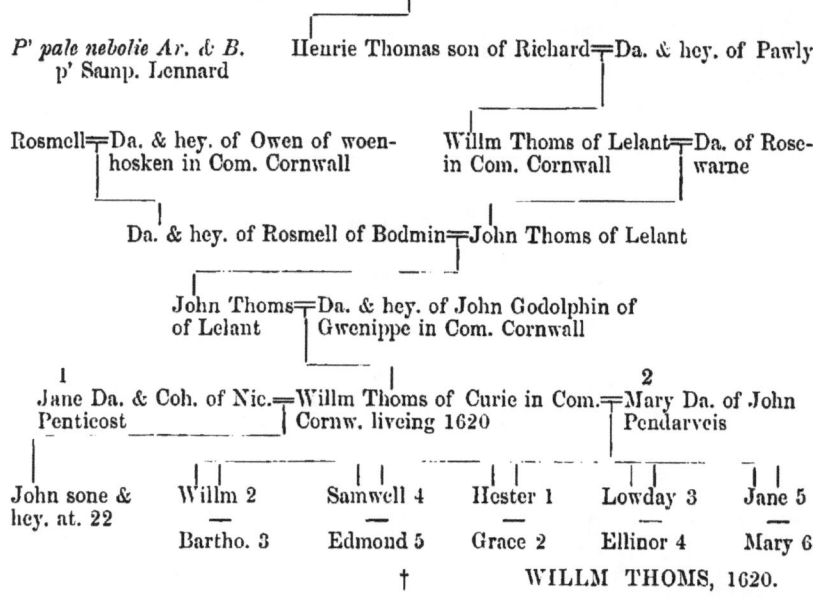

WILLM THOMS, 1620.

---

* Loveday, da. of Will. Thomas, gent., bap. at Constantine 6 Mar., 1601. } Bp. of Exeter's
Jane, wife „ „ bur. 1597. } Transcripts.
Ped. fin. Cornw. 8 Rich. II., No. 3. Roger Thomas of Fosuewith qu. Thomas Juyl of Treworgy and Celnance his wife def. Treworgy juxta Lanstenetha and Heye juxta Calington settled on Roger Thomas and Isabella his wife, rem. to Johana, da. of Isabella, rem. to John Treworgy and his heirs for ever.

† For continuation of this pedigree, see 'History of Trigg Minor.' vol. i., p. 306.

THE VISITATION OF THE COUNTY OF CORNWALL. 217

Thoms alias Carnsew.

Willm Thoms al's Carnsew of Carnsew=Mawd da. & heir of Drew of Tregny

[1] Henry Thoms al's=Julian da. of Tubb   Thomas Thoms=Sibell da. of Edw.
Carnsew of Carnsew | of St. Niott   al's Carnsew   Kestell of Kestell

    [1] Henry Thoms al's Carnsew of Treune=Charitie da. of James Tripcunny

Henry Thoms al's Carnsew   James 2   Grace wife   Ellynor 2   Johan 4
of Treune eldest sonne   sonne   to John   —
living 1620 ætat. 23   Chenowith   Julyan 3

HENRY THOMS AL'S CARNSEW.

*

Toinkein.

John Tonkin of Trevalack in St Kevern in Cornwall=

John Tonkin of Trevalack=Da. of Sandry Browne of
in St. Kevern | Logan in Cornwall

Julian Da. of Will. Pick-=Thomas Tonkin=Mary Da. of Hen. Dulyn of Newton
ford of Exeter ux. 2   of Trevalack   Ferrers in Devon ux. 1

Radigon mar. to Willm Braban of St. Cullum=

Filius unicus

†   THOMAS TOINKEIN.

---

   [1] Chanc. Pro. Elizab. (8 May, 1602), L. 1. 7, No. 44. Lovelis v. Thoms al's Carnsew and o'rs. Gives this descent.

   * Grace, da. of Henry Thoms al's Carnsew, mar. Walter Halamore of Penryn. See Hallamore ped., *ante*.

   For continuation of this pedigree, see 'Hist. of Trigg Minor,' vol. ii., pp. 174, 175.

   † Rev. Hugh Tonkin and Mrs. Prudence Williams mar. at Helstone 1726. ⎫ Archdeacon's
       Will. Tonkin, minister;   bur. at Mullion 7 Jan., 1719. ⎭ Transcripts.

[*Note continued on next page.*

2 F

Trebarfoote.

Tho. Trebarfoote of Poundstoke in Cornwall=Agnes Da. & hey. of Tole of Devon
|
John Trebarfoote of Poundstock=Marg{t} Da. of Wm. Penfound
in Com. Cornwall   of Poundstocke

Rich. 2 sone   Willm Trebarfoote of Trebar-=Mary Da. & Coh. of John
of Trebar-   foote in Com. Cornwall liveing   Bobage of Northtawton
foote   1620   in Com. Devon

Honor   Margt   Willm 2 sone   John sonne & heire at' 15
                           *   RICHARD TREBARFOOTE.

(*Note continued.*)

Michael,	son of Humph. Tonkin, gent.,	bap.	27 Feb.. 1654.	
James,	„ Thomas „ ..	..	1654.	
Sarah,	da. of Humph. „ „	..	1656.	
Sarah,	,. Thomas „ ..	„	1657.	
Henry,	son of John ..	..	1675.	
Stephen,	,. Stephen „	,.	1677.	
Mary,	da. of Willm. Tonkin Sen'r	„	1680.	St. Agnes
William,	son of William Tonkin	..	1681.	Par. Reg.
William,	„ „ „	„	1683.	
William,	„ John Tonkin,	„	1683.	
Temperance,	da. of Thomas Tonkin	..	1683.	
Frances,	„ Hugh Tonkin, Esq.,	..	11 Jan.. 1684.	
Humph.,	son of Humph. Tonkin	,.	30 Nov.. 1689.	
Humphry,	„ „	„	1694.	

Joseph May, clerk, and Elizab. Tauuking   mar. 22 Jan., 1697. } St. Austell Par. Reg.

William Tonkin and Elyzab. Erissy   mar.   1701.   Duloe Par. Reg.

Mr. Hugh Tonkin of Mullion and Elizb. Deane   mar. 22 June, 1687. } Mawgan in Men. Par. Reg.

John Tonkin and Loveday Vyvian .. 28 May, 1614. } St. Austell Par.
Philip Tonkin and Elizab. Halse .. 9 Aug., 1684. }   Reg.
William Cornish, gent., and Jane Tonkin, gent., mar. 12 Aug., 1675. { St. Breoke Par. Reg. } (J. M.)
Thomas Tonkin, Cornw. Will proved 1652, P. P. C. Bowyer, 93.
Edmund Tonkin, Cornw. Adm'n 1652. P. C. C.

* Olive Trebarfoot, wid., bur. 1686. St. Issey Par. Reg. See note 4 under Moyle ped., *ante*.
John Trebarfoot, gen., bur. 3 May. 1631, at Poundstock. Bp. of Exeter's Transcripts.
William, son of Digory Trebarfote, bap. 6 Jany., 1592. } Kilkhampton
Mary,   dau. of „ „ 14 Sep., 1594. } Par. Reg.
John, son of Arthur Trebarfote, bap. 27 May, 1676. } St. Columb Minor
Arthur, son of Arthur Trebarfote. „ 31 Aug., 1684. } Par. Reg.
Elizabeth, dau. of „ „ 24 Nov., 1686. }
Mar. lic. betw. Robert Martyn, of St. Gennys, gent., and ⎫
   Honour Trebarfoote of Poundstock, Jan. 26, 1634. ⎬   (J. M.)
Adm'n of goods, etc., of Simon Trebarfoote, late of ⎬ Act Books, Exeter.
   Newlyn, gent., who died intestate, granted to ⎪
   Nicholas Trebarfoot, his brother, Mar. 24, 1664. ⎪
Thomas Trebarfoot bur. at Poundstock 29 Aug., 1598. Bp. of Exeter's Trans. ⎭

Ped. fin. 31 Elizb., Mich., Devon. John Jollowe and Will. Trebarfoot qu. Rich. Clevedon
def.   250 acr. and ten'ts in Cleverton, 250 in Bradworthy.

Treffry.

ARMS.—*Sa. chev. ent. 3 trees arrashed Ar.*

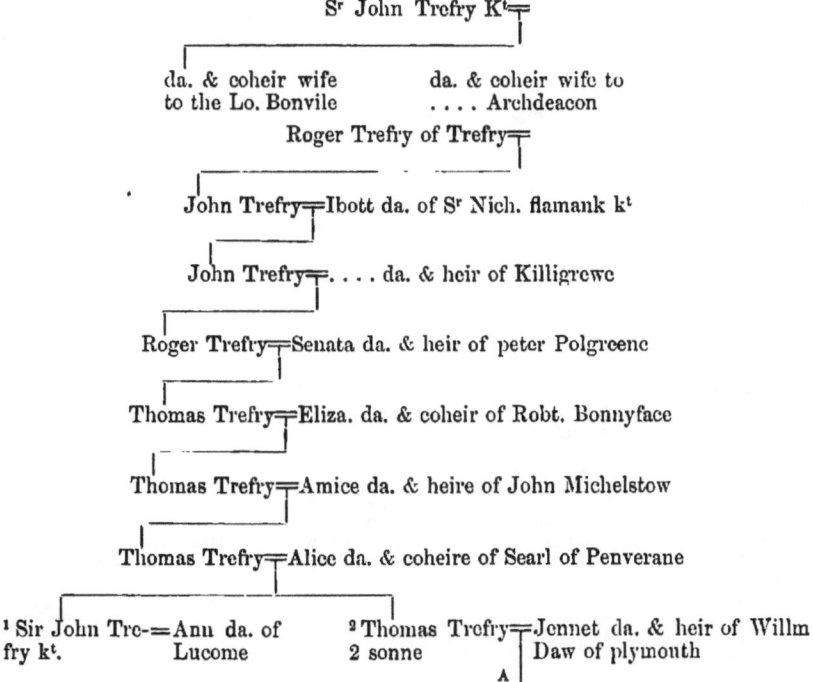

[1] Sir John Treffry, Knt., will P. P. C,, Moone 20. dat. 24 Jun., 1500. Legacies to the church of St. Fembaro at Fowey. " To the Prior and Convent of the Ho. of St. Andrew's at Tywardreath a goune of velvet without furre to make a Coope to thuse of the s'd House. Item, I beq. to the s'd Prior and Conv. a paxe and two cruetts of silver a pair of vestments of blewe velvet. Item 22 marcs for the paiment of the same, a basin and an ewer of silver, and money to the value of the s'd 22 marcs to thintent that the s'd Prior and Conv. of Tywardreath shall settle my name in the Mortelege w'th ther founders and so to say after my decesse iiij times placebo and diriges and 4 masses at 4 times in the year for my soul and all the soules that I am bound to pray for and after to be prayed for daily and yerely as ther founders be there prayed for, and that they shall be bound to me by the Convent seal for the performance of the same in £20." (This was duly observed; see Oliver's 'Monasticon.') A somewhat similar beq. to the Pbt. and Canons of St. German's, the freres of Truru and of Bodman, and to a priest to sing masses for his soul in the Lady Chapel of the Ch. of Saint Barry in Fowey. To his brother William Treffry, among several articles of plate, "a prang of silver for grene gynger," "a ringe of gold with a saffiour lope for the sight." To his nephew Wm. Trevanyon a furre of martres, etc. To his bro. Thos. Treffry a quart. of the 'George' (name of a vessel). To nephew Jno. Trevanyon a quart. of the 'Mary Hardford.' To his son-in-law John Tregorck and Anne his wife. To his sister Jane, wife of John Beckett. Executors were Sir Rob. Willoughby, Lo. de Broke. Wm. Trevanyon, ar., Peter Bevyll, ar., and Nicho. Penwarne. Witnesses Nicho. Kent, clerk, Rich. Harrington, Tho. Raby, Henry Pester, Rob. Poyle, and o'rs.

"*7th Sept. Obitus Johis Treffry militis bone memorie, qui obiit viii. id et. vii° die mensis Septembri MD. cujus a'ie p'picietur Deus, Amen.*" (*Calendar Tywardreath Priory.*)

[2] Named in will of Willm. Treffry of Fowey, P. P. C. Holgrave 21. 25 Nov., 1504. To be bur. in the Ch. of St. Barre of Fowey. " I beseech to convey a tombe out of ye yle of Porbeck

[*Note continued on next page.*

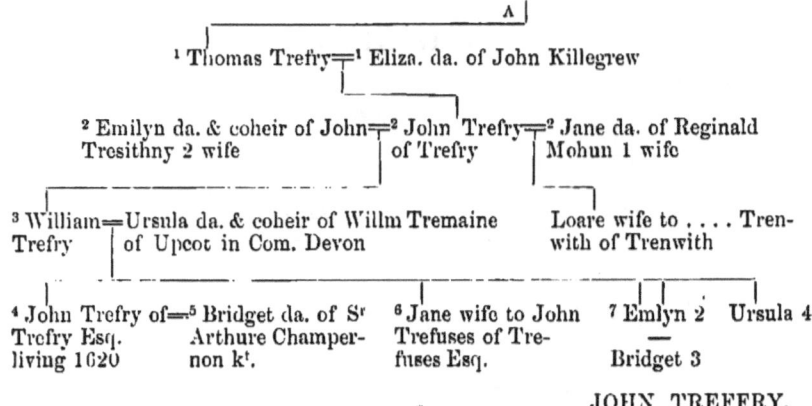

(Note continued.)

and send to Fowey, to be of the pattern of a tomb to Ar. Browne in the Croched Freers of Lond. Three images, my broder, me, and wyfe on tomb, with the portraits of St. Gregory and such sculpture as my Ex'or can devise after the apparell of the same." [There is a tomb in Fowey Ch. with figures of the three brothers. John, Wm., and Tho., which last died in 1509.—EDS.] Testator names his bro. and heir Thomas Treffry, his nephew John Treffry, nephew Jno. Trevanion, Lord Robt. Willoby de Broke, Sir Jno. Arundel of Cornw., and leaves his Chantry Priest of Barkley, Sir Tho. Holdman (Holman), to choose one of his Gildynes (geldings) and £3 to pray for him. Lands within Cornwall, Coventrie, and Barkley. Diamonds and rubies and much jewellery. (The originals of the above wills are lengthy, and worth the inspection of the antiquary.)

[1] M. I. Fowey Ch., date 31 Jan., 1563. Arms, TREFFRY *impaling* KILLEGREW.

[2] M. I. Fowey Ch. Jno. Treffry, ob. 28 Jan., 1590. He had nine sons and seven dau's by his second wife. One of the sons was Tho. Treffry, "Councell att Law," who mar. Kath'n, da. and coh. of Tho. Hellier al's Mayow, and ob. 1 Mar., 1635. M. I. Fowey Ch. Kath'n, wife of Tho. Treffry, Esq., bur. at Lostwithiel 1625. Bp. of Exeter's Transcripts.

[3] Willm., son of John Treffry.	bap.	18 Feb., 1559.
Willm. Treffry, Esq., and Ursula Tremaine	mar.	3 Ap., 1589.
[4] John, son of Willm. Treffry,	bap.	26 Jan., 1594.
[5] Bridget. ux. Jno. Treffry. Esq.,	bur.	15 Ap., 1650.
[6] Jane, da. of Willm. Treffry	bap.	5 Mar., 1591.
John Trefusis and Jane Treffry	mar.	29 May, 1611.
[7] Emblen. da. of Willm. Treffry,	bap.	15 Aug., 1596.
Mrs. Emblen Treffry	bur.	15 Ap., 1650.

Fowey Par. Reg.

* John Treffry of Place, Fowey, Esq. (Will Bodmin, 1716.) To poor of Foy £50. To children of cousin Thomas ten gold moydores. Cousin Mary Dagg. Godson John, son of Sir Rich. Vivian, Bart. To cousin John Toller, Lieut. of a man-of-war. Ratifies and confirms sale of Barton of Rooke to Mr. Edw. Treffry of Mevagizzy. The Three-Corner Park to Vicar of Fowey for ever. Annuity to wife Katherin. Trustees Sir Rich. Vivian, Bart., Major-General Charles Trelawney, and Charles Gryles. (Vivian and Gryles died, when Ph. Rashleigh of Menabilly and Joseph Sawle of Penrice were substituted.)

William Treffry and Thomazin Cecly	mar.	1682.	Broock Par. Reg.
Nicholas Trefry and Margaret Mill	,,	1610.	Egloshayle Par. Reg.
Nicholas Trefry and Thomazin Kestle	,,	1631.	
Anthony, son of Rob. Trevry	bap.	1658.	
Charles, ,, ,,	,,	1660.	
John, ,, ,,	,,	1664.	St. Issey Par. Reg.
William, ,, ,,	,,	1671.	
Walter Trefry and Elizab. Hambly	mar.	1686.	
John Trefry and Mary Williams	,,	1689.	

[*Note continued on next page.*]

Trefrie.

ARMS.—*Sa. a chev. betw. 3 trees Arg.*

John Trefrie of Foye=Emlyn Da. of Jo. Tresithny

Willm Trefrie of Foye 1 son

[1] Matthew Trefrie of Foye=Elizb. Da. of Jo. Somester of Peynsford in Com. Devon
3 sone liveing 1620

Thomas 1 sone at. 13, 1620

Willm 2 sone

John 3 sone *

Elizab. 1 Da.

Jane 2 Da.

Not signed.

(*Note continued.*)

Tho.,	son of John Treffry, Esq.,		bap.	16 June, 1563.
Debora,	da. of	,,	,,	1570.
Tresoney,	son of	,,	,,	23 July, 1571.
Martha,	da. of	,,	,,	1572.
Henry,	son of	,,	,,	Feb., 1575.
Rebecca,	da. of	,,	,,	1579.
Mary,	,,	,,	,,	1581.
Henry,	son of	,,	,,	20 June, 1583.
Mary,	da. of	,,	,,	1593.
Rebecca,	,,	,, ·	,,	1598.
Maud,	,,	,,	,,	1601.
John,	son of Justin Treffry,		,,	1677.
Maurice	,,	,,	,,	Ap. 6, 1681.
John,	,,	Thomas Treffry,	,,	20 July, 1684.
Mary,	da. of Mr. Justin Treffry		,,	1687.
Kat'n,	,,	Thos. Treffry,	,,	13 Sept., 1691.
Thos.,	son of	,,	,,	8 Sept., 1695.
Tho. Dickwood and Martha Treffry			mar.	June, 1594.

Fowey Par. Reg.

Otherwise *Hugh Peters, Chaplain and Adviser of Oliver Cromwell; b'h'd by Chas. II. on Tower Hill.*—J. J. T.
[A pencil note with the initials probably of Justin Treffry, clerk.—EDS.]

Tho. Treffry and Elizb. Morish	mar.	30 Nov., 1613.
Justin Treffry, clerk, and Susanna George	,,	14 Feb., 1669.
Tho. Treffry and Rose Major	,,	14 Oct., 1683.
Jno. Treffry, Esq.,	bur.	24 Sept., 1658.
Henry, son of Justin Treffry, clerk,	,,	1672.

Ped. fin. Cornw. 1 Rich. II., No. 3. Will Watta, Cappelanus, qu. William Treffry and Alicia his wife def. Hele, etc., settled on William and Alice, with rem. to right heirs of Alice.
Ped. fin. 13 Eliz., Ea., Cornw. John Treffry ar. qu. Wm. Lower ar. def. Polveyn juxta Fowey.

M. I. IN FOWEY CH.

Here in this Chancell do I ly,
Known by the name of John Treffry,
Being made and born for to dye.
So must thou, friend, as well as I.
Therefore Good works be Sure to try,
but chiefly love and Charity.
And still on them with faith rely :
So be happy Eternally.
Soli deo Gloria.

---

[1] Matthew, son of John Treffry, Esq., bap. 24 Feb., 1566. } Fowey
* Thomas Treffry and Jane his wife, da. of John Vivian of Trewan, mar. 1641. } Par. Reg.

For memoir of the family and continued ped. of Treffry, see 'Hist. of Trigg,' vol. ii., pp. 242, 256.

Trefusis.

ARMS. 1. TREFUSIS. *Arg. a chev. betw. 3 spindles Sa., a crescent for diff.* 2. MARTIN of Bodmin. 3. TREWANWELL. 4. PENKEVIL. 5. TRESITHNEY. 6. MILLITON.
CREST. *A Griffin sejant Or, winged B. The dexter claws resting on an escutcheon, Arg.*

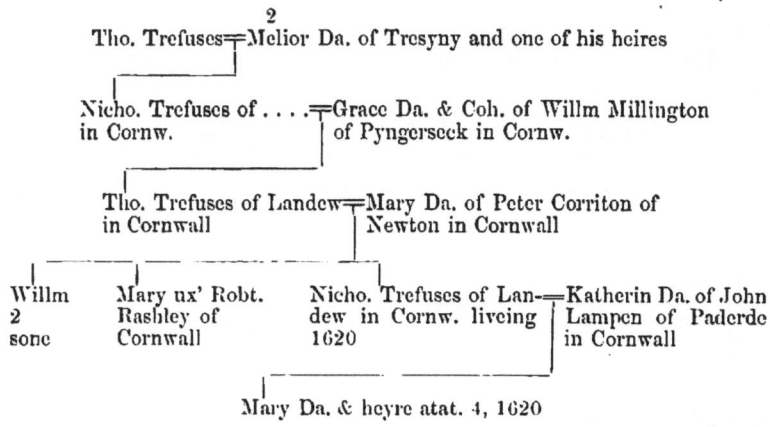

NICHOLAS TREFUSIS.

Trefusis.

Sciant p'sentes & futuri q^d ego Herveus de Lew dedi & concessi & hac presenti Carta mea confirmavi Ric'o filio Stephani de Trefuses p' homagio & servitio suo terr' in Villa de Trefuses cum p'tinent' sicut mete facta sunt & p'ambulati &c. usq'e ad ortum q^d fuit quondam Acei de Trefuses &c. Hijs Testib; Waltero de Penhergard, Herveo de Trewinse, Reginaldo de Killegabes, Willo de Benedict, Johe Clerico de Trefuses & alijs, sanz dat.

This Byll indented made at Westminster the 2 day of July in the 19 yeare of the raigne of our Soveraigne Lord King H. VII. witnesseth, that Mr John Wallis, Clark, hath received in the name & for the use & behoofe of our said Sov'aigne Lord of James Trefuses in the County of Cornwall Esq. in readye mony 5^l 6^s 8^d of Lawfull monye of England for his fine made & given to the king's Matie for his p'don to be released from the order of Knighthood of the Bath at the mariag. of my Lo. Arthure late prince. In witness, &c.

p' me JOHEM WALLES.

All this descent was exactly proved by evidences which remain in the Custody of John Trefuses, Esq., a^o Dnⁱ 1620, shewed unto us in this visitation.

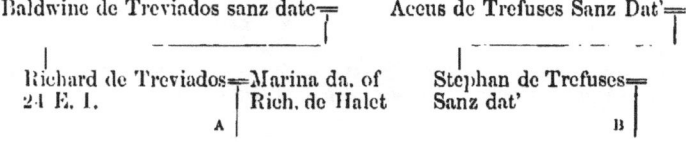

THE VISITATION OF THE COUNTY OF CORNWALL. 223

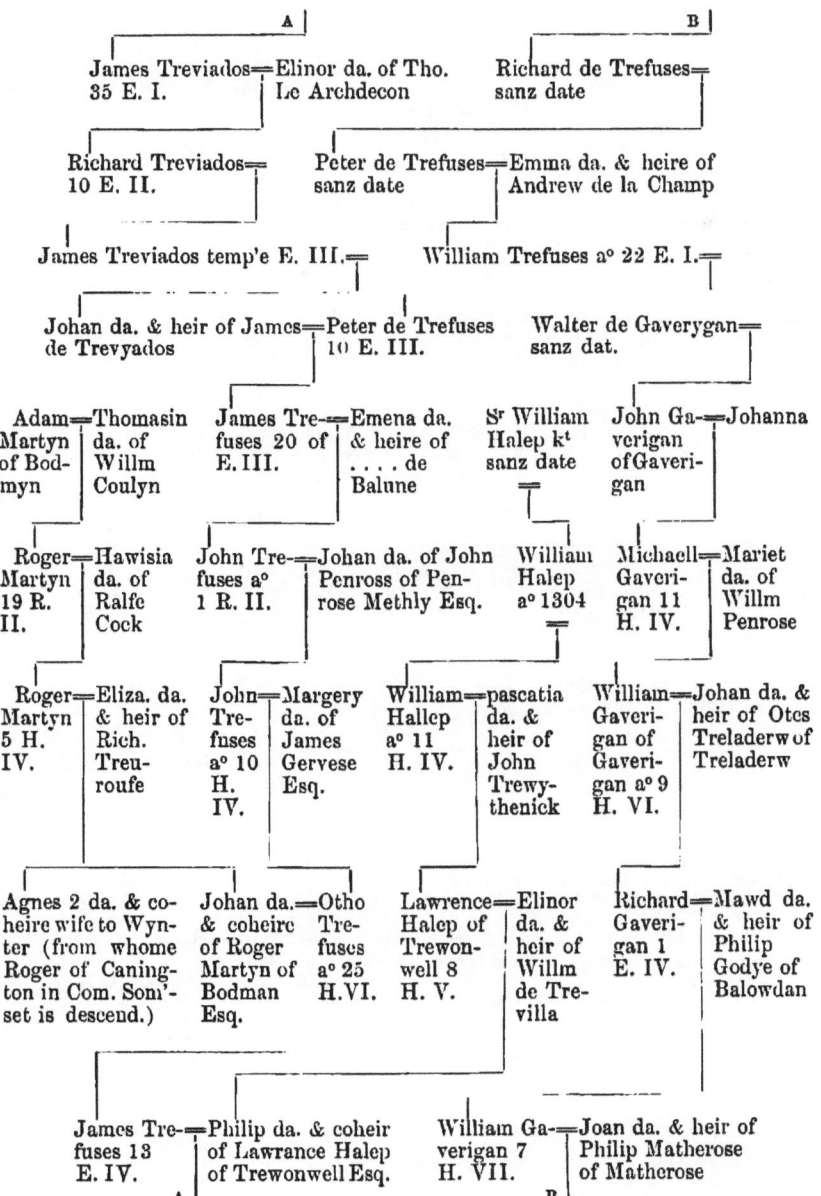

224   THE VISITATION OF THE COUNTY OF CORNWALL.

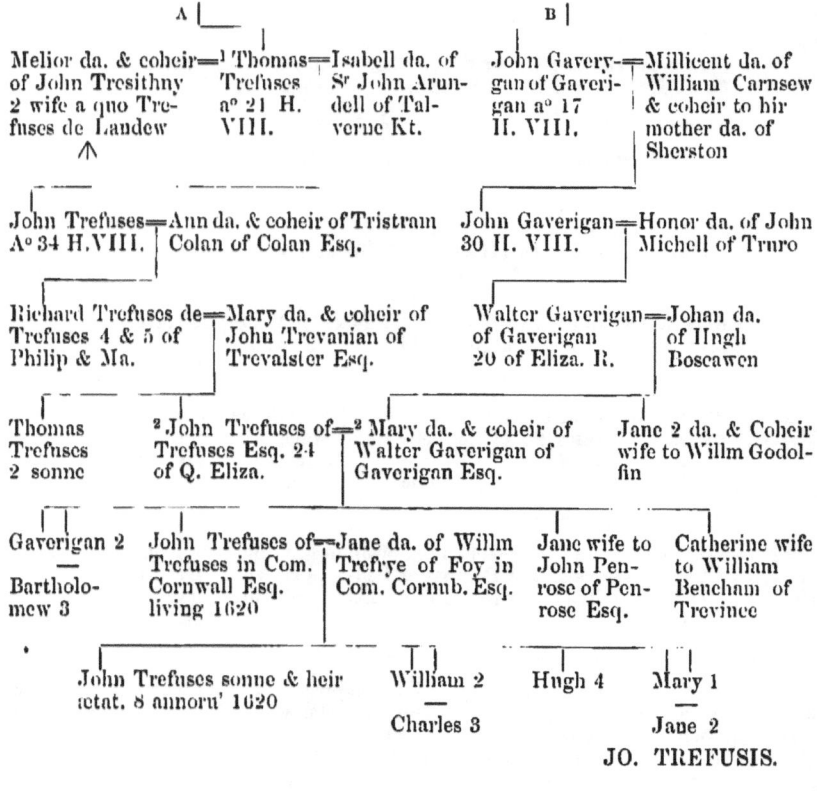

A |

Melior da. & coheir = ¹ Thomas = Isabell da. of
of John Tresithny   Trefuses   Sr John Arun-
2 wife a quo Tre-   aº 21 H.   dell of Tal-
fuses de Landew   VIII.   verne Kt.

B |

John Gavery- = Millicent da. of
gan of Gaveri-   William Carnsew
gan aº 17   & coheir to hir
H. VIII.   mother da. of
                 Sherston

John Trefuses = Ann da. & coheir of Tristram
Aº 34 H.VIII.   Colan of Colan Esq.

John Gaverigan = Honor da. of John
30 H. VIII.   Michell of Truro

Richard Trefuses de = Mary da. & coheir of
Trefuses 4 & 5 of   John Trevanian of
Philip & Ma.   Trevalster Esq.

Walter Gaverigan = Johan da.
of Gaverigan   of Hugh
20 of Eliza. R.   Boscawen

Thomas   ² John Trefuses of = ² Mary da. & coheir of
Trefuses   Trefuses Esq. 24   Walter Gaverigan of
2 sonne   of Q. Eliza.   Gaverigan Esq.

Jane 2 da. & Coheir
wife to Willm Godol-
fin

Gaverigan 2   John Trefuses of = Jane da. of Willm   Jane wife to   Catherine wife
—   Trefuses in Com.   Trefrye of Foy in   John Pen-   to William
Bartholo-   Cornwall Esq.   Com. Cornub. Esq.   rose of Pen-   Bencham of
mew 3   living 1620   rose Esq.   Trevince

John Trefuses sonne & heir   William 2   Hugh 4   Mary 1
ætat. 8 annoru' 1620   —   —
                                Charles 3   Jane 2

JO. TREFUSIS.

---

¹ Inq. p. m. 6 Edw. VI., part i., No. 10. Thomas Trefuses, ob. 14 April, 6 Edw. VI. Rich. Trefusis, son of his son John T., his grandson and heir. æt. 17 and more. Names his wife Melior, da. of John Tresithney, his dau'rs Mary, and Joanne, mar. to Rich. Garvis of Penhelleck, Esq., and son Thomas Trefusis.

² John Trefusis, gent., and Mary Gavergan mar. 17 June, 1583. St. Mabyn l'ar. Reg. (J.M.)

* John Trefusis, ar. of Milor, and D'nam Joanna Drake of Buck. Mon.,
    wid.,   mar. 6 Aug., 1639. } Buckland Mon.,
  John Trefusis, jun., of Milor, gen., and Elizb. Drake of Buck. Mon., } Devon. Par. Reg.
    spinster.   mar. 13 Feb., 1638.
  Edw. Herle, gent., and Maria Trefusis mar. 1634. (See mar. lic. p. 225.)
  John,   son of Tho. Trefusis, gent., and Mary,   bap. 1617.)
  Rich.,   "   "   "   „   1619.
  Thomas,   „   Henry Trefusis and Anne   „   1647.
  James,   „   „   "   „   1650.
  Thomas, 2nd of that name, son of Henry Trefusis and Anne   „   1654. } Constantine Par.
  William.   "   "   "   „   1658. } Reg.
  Thomas, son of Tho. Trefusis the elder, and Mary, da. of Wm.
    Mohown, Esq.,   mar. 1 Nov., 1626.
  Samuel, son of Tho. Trefusis, gent., and Lower Stone, wid., mar. 1635.
  Thomas Trefusis, gent.,   bur. 1642.
  Thomas Trefusis, gent., and Hannah Addis of Mevagizzy mar. 1716. St. Ewe Par. Reg.

[*Note continued on next page.*]

Tregeare.

The coate as they suppose of Tregonwell is a Chev' betweene 3 garbes.
The Armes of Tregonwell to be searched for at London in the office of Armes, & to be delivered to Mr Kinge & Mr Tregere.

Rich. Tregonwall══

Amond Tregonwall sonne of Rich.══Jone Da. of John Archard of Leysard E. II. 13.

Claris fil. et coheres ob. sine p'le   Alice maried to John Edward of Killyow══ A

(*Note continued.*)

John, son of John Trefusis, Esq.,	bap.	1612.	
Dorothy, da. of John Trefusis, gent.,	,,	7 Oct., 1646.	
John Trefusis and Jane Treffry	mar.	1611.	
Rich. Trefusis, gent.,	bur.	5 June, 1614.	Fowey Par. Reg.
Mrs. Ursula Trefusis, wid.,	,,	1660.	
Gaverigan Trefuses, gent.,	,,	—	
Mrs. Amy Trefusis	,,	1661.	
Chas. Trefusis	bur. in the church 19 July, 1681.		

Henry Trefusis, gent., and Anne, da. of James Trenarth, gent. both of Constantine   mar.   1642.   } Mawnan Par. Reg.

Nich. Munday, gent., and Mary, da. of Saml. Trefusis,   mar. 1657. { Mawnan and Constantine Par. Reg.

Jane, dau. of Samuel Trefusis, gent., by Lower his wife, bap. } Bp. of Exeter's
at Constantine   28 Jany., 1636. } Transcripts.

Grace, dau. of Thomas Trefusis, gent.,		bap.	30 Apl., 1607.	
Samuel, son of ,, and Mary,		,,	15 Sep., 1609.	
Ketheryn, dau. of ,, ,,		,,	23 Ap., 1611.	
James, son of Henry Trefuses and Anne		,,	14 Mar.,	
by 6 of the clock aft.,			1649.	
Mary, dau. of ,, ,,		,,	24 Sep., 1652.	
Mary, dau. of Samuel Trefusis and Lower		,,	13 July, 1639.	
Thomas, son of Mr. Henry Trefusis and Elizabeth, bap. 16				
Aug., by 6 of the clock aft.,			1687.	
Henry, son of Mr. Henry Trefusis and Elizab. bap.			6 July, 1690.	
Henry, ,, ,, ,,		born	2 July, 1697.	
Robert Quarme, gent., and Catherine, dau. of Thos. Trefusis,				Constantine
gent.,		mar.	24 Oct., 1632.	Par. Reg.
Mary, wife of Thomas Trefusis, gent.,		bur.	10 Nov., 1628.	
Thomas Trefusis, gent.,		,,	1 May, 1645.	
Jane, dau. of Samuel Trefusis, gent., bur. 17 Sept. (in chancel), 1656.				
Thomas Trefusis, gent.,		,,	11 May (in church), 1657.	(J. M.)
Loer, wife of Samuel Trefusis, gent.		,,	9 May, 1665.	
Henry Trefusis, gent.,		,,	23 Mar. (in church), 1687.	
Henry ,, ,,		bur.	13 Sep., 1690.	
Mrs. Ann ,, widow,		,,	17 Sep., 1692.	
Ann, dau. of Mr. Henry Trefusis,		,,	31 July, 1699.	
Henry, son of ,, ,,		,,	3 Aug., 1699.	
Samuel, ,, ,, ,,		,,	5 May, 1703.	
Ann, dau. of ,, ,,		,,	19 April, 1705.	

Mar. lic. betw. Nicholas Trefusis of Lezant and Katherine
      Lampen of Linkinhorne, gent.,   Nov. 22, 1615.
  ,,   ,,   betw. Robert Le Grys of Owby, co. Norfolk, Knt.,
      and Mary Trefusis of Lezant,   May 22, 1630.   } Act Books, Exeter.
  ,,   ,,   betw. Nicholas Trefusis of Lezant, Esq., and Phillipp Slanning of Tamerton Foliot, widow, April 5, 1632.
  ,,   ,,   betw. Edw. Hearle of Luxillian, gent., and Mary
      Trefusis of Lezant,   Feb. 5. 1634.

[*Note continued on next page.*

```
                    │ A
        Rich. Owrye of St. Maws═╤═Amy fil. et heres
                                │
         ¹ Rich. Owrye a° 2 Ri. II.═╤═Johanna fil. Rici Tregiskie
                                    │
Serlle Owrye al's Tregonwall de Tregiskie═╤═Milior Da. of John Treworga in Roseland
                                          │
Oliver Owry al's Tregonwall═╤═Amie Da. of John Michell al's Jagow of St. Collumb
                            │
        John Owry al's Tregonwall═╤═Udon Da. of John Tregithew
                                  │
   ┌──────────────────────┬───────┴────────────────┐
Jane the eldest Da. mar. to   Jane 2 fil. et Coh. mar. to   Amy 3 fil. et Coh. mar. to
Ric. Adam al's Polgwest       Rafe Liffnye of St. Ewe       John Tregere of Crowen
        ═╤═                        ═╤═                             ═╤═
         │                          │                                │
Thomas Adam al's Polgwest mar.   John Liffney mar. Joan Da. of
Mary Da. of Dowell               Walt' Herle of St. Blazie
     ═╤═                              ═╤═
   ┌──┴──────┬─────────┐        ┌──────┴──┬─────────────┐
George King of═Elizab. Da. & heyre  Jane ┐ Died both  Margaret mar. to
Manackan in    of Tho. Adam al's.         │ w'hout    Nicholas Kempe-
Corn.          Polgwest              Alice┘ Issue    thorne of Morestow
                                                          ═╤═
 ┌──────┬──────┬──────┬──────────┬───────────────┬─────────┴──────┐
Humphrie Joane  John   James  ═Maria fil.   Maude æt. 28 un-   John Kemp-
ob. s. p. mar.  2 fil.  Kinge  Will.         maried             thorn mar.
  —      to     æt.    fil.    Bowle of         —              ² . . . Da. of
George 3 Jona-  25     primo-  Miler in      Elizab. to be pre- Clifford
fil. æt. 15 tha.       genit.  Cornwal       sently maried to     ═╤═
annoru'  Bowle         ætat.                 Francis Tripconie
1620     of Miler      34                    of St. Keverne
         A ═╤═                       B                           C      D
```

Note continued.]
   Mar. lic. betw. John Trefusis of Myler. gent., and Elizab.
       Drake of Buckland Monachorum,   Feby. 13, 1638, } Act Books,
  „ „ betw. John Trefusis of Miler. Esq., and Lady Joanna } Exeter.
       Drake, widow, of Buckland Monachorum. Aug. 6, 1639. }

Wills.
John Trefusis, Cornw. Will proved 1648. Essex, 92.
John Trefusis, Cornw. Will proved 1654. Alchin, 309.

1594.	Trefusis.	Richard.	Myler.	Prob.	
1602.	„	Ann.	„	„	
1614.	„	John, Esq.	„	„	Exeter. (J. M.)
„	„	Mary.	„	„	
1660, Feb. 14.	„	Ursula.	Fowey.	—	
1661, Feb.	„	Gaverigan.	„	Adm.	
„ Mar.	„	Hugh.	„	—	Archd.
1662, June.	„	Ann.	„	Prob.	Cornw.
1688, April 30.	„	Henry.	Constantine.	„	
1692, April 21.	„	William.	„	„	
„ Oct. 13.	„	Ann, widow.	„	„	

    ¹ Ped. fin. Cornw. 3 Rich. II., No. 3. Rich. Oury and Johana, da. of Rich. Tregesky, qu. John Edwards of Kyllyou def. Kyllyou Edwards and Kyllyou settled on Rich. Ouryand Johana and their heirs, rem. to Will. Eyre and his heirs.
    ² Mawdlyn, da. of . . . Clifford. See ped. of Ley al's Kempthorne, *ante*.

THE VISITATION OF THE COUNTY OF CORNWALL. 227

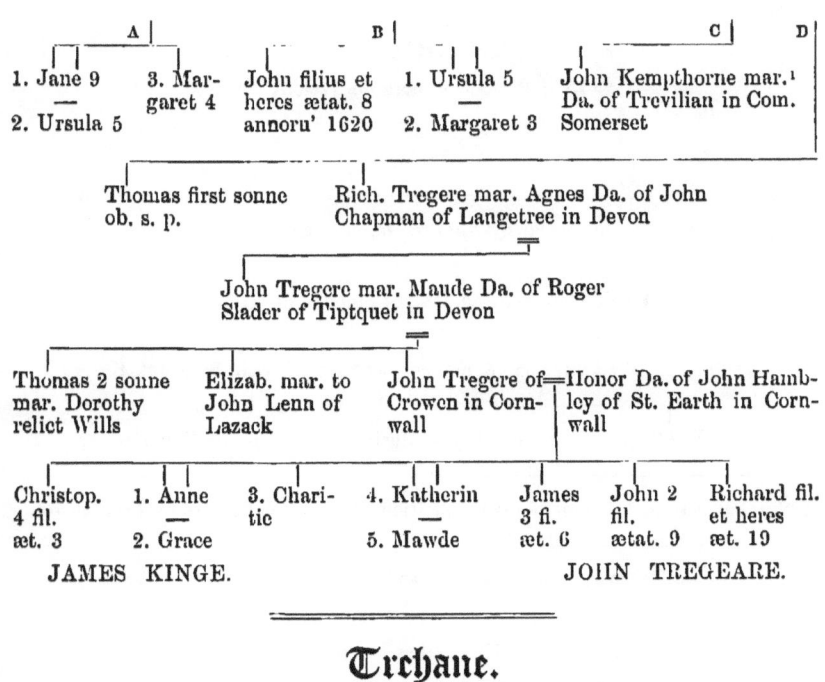

A	B	C	D
1. Jane 9 2. Ursula 5	3. Margaret 4	John filius et heres ætat. 8 annoru' 1620	1. Ursula 5 2. Margaret 3	John Kempthorne mar.[1] Da. of Trevilian in Com. Somerset

Thomas first sonne ob. s. p.

Rich. Tregere mar. Agnes Da. of John Chapman of Langetree in Devon

John Tregere mar. Maude Da. of Roger Slader of Tiptquet in Devon

| Thomas 2 sonne mar. Dorothy relict Wills | Elizab. mar. to John Lenn of Lazack | John Tregere of Crowen in Cornwall ═ Honor Da. of John Hambley of St. Earth in Cornwall |

| Christop. 4 fil. æt. 3 | 1. Anne
2. Grace | 3. Charitie | 4. Katherin
5. Mawde | James 3 fi. æt. 6 | John 2 fil. ætat. 9 | Richard fil. et heres æt. 19 |

JAMES KINGE.   JOHN TREGEARE.

Trehane.

Otes Trehane of Trehane in Cornwall═Daughter of Lahere

Mary   John Trehane of Trehane═Amy Da. & one of theires of .... Tregallost

| Agnes mar. to Stephe Polewheele | John Trehane of Trehane in Com. Cornw. liveinge 1620. ═ Elizb. Da. of John Merret of Probus in Cornw. gent. |

| 1 Elizb. uxor Jo. Scawyne[2] of Trehane | 2 Mary ux' Nicho. Kendall of Luxillian in Cornwall | 3 Amy uxor Pet' Courtney of Penkevell in Cornwall | 4 Katherin ux' Jo. Vermon of Lamarron | John liveing in 1640 |

JOHN TREHANE.

---

[1] Ursula, da. of Jno. Trevillian. See ped. of Ley al's Kempthorne, *ante.*

[2] Trehane, where this family was seated, is in the parish of Probus, and passed to Scawen with the eldest coheir. (J. M.)

* The addition in italic is in another handwriting.
Mr. John Carveth and Mrs. Jane Trehane mar. 1741. Menhenniot Par. Reg.
John Trehane of Linkinhorn and Martha Bellamy mar. at Probus ⎫ Archd.
    20 July, 1736.   ⎬ Transcripts. ⎫
Richard Ingram and Elizabeth Trehane mar. 25 Nov., 1567. St. Austell Par. Reg. ⎬ (J. M.)
Prob. of will of Thomas Trehane of Probus. Archd. Cornw., 26 Oct., 1570.   ⎪
Prob.   "   "   "   "   28 June, 1660.   ⎭

[*Note continued on next page.*

Trelawny.

Rich. Trelawny fuere de Trelony=

Wm Trelawny=

Jo. Trelawny=Joane Da. of Rich. Botterell

[1] Wm Trelawny=Jane Da. of Stephen de Trewynick

John de Trelawny sone & heyre=Laur Da. of Rich. Sergeaux K^t

Wm Trelawney sone & hey.=Margery Da. of Jo. de Reparijs

Wm Trelawny sone & heyre=Jone Da. of Rich. Doyngull & heire to hir brother John

John Trelawny sone & heyre K^t=Mawde Da. of Rob. Menwynick

S^r Jo. Trelawny K^t=Agnes Da. of Rob. Tregodack

[2] Rich. Trelawny sone & heyre obijt sine prole

[2] John Trelawny=Joane Da. & hey. of 2 sone & hey. | Nic. Helligan

(*Note continued.*)

Honour, dau. of George Trehane of Treworget, bap.		26 Dec., 1583.	
Stephen, son of „ „		8 Dec., 1588.	
George, „ „	[bap.?]	24 Oct., 1591.	
Katherine, dau. of „	Treworthen bap.	18 July, 1593.	
Penelope, „ John Trehane	,,	13 Nov., 1614.	
Phillippa, „ „	,,	5 Mar., 1616.	St. Kew
Grace, „ „	,,	10 Mar., 1619.	Par. Reg.
Jane, „ „	„	30 Apl., 1622.	
Nicholas Symons and Mary Trehane	mar.	28 Sept., 1653.	(J. M.)
Stephen Trehane of Treworthen	bur.	5 May, 1584.	
Honour, dau. of George Trehane	„	12 Mar., 1586.	
George, son of George Trehane,	,,	26 Mar., 1592.	
Johanna Trehane	,,	26 Feb., 1593.	
Christopher Trehane	,,	3 Jan., 1652.	
Honour, dau. of Rich. Trehane, clerk, and Margaret	bap.	March, 1624.	
Lawrence. son of Richard Trehane.	„	March, 1628.	St. Tudy
Christopher Trehane and Katherine Bennett	mar.	1603.	Par. Reg.
Richard Trehane. clerk, and Margaret Rowe	,,	1617.	
Katherine, wife of Christopher Trehane	bur.	1629.	

[1] Ped. fin. Cornw. 7 Edw. III., No. 4. Stephen de Trewint and Isabella his wife qu. William de Trelouney and Johanna que fuit uxor William de Walesbrew def.

[2] Ped. fin. Cornw. 13 Hen. IV., No. 5. John Trelouney and Rich. Trelouny qu. John Hendra of Lyskyrd and Elizabeth his wife and John Thomas and Johana his wife def. Lancrentyn settled on John Trelouny and Rich. T. and the heirs of Rich.

[*Note continued on next page.*

THE VISITATION OF THE COUNTY OF CORNWALL.   229

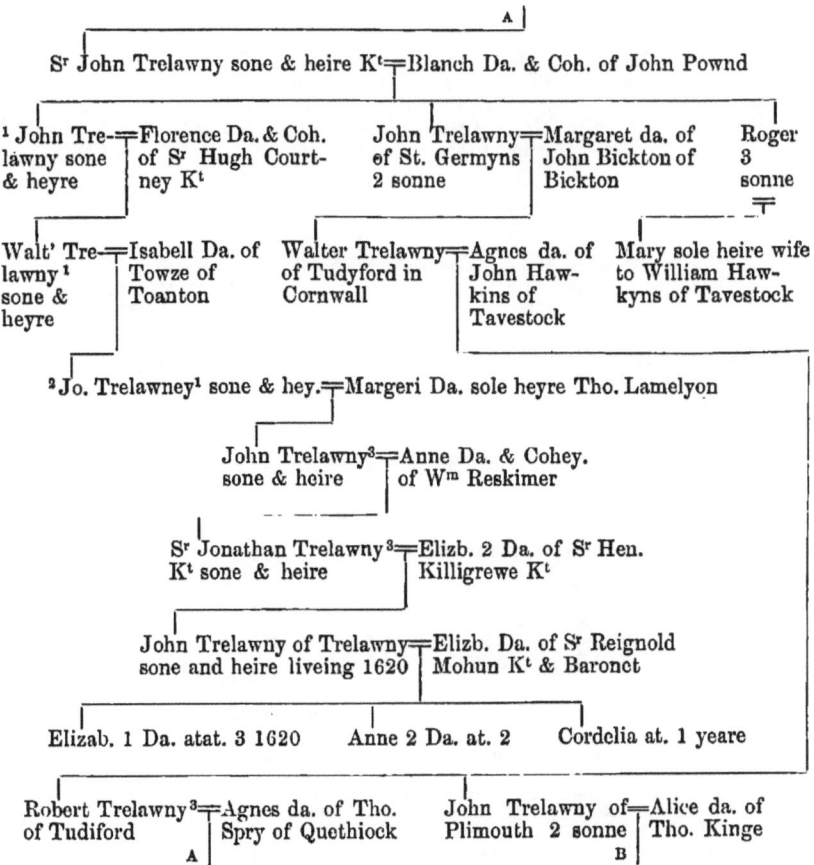

(Note continued.)
Ped. fin. Cornw. 9 Hen. V., No. 6. John Trelawny, junior, qu. Thos. Ricard and Johan his wife def. Northyeldelond.
Ped. fin. Cornw. 12 Hen. VI., No. 5. Eliam Upton and Reginald Toker qu. John Trelawny Chivaler and Thomas Edwards and Margery his wife def. Manor of Trewynnek, etc., held by John Trelawny and his heirs, rem. to Thos. Courtney, Earl of Devon, and his heirs.
Ped. fin. Cornw. 14 Hen. VI., No. 5. Rob. Arthorn and John Hameley qu. Rich. Trelauny and Johana his wife def. Penclwyn, etc., held by Richard and Johana, rem. to Margaret, wife of Thos. Edwards, rem. to Johana, wife of Roger Kelwa, rem. to Alex. Kenegy, rem. to right heirs of Johana Trelauny.
Ped. fin. 18 Hen. VI., No. 9. Rich. Trelauny qu. John Hendre of Lyskyryd and Elizabeth his wife def. Mess., etc., in Lancrentyn.
[1] Inq. p. m. Edw. Courtney, Earl of Devon, 3 and 4 Ph. and Mary, gives this descent to John Trelawney, one of the coheirs of Edw., Earl of Devon, and æt. 52.
[2] Ob. 29 Sept. 5 Eliz. Inq. p. m. 6 Eliz., No. 24. Recites his will, dat. 15 Feb. 5 Elizb., which names his wife Lore and his younger sons John and Reskymer T. John T., his eldest son and h., aged 30 and more. (*Lora Trecarrel*, 2nd wife, by whom 2nd son John m. Beatrix Trevanion.—ED.)
[3] Inq. p. m. 11 Eliz., No. 8. John Trelawney (s. and h. of John T., Esq.. of Menhenniot, dec'd), ob. 24 Oct. 10 Elizb. recites his father's will (note 2). His own will dat. 13 Oct. 10 Elizb., which names Lore his mother-in-law, Tho. T. al's Kellye, his bastard son, his dau. Anne, his brother John T. Robert T. of Tudeford. The child his wife "presently goeth with." John T., his s. and h. apparent, aged 4. (*The child unborn was Sir Jonathan, above.*—ED.)

230   THE VISITATION OF THE COUNTY OF CORNWALL.

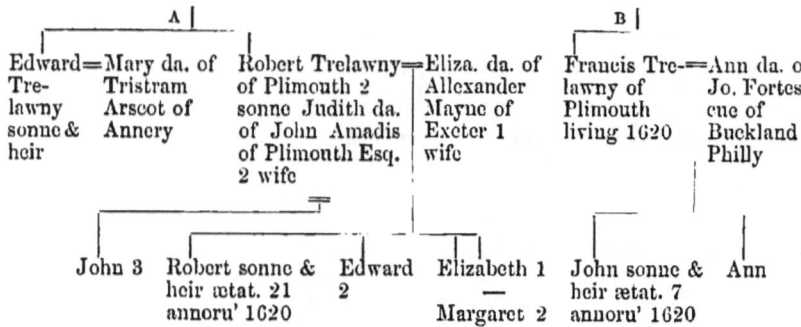

JOHN TRELAWNY.   ROBERT TRELAWNY.
                                  FRAUNCIS TRELAWNY.

* Edw., son of Jonathan, L'd Bp. of Exeter, and ye Lady Rebeca
  his wife,   bap.   9 July, 1699.
Mary, da. of Sir Jonat. Trelawney. Bar., Lo. B'p of Exeter, and
  Rebecca his wife,   bap.   1 Sept., 1700.
Jonathan, son of Sir Jonat. T., Bart., Lo. Bp. of Exeter,   bap. 1702.
John Fras. Buller, Esq., and Mrs. Rebecca Trelawney. 3rd da.
  of ye Hon. and Rt. Rev. Sir Jona. Trelawney, Bart., Ld.   } Archdeac. Tran-
  Bp. of Winchester, mar. in the chapel at Trelawne   22 July, 1716.}   scripts.
Kath., wife of John Trelawney, Esq., bur. at P'elynt   1677.
Sir John Trelawney, Bart.,   "   "   5 Mar., 1680.
The Coronell (sic) John Trelawney, Esq., "   "   9 Oct.. 1680.
Sir Jona. Trelawney, Bart., Lo. Bp. of Winchester bur. 10 Aug.. 1721.

Margery, da. of John Trelawny, gent., bap. at Pelint 19 Nov., 1620. }
Francis Trelawnie, gent., and Mrs. Anne Fortescue mar. at   } Bp. of Exeter's
  Weare Gifford   24 Dec., 1612.   }   Transcripts.
Francis Bassett of Illogan, Esq., and Anne, da. of Sir Jonathan   }
  Trelawney, dec.,   mar. at P'elint 31 Augt., 1620.   }
The Worshipful Sam. Trelawny, Esq., bur. at St. Tudy 1661.

Mr. Edw. Trelawney, clerk, and Mrs. Elizab. Darrell mar. 14 Nov., 1692.   } Egloshayle Par.
                                                                            Reg.
Jonathan, son of John Trelawney, Esq.,   bap. 19 Dec., 1568.   } Fowey Par. Reg.
John, son of Jonathan,   "   7 May, 1592.   }

Edw., son of Jonathan Trelawney, Esq.,   "   Aug., 1595.
Jonathan, son of Jonathan Trelawny, Esq., of Coldrenick, bap. 1648.
John, son of John Trelawney, Esq., and Ann Reskymer, gent.,
   da. of Alex. R.,   mar. 11 Dec., 1562. } Menheniot Par.
Sir Tho. Reynell, Knt., of E. Ogwell, Dev., and the Lady Elizb.   Reg.
   Trelawney of this p'ish   mar.   9 Feb., 1606.
John Trelawny, Esq.,   bur.   17 Oct., 1563.
Jonathan Trelawny, Esq.,   "   1705.

Rob. Trelawney and Anne Coga (or Crooke) mar. 5 Jan., 1623.   } Mevagizzy Par.
                                                                    Reg.
Edw. Trelawney of Lanteglos by Fowey, gen., and Ferdinanda Gorges
  of St. Budeaux. Mar. lic. 17 June, 1615.

Ellyn Trelawney   bur.   1573. } Bodmyn Par.
                                                                Reg.   }
Samuel Trelawny, gent., and Mrs. Elizabeth Billing mar. 22 } St. Breward   } (J. M.)
   Jan., 1651.   Par. Reg.   }
John Trelawny   bur.   30 Apl., 1631.   } St. Minver   }
                                                                Par. Reg.

[Note continued on next page.

Trenance.

John Trenance of Lastilion=Sist' & heyre of Tho. [1]Litleton of Lanhidrake

Blanch ux' Tho. Heliar of Lestithiell	.... ux^r Rawe 2 to Couch	Tho. Trenance of= Lanhidrak	Jone Da. of Nicho. Kendall of Peline

[2] Constance ux' George Courtney of Penkevill	Willmot ux' Rich. Gerveis of	Litleton Trenance= of Bodmin in Com. Cornwall liveinge 1620	Marg^t Da. of Tho. Roscarrock of Roscarrock	[3] Thomazin ux' John Coryn

A

(*Note continued.*)

Mr. Edward Trelawney instituted to Rectory of St. Tudy Oct. 12, 1677.
Jonathan, son of Edward Trelawney, bap. 1694.
Elizab., dau. of Hon. Charles Trelawney, Esq., by Elizab., bap. 30 Sep., 1700, and bur. 11 Dec., 1700.
John Trelawny, sometyme Minister of this Parish, mar.
.... Worthyvale at Lanevet 21 Oct., 1612.
Richard Lower and Elizabeth Trelawny mar. 7 Nov., 1666.
Captain Henry Davies and Madam Mary Trelawny, dau. of Sir Jonathan Trelawny, Bart., mar. 9 Nov., 1689.
Joan. wife of John Trelawny, Minister of St. Tudy, bur. 1607.
John Trelawny, Minister, bur. 13 Jan., 1615.
The Worshipful Samuel Trelawny, Esq. ,, 26 Apl., 1666.
Mrs. Ann Trelawney ,, 15 Oct., 1690.
Elizabeth, wife of the Hon. Charles Trelawney, Esq., bur. 28 May, 1701.

} St. Tudy Par. Reg.

Mar. lic. betw. John Cole of Sidbury, co. Dev., and Johanna Trelawny of Plymouth, gent., Aug. 28, 1610.
,, ,, betw. John Martyn of Plymouth and Margaret Trelawny of the same, Nov. 5, 1633.
,, ,, betw. John Billing of St. Tudye, gent., and Ann, daughter of Francis Trelawny of Plymouth, gent., Feb. 13, 1636.

} (J. M.)

Eulalia, dau. of Edward Trelawny, Esq., bap. at Pelynt 21 Jan., 1616.
Elizabeth, dau. of John Trelawny, Esq., bap. at Pelynt 2 Feb., 1616.
Mary, dau. of John Trelawny, Esq., and Elizab., bap. at Pelynt 24 Jan., 1620.
Dorothy, dau. of Sir John Trelawny, Knt. and Bart., and Dame Elizabeth, (bap. ?) at Pelynt 1638.
John, son of John Trelawney, bur. at Tywardreath 6 Nov., 1614.
Sir John Trelawny, Knt. and Baronet, bur. at Pelynt 26 Feb., 1664.

} Bishop's Transcripts.

[1] Tho. Littleton, Lanhydrock, will 1577, prob. Exon. Lands in Lanhydrock, St. Issey, St. Winnow, St. Vepe, Fowey, Tywardreath, St. Tua. St. Austel, St. Blazey, Lanivet, Lostwithiel, Cardinham, Luxylian, Ermington, Modbury, Stokenham, Withicomb, Colridge, Cornwithie, Hernefred, Harberford, Totnes, etc.

[2] Mar. 25 Jan., 1576.
[3] Thomazin Trenance bap. 1 Oct., 1569. } Lanhydrock } (J. M.)
John Corin and Thomazin Trenance mar. 1590. } Par. Reg.

| Mary 1 Da. atat. 24 | Jane 2 Da. | Tho. sone & hey. at. 22 1620 | Fran. 3 Da. | Katherin 4 Da. | [1] Cheston 5 Da. |

LITLETON TRENANCE.

---

[1] Christian, da. of Litleton Trenance, Esq., bap. 26 Jan., 1603. Lanhydrock Par. Reg. (J. M.)

* Will of Vivian Trenance, 19 Jan., 1506. proved at Lamehith (Lambeth) last day of Feb., 1507. Names his wife Pascacia, sons John, Reginald, Richard, Randulph, John, William, and Thomas, and dau'r Lucy. Wife and da. ex'ors. To be bur. in St. Austell Church. Leaves 6s. 8d. to church of the Convent and Priory of Bodmin for prayers for his soul.

Thomas Trenance and Ann Hawkyn mar. at Lanivet 21 July, 1641.		Bp. of Exeter's Transcripts.
William Trenance bur. at St. Ewe 16 Feb., 1613.		
Ann, dau. of John Trenance	bap. 24 Feb., 1565.	
Richard Trenance and Joanna Longge	mar. 24 Jan., 1568.	St. Austell Par. Reg.
Richard Trenance and Nichola Rawe	,, 19 June, 1581.	
Thomas Hellier and Blanche Trenance	,, 3 June, 1619.	
Mr. John Tredinnick and Petronel Trenance	,, 20 Dec., 1561.	St. Breoke Par. Reg.
Thomas Trenance of Withiel and Catherine Cock	mar. 1655.	St. Columb Major Par. Reg.
Loveday Trenance	bap. 3 June, 1561.	Lanhydrock Par. Reg.
Thomas Trenance	bur. 19 Jan., 1685.	Lanivet Par. Reg.
Elizabeth, dau. of John Trenance	born 16 July, 1657.	
Honour, ,, ,,	,, 24 Feb., 1659.	
Margaret, dau. of Thomas Trenance,	bap. 1 May, 1570.	
Richard, son of ,,	,, 28 Jan., 1571.	
John, ,, ,,	,, 29 Feb., 1573.	
Elizab., dau. of ,,	,, 4 Feb., 1575.	
Ralph, son of ,,	,, 5 Mar., 1577.	
Katherine, dau. of ,,	,, 13 Feb., 1580.	
Bawdon, son of ,,	,, 23 Oct., 1584.	
Thomas, ,, ,,	,, 15 Oct., 1586.	
Blanche, dau. of ,,	,, 10 Mar., 1586.	(J. M.)
Agnes, dau. of Richard Trenance	,, 2 July, 1600.	
Richard, son of ,,	,, 30 Nov., 1615.	
John, son of Thomas Trenance, jun.,	,, 19 Feb., 1615.	
Thomas, ,, ,,	,, 1 Apl., 1617.	
Elizabeth, dau. of ,,	,, 13 Feb., 1619.	
Thomazin, dau. of Philip Trenance	,, 20 Jan., 1620.	
Edward, son of Thomas Trenance	,, 6 July, 1623.	Withiel Par. Reg.
John, ,, Philip Trenance	,, 8 Jan., 1627.	
Joanna, dau. of John Trenance	,, 28 Sep., 1662.	
William Drake and Joanna Trenance	mar. 14 Nov., 1573.	
Thomas Bradley and Thomasine Trenance	,, 20 Jan., 1600.	
Philip Trenance and Elizab. Benford	,, 24 Apl., 1620.	
Wm. Randolph and Jane, dau. of John Trenance	,, 10 June, 1682.	
Joane Drake	bur. 1573.	
Phillippa Trenance	,, 1 May, 1576.	
Thomas Trenance	,, 20 July, 1593.	
Melliora, wife of Thomas Trenance, gent.,	,, 15 Dec., 1608.	
Blanche Trednance	,, 21 July, 1611.	
John, son of Thomas Trenance, jun.,	,, 26 Feb., 1615.	
Thomas Trenance	,, 4 Jan., 1623.	
Philip ,, ,,	,, 4 Dec., 1633.	
Warren ,,	,, 29 Dec., 1650.	
Richard ,,	,, 25 Feb., 1652.	
Katherine ,,	,, 21 Sept., 1661.	
Dorothy, dau. of John Trenance,	,, 17 Aug., 1663.	

Litleton is named on the appraismt with the will of Elizab. Drake. Note 1, p. 80.

Trenerth.

Gerans Trenerth of Trenerth=Mary Dau. of Edw. Kestell
in Com. Cornw. | in Com. Cornw.

John Trenerth of Trenerth=Mary Da. of Jo. Tresuggan

[1] Gawen Trenerth of Constentin=Amy Da. of Micha. Collerian
in Com. Cornw. | of Cornwall

James Trenerth of Constentin=Mary Da. of John Tooker
in Cornw. living 1620 | of Cardinha'

Anne a dau. at. half yeare 1620

*   JAMES TRENERTH.

Trengove als Nanse.

Alexander Trengove of Nance=. . . . da. of Gilly in
in Com. Cornwall | Com. Cornw.

Henry Trengove 2 sonne of=Cheston da. of Hen. Nanspyan of
Nance in Com. Cornwall | Powlsack in Com. Cornwall

[2] John Trengove of Nance=Margery da. of Sr John Arundell
in Com. Cornwall | of Trerise knight

| [2] Dorothy ux. Hen. Colthurst of Treley in Com. Cornwall | [2] Henry Trengove[3] of Nance in Com. Corn. æt. 64 liveing 1620 | =Margery da. of James Basset of Tehidy in Com. Cornwall | [2] Catherine ux. John Lawharne of Tregovethan |

A

[1] Gerance, son of Gawen Trenearth, gent., bap. at
    Constantine   12 Mar., 1599. ⎫ Bp. of Exeter's Transcripts.
* James Trenerth, gent.,   bur.   28 Mar., 1601. ⎭
  Marye, dau. of Mr. John Trenarth, bur.   21 Aug., 1564. ⎫
  Mrs. Elizabeth Trenarth   ,,   20 March, 1618. ⎬ Constantine Par. Reg. (J. M.)
  James Trenarth, gent.,   ,,   11 Nov., 1661. ⎪
  Gerrance   ,,   ,,   ,,   16 Aug., 1688. ⎭

[2] Named in will of John Arundell of Trerice, Esq., dated 14 Sept. 22 Eliz., P. P. C. 26 Nov., 1580, together with Richard Nannce, son of John N. and Margery Arundell.

[3] Esch. Eliz., Jas., and Chas., Pt. 14, No. 32. Henry Nance, gent., ob. 13 May 1 Chas. John Nance, his son and heir, æt. 11 years 10 months and ten days at his father's death.

234 THE VISITATION OF THE COUNTY OF CORNWALL.

A |

| John Trengove fil. et hæres æt. 6 | Arthure 2 fil. æt. 3 | Jane 1 da. æt. 8 | Margaret 2 daughter æt. 3 menses |

HENRYE TRENGOVE AL'S NANSE.

*

Tresaber.

ARMS.—*B. a chev. between 3 Talbots couchant (alibi currentes) sinister regardant Arg., quartering* PETIT *Arg. a lion ramp. Gu. with a crescent Sa. for difference.* (Harl. 1091, fo. 101.)
(In the Coll. of Arms the PETIT Lion is *Armed and langued Or.*)
CREST.—*A Demi-Talbot regard.*

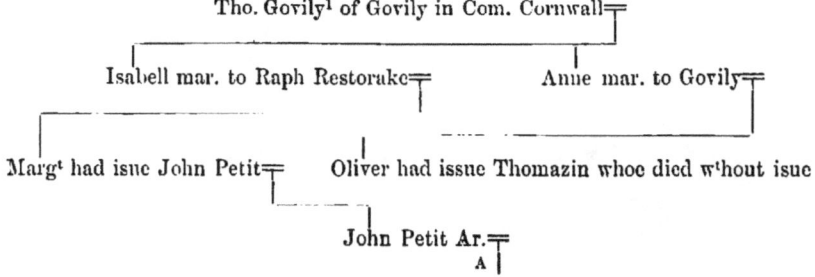

* Richard, son of Mr. John Nance, bap. at St. Keverne 9 Sep., 1610. ⎫ Bp. of Exeter's
 Henry Nance, Esq.,   bur. at Illogan   16 May, 1625. ⎬ Transcripts.
 Henry,   son of John Nance, Esq., by Dorothy, bap. 17 Feb., 1681.
 John,   „   „   „   „   21 Oct., 1684.
 John,   „·   „   „   „   21 Oct., 1686.
 William,   „   ··   „   ⎰   17 Aug., 1687. ⎱ Warleggan
                                        ⎱ bur. 11 Dec., ··   ⎰ Par. Reg.   (J. M.)
 Dorothy, dau. of   ··   ·,   bap.   8 Jan., 1690.
 John,   son of   ··   „   24 Jan., 1694.
 Luce.   dau. of   „   „   „   16 Nov., 1697. ⎭
 Mar. lic. betw. John Beaufort, clerk, and Ann, dau. of Henry Nance, 27 Jan., 1664.
 1686. Sep. 17. Prob. of will of Mary Trengoffe, widow. Archd. Cornw.

Mr. John Nans admitted to the church of St. Meriodoc, Camborne, on the free resignation of Alexander Penbyll, 5 June, 1501. (Bishop Redmayne's Reg., page 21. At page 22 is the permission of exchange between Mr. John Nans, Vicar of St. Thomas Collegiate Ch. of Glasney, and Mr. Alexander Penhall, of the parish of St. Meriodoc of Camborne.)

Ped. fin. Cornw. 1 and 2 Phil. and Mary, Pasch. John Courtney, gent., qu. Egidius Greynfeld. gent., and Margery his wife, one of the dau'rs and heirs of Richard Trengove al's Nans, def. Lands in Trengove. Pellawyne, St. Logan. Tretbarrope, Trespresyne, St. John's Parke, Helston, Sythney, St. Buryan, Trembrothcke, Trebuskan, and St. Paule.

Indenture made 15 Oct., 1677, betw. John Trengove al's Nance, of Trengove ⎫ Deed in
al's Trengoffe, co. Cornw., Esq., of the one part, and William Chester, of East ⎬ Collection of
Haddon, co. Northampton, and Dorothy his wife and others named. Recites a ⎰ Sir John
marriage between the said John Trengove and Dorothy his wife, daughter of the ⎰ Maclean.
said William Chester and Dorothy his wife, and settles Trengoffe and other lands.⎭
Seal of John Nance.

[1] The Ghivaile of Doomsday, Tregoney, Cornw.

THE VISITATION OF THE COUNTY OF CORNWALL. 235

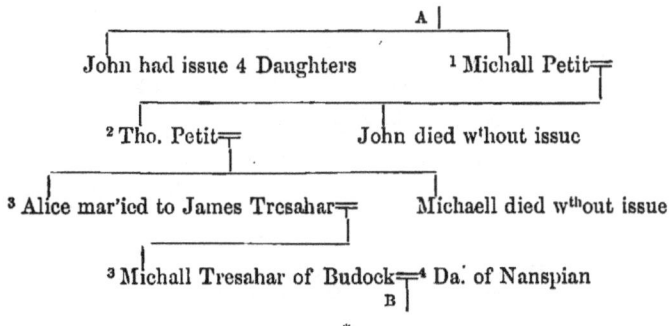

[1] Married Thomazin, da. of Tho. Leigh of Holsworthy; she afterwards married Peter Bevil, and in her will (P. P. C. Holder 36) bequeaths to "Elizb. Petytt a girdell with a golden corse of gold lyned with rede, a pair of beds of ambyr doble gawded with silver, a kirtell of tawny cloth." "Item, I beq. to Tho. Petyt, a gilt goblet, my best nutte and his cover, and the cover of the cup that was stole, and £20 in money on condicion that he clayme no more goods of his fadere nor of myn, etc. Item, I beq. to the dau. of Tho. Petyt a dymysent with a golde corsse." To Jane, dau. of Thos. P., and his other daus. now at home. "To John Pentyre's children begotten of my dau. Isabell." To Will. Gerves' children begotten of Emlyn. "My son Peers Bevill" and John Walsh, Exors., and "my son Tho. Petytt," Supervisor. Prob. 10 Nov., 1517.
Peter Bevill's will (P. P. C. Holder 13). "Item to Thomas Petytt my russet gowne furrd with foxe; to Wm. Gervys my best gowne lyned with sasnet." Names Sir John Treffry, Willm. Trevanion, John Arundell of Talverne, Marie Arundell, Matilda Greneffelde, John Bevil, his son's wife Thomazine, Michael Petyt, John Petyt, John and Rob. Fitz.

[2] Tho. Petit married Elizabeth, da. of John Godolphin, and had a son Thomas Petit, who married Jane, sole da. and heiress of Rob. Poyle, and their sole da. and heiress Alice married James Tresahar, as in the ped. above. One generation has been omitted. See 'Hist. of Trigg.'

[3] Chanc. Pro. Miscell., vol. ii. fo. 195. Temp. Elizb. To Rt. Hon. Sir Nich. Bacon, Kt., Lo. Keeper, etc. Orator Michell Tresagher of Trevithan, co. Cornw., gentleman; whereas James Tresagher, father to Orator, was seised in his demesne as of Fee of one-third of Manor of Trelowith, one-third of Govylie, Fentongorge, Soren, Carveynack Pettit; the same descended to your Orator within age as son and heir of s^d James. Alyse, wife of s^d James Tresaher, and mother of Orator, remarried one Edw. Cowche, who by reason of s^d marriage obtained custody of the evidences and writings which Cowche on his death bed directed should be delivered up to Orator. Plea for restoration by Exors.

[4] Agnes, da. of Nanspian. Heralds' Coll.

* Ped. fin. 25 Elizab., Easter, Cornw. Wm. Peres al's Pryske qu. Michael Tresagher al's Tresaugher, generos., and Anna, ux., def. Lands in Vounder Trewoone and Church Town, p'ish of Mullyan.
Ped. fin. 30 Elizab., Hil., Cornw. Rich. Rawlyn qu. Michael Tresagher, gen., and Anne, ux., def. 154 acres in Tregewe and Myler.
Ped. fin. 8 James, Mic., Cornw. Ralf Edwards, qu. Michael Tresahar, gen., and Tho. Tresahar, gen., def. 3^d part of Tregandallen and Mewan.
Ped. fin. 10 James, Hil., Cornw. Ant. Pye, gen., Hugh Trevanion, gen., qu. Tho. Tresahar, gen., and Anna, vid., def. Govyly Vean. Fentongock Tresoren, Kebye, Manor of Trelowith, and other lands in St. Ewe and St. Mewan. See under Pye, ante.
Ped. fin. 11 James, East., Cornw. Ralf Challons, gen., and Tho. Robyns, qu. Tho. Tresaher, gen., def. Ten't in Tregue and Mylor.
Ped. fin. 13 James, Mic., Cornw. Wm. Pracd, gen. qu. Tho. Tresahar, ar., and Geo. Williams, gen., def. Lands in St. Ives, Una juxta Lelant, and Illogan.
Ped. fin. 16 James, Mic., Cornw. Jno. Trefusis, ar., qu. Tho. Tresahar, gen., and Anne, ux., def. Lands in Tregewe and Mylor.
Ped. fin. 1655, Hil., Cornw. Wm. Oram and Xfer Ginn qu. Michael Tresahar, gent., and Elizab., ux. Lands in Smithick (Falmouth) al's Pennycomquick, Budock.
Ped. fin. 1656, East., Cornw. Peter Killegrew. Knt., qu. Tho. Hickes and Michael Tresahar, gen., and Elizb., ux., def. Lands in Trevethan, Trevethan Wartha, Trevethan Wollas, Cargamowe, The Cliffe Close, Smithick, and Budock.
Ped. fin. 13 Chas. II., Trin., Cornw. Hugh Boscawen, ar., qu. Michael Tresahar, genero., and Elizb., ux., def. Eastclose, Longclose, etc., and lands in Govilcy Vean and Fentongoth.
Ped. fin. 34 Chas. II., East., Cornw. Jno. Williams, gen., qu. Ezechiel Tresahar and Elizab., ux. 36 mess., 1 shop, 2 cellars, and 2 tortis, 30 gardens, 1 wharf, and 2 ac. land in town and parish of Falmouth.

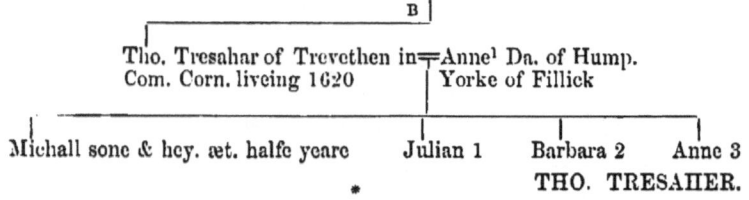

Tho. Tresahar of Trevethen in Com. Corn. liveing 1620 =Anne[1] Da. of Hump. Yorke of Fillick

Michall sone & hey. æt. halfe yeare | Julian 1 | Barbara 2 | Anne 3
* THO. TRESAHER.

[1] See Yorke ped., *post.*
* Rot. Claus. 25 Chas. II., 4383, 5th part. An Indenture, 4 Dec., 25 Chas. II., between Ezechiel Tresahar, bro. and heir to Michael Tresahar, late of Goviley, dec., co. Cornw., gent., first part, and Hugh Boscawen of Tregothnan, in s[d] co., Esq., of the other part. Ezechiel sold Boscawen, the Mansion, Barton, and demesne lands of Goviley or Goviley Vean, and Fentanguck al's Fentongock, etc., in p'ish of Cuby, then in tenure of Elizabeth Tresahar, widow, mother of Ezechiel, and relict of Michael Tresahar, father of s[d] Ezchiel, subject to certain reservations under the will of said Michael Tresahar.
Will of Michael Tresahar of Govyly, P. P. C. Bruce 106, A.D. 1664. To wife Elizb. £20 per ann. out of Barton of Govyly, and furniture of Green Chamber. Barton of Govylye to son Michael, he paying his mother the aforesaid annuity, and a debt to Hugh Boscawen. To three sons, Ezechiel, Gabriel, and Samuel. certain lands each. To daughters Carthrett, Elizab., Mary, Hannah, certain leases for term of 500 years.
Will of Richard Tresahar, prob. 1563, Exeter (Old Totnes collated). To wife Ann (? née Killegrew), sole executrix, Trevethan for life. To dau. Jane, lands in town of Tregoney, and lands in Mylor; rem. to rt. heirs of testator. To Elizb., Jane, and Chesten, daughters of his son James, legacies. Witnesses, John and Alexander Killegrew and John Denys, Vicar.
Will of John Tresahar of Constantine, yeom., P. P. C. Juxon, 86, A.D. 1663. To Bridget Pendarves, da. of Wm. P. of Roscrow, Esq., and o'rs. To his godson, son of Michael Tresahar of Smithicke, etc.
Will of Henry Tresahar, 1706, of H.M.S. Pembroke. Estate to sister Mary. Commission to Ezechiel Tresahar the father. Bodmin, and P. P. C.

Henry, the son of Ezekiel Tresahar, gent., and Elizabeth his wife,	bap. 13 June, 1683.	
Mary, the dafter of Ezechiel Tresahar,	„ 26 July, 1690.	
Richard, son of Michael and Mary Tresahar,	,. 1 April, 1712.	Cuby and Tregoney St. James' Par. Reg.
James, „ „ „	„ 13 May, 1714.	
Richard, „ James and Elizab. Tresahar,	„ 29 Dec., 1740.	
Mary, da. of „ „	„ 27 Dec., 1742.	
Richard, son of Michael and Mary Tresahar,	bur. 1714.	
Mary, wife of Michael Tresahar,	„ 26 May, 1724.	
Ezechiel Tresahar,	„ 17 April, 1734.	
Michael „	„ 30 Oct., 1744.	
Michael Tresahar & Mary Avent of Tregoney, mar. Ascension Day, 1701.		Lamorran Par. Reg.
James Tresaher of Tregony and Elizab. Chappel of this parish.	mar. 8 Dec., 1739.	Ruan Lanihorne Par. Reg.
Henry Holman and Mary Treshair,	„ 27 Aug., 1763.	Stoke Damarel Par. Reg.
James, son of Mr. John Tresahar,	bap. 20 Oct., 1613.	Gluvias Par. Reg.
Michell, „	.. 16 Dec., 1614.	
Michael, son of Mr. James and Mrs. Margery Tresahar,	bap. 30 July, 1655.	Budock Par. Reg.
Tho. Tresahar, gent., and Mrs. Matilda Pront, wid.,	mar. 1 May, 1665.	
Mrs. Anne Tresahar, wid.,	bur. 17 Nov., 1658.	
James Tresahar, gent.,	„ 15 Dec., 1667.	
Margery, wife of James Tresahar, gent.,	„ 25 Feb., 1669.	
Mr. James Tresahar,	„ 4 Feb., 1695.	
Ruth, wife of Mr. Jas. Tresahar of Falmo.,	„ 22 Jan., 1697.	
James, son of Tho. and Matilda Tresahar,	bap. 20 Jan., 1665.	Falmouth Par. Reg.
John, „ James and Ruth „	„ 2 July, 1679.	
James, „ „ „	„ 13 Apr., 1672.	
Thos., „ „ „	„ 11 Apr., 1674.	
Sampson „ ,. „ of Pendennis,	„ 7 Mar., 1675.	
Michael, son of James and Ruth Tresahar of Pendennis Castle,	,. 17 July, 1678.	

[*Note continued on next page.*]

Trethewy.

Omnibus Christi fidelibus ad quos p^rsent's l're p'venerint ego Henr' de Trethewy filius et hæres Hudone que fuit ux' Johis de Trethewy Salt'm in D'no sempiter.' Noveritis me relaxasse et penitus quietu' clamasse p' me et heredibʒ meis et assign' Willo de Tregodek her. suis et assig' &c. In cuius rei testimoniu' huic present' script' sigillu' meu' apposui. Hijs testibus Joh'e de Trenoda, Joh'e de Polgoner, Petro de Westmarch, Robt' de Carnedon, et aliis multis. Sans Dat'.

    SEAL.—*A chevron engr. betw. three goats statant.*

  Omnibus Xpi fidelibʒ ad quos p^rstus Scriptu' p'venerit ego Thomas Trethewy Armig' salt' in domino semp' noveritis me p^rfatu' Thoma' Remisisse relaxasse et omnino p' me et heredibus meis imperpetuu' clamasse Johe Lynam &c. In cuius rei testimoniu' Sigillu' meu' apposui hijs testibus Robt. Geffray maiore villæ predict. Johe Comitreff, Willo Bernard, Johe Haill, Johe Harvy et alijs. Dat' die lune in crastino S'ti Georgij martiris Anno regni regis E. IV. post conquest' 25.

    Tho. Trethewy Armiger 15 E. IV.

    James Trethewy of St. Stephens in=
    Branwell in Com. Devon (*sic*)

2. John   3. Thomas   Rich. Trethewy de St. Ste-=Jone Da. of Willm. Haw-
     —   phens in Com. Cornwall   kins of St. Wenne in
    4. Stephen   fil. primogenit.   Com. Cornwall

Hugh Trethewy   Robt. Trethewy de=Anne Da. of Tho. Burges   Anthonie
fil. primogenitus   St. Stephens in   of Truro in Com. Corn-   3 fil.
 =   Com. Cornwall   wall
A   B

(*Note continued.*)

Thos., son of John and Ursula Tresahar	bap. 28 Sept., 1678.	Falmouth Par. Reg.
Henry, ,, ,, ,,	,, 7 Apr., 1681.	
Ursula, wife of Mr. John Tresahar, ,,	bur. 1685.	
John Tresahare the elder,	bur. at Constantine 14 Aug., 1598.	Bp. of Exeter's Transcripts.
John ,, ,,	,, ,, 17 Mar., 1601.	
Barbara, da. of Tho. Tresahar, gent., bap. at Budock	8 Sept., 1625.	
... el, the son of Ezekiel Tresaheare and El . . . (Elizabeth)		
his wife, bap. at Cuhy, (*Partly torn and illegible*) 26 Mar., 1678.		
Mr. Tho. Tresahar & Mrs. Margt. Phillips, mar. at Camborne 7 June, 1730.		
,, bur. ,, 25 Oct., 1730.		Archdeacon's Transcripts.
Tho. Tresahar of Camborne and Mrs. Ann Treminhecre of		
Penzance, mar. at Madron, 22 Sept., 1730.		
Mary, da. of Gabriel Tresahar, bur. at St. Minver, 1698.		
Ann, da. of Ezekiel Tresaier, gent., and Elizb. his wife,		
bap. at Tregoney, 28 Mar., 1687.		
Margery, wife of Gabriel Tresahar, gent., bur. in the		Minster
Church of Minster, 3 July, 1694.		Par. Reg. (J. M.)
Tho. Tresahar of Falmo., gent., and Elizah. Phillips, mar. 17 Oct., 1689.		Poughill Par. Reg.
Elizb., da. of Gabriel Tresare, bap. 2 Feb., 1686.		St. Issey Par. Reg.
John, son of Thomas Tresare, gent., bap. 16 Oct., 1716.		
Mr. John Tozzare, bur. in the Church, 18 Aug., 1712.		Camborne Par. Reg.
Mistris Tresare, ,, ,, 17 Feb., 1718.		
,, Anne Tresare, ,. ,, 8 May, 1719.		

(The Camborne branch probably descended from James Tresahar of Gurlyn. See n. p. 155.)

  For continuation and extinction of male line of Tresahar, see Sir John Maclean's 'Hist. of Trigg,' vol. i., pp. 317–319. See also Petit ped., *post*, and Harl. MS. 1079, fo. 81.

238   THE VISITATION OF THE COUNTY OF CORNWALL.

A				B			
Hugh	2. Margerie	Elizab. mar. to Anthonie Pie of St. Stephens	John Trethewy fil. primogenit æt. 26	Thomas Trethewy 2 fil. æt. 24 w^t Mr Francis West silman in Cheepside	Barnard Richard gemelli ætat. 20 sup'stes 1620
John	3. Judith				
	4. Honor				
	5. Jone				

*

Entered, not signed.

Treunwith vel Trenwith.

Henry Treunwth de Trennwith=Elino^r Da. of Tho. Rosmadres
in Cornw. │ of St. Borian

Peter Treunwth fil. et her.=Elizab. fil. et her.   Johis Vincent   Otes 2 filius

Willm Treunwth=Jane Da. & her. Ri. Predency de St. Borian   Henry 2 fil.

Thomas fil.=Margerie of   Mathew Treunwith of Treun-=Elizab. da. & hey. of
et her.   James Erisey   with in Com. Cornwall   James Caskayes
                                      A

---

* Inq. p. m. 6 Edw. II., No. 20. William Trethewy fil. et her. Agnetiss de Nans. Nans. mess. and land in Moresk.

Ped. fin. Cornw. 3 Rich. II., No. 5. Philip Trethewy qu. Hugh Brendewoode and Alice his wife def. In Treledyk, Trehenford, and Bodmin.

Ped. fin. Cornw. 19 Rich. II., No. 3. John Trethewy qu. Walter Canford and Johana his wife def. In Trethewy.

Ped. fin. Cornw. 14 Hen. IV., No. 2. Rob. Bray and Johana his wife qu. John Trethewy and Cecilia his wife def. East Ashton, etc., settled on John and Cecilia, rem. to William Trethewy their son and his wife Cecilia.

Rich., son of Rich. Trethewye, bap. 11 Feb., 1582. } St. Ewe Par. Reg.
John   „   „   Trethewe,   „   12 June, 1585. }

Anne, dau. of Thomas Trethewy, gent., and Margery, bap. 3 Feb., 1632. Constantine Par. Reg.

John Trethewie, clerk, and Alse Marke, widow, mar. 15 May, 1623. Lanteglos by Camelford Par. Reg.

Licence to serve the cure of Lanteglos by Camelford granted to John Trethewy, clerk, 1634. (Act Book, Exeter.)

Robert Trethewy of St. Stephen's in Brannel and Loveday Avery of Truro. Mar. lic. 1681.

Ind're made 6 Jan. 1 Charles, betw. John Trethewy of St. Stephen's in Brannel, gent., of the one part, and Anthony Tanner of the same parish, gent., of the other part. Conveyance to the said Anthony Tanner and his heirs of two tenements called Trevenge (J. M.) in the said parish, which Richard Chiverton, by deed dated 1 Oct., 38 Elizab., granted to Robert Trethewy, gent., dec'd, father of the said John, and also certain lands in the same parish which William Carlighan of Illogan, by deed dated 18 Oct. 34 Eliz., granted to the aforesaid Robert Trethewy.

Seal.—A chev. engr. betw. three goats.

Ind're dated 2 March, 1680, betw. Anthony Trethewy, of St. Giles in the Fields, Middx., of the one part, and Sir John Baker, of St. Paul. Covent Garden, Knt., and William Baker, 2nd son of the said Sir John Baker, of the other part. Mortgage of lands in St. Stephen in Brannel for £1000.

(Penes Mr. Vosper Thomas of Wimborne, co. Dorset.)

THE VISITATION OF THE COUNTY OF CORNWALL. 239

A

[1] Willm 3 son mar. ye Da. of ═ Tho. Treunwith of Treunwith in Com. Cornwall ═ [2] Elizab. Da. & one of ye heyres of Willm Myllyton of Pengersick in Com. Cornwall

Rich. Treunwith of St. Earth in Com. Cornwall ═ Ann Da. of John Merrit of Probus in Com. Cornwall

Mary uxor Skott of Kent

Ann uxor Humphry Burgis of St. Earth

* RICHAR. TRENWITH.

Trevanion.

S^r Jo. Trevanion K^t ═ Jone Da. & hey. of Stephen de Belloprato

Rob. Trevanion mar. the Da. & hey. of Le Archdecon ═

S^r Jo. Trevanion K^t ═ Jone Da. of Rich. Le Sergiaux K^t
ob. sine prole

Rob. Trevanion ═ Jone Da. of Otho Arondell of Trembleth

Rob. Trevanion ═ Da. & heire of Carmynowe

Rob. Trevanion ═ Da. & hey. of Raph. Arondell of Caryhayes

Tho. Trevanion ═ Maude Da. & Cohey. of Jo. Petit Esq.

Jo. Trevanion temp. E. IV. 22 ═ Jennet Da. of Tho. Trefrie of Foye Esq.

John 2 sone from whome is descended Trevanion of Trevalster

Sr Wm Trevanion ═ Anne Da. of Sr Ric. K^t 1 sone | Edgcomb K^t

A

---

[1] Named, together with his son Thomas, in will of Jno. Bosustow of St. Leven (who mar. his sister Anne), dat. 8 July, 1604. P. P. C. 19 June, 1605.

[2] She afterwards mar. .... Arundell, and lastly Thos. Hearl of Prideaux. See ped. of Hearle, *ante*.

* Ezechiel Trenwith, gent., and Elizabeth Lanyon mar. 1614. St. Ives Par. Reg.
William Trenewith, gent., and Mary Pellamounter mar. 10 Nov., 1634, at Zennor. Bp. of Exeter's Transcripts. (J. M.)
Ped. fin. Cornw. 15 Rich. II., No. 3. Henry Treunwyth qu. Hugh Canas and Emma his wife def. Carbons and Carnyny.
Ped. fin. Cornw. 34 Hen. VI., No. 3. Otonem Treunwyth qu. John Velour, def. Porthyalananta, Carnesuwe, and Helston,
For more of Trenwith see Harl. MS. 1079, fo. 35.

240 THE VISITATION OF THE COUNTY OF CORNWALL.

A |

Jane ux' Reignold Mohun — S' Hugh Trevanion K'=Elizb. Da. of S' Lewis Pollard K'

John 2 ob. | Rich. 3=Margaret da. & cohcir of Tho. | Hugh Tre-=Sibell Da. of
sine p'le | Chamont sonne & heir of | vanion | Morgan of
 | S' Jo. Chamont | | Lockstowe

Elizab. | Hugh 1 | Willm 4 | Agnes wife | Sibell wife | Anne ux' | Beatrix
ux' | — | — | to John | to Hugh | Jo. Killi- | ux' John
Mallet | Richard 2 | Edward 5 | Madern | Tredin- | owe of | Tre-
= | — | | | ham | Lansallos | lawny
 | John 3 | | | *Esq'.* | | *Esq.*

Tho. Malet of The Midle Temple *Esq.*

Elizb. ux' S' | Kath. ux' | Marg' ux' | Edward 1 sonne | Charles=Jone Da. &
Rob. Cary | Jo. Ross- | S' John | — | Trevan- | hey. of
after made | carock of | Trevars K' | John 2 sone | ion of | Wichhalse
Erle of | Roscarrock | | — | Carry-
Munmouth | *Esq.* | | Hugh 3 sonne | hayes

Kath' 1 Da. | Charles Trevanion=Amye 1 Da. of S' Jo.
 | of Carryhayes | Mallet of Enmor

Mary a da. | John Trevanion sone & heir atat. 7 1620

* *Not signed.*

Trebanion.

S' Hugh Trevanion of Kerchayes=Elizab. Da of S' Lewis Pollard

John | ¹ S' Hughe Trevanion | Rich. Trevanion of=Marg' Da. of Chamond
 | 1 sonne | Tolverne in Com. | & widowe of Arondell
 | | Cornwall
 | | A |

* The additions in italic are in a different hand.
¹ Hugh Trevanion of St. Michael, Caerhais. Will prob. Exeter, 1571. Names brother Richard T., cousin Will. Mohun, Esq., and trusty friend John Davy of Restrewg trustees for his manors of Tolgarrock, Trebarthes, Penhale, Horwell, Grogoth; daughters Beatrice, Katherine, Elizabeth; his wife Sibill, and his youngest son Charles Trevanion. (For these see Harl. MS. 1079. fo. 158.)
Ped. fin. Cornw. 7 and 8 Eliz., Mich. Hugh Trevanyon, Esq., Will. Loveday. gent., qu. Rich. Trevanyon and Margaret his wife def. Glewyns al's Kenwyn, Keveran, and Lansallas settled on Rich. Trevanyon and Margaret his wife for life, rem. to Alice Arundell, da. of said Margaret, and her heirs, rem. to Rich. Trevanyon, second son of Rich. and Margaret, and his heirs, rem. to Thomas Arundell, son of said Margaret, and his heirs, rem. to right heirs of Margaret.

A

Hugh Trevanion of = Anne Da. & hey. of	Rich. Trevanion of = Mary Da. of Roll
Trelugan in Com.	Tho. Mayowe al's	St. Goran in Com.	of Heamton in
Cornw.	Hellier of Lost-	Cornwall liveinge	Devon
	withell	1620	

Hugh Trevanion = Suzan Da. of	Blanch. ux^r Jo.	Nathaniell Tre-	¹ Mary ux^r
of Trelugan	Robt. Ape-	Clyes of Pen-	vanion sone &	Richard Cros-
liveing 1620	ley of Bor-	sanz Gent.	hey. at. 20	man of Crosse
	stable		1620	

HU. TREVANION. * NATH. TREVANYON.

---

¹ Rich. Crosman, gent., and Mary Trevanyan, da. of Rich. Trevannion, Esq., mar. at Gorran 28 Jan., 1617. Bp. of Exeter's Transcripts.

* Nathaniel, son of Chas. Trevanion, gent., and Patience, bap. at
    Lanteglos by Fowey   2 Feb., 1713. ⎫
Mr. John Kemp and Mrs. Grace Trevanion mar. at Veryan   1699. ⎪
Sir Nich. Trevanion, Knt., and the Hon. Lady Coryton mar. at ⎪
    St. Stephen's by Ash   29 Mar., 1706. ⎬ Archdeacon's
Charles Trevanion and Mary Dodson of Pelint mar. at Lanteglos   Transcripts.
    by Fowey   1716. ⎪
Mr. Tho. Tresahar and Mrs. Ann Trevanion mar. at Veryan 16 July, 1717. ⎪
Grace Trevanion   bur. at Cuby 1700. ⎪
Eleanor, wife of Chas. Trevanion, bur. at Ruan Lanihorne 10 Mar., 1702. ⎪
Cath. Trevanion   "   "   1734. ⎭

Rich. Trevanyon. gent., and Katherine Nottell mar. at Ruan Lani- ⎫
    horne   3 July, 1610. ⎪
Fra. Godolphin and Kath. Trevanion   mar. 8 May, 1622. ⎪
John Trevannyon, Esq., and Mrs. Ann Arundell mar. at Newlyn ⎬ Bp. of Exeter's
     8 Dec.. 1634. ⎪ Transcripts.
Ann, wife of Hugh Trevanion, gen.,   bur. at Filley 6 Mar., 1613. ⎪
John Trevanyon, gent.,   bur. at St. Just in Roseland 1614. ⎪
Ric. Trevanyon, gent.,   bur. at Veryan 2 Nov., 1635. ⎭

Hugh, son of Hugh Trevanion,   bap.   1593. ⎫ Cuby Par. Reg.
Grace Trevanion   bur.   28 Ap., 1700. ⎭
John Trevanion   "   1602.   St. Ewe Par. Reg.
Nathaniel, son of Charles and Honor Trevanion   bap.   29 Oct., 1661. ⎫
Nathaniel, son of Nich. Trevanion, gent.,   "   1691. ⎪
Honor, da. of Charles Trevanion, gent., and Honor,   bur.   1662. ⎪
Honor, wife of   "   "   "   1665. ⎬ Gorran Par. Reg.
Nathaniel Trevanion, Esq.,   "   10 May, 1673. ⎪
Will. Trevanion, gent.,   "   12 Nov., 1681. ⎪
Nathaniel Trevanion, son of Chas. T., Esq.,   "   1684. ⎭

William, son of William Trevanion,   bap.   1661. ⎫ St. Issey Par.
John,   "   "   "   1666. ⎬ Reg.
William Trevanion and Honor Williams   mar.   1659. ⎭

Richard, son of Rich. Trevanion of Veryan, and Anne, dau. of John ⎫ Lamorran Par.
    Verman and Mary his wife, of Lamorran   6 Feb., 1694. ⎭ Reg.

Rich., son of Hugh Trevanion, gen.,   bur.   8 Nov., 1661. ⎱ St. Michael Pen-
                                                                 kivel Par. Reg.

Richard, son of Will. Trevanion and Honor,   bap,   1671. ⎱ Padstow Par.
Charles,   "   "   "   "   1676. ⎭ Reg.

Hugh Trevanion, gent., of Carhais died at Nuham in Kenwyn, bur. ⎱ Truro Par. Reg.
    in the church   20 Sept., 1696. ⎭

[*Note continued on next page*

Trevelyan.

John Trevelian of Nettlecomb=Eliza. da. & heire of Tho. Whalesbury
in Com. Som'set a° 9 H. VII. | of Whalesbury in Com. Cornub.

| S' John Trevelian of Nettlecomb Kt. sonne & heir | Thomas 2
Rich. 3
Nich. 4
Rich. 5
George 6
s. p. | Humfrey Tre-=Margaret da. of
vellian of   S' Rhice ap
Basill¹ in   Thomas K' of
Com. Corn.   the Garter
              tempe H. VII. |

John Trevellian of Basill=Eliza. da. of Peter   William Viell=Jane da. of S' John
sonne & heire   Corington of   of Trevarder   Arrundell of Trerice
                            Newton Esq.
                           A   B

(*Note continued.*)

Mr. Tho. Tresabar and Mrs. Anne Trevanion	mar.	16 July, 1717.
Jno. Trevanion	bur.	5 Dec., 1687.
Mr. Hugh Trevanion	,,	24 Mar., 1693.
Mrs. Grace Trevanion	,,	6 July, 1706. Veryan Par.
Mr. John ,,	,,	18 June, 1712. Reg.
Mr. Rich. ,,	,,	2 Nov., 1715.
Mrs. Anne ,,	,,	1716.
Mr. Tho. Tresabar	,,	1719.

Hugh Trevanion and Candace Carew of St. Just, spinster. mar. lic. 1665.

Sir Nich. Trevanion of Plymo. and Dame Sara Corriton, of St. Stephens by Ash, mar. lic. 3 Nov., 1716.

Duncombe Drake of Stoke Dam., Esq., and Grace Trevanion of same. mar. lic. 4 Dec., 1733.

Ric. Trevanion, " in the 87th year of my age." (Will 17 Ap., 1714, Bodmin.) Son Richard T. (Exor.). Son Charles T. to have Woodford in Lansalloes, he to pay his own dau. Jane £40 at 21. Charles' son John rem'r. Son Sir Nicholas T. a gold ring, and to his lady a gold ring, and each of his dau'rs £5. Daughters Elizb., Thomas, Grace Kemp, and Mary Kemp. Dau.-in-law Ann Trevanion.

Rich. Trevanion of Veryan, Governor of Pendennis Castle. Will prob. Bodmin, 15 Oct., 1717. Wife Ann Barton of Hay in Veryan. Lands of John Trevanion of Carhais "now in my possession." House and gardens at Tredinnick for her use. All residue of lands, etc., to his dau. Anne Tresabar, his sole executrix. See Chan. Pro., May, 1723.

Ped. fin. Cornw. 15 Rich. II., No. 4. Richard Trevanion qu. Ralph Soor def., etc.

Ped. fin. Cornw. 8 Hen. IV., No. 6. Carhays and other lands settled on Rich. Trevanyon and Johanna his wife, rem. to Stephen their son, rem. to Johanna their da., rem. to right heirs of Rich.

Ped. fin. Cornw. 8 Hen. IV., No. 10. Thos. Trevanyon qu. John Pascowe def. Lands in St. Enoder.

Ped. fin. 1656, Hil., Cornw. John Robins, gen. qu. Chas. Trevanion, gent. def. Lands Trenastell and Ruan Lanihorne.

Ped. fin. 26 Chas. II., Trin., Cornw. Rich. Seoble gen. and o'rs qu. Chas. Trevanion ar. def. Moiety of Tregarthen, etc.

Ped. fin. 15 Jas., Mic., Cornw. Ric. Trevanion ar. and Jno. Trefusis ar. qu. Chas. Trevanyon ar. Hugh Trevanion gen. def. Ardevora Vear and Filley.

Ped. fin. 4 Anne, Trin., Cornw. Stephen Robins ar. qu. Chas. Trevanion ar. def. Lands Trevethick.

¹ Basil in St. Cleather.

THE VISITATION OF THE COUNTY OF CORNWALL. 213

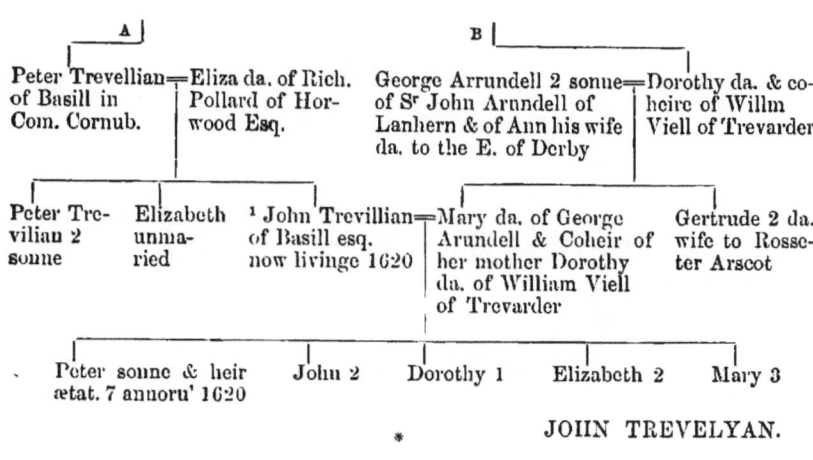

JOHN TREVELYAN.

---

[1] Jno. Trevillian, gent., and Mary Arundell, gent., mar. at Mawgan in Pider 31 Mar., 1608. Bp. of Exeter's Transcripts.

* Thomas Trevillian, gen., and Sarah Drake mar. 20 Feb., 1649. Buckland Mon. Par. Reg.
Jane, da. of Henry Trevillian, bap. 1682. Germoe Par. Reg.
Edward Trevillian „ 1575. Perranuthno Par. Reg.

James, son of Mr. James Trevillian and Lucy, bap. at Fowey 19 Feb., 1720.
Francis, son of Arthur and Jane Trevillian, bap. at Fowey 28 Jan., 1733.
Mr. James Trevilian bur. at Fowey 18 Oct., 1743.
Peter, son of John Trevelyan, Esq., bap. at St. Cleather 17 Feb., 1613.
William, son of Christopher Trevelian, Parson, bap. at Mawgan in Meneage 27 Ap., 1623.
} Archdeacon's Transcripts.
} Bp. of Exeter's Transcripts.

Nicholas Trevillyan and Mary Rogers mar. 29 Apl., 1605. } Blisland Par. Reg.
Stephen. son of Avis Trevellian „ 4 Mar., 1583. } St. Neot Par. Reg.
John Tomking and Avyes Trevillian mar. 28 Feb., 1591 } Withiel Par. Reg. (J. M.)

John Drew and Margery Trevylyan of St. Cleder, mar. lic. 8 Sept., 1568.
John Trevillian, jun., of Nettlecomb, co. Som., and Ann Courteney, widow, of Lazack, co. Cornw., mar. lic. 1 Oct., 1620.
Commend Garch of Nettlecomb, co. Som., and Cecilia Trevillian of Axmouth, mar. lic. 5 May, 1623.
Thomas Robinson of Helston, gent., and Mary Trevillian of Tiverton, mar. lic. 1 Oct., 1631.
Edward Morth of Talland, gent., and Elizabeth Trevillian of Morewinstow, mar. lic. 4 Oct., 1638.
Licence to preach within the Archdeaconry of Cornwall granted to James Trevillian, 5 Mar., 1662.
Hugh Trevillian and Mary Fane of Tavistock, mar. lic. 13 Oct., 1669.
Hugh Trevillian and Joanna Amery of Nymet Bishop, mar. lic. 7 Ap., 1670.

Ped. fin. Cornw. 26 Hen. VI., No. 1. John Trevillian qu. John Dunkyn and Cecilia his wife def. Trenevesack. etc.
Will of Jno. Trevelyan, Vicar of St. Peran in the Sands, 20 Mar., 1447, P.P.C. To be bur. in chancel of the ch. of St. Peran in the Sands. To several religious houses, etc. To the poor for meat and drink at his funeral. To his cousin John Wylle. Residue to his cousins John and Henry Trevelyan.
For enlarged pedigree see Trevelyan Papers. pt. iii., 1872, Camden Soc.

Trevisa.

Peter Trevisa of Crokadon == Elizb. base Da. of
in Com. Cornwall | Jo. Trelaunye

- Peter 2 — Andrew 3 ob. s. p.
- Edward & William Twinnes
- Elvazor Trevisa 2 sone liveing 1620
- ¹John Trevisa of Crokadon liveinge 1620 == ¹Margᵗ Da. of Petᵗ Courtney of Tretharlffe
- Anne a da. unmaried

Children of John Trevisa and Margt:
- ²Willm. 2 — Richard 3
- Dougles 4 — Jonathan 5
- Jo. Trevisa sone & heire atat. 16 1620
- Elizab. uxor Nicho. Battersbye of Caultock
- Anne 2 — Bridget 3 — Phillipa 4
- Mary 5 — Margᵗ 6 — Katherin 7

* ELEAZER TREVISA.

Trewolla.

Marke Trewola ==

Rich. Trewola ==

Thomas Trewola == Da. of Rosogan
A

---

¹ John Trevisa of St. Mellion and Margt. Courteney of Lazack (Laddock), mar. lic. 1 Dec., 1596.

² William, son of John Trevisa, gent., and Margt., bap. at St. Mellion 16 Dec., 1610.

* Jonathan, son of Peter Trevisa, Esq., and Hannah, bap. at St. Mellion — 1699. } Archdeac. Transcripts.

John Trevisa, gentleman, who was meaytayned by John Trevisa, Esq., bur. at St. Mellion — 1623.
Rich., son of Wm. Trevesa and Ursula Nancarowe. bap. at St. Martin's in Meneage — 27 Maᵣ, 1626.
John Trevisa, Esqᵣ, bur. at St. Mellion — 15 May, 1631.
Elizb., wife of Will. Trevisa, Esq., bur. at St. Mellion — 22 March, 1668.
} Bp. of Exeter's Transcripts.

John Hellyer of Harford and Jocosa Trevisa of St. Mellion, mar. lic. 12 May, 1621.

Ped. fin. 2 Hen. IV., No. 1. John Trethack qu. Walter Metheros and Johana his wife def. Various lands settled on Walter and Johana, rem. to heirs of Walter, rem. to Johana, wife of Will. Trethack, rem. to Johana, da. of Will. Trethack, rem. to Julia, da. of Galfrid Roskyr, rem. to John Trevysa, rem. to Juliana, sister of Jno. Trevysa, rem. to Nichola, sister of Juliana, rem. to Walter, son of Philip Trege, rem. to Roger, bro, of Walter, rem. to Rich. Tirell of St. Colan, rem. to Margery, wife of John Tregoys, rem. to right heirs of Walter Metheros.

Ped. fin. 14 Jas., Trin., Cornw. Edw. Courtney ar. and Jno. Trevisa ar. qu. Will. Courtney ar. and Douglas ux. def. *inter alia* Tresagher (Tresahar) estate, Constantine.

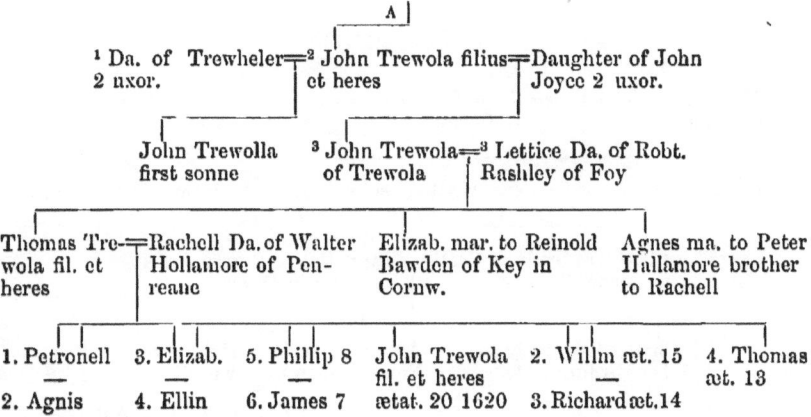

* THOMAS TREWOLLA.

[1] Alice, da. of Rich. Trewhilla of Trewhilla in St. Enoder. See note 2.

[2] Chan. Pro. 9 April, 1583, Eliz. K. k. 2, No. 33. Rich. Kendall and Katherine his wife v. John Trewolla and Jno. Higgowe. Names Alice, da. and b. of Rich. Trewhilla of Trewhilla in St. Enoder, wife of this John, together with John and William their sons, and Katherine, da. of William, mar. to Rich. Kendall.

[3] John Trewolly and Litty Rashligh mar. 5 Feb., 1570. Fowey Par. Reg.

* Will., son of John Trewolla	bap.	30 July, 1579.
Johanna, da. of Jno. Trewhela,	,,	20 Aug., 1584.
Thomas, son of Rich. Trewhela,	,,	24 Dec., ,,
Margaret, da. of Jno. Trewyla,	,,	16 Mar., 1586.
Jno. Trewolla, junior, and Agnes James	mar.	25 Oct., 1573.
Rich. Trewolla and Johanna James	,,	28 Oct., ,,
Jane, da. of Jno. Trewolla,	bur.	23 Jan., ,,
Rich. Trewolla	,,	20 Mar., 1585.
Jane, ux. Rich. Trewolla,	,,	25 Nov., 1587.
Rich. Trewolla	,,	31 Jan., 1588.
Margaret ,,	,,	28 Oct., ,,
Thomas ,,	,,	1 Mar., 1589.

St. Ewe Par. Reg.

George, son of John Trewhella,	bap.	27 Nov., 1608.
Will., ,, ,,	,,	21 Mar., 1610.

Gwinear Par. Reg.

James, son of Thos. Trewolla, gen., bap. at Gwennap		1614.
Tho., son of Tho. Trewalla, gen., ,,	,,	18 June, 1633.
Temperance, da. of Wm. Trewalla, ,,	,,	20 Aug, ,,
Tho., son of Tho. Trewalla, gen., bur.	,,	,,

Bp. of Exeter's Transcripts.

Tho., ,, John Trewolla and Margt., bap.		29 Oct., 1661.
John Trewolla, gent., .	bur.	13 Ap., 1679.

GorranPar.Reg.

Thomas, son of John Trewolla, gent.,	bur.	1676.
Margt., wife of Mr. John Trewolla,	,,	30 Oct., 1677.

Bodmin Par. Reg. (J. M.)

Ped. fin. 6 Chas. I., Mich., Cornw. Thos. Carthew qu. Thos. Trewolla gen. and o'rs def. Canclogic, etc.

Trewbody.

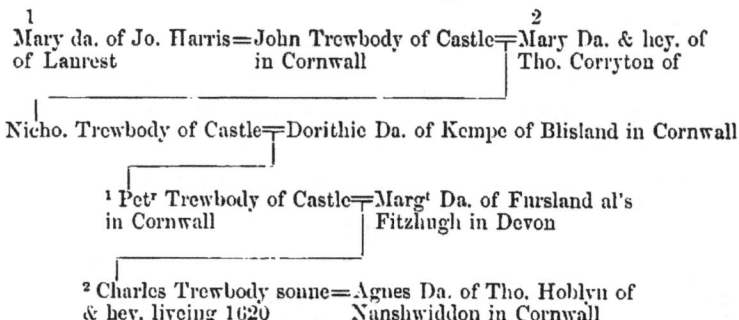

1. Mary da. of Jo. Harris of Laurest = John Trewbody of Castle in Cornwall = 2. Mary Da. & hey. of Tho. Corryton of

Nicho. Trewbody of Castle = Dorithie Da. of Kempe of Blisland in Cornwall

1. Pet^r Trewbody of Castle in Cornwall = Marg^t Da. of Fursland al's Fitzhugh in Devon

2. Charles Trewbody sonne & hey. liveing 1620 = Agnes Da. of Tho. Hoblyn of Nanshwiddon in Cornwall

* **CHARLES TREWBODY.**

---

[1] Peter Trewbody of Castle Laulivery. Will P.P.C. Stafford, 8, A.D. 1604. Names sons Charles, Tristeram, Thomas. To his wife Margaret all his lands in St. Austell called Boscovill during minority of Charles.

[2] Mar. at St. Columb Major 3 Aug.. 1620.
Mary, da. of Charles Trubody. gent., bap. 16 Sept.. 1621. } St. Columb Major Par. Reg.
Peter, son   „   „   13 Aug., 1622. } (J. M.)

* Stephen Trewbody and Anna Polwhele. wid. of Steph. P.,
  mar.   4 July, 1597. } St. Clement's Par. Reg.
Mark Truebody. clerk, and Elizb. Toller   „   1684. }
Mrs. Elizb. Trubody   bur.   „   „ } Fowey Par.Reg.
Mr. Mark Trubody, Vicar,   „   1700. }

Sybell, da. of Tho. Trewbodye,   „   1542. } Illogan Par. Reg.

John, son of Peter Trubody   bap.   1633. }
Thomas. son of John and Grace Trubody. ..   1686. }
Peter Trubody and Anne Mounsell   mar. Oct.. 1614. }
Peter Trubody, gent., and Sibella Tingcombe ..   1645. } Lansalloes Par.
Peter Trubody   bur.   1630. } Reg.
Walter   „   ..   14 Feb.. 1648. }
Peter   „   ..   1650. }
Susan   ..   ..   1679. }
John   „   „   1682. }
Peter Trewbody, gen. Rate Book, Laulivery, 1654.

Grace, da. of Tho. Trubody   bap.   1694. } Lanteglos by
Anne   „   „   „   1697. } Fowey Par.Reg.

Joan, wife of Xfer Trubody, gent.,   bur. 10 Aug.. 1689. } Pinnock Par. Reg.
Mr. Sam. Trewbody, Minister of St. German's, and Mrs.   } Sheviock Par.
  Elizb. Hancock of Hendra. wid.,   mar.   1729. } Reg.
William, son of Walter Trubody   bap.   1644. }
Mark.   „   „   „   1651. }
William, „ Mr.   „   1667. }
Philip.   „   Walter and Margt. Trubody „,   1674. } Tywardreath
Walter Trubody and Margt. Preston   mar. 25 Jan., 1667. } Par. Reg.
Mark Trubody and Sarah Carew   „   5 Feb.. 1693. }
Peter, son of Walter Trubody by Margt. his wife,
    bur. 15 May. 1613. }
John and Peter, sons of Walter Trubody,   „   1658. }

Tho. Hoblyn and Priscilla Trubody   mar.   1637. } St. Winnow Par. Reg.

[*Note continued on next page.*]

Trewren.

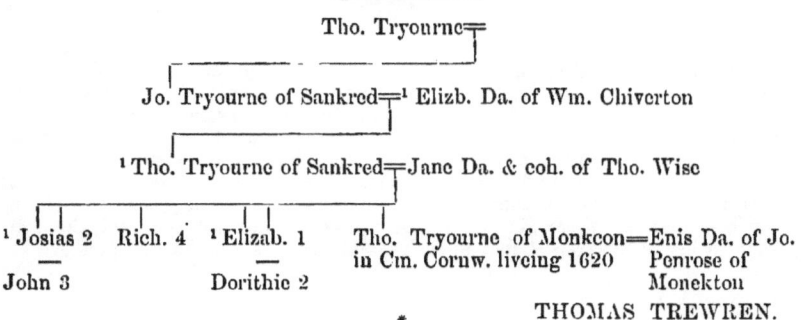

Tho. Tryourne =

Jo. Tryourne of Sankred = [1] Elizb. Da. of Wm. Chiverton

[1] Tho. Tryourne of Sankred = Jane Da. & coh. of Tho. Wise

- [1] Josias 2 — John 3
- Rich. 4
- [1] Elizab. 1 — Dorithie 2
- Tho. Tryourne of Monkeon in Cm. Cornw. liveing 1620 = Enis Da. of Jo. Penrose of Monekton

*

THOMAS TREWREN.

Tubb.

John Tubb of Trengoffe = Joane Da. & hey. of John Cullwaye

- George 1 sonne
- Roger 2 — John 3
- Willm Tubb of Gwennop 4 sone in Cornw. = Julian Da. of Bonithon of Curelew
- Tho. 5 sone a preist

Edm. Tubb of Guinop in Com. Cornwall liveing 1620 = Marg^t Da. of Rob. Rashley of Foye in Cornwall

- Germone 2 sonne
- Mary 1
- Jane 2
- Jo. Tubb sone & heyre liveing 1620
- Julian 3
- Sara 4

†

JOHN TUBB.

(*Note continued.*)

Charles Trubody, gent., and Katherine Allen mar. 27 Ap., 1680. } St. Austell Par. Reg.

Nicholas Harrye and Elizabeth Trubody mar. 20 Jan., 1611. } St. Kew Par. Reg. } (J. M.)

Mary, da. of John Treuren, jun., bap. at Sauccred 20 Aug., 1608.
Richard, son of Walter Trewren, „ „ 14 Jan., 1609.
William Trewren al's Tremearne bur. 21 Sep., 1636.
James „ „ 12 Nov., „
} Bp. of Exeter's Transcripts.

[1] Named in will of Thomas Chiverton of Paul, dat. 26 Aug., 1604, P.P.C. 7 Feb., 1604-5, together with Henry, John, and William Trewren, sons of John T. and Elizab. Chiverton.

* Ped. fin. Cornw. 24 Hen. VI., No. 2. John Treouran and Katherine his wife qu. Sampson Lucos and Alice his wife def. Mousehole, etc.

Ped. fin. Cornw. 37 Hen. VI., No. 2. Roger Treouran qu. Johana, who was wife of Adam Vyvyan, and William Fox and Agnes his wife def. Erth, Holewode, etc.

† George Robins and Agnes Tub mar. 1613. St. Austell Par. Reg.
Hugh, son of Henry Tubb. bur. 13 Oct., 1592. Cuby Par. Reg.

[*Note continued on next page.*

Tucker.

Henry R.

Henry, by the grace of god Kinge of England & of fraunce, & Lord of Ireland, To all manner our subiects, as well of the spetiall preheminence & dignitie as of temporall authoritie, theis our l'res hearing or seing greeting. forasmuch as we be credibly informed that our trustie subiect Stephin Tucker, of Lamartyn in Com. Devone, Gentleman, for certayne diseases and infirmities which he hath & dayly susteineth in his head, he cannot conveniently without his great Danger be discovered of the same. We let you wite that of our grace espetiall in tender consideration thereof, have by these presents licensed the said Stephen Tukker to use & wear his Bonet upon his said head, as well in our presence as

(*Note continued.*)

Stephen, son of John Tub,	bap.	28 Nov., 1562.	
Tobias, ,, ,,	,,	11 Oct., 1570.	
Robert Tubb and Jane Nicholls	mar.	20 Sept., 1565.	
Will. Tracher and Thomasine Tubbe	,,	25 Feb., 1578.	
George Tubb and Elizabeth Tredwene	,,	18 ,, 1583.	St. Ewe Par. Reg.
Jno. Tubbe and Johanna Batten	,,	3 Oct., 1585.	
Edward Prowte and Annys Tubbe	,,	12 Feb., 1586.	
Nicholas Tubb	bur.	10 Mar., 1588.	
George Tubb	,,	29 ,, ,,	
Katherine Tubb, widow,	,,	25 Sept., 1611.	
Hugh Popham and Jane Tubb mar. at Kilkhampton 17 Sept., 1608.			
John Roberts and Grace Tubb mar. at St. Allen		1612.	Bp. of Exeter's Transcripts.
Will. Tubb, gent., bur. at Warleggan		10 Jan., 1614.	
William Tubb and Loveday Mylton mar. at Sheviock 17 Jan., 1618.			
Blanch, wife of Jonathan Tub, gen., bur. at Padstow		1636.	
John, son of Mr. John Tobbe,	bap.	1571.	
Jonathan, ,, ,,	,,	1575.	Bodmin Par. Reg.
John, ,, ,,	,,	1582.	
John Tobb, gent.,	bur.	1603.	
Mrs. Agnes Tubb	,,	1611.	
Joanna, da. of John Tubb of Botreaux Castle, bur. 12 Feb., 1605.			Egloshayle Par. Reg.
Geo., son of Wm. Tubb, and Margt., da. of Walter Ford, mar. 1 Nov., 1683.			Lanivet Par. Reg.
Walter Tubbe, gent.,	bur.	21 Ap., 1630.	Lanreth Par. Reg.
Kath., da. of Rob. Tubb,	bap.	18 Nov., 1550.	
George, son of John Tubb,	,,	1587.	St. Neot Par. Reg.
Rob. Tubb, gent., and Jone Sloget, wid.,	mar.	11 Nov., 1589.	
Alice, wife of John Tubb, gent.,	bur.	4 Ap., 1623.	
John Tubb, gent.,	,,	19 Oct., 1623.	
Geo., son of John Tubb, gen.,	bap.	28 Sept., 1584.	
Elinor, wife of George Tubb, Esq.,	bur.	8 June, 1591.	Warleggan Par. Reg.
Geo. Tubbe, Esq.,	,,	1597.	
Will. Tubbe, gent.,	,,	1614.	

(J. M.)

John Tubb, of Mangan in Menage, gent., and Mary Bristow of Helston, widow, mar. lic. 1637.

Indenture dated 13 May, 20 Elizab., betw. John Bonython of Bouython, gent., of the one part, and William Tubbe of Gwynep, gent., of the other part. Grant of certain premises in Geare in the parish of Gwynep to William Tubb and his heirs.

Ind're made 9 June, 1619, betw. John Tubb of Gwennape, gent., of the one part, and George Husband, husbandman, of the other part. Lease of premises in Gwennape which late were the inheritance of William Tubbe, gent., grandfather of the said John Tubbe. Seal—*three tubs in pale naiant*.

By deed dated 25 Dec., 1652, Thomas Achim of Hall granted to John Lee of Lanreth, yeoman, certain premises in Trenay lately in the tenure of Thomas Olver by virtue of a lease made 29 Sept., 32 Elizab., by George Tubb, lord of Trenay, Eleanor his wife, and John Tubb their son, whose inheritance the premises late were.

elswheare at his liberty. Wherfore we will & com'and you and every of you to p'mitt & suffer him soe to doe without any your challenges letts or interruptions to the contrarye as yee & every of you tender our pleasure. Given under our signet at our mannor of Woodstock the 2 day of July in the 10 yeare of our Raigne.

Stephen Tocker.

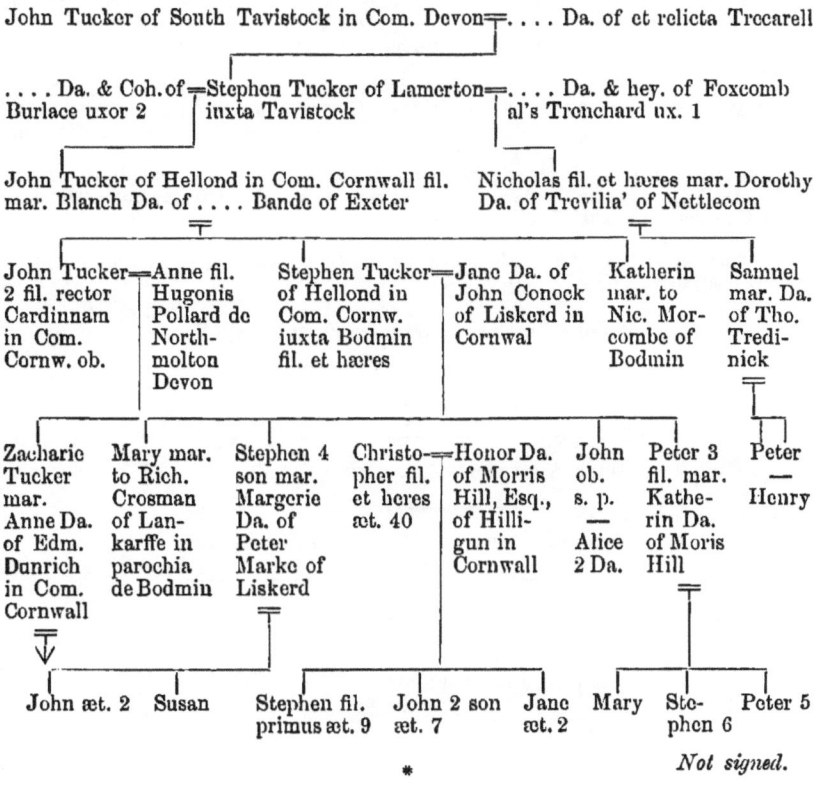

* John Williams and Joue, da. of Will. Tucker, mar. 14 Oct., 1574.
 John Tucker, said to have been bro. of the Mayor of Exeter, was last Abbot of Buckland Mon. Devon, pensioned on the Vicar of Buckland £60 per an.
 John Carveth al's Perguion and Emblin Tooker, mar. 1606. St. Breock Par. Reg.
 John Trenvroth, gent., and Mrs. Maria Tucker, mar. 1615. Mawnan Par. Reg.
 Henry Tucker, clerk, and Elizabeth Warrin mar. at St. Juliot 19 Jan., 1623. } Bp. of Exeter's Transcripts.
 John Toker, jun., gent., and Mrs. Probesia Pollard, mar. at St. Mabyn 1683. }
 Will, son of Mr. Stephen Toker and Susannah, bap. ,, 1697. } Archdeacon's
 Mr. Steven Toker, gent., bur. at Helland 1682. } Transcripts.
 Mr. John Toker, bur. at St. Mabyn 15 Mar., 1697. }
 Christopher Worthywell and Cath. Tucker of Cardinham, mar. lic. 1664.

[*Note continued on next page.*

Vacye.

ARMS. *Arg. on a chev. gu. 3 bezants.*

Sciant p'sent. et futuri q^d ego Theobaldus Vacy remise et om'ia p' me et heredibus meis sive assignat. meis imperpetuu' Waltero. Vacy fil. et hered. Will'mi Vacy et Augusta uxori suæ et hered' de corporibus coru' p'creat. totum jus meum et clamav. etc. Dat' die Sabbati prox post festu S'te Margarete Anno regni regis Ed'ri filij regis Edwardi 18.

Sciant p'sentes et futuri q^d ego Johis de Fenton remisi pro me et hered. meis et assignatis meis totu jus meu' q^d habui in Fenton Vacy cum om'ib. part'in suis Will'o de Vacy et hered' suis sive suis assign. imperpetu. etc. hijs testibus mag'ro Ramud Parloben D'no Rogero de Nononant D'no Reginaldo de Unvile Joh'e Gerner Will'o De Hollewey et alijs. dat. Lond. in Eccl'ia S'ci Pawli die mercurij prox post festu Conversionis Santi Pawli. Anno grac. 1291.

Remember to putt this Addition of the howse of Tredeage unto the discent of James Bonython. (*sic.*)

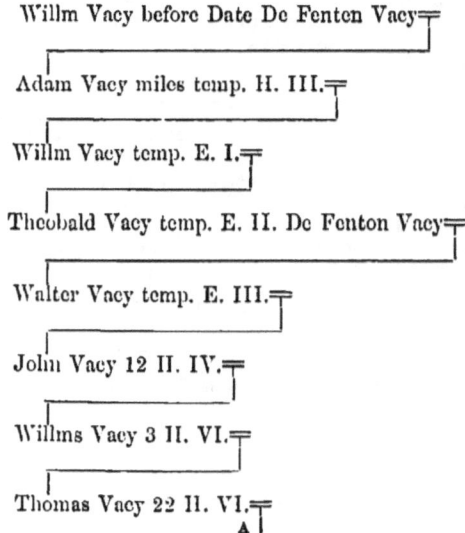

(*Note continued.*)

Ped. fin. Cornw. 12 Hen. IV. No. 4. Reginald Toker of Liskeard qu. John Geffery of Liskeard and Alice his wife def. Mess., etc., in Liskeard settled on Alice, da. of Reginald Toker.

Ped. fin. Cornw. 7 Hen. V. No. 5. Thos. Jeeche of Liskerd and Florence his wife qu. Rich. Toker of Liskerd and Alice his wife.

Ped. fin. Cornw. 18 Hen. VI. No. 10. John Toker qu. John Wade and Johana his wife def. In Camelford and Tregewe.

Ped. fin. 5 Eliz., East. Dev. John Toker, gen. qu. Jno. Wollye def. Tent. in Tavistock.

Ped. fin. 29-30 Eliz., Mich. Dev. Step. Toker, gen. qu. Samuel Toker, gen. and Anastasia, ux. def. Lands in Foxcomb, Lew Trenchard, Bradford.

See Memoir of the Family of Tucker, alias Toker, in 'History of Trigg Minor,' vol. ii., pp. 54-57.

THE VISITATION OF THE COUNTY OF CORNWALL. 251

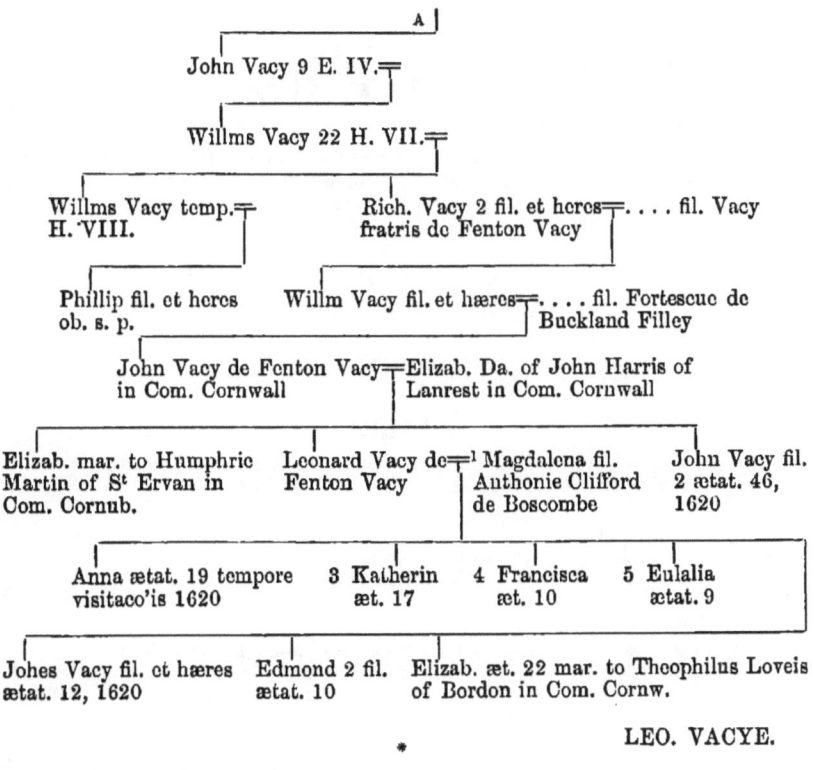

LEO. VACYE.

Verman.

Georg Verman of Ardeveray in Philley in Cornw.=Jane Da. of John Beaupre
│
Gerons Verman first son=² Agnis Da. of . . . Bonde of Earth
│
Mary │ Geo. Verman=Jane Da. & sol heire of Willm │ John 2 son
      │ of Lamorran │ Penant of Budock   │ ob. s. p.
                  A │

[1] Da. of Anthony Clifford of Descombe, co. Wilts., widow of John Ley al's Kempthorne of Tonacombe. See ped. of Kempthorne, *ante*.

* Eulalia, da. of Edmund Vacye, gent. and Jane, ux., bap. 30 June, 1647. } Anthony in Menenge Par. Reg.
Ped. fin. 3 John, No. 24. Walter de Vasol qu. Osbert de Escott def. In Escote.

[2] Da. of Thos. Bond. See ped. of Bond, *ante*.

252   THE VISITATION OF THE COUNTY OF CORNWALL.

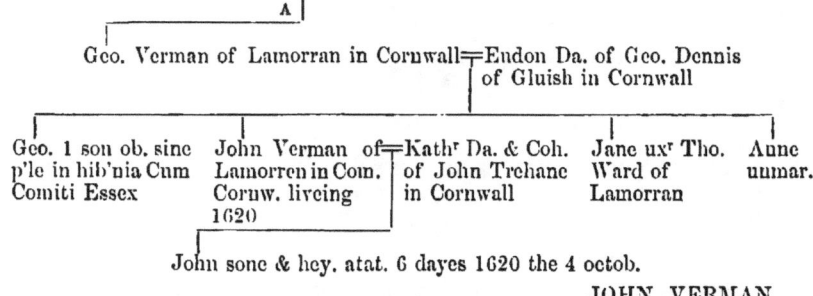

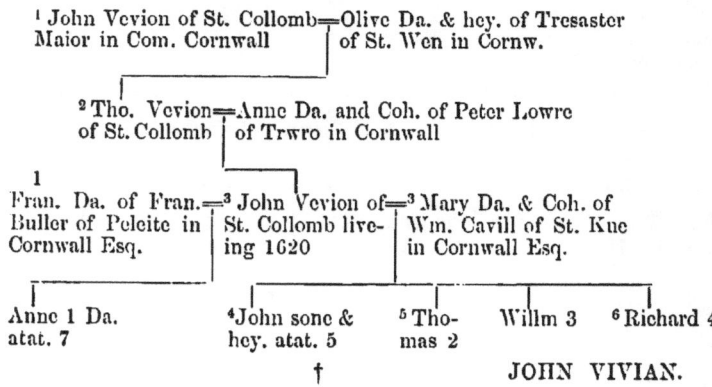

* John Verman de Lamorran et Maria Walrond filia Guillmi Walrond de Brad- ⎫
  field in comitat. Devon armigeri matr'onum contrax 5 July, 1660.   ⎬ Lamorran
  Rich. Trevanion, son of Rich. T., p'ish of Veryan, and Anne, da. of Jno. Ver- ⎭ Par. Reg.
  man and Mary his wife of Lamorran, mar. 6 Feb., 1693-4.

¹ Named in the will of his father Richard Vyvyan of Trenouth, dated 27 Sept., 1550.
P. P. C. together with his grandfather, John V., lately deceased, mother Elizabeth, brother Richard
V., and sister Emlyng V. (both under age). John Vyvyan, clerk, one of the overseers.
    John Vyvian and Ollyff Tacsalster (Tresaster) mar. 30 July, 1546. St. Columb Major
Par. Reg. His will as John Vivian of Trenouth, dated 4 June, 1587. P. P. C. 1589. Names his wife
Oliffe, sons Thomas, John. and l'ascaux, and dau'rs Johane and Emlin. (Johane mar. Jno. Carter
of St. Columb. See Carter ped., ante.)
    ² Thomas Vivian, gent., bur. 18 May, 1617. (St. Columb Major Par. Reg.) His will, as
Thomas Vyvyan of Trenouth, dated 8 May. 1617, P. P. C. Names his wife Anne, sons John,
Pascowe, Michael, Thomas, and Richard, dau'rs Olive, Barbara, Ursula, and Emlin mar. to
Moyle (see Moyle ped., ante), and Richard and John Vivian of St. Merryn. Inq. p. m. Wards
and Liv., 17 Jas., No. 110, Bund. 27, inter alia. Tho. V. held in Pollawyne (n. 17, p. 259),
Trenance, Skewys, Tresawell, Neweton, St. Anthony in Men., Towan Wartha, Towan Wolas, and
Tomyowe. See notes, p. 255.

[*Notes continued on next page.*]

THE VISITATION OF THE COUNTY OF CORNWALL. 253

(*Notes continued.*)
³ Johannes Vivian, gen., and Maria Cavell, filia Willmi Cavell, Ar., mar. at St. Kew 18 Ap., 1615. (Bp. of Exeter's Transcripts.) Named in will of John Pomeroy of St. Cleere, 16 June, 1618, P. P. C. 12 March, 1619. Witnesses Pascowe Vivian, Pascowe Vivian, jun., and Richard Vivian.
Will of John Vivian of Trewan, dated 18 Jan., 1641, P. P. C. 1647. Names his wife Mary, and her father and mother, Will. and Jane Cavell, sons John, Thomas, Richard, Francis, Mathew, Edward, and Peter, dau'rs Anne, Mary, and Jane, mar. to Treffry. His brothers Pascowe and Thomas V. and son John ex'ors. His son Thomas Vivian and Joseph Jane overseers.
⁴ Bap. 9 June, 1616. ⁵ Bap. 10 Aug., 1617. St. Columb Major Par. Reg.
⁶ For family of this Richard see Tavistock, Devon, Par. Reg.

* William Inch of St. Kew and Ursula Vivian of St. Columb Major, mar. lic. 18 Nov., 1612.
Francis Vivyan of St. Columb and Anna Maynard of Little Colon, mar. lic. 25 July, 1677. } Act Books, Exeter.

Degorie, son of Thomas Vivian, bap. at Crantock		21 July, 1598.
Thos., „ „ „ „		26 May, 1609.
John, „ Rich. Vivian and Grace, bap. at St. Merryn		13 Oct., 1633.
Thos. Vivian and Elyzabeth Jeffrie mar. at Crantock		13 Nov., 1597.
John Vivian and Margaret Minerd mar. at St. Mewan		1666.
John Vivian and Alsoa Jeffreye mar. at Crantock		10 Aug., 1612.
John Burlace and Thamson, da. of John Vivean, were mar. at Roche		30 April, 1622.
Thomas Carthewe and Amey Vivian mar. at St. Allen		1 Feb., 1624.
Richard Rownsewall and Elizabeth Vivian mar. at St. Winnow		3 Feb., 1630.
(This marriage is also entered in St. Minver, the same date, but her name is spelt Vyvyan.)		
Rich. Vivian and Grace Robbins mar. at St. Merryn		8 June, 1631.
John Vivian, Esq., of St. Columb, and Amy Nicolls of St. Tudy mar. at St. Stephen's in Brannel		4 May, 1671.
John, son of John Vivian, Esq., of St. Columb Major, and Mary, da. of Sir Joseph Sawle of St. Austell, mar. at St. Mewan		1684.
Henry Vivian the younger bur. at St. Ervan		7 Mar., 1602.
Johannes Vivian sepulta erat at St. Kew		25 July, 1615.

} Bp. of Exeter's Transcripts.

Rich. Carlyon and Letta Vivian	mar.	30 July, 1576.
John Yarde and Phillipa „	„	29 Jan., 1587.
Rich. Carlyon and Alice „	„	28 July, 1593.
Will. Carlyon and Blanche „	„	23 Nov., 1595.
Rich. Vyvian and Maria Mynars	„	2 Nov., 1614.
Will. „ and Phillipa Kestell	„	13 Jan., 1616.
John Courtney and Jane Vyvyan	„	1633.
Thomas Vyvyan and Mary Elliott	„	25 Sept., 1669.

} St. Austell Par. Reg.

Emblen, da. of Thos. Vivian,	bap.	31 Mar., 1580.
Peter, son of John and Mary Vivian,	„	12 Sept., 1630.
Elizab., da. of „ „	„	1634.
Francis, son of John Vivian and Mary,	„	1649.
Thomas, son of John Vivian, Esq., and Mary his wife	„	12 Sep., 1689.
Richard Vivian, gent., and Mary Flamocke	mar.	1601.
Richard Moyle and Emblen Vivian	„	30 Jan., 1602.
Robert Cocking and Margery Vivian	„	16 May, 1614.
James Moyle and Elizabeth Vivian	„	1616.
Walter Vivian and Loveday Carlyon	„	10 June, 1630.
Henry Roscorla and Alse Vivian	„	17 Jan., „
Walter Vivian and Ann Howe	„	20 Jan., 1684.
Rich., son of John Vivian, Esq.,	bur.	1660.
Pascowe Vivian, gent.,	„	6 Aug., 1634.
Peter, son of Rich. Vivian. gent.,	„	20 Dec., 1665.
Mrs. Olive Vivian	„	20 Aug., 1667.
Mary, wife of John Vivian, Esq.,	„	26 Mar., 1670.
Paskowe Vivian, gent.,	„	31 Mar., 1673.
John Vivian, jun., Esq.,	„	12 May, 1691.
Judith „ widow,	„	1700.

} St. Columb Major Par. Reg.

Emblyn, da. of John Vivian	bap.	20 Feb., 1593.
Thomazine, „ „	„	1594.
John, son of „	„	8 Mar., 1597.
Degorie, son of Degory Vivian	„	20 Mar., 1666.
Nicholas Warren and Thamson Vivian mar. at Mawgan in Pider		4 Aug., 1633.

} St. Columb Minor Par. Reg.

[*Notes continued on following page.*]

254   THE VISITATION OF THE COUNTY OF CORNWALL.

(*Notes continued.*)

Thomas Cock and Margery Vivian	mar.	21 July, 1634.	
Thomas Vivian and Franncis Robarts	,,	29 May, 1641.	
Digory Vivian and Mary Stone	,,	1644.	
William Vivian and Prudence Brewer,	.,	27 Dec., 1680.	St. Columb Minor
Thomas Hix and Prudence Vivian	,,	28 July, 1682.	Par. Reg.
Jone, wife of John Vivian,	bur.	1591.	
Will., son of Will. ,,	,,	1683.	
William V.		1692.	
John Vivian of St. Issey, jun., and Mary Carthew	mar.	1692.	
John Trebilcock, gent., and Elizabeth Vivian	,,	27 Dec., 1697.	
Sam Leche of St. Columb, gent., and Dorothy Vivian, da. of			St. Ervan Par. Reg.
Matthew Vivian of Advent, gent., deceased,	mar.	28 Nov., 1700.	
William Vivian, Rector,	bur.	1699.	
Michael Agus and Loveday Vivian	mar.	22 Oct., 1642.	
Mathew Vivian, gent., and Julyan Tanner, mar. published 20 May and 3 and 10 June,		1655.	
Jerome Mathew and Anne Vivian, mar. published 3, 10, and 24 Dec.,		1655.	St. Ewe Par. Reg.
Thomas Harris and Thomazin Viveon	mar.	27 April, 1681.	
John, son of Thomas Vyvian	bur.	10 June, 1572.	
John Vevinne, Esq.,	,,	1646.	Fowey Par. Reg.
Thomas, son of John Vivian.	bap.	27 May, 1665.	
John, ,, Rich. ,,	,,	11 Feb., 1695.	St. Issey Par. Reg.
Rich. Vivian and Elinor Hawkins	mar.	July, 1688.	
Stephen Vivian	bur.	1696.	
John Vivian, Esq., and Mrs. Mary Glanville	mar.	18 Oct., 1642.	Tavistock, Devon, Par. Reg.
Mr. Stephen Vivian and Mrs. Mary Slade	,,	8 Sept., 1685.	Veryan Par. Reg.
Thos. Hoblyn, gent., and Olyve Vivian, gent.,	,,	24 Nov., 1625.	St. Winnow Par. Reg.
Thomas Vyvian and Jane James,	,,	1 Oct., 1680.	Redruth Par. Reg.
Humphry Daniel and Jane Vivian,	,,	7 Nov., 1642.	
Hugh Harris and Margerie ,,	,,	16 Feb., 1652.	
Humphry, son of Hugh ,,	bap.	25 Sept., 1602.	
Jacobus, ,, ,, ,,	,,	23 Dec., 1603.	
Phillip, ,, ,, ,,	,,	2 Jan., 1607.	
Thomas, ,, Thomas Vivian,	,,	8 Sept., 1685.	
Rich., ,, ,, and Hannah.	,,	17 April, 1688.	
Walter, ,, ,, ,,	,,	17 Mar., 1689.	Truro Par. Reg.
Diggory, ,, ,, ,,	,,	16 Sept., 1694.	
John, ,, ,, ,,	,,	11 May, 1697.	
Hannah, da. of ,, ,,	,,	27 Feb., 1699.	
Humphry, son of Hugh Vivian,	bur.	1 Feb., 1602.	
Jacobus, ,, ,,	,,	4 Feb., 1604.	
Alice, wife of ,,	,,	28 Mar., 1605.	
Jane, wife of Thomas Vyvian,	,,	29 Dec., 1681.	

Will of John Vivian of St. Peter, Padstow, 9 Mar., 1505. Proved Lamehith (Lambeth) 8 May, 1506. Body to be buried in the Church of Carmelite brothers in the town of Bristol. Names his son John Vivian and dau'rs Johanna and Margaret ; Johanna his mother and Johanna his wife, Executors ; his cousin John Tregonwall. Overseer. (Dr. Tregonwall was retained as Counsel for the Rev. Tho. Vivian, bro. of the Prior, and Vic. of Bodmin v. the Parishioners, A.D. 1529.) William Taverner, gener. Tho., Harry, and o'rs. witnesses.

Will of Rich, Carter of St. Columb the Lower, 27 Nov., 1578. P. P. C. 5 Feb., 1582. Names Rich. Vyvyan of St. Meryn and Jane his wife, and their children Rich., John, and Olif.

Will of Rich. Vivian the elder, of St. Columb Major, gent., 18 April, 1653. P. P. C. 19 Nov., 1655. Names Thomas, John, and Francis, sons of John Vivian, Esq., his bro. Pascowe V., his nephew Richard, son of his bro. John Vivian, deceased, and Richard his son, his nephews Francis, Matthew, Edward, and Peter, sons of his bro. John Vivian, deceased, god-daughter Mary V., cousin Rich. Vosper, sister-in-law Mary V., sister Olive V., sister Inch, sister Vosper, Ann and Mary dau'rs of John V., Esq., cousins John V. of Truan, Jane Treffry, William Inch, Anne Tregose, Katherine Hore, David Moyle's wife, and Jonne Haweis, godsons Jno. Treffry, Sam. Moyle, and Edmond Beauford.

Will of Thomas Vivian of St. Martin's in the Fields, Surgeon, 13 Oct., 1690. P. P. C. 3 Dec. 1690. Names his sister Jane Vivian, uncle Thomas Vivian, cousins Robert Blewett, Edward Tregenna, ... Scoble, and Elizabeth Wrey. Brother John Vivian, sole Executor. Witness, Thos. Vivian.

Will of Thomas Vivian of St. Martin's in the Fields, Gent, 1 Oct., 1688. P. P. C. 2 Oct.,

[*Notes continued on following page.*

(*Notes continued.*)
1691. Da. Mary sole heir and Executrix. Witnesses Thos. Vivian, Elizabeth Blathwayte, and Mary Alexander.
Inq. p. m. 15 Jas. I., Wards and Liv., No. 184. John Vyvyan of St. Winnow, died 29 Jan., 1603. Olyve and Honor, his da.'s and coh.'s, aged 21 and 18.
Ped. fin. Cornw. 19 Hen. VI. No. 3. Jno. Bonde and Sibill his wife, a da. and coheir of Margaret, who was wife of Stephen Trenewyth, and Johanna, who was wife of Adam Vyvyan, the other da. and h. of said Margaret, qu. Michael Power, Esq., and Isabella his wife def. In Overa Penquyte, Fenne, Tremaylek, Carpenters, Peytevynespark, Coleford, Tremargh, Rowehill, Wolvecombe, Leskered, Weylonde, Penacadck, Staunton, Tredareppe, Trenewyth, Trethack, Wallelond, Tregadek, Shernepark, and Atte Water. Settled on Michael P. and Isabell his wife to hold of the said John Bond and Sibill his wife, and Johanna, rem. to Jno. and Sibill and Johanna, rem. to heirs of Sibill.
Ped. fin. Cornw. 21 Hen. VI. No. 1. Jno. Wydeslade qu. Odo Vyvyan and Matilda his wife def. Trewenhelek and appurtenances in Resgerans, Gluvyan Margh, and Treworrwale Vyan settled on Odo and his wife, rem. to Jno. Arundell, Esq., son of Jno. Arundell, late of Bydeford, rem. to Rich. Tregoys, Esq., rem. to Rich. Penpons and Amicia his wife, rem. to right heirs of Matilda.
Ped. fin. Cornw. 37 Hen. VI. No. 2. Roger Treouran qu. Johanna, who was wife of Adam Vyvyan, and Will. Fox and Agnes his wife def. In Erthholewode, Porthpigan, Orchard overa Saltash, Drussell, Tremalik overa Penquyte, Fen Carpenters, Paytevynespark, Coleford, Tremargh, Rowehill, Tredynnek, Furson, Neweton (Neweton was held by *Vivian of Trevidren*, Inq. 11, Rich. II., No. 83), Tretharup, etc., which Michael Power and Isabella his wife held for life; of the inheritance of Johanna in Treneweth, etc., settled on Roger; rem. to Johanna, who was wife of Adam Vyvyan, and her heirs.
Ped. fin. Cornw. 5 Edw. VI., Pasch. Jno. Connock, gent., qu. Stephen Vyvyan and Maria his wife def. In Penquyte al's Overa Penquyte, Fennesland, Tremaylek, Over Penquite al's Carpenters, Coleford, Tremargh, Rowehylle, Wolvecombe, Weylond, Pencradock, Staunton, Tredarope, Trenoweth, Tretharrop, Wallelond, Tregadock, Atte Water lands, and Lyskerd. Jno. C. paid Stephen £80. (These lands are named in Ped. fin. 37 Hen. VI. No. 2 as the inheritance of Johanna, widow of Adam Vyvyan, a coh. of Stephen Trenewyth, many of them were afterwards in the possession of Vivian of Trenouth and Trewan; Stephen Vyvyan also held lands in Luxulyan, Rosilion in St. Blasey, etc.)
Ped. fin. Cornw. 6 Edw. VI., Pasch. Jno. Collyns qu. Stephen Vyvyan def. In St. Austell, etc.
Ped. fin. „   „   „   „   Jno. Rashlegh qu. Stephen Vyvyan, gent., def. Penyllike, Foxholle, and Holewood.
Ped. fin. Pasch. Cornw. 6 Edw. VI. Will. Laa qu. Stephyn Vyvyan def. Porth Merthen, etc.
Ped. fin. 5 Edw. VI., Mich., Cornwall, No. 6. Rich. Roscarrock and Rich. Chamond qu. Stephen Vyvyan, gent., and Maria his wife, def. Trenans Austell, St. Austell, Castellgothan, Tregorrek, Trethyrgy, and Boscovey al's Boscavevyn. Settled on Stephen V. and wife, and their heirs, rem. to John V., bro. of Stephen, rem. to Francis Bluett, Hen. Chiverton, and John Courteney, rem. to right heirs of Stephen for ever.
Ped. fin. 7 and 8 Eliz. Mich. Cornwall. Jno. Robyn qu. Jno. Vyvyan, gent., bro. and heir of Stephyn Vyvyan, gent., defunct, def. In Trethyrgy.
Ped. fin. 8 Elizab., East., Cornw. John Vyvyan al's Trenoweth qu. Will. Tredenecke and Phillipa his wife, def. In Tredrym and St. Just in Roseland.
Ped. fin. 15 Eliz., East. Cornw. Roger Flamank and John Vyvyan, gents., qu. Otho and John Merefeild, gents., def. In St. Columb Major, Tresawell le over, Tresawell le lower (*Ralph Vivian of Trevidren*—Trelawarren family—held Tresawell, 11 Rich. II., in right of his wife, wid. of Tresawell, see Inq. p. m. 11 Rich. II., No. 83), Tomyowe, Luxulian, etc.
Ped. fin. Cornw. 16 Jas. I., Hill. John Prideaux qu. Rich. Vivyan and o'rs def. Trevemeder.
Ped. fin. Cornw. 17 Jas. I., Pasch. John Vivian, gent., qu. John Quych def. Manor of Retyn, etc.
Chancery proceedings, Elizab. P. p. 9, No. 56 (1590). Henry Penrose al's Nicholas, and Mary his wife, v. John Vyvyan al's Cooke, Richard Vivian al's Trenowithe, and o'rs. To recover lands called Trethias in St. Meryn and Porthvyan in Lower St. Columb. Vyvyan answers that one John Trethias was seized in his demesne as of fee in Trethias Towen and Towen Wolas in St. Meryn and Porthvyan in Lower St. Columb, and had issue two sons, John, Pascowe, and one da. Emmott, and intending to marry his son John to Joane, da. of one Will. Cooke, granted all his tenements in Trethias, Towen Wartha, and Towen Wolas, and Trevanenher to have and to hold to said Joane and her heirs by said John Trethias, etc., with rem. to Pascowe Trethias, with rem. to Emmott, sister of said John and Pascowe. John died unmarried, and Pascowe took to wife said Joane, and died without issue, and said Joane was seized for life. Emmott mar. one John Vivian, and had issue John V., who had issue James V., who had issue John Vivian, the present defendant, and Emmot died leaving Joane tenant for life, after whose death the said tenements descended of right to James V., father of defendant, etc. Def. Vivian is stated by Complainant to be a "very wealthy man, substantially and greatly allied in the County."
In the St. Columb 'Green Book' the Vivian's temp. Elizab. ,1580, spelt their name Vyvyan; but in 1598 Thomas spelt his name Vivian.

For additional information regarding this branch see ped. of Cavell, 'History of Trigg,' vol. ii., pp. 162-3.

Vyvyan.

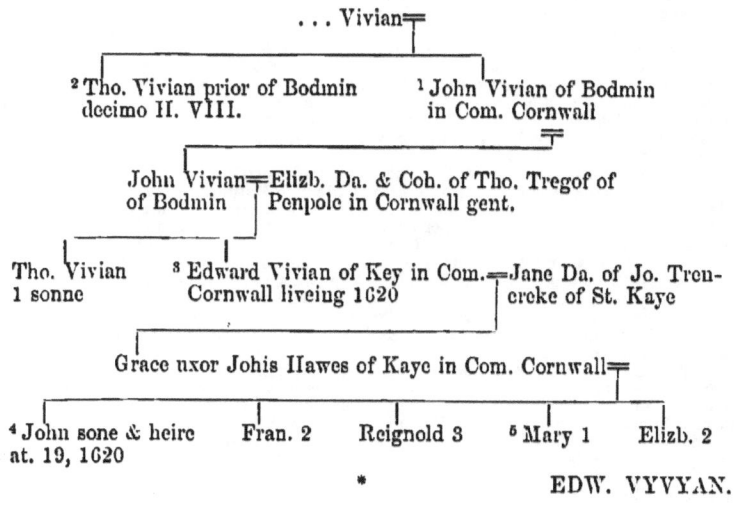

EDW. VYVYAN.

---

[1] Thomas Vivian. Bro. ord. and reg. of St. Augustine Friars, and Sub. Prior, elected Prior of Bodmin 30 April, 1507, on the death of William John. (Bp. Oldham's Reg., p. 22.) Prior Vivian received the Tonsor 15 Sept., 1493, and ordained Acolyth the same day, being then actually a Canon of Bodmin. Elected Suffragan Bishop of Megara, and as such held ordination in Exeter Cathedral 30 May, 1518. Died 1 June, 1533. Tomb in Bodmin Ch. He was second Prior of Bodmin of the name. Will Vyvyan having been elected 8 Oct., 1435.

[2] Rich. Coryn (of Kenwyn) mar. Elizabeth, da. of John Vivian, brother of the Prior. Coryn Ped. in Coll. of Arms.

[3] Mr. Edward Vivian was bur. at Kea 23 Feb., 1630. Bp. of Exeter's Transcripts.

[4] The will of Barbara Vosper of Kea (sister of John V. of St. Columb Major, who mar. Mary Cavell), 12 Aug., 1658. P. P. C. 30 Dec. 1658. Names her daughter Jane Hawcis, her son-in-law John Hawcis, her grandchildren Grace, Anne, Reginald, Jane, Mary, and John Hawcis.

[5] Bapt. at Kea 2 Feb., 1617. Bp. of Exeter's Transcripts.

* John Barges and Elizab. Vivyan, mar. 16 Jan., 1608. ⎫
Thomas Vivyan and Joane Harris, ,, 18 Oct., 1612. ⎪
John Nicholas and Johan Vivyan, ,, 24 Jan., 1615. ⎬ Kenwyn Par. Reg.
Degorye Vivian and Tamsen Beddlarke his wife were married ye five daye of Maye, 1616. ⎪
Thos. Husband and Miss Vivian mar. 1623. ⎪
Thomas Vivyan, bur. 29 Dec., 1614. ⎭

Trustrame, son of Degorye Viviane, bap. at Kea 3 Dec., 1617. ⎫
John, ,, Digorie ,, ,, 15 Sept., 1622. ⎪
Hugh, ,, John Hawcis, ,, 5 June, 1614. ⎬ Bp. of Exeter's
Anne, da. of ,, bur. at Kea 4 Oct., ,, ⎪ Transcripts.
John, son of Digorye Vivian and Thamsyne, his wife, was bur. at Kea 16 Dec., 1630. ⎭

Thomas Vivian, M.A., (brother of Prior V.) presented to the Vicarage of Bodmin 27 Nov., 1516, by the Prior and Convent, on death of Thos. Holwell, M.A.

Chan. Pro. Elizab. 9 May, 1597, M. m. 2, No. 51. Michell v. Challenor, Coryn, and o'rs. Sets forth that Thomas Vivian and Ann his wife were seized in right of his wife Ann for the life of the said Ann, of the moiety of Penventynes, or Penventennow, in Kenwyn, and certain lands, etc., thereunto belonging. (Ann was the da. of Rich. Singleton by Ann his wife, the da. and coh. of Richard Coryn of Kenwyn.—'Visit. Cornwall,1573,' Add. MS. 14, 315, and Harl. MS. 1079, fo. 5.)

For a memoir of this branch see 'History of Trigg,' vol. i., pp. 307-8.

Vivyan.

Arms. 1. Vivian. *A. a lion ramp. Gu., one foot on waves of the sea B.* 2. Ferrers. 3. Arundel. 4. Glyn. 5. Trethurf. 6. St. Aubyn. 7. Chalons. 8. Charlton. 9. Leigh. 10. Courtenay *and* Redvers *qrly*. 11. Trevisa.

Sʳ Vyell Vyvyan Kᵗ = Margaret da. of Christopher count of Kildare in Ireland

- Joane wife to Sʳ Bartholomew Greenevile Kᵗ
- Sʳ Raph Vivyan Kᵗ = Katherin d. of Reginald Farrers of Boswithegic
  - Umryell
  - ¹ Richard Vivyan of Trevedrian ob. a° 1331 = Constance d. of James Peferell ² or Sʳ Hugh Peverell
    - Hugh 2
    - ³ John 3
    - ⁴ Willm Vivyon sonn & heire ob. 1345 = Claryce ⁵ d. of Henry Le Forte of Pengersick ob. 1346
      - Raph Vivyan = Alice d. of Peter Kemple or Kemyll ⁶
        - ⁷ Roger Vivyan = Isabell d. of John Anthorne
          - Alice
          - Joane
          - Amor
          - ⁸ John Vivyan = Honor d. & h. of Rich. Ferrers of Trelawarren
            - ⁹ Richard Vivyan = Florence d. & h. of Rich. Arundell of Trerise ¹⁰
              - ¹¹ Robert Vivyan 2 sonne ¹² mar. Margret ¹¹ d. & coh. of John Durant of Trevanion
                - James
                - Michael ¹⁴
              - ¹¹ Michaell Vivyan sonne & heire = ¹¹ Thomazin ¹³ d. & h. of John Glyn of Morvale
                - ¹¹ Willm Vivyan eldest sonne served Charles Earle of Darby & was drowned on Passion Sunday a° 1520 s. p.
                - ¹⁵ John Vivyan of Trelawarren 2 sonne = Elizabeth d. & h. of Thomas Trethurfe ¹⁶
                  - ¹⁷ John Vivyan = ¹⁸ Ann d. of *Baldwin* Mallett of Devon
                    - 1. *Katherin mar. to John Bonithon of Carclew*
                    - 2. *Barbara mar. to Humphry Yorke of Devon*
                    - ¹⁹ Haniball Vivyan of Trelawarren = ²⁰ *Phillip* ²¹ da. & one of the heires of *Roger Tremaine of Devon*
                    - 3. *Anne mar. to John Kestell of Kestell*
                    - 4. *Christian* ²² *mar. to Willm Fortescue*
                    - 5. *Avis mar. to Ro. Ridge*
                - Margrett
                - Florence wife to John Fortescue of Sprylestou
              - Elizabeth ¹¹

[*Notes on next page.*]

258   THE VISITATION OF THE COUNTY OF CORNWALL.

| A

21 Sr Francis=Loweday d. of John	21 Michaell Vivyan 23=Katherin 23 2 da. of
Vivyan 25 K^t Connock of Treworgy	Barrester of the James Nanspian of
eldest sonne in the p'ish of St.	Middle Temple & Gurlyn in Com.
Cleere in Cornwall	now of Phillick in Cornwall Esq.
	Cornw. 2 sonne 26

3. *John* 21	1. *Margaret*	4. 21 *Edith* mar.	7. 21 *Phillip* mar. *Wal-*
4. 21 *Haniball* 27	2. 21 *Blanche* 24 mar.	*Phillip Mayou of*	*ler Coade of Morvall*
5. *Robert* 21	to *Fra. Tredenick* 24	*Cornw.*	8. 21 *Dorothy* 30 ma-
6. 21 *Roger* 28	3. *Anne sans issue*	5. *Avis sans issue*	*ried Nicholas Bogans*
7. 21 *Charles* 29		6. *Joane mar. to*	*of Treleague*
		Nicholas Connock of	
		Treworgie	
		*	*Not signed.*

---

[1] Jane, da. of Rich. Vivian of Trevidren, mar. John Erissey of Erissey, Esq., and died A.D. 1354; Isabella, da. of Rich. V., mar. John Aleth alias Abot of St. Martin's; and Deyones, another da., mar. Henry de Tresweswith (Harl. MS. 4031, ffo. 85, 86). Rich. Vivyan held in Trevenwyn of Joceus de Dynham. Inq. p. m. 29 Edw. I. No. 56.

[2] Sir James Peverell in Coll. of Arms.

[3] John Vivian of Boshavarne mar. Alice, da. of Francis Gwennow of Pordhenis, and died A.D. 1355. Harl. MS. 4031, fo. 86.

[4] Melior, da. of William Vivian of Trevidren, mar. Rich. Rosmadres; and Joane, another da., mar. Alan Trerencke. Harl. MS. 4031, ff. 85, 86.

[5] This marriage brought in a descent from Edward Godolphin of Pengersick.

[6] This match brought in a descent from Arundell and Helligan.

[7] Ralph in Coll. of Arms and all other pedigrees. Ralph and Thomas Vyvyan were indicted for killing John Trebner at Mousehole. Inq. 11 Rich. II., No. 83. Lands named as held by Vyvyan. Neweton, Trevudryn, Melynnewyth, Trethyn, Sendelowe, Trevorungowe, and Tresawell. Ralph Vyvyan held Tresawell in right of his wife Johanna, wid. of Robert Tresawell. Johanna, wid. of Adam Vyvian, held *Neweton*, ped. fin. 37 Hen. VI., No. 2. John Vyvyan held in Tresawell 15 Eliz., see ped. fin. 15 Eliz., Easter. in notes to Vivian of St. Columb, ped. *ante*.

[8] Pet. to Parl. 12 and 13 Edw. IV. John Vivian of Trelowarren, gent., sets forth that on the 2 Aug. 12 Edw. IV., when on his way to the Chapel of St. James, Tregours (? Tregoney), on pilgrimage, John Gerves, John Mayowe, jun., late of Fowey, Rob. Toker, and o'rs, servants unto Thos. Tretbewe, Esq., Coroner of Cornw., "arrayed in manner of werre, etc.," lay in wait to murder him and his, and wounded him, Anore, his wife, and Richard V. his son, and murdered "oon John Morthure, gent., nevewe and servaunte" to the said John Vivian. Rot. Parl., vol. vi., p. 54.

[9] Inq. p. m. 11 Hen. VIII. No. 39. Richard Vivian died 7 Aug. 9 Hen. VIII. William V., son of Michael V., dec., and Thomasine his wife, his grandson and heir, æt. 16 and more. The Inq. names his son Robert V. and Margaret his wife, and his da. Elizabeth, wife to William Cowlynge, and Will. C. their son. Rich. V. was called by Leland "a gallant courtier set forth by Somerset, Lord Herbert."

[10] This marriage brought in descents from Sergiaux, Seneschal, and the Earl of Arundell, according to Arundell ped., *post*.

[11] Named in Inq. p. m. 11 Hen. VIII., Note 9.

[12] He had a da., Margaret, mar. to Walter Kestell and Michael Hill, see Kestell and Hill peds., *ante*.

[13] She afterwards mar. Rich. Coode of Morval.

[14] Of Skyburiowe. Bur. at Mawgan in Men. 31 Jan., 1560-1. (Par. Reg.) He mar. Jane, da. of Robert Hill of Hellegan; she afterwards mar. Nicholas Fortescue of Mawgan (Fortescue ped., *ante*). Michael died 26 Jan., 3 Eliz., Christian V., his da. and h. (born 25 June, 1560). aged half a year and more. Inq. p. m. 4 Eliz., pt. i., No. 185.

[*Notes continued on next page.*

THE VISITATION OF THE COUNTY OF CORNWALL. 259

(*Notes continued.*)
    [15] John Vivian died 18 May, 4 Eliz. Inq. p. m. 4 Eliz. No. 183. (Henry V., one of the jurors.) John V., son and heir. æt. 36 and more. His da. Florence, wife of John Fortescue, his cousin James V. and Michael his brother, are named. He was ex'or to the will of Thomas Tretherffe, his father-in-law, dat. 20 Sept., 20 Hen. VIII. Proved in Archdeacon's Court of Cornwall, 26 Oct., 1529. Sir Nicholas Harris Nicolas, Testamenta Vetusta, 1826. Among other lands he held Tremaynone (note, p. 262), Tredencke, Fursdon, and Penquite.
    [16] This marriage brought into the Vivian family a royal descent through Courtney, Earl of Devon, by the daughter of Humphry de Bohun, Earl of Hereford and Essex, who mar. Elizabeth Plantagenet, da. of King Edward I.
    [17] He died 24 July, 19 Elizab., and was bur. at Mawgan in Men. 1 Aug.. 1577. (Par. Reg.) Inq. p. m. 20 Eliz., No. 22. Hauiball Vivian, son and heir, aged 23 and more. The Inq. recites an Indenture made 16 Aug., 4 and 5 Phil. and Mary, between him and John Mayow, alias Vivian, of Pollawyne. His eldest son John V. mar. Johanna Harrye in the ch. of St. Ladoc, and died at Arallas in St. Enoder, 28 Sept., 6 Eliz. (Inq. p. m. 15 Eliz., No. 159), leaving two dau'rs and coheirs, Johanna and Anna, twins, aged 11 years and more (in ward of John Cosgarne). Johanna, the widow, afterwards mar. Peter Bennett, and commenced a Chancery suit— " Peter Bennett and Joahne his wife, late wife of John Vyvyan, Esq., dec., v. Hanyball Vyvyan, Esq., and others." B. b. 25, No. 51. Claiming right of dower in one-eighth part of lands, etc., in Devon and Somerset. The proceedings set forth that the lands in question were the property of John Vyvyan, late husband of Joahne, and the elder brother of Haniball V., who after his brother's death had forcibly entered upon and taken possession of the said lands, etc. Ped. fin. Mich., 4 Eliz., set forth in the Inq. 20 Eliz. Thomas and Adam Mallet qu. John Vyvyan def. Settled lands in Devon upon Haniball V., second son of John V. and Ann his wife.
    [18] Bur. 13 May, 1592. Mawgan in Men. Par. Reg.
    [19] "Hannyball Vivian of Trelowarren, in the co. of Cornw., Esq., from Gibson's howse in the Friers." Bur. Feb. 20, 1609. St. Dunstan's in the West, London, Par. Reg. Will dated 30 Nov., 1608. P. P. C. 1609. Names his wife Phillipa, one of the dau'rs and coheirs of Roger Tremayne of Collacombe. Francis V., his eldest son and heir, who mar. Elizabeth, da. of John Rashleighe of Foye, Esq.; son Michael, "in consideration of his having been a very chargeable son, far above the proportion of any two of his younger brothers, etc." Sons John, Haniball, Robert, Roger, and Charles; dau'rs Phillip, Johane, Blanch Tredinyck, Judith Mayowe, and Dorothy Bogans. Son Francis V., sole ex'or. Sir Will. Godolphin and Sir Reginald Mohun, overseers, Chanc. Pro. Eliz. T. t. 11, No. 23. Hanibal Vivian, Esq., and o'rs v. Jno. Trejoskie. To protect rights in estates, etc. Trenhale in Newlin.
    [20] Bur. 8 April, 1612. Mawgan in Men. Par. Reg.
    [21] All named in will of Haniball V., note 19, but Mayow's wife is called Judith.
    [22] Mar. 14 Oct., 1591. Mawgan in Men. Par. Reg.
    [23] Mar. 14 Oct., 1603. St. Earth Par. Reg.
    [24] Bap. 1579, and mar. 26 Oct., 1596. Mawgan in Men. Par. Reg.
    [25] Francis Vivyan and Elizab. Raishleighe, mar. 13 Jan., 1605. Fowey Par. Reg.
    [26] Bap. 1576. (Mawgan in Men. Par. Reg.) Bur. 19 Oct., 1639. (St. Earth Par. Reg.) Will prob. Bodmin 1639. Inventory £279 : 16 : 4. Names his nephews, Sir Rich. and Michael Vivian, ex'ors.
    [27] Bap. 11 July, 1589, at Mawgan in Men. (Par. Reg.) Comptroller of the Coinage of Tin for the Duchy of Cornwall, and Keeper of the Gaol of Lostwithiel, Dom. Pap., Chas. I., Aug. 13, 1625. Mar. Anne, da. of John Munday of St. Columb Minor. Rich. Munday, gent. Will 6 Nov., 1643. P. P. C. 1647. Gives 20/- each to the children of his "brother-in-law, Haniball Vivian." King Chas. I. granted him a patent inasmuch as "The said Hannibal Vivyan hath, after much paynes and expences, invented and brought to p'fec'on an Engine of great use and p'ffitt both to us and our Subiects, Whereby one man alone can easily drawe as much water as otherwise ffower, and allsoe hoyse all weighty things out of the said Tynne Woorkes, etc." Pat. Roll. 10 Chas. I.. No. 12.
    [28] Bap. 1594 at Mawgan in Men. (Par. Reg.) One of the Tin Farmers, committed to Gaol 16 Jan., 1642, for refusing to pay over the money the House had ordered " unless the Receiver of the Duchy of Cornwall gave an acquittance, who as was informed was with the King's Army." State Pap. Ho. of Commons Journal, vol. ii., p. 929. He mar. Ellen Bennett 25 Oct., 1623, at Camborne. (Par. Reg.)
    [29] Bap. 1595. }
    [30] Bap. 1588. } Mawgan in Menege Par. Reg.

 * Sir Richard Vivian, Kt., of Trelowarren, and Mary Bulteele
        of Barum, mar. lic.   24 Sept., 1636. } Act Books, Exeter.
   Charles Vivyan. Esq., and Mary, da. of Richard Erisey of
        St. Nyott, mar. lic.   16 March, 1674. }

   Francis, son of Sir Viel Vyvyan, bap. at Mawgan in Pider
                                                   26 Feb., 1689. } Archdeacon's
   Sir Vyell Vyvyan and Mrs. Jane Coode mar.   „ 24 Jan., 1683. } Transcripts.
   Sir Vyel Vyvyan   bur. „ 27 Feb., 1696. }

[*Notes continued on next page.*

(*Notes continued.*)

Powle, son of James V. and Jane his wife, bap.	at Constantine	30 July, 1608.	
William, „ John and Honor Vivian „	„	10 July, 1612.	
William, „ James and Jane „ „	„	20 June, 1629.	
James Vivian	bur.	„ 2 May, 1636.	
Jane „ widow	„	27 Jan., 1637.	
Avice, da. of James and Jane Vivian, bap.	at Gluvias	10 May, 1625.	
Jone, da. of Hanniball Vivian, gent., bap.	at St. Just in Penw	26 Dec., 1597.	
Elizab., „ John Vivian	„ „	30 Mar., 1600.	
Jone Vevinne, widow,	bur.	„ 10 Sept., 1598.	
Thomas, son of John Vivian,	bap.	at. St. Keverne	30 Apl., 1599.
Tristram, „ „ „	„	„ 20 May, 1610.	Bp. of Exeter's Trans.
Avis, da. of Justinian V.,	„	„ 1 Jan., 1670.	
Justinian, son of „	„	„ 19 Oct., 1673.	
Thomas, „ Thomas V.,	„	„ 23 Nov., „	
John Vivian and Margaret Bolythoe mar.	„	26 Nov., 1670.	
Thomas. son of Thomas V.,	bur.	„ 24 Sept., 1664.	
Haniball, „ Hanniball Vivian, gent., bap.	at Lostwithiel	9 Feb., 1623.	
John, „ „ „ „	„	22 Feb., 1624.	
Thomas, „ „ „ „	„	15 Apl, 1628.	
Charles, „ Vyvyan Esq. & Anne „	„	11 July, 1630.	
Anne, wife of Hannyball Vyvian, Esq., bur.	„	3 Jan., 1635.	
Lovedaie, 2d da. of Sir Francis Vyvyan, Kt.	bap. at Mawgan in Meneage	8 Feb., 1623.	
Sir Rich. Vyvyan, Kt.,	bur.	„ 10 Nov., 1665.	
Roger Vivian and Ellen Bennett,	mar.	25 Oct., 1623.	
John Vivian, junior, and Jane Luke,	„	14 Feb., 1673.	
Johnson Vivian and Elizab. Davey,	„	24 Oct., 1685.	
John, son of Roger Vivian,	bap.	10 Sept., 1626.	
William, „ „	„	22 Feb., 1628.	
Francis, „ „	„	15 Jan., 1640.	
John, „ John Vivian,	„	5 Apl., 1651.	
Robert, „ „	„	7 May, 1653.	
Roger, „ „	born	22 June, 1655.	Camborne Par. Reg.
Francis, „ „	bap.	18 Nov., 1657.	
Johnson, „ „	„	1 Mar., 1659.	
John, „ Francis Vivian,	„	9 Jan., 1687.	
John, „ John Vivian,	„	20 Aug., 1689.	
John, „ Johnson Vivian,	„	29 Sept., „	
James, „ „	„	15 May, 1698.	
Johnson, „ „	„	16 Aug., 1701.	
Roger, „ John Vivian,	bur.	22 May, 1679.	
John Vivian,	„	Feb., 1689.	
Thomas, son of Annibal Vivian,	bap.	15 Apl., 1628.	St. Columb Minor Par. Reg.
Sir Viel Vyvyan and Thomazin, da. of James Robyns, gent.,	mar.	30 June, 1671.	Constantine Par. Reg.
Francis Vivian and Mary Childs,	„	1673.	St. Earth Par. Reg.
Francis Vevian,	bur.	9 April, 1693.	
Sir Richard Vivian of Trelowarren, and Mrs. Mary Vivian,	mar.	9 Nov., 1697.	St. Eval. Par. Reg.
Constance, wife of Vivian of Christeroy (?)	bur.	1 Aug., 1541.	Illogan Par. Reg.
Whillem. da. of Mr. Hannibal Vivian, Esquier.	bap.	1590.	
John, the eighth son of Sir Francis Vyvyan. Kt.	„	Jan., 1620.	
Viel, son and heir of the Rt. Worsh. Sir Rich. Vivian. Kt., and Lady Mary.	„	20 May, 1639.	Mawgan in Men. Par. Reg.
John, son of James and Phillip Vivian,	„	1640.	
Mr. James Vyvyan and Phillip Warne,	mar.	6 Oct., 1634.	
John Truran, Esq., and Mrs. Cordelia Vyvyan	„	3 Jan., 1673.	
Sir Vyell Vivian, Kt. & Bart., and his Lady Jane,	„	24 Feb., 1683.	
Francis Vyvyan, Esq.,	bur.	29 Nov., 1686.	
Michael Vivian, Esq., and Mary Erricke,	mar.	16 Jan., 1640.	
Michael Vyvyan, gent., and Grace Madderne,	„	31 Aug., 1652.	
John, son of Michael Vivian, gent., and Mary, bap.		1641.	
Loveday, da. of „ „ „ „		1653.	
Ann, „ „ „ „ „		1655.	Phillack Par. Reg.
Mary, „ „ „ „ „		1656.	
Grace, „ Michael Vyvyan, gent., „		1661.	
Elizab., „ „ „ „		1663.	
Francis, son of Michael Vivian, bap. 3 July, 1666, bur. 7 Mar., 1667.			
Michael Vyvyan, Esq.,	„	12 July, 1676.	

[*Notes continued on next page.*

THE VISITATION OF THE COUNTY OF CORNWALL. 261

(*Notes continued.*)
Henry Vivian and Alice Martyn mar. 20 Oct., 1600. Wendron Par. Reg.
Michael Vivyan of Pulsack, Cornw. Will, Bodmin, 1676. Inventory £882 13s. 4d. Names his wife Grace, daughters Loveday, Grace, and Elizabeth, and " Henry Polkinghorne, son and heir of Roger P., my son-in-law."
Will of Mary Vivian, spinster, 16 Dec., 1662, P.P.C. 1662. Names her brother Thankfull Owen's sons Thankfull and Philip, cousin Francis Howell, bro. Sir Rich. V., Kt. and Bart., bro. Michael V., cousin Haniball V., Anne Greatbatch, sister Loveday Owen. Thankfull Owen ex'or.
Will of Sir Rich. Vyvyan of Trelawarren, 1 Aug., 1665, P.P.C. 1666. Names his wife Mary, dau'rs Arabella, Elizabeth, Cordelia, Diana, and Anna, Charles V. his second son. Deed 15 Apl., 1651, conveyed to trustees certain lands in parishes of Cubert, Peransand, Mawgan in Menenge. St. Keverne, Constentine (Pollawin, etc.), Camborne, Cury, Budock, and Illogan for the use of himself and his heirs male, in default to the heirs male of his father, Sir Francis V., dec., in default to his own right heirs for ever. His first son Vyell V., his sister Loveday Owen. Son Vyell V. sole ex'or.
Francis Vivian of Cosowarth, gent. Will dat. 9 Ap., 1689, Archd. Court, Cornw. Names sisters Leach and Beauford, nephew John V., cousin Margt. Martyn. Devises all his lands to his child Mary Vivian, sole executrix. He desired his father, bro. Vivian, bro. John V., and cousins Richard Scobell and Francis Scobell (his son) to manage the estates for the good of the executrix, and to sell anything except the Barton of Cosowarth, to pay debts.
Will 1712, Archd. Court, Cornw. "I, Richard Vivian, of Trelowarren, Co. Cornw., Bart." Styled Richard Vivyan of Trelowarren in 1712 in the will, and Richard Vyvyan of Trelowarren in 1721 in the codicil.
Ped. fin. Cornw. 14 Hen. III., No. 1. Gilleb'm filiu' Viviani qu. Warin fil. Perlonis def. Advowson of the living of Queidike (Quethiock). Warin paid Gilleb. two marcs of silver quit claim.
Ped. fin. Cornw. 22 Hen. III., No. 9. Jordanus de Trevage qu. Vivian de Treviniel def. Trevathelek. Vivian paid one marc of silver quit claim.
Ped. fin. Cornw. 28 Hen. III., No. 16. Andrew de Trevagan qu. Vivianus de Treviniel def. In Rosalen.
Ped. fin. Cornw. 39 Hen. III., No. 1. Vivianus de Trevyniel pet. Andrea de Treverga ten. Trekurnel. Andrea paid V. four marks of silver.
Ped. fin. Cornw. 30 Edw. I., No. 9. Richard Vyvian de Trevydrun qu. Hervicus de Alta def. In Alta.
Ped. fin. Cornw. and Devon, 1 and 2 Ph. and Mary, Hill. James Vyvyan and Thos. Mallet, gents, qu. John Vyvyan, sen., Esq., and Elizabeth his wife def. Lands in Devon and Arrallas al's Argallas, Medeshole (Michell), Skewys, Reserens, Trenhale, Illogan, Gwynyer, etc., co. Cornw., settled on John Vivian, second son of Jno. and Elizabeth, rem. to Margaret Bouller, sister of said Elizabeth, and her heirs by Edw. Courtney, late her husband, rem. to John Tretherffe, rem. to Thomas T. his bro., rem. to right heirs of John V. and Elizabeth.
Ped. fin. Cornw. 13 Elizab., Mich. Jno. Cougan qu. Christopher Vyvyan def. Lands called Bodgall in Lanlivery.
Ped. fin. Cornw., Mich., 13 and 14 Elizab. Humphry Sydnam, Thomas Malet, Nicholas Flamock, John Collyns and or's qu. Humfry Vyvyan and Florence his wife def. In Tregoney Burgh and St. Kebye. Paid Humfry V. and Florence £40.
Ped. fin. Cornw., Hill., 38 Elizab. William Coode qu. Haniball Vivian and Phillipa his wife def. Lands in Morvall. William paid Haniball and Phillipa 130 marcs of silver.
Cor. Reg. Roll 1 Edw. I., Pasch., Cornwall, No. 3. Marcus le Cornwaleys v. Herveyus Vivien, Ranulphus de Treuronet, Alan de Treuronet, and others.
Cor. Reg. Roll 1 Edw. I., Pasch., Cornwall, No. 4. Peter de Nanscoct v. Radulphus de Vivien and Luca de Tremidren. Trespass in Rosplede.
Cor. Reg. Roll 30 Edw. I., Trin., Cornw., No. 170, case 14. Lucam Vyvyan and Vivianus Poer and Vivianus de Eskler named in suits.
Lay Subsidies, 1 Edw. III. Parish of Paul—John Vivian paid 4s., John Vivian 1s. St. Levan Par.—Viviano Poer, Viviano Bodeler. Sennan Par.—Viviano Ised, Viviano Trevergan.
Lay Subsidies, 29 Hen. VI., 87—92. Odo Vyvyan and John Vivian held in fee lands value of 100s.
The name of Vivian was used as a prenomen in England as early as Will. Conquer. (*Vide* Visitation of Lancashire, Harl. MS. 1468, fo. 78.) Vivian de Molynes, son of William de Molynes, temp. Will. Conq. Rot. Chart. King John. The Vivians held lands in co. Somerset A.D. 1200, and T. Vivian was Archdeacon of Derby A.D. 1199. Rot. Litt. Pat. King John. Ralph Vivian held lands in Lincolnshire, also Lucian Vivian and his two sons Thomas and Galfrid.
Rot. Litt. Pat. 14 King John. Rex Willo de Harecurt, etc. Sciatis quod Lucianus de Arquill' fine' fecit nobisc' per delibaco'e sua a prisona nostra in qua est eo q'd capt' fuit in Castro de Carickfergus per cent. marc' etc. Thom' filiu' suu' primogenitu' Galfrid' fil' suu' jun. et Radulphum fil' Viviani fratris sui primogenitus quos W. Com. de Warrem comisim' custodiendo etc. Grantham, 23 Feb., 14 John.
Rot. Hundredorum, vol. i. p. 13, Berkshire, 4 Edw. I. Dn't q'd Gervasius Vivien de Nuibyr' (Newbury) fecit duci lanas ad p'tes t'nsmarinos durante discord. etc. p' Johem Vivian filiu' suu' p' portu. Suht. et Portesmue sz nesciut' quo warranti necquot faceos. It. Will's Tabernar' cepit decc' marc' et alia dona de Joh'e de Dereby attach' cu' manupe' de magno latrocinio ut abire eum a prisona p'mitt'et.

[*Notes continued on next page.*

Webber.

Willm Webber de Amell in p'ochia de St. Kew = ... filia Willmi Mathew of St. Kew et Relicta of Harp of the same

John Webber of Amell in the p'ish of St. Kew in Com. Cornwall gent. = Jone Da. of .... Trwebody of Trengale in p'ochia de St. Cleere in Com. Devon (*sic*)

Susan Da. of Digorie Polewheele of Treworgan in Cornw. ux. 2 = John Webber of Amell in p'ochia de St. Kew gent. = Honor Da. of John Callwoodley de Padstow in Com. Cornwall Esq. ux. 1 — George Webber 2 fil. mar.

¹ Digorie Webber 3 fil. ætat. 4 annoru'

1. Katherin 9
—
2. Joane 6
—
3. Susan 3

Richard Webber fil. Primogenit. ætat. 21 annoru' 1620

Matheus fil. 2 ætat. 19 annoru' 1620

Honor fil. unica ob. s.p.

*

JOHN WEBBER.

White.

Oliver White of St. Stephens iuxta Launston in Cornwall =

John 2 sonne

Beaton 1 Da.

Jane ux' Jo. Cole of Linkinghorne in Cornw.

Oliv' White of St. Stephen's = Alice Da. of Pet' Mannaton of Mannaton Esq.

Anne ux' Jo. Hext of Launston

Marg' ux' Edw. Kempthorne of Hockland in Devon

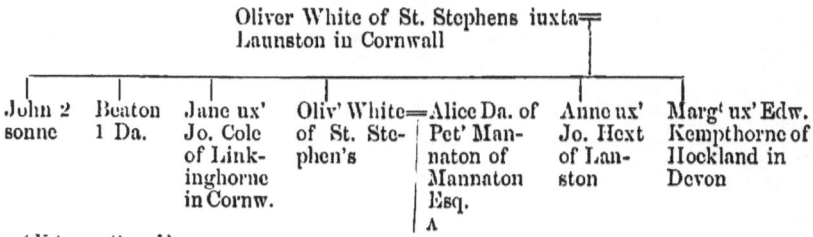

(*Notes continued.*)

Exchequer Depositions, 31 Elizab., Hillary, Cornwall, No. 24. Nich. Courtney v. Rich. Bennett, John Slade, and William Slade. Plea of lands in Tremaynon and Goolorock. Thomas Vyvyan dwelt at Tremaynon, and died suddenly in a field at Trevarrack (his property). His son William V. was slayne about a mile distant from the lands in question, and his three daughters and coheiresses were Christian, mar. to John Slade, Olyff, mar. to Rich. Polkinghorne, and Agnes, mar. to Perys al's Paris John of Helston, after their father's death.

For an account of the family of Vivonia or Vivian, see 'Collectanea Topographica et Genealogica,' vol. vii., p. 137.

The additions in italic are taken from Harl. MS. 1091, fo. 102, and the pedigree is continued in that MS. down to A.D. 1640.

We may note here that the name of Vivian has been spelt with *i* or *y* indifferently. The very earliest record of the name in England, temp. Will. Conq., gives it Vivian. The use of the *y* began about the time of Edw. I., and has since been adopted by different branches of the family.

¹ One of the Burgesses of Camelford, 12 Chas. II.

* Will of John Webber of Penponte in Parish of St. Kew, Yeoman, 7 March, 1607. P. P. C. 1610. Names his wife Phillipp. sons John, William, Samuel, Nicholas, Francis, James, and Digory. dau'rs Elizabeth, wife of Geo. Sheere of Plymouth, Johane Meacke, and Honor Tamline. Son John, sole ex'or.

For continuation of pedigree of the Family of Webber of Amell, and memoir of the Webbers of St. Kew, see 'History of Trigg,' vol. ii., pp. 166-168.

THE VISITATION OF THE COUNTY OF CORNWALL.

| A

Thomas 2 sonne   Samson 3 sonne   Willm 4 sone   Oliver White sone & hey. at. 17 at this p^rsent a ward

*   OLIVER WHITE.

Williams.

To enquire for the Coate of Williams of Dorsetsheir.

JO. ESTCOTT.

John Williams of Heringston in Dorsetsh.=Da. & sole hey Rich. of Trevervo
came to Trevervo in Com. Cornwall   in Com. Cornwall

Willm Willms of Trevervo=Da. of Jennings of Clemense in Cornwall

[1] John Williams of Trevervo=[1] Florence Da. of Pendarvers of Camborne in Cornw.

[2] Baltizer Williams=Elizb. Da. of Rich. Robts of
of Trevervo   Trwro in Com. Cornwall

[3] Rich. Williams of Trevervo in=[3] Ellin Da. of Willm Younge of
Com. Cornw. liveing 1620   Trent in Com. Som'set
                            A

* Grace, dau. of Oliver White, gent., and Audrey, bap. at   ⎫ Bishop's Tran-
   St. Stephen's by Launceston   1630. ⎬ scripts.
  Catherine, dau. of Mr. Oliver White and Jane, bap. Sep. 3, 1686. ⎫ Alternon Par.
  Mrs. Catherine White, widow,   bur.   Mar. 6, 1684. ⎬ Reg.
  Thomas, son of John White, gent.,   bap.   1605. ⎫ Bodmin Par.
  Richard,   „   „   „   „   1609. ⎬ Reg.
  John Billing and Bridget White   mar.   1683. ⎭
  Charles, son of Hugh White, clerk, and Jacket his   ⎫ Lantoglos by
    wife   bap.   Ap. 1, 1627. ⎬ Camelford Par.   ⎫ (J. M.)
                                                                ⎭ Reg.
  Hugh White, clerk,   bur. 25 Nov., 1679. ⎬ St. Minver Par.
                                                                ⎭ Reg.
  Robert White of Key, gent., and Jane Phillips mar. Mar. 28, 1690. ⎬ Poughill Par.
                                                                ⎭ Reg.
  John, son of Henry White, clerk, and Hannah, bap. 8 May, 1716. ⎬ Tintagel Par.
                                                                ⎭ Reg.
For a short descent of White, see Harl. MS. 1079, fo. 14.

   [1] John Williams of Probus and Florence Pendarves mar. 28 Sept., 1549.   Camborne Par. Reg.

  [2] Balthazar Williams generosus nup. Parochiæ de Probus sepult, fuit Decimo quarto die mensis Septembris 1608.   Truro Par. Reg.

  [3] Mr. Richard Williams and Mrs. Helen Younge mar. at Probus 6 Feb., 1608.   Bp. of Exeter's Transcripts.

THE VISITATION OF THE COUNTY OF CORNWALL.

A |

| Hugh 2 sonne | Henry 3 sone | Rich. 4 sone | ¹ Baltizer sone & heire atat. 11, 1620 | John 5 sone | Fran. 1 Da.at.12 | Radigund 2 Da. |

* RICHARD WILLIAMS.

---

¹ Balthazar Williams and Anne Paynter mar. 24 Nov., 1630, at Sithney. Bp. of Exeter's Transcripts.

* Elizb., da. of Courteney Williams, gent., bap. at Probus 18 Oct., 1715. ⎫
Rich., son of ,, Esq., ,, ,, 20 Feb., 1718. ⎬ Archd. Trans.
Rich., ,, ,, gent., bur. ,, 1715. ⎭
Mary, wife of Hugh Williams, gent., bur. 9 Feb., 1684. ⎫
Elizb., da. of ,, ,, ,, ,, ⎬ St. Austell Par. Reg.
Rich. Williams and Thomazin Clemence mar. 5 Feb., 1694. ⎭
Otes Willim and Tamson his wife mar. 19 Nov., 1540. ⎫
Harri ,, and Elizab. ,, ,, 11 Oct., 1546. ⎪
Jno. Williams, jun., and Kath. Lanion ,, 16 May, 1668. ⎬ Camborne Par. Reg.
Mr. Zachary Williams of Helston and Mrs. Cath. Pendarves
of Truro mar. 1718. ⎭

Rich., son of Rich. Williams, gent., and Elizb., bap. 1692. ⎱ St. Columb Major Par. Reg.

Michael Williams and Katherine Trewavas mar. 25 Feb., 1649. St. Erth Par. Reg.
John Williams and Martha Tremaine ,, 20 Jan., 1669. ⎫
John ,, gent. and Jana Maunder mar. (apud ⎬ St. Ewe Par. Reg.
St. Mewan) 29 Apr., 1699.
Tho. Pentire and Thomazine Williams mar. 1701. ⎭
Thos. Williams bap. 1543. ⎫
Edw., son of Michell Williams, ,, 8 Mar., 1570. ⎪
Davyd, ,, ,, ,, 1578. ⎬ Fowey Par. Reg.
Michael, ,, ,, ,, 10 June, 1615. ⎪
Michael Williams and Katherine mar. 1568. ⎪
Davy ,, ,, Margt. Dickwood ,, 1579. ⎭
Tho. Williams and Dorothy Harris ,, 7 Jan., 1672. Gorran Par. Reg.
Chas. Williams of St. Twin and Jane Nicholls of
Gulval ,, 27 Feb., 1676. ⎱ Gulval Par. Reg.
Walter, son of Tho. Williams bap. 1566. ⎫
Willyam, ,, Mr. Wm. Williams ,, 27 Nov., 1598. ⎪
Roger, 2nd ,, Wm. Williams, gent., ,, 24 July, 1600. ⎪
Otho, ,, Edw. ,, ,, 9 Mar., 1622. ⎪
Humphry, ,, Wm. ,, ,, 24 Ap., 1625. ⎪
Sciprian, ,, Otho ,, ,, 1656. ⎬ Gwinnear Par. Reg.
Michael, ,, John ,, and bur. 1658. ⎪
John, ,, Humphry Wyllyams, gent., at High ⎪
Bickington, Dev., 1660. ⎪
John Williams of Helston, gent., and Mary mar. 1689. ⎪
John, son of Jno. Williams of St. Tallin, bur. 5 Jan., 1658. ⎭
Michael, son of Henry Willim, bap. 10 Nov., 1566. ⎱ Gwithian Par. Reg.
Alis, da. of Humphre Willms, ,, 20 Jan., 1594. ⎰
William Williams of Probus and Christian, da. of Jno. Best
of Lamorran mar. 4 Oct., 1687. ⎱ Lamorran Par. Reg.
Peter, son of Mychael Willia, bur. 10 Sep., 1577. Ludgvan Par. Reg.
Hugh Williams, gent., and Jane mar. 22 Nov., 1637. Luxyllian Par. Reg.
Robt. Williams of Constantine and Eliz. Eriscy
of St. Nyott ,, 9 Jan., 1689. ⎱ Mabe Par. Reg.
Rich. Williams of Probus, gent., and Mary, da. of Wm. ⎱ St. Michael Penk.
Courtney, gent., dec., of this parish mar. 22 Dec., 1662. ⎰ Par. Reg.

[*Note continued on next page.*

Willoughby.

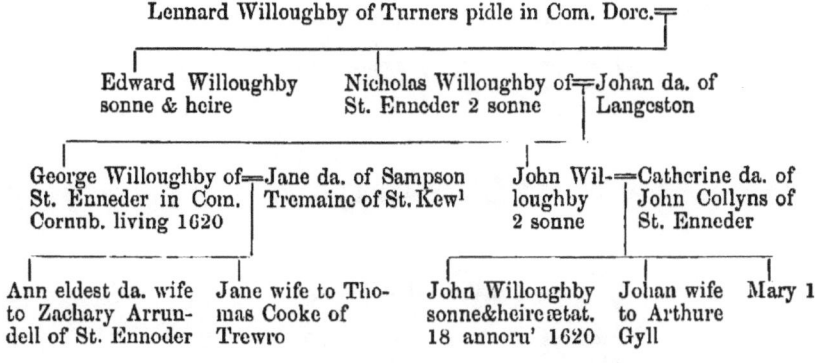

GEORGE WILLOUGHBY.

Wills.

Antho. Wills of Saltashe=Da. of Wootton of Ingleborn
in Cornwall   neare Totnes

Rich. Wills=Mary Da. of Wm. Carnsew

Digorie Wills=Mary Da. of Tho. Collyn
A

(*Note continued.*)

Erasmus, son of John Williams,	bap.	1587. }	Peranuthno Par. Reg.
Rich., son of Lewis Williams,	,,	1574.	Phillack Par. Reg.
John Robins and Jane Willyames	mar.	1 Oct., 1655. }	Tywardreath Par. Reg.
Hugh Williams	bur.	11 Ap., 1611. }	
Mr. Hugh Williams	,,	25 May, 1721. }	
Wm. Williams and Anne Tyncomb	mar.	8 July, 1673.	St.Winnow Par.Reg.

Besides the Herringstone branch, there appears to have been two or three respectable families of the name of Williams in Cornwall deriving from Devon and Wales, and rendering the identification very intricate, as these numerous specimen Registers will shew. The Gwinnear, Gwithian, and Phillack entries apply chiefly to the family seated at present at Carnanton. Michael was the prevailing name in a family now seated at Tregullow and Carhais Castle.

For more of Williams, see Harl. MS. 1079, fo. 85.

[1] ? St. Ewe.

* For another branch of Willoughby see Trevelyan Papers, pt. 3.

```
                                    A
              Rich. Wills of Boatesfleminge in==Anne Da. of Rog. Westcot of
              Com. Cornw. liveing 1620          Plimouth in Devon
        ┌──────────────┬────────────────────┬──────────────────┐
   Digorie      Rich. sone & heire    Anthonie 3 sonne atat.   Anne a dau.
   2 sonne      atat. 8, 1620         2 monthes 1620           at. 2

                                                            RIC. WILLS.
```

Wodenote.

```
              Lawrencius Woodnoth==Margaret filia Johis Rope
              2 filius Georgij      de Stapbley Armig'
        ┌───────────────────────────┬──────────────────────────┐
  Johes Wodenoth fil.==Elizab. fil.   Thomas Wodenoth==Francisca. fil. Henrici
  et hæres de Shaving-  Rog' Wal-     filius secundus   Clifford de Boscombe in
  ton                   then                            Com. Wilts
  ┌──────────────┬──────────────┐                ┌──────────────────────┐
 Prisilla uxor Chris-  Debora nupta   Theophilus Wodenoth==Maria fil. Jacobi Spicer
 topheri Oughe de   Hen. Fragle       de Linkenhorne in    of St. Gorrin in Cor-
 St. Cleere in      de Le Sante       Com. Corn. et rector nubia, who came out of
 Cornw.             in Cornub.        Ecclie ib'm.         the East Countrey

                              THEOPHILUS WODENOTE.
```

* Peter, son of Mr. William Wills and Bessie his wife, bur. at St. Stephen's juxta Saltashe 20 Aug., 1608. Bp. of Exeter's Transcripts.

Ambrosia, da. of Francis Wills, Esq., bap. at St. Stephen's by Saltash Mar. 31, 1633. Bp. of Exeter's Transcripts.

Mary, wife of Thomas Wills, gent., bur. 24 Nov., 1657. Week St. Mary Par. Reg. } (J. M.)

Francis Mannington, Clerk. Rector of St. Pinnock, and Joanna Wills of Saltash, mar. lic. 15 May, 1623. Exeter Act Books.

```
  Tho.,   son of Anthony Wills, gent., and Jenopheth,  bap.  15 Mar., 1661.
  John,     "          "              "         "       ,,    4 July, 1664.
  Rich.,    "          "              "         "       ,,             1665.
  Willm.,   ,,   Willm Wills and Lore           "       ,,             1665.
  Rich.,    ,,   Edm'd Wills and June,                  ,,             1680.
  James,    ,,   Willm Wills and Lore,                  ,,             1680.   Gorran Par.
  Rich.,    "          "              "         "       ,,             1682.   Reg.
  Rich. Wills and Winifred Longe                         mar.  Sept., 1670.
  Nathaniel Will and Florence Will                        ,,   24 Aug., 1702.
  William Wills and Elizb. Devonshire                     ,,             1723.
  John Andrew and Honour Wills                            ,,   2 Jan., 1745.
  Mrs. Susanna Wills                                     bur.            1682.
```

THE VISITATION OF THE COUNTY OF CORNWALL. 267

Worthevale.

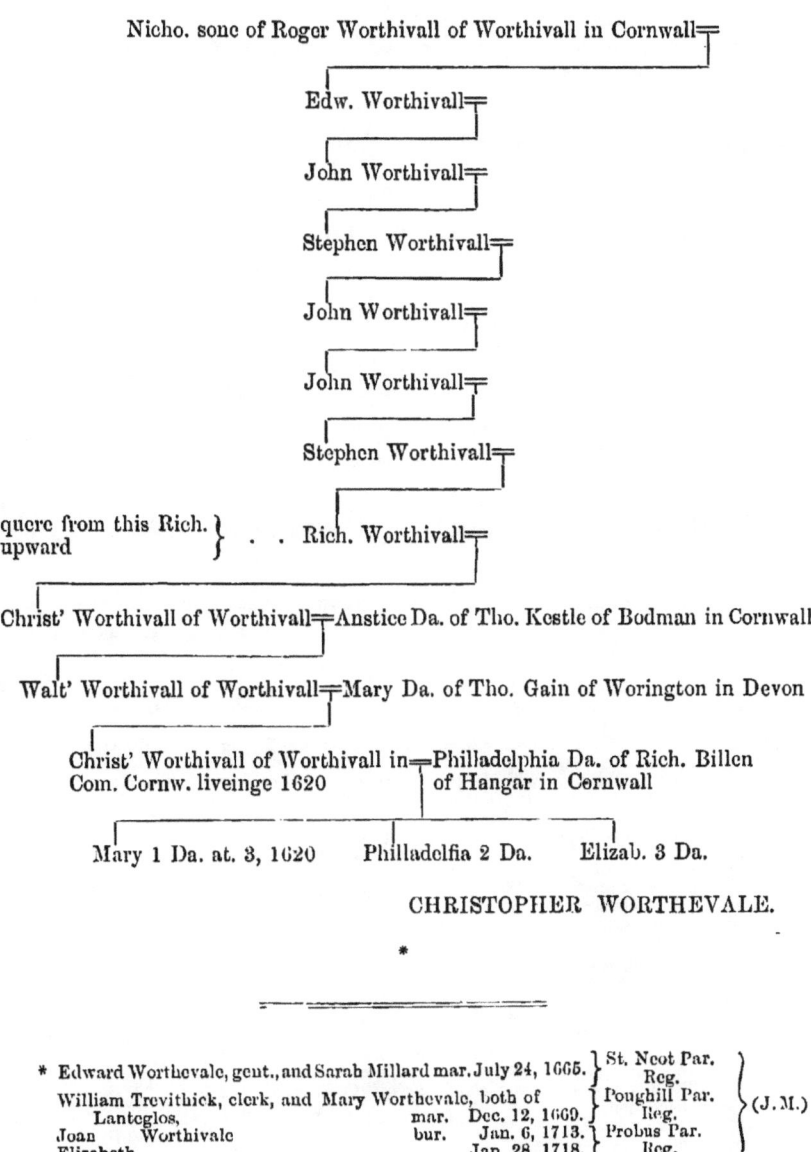

Nicho. sone of Roger Worthivall of Worthivall in Cornwall⊤

    Edw. Worthivall⊤

        John Worthivall⊤

            Stephen Worthivall⊤

                John Worthivall⊤

                    John Worthivall⊤

                        Stephen Worthivall⊤

quere from this Rich. } . . Rich. Worthivall⊤
upward

Christ' Worthivall of Worthivall=Anstice Da. of Tho. Kestle of Bodman in Cornwall

Walt' Worthivall of Worthivall⊤Mary Da. of Tho. Gain of Worington in Devon

    Christ' Worthivall of Worthivall in=Philladelphia Da. of Rich. Billen
    Com. Cornw. liveinge 1620   of Hangar in Cornwall

  Mary 1 Da. at. 3, 1620   Philladelfia 2 Da.   Elizab. 3 Da.

CHRISTOPHER WORTHEVALE.

*

---

* Edward Worthevale, gent., and Sarah Millard mar. July 24, 1665. } St. Neot Par. Reg.
William Trevithick, clerk, and Mary Worthevale, both of } Poughill Par.
   Lanteglos,   mar.   Dec. 12, 1669. } Reg.   } (J.M.)
Joan   Worthivale   bur.   Jan. 6, 1713. } Probus Par.
Elizabeth   ,,   ,,   Jan. 28, 1718. } Reg.

[*Note continued on following page.*

Wrey.

Henry Killigrew of Wolston=.... da. & Coheir of Trelawny

John Wrey of Northrusell=Blanch[1] da. & coheir of Henry Killigrew
in Com. Devon Esq. of Wolston in Com. Cornub.

Philippa wife to George= Upton of Puslich

Jane wife to= Peter Coriton

Arthure Wrey=Joyce da. & coheir of
3 sonne Tristram Harry

George 2   William Upton 1   William Coriton

John Wrey of=Elinor da. & heir to   Sr William Wrey of=Elizabeth da. of S^r
Northrusell Bernard Smith of   Northrusell in Com.   Wm Courtney of
Esq. ob. s. p. Totness & widow   Devon and of Tre-   Powderham k^t
             of Sr John Fulford   beigh in Com. of Corn- 2 wife
                                     wall k^t liveing 1620

William Wrey sonne & heir ætat. 20 annoru' 1620

Edmond Wrey 2 sonne=Catheryn da. of John Prys of Horwell

William sonne & heir æt. 21, 1620   John 2 sonne   5 daughters

*

W. WREY.

(*Note continued.*)

    Mar. lic. betw. John Baker of Tywardreth and Elizabeth Worthevale of the same,
      May 26, 1640.
  „   „ betw. Christopher Worthevale and Catherine Tucker of Cardinham,
      April 11, 1664.
  „   „ betw. William Williams of St. Juliot and Loveday Worthevale of
      Cambleford, spinster, Mar. 2, 1713.
  „   „ betw. Richard Worthevale of St. Lawrence, Exeter, Taylor, and Mary   (J. M.)
      Griflin of St. John's in same city, sp., May 16, 1737.
  „   „ betw. John Worthevale of Camelford, Taylor, and Ursula Masters of
      St. Bruard, sp., Feb. 26, 1742.
  „   „ betw. Christopher Worthevale of New Town, Ireland, and Mary Farn-
      ham of Camelford, widow, Dec. 26, 1746.
For account and continued ped. of Worthevale, see 'Hist. of Trigg,' vol. i., pp. 663, etc.

[1] Inq. p. m, 39 Eliz., Pt. 2, No. 157. Blanch Wrey, widow, died 14 Dec., 38 Eliz. John Wrey, son and heir, aged 40 and more.

  * Francis, son of Sir Wm. Wrey, Knt., and Elizb. ux, bap. 1633 at St. Ive. Bp. of Exeter's Transcripts.

    William, son of Sir William Wrey, Bart., and Lydia   } Bishop's Tran-
      Elizabeth his wife, bap. at St. Ive   May 17, 1631. } scripts.
    Colan Blewett, son of Colan Blewett of Little Colan,
      dec'd, and Elizabeth Wrey, the daughter of Sir   } St. Columb
      William Wrey, Knt. and Bart., dec'd. Contract   } Major Par.   (J. M.)
      published only.   1655,   } Reg.
    Jane Wraye, gent.,   bur.   Mar. 9, 1687. } Probus Par. Reg.
    John Wrey   „   Aug. 14, 1691. }
For more of Wrey see Harl. MS. 1079, fo. 141.

Wyvell.

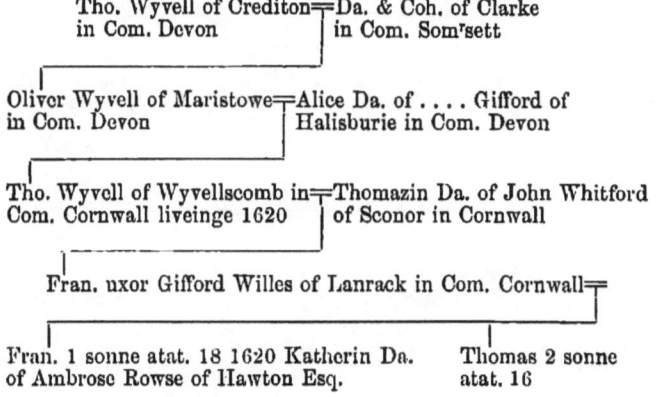

Tho. Wyvell of Crediton = Da. & Coh. of Clarke
in Com. Devon | in Com. Som'sett

Oliver Wyvell of Maristowe = Alice Da. of .... Gifford of
in Com. Devon | Halisburie in Com. Devon

Tho. Wyvell of Wyvellscomb in = Thomazin Da. of John Whitford
Com. Cornwall liveinge 1620 | of Sconor in Cornwall

Fran. uxor Gifford Willes of Lanrack in Com. Cornwall =

Fran. 1 sonne atat. 18 1620 Katherin Da. | Thomas 2 sonne
of Ambrose Rowse of Hawton Esq. | atat. 16

*

THO. WYVELL.

York.

[1] Rich. Yorke of Wellington = [2] Da. of Sr Andrew Lutterell
in Com. Som'set | de Dunster

A Da. mar. to .... | [3] Tho. Yorke of = Ellinor Da. of Hen. Waldron [3] of Brad-
Prediaux father to | Wellington in | feild & of his wife da. & hey. of Whiting
Sr Nich. Predeaux | Com. Som'set | of Devonsh.
A

---

* Mar. lic. between Thomas Wyvell of Wyvellscombe, in the parish of St. Stephen's } (J. M.)
by Saltash, and Joanna Wills of St. Stephen's aforesaid, 15 Dec., 1627.

[1] Should be Roger Yorke, Serjeant-at-Law.
Inq. p. m. Exch. 27-28 Hen. VIII. Rogeri Yorke, servientis ad legem, ob. Feb. 27 Hen. VIII. Thomas Yorke, son and heir, 15 years old at father's death. Names Sir Andrew Luttrell, bro.-in-law of Roger Yorke, and recites certain covenants in the event of Thomas York, s. & h., marrying Isabella Ernley, his step-mother's daughter. He married Eleanor Walrond as above. Roger York was called to be Serjeant-at-Law 1532.

[2] Should be Eleanor, dau. of Sir Hugh Lutterell of Dunster. Coll. of Arms 2 C. 22.

[3] Chan. Pro. B and A Eliz. Yorke v. Butler. Humphrie Yorke, gent., grandson of Roger Yorke, Serjeant-at-Law. Said Roger died 27 Hen. VIII., leaving a son and heir, Thomas, under guardianship of Henry Walrond of Bradfield, Devon, Esq. Names manor of Comb Ryall, and lands in Wellington, Kingsbridge, West Allington, Crediton, Exeter, and Sampford Arundel. Roger York married a second wife, Margaret, widow of Anthony Ernley.
Humphry York is named in will of Haniball Vivian of Trelowarren, 30 Nov., 1608, P. P. C. 1609.

```
     ┌─────────────────────────A─┴──────────────────────────┐
     │                           │                          │
¹ Humphrie=Barbara² Da. John Vivian    Mary Yorke mar.
  Yorke of  │ of Trelawarren in p'ochia    Francis Harvy Rector
  Fillack   │ de Mogan Esq.                de Breague
  ┌─────────┼──────────┬─────────────────┐
  │         │          │                 │ 2
1. Jane  2. Margt⁴  Anne mar. to ⁶ Tho.  ³ Sara mar. to Willm ⁵
   æt. 24    18      Tresaher              Noy of Burrian
```

                                                   HUMFRY YORK.

---

¹ See note 3. preceding page.
  Humphrie Yorke, gent. bur. 3 Sept., 1633.   } Gwinear Par. Reg.
² Barbara, wife of Humphrie Yorke, gent., bur. 1 March, 1631. }
  Humfrie York, gent., was married unto Barbara, the   } Mawgan in Meneage Par.
    da. of John Vivian, Esquire, the (sic) of the   }   Reg.
    month of   1585. }
  Blanche, da. of Mr. Humfrye Yeorcke,   bap. 18 Feb., 1586. ┐
³ Sara,   „   „   „   „ 24 Sept., 1589. │
  Christen, „   „   „   „ 16 Dec., 1593. │
⁴ Margt.,   „   „   „   „   2 Jan., 1603. ├ Phillack Par. Reg.
  Xtian,   „   „   „   bur. 18 Feb., 1608. │
⁵ Willm Noy, gent., and Sara, da. of   │
    Humph. York, gent.,   mar. 26 Nov., 1606. ┘
⁶ See Tresahar ped., *ante*.

* John Trewinnard, gent., of St. Ives, and Margaret, da. of Humphrye Yorke, gent., of Gwinnear, mar. 25 Ap., 1623, at Towednacke. Bp. of Exeter's Transcripts.
  Walter York, will prob. at Lambeth 2 Oct., 1505, Holgrave 36. Citz. and Mercht. of Exeter. To be buried in church outside the south gate of the city. Legacy to St. Gregory's, within the collegiate church of Crediton. Residue to Walter (Walthen) his wife, which Walthen after married Sir Hugh Lutterell, father-in-law of Roger Yorke.
  Roger Yorke married Eleanor, sister of Sir Andrew and da. of Sir Hugh Lutterell by Margaret, sister of Giles, Lo. Daubeney. (Coll. of Arms 2 C. 22, and Trevelyan Papers, pt. 3, p. ix.) Misc. Pap. Co. of Wards. temp. Hen. VIII., contains will of Sir Jno. Luttrell. Mention of lands as marriage jointure of "Welthian Luttrell, 2nd wief to Sir Hughe Luttercll," and a deed betw. Sir Tho. Windham and Roger Yorke touching the said lands and a payment of 300 marks to Roger Yorke and his wife.
  For continuation of Yorke, see 'Hist. of Trigg,' vol. i.

  It may be serviceable to the genealogical enquirer to remember that members of several of the Devonshire families migrated to Cornwall, following in the wake of relatives who acted as pioneers. Thus in St. Earth, adjoining Gwinear, is found the marriage of Tho. Whiting with Grace, the da. of Arthur Painter, Esq., in 1611, with a numerous issue. The Whitings were related to Yorke, as the pedigree explains. One Whiting was afterwards Vicar of St. Earth. The Devon name of Honichurch is also in the same parish. In Gwennap was a colony of names all previously connected by marriage in Devon, viz., Harris, Winter, Drake, and Crymes. The last two were successively "Ministers" of the parish during the Commonwealth. Another list of names is found in Gulval, viz. Harris, Drew, Davy, Newman, Stukeley, and Honichurch. In Ludgvan the same, with the addition of Talbot of Tavistock. Their peculiar Christian names indicate their Devonshire origin. In Duloe and Morval were branches of the Stukeleys of Affton and of the Fortescues, who were also in St. Winnow and Mevagizzy. Some county names extinct in Devon appear in various Parish Registers of Cornwall.—Eds.

ADDITIONS.

Arundell.

Raynulfe Lord of Albominster & Stratton 2^d son to John Earle of Arundell temp. H. III.

[1] Sr Oliver Arundell of Carshayes Knight temp. Hen. III. marryed = Margery the Daughter & heire of Raynulph de Arundell Lord of Albominster & Stratton 2 son to John Earle of Arundell

[2] Radulph Arundell marryed = Elizabeth y^e Da. & heire of Sr John Seneschall Kn^t lord of y^e Mannor of Trerise

John Arundell de Treres marryed = Jane Da. of Lupus of Tredannam

John Arundell de Treres marryed = Jane y^e Da. & Coheire of Sr Richard Sergeaunt Kn^t who marryed Phillip ye only child of Richard Earle of Arundell

[3] Nicholas Arundell de Treres marryed = Elizabeth Da. & Heire of Sr John Cheddore Kn^t

A

---

[1] Ex. è Rot. Fin. 55 Hen. III., m. 1, Cornw. Oliverus de Arundell et Margeria ux. eius, Joh'es de Kelerion et Johanna ux. eius dant dimid. manor, etc.
Ped. fin. Cornw., Hill., 2 Edw. I., No. 1. Olyver de Arundell qu. Robert Tyrel def. Tregenewe. Olyver gave one sparrowhawk quitclaim.

[2] Brev. Cornub. 31 Edw. I., 87/2. Ralph, son of Oliver de Arundell, held one knight's fee which his ancestors held in Trekynnen in Trigg.
Cor. Reg. Cornw. 31 Edw. I., Hill., m. 172. The jury present Roger de Ingepenue, Viscomes Cornubiæ, among other offences, for forcibly entering the house of Caryhayes and breaking open the coffer of Ralph, son of Oliver de Arundell, which was sealed with the seals of the Archdeacon of Cornwall and Lawrence de Arundell, and taking away one silver cup value 10s. and another value 40s., together with deeds, etc.
Ped. fin. Cornw., Mich., 18 Edw. II., No. 4. John de Carmenowe Chivaler qu. Ralph de Arundell of Karyhays def. Reskere, Dysard, Landu, and Treuryek next the village of St. Wenn, which Isabella de Buleghe held for life of the inheritance of Ralph, settled upon John de Carmenowe and John de C. his son, rem. to the right heirs of John de C.

[3] There is apparently confusion here. Segar says that Randell (Ralph) Arundell mar. Elizabeth, da. and h. of John Steward (Seneschall), and had a son Ralph, mar. to Jane, da. and h. of Michael Trerice, temp. Edw. III., whose son Nicholas continued the line. Harl. MS. 4031, fo. 274, attributes two wives to Ralph, son of Oliver Arundell, the first named; the name of the second agrees with Segar's account, but gives the descent as above, without mentioning a second Ralph, who, however, must have existed, as we find from proceedings Cor. Reg. Cornw., 50 Edw.

[*Note continued on next page.*]

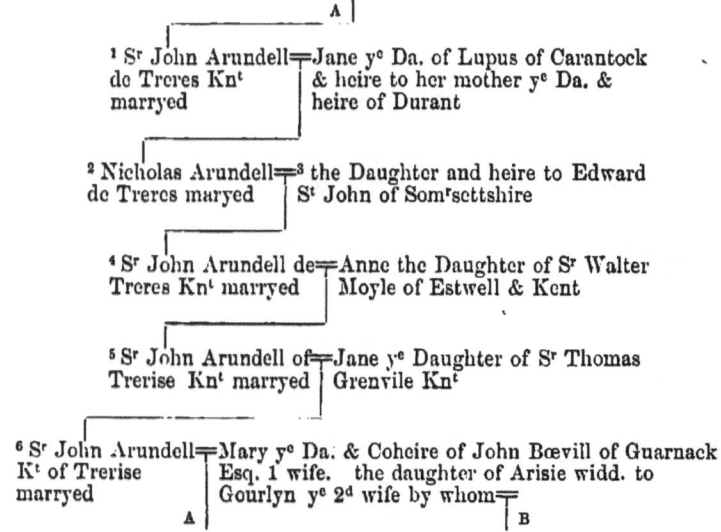

(*Note continued.*)

III., Trin. m. 120, John Tynton v. William Lambron Chivaler and Johanna his wife, that William and Johanna had abducted Nicholas, son and heir of Ralph Arundell of Trerice, a minor in ward of the said John T.
Ped. fin. Cornw. 33 Edw. III., No. 7. Ralph Arundell of Trerees and Johane his wife qu. Sir John Arundell and John Soor def. Govileymur, Govileybyhan, Fentongok, Polscoth, Trerees, Trenans, Trenewith, Trethygy, etc., settled on Ralph A. and Johane his wife and their heirs for ever, rem. to right heirs of Sir John A.
By deed, 2 Mar. 32 Ed. III., Sir Jno. Arundell of Lanherne granted to his *cousin* Ralph Arundel of Trerise lands in Caeruner and Dunsfeld.—*Communicated by Lo. Arundell of Wardour.*

[1] Ped. fin. 1 Hen. V., Cornw., No. 1. Sir Nicholas Trerys and Margaret his wife qu. Sir John Arundell of Trerys and Johana his wife def. Tregantallan, Trenans, etc.
Ped. fin. Cornw. and Devon 2 Hen. V., No. 18. John Cock qu. John Arundell and Johana his wife def. Efford, Thorlbeare, Lanest, Crugantallan al's Tregantallan and Alet, co. Cornw., Whitesday and Hundred of Blaketoriton, Lachebrook, and Hatherlegh, co. Devon. settled on John A. and Johanna his wife, rem. in part to Thomas Woyne and in part to the heirs of John Arundell.
Ped. fin. 12 Hen. VI., Cornw., No. 2. Baldwin Fulford qu. Sir John Arundell of Trerys, Kt., and Johanna his wife def. Marwynchurch.

[2] Inq. 3 Edw. IV., No. 26. Nicholas Arundell of Trerice, settlement of lands on Johanna his wife.

[3] Inq. p. m. 22 Edw. IV., No. 48. Johanna, who was wife of Nicholas Arundell of Trerice, Esq., died 5 July, 22 Edw. IV. Selworth, Luscombe, etc., in co. Somerset settled on Alice, late wife of William Seynt John, for life. Robert Arundell, son of John Arundell, son of Johanna, her grandson and heir, aged 15 and more. Inq. taken in Devon (attached). Manor and advowson of Lappeford, etc., settled on her son Alexander Arundell. Names her dau'r Johanna.

[4] Sheriff of Cornwall. Killed at the Mount when the Earl of Oxford surprised it, 10 Edw. IV. Inq. p. m. Y. O, 7 Hen. VII., No. 111. James Arundell died 31 Dec., 6 Hen. 7. John Arundell, cousin and heir, aged 21 and more.

[5] Inq. p. m. 3 Hen. VIII., No. 1. Sir John Arundell of Trerice, died 12 July, 3 Hen. VIII. Names his wife Johanna, brothers Walter and Robert A. and wife Helena, sons Richard and Edward, and da. Elizabeth. John A., son & h., aged 17 and more, mar. to Maria, da. and coh. of John Devill.

[6] Inq. p. m. 3 Elizab.. pt. 1, No. 8. Sir John Arundell of Trerice, died 25 Nov., 3 Elizab. Names his son John, dau'rs Margaret, Mary, Joane, Grace, and Margery. John A., son of Roger A. his son, his grandson and heir, aged 3 years and more.

THE VISITATION OF THE COUNTY OF CORNWALL. 273

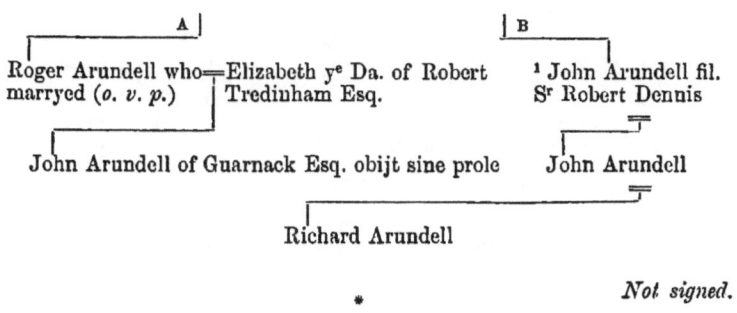

A
Roger Arundell who=Elizabeth yᵉ Da. of Robert
marryed (o. v. p.) | Tredinham Esq.

B
[1] John Arundell fil.
Sʳ Robert Dennis

John Arundell of Guarnack Esq. obijt sine prole

John Arundell

Richard Arundell

*

Not signed.

---

[1] Inq. p. m. 22 Elizab., Pt. i., No. 11. John Arundell of Trerice, Esq., died 22 Elizab. Names his dau'rs Julian, Dorothy, Mary, Anne, and Catherine. John A., his son and h., aged 3 years and more. Will dated 14 Sept., 22 Elizab. Names his late father Sir John A. of Trerice, "Gartbrewde," now his wife, Christopher, John, Robert, Richard, Marie, Jacquett, and Blanche, children of Robert Arundell, Esq., of Camborne, son John A., dau'rs Julian, mar. to Rich. Carew, Alice, Dorothy, Mary, Anne, and Catherine. Overseers Sir John Arundell of Lanherne, Sir John Chichester, Sir Richard Greynvele, and o'rs. Prob. London 26 Nov., 1580.

* John Arundel of North Tamerton, Devon, and Margaret Yeo of Brad-
  worthy, mar. lic. 2 June, 1671.
. Philip Arundel of West Anthony, scarlet dyer, and Elizabeth Deeble
  of same, spinster, mar. lic. 4 June, 1737.
} Act Books, Exeter.

Henry Somaster and Alice Arundell, gent., mar. at Anthony
  in the East   18 Dec., 1583.
James Tremerne and Catherine Arundell mar. at Breage
                                                                 19 Feb., 1600–1.
John Tresillian, gent., and Mary Arundell, gent., mar. at
  Mawgan in Pider   31 March, 1608.
Mr. William Carnsewe and Ann Arundell mar. at Newlyn in
  Pider   1 Dec., 1610.
Thomas Arundel of St. Columb Maj., gen., and Joanna Pyne
  of St. Goran, widow,   mar.   1625.
Edward Arundell, gent., and Jane Carmenowe mar. at St.
  Winnow   27 Nov., 1625.
Emanuel Arundell, clerk, Rector of Stoke Brewer, and Elizab.
  Hope of Sheviock mar. at Sheviock   1626.
John Arundell of Sithney, ar., and Margaret Cock mar. at
  St. Erme   20 July, 1636.
Henry Arundel, ar., bur. at Sithney   4 Dec., 1610.
Francis, son of Gabriel Arundel, bur. at Sheviock   1629.
Dorothy, da. of Geo. Arundle, Esq., bur. at Mawgan in Pider
                                                                 19 June, 1634.
William Arundell, gent., bur. at Newlyn in Pider   10 Maye, 1635.
Saberin, da. of Hugh Arundell, bur. at Mevagissey   2 July, 1636.
Mrs. Ann Arundel, wife of Rich. A. of Lanherne, Esq., bur.
  at St. Columb Minor   1718.
Ye Lady Ann Arundell bur. at St. Columb Minor   8 Sep., 1718.
} Bp. of Exeter's Transcripts.

Margery, da. of William Arundell,   bap.   14 Aug., 1612.
John,   son of   „   „   „   Feb., 1615–6.
Robert,   „   „   „   „   3 Aug., 1617.
John,   „   John   „   „   10 Sept., 1622.
James,   „   William   „   „   16 Nov., 1623.
Christopher, „   „   „   „   17 June, 1627.
Robye Trestene and Grace Arundell   mar. 17 Jan., 1574–5.
Robye Arundell and Elizabeth Trenwith   „   16 Apl., 1583.
John Arundell and Ann Pendarves   „   9 Sept., 1617.
Katherine, wife of Christopher Arundell,   bur. 1 Mar., 1617–8.
} Camborne Par. Reg.

[*Note continued on next page.*

(*Note continued.*)

Charles, son of Rich. Arundel, day labourer, bap.		1725.	St. Erme Par. Reg.
Hugh, son of Francis Arundell	,,	1 Oct., 1603.	St. Ewe Par. Reg.
Alexander Row and Jane Arundell	mar.	14 Nov., 1563.	
Capt. John Arundell	bur.	10 May, 1679.	Falmouth Par. Reg.
Bridget, da. of Sir Thos. Arundell, Knt.,	bap.	24 June, 1604.	Fowey Par. Reg.
Francis St. Aubyn of Crowan and Madron and Mrs. Anne Arundell	mar.	29 April, 1690.	Gulval Par. Reg.
Will. Arundell of Milor and Elizab., da. of Thomas Penwarne of Mawnan	mar.	1651.	Mawnan Par. Reg.
Ann, da. of Thos. Arundell, Esq., of Tolverne. bap.		27 June, 1602.	Menheniot Par. Reg.
Hugh Arundell and Jane Nance	mar.	3 Apl., 1632.	Mevagissy Par. Reg.
George Arundell, Rector		1629.	
Elizab., da. of Walter Arundel and Jone, bap.		1667.	
John, son of John ,, and Ursula, ,,		1668.	
Walter, ,, Rich. ,, and Bridget. ,,		11 Apl., 1684.	
Gregory and Michael, sons of Rich. Arundell and Joane, bap.		1695.	Sheviock Par. Reg.
Rich. Arundel and Bridget Balsou	mar.	19 June, 1683.	
Henry Austin and Mary Arundel	,,	1696.	
Mrs. Kate Arundel, widow,	bur.	1676.	
Walter ,,	,,	1689.	
Bridget ,,	,,	15 Feb., 1693.	
John, son of John Arundel and Elizabeth, bap.		7 May, 1670.	Sithney Par. Reg.
Susan, da. of ,, ,, ,,		1672.	
John Arundel	bur.	25 May, 1671.	
Mrs. Katherin Arundel	,,	19 Apl., 1688.	

Roger Arundell, described in Doomsday Book as holding manors in Dorsetshire and Somerset, 20 Will. Conqueror, had issue Gilbert de Arundell, first son, who mar. Rosamond, da. of John de Novant, and had issue Richard Arundell, who by his wife Juliana had issue Sir Reinfric Arundell, mar. to Alice, da. of Sir J. Lanherne of Lanherne, Cornw. (another pedigree says John de Umfravile mar. the widow of Sir J. Arundell, viz. Alice de Lauherne), by whom he had issue Sir Humphry A., who mar. a da. of John Umfravil and had a son, Sir Reinfric A., temp. H. III. Sir Ralph A., his son, Sheriff of Cornwall 44 Hen. III., mar. Eve, da. of Sir Richard de Rupe, Lord of Tremodrut, Cornwall, who by two deeds, dated Oct. 9, 1259, granted the manors of Trembleth and Tredreysowe to Sir Ralph de A. on his marriage with Eva, his da.—*Communicated by Lord Arundell of Wardour.*

Lay Subsidies, 31 Edw. I., 87/2. John de Umfravile held by Alice his wife one great fee in Lanherne.

Cor. Reg. Roll, Pasch., Edw. I. m. 13 d. Cornw. Ralph Arundell and John de Umfraville and o'rs, concerning a tenement in Conerton,

Inq. p. m. 11 Rich. 2, No. 1. Ralph Arundell, chivaler, son of John A., chivaler, son of John A. of Trembleth, chivaler. John A., bro. of said Ralph, his next heir, aged 22 years and more.

Inq. p. m. 19 Rich. II., No. 15. Johanna Carminowe died 21 Feb. John Arundell, son of Sir John Arundell, son of Elizabeth, da. of Sir Oliver Carminowe, one of her heirs, aged 28 years and more.

Inq. p. m. 35 Hen. VIII., War. and Liv., vol. i., p. 84. John Arundell of Tolfern. Esq., died 2 Mar., 34 Hen. VIII. Names his father John A., sons Thomas, Henry, Richard, and da. Marie, wife Matilda. Alexander A., his son and heir.

Inq. p. m. 16 Eliz., pt. ii., No. 19. Thomas Arundell of Ley, died 3 Mar., 15 Eliz. Alexander A., his son and h., aged 24 at his father's death. Names his sons John, Robert, Thomas, and Digory.

Inq. p. m. 13 Chas. I., pt. ii., No. 18. George Arundell died 29 Nov., 1636. Names his first wife Dorothy and second wife Elizabeth. Charles Arundell, son and h., aged 19 y'rs, 10 mo's, and 27 days. Lands in St. Eval, etc., co. Cornwall, Melcombe, etc., co. Devon.

1 Edw. III., Lay Sub., Cornub., 87/7. John de Arundell and John Arundell in Gorran. William Arundell in St. Michael's Mount.

Ped. fin. Cornw. 46 Hen. III., No. 5. Ralph de Arundell and Eva his wife qu. Rich. de la Roche def. Tremblyth and Tredreyses settled on Eva, rem. to Rich. de la Roche and his heirs.

Ped. fin. 8 Edw. III., Div. Co. Ligula 1, No. 151. John d'Arundell Chivaler qu. Radulphus d'Arundell Parsona eccl'ie de Colombe and John de Aldestowe def. In Manor de Morchard and Yeweton, co. Devon. Man. de Tremleth and Treiey. Medeshole, Tregenstock, Cacrennor, etc., co. Cornwall. John d'Arundell's for life, rem. in tail to John his son. Johann, who was wife of John d'Arundell, held Morchard for life.

Ped. fin. Cornw., 5 Hen. IV., No. 4. John and Edmund Bottreux qu. Ralph Soor of Tolvern def. Tolvern, Carlenuek, etc., settled on Ralph Soor, rem. to Ralph Arundell and Johanna his wife. rem. to Sir John Arundell and his heirs.

Ped. fin. 22 Edw. IV., No. 1. John Arundell, Esq., and Alice his wife qu. Emanuel Assanes Suffianus, Kt., and Amicia his wife def. Bosworgy, Tregose, etc.

[*Note continued on next page.*

(*Note continued.*)
Pipe Roll Cornw., 31 Hen. I. Rob. Arund. (Arundell) paid the sum of 12s. 4d.
Placita de quo Warrant. 30 Edw. I. John Arundell of Lanherne, after his father's death (Sir Ralph), proved his title to the manor of Medeshole (Mitchell) as that which descended to him from his ancestors.
Rot. Canc. K. John, Cornwall. Sibilla q. fuit ux. Willi. Arundell and Henry fil. Willi.
Rot. Litt. Claus. King John, m. 10. Umfrido de Arundell plenar' saisina' de terr'qua fuit Will'o de Arundell. Avunculi ipsius Umfrid. de qua Will's fil. ejusdem Will. de A. qui est cu' inimicis d'ni Reg' est saisana' h'uit et q'm idem Umfrid' die' ip'm. he'ditarie continge. Ap' Skelton viij. die Feb., A.D. 1216.
By deed dated 2 March, 32 Edw. III. (A.D. 1358), Sir John Arundell of Lanherne granted to his *cousin* Ralph Arundell of Trerice lands in Caeruner and Dontsfeld.—*Communicated by Lord Arundell of Wardour.*
Star Chamber 18° Hen. VIII. Lady Katherine Arundel, late wife of Sir John Arundel of Langerne, Knt., dec'd, complained that on September, 8 Hen. VIII., Nicholas Kendell, Wyllyam Vyell, Laurence Kendall, Stephen Kendall, all of the co. Cornw., gentlemen, "with dyvers other malefactors. mysgovernd p'rsons, to the numb. of 16 p'rsons, etc., and the s'd ryotouse p'rsons, etc., assembled about one of the clock of mydnight yn the snyde daye and yere with force of armes, that ys to saye, with bowes, arowes, byllys, stafys, swords, bucklers, hand gonnes, cross bowes, short daggers, and howndes, entyred into the deere parke of y'r snyde subject callyd Holsbery Park, broke down, etc., spoyled and kylled the deere of y'r s'd subject, etc."
Will of Sir John Arundell of Lanherne, dat. 8 Apl., 1433. Proved before Bishop Lacy at Chudlegh 7 June, 1433. Names his da. Johanne, cousin Isabella Bevylle, sons Renfrid and Sir Thomas Arundell.
Will of Sir Thos. Arundell of Lanherne, P. P. C. 1485, Mills 29, mentions "my Lord Dynham, my Lady my moder Dame Jana Dynham," Roger and Charles Dynham.
Will of John Arundell, Bishop of Exeter, 14 Mar., 1503, P. P. C. Names John Arundell, Peter Colsull, Walter Somaster, Humphry Arundell, and Thos. Whityndon, his cousin.
Will of Lady Elizabeth, wid. of Sir Jno. Arundell of Lanherne, 12 June, 1564, P. P. C. 9 Nov., 1564. Names her sons Sir John, Thomas, George, and Edward A., Lady Stourton, dau'rs Cicily, Mary, and Elizabeth, dau'r Katherine Tregian, sister Jane Arundell, bro. Thos. Danet, sister Medley, "little da." Dorothy," god-dau'r Eliz. Tregian. Mrs. Isabell St. Aubyn, Cicily, and Edward A. ex'ors.
Will of Thos. Arundell of Tremere, 29 May, 1571, P. P. C. 8 Nov., 1571, Names Elizabeth his wife and Thomas A. his son, ex'ors. Witnessed by his bro's and sisters, friends, and servants— Cecily Arundell, Eliz. A., George A., Edward A., Jas. Carter, physician, etc.
Will of Jane Arundell of Lanherne, 2 Sept., 1575, P. P. C. 31 Oct., 1577. Names nephew Sir John A., Lady Stourton, nephew and godson John, nephew George, niece Dorothy, nieces Eliz., Cyssell, Margaret, Gertrude, nephew Sir Matthew A., nephews Charles and Edward A., niece Kath. Tregian, niece Cecil the elder, niece and god-da. Mary, niece Eliz'th Hornell or Norwell, niece Isabell Arundell, nephew Thos. A., god-dau'r Eliz. St. Aubyn, niece Mary Tregian. Witnesses Mrs. Marie A. and o'rs.
Will of Edward Arundell of Lanherne, Esq., 15 Oct., 28 Eliz., P. P. C. 10 Nov., 1587. Names bro. Sir John A., Thomas A., son of his brother Thos. A. of Tremere, dec., sister Mrs. Katherine Tregian, nephews John, George, and Thomas A., niece Dorothy, god-d. Eliz'th A., nieces Cecil, Margaret, and Gertrude A., sister Isabell, nieces Turberville and Thomazin Buckland.

Bonnatre.

To all Nobles & Gentles these p'sent letters hereinge or seinge, Wm Hawkestow otherwise called Clarencieux kinge of Armes of the Southmarches of England sendeth humble & dwe recom'endac'on as ap'teyneth, for so much as John Bonnatre Gent. couragiouslie moved to exercise & use gentill & com'endable guyding in such laudable Mann' and forme as maye best sound unto Gentrie, by the wch he shall mowe wth godes grace to attayne unto honor & worshipp hath desired & prayed me the said kinge of Armes y^t by the power & Authoritie by the king's good grace to me in that behalf com'ited, should devise a conysaunce of Armes for the sayd Gent. wch he & his heires might boldly & vowably occupie, Challenge, & Inioy for ev'more w^thout anie p'iudice or rebuke of anie estate or gentill of this realme, at the Instaunce and request of whome I the sayd King of Armes takeinge respect & considerac'on unto the Godly entent & disposition of the sayd gent. have devised for him & his heires these Armes followeinge, that is to say, Gold & Asure p'tie in pale a Chev'on bataly, counter Bataly Gould and Azure, 3 lions enterchanged of the feild, Armyd Gu. a Cornish Chough in the Chev'on, a border Ermyn : wch Armes I of my sayd power and Authoritie, have appointed, given, & granted to and for the said Gent & his said heirs. And by this my p'sent letter appointe give and graunte unto them the same, To have occupie Challenge and enioye w^thout anie preindice or empechment for ev'more. In witnesse whereof I the said kinge of Armes to these p^rsents have sett my seale of Armes. given at London the first daye of the monthe of Aprill in the yeare of the reigne of Kinge Hen. the sixte, after the Conquest the 20th.

Petit.

Sr John Petit knt. who was Cosen & heire to Sr Otes Petit & Dame Eliz. his wife who was Daughter Isabell le Blanch sister to King Hen. III. marryed = Alice Daughter to Sr Michaell Beauchamp kn^t

Sr Michaell Petit kn^t marryed = Amitia Daughter to Sr Thomas Le Archdeacon kn^t

Sr John Petitt kn^t marryed = Marguerite eldest Daughter to Thomas Carminoe Esq.

Sr Michaell Petit knt. marryed = Julyan y^e Daughter of Sr William Talbot knt.

Sr John Petit kn^t marryed = Marguerite y^e Da. of John Trenoweth of Trenowith Esq.

John Petit Esq. marryed = Jane y^e Daughter of Wm Anthorne of Antorne Esq.

Ellen Petit Eldest Daughter & Coheire Marryed John Bœvill of Gwarnack Esq.

*

Not signed.

* A more reliable pedigree for several generations of this ancient family is given below from evidences :—

Sir Rob. Heligan ob. 1272 = Maude da. of Sir Roger Carminowe sister to Gervais C. ob. 1276

Sir Ric. Fitz Yva ob. 1207 = Isabella da. of King John, styled Isabell le Blanche Harl. MS. 4031, fo. 76, and elsewhere Isabel sist. of K. Hen. III.

Sir Wm. Heligan ob. 1286 = Margt. da. of Sir Wm. Dunstanville Lo. of Tchidy ob. 1285

Ric. Fitz Yva ob. 1281 ? =

John Le Petit. Ped. fin. 33 Hen. III. No. 1 Cornw.; Easter Assize Ro. 12 Ed. I. 1284 = Alice da. of Mirabell Durhall (*née* Beauchamp ?)

Sir Belym Heligan ob. 1312 = Isabell ob. 4 Ap., 1313

John Le Petit. Assize Ro. 30 Ed. I. 1302 = Laure da. of . . . . A

Ric. Helegan ob. 1326 = Margaret da. of Sir Roger Prideaux ob. 1302 B

THE VISITATION OF THE COUNTY OF CORNWALL.

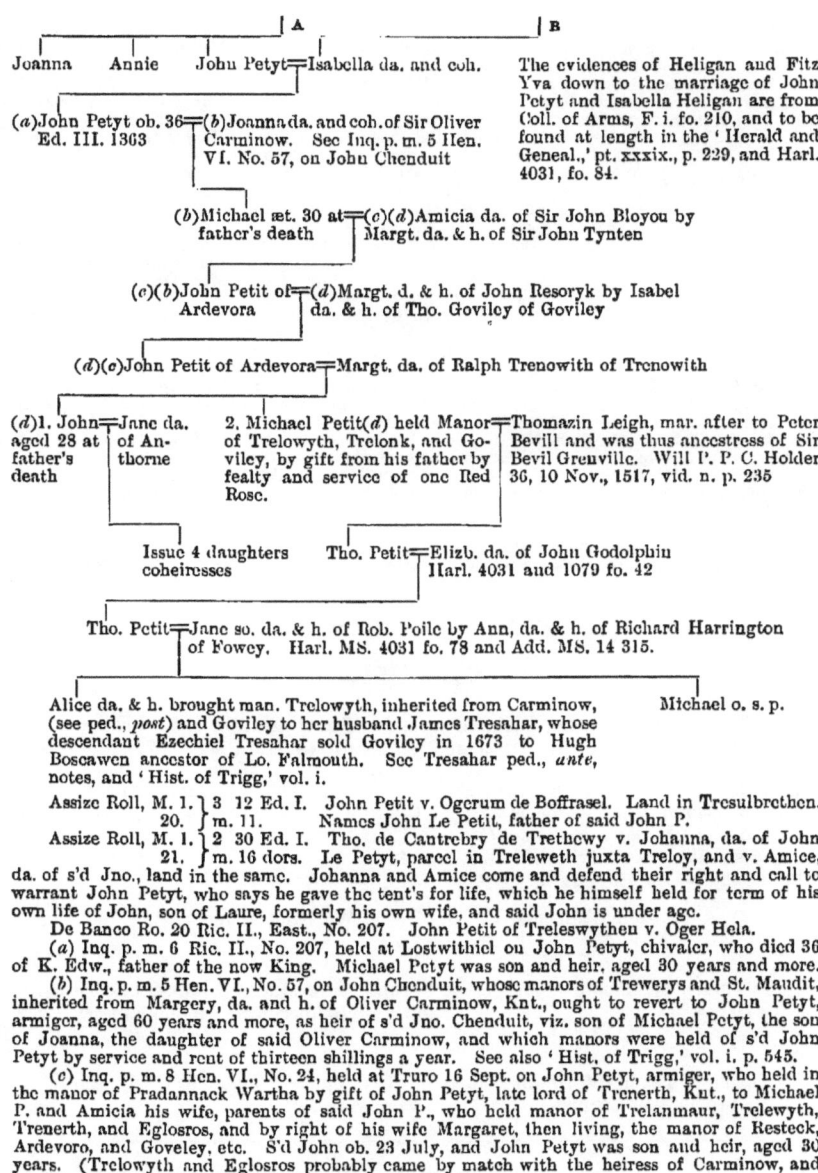

Alice da. & h. brought man. Trelowyth, inherited from Carminow, Michael o. s. p.
(see ped., *post*) and Goviley to her husband James Tresahar, whose
descendant Ezechiel Tresahar sold Goviley in 1673 to Hugh
Boscawen ancestor of Lo. Falmouth. See Tresahar ped., *ante*,
notes, and ' Hist. of Trigg,' vol. i.

Assize Roll, M. 1. } 3   12 Ed. I.   John Petit v. Ogerum de Boffrasel. Land in Tresulbrethon.
          20.   } m. 11.   Names John Le Petit, father of said John P.
Assize Roll, M. 1. } 2   30 Ed. I.   Tho. de Cantrebry de Trethewy v. Johanna, da. of John
          21.   } m. 16 dors.   Le Petyt, parcel in Treleweth juxta Treloy, and v. Amice,
da. of s'd Jno., land in the same. Johanna and Amice come and defend their right and call to
warrant John Petyt, who says he gave the tent's for life, which he himself held for term of his
own life of John, son of Laure, formerly his own wife, and said John is under age.
De Banco Ro. 20 Ric. II., East., No. 207.   John Petit of Treleswythen v. Oger Hela.
(*a*) Inq. p. m. 6 Ric. II., No. 207, held at Lostwithiel on John Petyt, chivaler, who died 36
of K. Edw., father of the now King. Michael Petyt was son and heir, aged 30 years and more.
(*b*) Inq. p. m. 5 Hen. VI., No. 57, on John Chenduit, whose manors of Trewerys and St. Maudit,
inherited from Margery, da. and h. of Oliver Carminow, Knt., ought to revert to John Petyt,
armiger, aged 60 years and more, as heir of s'd Jno. Chenduit, viz. son of Michael Petyt, the son
of Joanna, the daughter of said Oliver Carminow, and which manors were held of s'd John
Petyt by service and rent of thirteen shillings a year. See also ' Hist. of Trigg,' vol. i. p. 545.
(*c*) Inq. p. m. 8 Hen. VI., No. 24, held at Truro 16 Sept. on John Petyt, armiger, who held in
the manor of Pradannack Wartha by gift of John Petyt, late lord of Trenerth, Kut., to Michael
P. and Amicia his wife, parents of said John P., who held manor of Trelanmaur, Trelewyth,
Trenerth, and Eglosros, and by right of his wife Margaret, then living, the manor of Resteck,
Ardevoro, and Goveley, etc. S'd John ob. 23 July, and John Petyt was son and heir, aged 30
years. (Trelowyth and Eglosros probably came by match with the heiress of Carminow, and
were held under Dynham. See Carminow ped., *post*.)
Inquisit. Book of Hen. VI. Jno. Arundel held Treris and John Petyt held Predannck,
formerly held by Bp. of Exon.
Inquisit. Book of Hen. VI. Sir John Arundel of Trerys, John Petyt of Arworthell, and o'rs
held half a knight's fee in Trelonk, etc.
(*d*) Inq. p. m. 34 Hen. VI., No. 27, held at Leskeard 28 Oct., 34 H. VI., on John Petyt, ar.   S'd
[*Note continued on next page.*

(*Note continued.*)

John held parcel of manor of Predannack Wartha by gift of John Petyt, Knt., late lord of Trenerth, to Michael Petyt and Amicia his wife, etc., of whom s'd John in writ named was heir, viz. the son of John, the son of s'd Michael and Amicia, held of the King in puro socagio as of his Castle of Launceston as of Duchy of Cornw., etc. S'd John held land by gift of John Tynten, Knt., by ind're made to Margaret his daughter and her heirs, and s'd John Petyt was heir of said Margt., viz. son of John, son of Amicia, the daughter of aforesaid Margaret. And s'd John held by gift of Oto, lord of Bodrugan, to Ralph Resoryk and his heirs, of which Ralph s'd John was heir, viz. son of Margaret, the daughter of s'd Ralph. And further the said John P. gave the manor of Trelowyth and certain lands in Trelonk to his son Michael Petit, to be held of the same John by fealty and service of one red rose. S'd John P. ob. 10 June last, and John Petyt, son and heir, aged 28 years and more.

Parliam. Writs, A.D. 1297. Michael Le Petit returned for Cornw. as holding £20 in rents per an. sum. to perform mil. service with horses and arms beyond seas. Muster in Lond. Sunday next after Octave of St. John the Bap., 25 Ed. I.

" " " 1302. Michael le Petit Knight of Shire for Cornwall.
" " " 1311. Michael le Pedit, Petyt, Petit, Supervisor of the Army for Cornw., and also leader of the levies, 4 Ed. II.
" " " 1314. Michael le Petit Knt. of Shire for Cornw, 7 Ed. II.

Pat. Roll 1 Rich. III. Michael Petit on the Commission of Peace for Cornw.

Ped. fin. 33 Hen. III., No. 1, Easter, Cornw. John Le Petit and Alice his wife, who, with her sister Emma, were coh. of Mirabell. once wife of Roger Durhull.

Ped. fin. 47 Hen. III., Mich., No. 20. John Le Petit and Alice his wife pet. Steph. de Bellocampo. Said Stephen granted to John and Alice, Benherton and lands held of Rob. Carminow.

Ped. fin. 17 Ed. I., No. 6. Michael Le Petyt qu. John Le Petyt def. Lands in Trenerth, Predanckwartha, etc., which s'd John held of s'd Michael, and which s'd Michael had of gift of s'd John.

Ped. fin. 8 Hen. VII., Trin., Cornw. Rich. Harrington de Fowey mercat. qu. Tho. Glover and ux. def. Mess., yard, and wharf in Fowey.

For more on Petit, see Sir John Maclean's 'Hist. of Trigg,' vol. i., pp. 319, 546, 683; vol. ii., p. 252.

Tanner.

This and the following pedigree are indexed in Harl. MS. 1162, but are not to be found. They are therefore taken from Harl. MS. 1079.

ARMS. 1. TANNER. *Arg. on a chief Sa. 3 men's heads Or.* 2. TREGARTHAN. *Arg. a chevron betw. 3 escalops Sa.* 3. CORNEWALL. *Arg. a lion ramp. Gu. within a border engr. Sa. bezanté.* 4. CHAMBERLAIN.[1] *Arg. on a bend Sa. 5 bezants.* See Harl. MS. 1079, fo. 142 b.

CREST. *A demi-talbot Or, ears Arg.*

John Tanner=....d. of....Whitting of Wood

George Tanner of Colampton in Devon=Margret d. & coh. of....Tregartyn   This Margrett is descended as heire to Cornewall, Chamb'laine, & Pever

Anthonie Tanner of Brannell in St. Stphen's in Cornwall=Elizab. d. of....Tylley of Canington in Com. Som'sett

Joane wife to....Pomeroy   John Tanner of Brannell a⁰ 1620=Katherin d. of Tho. Roscarrok of Roscarrok   Robert 2 sonne

A

---

[1] The fourth quarter is assigned to Pever, who bore *Arg. on a chev. gu. 3 fleurs de lis, or.*

THE VISITATION OF THE COUNTY OF CORNWALL. 279

A

| Lewes 2 sonne | Barnard Tanner eldest sonne æt. 26 aº 1620 | Arther 3 sonne — John 4 sonne * | Jane wife to John Pye | Elizabeth — Dorothy | Ann — Mary |

Not signed.

Wallis al's Darte.

ARMS. *Gu. a fess and canton ermine.*
CREST. *A Bonfire ppr.*

p' Rob't Cooke Clar. aº 1590 32 Q. Eliz. to Lewes Wallis al's Darte

John Wallis al's Darte==Joane d. of Rob. Courtney
of Barstable │ of Molland in Devon

┌─────────────────────────┬─────────────────────────┬─────────────────────────┐

Lewes Wallis al's Darte of Meve-==Eliz. d. of Tho. Roscar-   Grace wife to Powle
gesie in Cornw. aº 1620   reck of Roscarrock   Worthe of Barstable

¹ Lewes 4 │ Phillip in Bohemia 3 sonne │ ² Jane wife to Jo. Tremayne of Tregonowe │ John eldest== sonne æt.32 aº 1620 │ ³ Charles 2 sonne of the Ynner Temple London

Not signed.

---

* Barnard Tanner, ar., and Julian, da. of Sir Rich. Buller, mar. 21 Nov., } Bp. of Exeter's
  1625, at St. Stephen's juxta Ash. } Transcripts.
Thomas Prowse of Taunton, gent., and Agnes, dau.
   of John Tanner, Rector of Offwell, mar. lic. July 3, 1628.
George Tanner of Farringdon, gent., and Edith
   Harlewyn of Sidmouth, mar. lic. Aug. 7, 1630. Act Books, Exeter.
Humphry Tanner of Crecombe and Johanna Park-
   house of Witheridge, mar. lic. Nov. 21, 1681.
John Masey of London, and Ann Tanner of St.
   Enedor, Cornwall, mar. lic. May 21, 1691.
Barnard, son of Barnard Tanner, Esq., bap. } Bp. of Exeter's
   at St. Stephen's by Ash 31 Mar., 1633. } Transcripts.
Anthony Tanner, gent., and Honor Sibly, mar. 19 Oct., 1704. St. Minver Par. Reg.
Elizab. ,, bur. 1652. St. Tudy Par. Reg.
Ind're dated 8 May, 26 Charles II. Between Richard Batten of Collombe Major, (J. M.)
Doctor of Physic, and Anthony Tanner of St. Enodoc, gent. Conveyance of premises
called Nampean in St. Enoder.—*Penes* Miles C. Seton, Esq.
For Anthony Tanner of Court, Esq., *vide* Abstracts of Deeds, *ante*, p. 238.
1669, Oct. 10. John Tanner of Court, Esq., one of the Trustees on settlement after
marriage of Chamond Roscarrock of Roscarrock, and Grace his wife.
   Ind're dated 23 Mar., 1675. Betw. Honor Carter the younger, one of the daughters
and coheirs of John Carter, late of St. Columb, Esq., decᵈ, of the one part, and Anthony
Tanner of the parish of St. Eneder, gent., and John Beauford of St. Columb, clerk.
Lease for a year of various manors and bartons, which descended to her as coheir of
John Carter, decᵈ. Seal of Arms, *two lions combattant.*
   Indorsed. Settlement upon the marriage of Honor Carter and William Silly.—*Penes*
Sir John Maclean.

¹ Bap. 10 Dec., 1597. ² Bap. 18 Dec., 1591 ; mar. 22 Nov., 1618. } Mevagizzy Par. Reg.
³ Bap. 19 May, 1590. } (J. M.)

Bodmin.

ARMS—none. A SEAL, representing *A King, crowned and sceptred, sitting under a canopy.*
INSCRIBED.—S. . COMMUNE . BURGI . ET . VILLÆ . BODMINÆ.

This is the Com'on seale of the Towne & ancient Borrough of Bodmin, wch hath beene enabled by his Maties most Noble progenitors wth divers lib'ties, priviledges, and greate immunities, the goverm^t Consistinge of a Maior & 36 Cheife Burgesses, wch are called the Com'on Counsell of the sayde Towne & Borroughe : the Election of the Maior being yearely the 24 day of Septemb. The Maior, Towne Clarke, & last Antecedent Maior, being Justices of the Peace wthin the sayd Borough. The Maior being Coroner wthin the Borrough. The Maior & Towne Clarke have power to take Recognizances of Debtors according to the Statute of Acton Burnell and Westm^r. they are to have a Com'on seale for all grauntes. forayne Justices of the peace are prohibited to intromit therein for causes wthin the sayd Borough. all wch priviledges & imunities were confirmed & ratified by o^r most gratious Sov'aigne Ladye Queen Elizab. of famous memorie, in the 36 yeare of hir raygne. And at the time of this p^{r}sent visitation, the 3 of Octob., 1620, was Wm Prist, Maior; Nicho. Sprye, Towne Clarke; Rob't Wilton, Thomas Helliar, Rob't Hartwell, John Stone, Nicho. Webber, Raph Turney, Rich. Durant, John Corey, Will'm Stone, and John Edye, 12 of the Cheife Burgesses wthin the sayd Towne and Borroughe of Bodmin.

WILLIM PRIST, Maiore.
NICHO. SPREY, Towne Clark.

the fee payd 40^s.   RICHARD DURANT.

Dunhevcd al's Launceston.

ARMS.—*A triple circular tower within a border charged with eight towers domed.*
CREST.—*A lion's head between two ostrich plumes, all rising out of a ducal coronet.*
INSCRIBED.—SIGILLUM . DUNHEVIDI . BOWROGH . ALIAS . LAUNCESTON.

This is the Com'on seale of the towne & Borroughe of Dunehened al's Launceston, wch by the auncient Kings of this land have beene endewed wth many previledgs, and great immunities, & incorporated in the 2 & 3 yeare of Kinge Phillip & Queene Mary, by the name of Maior, Aldermen, & Cominaltie of the

THE VISITATION OF THE COUNTY OF CORNWALL. 281

Borroughe of Dunhened al's Launcesto', & by that name to have perpetuall Succession, & enabled in Lawe to purchase Lands & Tenements & Likewize to assigne the same, and by the same name to plead & be impleaded, and that the Maior & Aldermen should have a Com'on Seale for their affairs, and that the Borroughe & Corporac'on should consist of eight Aldermen besides the Maior, wch should yearely be Chosen at the Nativitie of o^r Ladye in Septemb.; wch Maior & Aldermen shall be called the Com'on Counsell, & have power to Chose a Record^r, wch Maior & Recorder shalbe iustices of the peace wthin the sayd Borroughe, & no other Justice to intromitt therin, with manie other Priviledges & immunities, as by their Charter doth appeare. And at this present Visitac'on, the 27th daye of Septemb', 1620, was Thomas Morton, Maior; Sr Anthonie Rowse, Recorder; John Gennis, Rich. Estcott, Arthure Pypard, Nicho. Baker, Hugh Vygars, Hen. Cary, George Hexte, Oswold Cooke, Aldermen; and Phillip Kinge, Towne Clarke of the sayd Towne & Borrough of Dunheved al's Launceston.

THOMAS MORTON, Maior.

the fee payde	JOHN GENYS.	HENRY CARY.
£3 6s.	RIC. ESTCOTT.	GEORG HEAXTT.
	ARTHUR PIPARD.	OSWALD COOKE.
	HUGH VIGURES.	PHILLIPP KING.

East Lowe.

No Arms or Seal given.

This is the Common Seale of the towne and Borough of East Lowe in the Countye of Cornwall, incorporated the 8 day of January, in the 29 yeare of Queene Elizabeth, by the name of Maior and Burgesses, and by that name to have perpetuall succession, and enabled in lawe to purchas landes & tenements & likewise to assigne the same, and by the same name to pleade and be impleaded, & that the Borough & Corporac'on should consist of 9 Burgesses, whereof one of them should yearly be chosen for Maior. To have power to chouse a Recorder. And at this present Visitac'on, the 12 day of October, 1620, was John Eger, Maior; Sir Reginald Mohun, Knight and Barronet, Recorder, Phillip Fitz Williams, Edmond Fitz Williams. Henry Cloake, Tho. Egar, Dennis Fitz Williams, Daniell Chubb, Will'm Parris, Phillip Williams, Burgesses; and Joseph Bastard, Steward and towne Clerke of the same towne and borough.

JOHN EGER, meyr.

Grampound.

SEAL.—*A bridge of two arches over a river,—the dexter end shews the passage, and at the sinister end is a tree. Against the bridge a shield charged with a lion ramp. within a border bezantée. Inscribed* SIGILUM . COMMUNE . BURGI . GRAMPONI.E.

This is the Com'on Seale of ye towne and Boroughe of Grampound, wch was anciently incorporated by the name of Maior and 8 Burgesses, and at the time of this present Visitac'on, the sixt day of Octob., 1620, was Bennet Perdew, Maior, John Hawkins, Rich. Harison, John Sobye, Matthew Woldridge, Thomas Come, John Hawkins, Junio^r, Michaell Treglyne, & Thomas Hancock, Burgesses of the same Towne & Borroughe.

B. P., maior.
JOHN HAWKYNS.
MATTHEW WOULRYDGE.

Helstone.

No arms. A SEAL, representing *An angel winged, bearing a shield charged with the three lions of England, and thrusting a lance into the open mouth of a dragon at his feet, the whole flanked by two towers domed. Inscribed* SIGILLUM . COMUNITATIS . VILLE . DE . HELLESTONE . BURGTH.

This is the Com'on Seale of the Towne & Borroughe of Helstone in Cornwall, incorporated by Kinge John in the 2^d yeare of his raigne by the name of Maior & Burgesses. And at this present Visitac'on, the 9th day of October, 1620, was John Rowe, Maior; Tho. St. Aubin, Esquire, Will'm Robinson, Alexander Bolytho, John Harbert, John Allexander, Thomas James, Rob't Cock, Will'm Penhalurick, Daniell Bedford, Will'm Trewin, Patrick Pasemere, & John Cock, Burgesses; Fran. Godolphin of Godolphin, Esquire, Recorder; & Thomas Randall, Steward of the sayd Towne & Corporac'on.

The m'ke + of JOHN ROE, Maior.
THOMAS SEYNTAUBYN.
WILLIAM ROBINSON.
THOMAS JAMES.
JOHN HARBERT.

Liskerett al's Liskerd.

No Arms. SEAL.—*A fleur-de-lis between two birds. Inscribed* SIGILLUM . COM-MUN . BURGI . DE . LISKERTT.

This is the Com'on Seale of the Towne & borough of Liskerett al's Liskerd, anciently incorporated by the name of Maior and Burgesses of Liskerett al's Liskerd, and re-incorporated ye sixte daye of July in the 29th yeare of Queene Elizb. by the same name of Maior & Burgesses, & by that name to have p'petuall Succession, & enabled in Lawe to purchase Lands & Tennements & Liberties, & likewise to assigne the same, and by the same name to plead and be impleaded, and that the Borrough & Corporac'on shall consist of 9 Burgesses, wch shalbe called the Com'on Counsell of the sayd Boroughe, wherof one for the time beinge should be yearly Chosen for Maior, to have power to chose a steward and Recorder, and y^t the Mair & Burgesses should have a Com'on Seale for there affayres, & that the Maior, Recorder shalbe Justices of the peace within the sayd Borrough, which newe Corporac'on graunted by Queen Elizb. John Hunkin was the first Maior, wth divers other previledges and immunities, as by their Charter doth appeare. And at this present visitac'on, the 12 daye of Octob', 1620, was Edward Chapman, Maior; Sr William Wreye, Kt., Recorder; John Hunkin, gent., high Steward; Thomas Jane, John Vosper, Martin Sampson, John Pett, Jeffrie Clarke, John Taperell, and Will'm Fuge, Cheife Burgesses; and Walt' Nicholls, Towne Clark of the sayd Towne & Boroughe.

EDWARD CHEPMAN, Maior.

JO. HUNKYN.
THO. JANE.
MARTIN SAMPSON.

for GEFFERI ✠ CLARKE.
WILLIAM FUDGE.
WALTER NICHOLL.

Pensance.

SEAL.—*St. John the Baptist's head in a charger. Over the Inscription* ANNO . 1614. *Circumscribed* PENSANSE . DOMINI.

The Village of Pensance incorporated by o^r Sov'aigne Lord Kinge James, the 9 day of Maye in the 12 yeare of his highnes raigne, by the name of Maior, Aldermen, and Comunaltie of the village of Pensance, & by that name to be one bodie booth in name & deede, & to have p'petuall succession, & to be p'sons capable in Lawe to have, purchase, & posses laudes & Tennements, previledges & Jurisdictions, with divers other im'unities, & by that name of Maior, Aldermen, & Comunaltie to plead & be impleaded, & to have a com'on seale for their publick busines. That the Maior be chosen yearly, & 8 of the discretest sort to be Aldermen of the said Village, wch shalbe called of the Com'on Counsell, & 12 other men to be chosen wch shalbe called assistants, wth divers other priviledges & im'unities, as by their Charter doth appeare. And at the time of this p^{r}sent Visitac'on, the 9 day of Octob', 1620, was Will'm Noseworthie, Maior; John St. Aubin, Esq., Recorder; John Madderne, John Clyes, Rob't Dunkin, John Game, Rog. Polkinhorne, Will'm Madderne, Rob't Luke, Pasco Ellys, Aldermen and Nicho. Hixt, Towne Clarke of the said Village and Corporac'on.

JOHN MADDERN.
JAMES BONITHON.

Portbyan al's West Loe.

No Arms. Seal.—*A man wearing a sword, and carrying a bow in his right hand and an arrow in his left. Inscribed* s. . comune . burgi . portbian . als . west . lowe.

This is the Com'on Seale of the Towne & Borroughe of Portbyan al's West Loe, incorporated by the name of Maior & Burgesses the 14 daye of February in the 16 yeare of Queene Elizab. by the same name of Maior & Burgesses, to have p'petuall succession, & enabled in Lawe to purchasse lands & Tennem¹ˢ & likewize to assigne the same, & by the same name to plead & be impleaded, and that the Borroughe & corporac'on should consist of 12 Burgesses, wherof one for y⁰ time beinge shalbe yearely Chosen for Maior, and to have power to Chouse a Steward, & that the Maior & Burgesses shall have a Com'on seale for their affaires, wᵗʰ divers other priviledges & immunities, as by their Charter dothe appeare. And at this present visitac'on, the 12 day of Octob., 1620, was John Francis, Maior ; John Harris, Esq., Recorder ; John Sharpe al's Garrett, John Grove, Will'm Chanler, Stephen Gerre, Walter Whitt, Walter Lillyck, Walter Babbidge, John Grylls, Rob't Hearle, Ambrose White, Burgesses of the same towne and Boroughe ; & Thomas Jane, Towne Clarke of the same.

Saltashe.

Two Seals.—1. Sigillum Aquate Saltasche. *A three-masted ship riding at anchor.* 2. Sigillum Salteashe. *A shield charged with a lion ramp. within a border bezantée. The point of the shield rests on waves, over it is a prince's coronet, and on each side of it an ostrich feather.*

This is the Com'on Seale of the Towne & Borroughe of Saltashe in the Countie of Cornwall. And at this present Visitac'on, the 14 daye of Octob., 1620, was Hen. Cloberie, Maior ; Sʳ Rich. Buller, Kt., Recorder ; John Randall, Will'm Biele, Samson Bonde, Will'm Maynard, Will'm Wills, Hen. Martin, Will'm Michell, Rich. Furlonge, & Phillip Randall, Aldermen ; and Will'm Wills, Towne Clarke of the sayd Towne and Borroughe of Saltashe.

Henry Cloberye, Mayor.

William Biell. Sampson Bond.
Henrye Martyn. William Wylls.

THE VISITATION OF THE COUNTY OF CORNWALL. 285

Tregonny.

ARMS.—*A pomegranate seeded, slipped, and leaved.* Inscribed SIGILLUM . COM . BURGO . DO . TRIGONI.

This is the Com'on Seale of the Towne & Borroughe of Tregonny, incorporated by the name of Maior & Burgesses, and at the time of this present visitac'on, the first day of Octob', 1620, was Mr Henry Pomeroy, Maior; Phillip Jago, Hugh Munday, Rich. Carveigh, Arthure Osgood, John Jago, Will'm Cardew, John Collins, and Nicho. Bonithan, Nowe Burgesses of the sayd Towne & Borrough of Tregonye.

HENRY POMEROY, Maior.
HUGH MONDAY.
ARTHUR OSGOOD.

Trwro.

ARMS.—*On a base barry wavy of four, charged with two fish, a three-masted ship in full sail.*

Also two SEALS. One representing *A vessel with one mast sailing, one fish in the sea, and Inscribed* SIGILLUM . COMMUNITATIS . DE . TRURU. The other, *A one-masted vessel with no sail, two fishes in pale in the sea, and Inscribed* SIGILLUM . COMMUNE . TRURURIE.

fee payd £3 6^s.

These are the ancient Armes & Comon Seales of the Towne and Borroughe of Trwro, wch was incorporated by the name of Maior and Burgesses, by Reignold, Erle of Cornwall, Naturcall sonne to Henry the first, wch was done by Rich. Lucy al's Lacam, teste, Rogeri de Vallitort, Rob'te de Edunett Anuilla, Ricardo de Raddona, Alredo de S^{to} Martino, sealed wth an ancient seale wth a man on Horsbacke. And at the time of this present Visitac'on, the 9th daye of Octob., 1620, was Grigorie Frigens, Maior; Tho. Burgesse, Rich. Daniell, James Lawarren, Will'm Ketcher, Aldermen; Evarar. Edmondes, Hen. Will'ms, Edw. Kestell, Wm Avery, Walt' Penarth, Germain Grees, Fran. Noseworthie, Fran. Grevill, Cutbert Sidnam, Hump. Sidnam, Gawen Carverth, Tho. Burgesse, junior, Rich. Hill, John Adlington, Nicho. Paule, Edw. Grose, Robt. Kempe, Nicho. Stephens, John Parnall, & Will'm Cozen, Burgesses; Hugh Boscawen, Esq., Recorder; & John Michell, Towne Clarke of the sayd Borongh and Corporac'on. Wee finde also that the Maior of Trwro hath alwayes beene & still is Maior of Fallmouthe, as by an ancient graunt now in the Custodie of the said Maior & Burgesses as doth appeare.

GREGO. FRIGGENS, Mayor.   THOMAS BURGESSE.
HENRY WILLEAMS.   JAMES LESWAREN.

SUPPLEMENT.*

Arscott.

This descent of Mules to Dabernon, & from him to Battyn & soe to Arscott, was taken out of an antient pleadinge which was shewed unto us in our visitation by Mʳ Arthure Arscot of Dunsland, & is at this day remaining in his hand in Aº Dm' 1620.

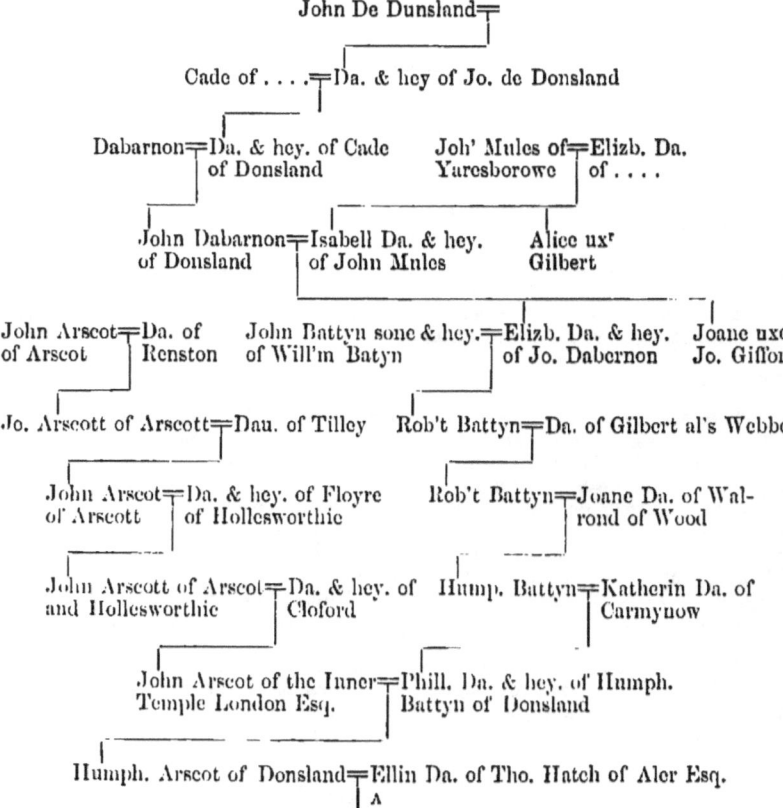

* All these pedigrees in the MS. are noted "This descent is to be entered in the Visitac'on of Devon."

THE VISITATION OF THE COUNTY OF CORNWALL.

A

John Arscot of Donsland liveing 1620 = Mary Da. of Tho. Monke of Powdridge Esq.

    Arthure Arscot of Donsland in = Ebbott Da. of Leonard
    Com. Devon liveing 1620   Yeo Esq.

    Mary 1 Da. at. 19, 1620   Grace 2 Da. atat. 18, 1620

Not signed.

Arscott.

John Arscott of Donsland =

Tho. Arscott of Hollisworthie in Com. Devon =

Willm Arscott of Hollisworthie =

Humph. Arscott of Hoieworthie = Elizb. Da. of Fran. Penkevill of Rossara

Julian   Rossackclea Arscott of Hollisworthie = Gartru. Da. of Geo. Arondell of
a da.   in Com. Devon liveing 1620   Lanherne in Com. Cornwall

ROSICLEER ARSCOTT.

Barkley.

John Barkeley of Kingsbridge = Joane Da. of Leigh of Leigh
in Com. Devon   in Com. Devon

Tho. Barkeley of Okenburye = Agnes Da. of Jo. Hele of Lucestow
in Com. Devon   in Com. Devon

Tho. Barkeley of Okenbury in = Elizb. Da. of Geo. Southcott
Com. Devon liveing 1620   of Bovy in Com. Devon

Hen. 2.   Elizab. 1   Tho. sone &   Mary 3   Joane 5   7. Margaret   9. Gar-
—   hey. atat. 16   —   —   —   trude
        Agnes 2   1620   Fran. 4   Jane 6   8. Bridget

THO. BARKLEY.

Blackall.

ARMS.—*Paly of six Or and Sa., on a chief Gu. 3 bezants.*

John Blackall of Exiter=Da. of Parrat of Dorsetsh.
|
Tho. Blackall of Cowick=Mary Da. of Geo. Southcott of
in Com. Devon | Callwoodley in Com. Devon
|
John Blackall of Cowick in=Jane Da. of Raphe
Com. Devon liveing 1620 | Haymer of London
|
John sone & heire at. 6 1620   Mary a dau. atat. 1 1620

JOHN BLACKALL.

Calmady.

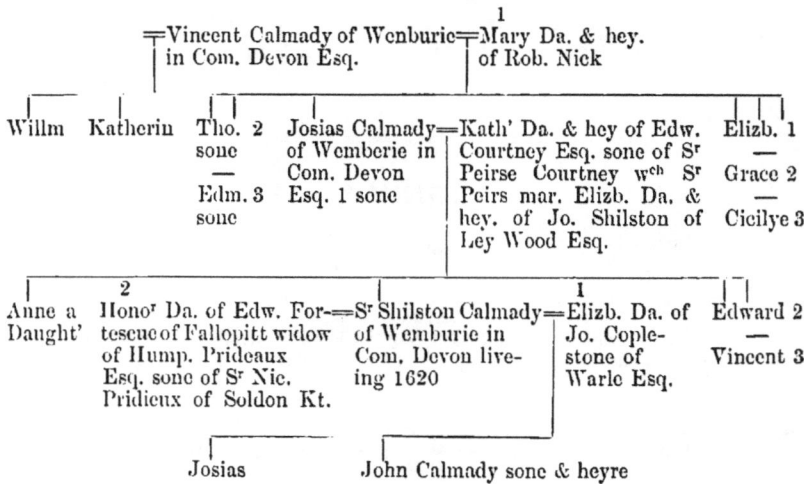

Not signed.

Fownes.

To Inquire for the Crest to this Coate in the Countie of Worcester.

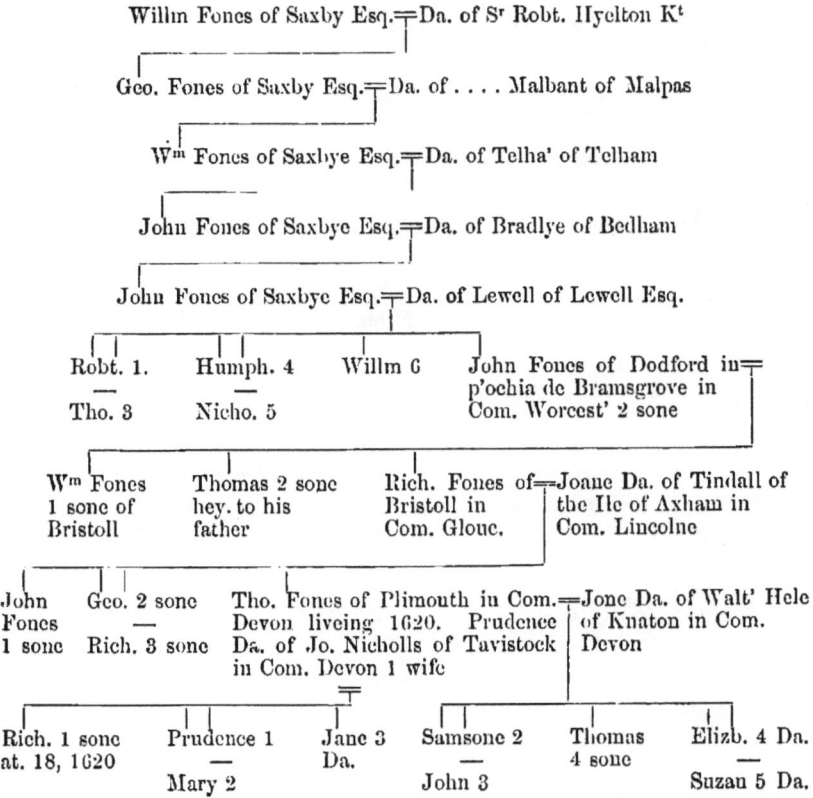

THO. FOWNES.

Hunkin.

Sciant p'sentx et futuri qd. ego Will's Boturnell dedi concessi et hac p'senti carta mea indent. confirmavi Willo Hunkin et Isabelle filie Thomæ Trenger om'ia messug. terr' et tent'a mea in Southkymbar & in Twelmona More que nup. habui ex dono et feoffamento eiusdem Will. Hunkyn &c. Hijs testibus Willo Devioke, Willo Littleton, Rico Clemens, Tho. Clemens, Nicho. Scheplyn, et alijs. Dat. apud Southkymbar die Sabbathi prox post festu' S'cti Luce Evangeliste a° Regni regis Hen. VI. post conquest' 27.

Willm's Hunkyn a° 27 H. VI. of South-=Isabella filia Tho.
kimbare in Com. Cornub.   Trenger

John Hunkin of Southkimbare=Elizab. filia Brendon 2 E. VI.

Ricus Hunkin filius et heres of Southkimbare=Matilda filia .... Alwin

John Hunkin of Liskerd=Lore filia Tho. Mayowe de
fil. et heres   Minheniott in Cornw.

Gracia filia Andrew Cloberie=John Hunkin de Gather-=Jana filia Johis Conock
of Bradston in Com. Devon | ley in Com. Devon fil. et | of Treworgay in Com.
uxor 1   her.   Cornw. ux. 2

Joseph fil. et heres   Radagunda   Ricus Hunkin 2   John 3 fil. ætat.   Maria
atatis 10 annoru'   ætat. 11   filius ætat. 5   unius. ann. 1620   ætat. 4

Not signed.

Roll.

John Cwthy=

Joane Da. & hey. of Jo. Cwthi=Rob. Stonard

John Stonord sone & heire=

Raph Kaill=Mawd Da. & hey. of John Stonord

Willm Kaill=
A

THE VISITATION OF THE COUNTY OF CORNWALL. 291

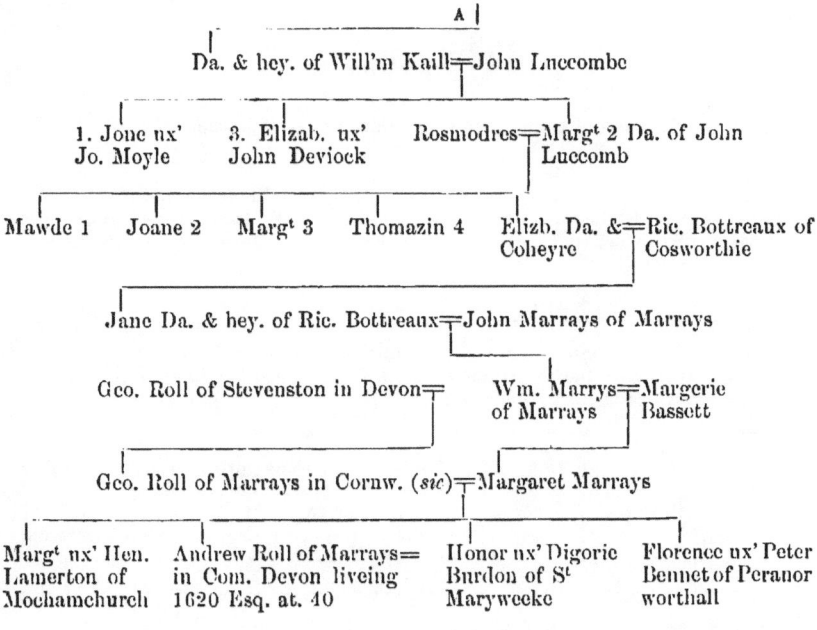

Not signed.

𝕌𝕡𝕡𝕖𝕥𝕠𝕟.

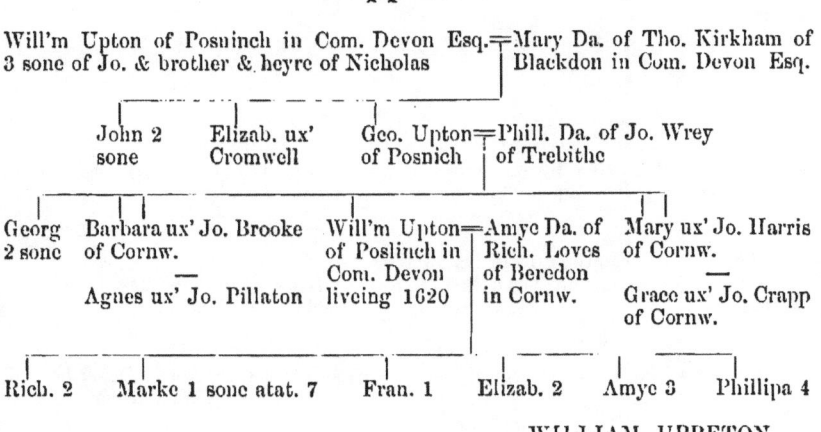

WILLIAM UPPETON.

292   THE VISITATION OF THE COUNTY OF CORNWALL.

Wychehalse.

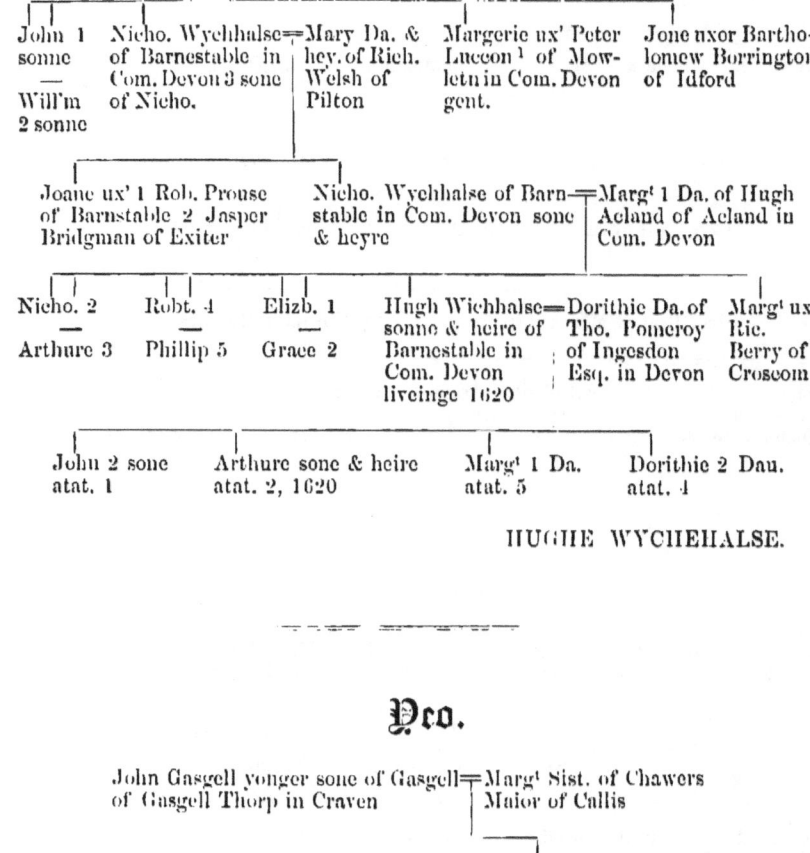

HUGHE WYCHEHALSE.

Yeo.

---

[1] Peter Lutton of Cofford in Parish of Kenton. Visit. Devon, 1620, Harl. MS. 1163, fo. 19.

THE VISITATION OF THE COUNTY OF CORNWALL. 293

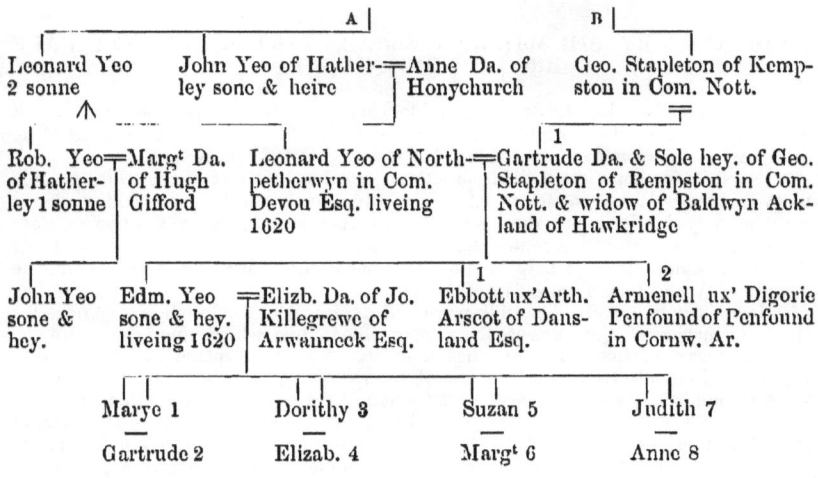

Not signed.

COMPLAINT BY SIR WILLIAM SEGAR, GARTER, AGAINST RALF BROOK, YORK HERALD.

Imprimis for that lowlye & humble cariag where he hath beene .... it generally knowne how proudly & audaciously he hath ever caried himself & especially to his own societte abusing & slandering the Kings Armes.

For his trecherie & devilish practises sufficiently appeared in that notable plott against Sr Wm Segar for the Armes of Brandon, whom he pretended was for a gentleman lyving in spaine the circumstances wherof being so well knowne, were tedious to repeate being intended for the subversion & utter undoing of the saide Sr Will'm Segar Garter principal King of Armes by his subtile practice to confirme a coate of Armes to the hangman of london.*

Item the like plotte he lately practised against the whole office of Armes for the confirmation of the like cote for one Renolds in Spaine for whom he had drawne a coate & crest of his owne devisinge & written the subscription himself naming the saide Reinolds to be the 3 sonne of an Esquier of Burford in Oxfordsh. the same Reinolds being there a meane tradesman & never reputed a gentleman.

Item for his further treacherie & abuses even towards his maiestie In that question of precedence betweene the Erles younger sonnes & the knights privie counsellors when we had received a special comande from his highnes to make a trewe collectione of all the p^rsidents in o^r office touching the right both of the one & the other. This Yorke secretlye under hand practised wth some of o^r companie to conseale all those that were most materiall & to produce but only one that was made in H. 7 time wch was most erronious & wch the kinge himself did utterly condemne, all wch was proved to his face before the king & other his misdemeans & also his being burnt in the hand, at wch time he beene kicte out of the place by some of the nobilitie had not the Kings presence bridled them.

Item his false reporte he lately made under his hand of Sr Tho. Bishop of sussex who was to receive a certificat fro' o^r office of the antiquitie of his gentrie to be a Barronett according to that order prescribed by his maiestie y^t evrie Baronett that should be made was to prove his gentillitie of 3 descents both by father & mother, this matter coming to o^r office to be testified we refusing the same, bycause we could not make a trewe certificate therof. This yorke notwithstanding wth Treswell his companion certified the same under booth thiere hands contrarie to the kings order & thier othe.

LIST OF PERSONS DISCLAIMED.

(HARL. MS. 1079.)

Disclaimed at Bodmyn 30 Septemb., 1620.

John Skinner of St. John's.
Sampson Bond of Salt Ashe.
John Vincent of Northill.
Anthony Furlong of Anthony.
Phillip Wallis of Shevioke.   Ignobilis.
John Hore of Landilp.
James Finch of St. Germins.
Will'm Bere of Linkinhorne.
Thomas Roberts of the same.

---

* It is said that for confirming a Coat to the Hangman, both Sir William and Ralf were put into the Marshalsea, where the latter was long detained. For the imprisonment of Yorke, etc., and "The Earl Marshall's demaunde of Yorke," see Harl. 4204. ff. 80-88.

John Squire of Lawannik.
Walter Harewood of Mariston.
George Drinnick of South Petherm.
John Mill of Lanist.
Will'm Squire of the same.
Thomas Vosper of Tamerton.
John Lucas of St. Cleere.
John Minors of Dulo.
John Mill of Lancells.
John Hoare of Dulo.
John Laukeston of Liskerd.
Lazarus Harris of St. Kaine.
Thomas Hawky of St. Winow. } Ignobilis.
Thomas Reswell of St. Pinnok.
Thomas Hoblin of the same.
Christopher Hendor of Minster.
Nicholas Hender of Tintagell.
Robert Mullis of Michelstow.
John Hockyn of Advyn.
John Taperell of Alternon.
Nicholas Axworthy of Treneglas.
Arthur Houlman of Poundstock.
John Murfield of the same.
Thomas Peirse of Dewstowe.
Abbot French of Otterham.

Disclaimed at Truro 6 October, 1620.

Walter Sweete of Lanlevery.
John Colquit of St. Samsons.
Walter Trewbody of Trewardreth.
Will'm Ludlow of the same.
Christopher Furlong of Fcoke.
Zachary Walter of St. Geron's.
Will'm Foote of St. Vivian (Veryan).
Edmond Candy of St. Allen.
John Tregagall of the same.
Walter Peirse of St. Erne.
John Garland of St. Cuby.
John Wymond of Lanhidrock. } Ignobilis.
Drew Perkins of St. Wenne.
John Marke of the same.
Thomas Daye of Collumb maior.
John Andrew of Cubert.
Will'm Smith of Newlin.
John Pellamounter of Cullomb Minor.
Richard Westcot.
Thomas Ricord of Enneder.
John Hockin of St. Esic.
Thomas Culley of St. Blasey.

COMPARATIVE PEDIGREE

OF

Carminowe.

(See Preface and p. 33.)

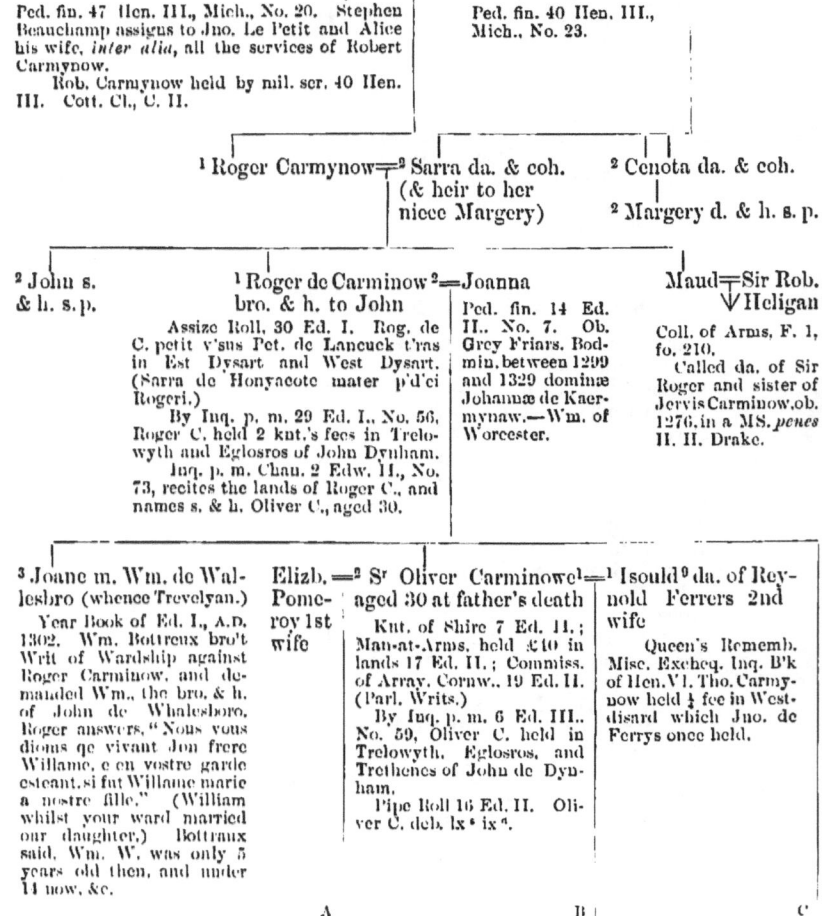

THE VISITATION OF THE COUNTY OF CORNWALL.   297

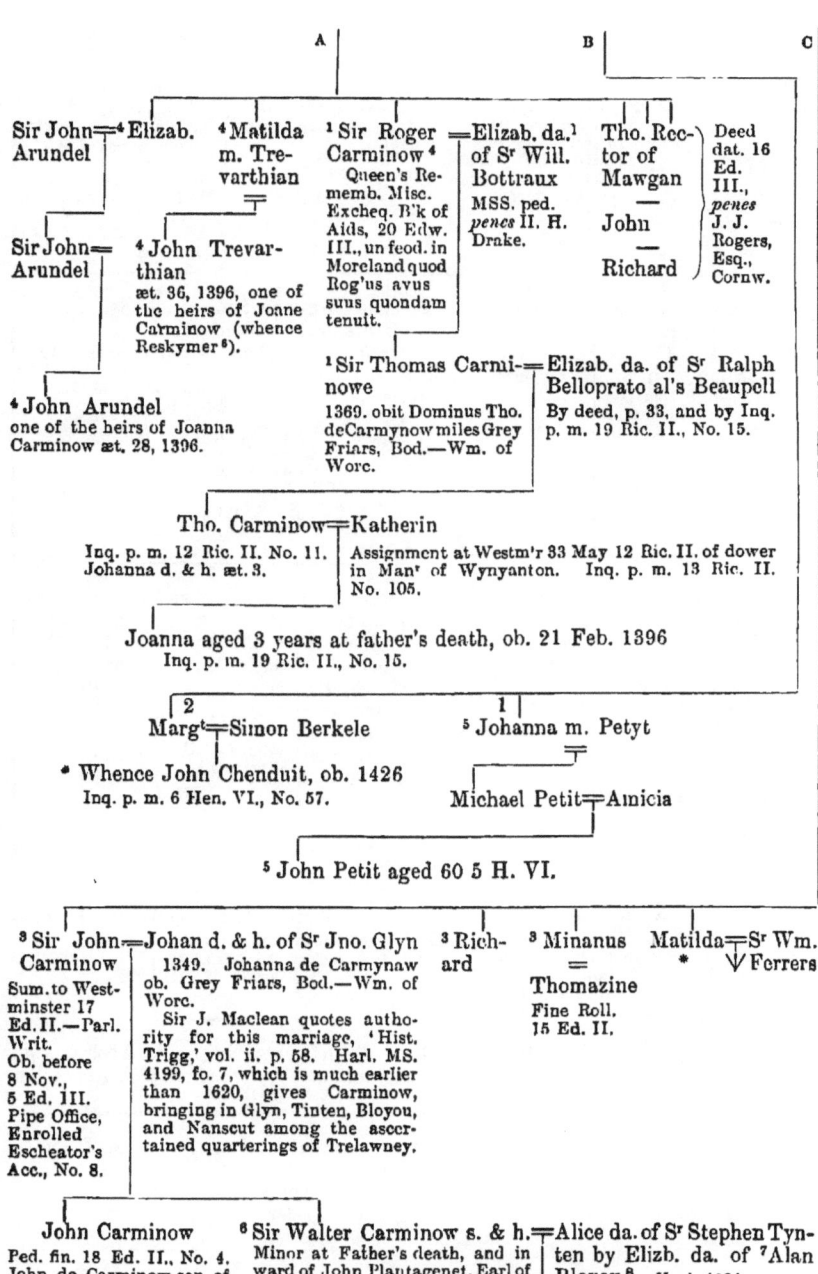

THE VISITATION OF THE COUNTY OF CORNWALL.

A

Sir Ralph Car- == Alice
minow s. & h. s. ↓ | Inq. p. m. 4 Hen.
p. m. | VI., No. 28. Will.
Inq. p. m. 10 Ric. | Bonville miles. filius
II., No. 11. names | Elizb. filie p'dct.
Will. C. as bro. and | Alicie que fuit ux.
heir, aged 31. Will | Ralf C. Cher.
June. 1386, names
Alice his wife.

b William Carminow == Margaret Kelly
bro. & h. of Ralph | Inq. p. m. 8 Hen. V.,
aged 31 at death of | No. 99, pt. 6. A certain
Ralph | Nich. Kelly, p'son of
Inq. p. m. 8 Hen. IV., | Laddock, etc., gave
No. 16, names John, s. | Manor of Ashwater to
& h. | Will. Carminow and Margaret his wife. Wm. C.
father of John C. and
Tho. C.

John Carminow s. &==Alice da.
h. aged 23 at father's | Sir Jno.
death 8 Hen. IV. | Dynham
Ob. 26 July, 1421. | Harl. 4031.
Inq. p. m. 8 Hen. V.,
No. 99. names his father
Wm. C. and his s. & h.
John.

² Thomas Carminow 2nd == Jane da. Rob.
heir to his nephew John | Hill
aged 25 at nephew's | Tho. C. enfeoffed
death 8 H. V. | Rob. Hill and o'rs
Ob. 21 H. VI. Inq. p. m. | p' Inq. p. m. 21 H.
No. 46. | VI., No. 46.
Inq. p. m. 5 H. VI., No. 57,
names Thomas, aged 30, s.
of Will. Carminowe, s. of
Alice, da. of Elizab,
Inq. a. q. d. Hen. VI., No.
1, recites will of Tho. C.

John C. s. & h. o.== Johanna
s. p. 6 May 8 H. V. | "ux. Stephen Bo-
a ward of Jno. Arun- | dulgate nup. ux.
del of Trerice | Johis Carmynow
Inq. p. m. 8 H. V., | fil. et her. Johis
No. 99. John C., s. & | Carmynow ar. frat.
h. of John, son of Will. | ipsius Thome C."
C. Tho. C., bro. of s'd | Her dower re-
John, son of Will., next | lated under Inq. p.
heir, æt. 25. | m. 21 Hen. VI., No.
Manors of Polrode, | 46.
Tynten, Dysert. Tamer-
ton, Boconnoc, Pen-
pent, and Glyn.

Johan aged == Sir Thomas | Margaret
15 and more | Carew, second- | aged 20
at time of | ly Sir Hal- | 21 H. VI.
Father's | nathe Male- | at father's
death 21 H. | verer 8 | death
VI. and was | Will of Sir H. | mar. Sir
then mar- | M. prob. 4 Ap., | Hugh
ried to Sir | 1502. P. P. C. | Cour-
Tho. Carew | Blamye 73. | teney
↓ | | ==↓

Nicho. Carminow ==
Inq. p. m. 11 Ed. IV., No. 44. Names his father
Will. C., and lands to revert to Joanna, aged
about 40, the wife of Halnathe Maleverer and
widow of Sir Tho. Carew, as d. & h. of Tho. C.,
the uncle and h. of John, s. and h. of John, s.
and h. of Sir Will. C.
Named also in will. of his bro. Thomas. Inq.
a. q. d. 24 H. VI.

Walter Carminow == Jane Resprin
All the descents from this
match are taken from an
old MSS. penes H. H.
Drake.

John Car- == Philippa da. & coh. of Jno.
minow | Trenowth of Fentongollan

Eliza. m	Elinor m.	Philippa	Catherine m.	Isabel m.	Jane m. Humfrey Calwood-
Jno. Bere	Nich. Opie	m. Peter	Humfrey	Jno. Viell	ley
of Pengelly	of Bodmin	Bevill	Baten Duns-	of Trevor-	
			land	der	==

Jane Calwoodley   A

THE VISITATION OF THE COUNTY OF CORNWALL. 299

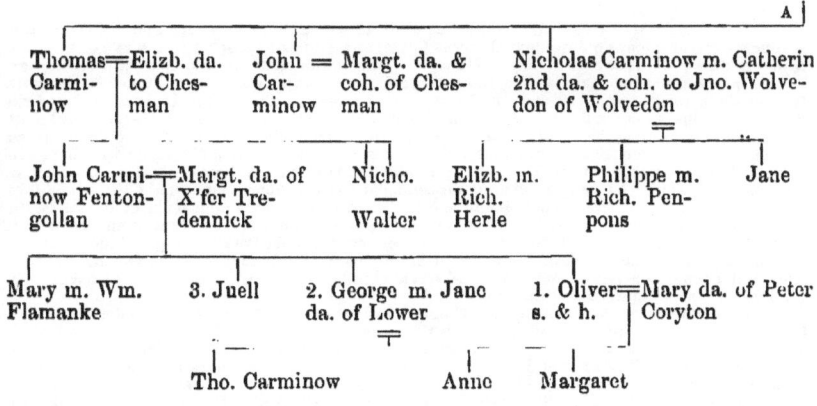

[1] These four generations follow in order according to a pedigree drawn up *temp.* Hen. VII. (Harl. 1074, fo. 320), supposed by Sir Harris Nicolas to have been the work of a Herald to prove several families to be " of the king's blood ; " also according to Harl. MS. 4031, fo. 221.

[2] Assize Roll, 30 Ed. I., Mich.

    M } 1 ⟩1 also M } 1 ⟩ 2 m. 21. In an Assize Roll 12 Ed. I. a Michael de Caer-
    21 }   21 }   minow is twice named.

,,   ,, 6 Ed. I.
            M } 1 ⟩4 m. 14. Rogerus de Kermynow plene ætatis et nondum miles.
            20 }

                  Roger tenet man'ia Wynyenton & Mervyn in excamb' maner' de
                  Bochyny & Tyntagel que comes modo tenet.

,,   ,, 30 Ed. I.
            M } 1 ⟩2 m. 22. Roger de Carminow, called to reply to the King for his man' of
            21 }   Wynyenton, said that Richard, formerly E. of Cornw., gave to a
certain Gervaise de Hornyngcote, his ancestor, the manor of Wynton, Merthyn, and Tam'ton in exchange for the manor of Bochym, wh' exchange King Henry, father of this King (Ed. I.), ratified, which same charter and deed Roger presents.

[3] Ped. fin. 12 Ed. II.
[4] Note 3, p. 30, under Carminow. Inq. p. m. 19 Ric. II., No. 15.
[5] Inq. p. m. 5 Hen. VI., No. 57. See under Petit, also Sir Jno. Maclean's ' Hist. of Trigg,' vol. i., p. 545. By Inq. p. m. 8 Hen. VI., No. 24, and 33 Hen. VI., No. 27, it is proved that Petit by inheritance held Trelowyth and Eglosros of Dynham. Trelowyth descended to and was sold by Tresaher. See under respective pedigrees, pp. 235, 277. (These manors were perhaps settled by Roger Carminow on his son Oliver and the issue of the marriage with Isould Ferrers.)
[6] Recites the exchange between Rich., bro. of Hen. III., and Gervais ⎫
Hornacote, and states that Jno. Arundel held Wynienton, the heirs of Reskimer⎪
held Merthyn, and Walter Carminow held Tamerton.   ⎪ Exch. Misc.
[7] Alan Bloyo held in cap. the manor of Polrode.   ⎬ Minister's Acc.
Tho. Carmynow, s. & h. of Will. C., held under the manor of Polrode. ⎪ 557. T. G.
[8] Extenta de ter' &c. que fuerunt Alani Bloyon. Manor de Polrode, etc.⎪ 13. 103.
34 Ed. III. Vic' Cornub' & recipi et t'ui de Tho. Carmynow ar. fil. et her.⎪
Will'i Carmynow ar. defuncti 68/70° p' rel'io de man'io de Polrode, &c., 6 Hen.⎪
VI. Halnathe Maleverer, who married Johan Carminow, the relict of Sir Tho.⎪
Carew, held part of manor of Polrode 6 Ed. IV.   ⎭
    Queen's Remembrancer, Excheq., vol. iii., 20 Ed. III. Book of Aids. Alice Carminow held in Polrode and Donnant q'd Alan Bloighou prius tenuit. Vol. iv., Inq. H. VI., Tho. Carmynow and o'rs held Polrode and Davanant ¼ fee which Alice Carmynow held. Vol. iv., also held in Hornccote, Reskere and Ashwater, wh' Roger Carminow held.

[9] By Harl. 4031, f. 221, Sir Oliver Carminow married also Elizb., da. of Pomeroy. Joanna Petit was issue by Ferrers, and the other children were by Pomeroy.

                                        [*Notes continued on next page.*

(*Notes continued.*)

* Inq. p. m. 6 H. VI., No. 57. John Chenduit, of whom John Petit, aged 60, is heir, in this manner :—" Jur' dicunt q'd quidam Oliverus Carmynowe miles nup' seisitus in d'm'cio suo ut de feod' de Maner' de Trewerys & Seynt Maudyt. Man'ia illa dedit pr'fato Simoni Berkeley ar. lib'rum maritagium cu' Marg'ia filia ipius Oliveri, virtute cujus doni idem Simon & Margeria fuerunt inde seisiti, tota vita sua, p' formam doni p'dicti. Et de ipis Simone et Margeria descendebat jus manor' cu' p'tin' Bartho' ut filio et hered' cor'dem Simonis et Margerie qui obiit inde seisitus p' formam doni p'dci. Et de ip'o Bartho' descendebat jus p'dcor' cu' p'tin Bened'co filio et hered' eiusdem Barth'i qui obit inde seisitus p' formam doni p'dci, et de ip'o Bened'co descendebat jus cor'dem manor' cu' p'tin, p'fate Johanne ut filie & heredi eiusdem Bened'ci p' formam doni p'dci. Et de ip'a Johanna descendebat jus coru'dem manor' cu' p'tin p'fato Johi Cheynduit, ut filio et hered' p'dce Johanne filie Bened'ci p' formam doni p'dci et de tali statu idem Johes obiit inde seisitus sine hered' de corpore suo exeunte et d'ca Maneria in Trewerys & Seynt Maudit cum p'tin rev'tebantur & rev'tere debent cuidam Johi Petyt, Armig°, adhuc superstiti ut consanguineo & hered' p'fati Johis videlt fil' Michis fil' Johanne filie ip'ius Oliveri. Et q'd Man'ia illa tenuit de p'fato Johe Petyt p' serviciu' reddendi ei xiij* p' an' o'mi s'v'cio &c. Et q'd Johes Petyt est etatis sexaginta annor' &c."

Also of the same John Chenduit, Thomas Carmynow, aged 30, is heir under the same Inquisition in the manner following : John Chenduit held at his death, being jointly enfeoffed with Joan his then wife, still living, of mess' and lands in Trymore and Penscras by gift of W. Aleyn, clerk, to s'd John and Joan and heirs of John's body, remainder in default to Thomas Carmynowe as kinsman and heir of s'd John. " Eidem Thome Carmynowe ut consanguineo & hered' ip'ius Joh'is videlt, ut filio Will'i Carmynowe fil' Alicie filie Elizabeth sororis Johanne matris Marg'ie matris Simonis Berkle patris Barth'i patris Benedicti patris perfate Johanne matris p'dci Joh'is Cheynduyt, idem John Cheynduyt obiit sine herede de corpore suo exeunte." This Inquisition, together with that taken at Michell 19 Ric. II., on the death of Johanna Carminowe, proves that Sir Oliver Carminowe left three daughters, who might be regarded eventually as his co-heirs. It is evident that Sir Oliver had at least two wives ; on the issue of the first marriage were settled the manors of Wynyanton, Merthyn, etc., and the issue of the second held certain other manors and lands by gift in libero maritagio. The first wife is said to have been Elizabeth Pomeroy (Harl. 4031, f. 221), and the Inquisition states that Joanna Carminow held of Sir Tho. de la Pomeray as of his manor of Tregony. The second wife, according to note 1, as well as Harl. MS. 4031, fo. 221, was Isould, daughter of Reginald Ferrers. The Harl. MS. mentions a Matilda Carminow, sister of Sir Oliver C. and wife of William Ferrers, " a quo descendunt, Baro de Slane Jo. Bonville, Champernon de Beer Ferris." Sir Wm. Pole aids this statement (' Devon,' p. 336) by saying that Sir Reginald Ferrers of Beere married Marget, sister and one of the heirs of Sir Rob. le Deneis of Pancrasewicke, by whom he had issue Sir William, which by *Matilda* his wife had, etc., whence Slane and Champernon, as before said.

ADDENDA.

BASSET, p. 5.

Carolus Basset, son of Francis B., ar., bur.	29 May, 1627.	Illogan Par. Reg.
Francis, ,, ,, ,, Esq., ,,	18 Jan., 1637.	
Tho. Carveth and Anne Bassett mar.	31 Dec., 1691, at St. Enoder.	
John Pendarves Basset a Squar (Esq.) and Ann Predeeks (Prideaux) mar. by licenss	12 Ap., 1737.	St. Stephen's in Bran. Par. Reg.

BEAUCHAMP, p. 8.

John Beauchamp, Esq., and Emblyn Edwards mar.	1684.	St. Collumb Major Par. Reg.
William Beauchamp, gent., and Mrs. Elizab. Courteney of Truro mar. at Kea	9 Ap., 1695.	Gwennap Par. Reg.

BEVIL.

Peter Bevill, Esq., and Mistress Grace Viel mar.	1591.	Breock Par. Reg.
Philip Bevil. Esq., bur. at Talland	1617.	Bp. of Exeter's Transcripts.

BULLER, p. 24.

Jane, da. of Matthew and Elizab. Buller, bap. at Lanreath	1694.	
Barnard Tanner, ar., and Julian, da. of Sir Ric. Buller, mar. at St. Stephen's in Brannel	21 Nov., 1625.	Bp. of Exeter's Transcripts.
Francis Tanner and Lady Carew mar. at Anthony	27 June, 1749.	
Francis Buller, Esq., bur. at Pelint	18 May, 1664.	
Tho. Dodson of St. Ive, Esq., and Mrs. Mary Buller, gent., mar.	16 May, 1584.	Morval Par. Reg.

CAREW, p. 33.

Weymond, son of Rich. Carew, ar., bap. at Anthony	7 Sept., 1623.	Bp. of Exeter's Transcripts.

CARY, p. 37.

William Carye, gent. and Elizab. Eddye (? Geyde) mar. at Menhenniott	21 Mar., 1621.	Bp. of Exeter's Transcripts.

COURTENEY, p. 54.

Peter Courteney and Grace Moor mar. at Creed	21 Ap., 1725.	Bp. of Exeter's Transcripts.

DENNIS, p. 61.

Ind., 20 Mar., 1657, betw. Augustyne Drake of Alphyngton, Exeter, gent., and Honor his wife, one of the daughters and co-heirs of Edmund Dennis of St. Nyott, Cornw., 1st part, and Edw. Champernon of Ide, Dev., gent., and Jno. Turner of Alphington, Dev., gent., other part. Lands in several parishes, Dev. and Cornw. } Deed *penes* Sir Charles Graves Sawle, Bart.. Penrice.

GODOLPHIN, pp. 80–83.

Sidney, son of Sir Wm. Godolphin,	bap.	16 Jan., 1609.	
William, son of Wm. Godolphin,	,,	1611.	
Elizb., da. Francis Godolphin. ar., and Dorothy,	,,	8 Feb., 1635.	
Sidney, son ,, ,,	,,	15 June, 1644.	
Henry, ,, ,, ,,	,,	15 Aug., 1648.	
Francis Godolphin, Esq., and Margaret, da. of John Killegrew,		mar. 24 June, 1652.	St. Breage Par. Reg.
George Kervyth, Esq., and Blanche, da. of Sir Francis Godolphin,		mar. 3 Dec., 1584.	
Walhelmus Godolphin miles	bur.	30 July, 1570.	
My Ladie Blanche Godolphin	,,	1583.	
Francis Godolphin miles	,,	22 Ap., 1608.	
William ,,	,,	21 Oct., 1611.	
William ,, miles	,,	5 Sept., 1613.	

Prudence, da. of Nicholas Godolphin, Esq., bap. 1613. St. Paul's Par. Reg.
Gentle, son of Gentle Godolphynne. bap. 21 Ju., 1614. Teingrace Par. Reg.

ST. AUBYN, p. 212.

John St. Aubyn, Esq., bur. 17 Jan., 1697, at Crowan. Bp. of Exeter's Transcripts.

TREVANION, p. 240.

Rich. Trevanion and Mary Pristwood. mar. 30 Jan., 1591. } Allhallows, Goldsmith Street, Exeter Par. Reg.

FACSIMILES FROM THE VISITATION OF 1620. HARL:MSS.1162

John Arundell of Trerise   Tho Carmynowe

Francis Godolphin   Geo: Carew.   Peter Courtney

Wm Courtenay   Reynell Mohun

John Vanssian   Antony Crowde

Edw: Cybyan   Reg Moyell   John Arscian

Tho Tresilder   George Spry   Nicholas Trefusis

John Gegrorgys   Humfrey Yorke

Thomas Denys.   Richard Erisey

Geo: Sayer: Nich: Boyle   John Hoyly:

William ffortescu   Peter ffolligh   Tho: munday

H.H.D

W. Beauchamp   Bev: Grenville   John Seawey

                                Richard Pendarves

Fr: Boscawen   Joseph Sawle   Jonas Robart

Hu: Prideaux   John Crobbe

nirjstib Carolo   Pierce Manington

J me Johanne Kyllygrue   John Trelawny

Nicholas Kendall   Richard Williams

Frith Butler   Christopher Wortheval

Jonathan Rashleigh   Ferdinando Lower

Walter Langdon   Thomas Polwheile

Edward Edgcombe   John Glanville

John Freffry   Ber: ff Lamankr

Hd: Molesworth   Jo: Borrython

BLAZON OF ARMS NOT ENTERED ON THE PEDIGREES.

In the following blazons, B stands for Azure.

Arscott.—Per chevron B. and Erm. in chief 2 bucks' heads cabossed Or.
Arundel.—Sa. 6 swallows arg.—3, 2, and 1.
Ayre (Devon).—Gu. on a bend betw. 6 crosses formée fitchée Ar., 3 mullets Sa.

Barkley.—Sa. a fess Erm., inter 3 cinqfoils Arg.
Barret of Penquite.—Ar. a chev. engr. betw. 3 bears pass. Sa., muzzled Or.
Barret of Tregarden.—Ar. a chev. eng. Gu. betw. 3 bears' heads Sa., muzzled Or.
Basset.—Barry undée of 8, Or and Gu.
Bastard.—Or a chevron B., charged with a martlet of the first.
Bawden.—B. a chev. betw. 3 griffins' heads couped Or, each transfixed with a dagger blade p'pr, pommel of the 2nd.
Beauchamp.—Vairé Ar. and B.
Beer.—Ar. a bear saliant Sable.
Bennett.—Gu. 3 demi-lions ramp., couped Ar.
Billing.—Or on a bend Sa. 3 bucks' heads erased of the first.
Blake.—Ar. a chev. betw. 3 garbs Sa.
Bligh.—B. a griffin segreant Or betw. 3 crescents Ar. Crest, an arm embowed per pale Or and B., cuffed A., hand p'pr, holding a battle-axe, blade Ar. helve B.
Bogans.—Sa. a cockatrice displ. Ar., crested, membered, and jelloped Gu.

Bonithon.—Ar. a chev. betw. 3 fleursde-lis Sa.
Bosaverne or Thomas.—Per pale nebulée Arg. and B.
Bosawsack.—A saltire engrailed (p' seal).
Boscawen.—Erm. a rose Gu., barbed Vert, seeded Or.
Bosusto.—B. 3 escalops Ar. (Harl.890).
Bosvargus.—Ar. on a fess B. 3 bezants betw. 2 chev. Gu.
Bray.—Quarterly Ar. and B., on a bend Gu. 3 fleurs-de-lis Or.
Buller.—Sa. on a cross Arg., pierced of the field, 4 eagles displayed of the first.
Burell.—Barry of 6 Ar. and Sa., on a chief Gu. 3 leopards' heads Or.
Burgess.—Chequy Gu. and Or, on a chief Ar. 3 cross-crosslets B.

Calmady.—B. a chevron betw. 3 pears Or.
Carew.—Or 3 lions pass. Sa.
Carnsew.—Sa. a goat pass. Or, attired, bearded, and ungued Or.
Carter.—B. 2 lions ramp. combattant Or.
Cavel.—Erm. a calf pass. Gu.
Ceely.—B. a chev. Or betw. 3 mullets Ar.
Chapman of Respryn or Whitstone.} Per chev. Ar. and Gu. a crescent counterch.
Chenouth.—Sa. on a fess Or 3 choughs' heads p'pr.
Cock, of Plymouth.—Ar. a chev. engr. betw. 3 cocks' heads eras. Sa., on a canton B. an anchor Or.

Connock.—Ar. a fess dancettée betw. 3 eagles displ. Gu.
Cooke of Trerice.—Erm. on a bend cotised Sa. 3 cats Or.
Coriton or Corynton.—Ar. a saltire Sa.
Cory.—Ar. a saltire Sa., on a chief B. 3 cinqfoils Or.
Cossen al's Maddern.—B. a lion ramp. Or, guttée de sang, ducally crowned of the 2nd.
Coswarth.—Ar. on a chev. betw. 3 falcons' wings B. 5 bezants.
Cowling.—Ar. a chev. Sa. betw. 3 Cornish choughs p'pr.
Crabb.—B. a chev. betw. 3 fleurs-de-lis Ar.
Crewes.—B. a bend per bend dancettée Gu. and Ar. betw. 2 escutcheons Or.
Croker.—Ar. a chev. engr. Gu. betw. 3 ravens p'pr.
Crookhays.—Party per pale Ar. and Sa., on a chevron 3 escalops, all counterchanged.

Dandy.—Ar. on a bend cotised Sa. 3 cinquefoils Or.
Darrell.—B. a lion ramp. Or., Ar. lang. and crowned Gu.
Dewin.—Gu. on a chev. Ar. 3 cinqfoils slipped Sa.
Dodson.—Ar. a bend engr. B. betw. 2 choughs p'pr.

Edmonds.—B. an eagle vol. Or.
Edwards.—Erm. an antelope ramp. Or.
Elford.—Q'rly 1 and 4. Per pale wavy Ar. and Sa. a lion ramp. Gu., crowned Or. 2 and 3. Gu. 3 stirrups Ar.
Erisey.—Sa. a chev. betw. 3 griffins segreant Or.

Ferrers.—Ar. on a chev. Sab. betw. 3 cinqfoils Gu. pierced of the field, 3 horse-shoes Or. (Harl. 4632.)
Ferrers.—Ar. on a bend Sa. 3 horse-shoes Or. (Harl. 4632.)
Fleming.—Chequy Or and Gu.
Fletcher.—Erm. a cross moline Sa.
Fortescue.—B. a bend engr. Ar. cotised Or.
Fownes.—B. two eagles displ. in chief, and a mullet in base Arg.

Gamon.—Ar. on a fess betw. 3 men's legs couped at the thigh Sa. a crescent.
George.—Ar. on a fess engr. Gu. betw. 3 doves volant B. 3 bezants charged each with a lion's head eras. Sa.
Gerveis.—Ar. a chev. betw. 3 garbs Sa.
Glynn.—Ar. 3 Salmon spears Sa.
Goode.—Gu. on a chev. betw. 3 lions ramp. Or 3 cinqfoils of the field.
Godolphin.—Gu. a double-headed eagle displ. Ar. betw. 3 fleurs-de-lis Or (sometimes Ar.).
Grose.—Q'rly Ar. and B. on a bend Sa. 3 martlets Or.

Harris.—Sa. 3 crescents within a border Ar.
Hatch.—Gu. 2 demi-lions pass. guard. Or.
Hawke.—Bendy of six B. and Or a chief Erm.
Hele.—Ar. 5 lozenges in pale Erm., the centre one charged with a leopard's face Or.
Hender.—B. a lion ramp. within an orle of escalops Or.
Herle.—Gu. a fess Or betw. 3 shovellers p'pr.
Herle.—Gu. 3 escalops and a bordure engr. Ar.
Hext or Hicks.—Or a tower triple-turreted betw. 3 battle-axes Sa.
Hill of Helligan.—Gu. a saltire vairé betw. 4 mullets Ar.
Hill of Hilltop.—Gu. a chev. Erm. betw. 3 garbs Or.
Hill of Shilston.—Ar. a chev. betw. 3 water bougets Sa. Crest, a dove, in the beak an olive branch Vert.
Hoare.—B. on a bend Arg. three torteaux.
Hoblyn.—B. a fess Or betw. 2 flanches Erm.
Hunkin.—Ar. a mascle Sa., over all a fess of the last.

Jenkins.—Or a lion ramp. regard. Sa.
Jennings.—Erm. a lion ramp. Gu.
Jope.—Ar. in chief 2 pheons, and in base a mullet Sable.

Keat.—Ar. 3 cats pass. in pale Sa.

Kempthorne.—Ar. a chev. betw. 3 bears' heads bendways, coup. Sa., muzzled Or. and Ar. 3 pine trees p'pr.
Kendall.—Ar. a chev. betw. 3 dolphins naiant, embowed Sa.
Kestle.—Ar. a chev. Sa. betw. 3 falcons close p'pr.
Kestle of Manaccan.—Or 3 castles Gu.
Killiow.—Or a chev. betw. 2 roses in chief and a mullet in base Sa.
Knevet.—Ar. a bend within a bord. Sa., in chief a crescent charged with a cresc. for diff.

Langdon of Keverell.—Ar. a chev. betw. 3 lizards' heads Sa.
Langdon of Langdon.—Ar. a chev. betw. 3 bears' heads eras. Sa.
Langford.—Paly of 6 Ar. and Gu., on a chief B. a lion pass. Or.
Langharne.—B. a chev. betw. 3 escalops Or.
Lampen.—Ar. on a chev. engr. Sa. 3 rams' heads caboshed of the first, attired Or.
Lanyon.—Gu. a square castle in perspective with a tower at each corner Or, a falcon p'pr rising from a mound Vert in the courtyard of the field.
Launce.—Or on a fess dancettée Sa. 3 roses of the field.
Leigh.—Ar. a lion ramp. Gu.
Loveis.—Or a chev. engr. Sa. betw. 3 sea pies p'pr.
Lowelis.—Ar. 3 calves' heads couped Gu.
Lower.—Sa. a chev. betw. 3 roses Ar.
Lyneham.—Ar. a chev. Gu. betw. 3 boars passant Sa.

Mark.—Gu. a lion ramp. within an orle of 8 fleurs-de-lis Or, a canton Erm.
Martin (St. Dominic).—Ar. 2 bars Gu.
Matthew of Milton.—Sa. a stork close Ar.
Matthew of Kew.—As above, within a bordure of the second.
Maynard.—Ar. 3 hands couped at the wrist Gu.
Mayow.—Gu. a chev. vair betw. 3 coronets Or. Crest, a bird Erm., also a falcon devouring a serpent.

Menwynick.—Sa. a chev. betw. 3 falcons rising Ar.
Michell of Truro.—Sa. an escalop betw. 3 birds' heads erased Or.
Mohun.—Or a cross engr. Sa.
Molesworth.—Gu. an escutcheon vairé betw. 8 cross-crosslets in orle Or.
Moyle of St. Austell.—Gu. a mule pass. Ar., in chief a mullet for diff.
Moyle of St. German's.—Same.
Munday.—Q'rly Gu. and Sa. on a cross engr. Ar. 5 lozenges B., on a chief Or 3 eagles' legs erased à la quise of the fourth.
Murth.—See Randall.

Nance al's Trengove.—Ar. a cross humettée Sa.
Nankevill.—Ar. a cross humettée voided Sa.
Nanspian.—Ar. 3 lozenges in fess Sa. a chief of the last.
Nicholls of Trewane.—Sa. 3 pheons Ar.
Noy.—B. 3 cross-crosslets in bend Ar.

Opie.—Sa. on a chev. betw. 3 garbs Or as many hurts p'pr.

Parker.—B. fretty Ar. a fess Or.
Paynter.—B. 3 billets Ar., each charged with an annulet Sa.
Pendarves.—Sa. a falcon rising betw. 3 mullets Or.
Penhalleck.—Sa. 3 butterflies volant Ar.
Penhallow.—Vert a coney Ar.
Penrose.—Ar. 3 bends Sa., each charged with as many roses of the field.
Penwarne.—Sa. a chev. Or betw. 3 fleurs-de-lis Ar.
Petit.—Ar. a lion saliant or ramp. Gu.
Plumlegh.—Erm. 6 lozenges in bend Gu.
Polkinghorn.—Ar. 3 bars Sa.
Pollard.—Ar. on a chev. Sa. betw. 3 escalops Gu., a cresc. for diff.
Polwhele.—Sa. a saltire engr. Erm.
Pomeray of Tregony.—Or a lion ramp. Gu. within a bordure engr. Sa.
Pomeray of St. Columb.—Same as above, with bordure Gu.
Porter of Lancells.—Gu. on a fess Or betw. 3 cherubs' wings Or a torteaux charged with a lion pass. guard. of the second.

Porter of St. Stephens.—Sa. 3 church bells, a canton Ar.

Poyle.—Arg. a pair of barnacles in pale Sa.

Pye.—Ar. on a fess B. 3 escalops of the first.

Quarme.—Barry lozengy Ar. and Gu. counterchanged.

Randall al's Murth.—Ar. a lion ramp. betw. 3 fleurs-de-lis Gu.

Rashleigh.—Q'rly Sa. a cross Or betw. a Cornish chough Ar., beaked and legged Gu., 1st q'r; in the 2nd q'r a text 𝕋 of the third; 3rd and 4th, a crescent of the last, on the cross in chief a rose.

Reskimer.—Ar. 3 bends Gu., in chief a wolf courant B. Crest, a lion ramp. Sa., holding a laurel branch Vert.

Roberts.—B. 3 estoiles and a chief wavy Or.

Roberts.—B. on a chev. Ar. 3 mullets pierced Sa.

Robinson.—Per pale Ar. and Gu. over all a bend engr. Sa.

Rogers.—Ar. a chev. betw. 3 bucks trippant Sa.

Rosearrock.—Ar. a chev. Gu., in chief 2 roses of the last, in base a fish naiant B.

Roscrow.—Ar. a chev. betw. 3 roses Gu, seeded Or.

Roscruge.—Ar. on a mound Vert. 3 red rose sprigs p'pr.

Rosewarne.—Ar. 3 Catherine wheels Gu. betw. 2 pales B.

Samuell.—Ar. 2 squirrels sejant, endorsed Gu. within a border Sa.

Sawle.—B. 3 falcons erased, 2 and 1, within a border Or.

Sayer.—Or on a bend cotised Sa. 3 cinqfoils of the field.

Scawen.—Ar. a chev. Gu. betw. 3 griffins' heads erased Sa., the 2 in chief respecting each other.

Scoble.—Ar. 3 fleurs-de-lis Gu., a label of 3 B.

Scoble of Tregonnan.—Per pale Ar. and Gu. 3 fleurs-de-lis, and a label in chief counterch.

Smith.—B. a saltire Ar. betw. 4 martlets Or.

Sparke.—Chequy Or and Vert, a bend Erm., an annulet Gu. for diff.

Sparnon.—B. 3 falcons' wings displayed, each standing on a staff couped raguled Ar.

Spoore.—Gu. on a chev. Or a rose of the first betw. 2 mullets pierced Sa.

Sprye.—B. 2 bars and a chev. in chief Or.

Sprye.—Party per saltier Arg. and Gu. 4 crescents countereh.

St. Aubyn.—Erm. on a cross Gu. 5 bezants.

Stephens.—Per chev. B. and Ar. in chief 2 falcons vol. Or.

Tanner.—Arg. on a chief Sa. 3 Moors' heads couped, banded about the temples Or.

Thomas.—Per pale nebulée Ar. and B.

Tonkin.—Sa. an eagle displ. Or, armed Gu.

Trebarfoot.—Sa. a chev. betw. 3 bears' feet erect and erased Or.

Tregeare.—Ar. a fess betw. 3 Cornish choughs p'pr.

Trelawney.—Ar. a chev. Sa., and Ar. a chev. Sa. betw. 2 oak leaves Vert.

Trenance.—Sa. a fess betw. 3 swords erect Ar., in chief a crescent for diff.

Trenerth.—A chev. betw. 3 horses' heads (?).

Tresaugher.—B. a chev. betw. 3 dogs pass. and regardant.

Trethewy.—Or a chev. Sa. betw. 3 trefoils slipped B.

Trevanion.—Ar. on a fess B. betw. 2 chevrons Gu. 3 escallops Or.

Trevillian.—Gu. the base undée of 5 Ar. and B. a demi-horse issuant of the 2nd, maned and hoofed Or.

Trevisa.—Gu. a garb Or.

Treunwith.—Ar. on a bend cotised Sa. 3 cinqfoils of the field.

Trewolla.—Sa. 3 owls Ar., beaked and legged Or.

Trewren.—B. a chev. Or. betw. 3 bezants.

Trubody.—Ar. on a fess cotised B. 3 fleurs-de-lis Or, on a chief Gu. a demi-lion ramp. of the third.

Tubb.—Ar. a chev. Sa. betw. 3 gurnets hauriant Gu.

Tucker.—Barry wavy of 10 Ar. and B. on a chev. embattled Or betw. 3 sea-horses naissant of the last, 5 guttées de poix.

Upton.—Sa. a cross moline Ar.

Verman.—Gu. on a bend cotised Ar. 3 eagles displayed of the last.
Vivian of Bodmin.—Or on a chev. B. betw. 3 lions' heads erased pur. as many annulets of the field, on a chief Gu. 3 martlets Ar.
Vivian of St. Columb.—Same as above, without the annulets and martlets (Coll. of Arms).

Webber.—Ar. on a chev. engr. betw. 3 hurts as many annulets Az.
White.—Ar. on a bend Sa. 3 griffins' heads erased of the first.

Wichalse.—Per fess Ar. and Sa. 6 crescents in pale counterch.
Williams of Trevervo.—Ar. a greyhound cour. Sa. betw. 3 Cornish choughs p'pr within a bordure engr. of the second, charged with 8 crosses formée Or, and as many bezants.
Willoughby.—Sa. a cross engr. Or.
Wills.—Ar. on a chev. engr. Vert betw. 3 martlets Sable 5 Ermine spots Or.
Wodenote.—Ar. a cross couped and voided Sa.
Worthivale.—Gu. 3 pheons Ar., ringed Or.
Wrey.—Sa. a fess betw. 3 pole-axes Ar., helved Gu.
Wyvel.—Ar. 3 mullets betw. 2 bars Sa. within a bordure engr. Gu.

Yorke.—Gu. a chev. betw. 3 hinds' heads erased Arg.

INDEX OF NAMES.

Names in *Italics* have their arms blazoned.
" in LARGE CAPITALS are headings of the Visitation Pedigrees.
" in SMALL CAPITALS are pedigrees incidental to the Visitation Pedigrees.
The letter M before the figures denotes "A Marriage."
The letter *n* after the figures means "Note."

Abbot, Abbott, Abbotte. Abigail, 211 *n*; Hanar, 132; Justinian, 85; William, 132.
Abbyngton, 24 *n*.
Abertivi, Stephen, Constable of, 30.
Abraham, Ann, 124.
Achim, Achym. Thomas, 248 *n*; William, 12, 184 *n*.
Ackland, Acland. Baldwyn, 293; Hugh, 292; Margaret, 292; Scipio, 127.
ADAM *alias* POLGWEST, 226.
Adams, M 203.
Addis, Anna, 146 *n*; Hannah, 224 *n*.
Adlington, John, 285.
Agus, Michael, 254 *n*.
Albalanda, 20.
ALBALANDA, 20. (See also De la Land, De la Launc.)
Aldestowe, John de, 274 *n*.
Aleigh, 1.
ALEIGH,1. (Alcc.) Lora,132*n*.
Aleth *alias* Abot, John, 258 *n*.
Alexander, John, 282; Mary, 255 *n*; William, 19.
Allder, M 57.
Allen, Alloyn, Allyn. Katherine, 247 *n*; Thomas, 74; Walter, 110; W., 300.
Ally, Abigail, 136 *n*; Elizabeth, 115.
Alta, Hervy de, 261.
Alwin, Matilda, 290.
Amadis, John, 230; Judith, 230.
Amerideth, Edward, 81, 120; Elizabeth, 120; Judith, 81.
Amery, Johanna, 243 *n*.
Andrew, Amy, 56; Isabella, 147; Joane, 136; John, 147, 153 *n*, 266 *n*, 295; Philippa, 181 *n*; William, 56.
Andrewe *alias* Hoop, Petronell, 122; Stephen, 122.
Anegos, Patricius Frisell, Earl of, 143.

Angers, M 116.
Anstis, Anna, 161 *n*; Edward, 161 *n*; Elizabeth, 161 *n*; Hugh, 161 *n*; John, 111 *n*, 161 *n*, 200 *n*; Mary, 111 *n*, 161 *n*; Philip, 161 *n*; Rachel, 161 *n*; Roger, 161 *n*; William, 161 *n*; Wilmot, 161 *n*.
ANTREWON, 75.
ANTRON, 162. (Anthorne.) Jane, 276, 277; John, 257; Isabell, 257; William, 276.
Anyon (? Lanyon), Walter, 154.
Ap Conwyn, Rywallon, Prince of Wales, 30; Gladys, his da., 30.
Apley, Apeley. J., 183; Mary, 101; Robert, 101, 241; Susan, 241.
Ap Griffith, Llewellyn, 180 *n*; Rhys, Prince of South Wales, 30.
Appledore or Appeldryffeld, Avice, 30; William, 30.
APSLEY, 32.
Ap Theodor Maur, Nesta, 30; Henry, 30; Rees, Prince of Wales, 30.
Ap Thomas, 216. Margaret, 242; Sir Rhice, 242; Sir William, 216.
Archar, Joan, 126; John, 126.
Archard, John, 225; Jone, 225; Richard, 156 *n*.
ARCHDECON, 31. (Archdeacon, Le Archdecon, Le Ercedekne.) M 219, 239. Alice, 75; Amitia, 276; Elinor, 223; Roger, 75; Sir Thomas, 276; Thomas, 180 *n*., 223.
Archedekne, 33 *n*.
Arquill', Galfrid de, 261 *n*; Lucian de, 261 *n*; Ralph de, 261 *n*; Thomas de, 261 *n*; Vivian de, 261 *n*.

Arscott, 303.
ARSCOTT, 286, 287. Agnes, 12; Anne, 116; Arthur, 109, 140, 293; Elizabeth, 109; Honor, 140; Humphry, 154; Joane, 193; John, 12; Katherine, 154; Mary, 230; Rosseter, 243; Thomas, 12; Tristram, 230; William, 116, 193.
Arthorn, Robert, 229 *n*.
Arthur, Prince, 222.
Arundel, 257, 303.
Arundell, 258 *n*.
ARUNDELL, 243, 297.
ARUNDELL, 2, 3, 271, 272, 273, 274 *n*, 275 *n*. (Arrundell, Arundle, Arondell, de Arundell, etc.) M 34,84,95, 239 *n*, 240. Agatha, 27; Alice, 19, 20, 240 *n*; Alexander, 100 *n*; Anne, 212 *n*, 241 *n*; Christopher, 17, 42, 89; Dorothy, 50; The Earl of, 31, 258 *n*; Elizabeth, 36, 64 *n*, 89, 185 *n*; Florence, 257; George, 287; Gertrude, 287; Humphry, 9, 37 *n*; Isabell, 224; Jacquet, 22; Jane, 40, 213 *n*, 242; Sir John, 19, 34 *n*, 35 *n*, 36, 40, 64 *n*, 81, 84 *n*, 213 *n*, 220 *n*, 224, 233, 242, 277 *n*; John, 27, 28, 29, 33 *n*, 34 *n*, 50, 68, 83, 164, 164 *n*, 189 *n*, 212, 233, 235 *n*, 255 *n*, 277 *n*, 298, 299 *n*; Jone, 239; Julian, 28; Katherine, 164 *n*, 212; Lady Elizabeth, 213 *n*; Sir Lawrence, 20; Lawrence, 19, 112; Margaret, 189 *n*, 240; Margery, 17, 233, 233 *n*; Maria, 85 *n*, 235 *n*; Mary, 243; Otho, 239; Philippa, 9; Ralph, 239; Richard, 257; Robert, 22, 39; Sir Thomas,

ARUNDELL—continued.
145, 185 n; Thomas, 85, 240 n; Thomasine, 85; William, 89, 171 n; Zachary, 265.
Arvos, Jane, 94; Joane, 94 n; Philip, 94; Richard, 94 n.
Ashe, Ash. Edward, 116 n; Henry, 149; Loveday, 149 n.
Ashford, M 194. Ann, 209, 211; Arthur, 209, 210, 211; Catherine, 210.
Aston, Julian, 4. Ralph de, 4. Sir Roger, 146.
At Comb, 69.
Atkins, M 207.
At Ley, Thomas, 6.
Atwill, At Will. John, 78 n; Ralph, 25.
Audley, Audeley, 86 n. Anne, 45: Blanch, 91; James, Lord, 91: Rowland, 91; Thomas, 45.
Auen, St. G., 43. Mary, 43.
Austin, Henry, 274 n.
Avent, Andrew, 180 n; Mary, 236 n.
Avery, Averie. Jenepher, 65; Johanna, 115 n; Loveday, 238 n; Michael, 65; William, 53, 53 n, 285.
Axworthy, Nicholas, 295.
Ayre, 303.
AYRE *alias* EYRE, 3. (See also Eare and Eyre.) M 182. Alice, 68.

Bab, Elizabeth, 10.
Babbidge, Walter, 281.
Bacon, Sir Nicholas, 235 n.
Badcock, John, 83 n.
Bagg, James, 215.
Bagnall, Dudley, 32.
BAKE, 150. Catherine, 209; John, 209; Margaret, 179.
Baker, 167 n. Abraham, 168; Avis, 73; Blandane, 168; Sir John, 238 n; John, 268 n; Margaret, 92 n; Nicholas, 281; Robert, 11; Thomas, 73; William, 238 n.
Baldewyne, Richard, 151 n.
Balson, Bridget, 274 n.
Balune, Emena de, 223.
Band, Bande. Blanch, 249; Elizabeth, 105 n.
Bancock, M 97.
BANT, 13.
Barber, M 108.
Bardfield, 108.
Barkley, 303.
BARKLEY, 287. (Barkly.) Lady Elizabeth, 87.
Barne, Johanna, 149 n.
Barnhouse, 193, 194.
BARNHOUSE, 194.
Barret, 303.
BARRET, BARET, 4, 5. (Barratt, Barrat, etc.) Grace, 81 n; John, 21, 47, 157 n; Nicholas, 180; William, 9, 71.
Barry, Barrye. Katherine, 72; The Lord, 30, 72.
Bartlet, Ellis, 142.
Basset, 20, 303.
BASSET, 5. M 75. Agnes, 92 n; Anne, 184, 301; Charles, 301; Francis, 123 n, 230 n, 301; Gilbert, 143; Isabella, 144; James, 52, 53 n, 81, 233; Jane, 20, 52, 53 n, 208; Sir John, 84, 92 n; John Pendarves, 301; Margaret, 104 n; Margery, 233, 291; Ralph, 180 n; Sir Robert, 184; William, 20, 208.
Bastard, 6.
BASTARD, 6. M 182. Anne, 129; Dorothy, 136; George, 178 n; Grace, 178 n; Joseph, 60 n, 129, 136, 281.
Bath, Bathe. Adam de (? Back), 150; Edmond, 48 n; James, 48 n; Tristram, 162 n; William, 188 n.
Battershye, 6.
BATTERSBYE, 6. Nicholas, 244.
BATTYN, 286. (Batin, Battin, Batten.) M 47, 84. Agnes, 179 n; Humphry, 298; Johana, 248 n; John, 179 n; Richard, 279 n; Richow, 95 n.
BAUGHTON, 39.
Bawden, 303. (Bowden.) George, 73; Hugh, 162 n; Nicholas, 191: Reginald, 245.
Bayley, M 202. Francis, 87 n.
Bealburye, Bealbery, Baberic. Alice, 56 n; Johan, 56 n; John, 56 n, 80 n; Jone, 56; Thomasine, 56 n, 80 n.
Beard, Katherine, 90 n; Sir Stephen, 6; Thomasine, 6.
Beate, Richard, 112 n.
Beauchamp, 86 n.
Beauchamp, 7, 303.
BEAUCHAMP, 7, 8. (Beaucham, Beawcham, Bello Campo, etc.) M 144. Alice, 142, 276; Hugh de, 124 n; John, 24, 85, 301; Sir Michael, 276; Pole, 142; Stephen, 278 n, 296; William, 126 n, 224, 301.
Beauford, Beaufort, 86 n, 261 n. Anne, 197 n; Edmund, 254 n; John, 234 n, 279 n; Mary, 197 n.
Beaumont, Jois, 84; Thomas, 84.
Beckett, x. Jane, 219 n; John, 219 n.
Becton, Bickton, Bycton. John, 135, 229; Margaret, 229; Richard, 4 n.
Bedford, Daniel, 282; The Duke of, 31.

Beddlarke, Tamsen, 256 n.
BEDOW, 98.
Bee, Edmund, 167; Mary, 167.
Beets, Ellinor, 28.
Bellamy, Martha, 227 n.
Bello Loco, Abbas de, 185 n.
Belloprato *alias* Beaupre, Beaupoll, etc. M 70. Elizabeth, 33, 297; Jane, 251; John, 251; Jone de, 239; Sir Ralph, 33, 297; Stephen de, 239.
Benarklick, Bauethlck. Alice, 75 n; John, 75, 75 n; Nicholea, 75.
Benedict, William de, 222.
Benford, Elizabeth, 232 n.
Bennett, 303.
BENNETT, 10. (Bennet, Benett.) Ellen, 259 n, 260 n; Jane, 104 n; Johan, 200 n, 259 n; Katherine, 228 n; Martha, 88; Peter, 259 n, 291; Richard, 262 n; Robert, 181 n; Thomas, 88.
Benny, Alice, 66.
Beorust, John, 113.
Bere, x, 303.
BERE, 9. (Beere, Beare.) M 47. Degory, 106 n; George, 116; Grace, 88; John, 101, 134, 298; Peter, 116; Robert, 114 n; Roger le, 88 n; Sephronia, 116; William, 74 n, 88, 294.
Berkele, Berkeley, Bartholomew, 300 n; Benedict, 300 n; Johanna, 300 n; Margery, 300 n; Simon, 297, 300 n.
Bernard, Benedict, 4; Margaret, 4; William, 237.
Berners, The Lord, 117.
Berry, x. Martha, 11; Richard, 292.
Bersey, Frances, 96 n.
Bertelet, Thomas, 215 n.
Best, Christian, 264 n; John, 264 n.
Bethever, John, 75 n.
Bett, Elizabeth, 96; Luke, 96.
Bettowe, Margery, 112 n; Michael, 112 n.
Betty, Giles, 172 n.
Bevill, x. (Beville, Bevile, Bevil, Bevyll, Bevyill, Bœvill, Bevylle). Agnes, 109, 111; Elizabeth, 85; Humphry, 69; Isabella, 275 n; Jane, 162; John, 9, 85, 85 n, 109, 111, 146 n, 162, 177, 235 n, 272, 276; Katherine, 42; Maria, 85 n, 177, 272; Matilda, 85, 85 n; Peers, 235 n; Peter, 76 n, 85 n, 171 n, 219 n, 235 n, 277 n, 298, 301; Philip, 85, 146 n, 301; Thomas, 42; Thomasine, 76 n, 235 n; Sir William, 146 n.
Bewes, Alice, 45 n.
Bice, Grace, 53 n.

INDEX OF NAMES. 311

Bickford, Thomasine, 140 n.
Biggs, Grace, 184 n.
Billing, 303.
BILLINGE, 10, 11. (Billin, Billyon, Billion *al's* Trelawder, Billen, etc.) Elizabeth, 72, 133 n, 230 n; John, 113, 133 n, 231 n, 263 n; Jone, 114; Margaret, 113; Philadelphia, 267; Richard, 9, 46, 113, 267; William, 72.
BIRRIE, 46.
Bishop, Sir Thomas, 294.
BLACKALL, 288. Christopher, 92.
Blackaller, M 137.
Blackdon, William, 69.
Blackston, Blaxton. Henry, 28; John, 125; Rebecca, 28, 125.
Blake, 303.
BLAKE, 11. Margaret, 95 n.
Blanchard, John, 214; Thomasine, 214.
Blanche, Isabell le, 276, 277 n.
Blanke, Alice, 91 n.
Blathwayte, Elizabeth, 255 n.
Blewett, Blewet, Bluett. M 10. Anne, 159 n; Colan, 131, 268 n; Emanuel, 54; Francis, 189 n, 255 n; Johan, 134; Maude, 203; Sir Richard, 203; Richard, 84; Robert, 254 n.
Bligh, 303.
BLIGHE, 12, 13. (Bligh, Blygh.) Anne, 88; Christopher, 88; Honor, 159 n; Philippa, 167, 168 n; Richard, 141 n; Thomas, 159 n, 167; William, 53 n.
Blompin, John, 209.
Bloy, Bloyou, Bloyo, Bloighou. Alan, 35 n, 297, 299. Alice, 34; Amicia, 277 n; Elizabeth, 297; Sir John, 277 n; Ralph, 35 n; Roger, 121 n.
Bobage, John, 218; Mary, 218.
Bockerell, 61.
Bodeler, Vivian, 261 n.
Boduan, Emma, 201 n.
Bodmin, 280. Thomas Munday, Prior of, 149 n, 151; Thomas Vivian, Prior of, 256.
Bodrigie, Gerance, 98; Jane, 98.
Bodrugan, Otho de, 213 n, 278 n.
Boduckshued, Budockshed, Butside, etc. Agnes, 99; Johanna, 42; Robert, 42; Roger, 99.
Bodulgate, Bodulgatt, Bodelesgat, etc. Anne, 107; Johanna, 298; John, 37; Jone, 49; Stephen, 49, 298.
Boffrasel, Oger de, 277 n.
Bogans, 303.
BOGANS, 14. (Bogins.) Dorothy, 259 n; John, 168; Nicholas, 258.

Bohun, 105 n. Humphry de, 31, 259 n; Margaret, 31.
Bois, Boys. John, 68 n, 173; Katherine, 68 n.
Bokelly, Alice, 108 n; Nicholas, 108 n.
Bolithoe, Bolytho, Bolythoe. Alexander, 282; Christian, 91 n; Grace, 168 n; Margaret, 260 n.
Bolson, Nicholas, 27.
Bond, 14, '15.
BOND, 36.
BOND, 14, 15. M 197. Agnes, 251; Jane, 126; John, 255 n; Sampson, 284, 294; Sibill, 255 n; Thomas, 126, 251 n.
Bonnatre, 275, 276. (Boniter.) Ephraim, 26; John, 275.
Bonnock, John, 47.
Bonnyface, Boniface. Elizabeth, 219; Jone, 37; Robert, 37, 219.
Bonvill, Bonville, Bonvile, Bondvile, Bovele, M 4. Elizabeth, 31, 102, 298; John, 194, 300 n; Katherine, 194; Lord, 84, 194, 219; Philippa, 84; Sir William, 31, 298; William, 102.
Bony, Stephen, 150 n.
Bonython, 303.
BONYTHON, 16, 17. (Bonithon, Bonython.) Alice, 183; Edmond, 68 n, 81, 83; Eliza, 177; Elizabeth, 68 n; James, 83 n, 250, 283; John, 68 n, 177, 212, 248 n, 257; Julian, 247; Katherine, 212; Margaret, 170; Nicholas, 285; Ralph, 68 n; Reskimer, 109; Richard, 68, 170; Thomas, 83n.
Boone, Boon, 105 n. Elizabeth, 163 n.
Borlase, Burlace, Burlassy. M 249. Elizabeth, 111 n; John, 253 n; Margery, 23; Mary, 42; Walter, 21, 23.
Boroughe, Borowe. Elizabeth, 125 n; John, 9; Thomasine, 9.
Borrington, Bartholomew, 292.
Bosavarne, 303.
BOSAVARNE, 17. (Bosavern.) John, 3; William, 65 n.
Boscawen, 303.
BOSCAWEN, 17, 18, 19, 20, 21. (Boscauin, Bascoyne, Boskawen, etc.) Alice, 111, 203; Bridget, 74 n; Christian, 169; Elizabeth, 180; Henry, 181 n; Hugh, 5, 28, 52, 74 n, 111, 167, 180, 224, 235 n, 236 n, 277 n, 285; Jane, 52; Joane, 5; Johan, 224; John, 52, 169; Lady Margaret, 74 n; Mary, 28; Sir Thomas, 203.
Boskennan, Ralph de, 195 n.

Bossawsacke, 303.
BOSSAWSACKE, 22; Richard, 116 n.
Bosustowe, 303.
BOSUSTOWE, 23; John, 239 n; Martin, 68.
Bosuysa, John, 167; Margaret, 167.
Bosvennon, Edward, 126; Elizabeth, 126.
Boswaro, M 190.
Boswathck, Boswarthick, Boswathick, John, 170 n; Katherine, 170 n; Margaret, 170 n; Penelope, 170 n.
Boteler, Matilda, 80.
BOTTREUX, 291. (Botreux, Botreus, Botterell.) Edmund, 274 n; Elizabeth, 297; Joane, 228; John, 274 n; Margaret, Lady Hungerford, 132 n; Richard, 228; William, Lord, 132 n; Sir William, 297; William, 120 n, 296.
Boturnell, Jane, 113; Richard, 113; William, 290.
Bowerman, Elizabeth, 52; Johanna, 177; Thomas, 177.
Boweyr, Bowyer. M 168. Alice, 167.
BOWLE, 226, 227.
Bowrd, John, 97; Jone, 97.
Boyle, Anna, 152 n.
Bozom, Elizabeth, 31.
BRABYN, 36, 217. (Brabin, Braban.) Frances, 151 n; John, 103; Katherine, 103.
Bradley, Bradlye. M 289. Thomas, 232 n.
Bragdon, Elynor, 90.
BRANDON, 61; Anne, 32; Charles, Duke of Suffolk, 32.
Brandon, 294.
Bray, 303.
BRAY, 23, 24; Alice, 131 n; Elizabeth, 38 n; Johanna, 238 n; Maria, 149 n; Robert, 131 n, 238 n; William, 38 n.
Brende, Johanna, 187 n.
Brendewoode, Alice, 238 n; Hugh, 238 n.
Brendon, Elizabeth, 290; Joane, 58; Joanna, 137 n.
Brentchurch, Baron, 30.
Brett, Rose, 19, 20; William, 19, 20.
Brewer, 61; Alice, 143; Prudence, 254 n; William de, 143.
Brewin, 65.
Brewys, Robert, 215 n.
Brian, Constance, 79, 80; John, 79, 80.
Bridges, Anne, 76; Richard, 76.
Bridgman, Jasper, 292.
Brightrixton, 193, 194; Johanna, 194; John, 194.
Bristol, Jonathan Trelawney, Bishop of, 110 n; Marquis of, 32.

Bristow, Mary, 218 n.
Brixston, 66.
Broadbridge, Bishop of Exeter, 10.
Broade, Joane, 177 n.
BROGRAVE. 61.
Broke, Willoughby de. See Willoughby.
Brokin, Broken. Alice, 6; Christopher, 6, 78; Elizabeth, 78.
Brooke, Brook. John, 291; Ralph, 294.
Brotherton, Thomas de, 64 n.
Browncowse, Christian, 22; John, 22.
Browne, GO n; Ar., 220 n; Elizabeth, 173 n; Frances, 81 n; Sandry, 217.
Browning, Browneing, Browninge. James, 41; Jane, 70; Katherine, 87; Richard, 7; Timothy, 128 n.
Bruin, Bruyne. Argent, 200 n; Margaret, 60; Richard, 60.
Bruysye, M 55.
Buckland, Thomasine, 275 n.
Bugges, Anne, 205; Edward, 205.
Buleghe, Isabella de, 271 n.
Bullen, Bullin. M 38. Anne 87 n; Mary, 87 n; Sir Thomas, 86 n, 87 n; Sir William, 86 n.
Buller, 303.
BULLER, 24, 25. (Boulter.) Elizabeth, 301; Eulin, 43; Frances, 252; Francis, 26, 43, 63, 112, 135, 252, 301; John, 47 n; John Francis, 230 n; Jane, 301; Katherine, 279 n, 301; Katherine, 161; Margaret, 112, 261 n; Margery, 135; Maria, 26; Mary, 301; Matthew, 301; Sir Richard, 26, 161, 279 n, 284, 301; Richard, 51 n, 161; Thomasine, 63.
Bulteele, Mary, 259 n.
Burdon, Burden. Digory, 291; Joane, 92; Margaret, 107; Peter, 210; Robert, 92, 123 n; Susan, 123 n.
Burell, 25, 303.
BURELL, 25, 26; Arthur, 25.
Burges, 303.
BURGES, 26. (Burgesse, Barges, etc.) Anne, 237; Grace, 187 n; Henry, 181; Humphry, 239; John 256 n; Thomas, 181, 237, 285.
Burgoyne, Brjwyn. Joane, 44; John, 66; Margaret, 66; Richard, 44.
Burnand, Peter, 54 n.
Burnbury, Edward, 150.
Burnell, Bridget, 49.
Burnevy, Thomas, 107 n.
Burnford, 13.
Burthogg, Martin, 110 n.

Burwash, Bartholomew, 144; Johanna, 144.
Bury, Gertrude, 207 n; Humphry, 207 n.
Buryngton, Robert, 125 n.
Bushel, M 20. Richard, 208.
Bussowe, Michael, 22.
Busvargus, 303.
BUSVARGUS, 27.
Butler, x. M 20. Anne, 86 n, 148; Baltizer, 148; Margaret, 86 n, 208; Thomas, Earl of Ormond, 86 n.
Butevant, (?) Viscount, 30.
Byll, 27.
BYLL, 27. (Bill, Boyle, Byle, Bile, Beele, Beile, Beill, Beale, Biell, etc.) M 209. John, 204 n; Margery, 46; Thomas, 46; William. 284.
BYRD, 28. (Bird.) William, 21.

CADE, 286.
Caflin, Mary, 178 n.
Call, Lawrence, 89.
Callard, Florence, 8; Jane, 215; Ralph, 8.
Callwaye, Joane, 247; John, 247.
Calmadow, Mary, 187 n.
Calmady, 303.
CALMADY, 288.
CALWOODLEY, 298. Honor, 262; John, 262.
Camborne alias Paynter, see Paynter.
Camden, William, 195.
Cammes, 113; Johanna, 112; John, 113; Meliar, 113.
Canas, Emma, 239 n; Hugh, 239 n.
Candy, Edmund, 295.
Canford, Johanna, 238 n; Walter, 238 n.
Cann, Can. Edmond, 37; Wilmot, 37; William, 89 n.
Canno, Nicholas, 138.
Cantrebry, Thomas de, 277 n.
Capell, Sir Gamaliel, 2; Mary, 2.
Cara, Francis, 162.
Cararthyn, Elizabeth, 82.
Carance, Alice, 98.
Carballa, William de, 55.
Cardew, William, 285.
Carew, 303.
CAREW, 28, 29, 30, 31, 32, 33. (Carowe, Caerau, Kaeryw, Karrew, etc.) Ann, 83, 83 n, 103 n; Bridget, 102 n, 163 n; Candace, 242 n; Elizabeth, 68, 68 n; Sir Gawen, 61 n; Sir George, 81; Jane, 110 n, 183 n; Johanna, 34 n; Sir John, 183 n; John, 102 n, 103 n, 143, 144, 215 n; Jone, 110 n, 111 n; Lady, 301; Martha, 195 n; Nicholas, 143; Peter, 68; Rachell,

CAREW—continued.
135 n; Richard, 2, 83, 83 n, 273 n, 301; Sarah, 216 n; Sir Thomas, 34 n, 298, 299 n; Thomas, 68, 110 n; Winnand, 19, 301.
Carkeete (Karkeke, Karkycke, etc.), 105 n; John, 118 n, 207 n; William, 102 n.
Carlyon. (Carlyan, Carlyone, Carlighan, etc.) Anne, 191; Barbara, 149 n, 201 n; John, 191 n; Loveday, 253 n; Nicholas, 79, 191, 191 n; Richard, 253 n; Thomasine, 79, 191 n; William, 109 n, 238, 253 n.
Carminowe, x, 33.
CARMINOWE, 33, 34, 35, 296, 297, 298, 299, 300 n. (Carmynow, de Carmyno, Carmyno, etc.) M 239. Blanche, 143 n; Catherine, 19; Elizabeth, 274 n; Gervais, 276 n; Jane, 273 n; Joane, 31; Johanna, 185 n, 274 n, 277 n; John, 72, 271 n; Katherine, 286; Margaret, 103, 276; Margery, 277 n; Mary, 72; Maude, 276 n; Matilda, 185 n; Nicholas, 19, 21, 80 n, 95; Sir Oliver, 185 n, 277 n; Oliver, 103; Philippa, 19, 21; Sir Roger, 20, 276 n; Roger de, 185 n; Robert, 20, 278 n; Thomas, 31, 276; Ralph, 38 n.
Carnarther, Elizabeth, 21; Thomas, 21.
CARNDOW, 46.
Carne, Elizabeth, 153 n; Roger, 153 n.
Carnedon, Robert de, 237.
Carnsew, 303.
CARNSEWE, 35; Alice, 37; George, 157 n; Gillian, 153 n; Jane, 7, 7 n; John, 100; Margaret, 100; Mary, 265; Millicent, 224; Thomas, 115; William, 2, 7, 7 n, 37, 224, 265, 273 n.
Carpenter, William, 204 n.
Carr, Edward, 46; Gabriell, 46.
Carswell, 66. (Kerswell.) Bridget, 66; Nicholas, 66 n.
Carter, 303.
CARTER, 36; Elizabeth, 204 n; Honor, 15, 279 n; James, 275 n; John, 15, 103, 103 n, 151 n, 252 n, 279 n; Katherine, 103; Mary, 103 n; Richard, 215 n, 254 n; William, 142 n.
Carthewe, Carthew. Anna, 91 n; Jane, 91 n, 197 n; John, 197 n; Mary, 254 n; Thomas, 245 n, 253 n.
Carvaddres, John, 155 n.
Carveigh, Carveighe. Barbara, 181 n; John, 181 n; Richard, 181 n, 285.

INDEX OF NAMES. 313

Carver, John, 147; Isabella, 147.
Carverth, Gawen, 285.
Carveth, Joan, 201 *n*; John, 227 *n*; Richard, 177 *n*; Thomas, 301.
Carveth *alias* Perguion, John, 249 *n*.
Carwytham, Richard, 131.
Cary, 37.
CARY, 87.
CARY, 37. (Carey, Carye.) Agnes, 106 *n*; Alice, 122 ; Anne, 64 ; Elizabeth, Lady Barkly, 87 *n* ; Sir George, 64, 87 *n*; George, 2, 13, 122; Henry Bozon, Lord Hunsdon, 31; Henry, Lord Hunsdon, 87 *n*; 281; James, 5 ; Margaret, 13 ; Mary, 2; Sir Robert, Earl of Monmouth, 240 ; Robert, 31, 94 *n*; Sir William, 87 *n*; William, 29, 301.
Cavell, 303.
CAVELL, 37, 38. (Cavill, etc.) M 68. Dorothy, 59; Jane, 253 *n*; Joane, 101 ; Johanna, 144 ; Mary, 87, 252, 253 *n*, 256 *n*; Nicholas, 59 ; William, 101, 177, 252, 253 *n*.
Caskayes, Elizabeth, 238 ; James 238.
Cason, John, 45 ; Margaret, 45.
Catcher, Dorothy, 170 *n*; William, 181.
Ceely, 303.
CEELYE, 38, 39 (Ceely, Celey, etc.) Thomas, 209; Thomasine, 220 *n* ; William, 170.
Chalons, 257 (Challons) ; Ralph, 235 *n* ; Sir Robert, 213 *n*.
Chamond, 40.
CHAMOND, 40. (Chamont, Chamon, etc.) M 165. Emanuel, 178 *n*; Gertrude, 178, 178 *n*; Jane, 165 *n*; Sir John, 165 *n*, 240 ; Margaret, 240; Richard, 178, 189 *n*, 255 *n*; Thomas, 240.
Chamberlaine, x, 278.
Champernon, (Champernown, Champnon) 31, 300 *n*; Arthur, 220 ; Bridget, 93, 220 ; Edward, 302 ; Henry, 64 *n*, 93 ; Margaret, 34 ; Sir Philip, 32 ; Philip, 170 ; Richard, 34.
Chanler, William, 284.
Chapman, 303.
CHAPMAN, 41 ; CHEPMAN, 40. M 62, 139. Abigail, 47 *n* ; Agnes, 227 ; Edward, 283 ; John, 227.
Chappel, Chappell. Elizabeth, 236 *n* ; Margery, 123.
Charfold, 7. (See Grenville.)
Charles, I., King, 259 *n*.
Charles II., King, 221.
Charles, Prince, 10.
Charlton, 257.

Chaterton, Elizabeth, 161 ; George, 161.
Chatley, John, 173.
Chawers, Margaret, 292.
Chedington, Ann, 24; Nicholas, 24.
Cheddore, Elizabeth, 271 ; Sir John, 271.
Chely, Jane, 54 *n*; Mary, 96 *n*.
Chenalls, Mary, 127 *n*.
Chenduit, Cheynduit, Chandit, etc. Alice, 20, 208 ; John, 277 *n*, 297, 300 ; William, 20, 208.
Chenouth, 303.
CHENOUTH, 41, 42. (Chenoweth, Chenowith, Chinoweth, Chenower, Chanough.) Anthony, 115 ; Ellen, 54; Ellinor, 192; Henry, 115; James, 54; John, 217 ; Temperance, 115 ; Thomas, 192.
Chesman, Elizabeth, 34, 299 ; Margaret, 299.
Chester, Dorothy, 234 *n*; William, 234 *n*.
Chichester, Christian, 41 ; Sir John, 273 *n*; John, 196; Mary, 196; Robert, 41.
Chidley, Dorothy, 145 ; John, 145.
Childs, Mary, 260 *n*.
Chiverton, 43, 303.
Chiverton, 176 *n*.
CHIVERTON, 42, 43 ; Elizabeth, 247, 247 *n*; Henry, 25, 189 *n*, 212, 255 *n*; Katherine, 3 ; Margaret, 191 ; Richard, 238 *n*; Thomas, 3 *n*, 17 *n*, 82 *n*, 247 *n* ; William, 3, 247.
Cholwell, Chollwell. Elizabeth, 128 ; Thomasine, 128 *n*.
Christenstow, 61.
Christopher, James, 168.
Chubbe, Chubb. M 6. Daniel, 281.
Chudleigh, Bridget, 29 ; John, 29.
Clarke, Clerk. M 269. Anne, 116; Arabella, 106 *n*; Elizabeth, 106 *n* ; Gefferi, 283 ; Thomas, 146 *n*.
Clare of Solgena, 80.
Clare, Gilbert de, Earl of Gloucester, 86 *n*.
Clapton, Clopton. Elizabeth, 3 ; Joyce, 32 ; Mr., 22 ; William, 3, 22 *n*, 32.
Claxton, M 97.
Clemence, Clemens. Richard, 290 ; Thomas, 290 ; Thomasine, 263 *n*.
Clement, Elizabeth, 204 *n* ; John, 205 ; Robert, 204 *n*.
Close, Clyes. Anne, 72 *n* ; John, 72 *n*, 241, 283.
Clevedon, Richard, 218 *n*.
Cleverton, Richard, 106 *n*.

Clickerd, Elizabeth, 207.
Clifford, M 226. Anthony, 128, 251, 251 *n*; Frances, 266 ; Henry, 266; Magdalen, 128 *n*, 251 ; Mawdelyn, 128, 226 *n*.
Clobery, Cloberie, Clowberie, Cloberye, etc. Alice, 119 ; Andrew, 290 ; Grace, 290 ; Henry, 119, 284; John, 55 ; Margaret, 55; Mary, 10; Oliver, 10, 109 *n*.
Cloford, M 286.
Cloke, Cloake. Cunstice, 145 *n*; Henry, 281.
Clotworthy, Clotworthie. Simon, 95 *n*, 183, 183 *n*.
Clowter, John, 213 ; Wilmot, 213.
Cock, 43 *n*, 303.
COCK, 43. (Cocke, Cok.) Catherine, 232 *n* ; Elizabeth, 72 ; Grace, 11 ; Gregory, 205 ; Hawisia, 223 ; Jane, 214 ; Joane, 255 *n*; John, 11, 119 *n*, 167, 204 *n*, 272 *n*, 282 ; Julian, 205 ; Katherine, 194 *n* ; Margaret, 273 *n*; Mary, 118 *n*; Milysent, 169 *n* ; Nicholas, 133 ; Ralph, 223 ; Robert, 282 ; Thomas, 72, 169 *n*, 194 *n*, 214, 254 *n* ; William, 255 *n*.
Cocke *alias* Lower. See Lower.
Cocking, Robert, 253 *n*.
Coffin, Ebit, 127 ; Jaqnet, 5, 114 ; John, 5 *n*, 67, 114; Peter, 21 ; Richard, 127, 130 *n*.
Coga (or Crooke), Anne, 230 *n*.
Coga, Richard, 180 *n*.
Cogan, Cougan. John, 261 *n* ; Miles, 30 *n*.
Coke (Cooke), 304.
COKE, 44. (Cooke.) Elizabeth, 43 ; Oswald, 281 ; Oswell, 43 ; John, 82 ; Margaret, 153 *n* ; Peter, 16 ; Radagund, 19 ; Robert, 108, 279 ; Thomas, 207 *n*, 265 ; Sir William, 19, 21.
COKEYNE, 46.
Colan, Ann, 223 ; Tristram, 223.
Cole, 199.
COLE, 13, 201. (Coles, Cooles.) Christian, 121, 121 *n* ; Humphry, 195 ; Joan, 137 *n* ; Johanna, 199 ; John, 121, 231 *n*, 262 ; Margaret, 103 ; Philip, 34, 103 ; Philippa, 195 ; Richard, 21 ; Roger, 199 ; Thomas, 85 ; Thomasine, 85.
Collard, Anstace, 101 ; Jane, 204 ; William, 101.
Collerian, Amy, 233 ; Michael, 233.
Collicotte, Joane, 214.
COLLING, 44.
Collings, Mary, 106 *n*.

2 S

Collin, Collyn. M 108. Geffery, 200 ; Jane, 108 ; John, 108, 158 n ; Mary, 265 ; Thomas, 265.
Collyer, Collier. William, 110 n.
Collyns, Collins. Catherine, 265 ; John, 255 n, 261 n, 265, 285 ; Oliver, 215.
Colman, Sophronia, 116 ; Johan, 59 ; Walter, 59.
Colquit, 45.
COLQUIT, 45. (Colquite, Coquit, etc.) M 116. Johanna, 12 ; John, 295.
Colscot, Daniel, 41.
Colsull, Peter, 275 n.
Colthurst, Henry, 233.
Combe, Richard, 206.
Come, Thomas, 282.
Comitreff, John, 237.
Commonwealth, Richard, Lord Protector of the, 106 n.
Condon, M 16.
Connock, 304.
CONNOCK, 46. (Conock.) Elizabeth, 10 ; Jane, 249, 290 ; John, 10, 249, 255 n, 258, 290 ; Loweday, 258 ; Nicholas, 258.
Constantin, Isabell de, 30 n.
Coode, 46.
COODE, 46, 47, 48. (Conde, Code, etc.) Anne, 49 ; Amicia, 145 ; Blanche, 159 n ; Edward, 115n ; Elizabeth, 4 ; Jane, 109, 109 n, 126, 259 n ; John, 4, 109 n, 123 n, 140 n ; Richard, 49, 145, 258 n ; Walter, 49, 126 n, 140 n, 258 ; William, 109, 111 n, 261 n.
Cooke, Vyvyan *alias*. See Vivian.
Copleston, Coplestone. Elizabeth, 288 ; Honor, 195 n ; John, 288 ; Susan, 195.
Corbet, Elizabeth, 31 ; Peter, 177 n.
Corey, 304. (Corry.) Andrew, 165n ; Hugh, 165n ; John, 280.
Cornish, Jane, 78 ; John, 78 ; Robert Kestell Kestell, 115 n ; William, 218 n.
Cornwaleys, Mark le, 261 n.
Cornwall, x. *Cornewall*, 278. Archdeacon of, 271 n ; John Plantagenet, Earl of, 297 ; Reginald, Earl of, 285 ; Richard, Earl of, 35 n, 299 n.
Coryn, Coryne, Corne, Corin. Ann, 256 n ; John, 231, 231 n ; Marian, 181 ; Richard, 181, 256 n.
CORYTON, 268.
Coryton, 14, 15, 304.
CORYTON, 49. (Coriton, Corryton, Corriton, Coringlon, Curington, etc.) M 212. Edith, 47 ; Elizabeth, 14, 15, 242 ; Grace, 100 ; Sir John,

CORYTON—*continued*. 43 n ; Lady, 241 n ; Lady Sarah, 242 n ; Margaret, 89 ; Mary, 34, 222, 246, 299 ; Nichol, 4 ; Peter, 34, 47, 100, 222, 242, 299 ; Richard, 47 ; Thomas, 4, 246.
Cosgarne, John, 200 n, 201 n, 259 n.
Cossen alias Madern, 304.
COSSEN *alias* MADERN, 51. (Cozen, Madderne, etc.) Grace, 260 n ; John, 240 ; William, 285.
Coswarth, 304.
COSWARTH, 50. (Cosworth, etc.) Alice, 102 n ; Catherine, 2 ; Dorothy, 112 ; Edward, 2 ; Henry, 139 n ; John, 2 n, 93 n ; Julyan, 139 ; Katherine, 28 ; Samuel, 93 ; Thomas, 112, 212.
Coswyne, Katherine, 174 ; Thomas, 174.
Coteeles, Mary, 64 ; Sir Thomas, 64.
Coterell, Judith, 170 n.
Cottell, M 206. Walter, 106 n ; William, 50.
Cotton, M 93. Dorothy, 101 n ; Reve, 106 n ; William, 93 n.
Coty, Johana, 186 n.
Couch, Couche, Cowche. M 231. Blanch, 58 ; Edward, 58, 135, 235 n ; Elizabeth, 10 ; Frances, 135 ; John, 96, 185 ; Ralph, 76 ; Robert, 10, 107 n, 141 n.
Courcye, Katherine, 30 ; Miles, Lord, 30.
Courtenay, Courtney, 52. 257.
COURTENAY, COURTENEY, COURTNEY, 51, 52, 53, 54 n. M 137. Ann, 108 n, 243 n ; Constance, 92 ; Douglas, 241n ; Earl of Devon, 259n ; Edward, 24 n, 108, 229 n, 288, 244 n, 261 n ; Edward, Earl of Devon, 21, 60 n, 145 n, 229n ; Sir Edward, 60n ; Elizabeth, 7 n, 268, 301 ; Florence, 229 ; Francis, 112 n, 118 n, 133, 133 n ; George, 92, 231 ; Henry, 152 n, 183 n ; Sir Hugh, 229, 298 ; Hugh, 84, 145 ; Humphry, 32 ; Isabella, 145 ; Joane, 32, 33, 279 ; Johanna, 207 ; John, 161 n, 189 n, 212, 234 n, 253 n, 255 n ; Katherine, 108, 127, 288 ; Lady, 74 n ; Lawrence, 21 n, 38 ; Lowday. 162 ; Margaret, 24 n, 84, 244, 244 n, 261 n ; Maria, 112 n, 207 ; Mary, 264 n ; Nan, 184 n ; Nicholas, 112 n, 262 n ; Sir Peirse, 127, 288 ; Peter, 24n, 207, 227, 244, 301 ; Philip, 137 n ; Philippa, 38, 112 n, 118 n ; Richard, 112 n, 162, 162 n, 207 ; Ro-

COURTENAY—*continued*. bert, 279 ; Thomas, Earl of Devon, 183 n, 229 n ; Ursula, 137 n ; Sir William, 32, 268 ; William, 5, 63 n, 80 n, 244 n, 264 n ; W., 107 n.
COURTNEY, 31.
Courtier, John, 160 ; Maria, 160.
Courtis, Curteis. John, 152 n ; Richard, 21.
Cowlin, Cowling, 304.
COWLIN, 54. (Cowling, Cowlinge, Coulyn, Cowlyngo, Cowlyn, etc.) M 174. Clarence, 42 ; Elizabeth, 99 n ; John, 42, 80, 127 n, 258 n ; Melior, 80 ; Richard, 102 ; Thomas, 127 n ; Thomasine, 223 ; William, 223, 258.
COWLING, 102.
Crab, 304.
CRAB, 55. (Crabb, Crabbe.) Agnes, 198, 200 ; Jane, 186 ; John, 200 ; Richard, 91.
Cradock, John, 59 ; Rose, 59.
Crago, Philipa, 111 n.
Crampporn, Thomas, 205.
Crancann, Crankan, or Carankan. M 82. Jane, 82 ; Nicholas, 82.
Crane, Sir Francis, 15 ; Jone, 15.
Crapp (? Crabb), John, 291.
Creber, Reskymer *alias*. See Reskymer.
Creswell, Henry, 60.
Crimes, 270 n.
CRIMES, 3. (Crymes.) Elizabeth, 78 n ; William, 90, 90 n.
Crispin (Crispine), M 182. Agnes, 182 ; Mary, 182 ; Robert, 182.
Crocker, 304.
CROCKER, 57 ; Agnes, 26, 165 ; Barbara, 66 ; John, 26, 66, 117 ; Mary, 57 n, 117.
Crockhay, 304.
CROCKHAY, 57.
Crook, Johanna, 63 ; Richard, 63.
Cromar, Elizabeth, 33 ; Sir James, 33.
Cromwell, M 291. Oliver, 221 n ; Richard, 106 n.
Crosman, 58.
CROSMAN, 58. (Crossman, Crasman.) Elizabeth, 54 n ; Richard, 152 n, 188, 241, 241 n, 249 n ; Richarda, 188 ; Thomas, 153 n.
Crowan, Margery de, 113 ; Richard de, 113.
CRESSEL, 55, 56 ; William, 198.
Crewes, 304.
CREWES, 56, 57 ; Anne, 80 ; Anthony, 80 ; John, 80 n.
Crudge, Honor, 159 n ; John, 81 ; Thomas, 72.
Crypse, Joanne, 140 n.

INDEX OF NAMES. 315

Cudlip, Elizabeth, 161 *n.*
Culland, Ann, 62*n*; Tristram, 62.
Culley, Thomas, 295.
Cullow, 58.
CULLOW, 58.
Cundye, Catherine, 209.
Cutland, 66.
Cutting, Anne, 213; Robert, 213.
CWTHY, 290.

DABARNON, 286.
Dabernon, 61.
DAGGE, 59. (Dagh, Dag, Dagg, etc.) M 154. Catherine, 168; John, 134; Mary, 220 *n*; Peter, 168; Philippa, 154 *n.*
Dallamayne, John, 180 *n.*
Dalley, Arthur, 105 *n*; Margaret, 105 *n.*
DAMERELL, 46. (D'Aumarle.) Robert, 180 *n.*
Danbye, M 97.
Dandy, 304.
DANDY, 60. (Danny.) Sir John, 198; Nicholea, 198.
Danet, Elizabeth, 2 *n*; Gerald, 2 *n*; Thomas, 275 *n.*
Danvers, Elizabeth, 24; Henry, 24; Sir John, 24.
Daniell, Danyell. Humphry, 122, 254 *n*; Jacob, 207; Jane, 122; John, 124 *n*; Jone, 166; Richard, 285; Roger, 166.
Dangrous, William, 20.
Darley, 60.
DARLEY, 60.
Darrell, 304.
DARRELL, 61. Elizabeth, 82 *n*, 230 *n.*
Darsie, Sir Edward, 124; Isabell, 124.
Dart. (See also Wallis *alias* Darte.) Charles, 201 *n*; Lewis, 190, 201 *n*; Philip, 201 *n.*
DASSELL, 214. Edward, 106 *n*; Margaret, 106 *n.*
Daubney, Ann, 24; Giles, Lord, 24, 270 *n*; Margaret, 270 *n.*
Davies, Davyes. Henry, 231 *n*; Samuel, 191 *n.*
Davilles, M 165. John, 90; Margaret, 90.
Davy, Davey, 270 *n.* Dorothy, 192; Elizabeth, 260 *n*; Emanuel, 125 *n*; Isabell, 69; John, 16, 170, 192, 240 *n*; Jone, 69; Nicholas, 16; William, 69.
Dawe, Daw. Jennet, 219; John, 101; Jone, 213; Margaret, 101; Robert, 213; Thomas, 215 *n*; William, 219.
Daye, Thomas, 295.
Deane, Elizabeth, 218 *n.*
De Broke. See Willoughby.
De Burgh, 86 *n.*
Dedicott, M 192.

Deeble, Debyll, Dible, Debell, Deble, etc. Elizabeth, 209, 211, 273 *n*; John, 209, 210, 211; Julian, 137; Margaret, 210.
De la Brigge, Richard, 55.
De la Champ, Andrew, 223; Emma, 223.
Delahay, x.
DE LA LAND, 19, 20, 203. (De la Landa, De la Laune; also Albalaudn.) Margaret, 18; Otho, 18.
De la Lande (see also Albalanda), 20, 204 *n.*
De la More or Mooringe, Alice, 83 *n*; Jane, 124; Richard, 83 *n*, 124.
De la Poyle, 180 *n.*
DE LA ROCHE, 31. (De Rupe.) Eve, 274 *n*; Sir Richard, 274 *n.*
Denny, Sir Edward, 64.
Denays, 61.
DENYS, 61, 62. (Dennis, Le Deneis, etc.) M 81. Alice, 79; Edmund, 302; Eudon, 251; George, 127 *n*, 251; Gertrude, 2; Honor, 82 *n*, 302 *n*; John, 236 *n*; Martha, 31; Philip, 118 *n*; Philippa, 118 *n*; Richard, 79; Sir Robert, 2, 273, 300 *n.*
Derby, Dereby. Anne, da. of the Earl of, 243; Charles, Earl of, 257; Isabella, da. of the Earl of, 143; John de, 261 *n*; The Earl of, 243; William, Earl of, 143.
Derwyn, Durwyn. Elizabeth, 91; Joan, 211 *n*; Roger, 211 *n*; Sibel, 211 *n*; William, 91.
Despencer, 86 *n.*
Deuse, Johanna, 171 *n.*
Devon, Edward Courtney, Earl of, 21, 60 *n*, 145 *n*; Thomas Courtney, Earl of, 183 *n*, 229 *n*; Courtney, Earl of, 259 *n.*
Devonshire, Elizabeth, 266 *n.*
Devreux, Robert, Earl of Essex, 31.
Devyok, Devioke, Deviock, Deviell, 37 *n*. Edmond, 37; Jane, 37, 52; John, 291; William, 290.
Dewen, 304.
DEWEN, 62. (Dewin, Duen.) M 23. Katherine, 174; Thomas, 174.
Dewhurst, M 202.
Dickwood, Margaret, 263 *n*; Thomas, 221 *n.*
Digby, Margaret, 197.
Diggow, Martin, 169 *n.*
DIMOCK, 317.
Dingley, M 47. William, 47 *n*.
Dinham, Dynham, Denham, de Dyncham. Alice, 298; Doro-

Dinham—*continued*.
thy, 101; Elizabeth, 99; George, 275 *n*; Lady Jane, 275 *n*; John, Lord, 31, 275 *n*; Sir John, 298; John, 99, 101, 296; Joseus, 84 *n*, 258 *n*; Margaret, 31; Margery, 84 *n*; Oliver, 2; Philippa, 96; Robert, 180 *n*; Roger, 275 *n*; William, 96.
Dodge, John, 78.
Dodson, 304.
DODSON, 63. (Dosten, Dosen, etc.) Mary, 46, 241 *n*; Robert, 25; Thomas, 46, 301.
Dodustow, Ralph de, 23; Richard de, 23; William de, 23.
Doe, Jane, 116.
Dolton, Roger, 68.
Donand, Warin, 59.
Donnet, x.
Donnet, 86 *n.*
Dowell, Mary, 226.
Downe, 66.
DOWNE, 206. M 16. Joane, 83 *n*; John, 83 *n.*
Downinge, Richard, 45.
Dowrish, Dourich, Dourishe, etc. Agnes, 60 *n*, 104 *n*; Anne, 64 *n*; Edmond, 60 *n*, 104 *n*, 173 *n*; Elizeus, 104 *n*; Hugh, 64 *n*; Johanna, 104 *n*; Lewis, 106 *n*; Margaret, 106 *n*; Walter, 32.
Dowse, Ellinor, 167; Richard, 167.
Doygnill, Walter, 55.
Doyngle, Doyngull. John, 9, 228; Jone, 228; Richard, 228; Sibbell, 9.
Drake, 270 *n.* M 119 *n.* Amy, 85 *n*; Augustyne, 302; Duncombe, 243; Edmund, 196 *n*; Elizabeth, 66 *n*, 80 *n*, 224 *n*, 226 *n*, 232 *n*; Sir Francis, 66 *n*, 68 *n*, 73 *n*, 85 *n*, 136 *n*, 195 *n*, 196 *n*; Francis, 106 *n*, 122 *n*; Henry, 159 *n*; Honor, 302; Joane, 232 *n*; Lady Johanna, 224 *n*, 226 *n*; John, 56 *n*, 80 *n*, 85, 143 *n*, 173 *n*; Margaret, 197 *n*; Sarah, 243 *n*; Thomas, 66 *n*, 78 *n*, 197 *n*, 199 *n*; Thomasine, 56 *n*; William, 56 *n*, 63 *n*, 80 *n*, 232 *n.*
Drew, Drewe, 270 *n.* M 92. Agneta, 169, 169 *n*; Emanuell, 169, 169 *n*; John, 243 *n*; Maude, 217.
Drinnick, George, 294.
Dubher, John, 112 *n*; Merauld, 112 *n.*
Ducket, M 108.
Ducton, Margaret, 4; Richard, 4.
Dulyn, Henry, 217; Mary, 217.
Dunheved alias Launceston, 280, 281.

INDEX OF NAMES.

Dunkyn, Cecilia, 243 n; John, 213 n; Robert, 283.
Dunn, Dunc, Donc. M 92. Margery, 92 n; Richard, 92 n; Richo, 104 n.
DUNSLAND, 286.
Dunrich, Anne, 249; Edmond, 249.
Dunstanville, Margaret, 276 n; Sir William, 276 n.
Durant, 67. M 272. Jane, 16; John, 16, 68, 257; Margaret, 68, 257; Richard, 280.
Durhall, Durhull. Alice, 276 n, 278 n; Emma, 278 n; Mirabell, 276 n, 278 n; Roger, 278 n.
Durham, John, Prior of, 94.
DURNFORD, 46, 47. (Dernford.) M 63. James, 63 n; Johanna, 63 n; Stephen, 63 n.
Dyer, John, 202 n.

E...., Margaret, 213.
Eare, 67. (Ere.) Alice, 68.
Eastchurch, M 171 n.
East Lowe, 281.
Eddye, Edye, Edy, Ede. Alice, 175; Elizabeth, 301; John, 153, 280; Otes, 175; William, 58.
Edgcombe, 63.
EDGCOMBE, 63, 64, 65. (Eggcombe, Edgcomb, Edgecombe, Edgcumb, Edgcumbe.) M 47, 139. Alice, 114; Anne, 135, 239; Elizabeth, 28; Francis, 211 n; Joan, 211 n; Sir Pierse, 47 n; Pierse, 135; Sir Richard, 28, 239.
Edmerston, 193.
EDMERSTON, 193, 194.
Edmondes, 304.
EDMONDES, 65. (Emondes.)
Everard, 285.
Ednuet Annilla, Robert de, 285.
Edward I., King, 180 n, 259 n, 299; Elizabeth, du. of, 259 n.
Edward III., King, 32.
Edwards, 304.
EDWARD, EDWARDS, 225, 226.
EDWARDES, 65. Emblyn, 301; Margery, 229 n; Ralph, 235 n; Thomas, 115, 192, 229 n.
Efford, Christopher, 136 n.
Eger, Egar. David, 17; John, 281; Martin, 17; Thomas, 281.
Eggloshcill, Eglos-hei, Egglesscil. Alice de, 113; Galfrid de, 113; John de, 113; Matthew de, 190 n; William de, 113.
Elford, 304.
ELFORD, 66. Alice, 211 n; Sarah, 179 n.
Elise, Blanch, 176 n.
Elizabeth, Queen, 73, 87 n.
Ellyott, 66.

ELLYOTT or ELIOT, 66. (Elliott, Elliot.) Mary, 253 n.
Ellys, Pascowe, 283.
Enedye, Thomas, 18.
Enis, 20 n.
ENIS, 169.
Enys, 67.
ENYS, 67. (Enis, Innis.) Margery, 63; Thomas, 185, 185 n; Samuel, 163 n.
Ercedekne. See Archdeacon.
Erisey, 67, 304.
ERISEY, 67, 68, 69. (Erisy, Erysy, Erisie, Erisi, Erisye, Erisa, Erysyc, Erissey, Herisi, Heris, Arisie, etc.) M 210, 272. Catherine, 171; Dionis, 158 n; Dorothy, 218, 98; Elizabeth, 218 n, 264 n; Florence, 169; James, 23, 28, 85, 98 n, 105 n, 171, 238; Johanna, 23; John, 23, 105 n, 258 n; Margery, 238; Martha, 210 n; Mary, 172, 259 n; Peter, 23; Richard, 98, 105 n, 259 n; Robert, 103 n; Thomas, 169.
Erlesman, Jane, 176; Richard, 176.
Erneetle, Joan, 197 n; John, 197 n.
Ernley, Anthony, 269 n; Isabella, 269 n; Margaret, 269 n.
Erricke, Mary, 260 n.
Eskler, Vivian de, 261 n.
Estcott, *Estcotte*, 69, 213.
ESTCOTT, 69, 70. (Estcote, Estcot, Escott.) Christian, 78; Joane, 120; John, 78, 204 n, 263; Osbert de, 251 n; Mr., 27, 58; Richard, 88, 215, 281.
Esse, x.
Essex, Robert Devereux, Earl of, 31, 259 n.
Eustace, Eustys. Alice, 48 n; John, 58.
Eustic, John, 132 n.
Eva, Evah. Anne, 164; John, 191 n; Thomas, 164.
Eyre. (See also Ayre and Eare.) M 182. William, 226 n.
Eyres, William, 38.
Exeter, Broadbridge, Bishop of, 10; William Cotton, Bishop of, 93 n.

Facy, Facie. (? Vacey.) Alice, 204 n; Jane, 58; Richard, 58.
Fairford, x.
Falmouth, Lord, 277 n.
Fantleroy, Brian, 112; Elizabeth, 112; Margaret, 100; Peter, 71.
Fane, Mary, 243 n.
Farnham, Mary, 268 n.
Favell, Bernard, 4 n.
Fayrfax, M 97.

Featey *alias* Fayrclowgh. Anna, 60; John, 60.
Fenton, John de, 250.
Ferrers, 299 n.
Ferrers, 257, 304. (Farrers, Ferrars, Ferrys.) Earl, 144, 144 n; Honor, 257; Isabella, 113; Isot, 49; Isould, 296, 300; Johanna, 144; John, 49, 296; Katherine, 257; Richard, 257; Sir Reginald, 300 n; Reginald, 257, 296, 300; Sir William, 297; William, 143 n, 300.
Fil Galfrid, Hawisia, 143; John, 143.
Fil Perlonis, Warin, 261 n.
Fil Petri, Alianora, 144; Beatrix, 143; Reginald, 143, 144.
Fil Wyhd, Richard, 195 n.
Finch, James, 294.
Firsdon, Auger de, 171 n; Margery de, 171 n.
Fitz, Fitze, Fites. Grace, 66, 122; Honor, 35; John, 14, 15, 35, 66, 85, 122, 235 n; Katherine, 14, 15; Robert, 235 n.
Fitz Alan, 86. Alice, 31; Sir Edmund, 31; Richard, Earl of Arundell, 31.
Fitzhugh. See Fursland *alias*.
Fitzmorice, Lord, 30.
Fitzpen alias Phippen, 71.
FITZPEN *alias* PHIPPEN, 71.
Fitz Pierse, William, 144 n.
Fitz Roger, Elizabeth, 144.
Fitz Stephen, Robert, 30.
Fitz Walter, Walter, 144.
Fitz Williams, Dennis, 281; Edmond, 281; Elizabeth, 144; Sir John, 144; Philip, 281.
Fitz Yva, 276 n.
Fitz Yee, x.
Flamanke, 71.
FLAMANKE, 71, 72. (Flamank, Flamanck, Flamick, Flamock, Flamocke, Flamoke.) M 100. Ibott, 219; John, 9; Mary, 253 n; Sir Nicholas, 219; Nicholas, 261 n; Oliver, 11; Richard, 76; Roger, 255 n; William, 299.
Fleming, 304.
FLEMINGE, 72. (Flemmyuge.) Doctor, 123 n.
Fletchar, 304.
FLETCHAR, 73. (Fletcher.) M 97. Godolphin, 140 n.
Floyer, Floyre. M 286. Francis, 39; William, 39.
Foalkroy, Margaret, 94; William, 94.
Foggins, Gregory, 123 n.
Foote, John, 138 n; Richard, 138; William, 295.

INDEX OF NAMES. 317

Ford, John, 114; Margaret, 114, 248 *n*; Roger, 11; Walter, 248 *n*.
Fornell, Thomas, 178 *n*.
Forster, Elyn, 117; Julian, 177; Richard, 117.
Fortescu, 304.
FORTESCU, 73, 74. (Fortescue, Foskew, Foscue, etc.) M 171, 251. Agnes, 215 *n*; Ann, 171 *n*, 230, 230 *n*; Arthur, 107 *n*; Charles, 201 *n*; Edmond, 158; Edward, 288; Elizabeth, 158; Florence, 259 *n*; George M., 86 *n*; Honor, 288; Humphry, 11; Jane, 258 *n*; John, 171 *n*, 230, 257, 258 *n*; Mary, 11, 176 *n*; Nicholas, 258 *n*; Richard, 215 *n*; William, 210 *n*, 257.
FORTESCUE, 150.
Fortescue, 270 *n*.
Fountaine, Margaret, 15; William, 194.
Fowey, Foye. Sir Adam de, 69; Asseria, 69; Vicar of, 180 *n*, 220 *n*.
Fowler, Joane, 105; Richard, 105.
Fownes, 304.
FOWNES, 289.
Fox, Agnes, 247 *n*, 255 *n*; Anthony, 133; Elizabeth, 133; William, 247 *n*, 255 *n*.
Foxcomb *alias* Trenchard, M 249.
Fragle, Henry, 266.
Francis, Johan, 104 *n*; William, 113; John, 284.
Frawn, Richard, 168.
Free, Elizabeth, 166.
French, Abbot, 295.
Frigens, Friggens. Robert, 207; Gregory, 285.
Frisell, Patricius, Earl of Anegos, 143.
Frye, Grace, 28; William, 28.
Fulford, M 47. Sir Baldwin, 31; Baldwin, 272 *n*; Elinor, 268; Elizabeth, 37; Sir John, 37, 268.
Furlonge, Richard, 284; Anthony, 294; Christopher, 295.
Furzland *alias* Fitzhugh, Margaret, 246.
Furzland, Fursland. Elizabeth, 137; John, 134 *n*, 137; Thomasine, 134.
Fursman, M 81. John, 135 *n*, 136 *n*.
Fuyge, Fudge, Fuge. Thomas, 179 *n*; William, 283.

Gabriel, William, 137 *n*.
Gache, Margaret, 13.
Gain, Mary, 267; Thomas, 267.
Gaire, Jone, 71; Reginold, 71.

Galis, Frances, 74; Richard, 74.
Game, John, 283.
Gamon, 304.
GAMON *alias* GAMBONE, 74.
Garch, Commend, 243 *n*.
Gardiner, Awdrey, 32; William, 32.
Garland, John, 295; Margaret, 44; Richard, 44.
Garrett. See Sharpe *alias*.
GASCOYNE, 174.
GASGELL, 292.
Gatliffe, Gatley, 105.
GAVERIGAN, 223, 224. (Gaverygan, Gaveregan, Gavrigan, etc.) Avis, 131 *n*; Jane, 81, 81 *n*, 83; John, 65, 131 *n*, 153, 186; Margaret, 65; Mary, 153; Philippa, 186; Walter, 21, 81, 83.
Gears, Theobald, 179.
Gedy, Gedye, Geyde. Elizabeth, 37 *n*, 301; Radigund, 66 *n*, 67; Richard, 21, 66 *n*, 67, 67 *n*.
Geere, Geare, Gere, Gerre. Alice, 62; John, 48; Margery, 23; Richard, 23; Stephen, 284; Thomas, 23; William, 62.
Geffery, Geffrey, Jeffery, Jeffric. Alice, 250 *n*, 253 *n*; Elizabeth, 253 *n*; Johan, 186; John, 250 *n*; Nicholas, 107 *n*; Robert, 237.
George, 304.
GEORGE, 75. (Gorges, Gorg, de Gorges.) Dorothy, 54 *n*; Duglas, 51; Elizabeth, 51, 53 *n*, 54 *n*, 84; Ferdinando, 230 *n*; Mary, 135; Susanna, 221 *n*; Sir Theobald, 84; Tristram, 51, 135.
Geirveis, 77, 304.
GEIRVEIS, 75, 76, 77; GEYRVEYS, 77. (Gerveis, Gerveys, Gervys, Gerves, Gearveis, Garvis, Jarvis.) M 70. Emlyn, 235 *n*; Grace, 182; James, 148 *n*, 223; John, 258 *n*; Margaret, 71; Margery, 223; Melior, 163, 164; Peter, 71; Richard, 162 *n*, 163, 164, 182, 224 *n*, 231; William, 235 *n*.
Genninge (? Jenning), Stephen, 57.
Gennis, Genys. John, 281.
Geraldines, 30.
Germayne, Joane, 202.
Gerner, John, 250.
Gerratt, Jane, 192; Thomas, 192.
Gerry, John, 173 *n*.
Giffard, X, 61.
GIFFORD, 206; Alice, 269; George, 185; Henry, 18; Hugh, 293; John, 58, 85,

GIFFORD—*continued*.
286; Leonard, 26; Margaret, 26, 185, 293; Mary, 185 *n*; Philippa, 58.
Gilbert, M 286. Geffry, 6 *n*; Isabell, 84, 87; Sir Oliver, 87; Otes, 6, 84; Richard, 40; Thomasine, 6, 40.
Gilbert *alias* Webber, see Webber.
Gill, 66. (Gyll.) Arthur, 265; John, 57; Margery, 57; William, 12.
Gillard, Margaret, 51.
Giles, M 52.
Gilly, M 233.
Ginn, Christopher, 235 *n*.
Glanville, 77; *Glanvile*, 78.
GLANVILLE, 77; GLANVILE, 78. (Glanvill, Glandville, Glandfield, etc.) Dioness, 173, 173 *n*; Duena, 173 *n*; Sir Francis, 196 *n*; Jane, 196 *n*; John, 70, 108, 173*n*, 197*n*; Mary, 108, 254*n*.
Glason, Thomas, 126.
Gloucester, Gilbert de Clare, Earl of, 86 *n*.
Glover, Thomas, 95 *n*, 278 *n*.
Glyn, 94 *n*.
Glyn, 257, 304.
GLYN, 79, 80. (Glinne, Glen, de Glen, etc.) George, 12; Johan, 56 *n*, 297; Sir John, 297; John, 47 *n*, 81, 83, 141, 257; Lowdy, 95; Margaret, 81, 83; Nicholas, 56 *n*, 95, 111 *n*; Thomas, 168 *n*, 175 *n*; Tomasin, 47, 191 *n*, 257.
Goddare, Goddard. Richard, 131, 131 *n*.
Godnesford, Johanna, 193; Robert, 193.
Godolphin, 304.
GODOLPHIN, 29.
GODOLPHIN, 80, 81, 82, 83. (Godolghan, Godolfyn, Godolfin, Godolphynne, Godolphyu, etc.) Alexander, 68; Lady Alice, 78 *n*; Blanch, 109; Catherine, 212 *n*; Edward, 258 *n*; Elizabeth, 119, 235 *n*, 277 *n*; Frances, 176 *n*; Sir Francis, 5, 28, 78, 78 *n*, 109; Francis, 212 *n*, 241 *n*, 282; Jane, 5; Johanna, 68; John, 38, 42, 68, 216, 235 *n*, 277 *n*; Nicholas, 156 *n*; Prudence, 44; Thomasine, 28, 38, 42, 205, 205 *n*; Sir William, 119, 259 *n*; William, 44, 127 *n*, 151 *n*, 224.
Godrewy, Joane, 155 *n*; William, 155 *n*.
Godye, Mawde, 223; Philip, 223.
Golopin (? Godolphin), Nicholas, 113; Johanna, 113.
Golston, John, 209.

INDEX OF NAMES.

Goode, 83, 304.
GOODE, 83.
Gough, M 85.
Gourdon, Jane, 69.
Gourlyn, Gerlyn, Gurland, M 272; Joane, 155 n; Johanna, 76; Nicholas, 131 n; Thomas, 155 n; William, 76.
GOURNY, 73. (Gourney.) M 24.
GOVILY, 234. (Goviley, Ghivaile.) Isabell, 277 n; Thomas, 277 n.
Grace, 30.
Grampound, 282.
Grandison, 86 n.
Gravenor, Gertrude, 69.
Greatbatch, Anne, 261 n.
Greby, Elizabeth, 141 n.
Grees, Germain, 285.
Gregory, Grigorie. Baldwin, 91; Elizabeth, 66 n, 91.
Grenvile, x, 40, 87.
GRENVILE, 84, 85, 86.
GREINEVILE, 87. (Greinvelle, Greenevile, Grenfeild, Greynvele, Greynvile, Grenoffelde, Greynfelde, de Greinvilla, etc.) M 165. Sir Bartholomew, 257; Sir Bernard, 146 n; Sir Bevile, 146 n, 277 n; Christian, 68; Digory, 178, 178 n; Ebbot, 195 n; Egidius, 234 n; Ellin, 292; George, 195 n; Grace, 74 n; Jane, 40, 272; Sir John, 146 n; John, 81, 83; Lady Mary Howard *alias*, 86 n; Margery, 234 n; Matilda, 235 n; Philippa, 178 n; Sir Richard, 273 n; Sir Roger, 7 n; Roger, 68; Susan, 178; Sir Thomas, 40, 272; Thomas, 69; William, 292.
Grevill, Sir Foulke, 90; Mary, 90; Francis, 285.
Grey, Gray, M 22. John, 144.
Griffin, Mary, 268 n.
Grills, 88.
GRILLS, 88. GRYLLS, 88, 89. (Gryles, Griles, de Grelles, etc.) Charles, 132 n, 199, 220 n; Elizabeth, 56, 199, 204 n; Jane, 132 n; John, 284; Mary, 96; Sampson, 70; William, 96; Willmot, 70.
Grimes (Crimes), William, 90.
Grimsbye, M., 97.
Grose, 304.
GROSSE, 89. David, 3, 127 n; Dorkis, 3; Edward, 123 n, 285; Jonathan, 108; Susan, 123 n; Thomas, 127 n, 133; William, 123 n; Zeakiell, 3.
Grove, John, 284.
Guavis, Anne, 51; John, 51.
Gubbes, Amy, 43; John, 43.
Guilford, Sir Henry, 32; Mary, 32.

Gunmaylek, Simon, 131 n.
Gwennow, Alice, 258 n; Francis, 258 n.
Gwinear (Winiore), Michael, Vicar of, 173.
Gye, Alice, 66; Robert, 66.

Haccomb, Cecilia de, 31. Jordan de, 31.
Haddon, M., 65.
Haigham, Sir John, 10. Lettice, 10.
Haill, John, 237.
Halep, 21.
HALEP, 223. (Hallop or Trewonwall.) Lawrence, 19, 21; Matilda, 19; Mawde, 21.
Halet, Marina de, 222; Richard de, 222.
Halke, Jane, 91.
Hall, Roger, 126.
HALLACOMBE, 150.
HALLAMORE, 90. (Hollamore.) Grace, 78; Peter, 78, 192 n, 245; Petronell, 162 n; Rachell, 245; Walter, 162 n, 217 n, 245.
Halse, Elizabeth, 218 n; Honor, 196; Richard, 196.
Haly, Robert, 45.
Hamle, Hameley, Hambly, Hamblie. Agnes, 154 n; Benedict, 189 n; Elizabeth, 220 n; Honor, 227; John, 227, 229 n.
Hamlyn, Jone, 201 n.
Hammett, Elizabeth, 45.
HAMMOND, 61. M., 97.
Hancock, Elizabeth, 246 n; Thomas, 282; William, 199.
Hankford, x. (Hankeforde.) Ann, 86 n; Sir Richard, 86 n; Sir William, 86 n.
Hankyn, Joseph, 131 n.
Hansam, Gregory, 88.
Hantkin, John, 40; Lore, 40.
Hanyon (? Lanyon), Alice, 183; William, 183.
Harding, Jane, 146 n.
Harecurt, William de, 261 n.
Harewood, Harwoode. Christian, 201 n; Walter, 294.
Harison, Gertrude, 69; Richard, 282.
Harlewyn, Edith, 279 n.
Harlisdon, John, 198.
Harp, M., 262.
HARRINGTON, 180 n. (Haryngton.) Anne, 95 n, 277 n; Richard, 94 n, 95 n, 219 n, 277 n, 278 n.
Harris, 270 n.
Harris, 304.
HARRIS, 90. (Harrys, Harryes, Harrice, etc.) M 76. Sir Christopher, 85; Christopher, 85; Dorothy, 264 n; Elizabeth, 101, 215, 251;

HARRIS—*continued*.
Frances, 114; Francis, 84; Henry, 181 n; Honour, 120 n; Hugh, 254 n; Joane, 256 n; Johan, 146 n; John, 101, 106 n, 114, 120 n, 197 n, 246, 251, 284, 291; Lazarus, 295; Mary, 72 n, 80 n, 246; Philippa, 80 n, 181 n; Pye, 181 n; Richard, 149 n; Thomas, 254 n; William, 120 n, 159 n, 215.
HARRY, 103. (Harrye.) Charles, 141 n; Joan, 126 n; Johanna, 259 n; Joyce, 268; Nicholas, 247 n; Parker, 159; Thomas, 254 n; Tristram, 268.
Harte, Hart. Jane, 90 n; John, 135; Katherine, 135.
Hartwell, Robert, 280.
Harry, 91.
HARVY, 91. (Harvey, Harvye.) Anne, 32; Francis, 270; George, 199 n; John, 97, 237; Jone, 97; Sir Nicholas, 32; Marquis of Bristol, 32.
Haston, M., 165.
Hatch, 304.
HATCH, 91, 92. Christopher, 53; Ellin, 286; Isabell, 31; Jane, 130, 131; Thomas, 286.
Hatherley, Anne, 144; Bartholomew, 144.
Haucksworthe, M 97.
Haughton. See Houghton.
Haward, Alice, 25; Sir Rowland, 25.
HAWES, 256. (Hawrys, Haweis.) Jane, 162; Joane, 254 n; John, 191 n; Reynold, 162.
Hawke, 304.
HAWKE, 92.
Hawkestow, William, 275.
Hawkins, Hawkyns, Haukins, Hawkin, Hawkyn. Ann, 232 n; Agnes, 139, 229; Barbara, 102 n, 200 n; Elinor, 254 n; Hugh, 179; John, 130, 220, 282; Jone, 237; Mary, 200 n; Richard, 135; William, 229, 237.
Hawky, Thomas, 295.
Haydon, Heydon. Ebit, 159; John, 188; Richard, 132 n; Thomasine, 188; William, 188.
Haymer, Jane, 288; Raphe, 288.
Hayne, Henry, 8; Wilmot, 8.
Hayre, Elizabeth, 144; Richard, 144.
Hoare, Cicily, 92; William, 92.
Hokinson, Elinor, 186; Richard, 186.
Hola, Ogor, 277 n.
Hele, 304.

INDEX OF NAMES. 319

HELE, 92, 93. (Heale.) Agnes, 287; Dulcebella, 50; John, 145, 287; Jone, 289; Philippa, 145; Thomas, 50; Walter, 289.
HELIGAN, 276 n, 277 n. (Helegan, Helligan.) Joane, 228; Nicholas, 228; Sir Robert, 296.
Helligan, 258 n.
HELL, 174.
Helleston, David de, 17. Martinus Eger, son of David, 17.
Helliard, Blanche, 34; Thomas, 34.
Hellier, Heliar, Hellyer. John, 244 n; Thomas, 231, 232 n, 280.
Hellier *alias* Mayow. See Mayow.
Hellinge, Mary, 92; Thomas, 92.
Helstone, 282.
Hender, x, 93 n, 304.
HENDER, 93. (Hendar, Hendor, Hinder, Hendre, Hendra, etc.) Catherine, 147; Christopher, 295; Edward, 186; Elizabeth, 228, 229 n; Frances, 186, 187; John, 147, 180 n, 187, 228, 229 n; Julyan, 116; Nicholas, 295; Richard, 191 n; William, 116, 172 n.
Hendy, John, 209.
Hennah, Richard, 210 n.
Henry I., King, 30, 285, 299; Henry, his son by Nesta, 30; Reginald, Earl of Cornwall, son of, 285.
Henry III., 276 n, 299 n; Richard, brother of, 299 n.
Henry VII., King, 63.
Henry VIII., King, 87 n.
Henry, Prince, 19.
Herbert, Harbert. John, 167, 282. Somerset, Lord, 258 n.
Hereford and Essex, Humphrey de Bohun, Earl of, 259 n.
Herle, 304.
HERLE, 94, 95. (Hearle, Hearell, Horrell, Horwell, etc.) Anne, 76, 77, 126, 180 n; Edward, 125, 224 n, 225 n; Elizabeth, 104 n; Jenophah, 125; Joan, 226; John, 76 n, 180 n; Loveday, 121 n; Margaret, 180 n; Nicholas, 76, 77; Richard, 299; Robert, 284; Sibell, 126; Thomas, 80, 121 n, 126, 239 n; Walter, 226; William, 173.
Horring, Edmond, 79 n.
Hext, 304.
HEXT, 96. (Hexte, Hexet, Hixt, Hix, Heaxtt, etc.) Digory, 177, 215; George, 281; Jane, 177; John, 262; Nicholas, 283; Thomas, 254; William, 182.

Hext, 105 n.
HEY, 63.
Hickes, 304.
HICKES, 96. (Hicks, Hickst.) Ephue, 101; Hannah, 120 n; Jane, 188; John, 188, 216; Richard, 188; Thomas, 101.
Hichins, Hitchins, Hitchings. Henry, 179; Johan, 140 n; Mary, 179; Thomasine, 101.
Hickinge, Elizabeth, 129 n.
Higgowe, John, 245 n.
Hill, 193, 304.
HILL, 73, 194.
HILL, 97, 98, 99. HYLL, 100. Agatha, 119; Agnes, 27; Francis, 183; Honor, 249; Jane, 258 n, 298; John, 27, 170; Katherine, 249; Michael, 258 n; Morris, 249; Pawle, 68; Philippa, 27; Richard, 285; Robert, 27, 119, 258 n, 298.
Hillersdon, Elizabeth, 26.
Hinckston, Elizabeth, 190; Thomas, 190.
Hoare, 304.
HOARE, 100, 101. (Hore.) M 76. Joane, 181 n; John, 38, 181 n, 294, 295; Katherine, 254 n.
Hobbes, Thomas, 19.
Hoblyn, 304.
HOBLYN, 101, 102, 103 n. (Hobelyn, Hoblynge, Hoblyng, etc.) Agnes, 246; Margorie, 9; Powley, 164; Thomas, 9, 50 n, 181 n, 246, 246 n, 254 n, 295.
Hockin, Hocking, Hocken, Hockyn. M 101. Elizabeth, 10; Jane, 29 n; John, 88, 101 n, 295; William, 133 n.
Hockings, Mileson, 72 n.
Hodgshonu, Philip, 165.
Hogge, John, 156 n; Mabel, 156 n; Stephen, 41.
Hole, Margaret, 160 n.
Holman, Helman, Hilman, Hillman, Holliman, Holdman, Houlman. Alice, 29; Arthur, 295; Fulke, 211 n; Honor, 211 n; John, 29, 105 n, 172 n; Lowdye, Louvdei, 11 n; Mary, 201 n; Sir Thomas, 220 n; Thomas, 6 n, 211 n; William, 120 n, 199 n.
Holmes, Joane, 28; William, 107 n.
Holland, 63. Roger, 31; Thomasine, 31.
Hollewey, William de, 250.
Holwell, Thomas, 256 n.
Honichurch, Honychurch, 270 n. Anne, 293.
Honnywood, Honywood. Sir Thomas, 25, 112 n.
Honstant, Joyce, 71. Sir Richard, 71.

Hoop. See Andrewe *alias*.
Hooper, Johan, 201 n; Jone, 45; Mary, 197 n; William, 207 n.
Hope, Elizabeth, 273 n.
Hora, Johanna, 158 n; John, 158 n.
Horde, Johanna, 141 n; William, 141 n.
HORNACOTE, 35 n, 296. (Hornicot, Hornyngecote, Hornyacote, etc.) Gervaise de, 299 n; Jarveis, 20; Mawd, 20.
Horndon, Grace, 135 n.
Hornell or Norwell. Elizabeth, 275 n.
Horsey, Katherine, 24, 145; Sir John, 24; John, 145; Sir Ralph, 145.
Houghton, Haughton. Maria, 60; Willmot, 14.
Howard, John, Duke of Norfolk, 60 n; Lady Mary (*alias* Grenfield), 86 n; Mary, 106 n.
Howe, Ann, 253 n.
Howell, Francis, 261 n; Mary, 179 n.
Howsaye, Johanna, 137 n.
Howse, Elizabeth, 154 n.
Huckmore, Elizabeth, 10.
Huddersfield, Catherine, 31; Sir William, 31.
Hudisland, Alice, 214; Robert, 214.
Humphrie, Humfry, Humphrey. Alice, 164; James, 56, 189 n; Jane, 56; John, 164.
Hungerford and Bottreaux, Margaret, Lady, 132 n.
Hungerford, x.
Hunicome, Dorothy, 88.
Hunkin, 304.
HUNKIN, 290. John, 46, 283.
Hunny, John, 134.
Hunsdon, Henry Bozon Cary, Lord, 31; Henry Carey, Lord, 87 n.
Hunt, John, 168; Peter, 15.
Huntingdon, Henry, Earl of, 170 n; Katherine, Countess of, 170 n.
Hurst, M 70. Anne, 31; Robert, 194.
Husband, George, 248 n; Thomas, 256 n; John, 119; Maria, 137 n.
Hussie, M 75.
Hutchins, Thomas, 23.
Huthnans, Anna, 89 n.
Hyelton, Sir Robert, 289.

Ilcomb, x.
Inch. Elizabeth, 121; Philip, 121; William, 253 n, 254 n.
Ingpenny, Ingepenne. Alice, 33; Roger de, 271.

INDEX OF NAMES.

Ingram, Mary, 48 n; Richard, 227 n; Robert, 117.
Inkleton, M 177.
Innis, 21 n.
Irishe, Robert, 104 n.
Isack, Isseck. M 126. Edward, 182.
Isam, Katherine, 23; William, 23.
Ised, Vivian, 261 n.

Jackman, Jane, 206; Johanna, 139; John, 206.
Jago, Jagow. Alice. 166, 166 n; George, 122 n; Henry, 166; John, 285; Philip, 285; Robert, 72.
Jagow, Michell alias. See Michell.
James, Agnes, 245 n; Jane, 254 n; Johanna, 245 n; John, 24; Thomas, 282.
Jane, Christian, 105 n; John, 199; Thomas, 283, 284.
Jenkin (Jenkins), 304.
JENKYN, 36.
JENKYN, 103, 104 n. (Jenken, Jenkin.) Anne, 212 n; James, 212 n; Johanna, 155 n; John, 159; Patrick, 160; Walter, 177 n.
Jennings, 304.
JEYNENES, 104. (Jenneus, Jennyngs, Jennynge, Jennings.) M 263. Alice, 179 n.
Jewell, Joane, 3; John, 3.
Joeelie, Florence, 250 n; Thomas, 250 n.
John, King, 276 n; Isabell his da., 276 n.
John, Ellenor, 150 n; Florence, 152 n; Paris, 262 n; William, 256 n.
Jollar (? Jollowe). Ellinor, 120; Thomas, 120.
JOLLYFE, 105, 106, 107. (Jollye, Joll, Jole, Jowl, Joyliffe, Jollowe, etc.) Joan, 141 n; John, 35, 218 n; Katherine, 120 n; Leonard, 141, 141 n; Nathaniah, 141; Nicholas, 207 n; Peter, 207, 207 n; William, 120 n, 122 n, 140 n.
Jon, Thomas, 76 n.
Jones, Rebecca, 138.
Jouwan, Roger, 76.
Jope, 304.
JOPE, 108. (Jop.) John, 10, 78.
Jordan de Haccombe. See Haccombe.
Jordan, Jordon. Cicilie, 71; Robert, 129; Thomas, 71; Thomasine, 127, 129.
Josselin, see Mont Tregomynion
Joyce, John, 245.
Joye, Richard, 38.

Juyl, Celnance, 216 n; Thomas, 216 n.

KAILL, 290, 291. (Kayell.) Margerie, 20; Ralph, 20.
Karkeek. See Carkeete.
Keagle, Elizabeth, 74 n.
Keigwin, Elizabeth, 72; Jenkin, 72; Mrs., 124 n.
Kekewich, 108.
KEKEWICH, 108, 109. (Keckwich, Keckwych, Ketchwich.) Edward, 47; George, 81; Samuel, 107 n; William, 48.
Kelerion, Johanna de, 271 n; John de, 271 n.
Kelloway, x. (Kellaway, Kelwa.) M 165. Catherine, 206; Dorothy, 24; Florence, 86; Johanna, 229 n; Sir John, 24; John, 206; Roger, 229 n; William, 70.
Kelly, Kelley, M 150. Anne, 200; John of, 58; Katherine, 130; Lore, 133; Margaret, 34, 298; Nicholas, 298; Thomas, 90, 200; Walthen, 58; William, 46, 130, 133; Wilmot, 130.
Kellye, Trelawney alias, see Trelawney.
Kelverth, Henry, 192.
Kempe, Kemp, Kympe. Dorothy, 246; Grace, 212 n; Humphry, 107 n; John, 210, 215, 241 n; Mary, 242 n; Robert, 117, 285; William, 21.
Kemple or Kemyll. Alice, 257; Peter, 257.
Kempthorne, 305.
KEMPTHORNE, 226, 227 (see also *Ley alias*): Edward, 262; John, 53 n; Richard, 6.
Kendall, 305.
KENDALL, 109, 110, 111, 112. (Kendale, Kendell, Kendle. de Kendale.) M 197. Anne, 118; Blanch, 4; Constance, 129; Jane, 80, 196, 203 n; Jone, 231; Katherine, 151 n, 245 n; Lawrence, 119, 151 n, 152 n, 275 n; Leodiu, 47; Lowday, 17; Margery, 148; Mary, 47 n, 119; Nicholas, 4, 52, 196, 227, 231, 275 n; Philippa, 142; Richard, 21, 25, 203 n, 245 n; Stephen, 80 n, 141 n, 275 n; Thomas, 118, 129, 151; Thomasine, 52; Walter, 47, 80, 142, 143 n, 152 n; William, 17, 148, 195 n, 197 n.
Kenegy, Kenege. Alexander, 229 n; Honor, 7.
Kensham, Richard, 153.
Kent, Nicholas, 219 n; Thomas, 114.

Kerne *alias* Tresilian, Jane, 205; John, 16; Margery, 16; Pasco, 205.
Kerrise, Ralph de, 17.
Kervyth, George, 302.
Keste, George, 152 n; Robert, 152 n.
Kestell, 113, 305.
KESTELL, 112, 113, 114, 115. (Kestle, Kestill, Castell, Castle, etc.) M 10, 183. Anstice, 267; Edward, 53, 217, 233, 285; James, 42; Jaquet, 9; John, 9, 10 n, 257; Mary, 42, 170 n, 233; Philippa, 253 n; Robert, 131 n; Sibell, 217; Thomas, 267; Thomasine, 220 n; Walter, 42, 258 n; William, 159 n.
Ketcher, William, 285.
Kete, 304.
KETE, 116, 117 n. (Keat, Keet, etc.) M 150. Ralph, 22; Sara, 22.
Keynwood, John, 76.
Kidbroke, Baron, 32.
Kildare, Christopher, Count of, 257; Margaret his da., 257.
Killegabes, Reginald de, 222.
Killigollan, John, 191 n.
Killegrath, x.
Killegrew, 220.
KILLEGREW, 268. (Kyllygrew, Killygrewe, Killigrey, etc.) M 149. Agneta, 169, 169 n; Alexander, 236 n; Elizabeth, 220, 229, 293; Sir Henry, 145, 229; Jane, 142; Joane, 204; John, 81, 83, 86, 142, 169, 169 n, 220, 236 n, 293, 302; Margaret, 81, 83, 302; Margery, 172; Maria, 86, 145, Sir Peter, 235 n; Robert, 204; Walter, 172.
Killyowe, 305.
KILLYOWE, 117, 118. (Killyawe, Kyllow, Killiowe, Kelow, Kellowe, etc.) Anne, 6; Florence, 154 n; John, 6, 109, 111, 111 n, 158, 240; Loveday, 109, 111; Richard, 119 n; Sibell, 158.
Killivorne, Jenkyn, 167; Thomasin, 167.
Kilquite, John, 198; Sibilla, 198.
Kingdon, Kindon. Alice, 43, 43 n; John, 135.
KINGE, 226, 227. (King.) Agnes, 101; Alice, 229; Mr., 225; Philip, 281; Thomas, 229; William, 101.
Kirkham (Kerkham), 193.
KIRKHAM, 194. Mary, 291; Thomas, 32, 291.
Kittow, Elizabeth, 207.
Knapman, M 47.
Knight, Constance, 147; John, 147; William, 38.

INDEX OF NAMES. 321

Knighton, John, 119 *n*; Richard, 211 *n*.
Knoles, Margerie, 65; Richard, 65.
Knyvett, 305.
Knyvett, 86 *n*.
KNYVETT, 117. Henry, 57 *n*.

Laa, William, 255 *n*.
Lacy, Bishop, 275 *n*.
Lagher, Elizabeth, 166.
Lahere, M 227.
Lambe, John, 45.
LAMBERT, 187. Richard, 179.
Lambron, Johanna, 272 *n*; William, 272 *n*.
Lamelyon, Margery, 229; Thomas, 229.
Lamerton, Henry, 291.
Lampen, 305.
LAMPEN, 119. (Lampene.) John, 222; Katherine, 222, 225 *n*; Robert, 138.
Lancaster, 86 *n*.
Lancuck, Peter de, 35 *n*, 296; William, 35 *n*.
Lander, Laudare. Honor, 149*n*; Susan, 173 *n*.
Landrey, John, 119; Wilmot, 119.
Langdon, 305.
LANGDON, 119, 120. (Landon, de Langdon, etc.) Blanch, 13, 81, 83; Elizabeth, 139; John, 13, 81, 83; Mary, 188; Robert, 83 *n*; Walter, 139, 154; William, 188.
Langeston, Johanna, 265.
Langford, Langeford, 122, 122*n*, 305.
LANGFORD, 121. LANGEFORD, 122. (Langefford, etc.) Emanuell, 107 *n*; Grace, 47 *n*; Margery, 66; Roger, 66.
Langharne, 305.
LANGHARNE, 122, 123. (Lawharne.) John, 233.
Langollan, Langollen. Ann, 179 *n*; Walter, 178 *n*.
Langmaid, Nicholas, 153 *n*.
Langson, Thomasine, 146 *n*.
Langworthy, Elizabeth, 66 *n*; Frances, 66 *n*; Richard, 66 *n*.
Lanhergy, x.
Lanherne, Alice, 274 *n*; Sir John, 274 *n*.
Lankeston, John, 295.
Lanyon, 204 *n*, 305.
LANYON, 123, 124. (Lanion, Linyine, Lanian, Lanyne, etc.) Elizabeth, 239 *n*; Katherine, 263 *n*; Margaret, 48, 203; Margery, 120 *n*; Maria, 187 *n*; Mary, 42; Philippa, 158; Ralph, 127 *n*; Richard, 75; Robert, 203; Thomas, 127 *n*; Tho-

LANYON—*continued.*
  masine, 75; Walter, 155 *n*; William, 42, 48.
Lap, Walter, 113.
Lapfeild, M 97.
Launce, 305.
LAUNCE, 124, 125. (Lawnce, etc.) John, 65; Matilda, 65; Thomas, 130.
Launcelles, Basilia, 69; William, 69.
Lavers, Nicholas, 104.
Lawharne, see Langherne.
Lawse, Ralph, 138.
Leach, 261 *n*.
Leache, 125.
LEACHE, 125. (Leach, Leche.) Charity, 70; John, 70; Nicholas, 95; Samuel, 254 *n*.
Le Archdecon, Le Ercedekne, etc. See Archdeacon.
Lee, M 47. John, 248 *n*; Sir Richard, 85.
Le Fort, Claryce, 257; Henry, 257.
Legg, Jane, 195.
Le Grys, Robert, 225 *n*.
Leigh, 193, 194, 257, 305.
LEIGH, 194.
LEIGH, 125, 126. (Leighe, Leygh, de Leghe, etc.) M 47, 88. Barnaby, 178 *n*; Genet, 183; Grace, 62; Joane, 287; Mabell, 91; Nicholas, 133; Thomas, 91, 183, 235 *n*; Thomasine, 235 *n*, 277 *n*; William, 62, 177, 178 *n*.
Leigh, Aleigh *alias*. See Aleigh.
Lenn, John, 227.
Lennard, Sampson, 216; William, 215.
Lentall, Mary, 204. Sir —, 204.
Leswaren or Lawarren. James, 285.
Le Tailleur, x.
Levelis, 127 *n*. *Lowelis*, 305.
LEVELIS, 126, 127. (Loveales, Lavelys, Lavelis, Lowelis, etc.) John, 100 *n*; Katherine, 54; William, 54.
LEVENTHORP, 61.
Lew, Hervey de, 222.
Lewell, M 289.
Lewis, John, 201.
Ley, Sir James, 68; Mary, 68.
Ley, 127. *Kempthorne*, 305.
LEY *alias* KEMPTHORNE, 127, 128, 129, 130 *n*. (See also Kempthorne.) Christian, 214; Edward, 262; Elizabeth, 123; John, 53 *n*, 251 *n*; Magdalen, 251 *n*; Richard, 6, 123.
Lickfald, Joane, 28.
LIFFNEY (or Luney), 226. John, 128; Margaret, 128.
Lillyck, Walter, 284.

Linan, John, 138.
Lipkencott, John, 72; Mary, 72.
Liskerett alias Liskerd, 283.
Lisly, Arthur, Lord, see Plantagenet.
Littleher, M 100.
Littleton, Thomas, 231, 231 *n*; William, 290.
Lock, Anne, 151; Dorothy, 50; Henry, 151; Sir William, 50.
Longe, Longge. Joanna, 232*n*; Winifred, 266 *n*.
Longman, see Langmaid.
Louis, Joane, 57.
Lovday, Loveday. Jennor, 61; Philip, 61; William, 240 *n*.
Lovelace, Leonard, 130 *n*.
Lovell, Elinor, 215 *n*.
Loveys (Loveis), 305.
LOVEYS, 130, 131. (Loves, Lowis, etc.) Amye, 291; Grace, 124 *n*; Leonard, 124 *n*; Richard, 291; Theophilus, 128 *n*, 251.
Lower, 132, 133, 305.
LOWER, 132, 133. (Loure, Lowre, etc.) Anne, 251; Barbara, 126; Catherine, 52; Edward, 52; Elizabeth, 19, 21; Ferdinando, 126; Grace, 172; Jane, 34, 119, 299; John, 34, 197 *n*; Margery, 194; Nicholas, 19, 21, 119; Peter, 108 *n*, 251; Richard, 202 *n*, 231 *n*; Thomas, 89 *n*, 108 *n*; William, 194, 221 *n*.
Lucas, Lucos. Alice, 247 *n*; John, 295; Lettice, 85; Sampson, 247 *n*.
LUCCOMBE, 291. (Lucome.) Ann, 219.
Luccon, see Lutton.
Lucy *alias* Lacam, Richard, 285.
Ludlow, William, 295.
Lugar, Elizabeth, 11; Robert, 11.
Lugie, Thomas, 192.
Luke, Jane, 260 *n*; Robert, 283.
Lukie, Lukye, Luky, Lukey, etc. M 114. Alice, 123; Ellyn, 57; Johanna, 158 *n*; John, 35, 158 *n*; Otes, 172; Thomas, 57, 167 *n*, 170.
Luney, see Liffney.
Lupus, Jane, 271, 272.
Luscombe, Agnes, 179; Henry, 179.
Lutton, Luccon. Peter, 292, 292 *n*.
Luttrell, Lutterell, Luterell. Sir Andrew, 64, 64 *n*, 65, 269, 269 *n*, 270 *n*; Andrew, 130, 131; Eleanor, 269 *n*, 270 *n*; Grace, 130, 131; Sir Hugh, 269 *n*, 270 *n*; Hugh, 160 *n*; Sir John, 270 *n*; Margaret, 64, 64 *n*, 65; Walthen, 270 *n*.
Lycheborowe, Johanna, 158 *n*; Thomas, 158 *n*.

2 T

Lynam, 305.
LYNAM, 134. (Lyncham, Lynham, etc.) Agnes, 9; Dorothy, 59; George, 138 n; John, 9, 237; Richard, 59; Sara, 138 n; Ursula, 138 n.

Mac Morrough, Dermot, 30.
Madern, Madderne (see also Cossen alias). John, 240, 283; William, 283.
Madocke, Alice, 56 n; John, 56 n.
Maior (? Maioe), Jane, 184 n.
Major, Rose, 221 n.
Malbant, M 289.
Malerbe, Cristina, 112 n; John, 112 n.
Maleverer, Sir Halnathe, 298; Halnathe, 31, 34 n, 299; Johanna, 34 n, 298.
Mallet, x.
MALLET, 240. (Malet.) Adam, 259 n; Ann, 257; Baldwin, 92, 257; Elizabeth, 53 n; John, 212; Robert, 180 n; Thomas, 259 n, 261 n; William, 107 n, 207 n; Zenobia, 212.
Man, Joan, 151; J., 151.
Manington, 134.
MANINGTON, 134, 135, 136 n. (Manyngton, Manaton, etc.) Alice, 262; Ambrose, 64; Anthony, 207; Francis, 266 n; Henry, 44; Katherine, 44; Peter, 262; Piers, 25; Samson, 21.
MANNING, 214. (Maning, etc.) Anne, 70; Hugh, 213; Philippa, 213.
Marat al's Treludders, M 114.
Marchant, Avis, 38.
Marifeild, Merefield, Merrifield. M 97. John, 72 n, 170 n, 255 n; Otho, 72 n, 255 n.
Marke, 305.
MARKE, 136, 137 n. (Marrke, Marok, etc.) Alice, 238 n; James, 6; John, 46, 295; Joseph, 127 n; Margerie, 249; Peter, 46, 103 n, 169 n, 249.
Marlborough, The Duke of, 81 n; Henrietta, Duchess of, 81 n.
Marquille, Ermano de le, 55.
MARRAYS, 291. (Mareys.) John, 74 n; Richard, 112 n.
Martyn, Martin, 222, 305.
MARTYN, 223.
MARTYN, 137. (Martin.) M 183. Agnes, 31; Alice, 261 n; Charles Wykeham, 87 n; David, Bp. of St. David's, 30; Henry, 284; Humphry, 251; John, 153, 153 n, 205, 231 n; Margaret, 205, 261 n; Mary, 105 n, 201 n; Robert, 218 n; Thomas, 57, 90; Sir Wil-

MARTYN—continued.
liam, 31, 144 n; William, 183 n.
Maruni, Sir Edmund, 194; Elinor, 194.
Marwood, Jaquet, 41.
Maryett, Ann, 34.
Masey, John, 279 n.
Mason, Adryan, 28; Ann, 191 n; Cicily, 28.
Masters, Ursula, 268 n.
Mathedarra, x.
Mathew, 305.
MATHEW, 137, 138, 139. (Mathewe, Matthew, etc.) Anne, 176; Elizabeth, 131 n, 203; Sir George, 176; John, 215; Jerome, 254 n; Richard, 134 n, 154, 189 n, 203 n; William, 131 n, 134 n, 155 n, 189, 190, 203, 262; Wilmot, 120 n.
Maude, M 97.
Maunder, Jane, 263 n.
May, Joseph, 182 n, 218 n.
Maynard, 14, 15, 305.
MAYNARD, 50 n, 143.
MAYNARD, 139, 140. (Minerd, Mainard.) Anna, 253 n; Bridget, 197 n; Margaret, 253 n; Nicholas, 120; William, 284.
Mayne, Alexander, 230; Elizabeth, 230.
Mayow, 305.
MAYOW, 140, 141 n. (Mahow, Mayo, etc.) Ann, 73, 152, 152 n; Cecilia, 112 n; Elizabeth, 44; John, 73, 118 n, 183, 258 n; Judith, 259 n; Lore, 290; Margaret, 60; Margery, 47, 47 n; Nicholas, 107; Peter, 21, 44; Philip, 47, 47 n; Thomas, 60, 152, 152 n, 290; Walter, 112 n.
Mayow alias Hellier. Anne, 241; Katherine, 220 n; Thomas, 220 n, 241.
Mayow alias Vivian. John, 259 n.
Meacke, Johanna, 262 n.
Melhuise, John, 16; Margery, 16.
Melton, M 97.
Menwynick, 305.
MENWYNICK, 141. (Menwynecke, Menwynuyk, Menwincke, etc.) Anne, 79; Joanna, 146 n; Matilda, 70; Maude, 228; Robert, 79, 228; William, 70, 190.
Meriett, John, 143, 210.
Merritt, Merrett. Anne, 239; Elizabeth, 227; John, 227, 239.
METHEROS, 169. (Matherose, etc.) Joan, 223; Johanna, 244 n; Philip, 223; Walter, 244 n.

Mewthing, Margaret, 76; William, 76.
Michell, 142, 305.
MICHELL, 142, 143. M 121. Gilbert, 139 n, 190; Honor, 224; Jane, 139; John, 52, 186, 224, 285; Lawrence, 153 n; Maude 52; Richard, 111 n; Sibill, 197 n; William, 284.
Michell alias Jagow. Amie, 226; John, 226.
Michelstow, Amice, 219; John, 219.
Mill, Myll. Benett, 165 n; John, 295; Margaret, 220 n.
Millard, Sarah, 267 n.
Milleton, 67. Milliton, 222. (Millington, Mylyton, etc.) Avice, 68; Elianor, 16; Elizabeth, 95, 239; Grace, 222; Mary, 168; Philippa, 123; William, 16, 68, 81, 95, 123, 168, 222, 239.
Millionick, Florence, 7; Richard, 7.
Mohun, 305.
MOHUN, 143, 144, 145, 146. (Mowhown, Mohen, Moone, etc.) Bridget, 158 n; Dorothy, 140 n; Elinor, 30; Elizabeth, 229; Jane, 220; John, 31, 47, 47 n, 141 n; Margaret, 31, 70; Mary, 224 n; Sir Reginald, 158 n, 229, 259 n, 281; Reginald, 220, 240; Richard, 70; William, 30, 140 n, 141 n, 224 n, 240 n.
Mohun, 105 n.
Molesworth, 305.
MOLESWORTH, 147. (Mollesworth, Molsworth, etc.) John, 93; Mary, 178 n.
Molynes, Molyns. M 63. Vivian de, 261 n; William de, 261 n.
Mouke, Mary, 287; Thomas, 287.
Monmouth, Robert Cary, Earl of, 240.
Monpesson, Sir Giles, 2; Rachell, 2.
Montacute, 86 n; William, Earl of Salisbury, 31.
Montague, William, 144.
Montgomery, Adam de, 30; Robert de, 30; Thomas de, 30.
Mont Tregomynion, Isabell de, 84; Josselin de, 84.
Moor, Moore. Anne, 137; Grace, 301; Jane, 205; Robert, 137; Susan, 215; Thomas, 215; Tristram, 191 n; William, 146 n.
Mooringe. See De la More.
Morden, Barney, 106 n.
Morecombe, Morcombe. Nicholas, 249; Philippa, 131 n.

INDEX OF NAMES. 323

Morgan, Sibell, 240.
Morice, Catherine, 212 n; Sir Nicholas, 212 n.
Morish, Elizabeth, 221 n.
Morley, Edward, Lord, 2.
Morris, M 165.
Morshead, Robert, 146 n.
Morthe, see *Randall*, 306.
MORTHE, 147, 148. (Murthe, Morthure, etc.) Edward, 243 n; John, 258 n.
MORTON, 148. Thomas, 281.
Moulton, William, 60 n.
Mounsell, Anne, 246 n.
Mount Edgcumb, Earl of, 31.
Moyle, 305.
MOYLE, 103.
MOYELL, 149. MOYLE, 150, 151. (Moule, Moile, Mule, etc.) M 252 n. Anne, 272; Constantine, 182 n; David, 254 n; Elizabeth, 102 n; Jane, 96 n; James, 253 n; Joane, 112; John, 291; Mary, 36; Olivia, 90 n; Richard, 112, 253 n; Robert, 36; Samuel, 254 n; Sir Thomas, 19; Sir Walter, 272.
Moyse, Honour, 156 n.
MULES, 286.
Mullis, Robert, 295.
Munday, 305.
MUNDAY, 151, 152, 153. (Monday, Mundaye, Mundye al's Wansworth, etc.) Anne, 16, 259 n; Edward, 72; Elizabeth, 180; Hugh, 16, 180, 180 n, 285; John, 259 n; Katherine, 149 n; Nicholas, 225 n; Richard, 259 n; Thomas, 149 n.
Murdoke, Guinthian, 91; Sir John, 91.
Murfield, John, 295.
Muschamp, Katherine, 186.
Myler, 30.
Mylton, Loveday, 248 n.
Myners, Mynars, Minors. M 45. John, 295; Margaret, 58; Maria, 253 n; Richard, 58, 80 n.

Nancarowe, Ursula, 244 n.
Nance, 305, see also Trengove *alias* Nanse. Jane 274 n; Richard, 124 n.
Nanconan, Nanconnan. Elizabeth, 104 n; Jane, 36.
Nancoras, Katherine, 126.
NANCOTHON, 174 (Nancothan). Elizabeth, 167; John, 167.
Nankevell, 305.
NANKEVELL *alias* TIPPETT, 153, 154; John, 118 n.
Nanfan, Jane, 208; Jacob, 208; Johanna, 20; James, 20.
NANGOTHAN, 167.
Nans, Agnes de, 238 n.

Nanscaven, M 21.
Nanscut, Nanscoet, 297; Peter de, 261 n.
Nanspian, 305.
NANSPIAN, 154, 155, 156 n. (Nanspean,etc.) M 235. Agnes, 235 n; Cheston, 233; Henry, 186, 233; James, 138 n, 258; Katherine, 258; Wilmot, 138 n.
Nantian, x.
Nappar, Napper. Alexander, 125; Baronet, 125; Elizabeth, 125.
Newcastle - on - Tyne, Robert Whelpington, Mayor of, 94.
Newcourt, Newcort. Agnes, 93; Johanna, 12; John, 12, 93, 215; Mary, 215; Tobias, 90.
NEWMAN, 36; William, 5.
Newman, 270 n.
Newminster, William, Abbot of, 94.
Newton, Jane, 114; John, 114, 134.
Nevill, 86 n; Anne, 292; Auxillia, 292; Elizabeth, 82; John, 292; Richard, 82.
Nicholas, Penrose *alias*, see Penrose.
Nicholls, 305.
NICHOLLS, 157, 158. (Nicholles, Nicholl, Nicholas, etc.) Anne, 200; Jane, 248 n, 263 n; John, 35, 46 n; 145, 145 n, 168, 191 n, 200, 256 n, 289; Margaret, 107; Prudence, 289; Robert, 117; Sibilla, 165 n; Thomas, 10; Thomazin, 35; Walter, 283.
Nicoll, 156, 199.
NICOLL, 156, 157. (Nicholls, Nicolls, etc.) Amy, 253 n; Humphry, 82, 133, 195, 199; Isabella, 199; Mary, 133; Philippa, 82.
Nick, Mary, 288; Robert, 288.
Ninnis (? Innis), Thomas, 21.
Noble, M 69. Johanna, 79 n.
Nononant, Roger de, 250.
Norbrooke, Joane, 66; John, 66.
Norfolk, John Howard, Duke of, 64 n.
Norreys, Henry, Lord, 32.
Norrish, Elizabeth, 32; Sir John, 32.
North, Frances, 136; Francis, 136.
Northcott, John, 195.
Northumberland, Roger Wodrington, Sheriff of, 94.
Nosworthy, Nosworthie. Alice, 89 n; Francis, 285; William, 89 n, 283.
Nottell, Katherine, 241 n.
Novant, John de, 274 n; Rosamund de, 274 n.
Noy, 305.

NOYE, 158, 159 n. (Noie, etc.) Barbara, 186; Edward, 48, 186; Philip, 104 n; Richard, 104 n; William, 104 n, 123 n, 186, 270, 270 n.
Odrone, Digon, Baron of, 30; Avice, his da., 30.
Oglethorpe, M 116.
Oliver, Olliver, Olver. M 174. Elizabeth, 175, 175 n; Jane, 53 n; John, 119 n, 172 n; Thomas, 175, 175 n, 248 n.
Opie, 305.
OPY, 159, 160. M 174. Nicholas, 12, 298.
Oram, William, 235 n.
Orchard, Thamasine, 24.
Ormond, Thomas Butler, Earl of, 86 n; Anne, Countess of, 86 n. (See Butler.)
Orwell, Sara, 109.
Osborne, 195; John, 195; Magdalen, 195.
Osgood, Arthur, 285.
Osmond, Christopher, 179 n.
OUGHE, 160; Christopher, 266.
Owen, M 216. Loveday, 261 n; Philip, 261 n; Thankfull, 261 n.
OWRYE, 226. (Owry *alias* Tregonwall, etc.)
Oxford, The Earl of, 31.

Packer, Mary, 133 n.
Padarda, Paderda, Padreda. Matilda, 150 n; Nicholas de, 55; Noel, 100 n; Ralph, 150 n; Thomas, 55, 198.
Pafford, M 150.
Palke, Mary, 201 n.
Palmer, M 160; Sir William, 106 n.
Panchard, Johanna, 161.
Parker, 305.
PARKER, 161; Anne, 137; James, 25; Sir Nicholas, 68 n; Thomas, 137.
Parkhouse, Johanna, 279 n.
Parkyng, William, 179.
Parloben, Ramund, 250.
Parmere, Alice, 54; John, 54.
Parnell, Parnall. Constance, 129 n; John, 39, 285; William, 172 n.
Parrat, M 288.
Parris, William, 281.
Parsons, John, 139; Susan, 139.
Pascoe, Pascowe. Elizabeth, 179; John, 179, 242 n.
Pascmere, Patrick, 282.
Paule, Nicholas, 285.
Pawlet, Elizabeth, 141; Giles, 141.
Pawley. M 216. James, 16.
Paulherman, 66.
Paynell, William, 143.

INDEX OF NAMES.

Paynter, 305.
PAYNTER, 162. (Penter, Painter, etc.) Anne, 263 n; Arthur, 270 n: Edmond, 58; Ellinor, 215; George, 90; Grace, 270 n; William, 52, 215.
Pearce, Pearse. Degory, 136 n; John, 106 n; Mary, 163 n.
Peard, Rachell, 159 n.
Pearne, Frances, 105 n.
Peck, Pecke. Elizabeth, 197 n; Joan, 201 n.
Peirse, Pierse, Peirs. Agnes, 168; Alice, 71; Jane, 59; John, 59, 114; Nicholas, 11; Richard, 160; Thomas, 168, 295; Tristram, 79; Walter, 295; William, 160.
Pellamounter, Catherine, 175; John, 295; Mary, 239 n; Richard, 175.
Pembroke, Richard, Earl of, see Strongbow.
Penant, Jane, 251; William, 251.
Penarth, Walter, 285.
Pencarowe, Jane, 191; Ralph, 191.
Pendarves, 305.
PENDARVES, 163, 164; PENDARVIS, 164. (Pendarvers, etc.) Alexander, 3; Ann, 273 n; Bridget, 236 n; Catherine, 264 n; Dorothy, 53 n; Elizabeth, 79 n; Florence, 263, 263 n; Grace, 187 n; John, 76 n, 216; Mary, 216; Mellior, 76 n; Peter, 79 n; Samuel, 187 n; William, 236 n.
Pender, Pendre. Ellinor, 8; Martin, 8; Richard, 23.
Pendergast, 30.
PENFOUN, 164, 165. (Penfound, Penfownd, etc.) Digory, 293; Elizabeth, 105; Margaret, 218; William, 105, 218.
Pengelley, x; Richard, 181 n.
Penhalurick, William, 282.
Penhallow, 305.
PENHALLOW, 166. (Penhaloo, etc.)
Penhellick, 305.
PENHELLICK, 167, 168. (Penhillick, etc.) Alexander, 14; Alice, 14; John, 12.
Penhergard, Walter de, 222.
Penhergie, Edith, 4; Henry, 4.
Penhyll, Alexander, 234 n.
Penkeril, 222. (Penkevell, etc.) M 83. Catherine, 100; Dorothy, 83 n; Elizabeth, 287; Francis, 12, 287; Jane, 12, 159; Philip, 100.
Pennance, Penans. Annora, 189 n; John, 22, 189 n; William, 189 n.

Penpons, 21. (Penpan.) M 21. Amicia, 255 n; John, 22; Richard, 255 n, 299.
Penqnit, William de, 55.
Pe ose, 305.
PENROSE, 168, 169. PENROS, 169, 170. (Penrosse, Penrees, Penrise, etc.) Alice, 98; Anne, 38; Enis, 247; Grace, 154, 155n; Johan, 223; John, 154, 155 n, 223, 224, 247; Katherine, 188; Mariet, 223; Margerie, 18; Thomas, 38, 98, 188; Vivian, 18; William, 223.
Penrose alias Nicholas, Henry, 169 n, 255 n: Margaret, 169 n; Mary, 255 n.
Penrose alias Treveare, Henry, 170 n.
Pensance (Penzance). 283.
Penticost, Gertrude, 182; Jane, 216; Nicholas, 182, 216.
Pentier, Pentire, Pentyre. Elynor, 133; Jane, 189, 190; John, 8, 69, 70, 235 n; Mary, 8; Richard, 70, 152; Samuel, 152 n; Thomas, 264 n; William, 189, 190.
Penvrane, Lawrence, 113; Margaret, 113.
Penwarne, 305.
PENWARNE, 170, 171. (Penwarren, Penwerin, Penwarn, etc.) Anne, 211 n; Elizabeth, 274 n; John, 22; Mary, 166; Nicholas, 219 n; Richard, 180 n, 211 n; Thomas, 69, 274 n; Vivinn, 166.
Percivall, Margaret, 132.
Percy, 86 n.
Perdew, Bennet, 282.
Peres alias Pryske, William, 235 n.
Perkins, Drew, 295.
Perne, Josias, 192.
Perrie, Perrye. Agnes, 188; Elizabeth, 201; Thomas, 188; William, 201.
Perrow, Susan, 150 n; William, 150 n.
Peryam, Christian, 170.
Pester, Henry, 180 n, 219 n.
Peters, Hugh, 221 n; Thomas, 81.
Petherbridge, Alice, 56 n; John, 56 n.
Petit, x, 234, 305.
PETIT, 180 n, 234, 235, 297.
PETIT, 276, 277 n, 278 n. (Pedyt, Petyt, le Petit, etc.) Alice, 296; Emlin, 76, 76 n; Johanna, 299 n; John, 239, 296, 300 n; Maude, 239; Michael, 76, 76 n, 300 n; Thomas, 95 n; Thomasine, 76 n.
Pett, John, 283.
Pever, x, 278 n.

Peverell, 71. (Peferell.) Amicia or Avice, 30 n; Constance, 257; Sir Hugh, 257; Hugh, 30 n, 75; Sir James, 258 n; James, 257; John, 30 n.
Phillipa, Queen, 32.
Phillips, Elizabeth, 237 n; Jane, 263 n; Margaret, 237 n; Rebecca, 192 n.
Philpott, Mr., 134.
Phippen, George, 170 n.
Picford, Julian, 217; William, 217.
Pike, Anne, 150 n.
Pillaton, John, 291.
Pim, Pime, Pym. Alexander, 195; Jane, 195; Philippa, 195.
Pipard, Pypard. Arthur, 281.
Piper, Elizabeth, 63; William, 63.
Pitchard, Elinor, 188.
Pitford, M 177.
Pitt, Pitts. John, 101, 153 n.
Plantagenet, Arthur, Lord Lisly, 84; Elizabeth, 31, 259 n; John, Earl of Cornwall, 297.
Plumleigh, 305.
PLUMLEIGHE, 171, 172 n. (Plumley, etc.) Mary, 138; Thomas, 138.
Poher, Poer. Florence, 20; Vivian, 261 n: Walter, 20.
Poldresak, Vincent de, 55.
Poleglasse, William, 94.
Polgoner, John de, 237.
Polgreene, Peter, 219; Senata, 219.
Polgwest, Adam alias. See Adam.
Polhelon, Walter de, 55.
Polkinghorne, 305.
POLKINGHORNE, 173, 174. POLKINHORNE, 175, 176 n. Alexander, 162; Henry, 261 n; John, 62 n; Mary, 79 n, 168 n; Otho, 79 n, 168 n; Richard, 262 n; Roger, 51, 261 n, 283.
Polland, Christopher, 137 n.
Pollard, 305.
POLLARD, 176. M 165. Anne, 249; Elizabeth, 240, 243; Sir Hugh, 63, 195; Hugh, 249; Isat, 76; Sir Lewis, 240; Mary, 63; Probesia, 249 n; Sir Richard, 32; Richard, 76, 243; Susan, 195.
Pollexfen, Ann, 165.
Pollowyn, Furnifell, 110 n.
Polsewe, Poulsewe. Edward, 108; Katherin, 89 n.
Polsulsack, Cheston, 155 n; John, 155 n.
Polmarva, Alice, 34.
Polwhele, 305.
POLWHELE, 172, 173. (Polwhile, Polewheele, etc.)

INDEX OF NAMES.

POLWHEILE—*continued.*
Anna, 246 *n*; Digory, 262; Grace, 62; John, 62; Isabell, 43; Mary, 124; Stephen, 227; Susan, 262.
Pomeroy, 305.
POMEROY, 176, 177. (Pomery, Pomeroi, etc.) M 278.
Andrew, 1, 103 *n*; Anne, 103 *n*; Christopher, 204 *n*; Constance, 158; Dorothy, 292; Elizabeth, 299, 300 *n*; Henry, 17, 285; Hugh, 158; Jane, 38; John, 38 *n*, 253 *n*; Mary, 1; Richard, 119 *n*; Stephen, 137 *n*; Sir Thomas, 300 *n*; Thomas, 292; William, 38.
Pope, 194. Jane, 194; John, 194; George, 119 *n*.
Popham, Hugh, 248 *n*.
Portbyan alias *West Loe,* 284.
Porter, 305, 306.
PORTER, 178, 179. Christian, 131 *n*; Mary, 166; Thomas, 131 *n*; Walter, 130, 166.
Post, Robert, 113.
Pound, Pownd. Blanch, 229; Constance, 181; John, 229; William, 181.
Power, Isabella, 255 *n*; Michael, 255 *n*.
Poyle, 180, 180 *n*, 306.
POYLE, 180. (Poile, de la Poyle, etc.) Jane, 126, 235 *n*, 277 *n*; Richard, 21; Robert, 95 *n*, 126, 219 *n*, 235 *n*, 277 *n*; Thomas, 171 *n*.
Prade, Praed. James, 36, 103; Jane, 48; William, 48, 103, 235 *n*.
Prawle, 66.
Predency, Jane, 238; Richard, 238.
Preston, Margaret, 246 *n*.
Prideaux, Pridiux, Prideis, Predecks, etc., 31, 32. M 47, 210.
Admonition, 151, 151*n*, 164*n*; Ann, 301; Charitie, 134; Edmund, 64, 151, 151 *n*; Edward, 164 *n*; Elizabeth, 152 *n*, 288; John, 151 *n*, 156 *n*, 201 *n*, 255 *n*; Margaret, 276 *n*; Milicent, 74 *n*; 41, 133 *n*, 151 *n*; Honor, 288; Humphry, 134, 151 *n*, Sir Nicholas, 269, 288; Nicholas, 107 *n*; Peter, 86; Richard, 41, 74 *n*, 154, 155 *n*, 156 *n*, 210; Sir Roger, 276 *n*; Thomas de, 18; William, 152 *n*, 199 *n*; Zenobia, 155 *n*, 156 *n*.
Prisk, William, 73.
Pristwood, Mary, 302.
Prosoper, John, 55; Margerie, 55.
PROUTE, 87. (Prowt, etc.)

PROUTE—*continued.*
Digory, 70; Edward, 248; Matilda, 236.
Prowse, Prouse, Prouze, etc. Elizabeth, 121*n*; Hugh, 121*n*; Humphry, 54 *n*; Philippa, 54 *n*; Prudence, 49; Robert, 292; Thomas, 279 *n*; Ursula, 105 *n*.
Prust, Prost, Prist, etc. Charles, 70, 92, 215; Henry, 37; Honor, 70; Hugh, 35, 115 *n*, 178 *n*; Lawrence, 214; Margaret, 214; Maria, 70; Philippa, 178 *n*; Temperance, 92; William, 280.
Pryor, Warne, 175.
Prys, Catherine, 268; John, 268.
Pube, Katherine, 104 *n*.
Purfrey, Purefoy, Purforoy. Alice, 16; Joanna, 39; Thomas, 39.
Putt, Mary, 196 *n*; Nicholas, 205.
Pye, 306.
PYE, 181, 182 *n*. (Pie.) Anthony, 26, 235 *n*, 238; Elizabeth, 26; Jane, 26; John, 101, 279; Philippa, 101.
Pyne, Elizabeth, 209; Hugh, 209; Johanna, 273 *n*.

Quarme, 306.
QUARME, 182. Abigail, 96; Robert, 96, 225 *n*.
Quarton, Dorothy, 97; William, 97.
Quych, John, 255 *n*.

Raby, Thomas, 219 *n*.
Radcliffe, Martha, 135 *n*, 136 *n*.
Raddona, Richard de, 285.
Raleigh, Ralegh. M 84. Henry de, 180; Sir Walter, 31.
Ramesland, 193. Rose of, 194; William of, 194.
Randall, 306.
RANDALL, 182, 183. Alice, 151 *n*; Grace, 98; Jane, 139; John, 74, 139, 284; Mary, 27; Thomas, 27, 98, 282; Philip, 284.
Randolph, William, 232 *n*.
Raoll, Margery, 19; Ralph, 19.
Rashleigh, 306.
RASHLEIGH, 183, 184. (Rayssbleigh, Rayshley, Rushley, etc.) Agneta, 169; Alice, 54 *n*, 196; Avis, 115; Deborah, 205; Elizabeth, 259 *n*; Jane, 139; John, 23, 115, 139, 140, 169, 196, 205, 255 *n*, 259 *n*; Jonathan, 54 *n*; Jone, 45 *n*, 140; Lettice, 245, 245 *n*; Margaret, 247; Mary, 90 *n*; Philip, 220 *n*; Robert, 45, 222, 245, 247.

Ravell, see Revell.
Rawfis, Joane, 8; John, 8.
Rawle, see Roll.
Rawlyn, Richard, 235 *n*.
Rawton, M 97.
RAYNFRY, 13.
Reade, Reede. Edward, 108 *n*; John, 70.
Redris, Grace, 203; Robert, 203.
Redvers, 52, 257.
RENCIE, 80.
Renolds, Reinolds, 294; Elizabeth, 174; John, 174; Redygan, 119.
Rensby, M 97.
Renston, M 286.
Reparijs, John de, 228; Margery de, 228.
Reprin, or *Wroughton,* X.
Reskimer, 306.
RESKIMER, 185. (Reskimmer, Reskemer, Reskemore, etc.) Alexander, 230 *n*; Anne, 145, 229, 230 *n*; Eusada, 20; John, 19, 20, 67, 212; Katherine, 51, 67; Margaret, 145 *n*; Matilda, 19; Philippa, 216; Roger, 19; William, 51, 76 *n*, 145, 206, 216, 229.
Reskimer, 35 *n*, 297, 299 *n*.
Resprin, Jane, 34, 298; Richard, 34.
RESTORAKE (Roscarrock), 234.
Reswell, Thomas, 295.
Retallack, Retallick, Edward, 201 *n*; Elinor, 201 *n*; John, 183.
RETALLER, 103.
Revell, 193.
REVELL, 194. (Ravell.)
Reynell, Alice, 6; Edmond, 6; Sir Thomas, 230 *n*.
Reyney, Elizabeth, 49; John, 49.
Ricard, Ricord. Johanna, 229*n*; Thomas, 229 *n*, 295.
Rich, Riche. Hugh, 188 *n*; Sir Richard, 19.
Richardes, Jane, 96; Joan, 96*n*; Richard, 162; William, 96.
Richowe, Elizabeth, 7; Nicholas, 7.
Ridge, Roger, 257.
Ridgwaye, Philippa, 9; Thomas, 195.
Rilston, Anna, 77; Elizabeth, 74; Jacob, 77; James, 74.
RISDON, 147. (Risden.) Elizabeth, 107; Prudence, 79; Thomas, 107.
Rise, Thomas, 67; Wynifred, 67.
Rivers, Sir John, 33.
Ritt, John, 150.
Robarts, 186. *Roberts,* 306.
ROBARTS, 186. ROBERTS, 187. (Roberds, Robartes,

ROBARTS—*continued.*
etc.) Cristobel, 142; Dorothy, 137 *n*; Elizabeth, 263; Frances, 254 *n*; Grace, 163, 163 *n*; Jane, 17, 153 *n*; John, 163, 248 *n*; Margaret, 154, 155 *n*; Maria, 195*n*; Philippa, 141 *n*; Sir Richard, 93, 93*n*; Richard, 15, 17, 137 *n*, 142, 154, 155 *n*, 263; Thomas, 294; William, 163 *n*.
Robins, Robyns. M 139. George, 247 *n*; Grace, 111 *n*, 253 *n*; James, 260 *n*; Jane, 38 *n*; John, 242 *n*, 255 *n*, 265 *n*; Robert, 96 *n*, 188; Stephen, 210 *n*, 242 *n*; Thomas, 155 *n*; 235 *n*.
Robinson, 306.
ROBINSON, 188; Anne, 129*n*; Thomas, 243 *n*; William, 170, 282.
Rockwood, M 97.
Rodd, James, 207 *n*; Mary, 207 *n*.
Rogers, 306.
ROGERS, 214.
ROGERS, 188; Christopher, 120 *n*; Elizabeth, 25; Sir John, 25; Mary, 243 *n*.
ROLL, 290. (Rolls, Rawle, etc.) Frances, 130, 130 *n*, 131; Francis, 153, 153 *n*; Henry, 130, 131, 147; John, 107 *n*; Mary, 241; Miss, 29; Moris, 147 *n*; Philippa, 147; Robert, 92 *n*.
Ronnell, Edward, 101; Sibell, 101.
Roope, Rope. Barbara, 152; John, 152, 266; Margaret, 266.
Roscarrock, 306.
ROSCARROCK, 189, 190. (Roscowreake, Resoryk, de Roskareo, etc.) Agnes, 141; Anthony, 142, 215; Chamond, 279 *n*; Charles, 146 *n*; Elizabeth, 100, 279; Frances, 142; Grace, 279 *n*; Jane, 156; John, 84, 100, 138, 240, 277 *n*; Katherine, 278; Margaret, 231, 277 *n*, 278 *n*; Mary, 87; Ralph, 278 *n*; Richard, 156, 255 *n*; Sibilla, 138; Thomas, 20, 141, 208, 231, 278, 279; Walter, 17.
Roscorla, Roscorly. George, 45; Henry, 253 *n*.
Rose, Faith, 39; Judith, 39.
Rosewarun, 306.
ROSEWARAN, 191. (Rosewarne.) M 216. Jane, 156 *n*; Steven, 156 *n*; Thomas, 53.
Rositer, Rosetor. Christian, 54; Hugh, 14; Robert, 54.
Rosiwike, June, 98; Reginald, 98.

Roskrow, 306.
ROSKROWE, 192.
Roskruge, 306.
ROSKRUGE, 192. (Roseruge, Roskirke, Reskrcek, etc.) Christian, 210 *n*; Grace, 162, 162 *n*; Jane, 65; John, 41, 41 *n*, 65, 162, 162 *n*, 210 *n*; Richard, 174.
Roskyr, Reskere. Elizabeth, 59; Galfrid, 244 *n*; John, 59; Julia, 244 *n*.
ROSMELL, 216.
ROSMODRES, 291. (Rosmadres, Rosmoders, etc.) Elinor, 238; Johanna de, 18; Richard, 258 *n*; Thomas de, 18; Thomas, 23, 238.
Rosuggan, 193.
ROSUGGAN, 193. (Rosogan, Resuggan, etc.) M 145, 244. Katherine, 193 *n*; Robert, 193 *n*.
Rous, 193.
ROUS, 193, 194, 195. (Rows, Rufus, etc.) Ambrose, 269; Sir Anthony, 281; Anthony, 119, 119 *n*, 156; Blanch, 114; Emlin, 138; Jane, 119; Katherine, 269; Philippa, 156, 156 *n*; Richard, 11; W., 107 *n*; William, 107 *n*, 114, 187 *n*.
ROWSE, ROUSE, 187, 206.
Rowe, Rawe, Roe. M 231. Alexander, 274 *n*; Alice, 112; Digory, 12; Elizabeth, 12, 125 *n*, 201 *n*; Johan, 46, 115 *n*; John, 112, 123, 123 *n*, 125 *n*, 282; Margaret, 228 *n*; Mary, 54 *n*; Nichola, 232 *n*; William, 46.
Rowland, Jane, 214; John, 214.
Rownsewall, Richard, 253 *n*.
Rumoe, William, 183.
Rupe. See De la Roche.
Russell, Andrew, 112; Anne, 156; John, 177 *n*; Nicholas, 112; Rohaysia, 177 *n*.
Rutter, Matthew, 162 *n*; Nicholas, 107, 107 *n*; Richard, 107 *n*.
Ryder, Thomas, 56 *n*; Thomasine, 56 *n*.

St. Clair, M 32.
St. David's, David Martyn, Bishop of, 30.
St. John, Seynt John. Alice, 272 *n*; Edward, 272, 272 *n*; Johanna, 272 *n*; William, 272 *n*.
St. Leger, x. Anne, 87 *n*; Sir George, 86 *n*, 87 *n*; Sir James, 86 *n*; Sir John, 85, 87 *n*; John, 87 *n*; Mary, 85.
St. Tavy (St. Aubyn), Ann, 151, 151 *n*; Thomas, 151, 151 *n*.

Sakfen, Joan, 135 *n*.
Salisbury, Salisburie, Salisberie. Alice, 41; Jane, 213; John, 41; William Montacute, Earl of, 31; William, 213.
Sallamon, Rose, 196.
Saltashe, 284.
Salter, Anne, 180 *n*; Elizabeth, 94; John, 94, 180 *n*; William, 34.
Samford, M 65.
Sampson, Bethseba, 142 *n*; Martin, 283; Robert, 80 *n*.
Samuell, 306.
SAMUELL, 196. (Samwell.) Elizabeth, 204; John, 73; Lower, 73; Margaret, 160; William, 160, 204.
Sancto Martino, Alred de, 285.
Sanders, Elizabeth, 61; John, 142, 190.
Sapcot, Johanna, 177 *n*; Sir John, 177 *n*.
Savell, M 97.
Savory, Savery. Christopher, 14; Jane, 139; Margaret, 14.
Sawle, 306.
SAWLE, 196, 197 *n*. (Sawell, Sawl, Saull, etc.) Amy, 90 *n*; Sir Joseph, 253 *n*; Joseph, 220 *n*; Mary, 253 *n*; Nicholas, 184; Oliver, 78 *n*.
Sawle, 29 *n*.
Sayer, 306.
SAYER, 197.
Scafe, M 97.
Scawen, 198, 306.
SCAWEN, 198, 199.
SCAWNE, 200. (Scawyne, etc.) Agnes, 56; Christian, 60; Edward, 56; John, 55, 227; Margerie, 55; Robert, 156 *n*; William, 55, 60.
Scheplyn, Nicholas, 290.
Scobell (*Scoble*), 306.
SCOBELL, 200, 201. (Scobbell, Skobell, etc.) Francis, 50 *n*, 261 *n*; Richard, 50 *n*, 149, 242 *n*, 261 *n*.
Scoble, 254 *n*.
Scutoris, Nicholas, 18; William, 18.
Searle, 202.
SEARLE, 202. (Sorrell, Searell, etc.) Alice, 219; Elizabeth, 1; Jane, 74 *n*; Philadelphia, 133 *n*; Wymund, 1.
Secom, Thomas, 118 *n*.
Segar, Sir William, 294.
Segrave, Christian, 144; John, 144.
Sele, Margaret, 183 *n*; Thomas, 183 *n*.
Seler, John, 76.
Selman, M 1. Thomasine, 92; William, 92.
Seneschall, Seneshall, Steward, 258 *n*. Elizabeth, 271, 271 *n*;

INDEX OF NAMES. 327

Seneschall—*continued*.
Jane, 98 : Sir John, 271 ;
John, 271 ; Richard, 98.
Sergiaux, Le Sergeaux, Sergeant, Sargeant, 258 *n*.
Alice, 213 ; Jane, 271 ; Jone, 239 ; Katherine, 213 *n* ;
Laura, 228 ; Philippa, 213 *n* ;
Sir Richard, 228, 239, 271 ;
Richard, 213 *n*.
Seward, Judith, 28.
Seymour, Seamour. Sir Edward, 200 *n* ; Mary, 200 *n* ;
John, 70, 107 *n*.
Seyntaubyn (*St. Aubyn*), 257, 306.
SEYNTAUBYN *vel* ST. AUBIN, 212, 213 *n*. (Sancto Albino, St. Albone, St. Albyn, St. Ablyn, St. Aybyn, etc.)
M 84. 151 *n*. Agnes, 50 ;
Anne, 54 *n*; Elizabeth, 21, 275 *n*; Francis, 274 *n*; Geofrey, 21 ; Grace, 185 ; Isabell, 275 *n* ; Jane, 90 *n* ; Johanna, 144 ; John, 2, 2 *n*, 43 *n*, 50, 104 *n*, 185, 288, 302 ; Mary, 43 *n* ; Thomas, 185 *n*, 282.
Sharpe *alias* Garrett, John, 284.
Shapley, Shapleigh. M 41.
Elizabeth, 171 ; Robert, 171.
Sheere, Grace, 43 ; George, 262 *n*.
Shelton, 203 *n*. Anne, 189, 190 ; Maria, 203 *n* ; Thomas, 203 *n*.
Sherley, Katherine, 33.
Shern, John, 11.
Sherston, Jane, 7 *n* ; Lawrence, 7 *n*.
Shillstone, Shilstone. Anne, 32, 61 *n* ; Elizabeth, 288 ; Sir John, 32, 61 *n*; John, 288.
Shirwill, John, 39.
Shoote, Shute. Thomas, 197 *n* ; Timothy, 197 *n*.
SHORROCK, 202, 203. (Sharrock, Sharock.) Anne, 138 *n* ;
John, 138, 138 *n*; Philip, 138 *n*.
Short, Joanna, 207 *n*.
Sibly, Honor, 279 *n*.
Sidenham, Sidnam, Sydnam.
Alice, 24 ; Cuthbert, 285 ;
Honor, 26 ; Humphry, 26, 261 *n*, 285 ; Sir John, 81.
Sidney, Thomas, 81 ; Thomasine, 81.
Sillye, John, 156 *n* ; Richard, 156 *n* ; William, 279 *n*.
Singleton, Ann, 256 *n* ; Richard, 256 *n*.
Skelton, Skellton. Elizabeth, 58 ; Nicholas, 58, 210 *n*.
Skenoke, Isabell, 27 ; John, 27.
Skerrett, Skirrett, Skirritt, etc.
Alice, 78 *n* ; Edward, 173 *n* ;
John, 78, 78 *n* ; Mary, 78.
Skewys, John, 76.

Skinner, Agnes, 12 ; John, 294 ;
Walter, 13.
Skipwith, Margaret, 32 ; Sir William, 32.
Skory (*Scory*), 204 *n*.
SKORY, 203, 204. (Score, Skore, etc.)
Skott, M 239.
Slade, John, 262 *n* ; Mary, 254 *n* ; William, 262 *n*.
Slader, Maude, 227 ; Roger, 227.
Slane, Baro de, 300 *n*.
Slaninge, Slanning, Slannig, etc.
Elizabeth, 11 ; John, 11, 177 ;
Mary, 177 ; Sir Nicholas, 104 *n* ; Philippa, 225 *n*.
Slarder, Henry, 128 *n*.
Sleeman, Eliza, 73 ; Mary, 212 *n* ; Roger, 73.
Slogot, Jone, 248 *n*.
Small, George, 107 *n*.
Smith, 306.
SMYTH, 204. Bernard, 268 ;
Elinor, 268 ; Sir George, 85 ;
George, 107 *n*, 111 *n* ; Grace, 85 ; Jennet, 59 ; John, 209 ; John, 59, 92 ; Julian, 92 ; Katherine, 88 ; Lucy, 59 ; Margaret, 140 ; Mary, 111 *n* ; Richard, 59 ; Walter, 198 ; William, 88, 295.
Snelling, M 47. Thomas, 47 *n*.
Snith, Margaret, 140.
Sobye, John, 282.
Solgena, Clare of, 80.
Soor, Soar. John, 272 *n* ;
Melior, 20 ; Sir Osbert, 20 ;
Ralph, 242 *n*, 274 *n*.
Somer, Thomas, 115.
Somerset, Lord Herbert, 258 *n*.
Somester, Somaster. Elizabeth, 221 ; Henry, 2, 273 *n* ; John, 69, 91, 221 ; Mary, 91 ; Walter, 275 *n*.
Soper, Wilmot, 201 *n*.
Souch, Charles, 23.
Soughte, Richard, 104 *n*.
SOUTHCOT, 194, 195. Cicily, 83 *n* ; Elizabeth, 287 ;
George, 83 *n*, 287, 288 ;
Margaret, 99 ; Mary, 288 ;
Thomas, 57, 99.
Southwell, Sir Robert, 19.
Sowden, Margaret, 95 *n*.
Sparke, 306.
SPARKE, 205. John, 184.
Sparnon, 306.
SPARNON, 205. (Sparnan, Spernon.) Jenefer, 27 ; John, 27 ; Mary, 163 ; Thomas, 82.
Speccot, Specot, Speckett. M 68.
Amy, 157, 157 *n* ; Edmond, 120 ; Humphry, 130 ; Ibott, 130 ; Johanna, 193 ; Sir John, 64, 145 ; Katherine, 120 ; Peter, 157, 157 *n* ; Sir Richard, 193.
Speeke, Alice, 61.

Spent, Edmond, 85.
Spicer, James, 266 ; Maria, 266.
Spoore, 306.
SPOORE, 206, 207. (Spoure, Speur, Spurre, etc.) M 107 *n*.
Anna, 107 ; Elinor, 185 ;
Elizabeth, 104 ; Grace, 41 ;
Henry, 104, 107 *n*, 185 ;
Jane, 14 ; Katherine, 87 ;
Richard, 107 ; Thomas, 14, 41, 87 ; Widow of, 107 *n*.
Spry, 208, 306.
SPRY, 208, 209, 210, 211.
(Sprie, etc.) Agnes, 229 ;
Alice, 66, 199, 200 ; Edward, 66 ; Oliver, 38 ; Peter, 69, 192 ; Thomas, 199, 200, 229 ;
Thomasine, 38 *n*.
SPREY, 207. (Spray, etc.)
Christopher, 52 ; Ursula, 104 *n* ; Nicholas, 280.
Squire, John, 148, 295 ; Mawd, 148 ; William, 295.
Stafford, 86 *n*.
Staly, 24 ; Ann, 24 ; Roger, 24.
Stanberye, 213.
STANBERYE *vel* STANBURYE, 213, 214.
Stapledon, X.
Staplehill, Gilbert, 168 *n*.
STAPLETON, 292, 293.
START (Stearte), 74. Thomasine, 202 ; Walter, 202.
Stening, M, 84.
Stephen of Abertivi, 30.
Stephens, 306.
STEPHENS, 214, 215 *n*. (Stevens, Stephyn, etc.) M 65.
Anthony, 212 ; Jane, 176 *n* ;
Nicholas, 9, 285 ; Henry, 172 *n* ; Humphry, 37.
Stewert ? Jane, 129 *n*.
Stiler, M. 210.
Stoford, Katherine, 49 ; Philip, 49 ; Walter, 70.
Stoke, Thomas, 74 *n*.
STONARD, 290.
Stone, 215.
STONE, 215 ; Elizabeth, 93 *n* ;
Honor, 70 ; Isabella, 190 ;
John, 70, 138, 190, 280 ;
Lower, 224 *n* ; Mary, 254 *n* ;
Thomas, 90 ; William, 280 ;
Winifred, 138.
Stourton, Lady, 275 *n*.
Stradling, Jane, 35 ; Edmund, 35.
Strange, John, Lord, 144.
Strechly, Andrew, 99 *n* ; Joane, 99 *n*.
Strike, Nicholas, 198.
Stronge, Argent, 15 ; John, 15, 183 ; Katherine, 183.
Strongbow, Richard, Earl of Pembroke, 30 ; Pricilla, his sister, 30.
Stroud, Strowd, Stroude. M 176.
Julyan, 45 ; Philip, 14 ; William, 45 ; Willmot, 14.

INDEX OF NAMES.

Stuart, Anne, 160 n.
Stubb, Agnes, 88; George, 88.
Stubley, Gregory, 173 n.
Stukeley, Stuckley, 270n; Anna, 47; Frances, 141 n; John, 47, 141 n; Katherine, 32; Lewis, 47 n.
Sturbridge, Peter, 118 n.
Sture, John, 171; Joue, 171.
Suffianus, Sir Emanuel Assanes, 274 n; Amicia, 274 n.
Suffolk, Charles Brandon, Duke of, 32.
Sulyn, Nicha de, 20.
Sutton, Walter de, 212 n.
Sweete, Walter, 295.
Symons, Nicholas, 228 n; Richard, 104 n.

Tabernar, William, 261 n.
Tailleur, John le, 139 n; Richard le, 139 n.
Taland, Joanna, 148; John, 148.
Talbois, George Lord, 32; Margaret, his wife, 32.
Talbot, 105 n, 270 n; Elinor, 31; Elizabeth, 31; Sir Gilbert, 30; Joan, 30; Sir John, 31; Julyan, 276; Margaret, 94; Richard, Lord, 31; Sir William, 94, 276.
Talverne, Sir Osbert de, 208; Melior, 208.
Tamline, Honor, 262 n.
Tancred, Tankred, Isabell, 12; Margaret, 30; Richard, 30.
Tanner, 278, 306.
TANNER, 278, 279; Anthony, 238 n; Barnard, 301; Francis, 301; Jane, 181; John, 181, 190; Julian, 254 n; Michael, 168.
Taperell, John, 295.
Tapson, Joan, 201 n.
Taverner, Alice, 178 n; William, 254 n.
Taylor, Agnes, 41.
Telham, M 289.
TEMPEST, 57.
Thinn, Thynne. Dorothy, 189, 190; Sir John, 190; Sir Thomas, 189.
Thomas *alias* Bosaveron, Martyn, 186. See Bosavarne.
Thomas, 306. *Thoms*, 216.
THOMAS, THOMS, 215, 216; Johanna, 228 n; John, 62, 228 n; Margaret, 62; William, 163, 163 n.
THOMS *alias* CARNSEW, 217; Grace, 42, 90; Henry, 42, 90, 126 n; Maria, 62 n.
Thorne, M 93, 141. Zenobia, 131 n.
Thorning, Robert, 11.
Thorp, Robert de, 18.
Thurlbere, John de, 126 n.
Ties, Joan, 8; Henry, 8.

Tindall, Joane, 289.
Tingcombe, Tinkcombe, Tyncomb. Anne, 265 n; Philip, 118, 118 n; Sibilla, 246 n.
Tinmouth, Thomas, Prior of, 94.
Tippett, *see* Nankevell *alias*.
Tiptoft, Ada, 144; Pagauns, 144.
Tirrell, Tirell, Tyrel. Elinor, 150; Elizabeth, 41; John, 41; Richard, 244 n; Robert, 271 n; William, 150.
Todiford, Nicholas de, 55.
Toinkein, 306.
TOINKEIN, 217, 218 n. (Tonkin, Tonken, Tonckin.) Anne, 129 n; John, 124; Philip, 192 n.
Tolkarne, 108. (Tolcarn, Talkarn, etc.) Elizabeth, 79, 80; Johanna, 198 n; John, 79, 80, 198, 198 n.
Toll, Tole, Toule. Agnes, 218; Elizabeth, 205; Henry, 122; John, 205; Wilmot, 122.
Toller, Elizabeth, 246 n; John, 220 n.
Tom, Tome. Gregory, 138; Jone, 14; T., 14.
Tomking, John, 243 n.
Tone, Florence, 167; William, 167.
Totworthy, 69.
TOTWORTHY, 69, 70.
Towse, Isabell, 229.
Tracher, William, 248 n.
Trafford, M 36.
Travais, M 207.
Trebarfoot, 306.
TREBARFOOTE, 218. (Trebarfett.) Olive, 149 n; William, 106 n.
TREBARTHA, 206.
Trebilcock, John, 254 n.
Trebner, John, 258 n.
Trecarrel, Trecarl. M 249.
John, 135; Lora, 229 n; Richard de, 69 n.
Trecarren, Alice, 37; John, 37.
TREDIDON, 105, 106.
Tredinham, Tredenham. Elizabeth, 273; Hugh, 240; John, 147; Sir Joseph, 200 n; Mary, 200 n; Robert, 273.
TREDINICK, 150. (Tredeneck, Treddennick, etc.) Amicia de, 151 n; Blanche, 259 n; Charles, 151 n; Christopher, 34, 56 n. 299; Constantia, 151 n; Dorothy, 114; Elizabeth, 114; Francis, 258; Henry, 249; Jane, 82, 151 n; John, 82, 151 n, 232 n; Margaret, 34, 299; Marose, 152; Mary, 21; Nicholas, 151 n; Peter, 249; Philippa, 110 n, 255 n; Ralph de, 151 n; Robert, 114; Thomas, 21, 249; William, 255 n.

Tredwene, Elizabeth, 248 n.
Treffry, 219, 221.
TREFFRY, 219, 220. TREFRIE, 221. (Trevroi, Trevry, etc.) M 59. Agnes, 133; Anne, 95; Elizabeth, 93, 148; Jane, 224, 225 n, 253 n, 254 n; Jennet, 239; Sir John, 171 n, 180 n, 235 n; John, 93, 95, 145 n, 148, 214 n, 254 n; Thomas, 133, 180 n, 239; William, 224.
Trefusis, 222.
TREFUSIS, 222, 223, 224, 225n, 226 n. (Trefuses, etc.) Jane, 76, 76 n, 98, 145 n, 170; John, 7, 76, 170, 220, 235 n, 212 n; Katherine, 7, 182 n; Marin, 95 n; Mary, 152 n; Nicholas, 119, 119 n; Otes, 98; Richard, 64, 135 n; Samuel, 152 n; Thomas, 76, 76 n, 145 n, 182 n.
Trefyns, Trevince, Trewinse. Henry, 7, 7 n; Hervy de, 222; Margaret, 7.
Tregagall, John, 295.
Tregallest, Amy, 227.
Tregarick, 20. (Tregorck.) Anne, 219n; John, 20, 219n; Mawde, 20.
Tregarthan, 40, 278. (Tregartyn etc.) Honor, 21, 208; Margaret, 40, 278; Sir Thomas, 180; Thomas, 40; William, 21, 208.
Tregasaw, Tregasow, Tregasse. M 150. John, 49; Jone, 49; Margaret, 137 n; Walter, 137 n.
Trege, Philip, 244 n; Roger, 244 n; Walter, 244 n.
Tregeare, 306.
TREGEARE, 225.
TREGENDER, 155.
Tregenna, Edward, 254 n.
Tregennowe, Richard, 176 n.
Tregian, M 64. Elizabeth, 275n; Katherine, 275 n; Mary, 275 n.
Tregiskie, Tregesky. Johanna, 226, 226 n; Richard, 226, 226 n.
Tregithew, Tregetho. John, 168, 226; Nora, 168; Udon, 226.
Treglethenck, Roger, 113.
Treglyne, Michael, 282.
Tregodnck, Tregodeck. Agnes, 228; Robert, 228; William de, 237.
Tregof (? Tregose), Elizabeth, 256; Thomas, 256.
Tregolles, Tregolse. M 16. Richard, 152.
Tregouell, Alice, 204; John, 204.
Tregonny, 285.
Tregonwall, 225.

INDEX OF NAMES. 329

Tregoswall, 225; Doctor, 25¼ n; John, 254 n.
Tregose, Tregos, Tregosa, etc. Ann, 41, 254 n; Catherine, 23; Elizabeth, 7, 7 n; Joane, 154, 155 n; Richard, 7 n; Thomas, 41, 154, 155 n, 215 n; Walter, 23.
Tregost, 39; Walter, 68.
Tregothnan, 20. (Treguthnan.) Joan, 20; John, 18, 20.
Tregoys, John, 244 n; Margery, 244 n; Richard, 255 n.
Tregrilla, Richard de, 55.
TREHANE, 227, 228 n. (Trehayne, etc.) Amye, 53; Elizabeth, 199; John, 53, 111, 199, 252; Katherine, 252; Lawrence, 88; Mary, 111.
Trehake, Trehauke. Elinor, 106; John, 106; June, 117; Richard, 117.
Trehaverock, John, 37; Sibell, 37.
Trehey, Alice, 167; John, 167.
Treiagow, 20, 208. (Trejeagowe, Treagowe, etc.) Joane, 118 n, John, 22.
Trejoskie, John, 259 n.
Treladerw, Johanna, 223; Otes, 223.
Trelawny, 306.
TRELAWNY, 228, 229, 230. (Treloney, Trelaue, etc.) M 268. Ann, 5, 185 n; Charles, 220 n; Elizabeth, 71, 133 n, 244; Sir Jonathan, 5; Jonathan, Bp. of Bristol, 110 n; John, 71, 146, 185 n, 201, 240, 244; Jone, 201; Robert, 210; Samuel, 133 n.
Treledris, Margaret, 89; Richard, 89.
Trelother, Otes, 160 n.
Trelowarren, x.
Treludders, see Marat *alias*.
Tremayne, Tremain. Agnes, 49; Arthur, 85, 85 n, 132, 132 n; Edmund, 132 n; Eulalia, 132, 132 n; James, 47 n; Jane, 156 n, 265; John, 18, 85 n, 180 n, 279; Lewis, 201 n; Margaret, 61; Martha, 263 n; Mary, 196; Philippa, 257, 259 n; Richard, 85 n, 135, 196 n; Roger, 204, 257, 259 n; Sampson, 265; Thomas, 61, 85, 196; Ursula, 220, 220 n; William, 156 n, 181 n, 220; Wilmot, 204.
Tremearne, Trewren *als.*, see Trewren.
Tremerne, James, 273 n.
Tremidren, Luke de, 261 n.
Treminheere, Tremenhere. Ann, 237 n; Ellyn, 57; Thomas, 57.
Tremlet, 107 n.
Tremouth, John, 108; Katherine, 108.

Tremrow, John, 80; Marion, 80.
Trenance, 306.
TRENANCE, 231, 232; Constance, 53; Johanna, 208; Littleton, 190; Richard, 208; Thomas, 53, 76; Wilmot, 76.
Trenant, Alice, 113; John, 113; Luke de, 113.
Trenchard, Nicholas, 113.
Trenchard, see Foxcomb *alias*.
Trencreke, Taucreke. Ann, 210; Honor, 145; Jane, 171, 256; John, 145, 256; Katherine, 172; Robert, 80 n, 171, 172.
Trenerth, 306.
TRENERTH, 233. (Trenarth, etc.) Anne, 225 n; James, 225 n.
Trenger, Isabella, 290; John, 69; Thomas, 290.
Trengove alias Nanse, 305.
TRENGOVE *alias* NANSE, 233, 234. (Tringove, Trengoffe, etc.) Catherine, 123; Elizabeth, 2, 52; Henry, 5; Jane, 274 n; John, 123 n; Richard, 52, 124 n.
Trenhall, James, 162.
Trenoda, John de, 237.
Trenouth, 20. *Trenowith*, 208.
TRENOUTH, 20, 21. TRENOWITH, 208, 209. (Trenowth, Trenoweth, Trenewyth, etc.) M 68, 169. Johanna de, 19, 255 n; John, 276, 298; Margaret, 255 n, 276, 277 n; Philippa, 298; Ralph, 19, 277 n; Stephen, 255 n; Thomas, 68 n.
Trenowithe, see Vivian *alias*.
Trerice, Trerys, Trerise. Jane, 271 n; Joan, 126; Margaret, 272 n; Michael, 271 n; Sir Nicholas, 272 n; Renold, 126.
Trenthall, John, 185 n.
Trenvroth, John, 249 n.
Trenwith vel Treunwith, 306.
TRENWITH *vel* TREUNWITH, 238, 239. (Treunwyth, Treanwith, etc.) M 220. Ann, 23; Elizabeth, 95, 273 n; Ezechiel, 123 n; John, 34, 89, 89 n; Mathew, 23; Philippa, 34; Thomas, 89, 89 n.
Treroncke, Alan, 258 n.
Treruf, Trenroufe, Trerraffe *alias* Treruthe, 169 n, 193 n. Elzabeth, 223; Richard, 223; William, 72.
Tresaher, 234. *Tresaugher*, 306.
TRESAHER, 234, 235, 236, 237 n. (Tresahare, etc.) Anne, 181 n, 242 n; Ezechiel, 277 n; James, 155 n, 160 n, 277 n; John, 163 n; Michael,

TRESAHER—*continued.* 65 n, 155 n; Thomas, 65 n, 181 n, 241 n, 242 n, 270.
Tresaster, Taesalster. Olive, 36, 252, 252 n.
Tresawell, Treswell. M 255 n. Johanna, 258 n; Robert, 199, 258 n.
Tresilian, Jane, 124 n; John, 273 n; Robert de, 126 n.
Tresithney, x, 222. (Tresyney.) Emlyn, 220, 221; John, 76, 220, 221, 224, 224 n; Melior, 76, 222, 224, 224 n.
Treskillard, Margaret, 123; Thomas, 123.
Tresole, Tresula. M 18. Mabel de, 17.
Tresoye, M 172.
Tresteue, Robye, 273 n.
Trestrale, Agnes, 75; John, 75.
Tresuggan, John, 233; Mary, 233.
Tresulgan, Henry, 55.
Tresungar, M 134 n, 138.
Tresweswoth, Henry de, 258 n.
Trethack, Johanna, 244 n; John, 244 n; William, 244 n.
Tretherf (Trethurf), 257.
TRETHERF, 169. (Tredurff, Trethref, etc.) Elizabeth, 257; John, 155 n, 261 n; Margaret, 21, 24 n, 51; Reginald, 213 n; Thomas, 21, 24 n, 51 257, 259 n, 261 n.
Trethewy, 237, 238 n, 306.
TRETHEWY, 237, 238. (Trethewe, Tredewey, Trethewye, etc.) Elizabeth, 181; Robert, 26, 181; Thomas, 148 n, 258 n.
Trethias, Emmott, 255 n; John, 169 n, 255 n; Margaret, 169 n, 255 n; Mellyar, 169 n; Pascowe, 255 n.
Trethowen, John, 67.
Treughans, Elizabeth, 40; Thomas, 40.
Treuronet, Alan de, 261 n; Ranulph de, 261 n.
Trevagan, Trevegan. Andrew de, 261 n; Philip, 113.
Trevage, Jordan de, 261 n.
Trevail, Trevaile. Alice de, 19, 20; Elizabeth, 91 n; Odo de, 19, 20.
Trevais, M 207.
Trevalseus, Trevalscois. Christian, 166; Edward, 101; Judith, 101.
Trevanion, 306.
TREVANION, 239, 240, 241, 242 n. (Trevanyan, Trevanian, etc.) Alice, 19, 21; Amy, 197 n; Anne, 51, 117, Beatrix, 229 n; Charles, 201 n; Elizabeth, 183 n, 184 n, 189; Sir Hugh, 95, 117, 145; Hugh, 181 n, 189, 189 n,

2 U

INDEX OF NAMES.

TREVANION—continued.
190, 235 n; Jane, 208;
Jenophes, 95; Johanna. 115;
Sir John, 20; John, 13, 19,
21, 208, 219 n, 220 n, 224;
Jone, 13, 20, 76, 77; Katherine, 81 n, 189 n, 190; Mary,
58, 224; Richard, 51, 58,
183 n, 252 n, 302; William,
77, 219 n, 235 n.
Trevars, Sir John, 240.
TREVARTHIAN, 297. (Trevertheu. Sir John, 34; John,
34 n, 185 n.
Trevasco, M 47.
Treveare, see Penrose alias.
Treveglos, Isabella, 75 n; Roger, 75 n.
Trevelizek, John, 41.
Trerelynn, 306.
TREVELYAN, 242, 213. (Trevillian, Trevillion, etc.) M
164, 227. Dorothy, 249;
Hugh, 197; John, 38, 69, 128,
227 n; Richard, 21; Thomasine, 197 n; Ursula, 128,
197, 227 n.
Trevener, 40.
TREVENOUR, 169. (Trevener
alias Dewy, Trevenor, etc.)
Grace, 203; Hugh, 203; Isabella, 189, 190; Margaret, 40;
Richard, 21, 40, 189, 190;
William, 189 n.
Treverga, Andrew de, 261 n.
Trevergan, Vivian, 261 n.
Trevervo, Richard, 263.
Trevethwane, Trevythvan.
John, 80 n; Thomas, 80 n;
William, 80 n.
TREVIADOS, 222, 223.
Trevilla, Treville, Trevilli, Trevill, etc. M 114. Elinor, 19,
21, 223; Philip de, 18;
Rodolph de, 18; William de,
19, 21, 223.
Treviniel, Vivian de, 261 n.
Trevisa, 257, 306.
TREVISA, 214. (Trevisa.)
Elizabeth, 6; Henry, 203;
John, 6; Katherine, 203.
Trevithick, William, 267 n.
Treviwen, Robert de, 55.
Trewanwell, 222. (See Halep.)
Trewartheniek, 20, 208.
TREWARTHENICK, 20, 208.
(Trewarthenek, Trewarthenik, Trewythenick, etc.)
John, 223; Pascatia, 223.
Trewavas, Trewawas. M 188.
Katherine, 263 n.
Trewbody, 306.
TREWBODY, 246, 247 n.
(Trwbody, Trubody, Trubodie, etc.) Charles, 101;
Elizabeth, 204; John, 119 n,
204, 209; Jone, 262; Walter,
295.
Trewenhelek, William, 112 n.

Trewethy, John de, 23.
TREWIKE, 7. (Treweike, etc.)
Mary, 79; Robert, 79.
Trewin, William, 282.
Trewinard, Trewynard, Trewinnard, Trewinward, etc. M
192. Henry, 71; Jane, 71;
John, 76, 270 n; Joseph,
87 n; Matthew, 145; Mary,
87 n.
Trewint, Trewent, Trewynt.
M 203 n. Isabella, 228 n;
Jane, 84; Stephen de, 228 n;
William, 84.
Trewolla, 306.
TREWOLLA, 244, 245. (Trewalla, Trewolly, Trewyla, Trewhilla, Trewhella, Trewhela,
Trewheler, etc.) Agnes, 90 n;
Ann, 90; John, 90, 111 n;
Katherine, 111; Richard,
111 n; Thomas, 90, 111;
William, 111.
Trewoof, Trewoofe. Joan, 126;
Hawise, 20; Thomas de, 18;
William, 20.
Treworgy, Treworga. John,
216 n, 226; Melior, 226.
Trewren, 268.
TREWREN, 247. (Treuren,
Truran, Treowran, Tryourne,
etc.) Alice, 123; John, 42,
123, 183, 260 n; Thomas,
169; Roger, 255 n.
Trewynick, Jane de, 228; Stephen de, 228; William, 183.
Triggs, Triggos. Catherine,
108; Thomas, 72.
Tripcouney, Tripconie, Trepconye, etc. Alexander, 141;
Alice, 193; Charity, 217;
Elizabeth, 22; Francis, 226;
Jane, 115; John, 22, 115, 217.
Trithwall, Agnes, 155; John,
155, 185.
Triwancamstell, Reginald de,
18.
Troblefeild, Jone, 116.
Trochynock, Richard de, 55.
Trowbridge, Trobridg. Catherine, 157; John, 157; Judith,
39.
Trowte, Elinor, 140 n.
Trwro (Truro), 285.
Tubb, 248 n, 306.
TUBB, 247, 248 n. (Tub,
Tubbe, etc.) Anne, 103 n;
George, 9, 16, 124; Joanne,
7, 9; John, 155 n; Julian,
217; Mary, 46; Robert,
158 n, 174; Susan, 124;
William, 7.
Tucker, 307.
TUCKER, 218, 249, 250 n.
(Tocker, Toker, Tooker.)
Catherine, 268 n; Christopher, 100; George, 154 n;
John, 176 n, 203, 233; Mary,
233; Peter, 100; Reginald,

TUCKER—continued.
229 n; Robert, 148, 258 n;
William, 68; Stephen, 46;
William, 68.
Tuitt, Avice, 30; Richard, 30.
Tully, John, 18.
Turberville, 275 n. Katherine,
125 n.
Turnavyue, John, 153.
Turner, John, 302; Thomas,
156 n.
Turney, Ralph, 280.
Tylley, Tilley. M 286. Elizabeth, 278.
Tynton, Tynten, Tinten. Alice,
297; Sir John, 277, 278 n;
John, 272 n; Margaret, 277,
278 n; Sir Stephen, 297.
Tyrack, Henry, 67.

Udey, x.
Ugler, John, 153 n.
Uglow, George, 107 n.
Umfravile, Alice de, 274 n;
John de, 274 n.
Unvile, Reginald de, 250.
Upcott, Upcote. Jane, 130, 131.
Upton, 307.
UPTON, 268.
UPPETON, 291. (Upeton,
Upton.) Eliam, 229 n;
John, 195; William, 131.
Urban, Anna, 199 n.

Vacye, 250.
VACYE, 128. (Vasie.)
VACYE, 250, 251. (Vacey,
Vasie, Vesie, and Facey.)
Elizabeth, 131, 131 n; Leonard, 131, 131 n.
Vallet, William, 70.
Vallitort, Valle Torte. Ralph
de, 211 n; Roger de, 285.
Vanson, Elizabeth, 110 n.
Vashment, Ann, 210; John,
209, 210.
Velour, John, 239 n.
Vere, Sir Robert, 31.
Verman, 307.
VERMAN, 251, 252. (Vermon.) Anne, 241 n; John,
227, 241 n; Mary, 241 n.
Verney, Sir Edmond, 32.
VIELL, 242, 243. (Viall, Vyell.)
M 10. George, 10 n; Grace,
301; John, 298; Julyan, 86;
Thomas, 69; William, 85,
86, 275 n.
Vigurs, Vygars. Hugh, 281;
Thomas, 106 n.
Vincent, Vyncent. Anne, 47 n;
Elizabeth, 238; Henry, 47 n;
John, 151 n, 238, 294; Margery, 123; Thomas, 123.
Vine, Michael, 45.
Vivian, 307. Viryan, 257.
VIVIAN, 36, 50 n.
VIVIAN, 252, 253 n, 254 n.
VYVYAN, 256. VIVYAN,

INDEX OF NAMES. 331

VIVIAN—*continued.*
257, 258, 259 n, 260 n, 261 n, 262 n. (Vyvian, Vivion, Vavion, Viveon, Vivean, Vivyon, de Vivien, de Vivonia, Vivian *alias* Cooke, Vivian *alias* Trenoweth, etc. M 138, 197. Adam, 247 n; Agnes, 149 n; Anne, 114; Anor, 148 n; Barbara, 270, 270 n; Bridget, 197 n; Charles, 68 n; Christian, 73; Dorothy, 14, 125 n; Edeth, 140; Edward, 173 n; Elizabeth, 149 n; Emlyn, 136, 138 n, 149, 149 n; Sir Francis, 46; Francis, 139 n, 184 n, 200 n; Hanibal, 14, 14 n, 47 n, 90 n, 140, 140 n, 269 n; Henry, 214 n; Ina, 107 n; Jane, 53 n, 73, 221 n; Joane, 68 n; Johanna, 84; 247 n; John, 25, 38, 38 n, 72 n, 73, 114, 139 n, 148 n, 149 n, 156 n, 157 n, 164 n, 169 n, 181 n, 189 n, 197 n, 220 n, 221 n, 270, 270 n; Judith, 140 n; Katherine, 155 n; Loveday, 218 n; Margerie, 98, 115; Maria, 181 n, 189 n; Mary, 38 n, 197 n, 211 n; Matilda, 149 n; Matthew, 125 n; Michael, 47, 73, 154, 154 n, 155 n, 156 n; Miss, 214 n; Odo, 149 n; Olive, 102 n; Pascowe, 177 n; Peter, 186 n, Philippa, 47 n, 104 n; Sir Richard, 220 n; Richard, 23, 68 n, 72 n, 138 n, 139 n, 177 n; Robert, 98, 115; Stephen, 184 n, 189 n; Thomas, 136, 148 n, 149, 197 n; Thomasine, 90 n; William, 114 n; Sir Viell, 84.
Voly, Nicholas, 70.
Vosper, 254 n. Arthur, 127 n; Barbara, 256 n; Elizabeth, 127 n; John, 283; Prudence, 127 n; Richard, 127 n, 254 n; Thomas, 295.
Vowell, Sibil, 194; William, 194.

Waddon, M 39.
Wade, Johanna, 250; John, 250 n.
Wadham, Wadda. Dorothy, 123; Frances, 77; George, 77; William, 68.
Waff (?), x.
Wainwright, James, 106 n.
Wales, Prince of. See Ap Conwyn, Ap Griffith, and Ap Theodor Mawr.
WALKER, 207.
Wallacomb, Jenor, 5; John, 2.
Waller, Erasmus, 17; Francis, 17.

Wallis, Wallys. Christopher, 13; Henry, 128 n; John, 222; Margaret, 102; Philip, 294.
Wallis alias Darte, 279.
WALLIS *alias* DARTE, 279. See also Dart.
Walrond, Waldron. Elinor, 269, 269 n; Joane, 286; Henry, 269, 269 n; Maria, 252 n; William, 252 n.
Walsbury, Walesbrew, Whalesbury, Whalisborough. M 42. Elizabeth, 242; Jane, 34; Johanna, 228 n; John, 296; Thomas, 242; William de, 228 n, 296.
Walsh, John, 235 n.
Walter, Zachary, 295.
Walthen, Elizabeth, 266; Roger, 266.
Walton, Thomas, 37.
Ward, Thomas, 252.
Wardon, Stephen, 88.
Warne, Elizabeth, 102 n; Philippa, 260 n.
Warren, Warrin. Christopher, 160 n; Elizabeth, 249 n; John, 114; Nicholas, 253 n; Richarda, 201 n.
Warwick, Richard, Earl of, 186; Lucy, da. of the Earl of, 186.
Watt (? Harry). See Harry.
Watta, William, 221 n.
Way, Waye, Wey. Alice, 159; Emlyn, 152; John, 105 n; Temperance, 109, 111; William, 109, 111, 152, 159.
Webb, M 140. Jone, 118 n; Thomas, 107 n; Walter, 139.
Webber, 307.
WEBBER, 262. M 286. Bridget, 182; Jane, 90 n; John, 35, 173; Margery, 59, 200; Mary, 35; Nicholas, 280; Robert, 182; William, 59, 200.
Weekes, Weeke. Elizabeth, 197 n; Hugh, 98; John, 11; Justian, 137; Lora, 99; S^{n}volla, 11.
Wellington, Willington. M 138. Ralph de, 144.
Welsh, Mary, 292; Richard, 292.
Wenmouth, Wenemouth. Anastacia, 198, 200; Joan, 102 n; John, 102 n; Robert de, 198, 200.
West, Francis, 238.
Westcot, Agnes, 200; Alice, 199; Anne, 266; John, 199, 200; Margaret, 147; Richard, 295; Roger, 266; William, 147.
Westlake, Christian, 107 n; Richard, 107 n.
Westmarch, Peter de, 237.
Weston, M 74.

Whelpington, Robert, 94.
Whethall, Robert, 85.
Whiddon, William, 119 n.
White, 307.
WHITE, 262, 263. Ambrose, 284; Anne, 99; Jane, 21; Richard, 99; William, 21.
Whitfeld, Thomas, 117.
Whitford, John, 269; Thomasine, 269.
Whiting, Whitinge, Whitting. M 278. Nicholas, 82; Thomas, 270 n.
Whitleigh, x. (Whitleygh, Whetleighe.) Margaret, 84, 87; Richard, 84, 87.
Whitt, Walter, 284.
Whittington, Whityndon. Blanche, 212, 212 n; Thomas, 212, 212 n, 275 n.
Wiat, Richard, 12.
Wilcock, Katherine, 152.
Wilford, Sir Thomas, 32; William, 32.
William, Peter, 186 n.
Williams, 307.
WILLIAMS, 39.
WILLIAMS, 263, 264, 265 n. (Willeams, Willyams, etc.) M 65. Anne, 91 n; Balthazer, 162 n, 186; Bartholomew, 103 n; Charles, 158 n; Frances, 170 n; George, 235 n; Henry, 285; Honor, 63 n, 241 n; Hugh, 197 n; James, 176 n; Jane, 197 n; John, 103 n, 123 n, 164 n, 168 n, 235 n, 249 n; Mary, 220 n; Michael, 215 n; Patience, 91 n; Prudence, 217 n; Rebecca, 109 n; Richard, 53 n, 104 n; Ruth, 109 n; Thomas, 24; Thomasine, 24; Warren, 151 n; William, 12, 103 n, 214 n, 268 n.
Williams *alias* Boswathick. See Boswathek.
Willoughby, 307.
WILLOUGHBY, 265.
Willoughby de Broke. M 31. Sir Robert, Lord de Broke, 219 n; Lord, 171 n; Robert, Lord, 220 n.
Wills, 307.
WILLS, 269.
WILLS, 265, 266. (Wylles, Wylls, Willes.) Dorothy, 227; George, 165 n; Hugh, 188; Joanna, 136 n; Margery, 186; Richard, 199; William, 284.
Wilshman, Cecilia, 198; John, 198.
Wilson, Jane, 185; John, 61, 185.
Wilton, Elizabeth, 162; Robert, 280; William, 60.
Winard, x.

INDEX OF NAMES.

Windham, Wyndham. Margaret, 64 n; Sir Thomas, 64 n, 270 n.
WINDSOR, 106, 150. The Lord, 30.
WINTER (Wynter), 120, 270 n. M 223. Philippa, 100.
Wise, Wyse. Constance, 80; Jane, 247; John, 64 n; Thomas, 24, 247; William, 80.
WODELAND, 25.
Wodenote, 307.
WODENOTE, 266. (Woodnott.) Prisilla, 160; Thomas, 160.
Wodman, M 139.
Wodrington, Sir John, 94; Roger, 94.
Wolcott, Wolcot. Barbara, 141; Katherine, 174; Peter, 142; Thomas, 174.
Woldridge, Woulrydge. Matthew, 67, 282.
Wollesdon, Joane, 55; Thomas, 55.
Wollye, John, 250 n.
Wolvedon, Catherine, 19, 299; John, 19, 299.
Wolverston, Mary, 117.

Woode, Wood, Waade. Alice, 146 n; Dorothie, 11; Henry, 102; Jane, 160, 160 n; Johan, 102; John, 11, 160, 160 n.
Worlington, Jane, 91; Sir Matthew, 91; William, 91.
Wortham, x; Joanna, 81.
Worthe, 40. (Worth, Writhe.) Agnes, 40; Isabell, 194; Powle, 279; Thomas, 40.
Worthevale, 307.
WORTHEVALE, 267, 268 n. (Worthivale, Worthyvale, Warthewale, Worthywell, Worthwale, etc.) M 231 n. Christopher, 11, 114 n, 249 n.
Wotton, Wotten, Wootton. M 265. Alice, 51; John, 3, 51; Margaret, 3; Mary, 32 n.
Woyne, Thomas, 272 n.
Wrey, 193, 307.
WREY, 268. (Wray.) Elizabeth, 254 n; Johanna, 194; John, 194, 291; Philippa, 291; Sir William, 132 n, 283.
Wroughton or *Reprin*, x.
Wychehalse, 307.

WYCHEHALSE, 292. (Wichhalse.) Jone, 240.
Wydeslade, Widdeslade. John, 255 n; Mary, 92; William, 92.
Wykkett, Wyket. Elizabeth, 165 n; Johanna, 215 n; Nicholas, 165 n; Richard, 215 n.
Wylle, John, 243 n.
Wymond, John, 295.
Wyrel, 307.
WYVELL, 269.
Wythyby, Thomasine, 200.

Yarde, John, 253 n.
YEO, 292, 293; Alice, 91; Ebbott, 285; George, 162 n; John, 91, 128 n; Leonard, 115 n, 165, 285; Margaret, 273 n; Robert, 7; Sara, 162 n; William, 84 n.
York, Edward, Duke of, 144.
York, 307.
YORKE, 269, 270. (York, Yeorcke.) Anne, 236; Humphry, 155 n, 158, 158 n, 236, 257; Sara, 158, 158 n.
Young, Yonge. Ellin, 263. Helen, 263 n; William, 142, 263.

OMISSIONS IN INDEX.

Carter, 279 n.
Essex, The Earl of, 252.
Hender, 186.
Hill, 194. M 84.

Incledon, John, 80 n.
John, Martha, 150 n.
Revel, 194.
Rochford, x.

Trecarrel alias Esse, x.
Tredignie, x.
Trefonis, x.
Tregarthan, x.

INDEX OF PLACES.

Abbotsham, 78.
Abraham Hall, Lancashire, 124.
Acland, 292.
Acton, Middlesex, 151.
Addeston, Devon, 6.
Advent, Adven, etc., Cornwall, 125 n, 133 n, 200, 254 n, 295.
Afton, 141 n, 270 n.
Albominster, 271.
Aldercombe, 87.
Aler, 286.
Alet, 272 n.
Aliscomb, 107 n.
Allington, Devon, 87, 205.
Alphyngton, Devon, 302.
Alta, 261 n.
Alternon, 92, 105 n, 107 n, 108 n, 141 n, 295.
Amell, St. Kew, 262, 262 n.
Ampthill, Bedfordshire, 106 n.
Anglesea, 30.
Annery, 230.
Anthony, Authonie, 1, 2, 28, 29, 29 n, 31, 68, 83, 83 n, 118 n, 135 n, 210 n, 211 n, 294.
Antron, Antorne, Cornwall, 162, 162 n, 276.
Apledrum, Sussex, 28.
Ardevora Vear, 242 n.
Ardevoro, Ardeverey, 251, 277, 277 n.
Arrallas, Argallas, in St. Enoder, 212 n, 259 n, 261 n.
Arrington, Berks, 116.
Arscott, 286.
Arundell, 31.
Arundell Street, London, 161 n.
Arwanneck, Arwenneck, Arwanick, 81, 86, 293.
Arworthell, 277 n.
Ashwater, 63 n, 207 n, 298, 299 n.
Ashwell Thorp, Norfolk, 117.
Aston, Devon, 47, 79.
Atte hole, 204 n.

Atte Water, 255 n.
Austell, see St. Austell.
Austle *alias* Hawsewell Park, Alternon, 122 n.
Axham, Lincolnshire, Isle of, 289.
Axmouth or Exmouth, 243 n.

Babligh, 106.
Bake, Cornwall, 150, 151, 179.
Balowdan, 223.
Barkley, 220 n.
Barne, Dorset, 28.
Barnstaple, Barstable, Borstable, Devon, 45, 101, 159 n, 207, 241, 279, 292.
Barowhall, Suffolk, 10.
Barum, 259 n.
Basill, Cornwall, 242, 243.
Barley, Exeter, 29 n.
Battersby Hall, Yorkshire, 6.
Beaga-Cubie, 180 n.
Beard Hill, Sussex, 6.
Beardon, Beredon, Bordon, 131, 251, 291.
Beauchamp Court, Warwickshire, 90.
Beckles, Suffolk, 60.
Bedham, 289.
Bednall Greene, 186.
Beere, 300 n.
Beill, 46.
Belenick, see Meleneck.
Benethewood, 9.
Benunlack, Benathleck, Banethlek, Bonathlek, 75 n, 76, 76 n, 150 n, 162 n.
Berican erber, Devon, 134, 173.
Berie, Devon, 170.
Berkshire, 30, 116.
Bickingham, 61.
Bickington, Devon, 134, 137.
Bickley, Devon, 32, 68.
Bickton, Bicton, Cornwall, 119, 229.

Bickwel, Devon, 90.
Biddiford, Bitellford, Bydeford, Devon, 70, 107, 209, 255 n.
Binnerton, Benherton, 7, 278 n.
Blaboll, 18.
Blackawton, 199 n.
Blackdon, Blackdoune, Devon, 194, 291.
Black Torrington, Blaketoriton, Black Torrinton, 107 n, 131 n, 139, 272 n.
Blasey, see St. Blazey.
Blaxton Hall, Durham, 28.
Blisland, Cornwall, 21, 25, 96, 161, 188, 204 n, 246.
Bliston, 27.
Blowfleming, 186.
Boatesfleminge, Botusfleming, 54 n, 266.
Bocarren, 146 n.
Bochym, 35 n, 299 n.
Bochyny, 299 n.
Boconnoc, Bokonock, etc., Cornwall, 144, 146 n, 158, 160 n, 298.
Boddrane, Bodreyn, 101, 102.
Bodgall in Lanlivery, 261 n.
Bodinick-Veor, Cornwall, 181.
Bodinnick, Cornwall, 56 n.
Bodmalgan, 150 n.
Bodmin, Bodmyn, Bodman, Badman, Cornwall, 11 n, 12, 42 n, 46 n, 48 n, 52, 56 n, 59 n, 72, 88 n, 111 n, 112 n, 114, 139 n, 142, 143, 143 n, 146 n, 150 n, 153, 158 n, 159, 159 n, 160 n, 163 n, 167, 174, 175, 180 n, 190, 207, 214, 216, 219 n, 223, 231, 232 n, 238, 249, 254 n, 256, 256 n, 267, 298.
Bodrennek, 156 n.
Bodrigan, Bodringham, 64, 64 n, 65, 65 n, 278 n.
Bodriggey, 79 n.
Bohemia, 279.

INDEX OF PLACES.

Bokedock in Lanivet, 114.
Boleth, 18.
Bonithan, Bonythan in Cury, Cornwall, 16, 17, 109, 248 n.
Borlawren, Barlawren in Egleshevle, 9, 114 n.
Bosawsnke, Bossawsack, 22.
Boscawen Rose, 17, 18.
Boscombe, Wilts, 251, 266.
Boscovey *alias* Boscavevyn, in St. Austell, 189 n, 255 n.
Boscovill in St. Austell, 246 n.
Boshavarne, 258 n.
Bosiron, 9.
Boskenna in St. Buryan, 162 n.
Boskennan, 79 n.
Boskerin in Bodmin, 195 n.
Bosmawgan, Cornwall, 104.
Bossagran, 50 n.
Bossiney, 107 n.
Bossinver, 181 n.
Boswednock in Senar (Zennor), 22.
Boswithegio, 257.
Bosworgy, 274 n.
Botadon, Botaden, Botathan, 13.
Botallack in St. Just, 169 n.
Botnole Biehan, 124 n.
Botreaux Castle, 93, 93 n, 116, 147, 186, 187, 248 n.
Bovey, Bovye, Devon, 99, 287.
Bowrings Lee, 182.
Boyton, Cornwall, 79, 79 n, 80 n, 141.
Bradfield, Devon, 252 n, 269, 269 n.
Bradford, Devon, 250.
Bradston, Devon, 11, 290.
Bradworthy, 107 n, 218 n, 273 n.
Brampton, 24.
Brannell, 278.
Branton, 91.
Bratton, 80 n.
Bread Street, London, 160.
Breage, Breague, Boreage, etc., Cornwall, 48, 48 n, 77, 82, 93, 123 n, 152, 174, 205, 270, 273.
Brembowel, 46.
Breward, see St. Breward.
Broock, see St. Breock.
Brewery, 16.
Brey in Morvall, Cornwall, 140.
Bridge, 107 n, 207 n.
Bridgend juxta Lostwithiel, 112 n.
Bridgerule, 107 n.
Brightley, 85.
Bristol, Bristow, Glostershire, 38, 38 n, 57, 72, 214, 254 n, 289.
Brixton, Devon, 11.
Broadstone, 55.
Broadwood, 213.
Brousholm in Bolland, Yorkshire, 161.
Browularsh, 60 n.
Brown Park, 207 n.
Bryggend, 158 n.

Buckelley, Bokally, 2, 100.
Buckish, Devon, 21.
Buckland Bruer, Devon, 41, 213.
Buckland Monachorum, Devon, 90, 226 n, 249 n.
Buckland Philly, 230, 251.
Budcox, see St. Budeaux.
Budock, 42, 235, 235 n, 251, 261 n.
Budokeshed, Budeuxshed, Budside, Butshed, etc. 51, 54 n, 99, 135.
Budyn, 23.
Bukian, Cornwall, 71.
Burford, Oxfordshire, 294.
Burye, 31.
Burian, Buryan, Borian, Berian, St. Burian, Cornwall, 74, 89, 123 n, 126 n, 158, 159 n, 170 n, 234 n, 238, 270.
Burncoose in Stithians, 22 n.
Burrell juxta Saltash, 25 n, 26.
Bury Pomeroy, Devon, 177.
Buscane, Cornwall, 71, 72.
Buswistock, Cornwall, 92.
Buttercram, Yorkshire, 60.

Cadley, 125 n.
Caerumer, 272 n, 274 n, 275 n.
Callard, Devon, 215.
Callington, Killington, 135 n, 199, 200.
Callis, 85, 292.
Callwoodley, Devon, 83 n, 288.
Caistock, Cawlstock, Cornwall, 88, 135 n, 136 n.
Camborne, Cornwall, 3, 17, 42, 89, 123, 123 n, 164, 191, 234 n, 237 n, 261 n, 263, 273 n.
Camelford, Cambelford, etc., Cornwall, 11, 29 n, 250 n, 262 n, 268 n.
Camerton, see Connerton.
Canelogie, 245 n.
Canington, Somersetshire, 223, 278.
Carbons, 239 n.
Carclew, Calclew, Crneeleu, Kertleowe, etc., 20, 68, 183, 212, 247, 257.
Cardigan, 30.
Cardinham, Cornwall, 231 n, 233, 249, 249 n, 268 n.
Cargamowe, 235 n.
Cargreene, 199.
Carhais Castle, 265 n.
Carheis, Carhayes, Cary Hayes, Kerehayes, etc., 51, 117, 189, 190, 239, 240, 241 n, 242 n, 271, 271 n.
Carickfergus, Castro de, 261 n.
Carlenuck, 274 n.
Carlyan, Carlighan, Carlyon Key, Cornwall, 79, 191, 191 n.
Carminowe, 33, 212 n.
Carnanton, Carnington, 186, 265 n.
Carno Greowe, 148 n.

Carnewrynek Wartha, 151 n.
Carnsew, Carnesuwe, 217, 239 n.
Carnworthy in Warbstow, 120n.
Carnyny, 239 n.
Carpenters, 255 n.
Carver, Cornwall, 147.
Carveynnek Pettit, 235 n.
Carwin, 89 n.
Cary, Devon, 37.
Castle, Castell, in Lanlivery, Cornwall, 101, 246, 246 n.
Castle Gotham, 189 n, 255 n.
Castle Horneck, Cornwall, 126.
Castlesance, Castlezans, etc., Cornwall, 180, 180 n.
Castlewich, Cornwall, 55.
Catherloghe, Ireland, 32.
Caultock, 244.
Cavan, Ireland, 187.
Cayrowe, 112 n.
Chafard, 119 n.
Chagford, 54 n, 121 n.
Chalton, 195.
Chappell in Winklye Tracy, Devon, 127.
Cheepside, Chepeside, London, 16, 238.
Chekington, Berks, 116.
Chelsea, 187 n.
Cheshire, 202.
Cheston, Suffolk, 61.
Chestow, Devon, 200.
Chichester, 28.
Chidown, 177 n.
Chinals, 23.
Chipons, 149 n.
Christeroy, 260 n.
Chiton, Cornwall, 7, 8.
Chiverton, 191 n.
Chudleigh Chudley, Devon, 29, 292.
Clearzarn, 162.
Cleere, see St. Cleere.
Clemense, Clements, Cornwall, 173 n, 180 n, 263. See also St. Clements.
Cleverton, 106 n, 218 n.
Clopton, Warwickshire, 32.
Cloveley, Devon, 2, 13, 29, 41, 122.
Clowance, Clowans, St. Clowins, Cornwall, 2, 2 n, 43 n, 50, 185, 185 n, 212.
Cliffe, 213.
Cliffe Close, The, 235 n.
Cockington, 5, 64.
Codner, 144.
Cofford in Kenton, Devon, 292 n.
Colampton, Devon, 278.
Colan, Colon, 50 n, 139 n, 224.
Cold Ashby, Northamptonshire, 65.
Coldrenick, 230 n.
Coleford, 255 n.
Colewood in St. Nightons, Bodmin, 56 n.
Collacombe, Cullacombe, Devon, 85, 132, 132, n 196, 259 n.

INDEX OF PLACES.   335

Colliton, Coleton in Newton Ferrers, Devon, 49, 176, 177.
Colridge, 231 n.
Colshull, 197.
Combe, Devon, 11.
Combesberie, Somersetshire, 38.
Combeshed, Cornwall, 135.
Comb Ryall, 269 n.
Connerton, 80, 274 n.
Constantine, Constenton, Kestenton, etc., Cornwall, 22, 48 n, 54, 54 n, 77, 96, 107, 107 n, 152 n, 163 n, 164, 182, 187 n, 225 n, 233, 236 n, 261 n, 264 n.
Coome Florie, Somersetshire, 65.
Coriton, Devon, 49.
Cork, 30, 32.
Corkington, 31.
Cornelly, 180 n.
Cornwithie, 231 n.
Cornwood, Devon, 92.
Corry Mallet, 73.
Coswarth, Cosworth, Cornwall, 2, 50, 50 n, 112, 197 n, 200 n, 261 n.
Cosworthie, 291.
Coswyn, 68 n.
Court, 181, 279 n.
Coventrie, 220 n.
Cowick, Devon, 288.
Craford, Kent, 74.
Crantock, Carantock, Cornwall, 22, 130, 272.
Crecombe, 279 n.
Crediton, Devon, 70, 125 n, 170, 269, 269 n, 270 n.
Creede, Cornwall, 61, 138.
Cressell, Cressoll, etc., Cornwall, 55, 56.
Crofthole, 204 n.
Crokadon, Cornwall, 6, 244.
Croscom, 292.
Crosse, Cornwall, 58, 241.
Crowan, Cornwall, 54 n, 61, 62, 142, 154, 155, 155 n, 163, 164, 185 n, 186, 190, 212 n, 215, 226, 227, 274 n.
Crugantallan, see Tregantallan.
Cruse Morchard, Devon, 56 n.
Crutched Friars, London, 220 n.
Cubert, Cuthbert, 173 n, 107 n, 261 n, 295.
Cuby, Kebye, etc., 181 n, 235 n, 261 n, 295.
Culleton in Chumleigh, 207 n.
Cury, Kewry, Cornwall, 48 n, 73, 163, 177, 216, 261 n.
Cuterew, Cornwall, 209, 211.
Cutland, Devon, 66.
Cutparrot, 111 n.

Dalverton, Somerset, 205.
Dancy, Wiltshire, 24.
Danet's Hall, 2 n.
Dartford, Kent, 124.
Dartmouth, Devon, 6, 138, 168 n, 171.

Dassell in Morewinstow, Cornwall, 213.
Davanant, 299.
Davies, 69.
Deliobell, 190 n.
Derby, 151, 261 n.
Descombe, Wiltshire, 128, 251 n.
Desmond, 32.
Deverell, 162.
Deviok, 52, 80 n,
Devon, 5, 6, 9, 10, 14, 29 n, 31, 32, 34, 35, 47, 54, 70, 70 n, 81, 83, 90, 93, 107 n, 122, 124, 130, 131, 138, 142, 160, 168, 169, 183, 184, 200 n, 205, 218, 246, 257, 259 n, 261 n, 265 n, 270 n.
Dewstock, 138.
Dewston, 134.
Dewstowe, Cornwall, 3, 295.
Dinham, 114.
Dodacomb, 207 n.
Dodbroke, Devon, 137.
Dodford in Bramsgrove, Worcestershire, 289.
Dodustow, 23.
Dominock, see St. Dominick.
Donnant, 299 n.
Dorsetshire, 34, 38, 71, 263, 288.
Dotington, Devon, 137.
Downend, East, 106 n.
Dowrish, Devon, 32, 106 n.
Drannek, 158 n.
Drussell, 255 n.
Dublin, Ireland, 32, 202.
Dunheved, 13, 107 n, 126 n.
Dulo, Duloe, Dewlo, Cornwall, 6, 136, 161 n, 214, 270 n, 295.
Dunsfeld, Dontsfeld, 272 n, 275 n.
Dunsland, Donsland, Devon, 12, 286, 287, 293, 298.
Dunster, 31, 143, 269, 269 n.
Durworthy, 190.
Dynasia, 174.
Dysard, Dysert, 271 n, 298.
Dysart, East, 35 n.
Dysart, West, 35 n.

Earth juxta Saltash, 14, 15, 36, 251.
East Allington, Devon, 153 n.
East Ashton, 238 n.
Eastclose, 235 n.
East Down, Devon, 209.
East Downend, 106 n.
East Haddon, Northamptonshire, 234 n.
Easthendra in St. Kew, 56 n.
East Indies, 88, 182.
East Lowe, Eastlow, 73, 73 n, 181 n.
East Ogwell, Devon, 230 n.
Easton, Worcester, 106 n.
East Stonehouse, 63 n.
Ebbeford, 69 n.
Edgcomb, Cornwall, 28, 64.

Efford, 272 n.
Egglesford, Devon, 49.
Egloshaile, Eglesychle, Egglosheile, Egloshey, etc., Cornwall, 9, 112, 113, 114, 134.
Egloskerry, Egleskerrie, 45, 105 n, 106 n.
Eglosros, 277 n, 296, 299 n.
Elam, Kent, 74.
Elerkie alias Verian, 180 n.
Empingham, Lincolnshire, 65.
Endellion, 11, 120 n, 189 n.
Enis, Eneys, Cornwall, 21 n, 67, 185.
Enmor, 240.
Enneder, see St. Enoder.
Erisey, Erysy, Erisa, etc., Cornwall, 23, 28, 68, 258 n.
Ermington, 231 n.
Ernsettle on the Tamar, near Saltash, 197 n.
Erthholewood, 247 n, 255 n.
Ervin, see St. Ervan.
Escote, 251 n.
Essex, 100.
Essex Street, London, 161 n.
Estwell, 272.
Ethye, 118 n.
Eton, 195 n.
Exeter, Exiter, 12, 32, 61 n, 66, 68, 85, 85 n, 92, 125, 135 n, 136 n, 142, 156 n, 159 n, 207 n, 217, 230, 249, 249 n, 256 n, 269 n, 270 n, 288, 292.
Exeter College, Oxford, 203.

Falmouth, 67 n, 235 n, 236 n, 237 n, 285.
Falopit, 73, 158, 171, 171 n. See also Vallopit.
Farringdon, 279 n.
Farway, 151 n.
Favant, Wiltshire, 215.
Fellick, see Phillack.
Fen Carpenters, 255 n.
Feune, 255 n.
Fennesland, 255 n.
Fenton, 69.
Fentongeock, Fentongok, Fentongoeth, etc., in Cuby, 181 n, 235 n, 236 n, 272 n.
Fentongollan, Fentongollen, Cornwall, 34, 72, 298, 299.
Fentongorge, 235 n.
Fenton Vacy, 250, 251.
Feock, Feok, etc., 181 n, 191 n, 295.
Filley, see Philleigh.
Fitz Ford, Devon, 15.
Fleete, Devon, 50, 92, 92 n, 93, 93 n, 194.
Fodringay, 147.
Forde, 125 n.
Forde in Hartland, 207 n.
Forest of Knavesbury, 97.
Fosnewyth, Fosnewith, 100 n, 216 n.
Fowelscombe, 194.

INDEX OF PLACES.

Fowey, Foye, etc., Cornwall, 21, 45, 54 n, 57, 93, 94 n, 95 n, 115, 116, 133, 140, 145 n, 146, 148, 148 n, 169, 180 n, 183, 183 n, 196, 204 n, 205, 205 n, 219 n, 220 n, 221, 224, 231 n, 239, 245, 247, 277, 278 n.
Foxcomb, 250 n.
Foxehall, 184 n.
Foxholle, 255 n.
Foy Moor, 107 n.
Fulham, 161 n.
Fulford, Devon, 37.
Furland, 29.
Fursdon, 259 n.
Furson, 255 n.

Gamon House by Padstow, 74.
Gatherley, Devon, 46. 290.
Gasgell Thorp in Craven, 292.
Gaverigan, Gavrigan, etc., Cornwall, 65, 83, 185, 223, 224.
Geare in Gwennap, 218 n.
George Come, Gloucestershire, 75.
Gerrans, Garrens, St. Garons, etc., Cornwall, 56, 57, 197 n, 295.
Gidley, Goodleigh, 47 n, 63 n.
Glewyas *alias* Kenwyn, 240 n.
Glin, 12.
Gluvias, Gluish, Glwvies, etc., Cornwall, 7, 185 n, 192, 203 n, 252.
Gluvyan Margh, 255 n.
Glynn, Glin, etc., in Cardinham, Cornwall, 79, 79 n, 80, 80 n, 95, 111 n, 298.
Godolphin, Godolphyn, 5, 81, 82, 83, 109, 214 n.
Golden, 64.
Gollant, 4.
Golocotte, Godacote, 79, 80.
Goodorock, 262 n.
Gorran, St. Gorna, etc., Cornwall, 55, 180 n, 181 n, 241, 274 n.
Gorwena, Cornwall, 156 n.
Goviley, 234, 235 n, 236 n, 277, 277 n.
Govileybyhan, 272 n.
Govileymur, 272 n.
Govyley Vean, 181 n, 235 n.
Grampound, 181 n, 215.
Grantham, 261 n.
Grayston, 80.
Great Woodstock Street, in St. Michael's, London, 106 n.
Grenway, Devon, 6.
Grey's Inn, Middlesex, 106 n.
Grindreth, 68.
Grogoth, 240 n.
Grove, Buckinghamshire, 32.
Grymsbye, 97.
Guernsey, Isle of, 156 n.
Gulval, Gowlvale, Gulver, 22, 82, 115, 158 n, 264 n, 270 n.
Gurlyn Lountha *alias* St. Earthe Church Town, 155 n.

Gurlyn, Garlyn, Gurland, Cornwall, 138 n, 154, 155 n, 156 n, 237 n. 258.
Gurlyn Rebah, 155 n.
Gunwalloe, 184 n.
Gweek Wood, 167 n.
Gwendron, see Wendron.
Gwennap, Gwinhop, Gwenip, etc., Cornwall, 8. 46 n, 68, 126 n, 216, 247, 248 n, 270 n.
Gwinear, Gwynnyer, Gwiniard, Wynier, etc., Cornwall, 23, 23 n, 62, 73, 158, 168 n, 173 n, 174, 175, 261 n, 270 n.
Gwarnack, Guarnack, 42 n, 272, 273, 276.

Haccombe, 31.
Hale in Linkinghorne, Cornwall, 91.
Hall, Devon, 41, 47, 196, 248 n.
Hallisburie, Devon, 58, 269.
Hallivick, in St. Stephen's in Branwell, 181 n.
Halton, 187.
Hamond Aley, 97.
Hampte, 44.
Hampton Poyle, Oxfordshire, 180 n.
Hanckford, Devon, 41.
Handsaker, Staffordshire, 147.
Hanger, Hengar in St. Tudy, Cornwall, 10, 46, 72 n, 133 n, 267.
Harberford, 231 n.
Harclesdon, 55.
Harford, 244 n.
Harlow, Essex, 205.
Harmbeare, Harraver, Cornwall, 6.
Harroboro, 110 n.
Hartland, Devon, 35, 85, 92, 131, 132, 207 n.
Harvena *alias* Harmera in St. Enoder, 170 n.
Harwood, 97.
Hatch, 66, 144.
Hatch Arundell, 66 n.
Hatherlegh, Devon, 272 n.
Hatherley, Heatherley, 292, 293.
Haucksworthe, 97.
Haughton Tower, Lancashire, 14.
Havenant, 190 n.
Hawcombe in Beer Ferris, 197 n.
Hawkridge, 293.
Hawsewell Park, see Austle *alias*.
Hawton, 269.
Hay in Veryan, 242 n.
Haye, Hey in St. Ive, 25, 63, 63 n.
Hayne, Devon, 90, 215.
Heampton, Heanton, Heanton, Devon, 29 n, 92 n, 131, 147, 241.
Heamton Sackvile, 292.
Hedswell, 182.

Heldrop, Wiltshire, 116.
Hele, 221 n.
Helland, Hellon, Hellond, Cornwall, 35, 72, 100, 188, 249.
Hellegan, Helligan *alias* Heligan, etc., Cornwall, 27, 73, 100, 119, 180 n, 249, 258 n.
Helligau in St. Mabyn, 157 n.
Hellond juxta Bodmin, Cornwall, 249.
Helman Tor, Lanlivery, 211 n.
Helpeston, Northamptonshire, 117.
Helsbery Park, 275 n.
Helston, Cornwall, 11, 12, 14, 17, 75, 75 n, 76, 76 n, 77, 79 n, 82, 167, 167 n, 168, 168 n, 173 n, 175 n, 188, 188 n, 189 n, 212, 234 n, 239 n, 243 n, 248 n, 262 n, 264 n.
Hempshill, 97.
Hender, Hendra, Hendre, 120 n, 199, 216 n.
Hereford, 204 n, 213.
Heringston, Dorsetshire, 263.
Hernefred, 231 n.
Herston, Devon, 160.
Hertfordshire, 28.
Hewgose Wood in Kea, 126 n.
Heybullien, 201 n.
Heydon in Jacobstowe, Cornwall, 188.
Heye juxta Calington, 216 n.
Heywartha, 201 n.
Higher Millcombe, 119 n.
Highhampton, Devon, 133.
Highleigh, Cheshire, 1.
Highnam, Hinam, Gloucestershire, 19, 21.
Highweeke, Devon, 11.
Hill Tope, 97.
Hinderthyn, 13.
Hockland, Devon, 262.
Holberton, Devon, 45, 99 n, 195 n.
Holcombe, Devon, 2, 61.
Holesworthy, Hollsworthy, etc., Devon, 12, 69, 92 n, 93, 116, 193, 286, 287.
Holowood, Holowode, Cornwall, 14, 184 n, 217 n, 255 n.
Hollocombe, 150.
Hornecote, 299 n.
Horwell, 240 n, 268.
Horwood, 119 n, 213.
Horwood House, Wiltshire, 165.
Hoton Conquest, Bedfordshire, 45.
Houghton, 60, 135.
Hugborne, Berkshire, 116.
Huish, Devon, 162 n, 171.
Hurledith, 68.

Idderlegh, 107 n.
Iddeslegh, 207 n.
Ide, Devon, 302.
Idford, 292.
Ilbruers, Somersetshire, 23.

INDEX OF PLACES. 337

Illogan, Cornwall, 167, 230 n, 235 n, 238 n, 261 n.
Ilmister, Illmester, Somersetshire, 14, 186.
Ilstor, 144.
Indies, The, 85 n.
Ingesdon, Devon, 292.
Ingleborne, near Totnes, Devon, 3, 265.
Inner Temple, London, 279, 286.
Insworth, Insworke, Cornwall, 209, 210, 210 n, 211.
Ireland, 30, 68, 71, 72, 177.
Isle of Axham, Lincolnshire, 289.
Isle of Guernsey, 156 n.
Isle of Wight, 176, 177.
Islington, Middlesex, 186.

Jacobstowe, Cornwall, 120

Karlunyck, 189 n.
Kea, Key, St. Kaye, Cornwall, 7, 119 n, 162 n, 173 n, 191, 245, 256, 256 n, 263 n, 301.
Kebye, see Cuby.
Kelley, Devon, 46, 90, 200.
Kellygarth, Killgarth, etc., Cornwall, 9, 85, 177.
Kempston or Rempston, Nottinghamshire, 293.
Kempthorne, Devon, 127, 129.
Kenal in Stithians, 48 n.
Kenegy, Keneg, 7, 215 n.
Keneton, Devon, 196.
Kent, 25, 32, 52, 106 n, 112 n, 239, 272.
Kenwyn, 107 n, 123, 173 n, 256 n.
Kernick, 70.
Kerry, 30, 32.
Kerrys in Paul, 42 n.
Kestell, Kestle, Cornwall, 112, 113, 114, 115, 180 n, 217, 257.
Ketchfronch, 48, 81, 109.
Keverell in St. Martins, Cornwall, 119, 119 n, 120, 120 n, 139, 154, 305.
Keverne, see St. Keverne.
Kew, see St. Kew.
Kildare, Ireland, 257.
Kilkenny, 30.
Kilkhampton, Cornwall, 41, 84 n, 86 n, 168, 199 n.
Killiowe, 225, 226, 226 n.
Killiver, 135 n.
Kilquite in Mabin, 198, 213 n.
Kingsale, Ireland, 203.
Kingsbridge, Devon, 66, 269 n, 287.
Kingston-upon-Hull, 57.
Kirthou, 42.
Kirton, Devon, 116, 134.
Knaton, Devon, 289.
Knoll, 107 n, 207 n.
Krabrill, 107 n.
Kyllyou Edwards, 226 n.

Lachebrook, Devon, 272.
Ladock, Laddock, Lazack, Cornwall, 54 n, 103 n, 212, 212 n, 227, 243 n, 244 n, 298.
Lamaclt, Lamaylo, 18, 20.
Lamartyn, Devon, 248.
Lamerton, 132 n, 136 n.
Lamerton juxta Tavistock, 249.
Lammoran, Cornwall, 170 n, 227, 251, 252, 252 n, 264 n.
Lampeno, Cornwall, 119.
Lancashire, 202.
Lancrentyn, 228 n, 229 n.
Landew, Landu, Cornwall, 18, 119, 222, 224, 271 n.
Landithe in Maderne, Cornwall, 72.
Landrake, Laurack, etc., Cornwall, 15, 24 n, 46, 51, 108, 209, 269.
Landulph, Landilp, Landilt, Cornwall, 58, 294.
Lancast, Lanist, 272 n, 295.
Langdon in Jacobstowe, Cornwall, 120 n, 188, 305.
Langetree, Devon, 227.
Langford, Devon, 121, 122.
Langford Hill, Cornwall, 121, 121 n.
Langles, Devon, 76.
Lanherne, Cornwall, 2, 2 n, 34, 84, 213 n, 242, 273 n, 274 n, 275 n, 287.
Lanhidrock, Lanhydrock, 80 n, 231, 231 n, 295.
Lanion, Lanyan, Cornwall, 123, 124.
Lanivet, Lanhoved, etc., Cornwall, 12, 18, 51, 52, 54 n, 133, 160, 162, 207, 231 n.
Lankarffe in Bodmin, Cornwall, 188, 249.
Lanke, Cornwall, 120 n, 188.
Lanlivery, Lanlevery, Cornwall, 80 n, 96 n, 110 n, 172 n, 204, 295.
Lannergh, 185 n.
Lanowemore, 159 n.
Lanreath, Landreyth, Lanrethoe, etc., Cornwall, 58, 60, 88, 126, 199.
Lanrest, Landrost, Cornwall, 90 n, 101, 114, 246, 251.
Lansallos, Cornwall, 111 n, 117, 118, 118 n, 158, 240, 240 n.
Lanteglos by Camelford, 238 n.
Lanteglos by Fowey, 47 n, 86 n, 230 n.
Lanteglos, Cornwall, 9, 86 n, 178 n, 267 n.
Lappeford, 272 n.
Lastilion, 231.
Latchford, Oxfordshire, 204.
Launcells, Lancolls, Cornwall, 40, 107 n, 111, 128 n, 178, 178 n, 179 n, 295, 305.
Launceston, Lanston, Cornwall, 5 n, 27 n, 37, 43, 70, 70 n, 78,

Launceston—continued.
88, 101, 108, 108 n, 135 n, 148, 177, 178 n, 179 n, 181, 215, 262, 278 n.
Lavaren, 196.
Lawhitton, Lawhidon, Cornwall, 10, 197 n.
Lee, 85.
Leicester, 16, 73.
Loigh, 177, 194.
Leigh, Cornwall, 126.
Loiuh, Devon, 287.
Lelant, Lenant in Penwith, Cornwall, 65, 78 n, 216.
Lescarwell, 101.
Lesnewth, 74 n, 106 n, 108.
Loviston, 96.
Lewannik, Lewannack, etc., 105 n, 132 n, 295.
Lowell, 289.
Lowhire in Foy, 45.
Low Trenchard, 250 n.
Loy, 11, 275 n.
Loyante, 10.
Loy Wood, 288.
Lezant, Le Sante, Cornwall, 45, 119 n, 133, 225 n, 266.
Lidington, Rutland, 65.
Lifton, 131 n.
Ligorno, Italy, 106 n.
Lillesdon, Somersetshire, 24, 25.
Liucoln, 161.
Lincoln's Inn, 70, 85, 88, 186.
Lincolnshire, 261 n.
Linkinghorne, Cornwall, 91, 119 n, 160, 207 n, 225 n, 262, 294.
Liskeard, Leskerdo, Liscard, etc., Cornwall, 6, 11 n, 15, 40, 46, 46 n, 47, 47 n, 56, 56 n, 71, 80 n, 89, 102, 122, 127 n, 133, 136, 137 n, 141 n, 146 n, 169 n, 202 n, 215 n, 228 n, 249, 250 n, 255 n, 295.
Little Colan, 93 n, 253 n, 268 n.
Little Collom, Cornwall, 131.
Littlecote, 215 n.
Little Dartmouth, Devon, 152.
Little Peran, 191.
Little Potherick, 138.
Little Torington, 83 n.
Lizard, Leysard, 126, 126 n, 225.
Lockage, Berkshire, 116.
Lockstowe, 240.
Logan, Cornwall, 217.
London, 11, 17, 25, 43 n, 45, 46, 50, 50 n, 53 n, 60, 64, 74, 76, 95, 97, 106 n, 160, 160 n, 164 n, 173, 190, 278, 279 n, 288.
Longclose, 235 n.
Lostwithiel, Lostithell, Listidiall, Lostwithian, etc., Cornwall, 17, 17 n, 34, 52, 109, 111, 111 n, 112 n, 143 n, 150 n, 152, 158 n, 159, 197 n, 231, 231 n, 241, 259.
Low Countries, The, 120, 210.

2 X

338 INDEX OF PLACES.

Lowe, Loowe, Cornwall, 47, 140.
Lucestow, Devon, 287.
Ludgvan, 159 *n*, 270 *n*.
Lnney, Lewney, Luna, 111 *n*, 128, 128 *n*, 146 *n*.
Lupton. 195.
Luscombe, Somersetshire, 272*n*.
Luxulyan, Luxillian, Cornwall, 72 *n*, 95, 96, 96 *n*, 225 *n*, 227, 231 *n*, 255 *n*.
Lyme, 39.
Lynam, Linham, Devon, 26, 57, 57 *n*, 117.

Mabe, Cornwall, 115.
Madagascar, 115.
Madron, Madderne, Cornwall, etc., 54, 72, 176 *n*, 212 *n*, 274 *n*.
Maker, 210 *n*, 211 *n*.
Malpas, 289.
Malston, Devon, 6.
Malta, 32.
Manuccan, Monnaccon, etc., Cornwall, 42, 148 *n*, 168, 169, 226, 247, 305.
Mannington, Maunaton, Cornwall, 44, 134, 135, 262.
Manoid *alias* Manor Mylls, 148 *n*.
Marazion, Market Jew *alias* Marasion, Marrasow, 51, 62, 62 *n*.
Marham Church, 128 *n*.
Mariston, 295.
Maristowe, Devon, 269.
Markand, Devon, 90.
Marrays, Devon, 291.
Marsh, Devon, 194.
Marshwood, Somersetshire, 160 *n*.
Marston, Marston Tute, 30, 32.
Martin in Meneage, see St. M.
Marwynchurch, 272 *n*.
Maryweek, Cornwall, 37.
Matherose, Medrose, 111, 223.
Maugan in Pyder, 159 *n*.
Mawgan, Cornwall, 73, 74, 258*n*.
Mawgan in Meneage, Mogian, 41, 41 *n*, 42, 73, 248 *n*, 261 *n*.
Mawnan, Cornwall, 65 *n*, 66, 87 *n*, 152 *n*, 192, 274 *n*.
Medeshole (Michell), 212 *n*, 261 *n*, 274 *n*, 275 *n*.
Megara, 256.
Melcombe, Devon, 274 *n*.
Melcombe Regis, 107 *n*.
Meleneck, Meneleck, Beleneck, Molinick, etc., 55, 198, 200.
Mellydar, 111.
Mellyn, 155 *n*.
Melynnewyth, 258 *n*.
Memland, Devon, 26.
Menabilley, Menabilie, etc., 183 *n*, 184 *n*, 220 *n*.
Menadarvy, 89.
Menaguins, 149 *n*.

Menheniot, Menhenet, Minhenuit, etc., Cornwall, 48, 60, 62, 107, 229 *n*, 290.
Menver, see St. Minver.
Menwynnick, Minwenick, etc., Cornwall, 71, 79, 141.
Merkwell, 179.
Merthen, Cornwall, 35 *n*, 67, 76*n*, 185, 185 *n*, 206, 216.
Merther, Cornwall, 6, 127, 129, 130 *n*, 183 *n*.
Merthyn, Mervyn, 299 *n*, 300 *n*.
Meryfeild in Stokeclymsland, Cornwall, 78, 108.
Methe (Meath), Ireland, 32.
Methlowe, 155 *n*.
Mevagissey, Mevagesye, 29 *n*, 89 *n*, 108, 170, 209, 220 *n*, 224 *n*, 270 *n*.
Mevey, Devon, 3.
Mevy, Cornwall, 183.
Mewan, see St. Mewan.
Mewden in Mawnan, 210
Michelstow, Cornwall, 136, 147, 295.
Midd-londe, 112 *n*.
Middle Temple, London, 13, 101, 116, 140, 155 *n*, 246, 258.
Middlesex, 203.
Milbrook, Millbroke, 119 *n*, 209, 210 *n*.
Miler, 170, 171 *n*, 224 *n*, 226, 226 *n*, 235 *n*, 236 *n*, 274 *n*.
Milton, Devon, 139.
Milton in Lanlivery, Cornwall, 138, 139.
Minster, 154 *n*, 295.
Misterton, Somersetshire, 206.
Mochamchurch, 291.
Modbury, Devon, 11, 136 *n*, 231 *n*.
Mohuns Ottery, 31, 143.
Molana Abbey, near Youghal, 30.
Molland, Devon, 137, 279.
Monkhampton, 207 *n*.
Monk Okehampton, 106*n*, 107*n*.
Monster (Munster), Ireland, 72.
Morchard, Devon, 56, 274 *n*.
Moresk, 238 *n*.
Morestow, 226.
Moristow, 121.
Mortlake, Surrey, 161 *n*.
Morvall, Morevale, Morle, etc., 47, 49, 81, 83, 109, 109 *n*, 111 *n*, 126, 140 *n*, 257, 258, 258 *n*, 261 *n*, 270 *n*.
Morwinstow, Cornwall, 11, 106*n*, 108, 127 *n*, 128 *n*, 213, 243 *n*.
Mount Edgcombe *al's* West Stonehouse, Mont Edgcomb, Devon, 63, 64, 64 *n*, 65 *n*, 135.
Mousehole, 124 *n*, 247 *n*, 258 *n*.
Mowleton, Devon, 292.
Mulesford, Moulesford, Berkshire, 29 *n*, 30, 30 *n*, 31.
Mullion, 130 *n*, 152 *n*, 171, 218 *n*, 235 *n*.
Murthe, Cornwall, 147.

Musbery, Devon, 85 *n*.
Mylton Abbott, Devon, 143.
Nampean in St. Enoder, 279 *n*.
Nance, Nans in Illogan, Cornwall, 2, 2 *n*, 233, 238 *n*.
Nausarth, Cornwall, 181.
Nansavallen, 18.
Nanspellye in St. Gernas, 189 *n*.
Nanswhiddon, Nanswedon, Cornwall, 101, 102, 102 *n*, 246.
Nantwich, Cheshire, 205.
Naphissick, 181 *n*.
Netherlands, 76, 114.
Nether Polscoth, 158 *n*.
Netherton, Devon, 64, 151.
Netleham, 128.
Nettlecomb, Somersetshire, 242, 243 *n*, 249.
Newbury, Berkshire, 261 *n*.
Newcastle-on-Tyne, 94.
Neweton, 252 *n*, 255 *n*, 258 *n*.
Newham in Axminster, 143.
Newlyn, Cornwall, 23, 173, 218 *n*, 295.
Newminster, 94.
Newport, Cornwall, 3 *n*.
Newton Abbott, Devon, 195.
Newton, Cornwall, 47, 100, 222, 242.
Newton, Durham, 125.
Newton Ferrers, etc., Devon, 2, 2 *n*, 131, 217.
Newtown, Ireland, 268 *n*.
Ninnis (? Innis or Ennis), 21 *n*.
Norfolk, 89, 203 *n*.
Northam, 69, 72.
Northamptonshire, 65, 91, 93.
Northdowne, 69.
North Huish, 106 *n*.
Northill, Cornwall, 14, 60, 107, 119, 185, 206, 207 *n*, 294.
Northlew, Devon, 99, 133.
Northmolton, Devon, 137, 249.
North Paderda, 100 *n*.
North Petherwin, 115 *n*.
North Petherwyn, Cornwall, 40.
Northpetherwyn, Devon, 92, 115 *n*, 293.
Northrussell, Devon, 268.
North Tamerton, Devon, 273 *n*.
Northtawton, Devon, 218.
Northumberland, 94.
Northyeldelond, 229.
Nuham in Kenwyn, 241 *n*.
Nuthurst, Lancashire, 161.
Nymet, Bishop, 243 *n*.

Odrone or Idrone, Ireland, 30, 30 *n*, 32, 32 *n*.
Offwell, 279 *n*.
Ogbeare, Cornwall, 130, 131.
Oglethorp, Berkshire, 116.
Okehampton, Devon, 37, 81, 106 *n*.
Okenburye, Devon, 287.
Orchard overa Saltash, 255 *n*.

INDEX OF PLACES. 339

Osmondton, Dorsetshire, 75.
Otterham, 295.
Ottery, 30.
Ottery Mohun, 32.
Over Bichan, 124 n.
Over Penquite alias Carpenters, 255 n.
Overa Penquyte, 255 n.
Oxford, 60, 139.
Oxford Park, 180 n.
Owby, Norfolk, 225 n.

Paderda, Padardaye, Padreda, etc., Cornwall, 119, 222.
Padstow, 31, 32, 74, 90 n, 104 n, 107 n, 130, 164 n, 190, 215, 262.
Painsford, Peynsford, Devon, 2, 221.
Pancrasewicke, 300 n.
Pauston, Devon, 131.
Pardnon, 176.
Park, 9.
Parkgate, 190.
Park in Bodmin and Eglosheile, 160 n.
Parva Modberie, 193.
Paul, Pawle, etc., Cornwall, 3, 3 n, 17 n, 18, 27, 42, 42 n, 48, 72, 82 n, 159 n, 234 n, 247 n.
Pawntley, Gloucestershire, 212.
Peccam, Surrey, 185.
Peleite, Cornwall, 252.
Peline, Pelyn, etc., 80, 109, 109 n, 111, 142, 231.
Pelint, 12, 203 n, 241 n.
Pellawyne, Pollawyne, 234 n, 252 n, 259 n, 261 n.
Pembroke, 30, 31.
Penboghe, 180 n.
Penborgard, Cornwall, 160.
Penearrow, Cornwall, 147.
Pencorse, 107 n.
Pencradock, 255 n.
Pendarves in Camborne, Cornwall, 164.
Pendennis Castle, 197 n, 236 n, 242 n.
Pendevy, Cornwall, 114.
Penelwyn, 229.
Penere, Peneare, Pennare, Cornwall, 8, 123 n, 125.
Penfound in Poundstock, Lesnuth, Cornwall, 105, 164, 165, 293.
Pengelley, 9, 100 n, 298.
Pengersick, Pengarsick, etc., Cornwall, 68, 81, 168, 222, 239, 257, 258 n, 259.
Penbalow in Filley, 166.
Penhargard, 160 n.
Penheale, Penhale, 40, 85, 87, 195 n.
Penhellick, 167, 224 n.
Penhollick in Pelynt, 184 n.
Penhergie, 4.
Penishill, Pewishill in Abbotsham, Devon, 70.

Penkevell, Penkivel, Cornwall, 52, 53, 92, 227, 231.
Pennaguinnell, 113.
Penpole, Cornwall, 106 n, 148, 256.
Penpol Melyn, 148 n.
Penpons, 155 n.
Penpons Alverton in Madron, 104 n, 159 n.
Penponte in St. Kew, 262n, 298.
Penquite, Cornwall, 4, 4 n, 47, 112 n, 194, 259 n.
Penrise, 29 n, 196, 197 n, 220 n.
Penrose, etc., Cornwall, 38, 152 n, 195, 224.
Penrose in St. Breward, 188 n.
Penrose Metheley, Cornwall, 169, 170 n, 223.
Penryn, Perin, Peryn alias Penryn, Cornwall, 57, 71, 71 n, 78, 90, 91, 107 n, 152 n, 155 n, 162, 170, 182, 185, 192 n, 217 n, 245.
Pensinans, Pensinguns, Cornwall, 16, 68.
Pentewan, 201 n.
Pentier, Pentiene, Pentune, Cornwall, 189, 190.
Penventynes or Penventennow in Kenwyn, 256 n.
Penveraue, 219.
Penvose, Cornwall, 156, 157 n.
Penvose in St. Tudy, 82.
Penwarren, Penwarne, Peuorne, in Mawnan, 69, 74 n, 102 n, 103 n, 170, 171, 177 n.
Penwithes, 18.
Penyllike, 255 n.
Penytenny, Penetenny, 138.
Penzance, Pensance, etc., 7, 51, 124, 127 n, 237 n, 241.
Peranorworthall, 291.
Peransand, 261.
Peterwthk in Pider, 152 n.
Petroke Stowe, Devon, 61.
Peytevynespark, 255 n.
Phillack, Fillick, etc., Cornwall, 39, 39 n. 158, 236, 258, 270.
Philleigh, Filley, Cornwall, 35, 74 n, 167 n, 242 n, 251.
Pickwell, Devon, 215.
Pill, Pembroke, 31.
Pilton, 83 n, 292.
Pinnock, see St. Pinnock.
Place, Fowey, 220 n.
Plemyn, 5.
Plimpton, 11.
Plymouth, Devon, 38, 39, 43, 43 n, 66, 83 n, 97, 146 n, 160 n, 179 n, 200, 201, 204 n, 205, 209, 214, 215, 219, 229 n, 230, 231 n, 242, 262 n, 266, 289, 303.
Plympton St. Mary, Devon, 66 n, 177, 201 n.
Plympton St. Maurice, Devon, 205.
Polewheele, Cornwall, 62, 124, 172, 173.

Polkinhorne, Polkinghorne, Cornwall, 79 n, 141 n, 173, 174, 175, 175 n.
Polmagan, Cornwall, 34.
Polneder, 201 n.
Polrode, 35 n, 298, 299 n.
Polruddan Port, 173, 174, 175, 175 n, 201 n.
Polscoth, 150 n, 272 n.
Polveyn juxta Fowey, 221 n.
Pordhenis, 258 n.
Porghol, 112 n.
Port Eliott, Cornwall, 66, 67.
Portheast in St. Goran, 181 n.
Porthenes, 18.
Porthledge, Portlage, Porthlich, Devon, 5, 5 n, 114, 127.
Porth Merthen, 255 n.
Porthpigan, 255 n.
Porthvean, 152 n.
Porthvyan in Lower St. Columb, 169 n, 255 n.
Porthyalananta, 239 n.
Portsmouth, 261 n.
Posninch, Devon, 291.
Poughill, 106 n.
Poules Church Yard, London, 10.
Poundstock, Cornwall, 165 n, 218, 218 n, 295.
Powderham, Devon, 31, 32, 52, 268.
Powdridge, 287.
Pradannack Wartha, 277 n, 278 n.
Preston, Devon, 150.
Prideaux Hearle, Cornwall, 94n, 95, 121 n, 180 n, 239 n.
Prideaux Place, Padstow, 32.
Pritwell, 61.
Probus, Cornwall, 53 n, 78 n, 89 n, 173 n, 227, 227 n, 239, 263 n, 264 n.
Pulsack, 155 n, 261 n.
Puslich, 268.
Putford, Devon, 41.
Pyeworthy, Puerthy, 58, 107 n.
Pyran in Powder, 104 n.

Quethiock, Cornwall, 49, 102 n, 133, 184 n, 229, 261 n.
Quotoule, 75.

Radford, Devon, 90 n, 197 n.
Rashleigh, 183.
Rayles, 181 n.
Redrife juxta London, 193.
Redruth, 162.
Rescradock, 60 n.
Rescrens, 261 n.
Reskere, 59, 299 n.
Resprin, Cornwall, 41.
Restock, 277 n.
Restormel, Cornwall, 160, 196.
Restrewg, 240 n.
Retyn, 255 n.
Rialton, 151, 152, 152 n, 153 n,

INDEX OF PLACES.

Ribblesdale, Lancashire, 202.
Richard's Castle, 31.
Roche, Cornwall, 56 n, 80 n.
Roche, Pembrokeshire, 31.
Rockwood, 97.
Rodeland, 4.
Rooke, 220 n.
Rosalen, 261 n.
Roscarrock, Cornwall, 117, 138, 141, 146 n, 189, 190, 231, 240, 278, 279 n.
Roscrowe, Cornwall, 163, 163 n, 192.
Roserude, 65.
Roseland, 226.
Roselion, in St. Blazey, Cornwall, 118 n, 255 n.
Rosemeryn, 117.
Roseverth, Cornwall, 123 n.
Rosgerence, etc., 149 n, 255 n.
Rosplede, 261 n.
Rossara, 287.
Rowehill, 255 n.
Ruan, 166.
Ruan Lanihorne, 242 n.
Rye, 90.

Saffron Walden, Essex, 28.
St. Agnes, St. Ann's, 57, 212 n.
St. Allen, 163 n, 187 n, 197 n, 264 n, 295.
St. Andrew's, Tywardreath, 219 n.
St. Anthony, Cornwall, 48 n, 148 n, 182, 192.
St. Anthony in Meneage, 252 n.
St. Austell, Cornwall, 50 n, 107 n, 149, 149 n, 189 n, 196 n, 197 n, 200 n, 201 n, 231 n, 232 n, 253 n, 255 n, 305.
St. Barre, Fowey, 219 n.
St. Blasey, Cornwall, 117, 189 n, 201 n, 226, 231 n, 295.
St. Breague, 82, 186.
St. Breock, 56 n, 74, 107 n.
St. Breward, 10, 10 n, 268 n.
St. Budeaux, Devon, 54 n, 106 n, 120 n, 230 n.
St. Burian, see Burian.
St. Catherine's, Devon, 178 n.
St. Cleather, Cleder, etc., 92, 243 n.
St. Clements juxta Truro, St. Clements, 65, 99 n, 139 n.
St. Cleere, Cornwall, 10, 38 n, 122 n, 160, 177 n, 253 n, 266, 295.
St. Colan, 52 n.
St. Columb, Cornwall, 9, 25, 36, 36 n, 37, 38, 50 n, 102, 116, 125 n, 136, 139, 142, 149, 149 n, 177, 217, 226, 252, 253 n, 254 n, 279 n, 305, 307.
St. Columb Major, St. Collumbe the higher, etc., Cornwall, 15, 36, 36 n, 72 n, 103 n, 149 n, 153, 197 n, 204 n, 252, 253 n, 254 n, 255 n, 256 n, 273 n, 279 n, 295.

St. Columb Minor, Lower St. Colomb, etc., 16, 152 n, 153 n, 212 n, 215 n, 254 n, 259 n, 295.
St. David's, 30.
St. Dominick, Cornwall, 137, 137 n, 195 n, 199, 305.
St. Donnett's, Wales, 35.
St. Dunstan's in the West, London, 33.
St. Earth, Cornwall, 41, 154, 162 n, 168 n, 215, 227, 239.
St. Endellion, see Endellion.
St. Enoder, 103 n, 107 n, 242 n, 265, 279 n, 295.
St. Erme, Cornwall, 22, 53 n, 72, 123, 173 n, 193.
St. Erney, Erne, 295.
St. Ervan, Ervin, etc., Cornwall, 76, 116, 153, 210 n, 251.
St. Eval, Cornwall, 210 n, 274 n.
St. Ewe, St. Tua, etc., Cornwall, 141, 180 n, 181 n, 226, 231 n, 235 n, 265 n.
St. Fembaron in Fowey, 180 n, 219 n.
St. Gees, 76 n.
St. Gennys, Cornwall, 88, 165 n, 218 n.
St. Germans, Germins, etc., Cornwall, 36, 38, 56, 60, 66, 149 n, 151 n, 204 n, 219, 229, 246 n, 294, 305.
St. Giles in the Fields, Middlesex, 238 n.
St. Gilt, Cornwall, 153.
St. Gorran, 181 n, 266, 273 n, 274 n.
St. Gregory's, Crediton, 270 n.
St. Hillary near the Mount, 83 n, 176 n, 212 n.
St. Issey, Tissey, etc., Cornwall, 12, 76 n, 90 n, 96, 149 n, 231 n, 254 n, 295.
St. Ive, near Liskeard, 46, 16 n, 49.
St. Ives, Cornwall, 23, 38, 39, 96 n, 159 n, 174, 235 n, 270 n.
St. James, Poole, 105 n.
St. James, Tregours (? Tregoney), 148 n, 258 n.
St. John, Exeter, 268 n.
St. John's, 79, 294.
St. John's Park, 234 n.
St. Juliot, 107 n, 268 n.
St. Just, Cornwall, 17, 27, 164, 242 n.
St. Just in Roseland, 255 n.
St. Kaine, 295.
St. Katherin's, Cornwall, 62.
St. Keverne, Cornwall, 14, 48, 48 n, 99, 148 n, 153, 168, 182, 185 n, 226, 240 n, 261 n.
St. Kew, Cue, etc., Cornwall, 3, 9, 35, 35 n, 59, 59 n, 82 n, 101, 117, 121, 134, 138, 165 n, 173, 203, 215, 252, 253 n, 262, 265.
St. Lawrence, Exeter, 268 n.

St. Levan, Cornwall, 23.
St. Leonard's by Exeter, 52.
St. Logan, 234 n.
St. Mabyn, Cornwall, 81 n, 100 n, 137 n, 172 n, 179.
St. Martin, 54, 192.
St. Martin's, Cornwall, 120 n, 258 n.
St. Martin in the Fields, 254 n.
St. Mary Ov'y, Devon, 71.
St. Mary Tavey, 47 n.
St. Maudyt, 300 n.
St. Maws, 226.
St. Mellion, 244 n.
St. Meriodoc, Camborne, 234 n.
St. Merryn, 36 n, 254 n, 255 n.
St. Mewan, 65 n, 149 n, 181 n, 235 n.
St. Michael, Caerhais, 240 n.
St. Michael Penkivel, 54 n, 197.
St. Michael's, 106 n.
St. Michael's Mount, 90 n, 274 n.
St. Minver, 8, 12, 110 n, 182 n.
St. Neott's, Nyott, etc., 68 n, 79 n, 88, 105 n, 152 n, 217, 264 n, 302.
St. Paul, Covent Garden, 238 n.
St. Paul. See Paul.
St. Peran in the Sands, 243 n.
St. Peter, Padstow, 254 n.
St. Peter's, Bodmin, 215 n.
St. Peter's, Exeter, 125 n.
St. Pinnock, Penioke, etc., Cornwall, 58, 136 n, 266 n, 295.
St. Sampson's, Cornwall, 4, 45, 295.
St. Stephen's, 27, 58, 103 n, 106 n.
St. Stephen's in Brannell, 180 n, 181 n, 182 n, 237, 238 n.
St. Stephen's juxta Saltash, Cornwall, 179, 242 n.
St. Stephens, St. Steven's, Cornwall, 27, 58, 68, 103 n, 181, 238, 306.
St. Stephen's, Stevens juxta Launston, Cornwall, 87, 262.
St. Teath, St. Eath, etc., Cornwall, 59, 59 n, 117 n, 168, 190 n.
St. Thomas, 107 n.
St. Thomas, Glasney, 204 n.
St. Tudy, Tidy, etc., Cornwall, 5, 72 n, 133, 133 n, 199, 231 n, 253 n.
St. Veepe, 231 n.
St. Wenn, St. Twin, etc., Cornwall, 74 n, 152 n, 153, 154, 158 n, 237, 252, 295.
St. Winnow, St. Wynowe, etc., Cornwall, 19, 132 n, 133, 231 n, 255 n, 270 n, 295.
Salt Ashe, Cornwall, 14, 15, 25 n, 60 n, 104 n, 119, 136 n, 183, 186, 255 n, 265, 266 n, 294.
Samford, Devon, 192.

INDEX OF PLACES. 341

Sampford Arundel, 269 n.
Sancreed, Sancret, etc., Cornwall, 123, 124 n, 126, 159 n, 247.
Sandford, Devon, 32, 106 n, 125 n.
Santon, 27.
Savoye, London, 157 n.
Saxbye, 289.
Scobell, Devon, 156 n.
Sconer, Cornwall, 269.
Selworth, Somersetshire, 272 n.
Sendelowe, 258 n.
Sendy, 156 n, 191 n.
Senobell, 8.
Shavington, 266.
Shebeare, Devon, 200.
Sheepwash, 131 n.
Shelton, Cornwall, 189.
Sherford, 165 n.
Shernepark, 255 n.
Sheviock, Cornwall, etc., 56, 60, 60 n, 196, 273n, 294.
Shillingham, 24, 25, 42, 63.
Shilston, 14, 99.
Shippesford, 66.
Shippester, Devon, 66.
Shropshire, 97, 104.
Shute, 31.
Sidbury, Devon, 231 n.
Sidenham, 24.
Sidmouth, 279 n.
Silloy, Seelye, 81 n, 82.
Sithney, Sceny, etc., Cornwall, 48 n, 51, 168, 170 n, 188, 234 n, 273 n.
Skyberio, 73 n, 258 n.
Skewys, 252 n, 261 n.
Skynter, 56 n.
Slade, 85.
Slapton, 120.
Slasney (? Glasney), 76.
Smithick alias Pennycomquick, Falmouth, 235 n, 236 n.
Soldon, 288.
Somersetshire, 28, 37, 90, 132, 137, 142, 188, 213 n, 227, 259 n, 261 n, 269, 272.
Soren, 235.
Southampton, 28, 261 n.
Southhill, Cornwall, 88.
Southkymbar, 290.
South Petherwin, Cornwall, 64, 133, 135, 213, 295.
South Tavistock, Devon, 249.
Southweek, 150.
Sowton, Devon, 149.
Spain, 294.
Sparnon, Cornwall, 205.
Spryleston, 257.
Spurwaye, 11.
Stafford, 3, 22.
Stanberye, Stanburye in Morewinstow, Cornwall, 213, 214.
Stapbley, 266.
Staunton, 255 n.
Stellonorgan, Dublin, 32.
Stevenston, Devon, 291.
Stithians, Stediens, etc., 79, 148.

Stoford, Devon, 49, 70.
Stoke, 108, 209.
Stoke Brewer, 273 n.
Stokeclymsland, Cornwall, 88, 95, 108, 125, 200, 206.
Stoke, Cornwall, 27.
Stoke Damerel juxta Plymouth, Devon, 146 n, 242 n.
Stoke Flemynge, 199 n.
Stoke, Sussex, 28.
Stokenham, 231 n.
Stoliford, 194.
Stonarton (Staverton), Devon, 96, 194.
Stone, Devon, 148.
Stowe, Cornwall, 7 n, 18, 146 n, 292.
Stratton, Statton, 70, 271.
Streete, 181 n.
Strete alias Trevervyn, 199 n.
Strevigo. See Trevigo.
Surrey, 204 n.
Sussex, 10, 28.
Swandrop, Hampshire, 141.

Talland, Tilland, etc., Cornwall, 148, 199, 200, 209, 210, 243 n.
Tamerton, 35 n, 69, 70, 79, 131, 213, 298, 299 n.
Tamerton Foliot, 225 n.
Taunton, Toanton, Somerset, 73, 84, 229, 279 n.
Tavistock, Tavestock, etc., Devon, 25, 35, 47, 57, 60, 66, 77, 78, 78 n, 81, 85, 86 n, 88, 96, 119 n, 137, 139, 140, 144 n, 173, 173 n, 197 n, 211 n, 229, 243, 250 n, 289.
Tehidy, Tchiddye, Cornwall, 5, 52, 53 n, 233, 276 n.
Telham, 289.
Temple, 118.
Tencreke, 210.
Tendeyll, 155 n.
Terris in St. Stephen's in Brannell, 181 n.
Thanks, Cornwall, 202.
Thankes, Cornwall, 202.
Thewborow, Thewburie, Devon, 41, 210.
Thorlbeare, 272 n.
Thornborowe, Devon, 120.
Thornbury, Devon, 157.
Thorne, Devon, 44, 44 n, 141.
Thory, Thori in Hartland, 70, 214.
Tingrase, Devon, 10.
Tinmouth, 94.
Tinnyo, 69.
Tintagell, Tintodgwell, Cornwall, 35 n, 58, 58 n, 139, 172 n, 295, 299 n.
Tintenhall, Somersetshire, 136 n.
Tiptquet, Devon, 227.
Tisick. See St. Issey.
Titcott, Telcot, Devon, 109, 140.
Tiverton, 185, 243 n.
Toba alias Gyllyn Wolla, 148 n.

Tolcarne, Talcarn, etc., 159 n
Tolgarrock, 240 n.
Tolverne, Talverne, etc., 20, 29, 36, 51, 81, 224, 235 n, 240, 274 n.
Tomyowe, 252 n, 255 n.
Tonacombe, Tohacombe, etc., Cornwall, 127, 128, 129, 251.
Torr, Cornwall, 44, 179.
Torry, 143.
Totnes, Devon, 6, 13, 14 n, 78, 140 n, 167, 168, 183, 231 n, 268.
Tottin Mill, Lancashire, 104 n.
Totworthy, 69, 70.
Towan Wartha in St. Merryn, 252 n, 255 n.
Towan Wollas in St. Merryn, 252 n, 255 n.
Tower Hill, 221 n.
Townstall juxta Dartmouth, 171.
Toye, 28.
Traytor in Padstowe, 175 n.
Trebarfoote, Cornwall, 218.
Trebathe, Trebarthe, 87, 104.
Trebeigh, Cornwall, 268.
Trebigh in Eggloskerry, 188 n.
Trebuskan, 234 n.
Treberthes (? Treverthes), 189n, 240 n.
Trebisker, 210 n.
Trebithe, 291.
Tredareppe, 255 n.
Tredawle, 107 n.
Tredeage, 250.
Tredannum, 271.
Tredewi, 195 n.
Tredidon in Egloskerry, Cornwall, 69 n, 105, 106, 107, 207.
Tredinnick, Tredynnek, Tredynek, etc., 242 n, 255 n, 259 n.
Tredinnyal, 169 n.
Tredreysowe, Tredreyses, 274 n.
Tredrym, 255 n.
Tredurff, Cornwall, 207.
Trefry, 219, 220.
Trefuses, etc., Cornwall, 7, 76, 220, 224 n.
Tregadek, 255 n.
Tregagelwales, 158 n.
Tregagelwortha, 158 n.
Tregaminion juxta Liscard, 195 n.
Treganaw, 147.
Tregantallan, Tregandallion, etc. 65 n, 112 n, 181 n, 235 n, 272 n.
Tregarne, Tregarin, Tregardon, etc., 5, 71, 180.
Tregarrock, 180 n.
Tregarthen, 201, 242 n.
Tregasow, Tregaso, Cornwall, 49, 186.
Tregearchapell, 158 n.
Tregellas, 164 n.

INDEX OF PLACES.

Tregellas in Probus, 53 n.
Tregender, 155 n.
Tregenha, near St. Ives, 22.
Treg ustock, 274 n.
Tregerthick, 181 n.
Tregethowe, 168 n.
Tregewe, 235 n, 250 n.
Tregiddin, 19.
Tregiskie, 226.
Tregolse, 152.
Tregon John, Cornwall, 203.
Tregonake in St. Germayns, 204.
Tregoney, Tregonie, etc., 16, 17, 26, 72, 152 n, 158, 167, 173 n, 177, 177 n, 180, 180 n, 214, 217, 234 n, 236 n, 261 n.
Tregonnan, 306.
Tregonowe, Tregenewe, 155 n, 271 n, 279.
Tregorrek. 189 n, 255 n.
Tregorthian, 108 n.
Tregose, Tregos, 7, 7 n, 274 n.
Tregothnan. Treguthnan, etc., 18, 19, 236 n.
Tregovethan, 122, 233.
Tregownan, 28.
Treguden, 18.
Tregullow. 265 n.
Trehane, Trehayne in Probus, Cornwall, 111, 199, 227, 227n.
Trehanke, 47, 106.
Trehaverock alias Trebarrock, etc., 37 n, 38, 59.
Trehenford, 238 n.
Trehunsey, Trehunsie in Quethiock, 43, 43 n.
Treire, 101.
Trekurnel, 261 n.
Trekynnen in Trigg, 271 n.
Treladerw, 223.
Trelanmaur, 277 n.
Trelawarren, Trelaworen, etc., in Mawgan, Cornwall, 14, 14 n, 46, 47 n, 73, 90 n, 114, 116, 148 n, 257, 258 n, 259 n, 260 n, 261 n, 269 n, 270.
Trelaske, Treloske, etc., Cornwall, 108 n, 132, 132 n, 172.
Trelawny, Treloney, Trelani, Trelaune, etc., Cornwall, 5, 94, 146, 228, 229.
Treleague, 258.
Treledyk, 238 n.
Trelege Vean, 148 n.
Trelewythen, 277 n.
Treleven, 17 n.
Treleweth juxta Treloy, 277 n.
Treley, Cornwall, 233, 274 n.
Treloddrow, 155 n.
Trelonk, 277, 278 n.
Trelowith the Lower, 181 n.
Trelowyth, 181 n, 235 n, 277, 277 n, 278 n, 296, 299 n.
Trelugan, Cornwall, 211.
Tremage, Tremade, Cornwall, 122, 122 n.
Tremargh, 255 n.
Trematon, 25 n, 56 n.

Tremaylek, Tremalik overa Penquyte, 255, 255 n.
Tremaynon, 262 n.
Trembath, 41.
Trembleth, Tremblyth, Tremleth, etc.. 239, 274 n.
Trembrase, 56 n.
Trembrotheke, 234 n.
Tremedow in Senar (Zennor), 22.
Tremeer, Tremeere, Tremere, Tremure, etc., Cornwall, 5, 28, 52, 86 n, 133 n, 156 n, 275 n.
Tremerake, Cornwall, 49.
Tremodrut, Cornwall, 274 n.
Trenaek, 151 n.
Trenale, 158 n.
Trenance, 252 n.
Trenancmoor, 18.
Trenauns, 272 n.
Trenans Austell, 189 n, 255 n.
Trenart, 113.
Trenastell, 242 n.
Trenny, 248 n.
Treneglas, 295.
Trenerth, Cornwall, 233, 277 n, 278 n.
Trenevesack, 243 n.
Trenewyth, Trenowith, 255 n, 272 n, 276, 277.
Trengale in St. Cleere, 100 n, 262.
Trengove alias Trengoffe, Tringoff, and Trangoe, Cornwall, 7, 46, 124, 234 n, 247.
Trengwainton, Trenguenthen, in Madren, 54, 54 n, 127 n.
Trenhale in Newlin, 259 n, 261 n.
Trenouth, Trenowthe, etc., Cornwall, 38, 68, 75, 76, 80, 100, 125, 126, 138, 138 n, 252 n.
Trenowre, 18.
Trent, Somersetshire, 112, 263.
Trenwith, Trennwith, Cornwall, 89, 220, 238, 239.
Trenyne in Myuver, Cornwall, 91.
Trenynnock, 181 n.
Trenytheu in Probus, 215 n.
Trerice, Trerise, Trerys, etc., in St. Allen, Cornwall, 2, 3 n, 19, 28, 40, 44, 50, 68, 82, 83 n, 84, 84 n, 212, 233, 233 n, 242, 257, 271, 272, 272 n, 273 n, 275 n, 277 n, 298, 304.
Treriven, Cornwall, 92.
Tresagher, Constantine, 244 n.
Tresawell, 252 n, 258 n.
Tresawell le Lower, 255 n.
Tresawell le Over, 255 n.
Treseles, 179 n.
Tresilian, Cornwall, 16, 118, 205.
Tresoren alias Soren, 181 n. 235 n.
Tresoye, 172.
Trespresyne, 234 n.
Tresula, 186 n.
Tresulbrethen, 277 n.

Tresungar, Cornwall, 134, 138, 138 n, 189, 190, 203 n.
Treswithen, Tresudyan in Camborne, 23, 23 n, 24.
Trethack, 255 n.
Trethake in St. Cleere, 118 n.
Trethank, 109 n.
Trethannicke, 114 n.
Tretharas, 153 n.
Tretharlffe, Tredurfe, etc., Cornwall, 207, 244.
Tretharrope, Tretharup, 234 n, 255 n.
Trethyn, 258 n.
Trithell juxta Crofthole, 204 n.
Trethenes, 296.
Trethewy. 238 n, 277 n.
Trethias Towen in St. Merryn, 255 n.
Trethias in St. Merryn, 169 n, 255 n.
Trethowen, 67.
Trethyrgy, Trethrygy, Trethygy, 189 n, 255 n, 272 n.
Treune, 217.
Treuryek, next the village of St. Wenn, 271 n.
Trevagethyghan, 185 n.
Trevagetmur, 185 n.
Trevaile, 18.
Trevalnck in St. Keverne, Cornwall, 217.
Trevalane, 191.
Trevalgn, 136 n.
Trevalla Vean, 180 n.
Trevalster, 224, 239.
Trevalster, Cornwall, 13, 224, 239.
Trevanhener, 255 n.
Trevanion, 257.
Trevarrack, 262 n.
Trevathelek, 261 n.
Trevedowe, Trevedo, 9, 101, 118 n.
Trevegles, Treveglas, 54, 75 n.
Trevelli, 18.
Trevemeder, 255 n.
Trevencage, Treverege, etc., Cornwall, 29, 81, 83.
Trevenethcke, 98.
Trevenege, 238 n.
Trevenhedee, 8.
Treveniel, 79 n.
Trevenwyn, 258 n.
Treverbon, 8.
Trevervn, Trevorvoe in Probus, Cornwall, 186, 263.
Trevethan, Cornwall, 180 n, 235 n, 236, 236 n.
Trevethan Wartha, 235 n.
Trevethan Wollas, 235 n.
Trevidren, Trevudren, etc., 68, 255 n, 257, 258 n.
Trevigo, 70, 215.
Trevince, Trefius in Gwinop, 7, 7 n, 224.
Trevithan, Trevethan, Cornwall, 180 n, 235 n.
Trevithick, 242 n.

INDEX OF PLACES. 343

Trevorder, Trevourder, etc., Cornwall, 10, 113, 118 n, 242, 243, 298.
Trevorungowe, 258 n.
Trevyan, 23.
Trewan, Trewen, 56 n, 157 n, 221 n, 253 n, 255 n.
Trewand, 170 n.
Trewane in St. Kew, Cornwall, 145, 157, 158 n.
Trewardrevah, 67.
Trewarcton Hale, Cornwall, 75.
Trewarnon, 54 n, 80.
Trewarveneth, Trewarvenner, etc., in Paule, Cornwall, 44, 82, 127 n, 156 n, 205.
Trewaythe, 100 n.
Trewegett, Trewegit, 59, 134.
Trewenhelek, etc., in Resgerens, 255 n.
Trewerys, 277 n, 300 n.
Trewethock, 68.
Trowhilla in St. Enoder, 245 n.
Trewidlonde, 56 n.
Trewinny in Mevagesy, 209.
Trewola, Trewolley, 111, 245.
Trewolla-Vean, 180 n.
Trewonwell, Trewonwall, 21, 223.
Trewooffe, 126, 127 n.
Treworgan, Cornwall, 171, 173 n, 262.
Treworget, 228 n.
Treworgie Skorie, Cornwall, 204.
Treworgy, Treworgie, etc., 25, 111 n, 112, 112 n, 118, 129, 151, 216 n, 290.
Treworgy in St. Cleere, Cornwall, 46, 258.
Treworgy in St. Gennys, Cornwall, 88.
Treworgy juxta Lansteuetha, 216 n.
Treworles, 38 n.
Treworrek, Treworricke, 119 n, 209.
Treworthen, 228 n.
Treworwale Vyan, 255 n.
Trewthand, 46.
Trewynt in Alternon, 107 n.
Trewynt in Blisland, Cornwall, 204.
Trey, 152.
Trimerton in St. Stephen's, 179.
Trink, 185.
Trobridge, Devon, 157.
Truro, Trwro, Trewro, etc., 7 n, 17, 26, 26 n, 48 n, 65, 71, 71 n, 93, 99, 142, 154, 155 n, 163, 163, 173, 173 n, 181, 186, 187, 187 n, 189 n, 207, 215 n, 219 n, 224, 237, 238 n, 252, 263, 264 n, 301.
Truro Merther, 16.
Trworbonett, 82.
Trymore, 300 n.
Tudyford, Cornwall, 229, 229 n, 230 n.

Tunsted, Kent, 33.
Turner's Pidle, Dorsetshire, 265.
Turkey, 39.
Twelmona More, 290.
Twynyo, 105.
Tynten, 298.
Tywardreath, Trewardreth, etc., 11, 95 n, 231 n, 268 n, 295.

Ugborough, Devon, 15.
Umberleigh, Umberley, Devon, 5, 92 n.
Uny Lelant, Uni juxta Lelant, Cornwall, 48, 192, 235 n.
Upchurch, Kent, 196.
Upcott, Upcote, Devon, 156 n, 220.

Valapit, 288.
Vallopit, Devon, 73, 288.
Vasie, 128.
Veep, see St. Veep.
Ventogou, 120 n.
Veryan, Cornwall, 75, 93, 241 n, 242, 252 n, 295.
Vileston, Devon, 147.
Vounder, Trewoone, 235 n.

Wadefast, 158 n.
Wadeford, 171 n.
Wadham College, Oxford, 72.
Wales, 30, 176, 216, 265 n.
Wallelond, Weylonde, 255 n.
Walton-on-Thames, 106 n.
Warle, 288.
Warleggan, 118 n.
Warwickshire, 22, 39.
Washfield, 40.
Waterford, 32.
Wellington, Somersetshire, 269, 269 n.
Wemburie, Devon, 288.
Wembworthy, 95 n.
Wenbury, Devon, 108 n, 288.
Wendron, Gwendron, etc., Cornwall, 168, 170, 173 n.
Wennet, 97.
Werrestone, 107 n.
Werrington, 79 n.
West Allington, 269 n.
West Anthony, 273 n.
Westburie, Wiltshire, 68.
Westcott, Devon, 41.
West Disard, 296.
West Herle, Northumberland, 94.
West Langdon, 181 n.
Westley, Devon, 41.
Westmarker in Dwlo, Cornwall, 129.
Westminster Abbey, 31.
Westmoreland, 22.
West Newton, Cornwall, 49.
Westnorth in Duloe, 6 n.
Weston Peverell juxta Plymouth, 30.
West Putford, or Pudford, Devon, 41, 106 n.
Weststanbery, 213.

Westwillesworth, 69.
Wexford, 30.
Weymouth, Wamouth, Dorsetshire, 71, 107 n.
Whaddon prope Sarum, Wiltshire, 116.
Whalesbury, Cornwall, 203, 203 n. 242.
Whetstone, Whitston, Cornwall, 40, 83, 83 n, 165, 206, 212 n.
Whitechurch, 78, 173 n.
Whitehall, 43 n, 64 n, 67 n.
Whitesday, 272 n.
Whitfeld, 44.
Wibberie, Devon, 72.
Wideslade, 92.
Widicomb, Devon, 11.
Wight, the Isle of, Southampton, 176, 177.
Wilcombe, Cornwall, 119.
Wiltshire, 38, 131, 161, 189, 190.
Windsor, 30, 32, 74, 81.
Winscott in Puerthy, 58.
Witchampton, Dorsetshire, 201.
Witheridge, 279 n.
Withicomb, 231 n.
Withiel, 77, 78 n.
Wodeland, 25, 26.
Woenbosken, Cornwall, 216.
Wollesdon, 55.
Wolley, 212.
Wolston, 268.
Wolvecombe, 255 n.
Wolvedon, 299.
Wonewell, Wonwell, Devon, 194, 209, 210, 211.
Wood, 10 n, 24, 32, 74 n, 278, 286.
Woodford in Lausalloes, 242 n.
Woodhill, 127 n, 137 n.
Woodhouse, Devon, 182.
Worcester, 106 n, 180 n, 188, 192, 289.
Worington, Devon, 267.
Wortham, Devon, 99.
Worthevale, Worthivall, Cornwall, 11, 267.
Wotton, Cornwall, 119.
Wrighton, Norfolk, 81.
Wyk St. Mary, St. Mary Week, Cornwall, 1, 212 n, 291.
Wynyanton, 35 n, 297, 299 n, 300 n.
Wynyard (Gwinear), 123.
Wyvellscombe in St. Stephen's by Saltash, Cornwall, 269, 269 n.

Yalwelegh, 126 n.
Yareslorowe, 286.
Yarmouth, 72.
Yarnescombe, 197.
Yewoton, Devon, 274 n.
Yoe, 26.
York, 144.

Zennor, Sunner, etc., 54, 54 n, 159 n.

www.ingramcontent.com/pod-product-compliance
Lightning Source LLC
Chambersburg PA
CBHW020325240426
43673CB00039B/926